The Soviet Rural Community

A SYMPOSIUM

The Soviet

Edited and

Rural Community

ith an Introduction by **James R. Millar**

UNIVERSITY OF ILLINOIS PRESS
Urbana : Chicago : London

ACKNOWLEDGMENTS

The papers collected in this volume were presented at a symposium held at Allerton House of the University of Illinois in April, 1969. The symposium was jointly sponsored by the University's Russian and East European Center, the James Buchanan Duke Memorial Fund, and the Center for International Comparative Studies of the University of Illinois at Urbana-Champaign as a means to bring together specialists in the various disciplines to consider, discuss, and appraise the changing characteristics of the Soviet rural community. I would like to express my appreciation for the generous support and encouragement provided by these organizations. The Russian and East European Center has also supplied essential assistance in preparing the proceedings for publication. I am certain that the other participants join me in praise of Miss Corinne Guntzel, whose efficiency, unstinting efforts, and expert trouble-shooting have made both the symposium and the publication of its proceedings possible, expeditious, and carefree for the rest of us.

Contents

PART III : Recent Trends in the Rural Economy

PART IV : The Texture of Rural Life

Introduction : Themes and Counter-Themes in the Changing Rural Community

James R. Millar

The fifteen essays that compose this volume were presented as original research studies to a symposium that was held at the University of Illinois in the spring of 1969. The purpose of the symposium was to foster a cross-disciplinary examination and appraisal of the changing nature of rural life and work in the Soviet Union. The essays range over the whole of the Soviet period, with considerably greater concentration upon the post-Stalin years. Comprehensive coverage was not, however, a primary goal. Emphasis was instead placed upon the exploitation of the most recent sources of data, the exploration of hitherto neglected topics, and the formulation of new interpretations of the Soviet experience. The salient and unifying theme that emerges from this collection is the issue of rural modernization, particularly its relative belatedness for this sector of the Soviet society.

Under the various Soviet administrations, modernization of the rural community has meant both progress toward minimization of the weather-dominance of agricultural production and progress toward the elimination of a peasant-dominant economy, polity, and society. However, given this common policy theme, three quite distinct phases can readily be identified in the evolution of the Soviet rural community, each the product of specific policy decisions associated with the prominent political figure of the period: the New Economic Policy (NEP) with Lenin; mass collectivization with Stalin; and belated modernization with Khrushchev.

The New Economic Policy represented an accommodation by the Bolsheviks to a rural-dominant society and economy. Fully 85 percent of the population of Soviet Russia lived and worked in the rural community, and perhaps a larger share could have been classified as peasants on sociological criteria.[1] Moreover, better than one-half of Soviet national income orginated in the agricultural sector.[2] Given the urban-industrial orientation of Soviet leadership, the NEP was necessarily viewed as an uneasy and impermanent accommodation to the political and economic facts of life. If, following Isaac Deutscher,[3] the successful attainment of Soviet power represented the harnessing of an urban and collectivist proletarian revolution with a rural and individualistic agrarian revolution, then the prime question of the immediate postrevolutionary period of necessity involved which was to lead if the two revolutionary forces were subsequently to work in tandem.

The answer was not at all obvious, given the ideological preconceptions of the Bolsheviks and the institutional premises of the NEP. The NEP presupposed small-scale peasant enterprise, open agricultural product, and labor- and land-hire markets, and thus it left determination of the level, composition, and marketed share of agricultural output in private hands. It offered opportunities for economic, social, and thus political differentiation in the rural community. These institutions also necessarily restricted the possibilities for direct state intervention in the rural sector. State policy had to be framed, instead, in terms of indirect instruments of control such as price and financial policies. There were doubts about both the effectiveness and the appropriateness of policy instruments such as these in the budding socialist economy. Moreover, the main direct link between the state and the peasantry was the agricultural specialist. More often than not, the agricultural specialist was not a Bolshevik, and he carried out his work under what George Yaney calls an "alliance of rhetoric" with the Bolsheviks (see Chapter 1). The specialist, in effect, translated the revolutionary rhetoric of Soviet agricultural pronouncements into a continuation of the land settlement and adjustment measures originally instituted by the tsarist regime.

The attempt to accommodate the social and economic institutions favored by the peasantry failed, and the second phase was initiated by the "emergency measures" Stalin introduced in response to the "grain crisis" of 1928 and was confirmed by the subsequent collectivization drive. The Stalinist phase substituted collective for private enterprise, the large-scale farm for the small, bureaucratic arrangements for open markets, and the administrator for the agricultural specialist. Exhortation and administrative pressure became, therefore, the principal instruments for central management of agricultural production and the distribution of its fruits between urban and ru-

[1] Maurice Dobb, *Soviet Economic Development Since 1917*, rev. ed. (New York: International Publishers, 1966), p. 36.

[2] Naum Jasny, *Soviet Industrialization, 1928–1952* (Chicago: University of Chicago Press, 1961), p. 43.

[3] Isaac Deutscher, *The Unfinished Revolution Russia 1917–1967* (London: Oxford University Press, 1967), pp. 22–26.

ral sectors (for a model of Soviet agricultural administrative behavior, see Chapter 3).

Although, in terms of scale and the organization of farm work, these changes made the agricultural production unit look a good deal more like an industrial establishment, they were also coupled with measures which led to a de facto depecuniarization of the agricultural sector. Pecuniary and other material incentives to work on the collectives were neglected and other restrictions were imposed upon the sector's access to the Soviet main income and money circuit, and thus to the more progressive sectors of the economy. The economic budgeting and accounting procedures (*khozraschet*) standard for all state enterprises, for example, were not even introduced on the kolkhoz.

It has been widely believed that the institutions that replaced those destroyed in the process of collectivization played critical political and economic roles in support of Stalin's industrialization drive of the 1930's. The argument, in brief, has run in terms of the establishment of central control over a restless and potentially hostile petty-capitalist class on the political side, and in terms of the "extraction" of necessary resources from the agricultural sector on the economic side. Jerzy Karcz raises some important questions with respect to the economic rationale for collectivization in his contribution to this collection (Chapter 2),[4] and the political rationale has been seriously challenged elsewhere recently.[5]

If the short-run merits of Stalin's agricultural policies remain somewhat controversial, there can be no question that the long-run effects have been extremely deleterious and extraordinarily difficult and costly to reverse. The relatively poor performance of agricultural enterprises today and the persisting backwardness of the contemporary rural community are direct consequences of both what was done and what was left undone in the way of agricultural policy during the Stalinist phase. The Stalinist phase did destroy thoroughly and irrevocably rural-agricultural dominance of Soviet economic, political, and social institutions. It did so partly through the success of rapid industrialization, which sharply increased the share of GNP originating in nonagriculture and thus also the urban-worker share of the total population. But rural-agricultural dominance was also undermined by a deliberate policy of excluding the rural sector from the main sources

[4] See also James R. Millar, "Soviet Rapid Development and the Agricultural Surplus Hypothesis," *Soviet Studies*, XXII, no. 1 (July, 1970), 77–93.

[5] Moshe Lewin, *Russian Peasants and Soviet Power: A Study of Collectivization*, trans. Irene Nove with the assistance of John Biggart (Evanston, Ill.: Northwestern University Press, 1968); James R. Millar and Corinne Guntzel, "The Economics and Politics of Mass Collectivization Reconsidered: A Review Article," *Explorations in Economic History* (forthcoming).

as well as the benefits of economic development, which served to perpetuate the traditional social, economic, and religious institutions of rural life in the peasant isolate thereby created (see Chapters 7, 12, 13, and 14).

The differential impact of industrialization upon the urban-industrial and rural-agricultural sectors during the Stalinist phase differs from the development experience of other successfully industrializing economies only in degree, perhaps, but the difference is nonetheless a significant one. The third phase in the evolution of the contemporary Soviet rural community has been characterized by attempts to close the gap between the urban-industrial and rural-agricultural sectors. Khrushchev began as a reformist tinkerer, attempting to make the institutions of Stalinist agriculture work through the restoration of "socialist legality" in the relations between state agencies and the enterprises and members of the rural community, by improving material incentives to work on the agricultural collectives, and by increasing the share of investment funds allocated to the rural sector. However, the cumulative impact of these reforms, taken together with the abolition of the Machine Tractor Station system and the discriminatory, multichannel state procurement system in 1958, fully justifies labelling the third phase Khrushchevian. Besides, his successors have altered neither the direction nor the premises of the process of rural modernization belatedly set in motion in the post-Stalin period.

The large-scale, factory-farm organization of agricultural production represents, perhaps, the single most important permanent legacy of collectivization. For, where Stalin rejected open market institutions and reliance upon pecuniary and other indirect policy instruments in favor of an extension of the state bureaucracy and direct central control devices to the countryside, a contrary process has been taking place during the contemporary phase—one that has involved also the substitution of material incentives and socialist legality for force and fraud in the administration of agricultural production. Institutionally, the contemporary Soviet agricultural economy combines elements of both preceding stages: the large-scale factory-farm created by collectivization and a socialist variant of the pecuniary and market institutions of the NEP. The Khrushchev phase represents a reversal of the Stalinist in the sense that it has been characterized by complementary processes of pecuniarization and debureaucratization; and it represents a reversal in the sense that the relative priority of the rural sector has been greatly enhanced.

Substantial progress has been made in the years since Stalin's death toward modernization of the Soviet rural sector. The agricultural capital stock, both productive and "nonproductive," has increased and been modernized (see Chapter 10). Progress has also been made toward creating the conditions necessary to bring into being a competent, reliable, and disciplined agricultural work force. Total personal income earned in agricultural employment increased five-fold between 1953 and 1966. Increased income from work on collective and state farm enterprises accounts for the greater part of this expansion in earnings, and the share of income generated by private plot production has declined accordingly. Moreover, the share of money pay in total pay for collective work has increased sharply, minimum and regular payment for work on collective farms has been introduced, and many of the fringe benefits previously available only to state enterprise employees have been extended to collective farm workers as well (see Chapters 9 and 11).

Management and staff-specialist personnel of agricultural enterprises have improved quantitatively and qualitatively. Educational attainment levels are up, the number of agricultural specialists working at the enterprise level has increased, and Party membership in the countryside is greater than ever before (see Chapters 4, 5, and 8).

Although the collective farm retains certain features indicative of its status as a "producer cooperative," especially with respect to the financing of investment expenditures and operating losses, determination of the total wage bill, and the legal status of its membership, the main structural and organizational differences between kolkhozy and sovkhozy have disappeared (see Chapters 6, 9, and 11). Changes introduced in sovkhozy and those implied for all state enterprises by the 1965 Kosygin reforms suggest a process of mutual convergence that will ultimately eliminate the remaining differences among kolkhozy, sovkhozy, and other state enterprises.

Despite the radical character and extent of the post-Stalin agricultural reform movement, thus far the results of these costly changes have been somewhat disappointing to the Soviet leadership, whether measured in terms of capital and labor productivity, the level, composition, and rate of growth of agricultural output, or the overall efficiency of agricultural production. Part of the explanation for this disappointing rate of improvement in the performance of agricultural enterprises is to be found in the sheer magnitude of the task required to overcome the neglect and abuse Stalinist agricultural policies imposed upon the sector. Relatively, if not absolutely, the Soviet rural community was more backward both technically and socially in 1953 than had been the case at the close of the NEP. What this suggests is that the outlays necessary to modernize the rural sector were compounded during the period of their postponement. Belated modernization of an agricultural sector is apparently more difficult and costly than advocates of unbalanced growth have led us to believe. Nonetheless, there is no reason to suppose that the remaining obstacles to modernization of the rural community cannot be removed, given a continuation of the reform movement.

However, the sluggishness of the response to reform is only partly due to the magnitude of the task involved. It has also been due to the way in which the reform effort has been carried out. If the general strategy of reform has been clear, bold, and essentially correct—to increase the agricultural capital stock, the level of skills, and material incentives in agricultural production—reform tactics appear on the contrary often to have been hesitant, piecemeal, niggardly, and sometimes self-defeating. This suggests that a remedy will also require better articulation of the reform program as a whole, greater realism in the setting of reform goals and requirements, and more effective implementation of the general reform strategy at the local level.

The "modernization drive" of the third phase in the evolution of the contemporary Soviet rural community has required not merely diverting scarce human and material resources to the rural sector, but overcoming resistances generated by certain ideological preconceptions and organizational preferences which have shaped Soviet agricultural policy and practice from the outset. An enduring contempt for "the idiocy of rural life,"[6] the traditional low priority of the rural-agricultural sector in the planning process, the long-standing mistrust of decentralized exercise of economic discretion, and an ideologically ingrained, but clearly outmoded, hostility to the idea of relying upon pecuniary and other indirect central planning and management instruments have served as mutually reinforcing obstacles to modernization of the rural community. Coupled with the "impatience for results" that has always characterized Soviet leadership, these features contributed to the bureaucratic hypertrophy of Soviet political and economic administration. The main sweep of the institutional reforms of the third phase is closely connected, therefore, with the more general reform of Soviet central planning and management procedures that has been underway during roughly the same period, and it has encountered similar obstacles.

In the concluding Chapter 15, Professor Gleb Žekulin indicates that an interesting and important branch of the "oppositionist" literary establishment seems to be formulating a somewhat romantic conception of the con-

---

[6] Karl Marx and Frederich Engels, "Manifesto of the Communist Party," in Lewis Feuer (ed.), *Basic Writings on Politics and Philosophy* (New York: Anchor Books, 1959), p. 11.

temporary Soviet peasant. The peasant has somehow endured Soviet power, as he did the hardships imposed by earlier regimes, by and with his own peculiar bucolic values and a distinctive conception of the world. Perhaps so, but might this not be, instead, a mythopoetic harbinger of the close of the peasant era in Russia?

PART I

Agricultural Policy in Historical Perspective

1 : Agricultural Administration in Russia from the Stolypin Land Reform to Forced Collectivization: An Interpretive Study

George L. Yaney

I

This essay seeks to reconsider the development of agricultural administration in the Soviet Union in the 1920's and its destruction in 1930–1933 in the light of a perplexing fact: namely, that in 1928–1929 the Soviet government's rural agencies were not actually collectivizing the peasants' land or even trying to but instead were devoting their efforts to programs that resembled very closely those set forth in the so-called Stolypin land reform of 1906–1917. Ordinarily, the best method of presenting such a reconsideration would be to begin with the new evidence and proceed thence to the reconsiderations that it suggests. The evidence, however, relates to the late 1920's, whereas the reconsideration extends back to 1906. I have thought it best, therefore, to sacrifice the proper order of inductive reasoning for the sake of chronology and to begin the account with the historical background rather than the data. In this way the historical significance that I attach to the data will be apparent before they are presented.

In 1906, the Russian government launched a sweeping agrarian reform that brought large numbers of technical specialists to the peasant villages under the aegis of a bureaucratic executive organization.[1] Some of the peasants had seen individual specialists before, but this was the first time in Russia's history that they encountered a bureaucracy head on and actu-

[1] The development of the administration of the so-called Stolypin land reform is described in G. L. Yaney, "The Imperial Russian Government and the Stolypin Land Reform" (Ph.D. dissertation, Princeton University, 1961), pp. 177–220.

ally interacted with it. The relationships that arose from this encounter constituted a unique and unprecedented social development, and by 1914, when World War I interrupted the agrarian reform, the Russian terms for agricultural specialist (*agronom, agrarnik, spetsialist, zemleustroitel'*) had acquired associations and implications of a social and historical nature that went beyond the purely functional capacities they describe. Interaction between peasants and specialists had become, as A. V. Chayanov put it, a "mass phenomenon." On the one hand, the rapid increase in the quantity of agricultural specialists produced a qualitative change in rural society that derived primarily from the specialists' efforts "to build a new Russian countryside by means of their molecular work."[2] On the other hand, the specialists themselves derived attitudes and purposes from their involvement in the villages that gave their work a momentum of its own. They worked within the formal structure of the government and accepted the commands that came down from the central offices, but what they actually did and tried to do was rooted in their own experiences with the villages. The bureaucracy of the agrarian reform that began to interact with the peasants on a massive scale after 1906 was both a formal structure and a practical experience, and these two elements in its nature followed somewhat separate paths.

The interaction between peasant village and the bureaucracy of specialists continued until the winter of 1929–1930, a period of approximately 23 years, during which time groups of specialists worked in the villages in coordination with each other and in cooperation with the peasants. Until 1929, the specialists who operated in active contact with the villages were able to impose their beliefs on each of the regimes under which they worked, outlasting the one under which they began. I have described the development of this "movement" in tsarist times elsewhere.[3] The main purpose of this essay is to trace the specialist movement's relationship with the Soviet regime up to the time of its destruction in 1930.

A movement of agricultural specialists is necessarily an ambiguous concept. Interaction with the peasants did not produce the same effects on all the specialists who were involved in it, and therefore the movement did not include all of them or even, necessarily, a majority of them. Those specialists who did act as if they were part of a movement rarely spoke of it openly, mainly because their common sense of purpose and their awareness of

[2] A. V. Chayanov, *The Theory of Peasant Economy* (Homewood, Ill.: Richard D. Irwin, Inc., 1966), pp. 35–36.

[3] See G. L. Yaney, "The Concept of the Stolypin Land Reform," *Slavic Review*, XXIII (June, 1964), 275–293.

a shared experience in relation to the peasants did not require articulation. To make a trivial but instructive comparison, all the football coaches in the United States can be said to constitute a "movement," and they share certain experiences, attitudes, and purposes; yet they feel no great need to articulate their sense of solidarity, and when one of them does articulate it, the rest are likely to disagree with what he says. Likewise, the Russian agricultural specialists of the 1920's could act and align themselves as if they were a part of a movement without having to announce it publicly, and when one of them did make such an announcement, it did not necessarily constitute a description of the specialists' general state of mind, only an expression of it. The specialists were government servitors, and when they were in public they generally said what they thought their various superiors expected them to say. In the writings of the 1920's, it is often difficult to distinguish an agrarian reformer who was dissembling from a straight Party activist who opposed the specialists' procedures and wished to impose restraints on their informal movement. This essay, then, cannot pretend to measure unambiguously just how many specialists actually felt themselves to be a part of a movement, nor can it establish that any given individual did or did not consider himself first and foremost an agrarian reformer. The essential point that can be made is that the activities and accomplishments of the agricultural specialists *on the whole* indicate that a considerable number of them acted as if they were motivated by a common set of attitudes and were able to cooperate within commonly understood patterns of behavior, even when these patterns were not expressed in any formal organizational structure.

II

Given the unreliability of public expressions of beliefs and attitudes, the clearest way to begin a description of the agricultural specialists as a historical movement is to describe what they achieved during the period 1906–1929. There are some who would set the beginning of the movement earlier than 1906. Chayanov, who began work as a zemstvo statistician in the early 1900's, traced the relationship between the agricultural specialists and the peasants back to 1900, and he notes further that usable statistics on the rural economy, one of the key elements in the movement, began to be accumulated even earlier, in the 1880's.[4] B. Veselovskii would have it that the zemstvo administrations began to show active concern for the peasants

[4] Chayanov, pp. 35–36, 67–68.

in the 1890's.[5] Be this as it may, contact between agricultural specialists and peasants did not develop on a large scale under the aegis of bureaucratic programs until after 1906. In that year, there were only ten zemstvo agronomists working with the peasants, and the central government employed a total of 200 surveyors in European Russia to carry out whatever pretensions it made to achieving land reforms.[6] From then on, the number of agricultural specialists working with the peasants increased rapidly, and by 1914, about 5,000 agronomists and 7,600 surveyors were active in peasant agriculture. Most of them were the servitors of the various ministries. The surveyors worked for the Ministry of Justice, and the administrative directors and agronomists were under the Ministries of Agriculture and Internal Affairs.[7] About one-fifth of the agronomists worked for the zemstvos, but their work, their relationships with the bureaucratic reform administration, and their attitudes did not differ observably from those employed by the central government.

World War I brought an end to active land reform on a large scale, and the revolution brought an end to tsarist government and zemstvos alike; but the agricultural specialists survived. In the early 1920's, an estimated 7,000[8] of them were again at work under the auspices of the Soviet government, i.e., the People's Commissariat of Agriculture (hereinafter referred to as the NKZ); and by 1928, their number may have swelled to over 17,000.[9] That the specialists of the 1920's were mostly survivors of the earlier reform period is indicated by the fact that in January, 1928, 55.5 percent of those working on the guberniia level had begun their careers as agricultural agents of the tsarist government in the time of the so-called Stolypin land reform, and 43.5 percent of those working on the uezd level had similar origins.[10]

What did the specialists do? From 1906 through 1914 and from about 1921 through 1929, they carried out land settlement (*zemleustroistvo*). Land settlement was a broad term that included all measures designed to

---

[5] B. Veselovskii, *Istoriia zemstva za sorok let* (4 vols., St. Petersburg, 1909), I, 585–587.

[6] The number of agronomists is from V. Trutovskii, *Sovremennoe zemstvo* (Petrograd, 1914), p. 115. For the surveyors, see *Desiatiletie zavedyvaniia mezhevym upravleniem zemlemernoiu chastiu zemleustroitel'nykh kommissii 1906–1916* (Petrograd, 1916), p. 6.

[7] Trutovskii, pp. 112, 115; *Desiatiletie*, pp. 25–26.

[8] N. V. Bochkov, *Istoriia zemel'nykh otnoshenii i zemleustroistva* (Moscow, 1956), p. 151. I am indebted to Mr. Ihor Stebelsky for calling my attention to this very valuable book.

[9] *Spravochnik zemleustroitelia* (Moscow, 1928), p. 223. But an estimate of January, 1929, gives the number of specialists in operation as 7,900. See *Stenograficheskii otchet IV soveshchaniia zemorganov 5–12 ianvaria 1929 goda* (Moscow, 1929), p. 40.

[10] *Sprav. zem.*, pp. 226–227.

eliminate the many narrow strips into which the peasants were fond of dividing their fields and to replace them with larger, wider plots that lent themselves to rational farming. Conditions varied from one area to another, but according to traditional arrangements in just about all of European Russia, each peasant household held between 30 and 50 separate strips, one in each cultivated field. Ordinarily, the meadows and forest lands were held in common, but sometimes these too were divided. In southern Russia, there were not so many strips, but the villages were much larger and the strips much farther apart. The confusion grew worse when the villages themselves got intertangled. It often happened that a field fell into common ownership between more than one village, in which case it would normally be divided into strips for the households in all the villages concerned. Not infrequently, a single village was spread out over separate lots, sometimes as many as 20 or 30 of them, with fields belonging to other villages and/or private owners in between.[11] Land settlement, then, had to cover a wide variety of measures: any rearrangement of the land that was acceptable to the peasants and would enable them to use the land more efficiently.

At the outset of the agrarian reform, the leading officials of the government had made it their ultimate aim to bring the peasants to full consolidation of their lands, with each peasant household settled on its own, single, separate lot. This arrangement was called a khutor, an ideal form that some tsarist officials continued to insist upon right up to the revolution.[12] The specialists in the field, however, were generally more flexible, and in practice they carried out land settlement projects pretty much as the peasants wanted them. Only in the Lithuanian and Belorussian guberniias did large numbers of peasants express a demand for khutory; consequently, it was only there that any significant number was formed on village lands.

Land settlement continued to be the major preoccupation of the specialists throughout the period 1906–1929, and it seems to have gone forward at a much faster pace in the 1920's than it did in 1906–1914. Land settlement projects of the seven-year period from 1907 to 1913 covered a total area of less than 20 million hectares, of which 4.8 million were completed in 1913, when the number of land settlement workers reached its prewar peak.[13] Had the specialists of the 1920's performed at the 1913 level, they would have covered 24 million hectares in 1921–1925. A recent Soviet study, however,

[11] So far as I know, the best descriptions of peasant landholding systems, complete with diagrams, are in P. N. Pershin, *Zemel'noe ustroistvo dorevoliutsionnoi derevni* (Moscow, 1928).

[12] Especially A. A. Kofod, the chief inspector of the land reform organization. One of his more dogmatic assertions, claiming that all peasants should be put on khutory, is in *Russkoe zemleustroistvo* (St. Petersburg, 1914), pp. 66–69.

[13] S. M. Dubrovskii, *Stolypinskaia reforma* (Leningrad, 1925), pp. 138–140.

sets the area covered in these years at 77 million hectares,[14] and this is close to what the specialists were claiming at the time. Indeed, according to a report made in 1929, the area covered in the RSFSR alone by the end of 1928 totalled 152.6 million hectares.[15]

The data for the 1920's are extremely doubtful. In part they reflect the Soviet government's small concern for the intricacics of land rights, which made things simpler for land reformers, and in part they reflect the generally more modest nature of the projects undertaken in the 1920's. Prior to 1928, many seem to have involved only minor readjustments of the boundaries between villages.[16] The main reason the figures for the 1920's are so high, however, is probably simply exaggeration, which seems to have been a habit among government officials at that time, doubtless partly as a heritage of civil war days. To take only one example, a 1920 publication of the NKZ claimed that 16,000 agricultural specialists were on the job in that year, and that they had carried out land settlement work on 3.7 million hectares in 1919.[17] A recent Soviet book, on the other hand, has only 7,000 specialists working in the period 1921–1925, but they allegedly covered 19 million hectares in 1919.[18] The statistics, then, are grossly inaccurate. They do indicate, however, that in the 1920's agricultural specialists were working actively on land settlement *and that they were very proud of it*. If they completed only one-third of the projects they claimed, the programs that began in 1906 under the Stolypin land reform went forward in the 1920's at least as rapidly as they had in 1913, the most productive prewar year.

The specialists of the 1920's did not confine themselves to operations in the villages. Shortly after the revolution, they moved into the higher levels of the Soviet government. The NKZ of the RSFSR came under their effective control in 1918 at about the time S. P. Sereda, an erstwhile zemstvo statisti-

[14] Bochkov, pp. 147–148.
[15] *Sten. ot.*, p. 492. When the same land area was subject to some sort of reform more than once, it seems that it was counted into the above total more than once (p. 493). Thus, the net area covered in the 1920's had to be less than 152.6 million hectares.
[16] Bochkov, p. 149, gives a diagram showing a typical intervillage project.
[17] B. N. Knipovich, *Ocherki deiatel'nosti narodnogo kommissariata zemledeliia za tri goda: 1917–1920* (Moscow, 1920), pp. 24, 38. Not content merely to claim the 16,000 specialists, Knipovich also gives their educational backgrounds.
[18] Bochkov, pp. 130–131, 151. Pershin, writing in 1922, says that although land settlement spread among the peasants themselves from 1918 on, the government actually discouraged it in the civil war period. See his *Uchastkovoe zemlepol'zovanie v Rossii* (Moscow, 1922), pp. 39–42. An unusually frank Soviet statement on the value of early Soviet statistics—A. K. Kasian's comment in *Istoriia sovetskogo krest'ianstva i kolkhoznogo stroitel'stva v SSSR* (Moscow, 1963), pp. 147–148—says that statistics from the period 1917–1920 do not justify any conclusions whatever regarding land division, let alone land settlement.

cian, took it over.[19] In May, 1918, when the NKZ took up the supervision of crop planting, it immediately began, according to its own report, to use its resources to initiate once again the old campaign for land settlement that had been abandoned in 1914.[20] The edict of February 14, 1919, gave the NKZ formal responsibility for the management and development of the sovkhozy (state farms) and the kolkhozy (collective farms) and also set forth the Soviet government's first general regulations for land settlement.[21] Armed with these formidable authorizations the NKZ began immediately to organize itself to carry out land settlement and virtually to ignore the sovkhozy and kolkhozy (see below, pp. 16–18). From then on, scholars and experts of the NKZ and other organs of agricultural administration wrote the laws, circulars, and plans that expressed the government's agricultural policies, and they staffed the faculties of agronomic science and economics in the institutions of higher and middle education.[22] They ran the agricultural section of the State Planning Commission, and in 1927–1928, it was they who turned out the first Five-Year Plan for agriculture—the relatively moderate one that the Communists were to accept in the spring of 1929 and subsequently to reject in August.[23]

III

Judging from the success of land settlement in the 1920's, the specialist movement was much more influential in the countryside and better able to operate in conjunction with the peasants than was the Communist Party, which suffered throughout the period from an almost complete lack of operational relationships with the peasantry. To be sure, there were peasant Party members at work in the countryside, but the vast majority of them were petty administrators holding positions in raion and volost' organizations far from their own home villages. In Tula guberniia in the early 1920's, 93 percent of the peasant Party members came from areas other than those in

[19] Sereda's lack of Bolshevik enthusiasm and his typically specialist passion for practical programs based on accurate statistics are reflected in his foreword to *The Restoration of Agriculture in the Famine Area of Russia* (London, 1922), pp. 9–11.
[20] Knipovich, p. 21.
[21] *Ibid.*, pp. 11, 22–24. Concerning the general nature of the sovkhozy and kolkhozy, see below, n. 60.
[22] It is worth mentioning that the specialists were very active throughout the 1920's in producing scholarly works. Pershin published his book on the Stolypin land reform in 1928 (see above, n. 11) and the contributions of the Russian agricultural economists ranked them with the world's best (Chayanov, pp. v–vi, xxx–xxxiii).
[23] Iu. A. Moshkov, *Zernovaia problema v gody sploshnoi kollektivizatsii sel'skogo khoziaistva SSSR 1929–1932 gg.* (Moscow, 1966), pp. 67–68. I am indebted to Professor Alec Nove for calling my attention to this work.

which they held office, and this was typical of the RSFSR in general.[24] It seems that when peasants joined the Party they lost contact *and any desire for contact* with their own villages and with peasant society in general. Working as alien administrators, they rarely went out even to visit the villages under their official jurisdiction, let alone participate in their development.[25] By 1929, the situation may have improved slightly. Of 333,000 Party members in the rural cells, 124,000 were actually practicing farmers. Nevertheless, the Party still regarded its connections with the peasants as very weak, and so they seem to have been.[26] What was true of the "peasant" Party cells was equally true of the formal apparatus of "peasant" administration. Village, volost', and raion soviets and executive committees (*ispolkomy*) generally left the villages to themselves, interfering only when someone made a specific complaint or openly opposed their authority. Rural officials had neither the desire nor the ability to lead the peasants or to organize them around a program of action.[27] Indeed, as Maynard has pointed out, they could not even set up an orderly system of tax assessment.[28]

If the government and Party organs played no active role in the countryside in the 1920's, it was partly due to the inability of the traditional peasant villages to organize their members to do anything outside their customary routines. True, there were individual peasants who desired change and worked to improve their own conditions. In both tsarist and Soviet times, a few peasants proved themselves capable of dealing with the world by acquiring wealth, influence in the administration, and/or knowledge of the workings of the law and the administration. Generally speaking, the mass of the peasants looked up to them,[29] and if anyone could have led the peasants through the tribulations of social change it would have been these men—the *kulaki* of both tsarist and Soviet mythology. These potential leaders, however, rarely showed any inclination to organize whole villages and volosti for

[24] Ia. A. Iakovlev, *Nasha derevnia* (Moscow, 1924), p. 163.

[25] *Ibid.*, pp. 109–166.

[26] M. Lewin, *La paysannerie et le pouvoir soviétique, 1928–1930* (Paris: Mouton and Co., 1966), pp. 111–117.

[27] Many observers noted the inertness of local rural administration throughout the 1920's. See, e.g., M. Ia. Fenomenov, *Sovremennaia derevnia* (2 vols., Moscow, 1925), II, 32–34, 95; Ia. Burov, *Derevnia na perelome* (Moscow, 1926), pp. 26–27, 57–58, 179–181, 236–241; Iakovlev, *Nasha*, pp. 33–46, 109–110, 143–166; and especially a collection of articles edited by Iakovlev, *Sel'sovety i volispolkomy* (Moscow, 1925), pp. 3–11, 50–62, and 75–79. For the late 1920's, see Iakovlev's *Bor'ba za urozhai*, 2nd ed. (Moscow, 1929), pp. 62, 95.

[28] J. Maynard, *The Russian Peasant* (New York: Macmillan, 1962), pp. 165–167. His source was probably A. L. Weinstein, *Oblozhenie i platezhi kres'tianstva v dovoennoe i revoliutsionnoe vremia* (Moscow, 1924).

[29] Fenomenov, I, 117–119, II, 34–36; Iakovlev, *Derevnia kak ona est'* (Moscow, 1924), p. 127.

programs of development. Generally speaking, they showed the same tendency to isolate themselves from their village communities as did the peasants who joined the Party. When they did organize themselves, it was usually only for private, business purposes; and when they led people, it was generally by individual arrangements such as hiring, renting, buying, or bribing.[30] Thus, without any political leadership or any basis for political organization in peasant society itself other than the family-type hierarchies that held together the customary arrangements of everyday life, the organs of government would have had great difficulty leading the peasants, even if they had wanted to.[31]

The Communists' failure to make contact with the peasants was due not only to the nature of village society but also to their own situation. Their very possession of political power and their need to devise a practical political program *for the whole country* made it very difficult for them to find common ground with the peasants. Unlike the specialists, who had only to carry out a land reform and did not have to concern themselves with other problems of state, the Party organization had to look after foreign affairs, defense, finance, and the problems of industrial development. Not only was it unable to respond adequately to peasant needs; it had, like the tsarist government before it, to impose demands on the peasants that aroused their resentment.[32]

Consider the situation of 1917–1920. The only rural institutions that had ever played an active role in government—the gentry and the zemstvos—had disappeared from the scene and with them all effective contact (except for the recalcitrant specialists) that the central administration had ever had with rural society. There remained no means by which the government could mobilize or organize the villages to support it or to serve its purposes. Of course, the peasantry could still be cowed by military force, but for *active* support, the government would have to depend entirely on the cities. In the

[30] Iakovlev gives a number of descriptions of *kulaks* in *Derevnia*, pp. 13–23, 52–56. See also Fenomenov, I, 24, 66–70, II, 35; and Lewin, pp. 417–418.

[31] T. Bernstein, "Leadership and Mass Mobilization in the Soviet and Chinese Collectivization Campaigns of 1929–30 and 1955–56; a Comparison," *China Quarterly,* XXXII (July–September, 1967), 9–12, 17–18, 22–23, notes that the weakness in rural leadership in the Soviet Union was one of the crucial distinctions between the collectivization in Russia and that which went forward in the 1950's in China.

[32] S. Iu. Witte, Minister of Finance from 1892 to 1903, once pointed out that the needs of industrialization caused the government to inflict burdens on the peasantry, even in a time when foreign capital was available. In a memorandum to the tsar, he acknowledged "that the customs duties fall as a particularly heavy burden upon the impoverished landowners and peasants, particularly in a year of crop failure. These imposts are a heavy sacrifice made by the entire population, and not from surplus but out of current necessities." Quoted in T. Von Laue, "A Secret Memorandum of Sergei Witte on the Industrialization of Imperial Russia," *Journal of Modern History*, XXXI (March, 1954), 67.

period 1917–1920, however, the very existence of the cities was threatened by the general economic collapse. Trade and industry virtually ceased, transportation fell into profound irregularity, and foreign capital became unavailable. The cities suffered such a critical shortage of food and fuel that large numbers of their inhabitants abandoned them. Consequently, the most urgent necessity that the Bolshevik government (or any kind of government) faced was to re-establish the supply of food and fuel to the cities in the absence of all the administrative, financial, and commercial means that had been available to the tsarist regime. Under these circumstances, there could be no talk of relying on the natural operation of the market. If the price of bread in the cities was allowed to rise high enough to bring in grain, the city population would not be able to pay it. Thus, it is at least understandable that the Communists should have begun their reign by resorting to the most primitive methods to force the peasants to supply the cities with grain, and that this should have tended to alienate the peasants from the Soviet regime at the outset. It is worth mentioning in this regard that the first law that authorized grain seizures was not the product of the Bolsheviks but of the Provisional government.[33]

To sum up the remarks on the Party's weakness in the countryside, the rural organs of Party and government failed to organize the peasants or even to influence them in the 1920's, partly because of the traditional social isolation of the peasantry and partly because the Communist government had inherited in much more drastic form those harsh responsibilities—political, military, and financial—that had always alienated the Russian people from their government. This left the agricultural specialists as the only administrative group in Soviet Russia with any basis for acting to bring the peasantry into effective communication with the state organization. The Communists needed the specialists, and this need was the foundation for the unlikely and patently self-contradictory alliance from 1918 on between the dictatorship of the proletariat and agrarian reform.

IV

The alliance began in the midst of civil war and general economic disintegration, a time of such confusion that no one in Russia worried much about the absurdity of what he was doing or saying. The Communists were desperately striking about to find or form some sort of organized support in the country-

---

[33] See the excerpts from the statute on the grain monopoly, dated March 25, 1917, in R. Browder and A. Kerensky, *The Russian Provisional Government, 1917* (3 vols., Stanford, Calif.: Hoover Institution, Stanford University, 1961), II, 619.

side, and in the process they concocted, among other things, a vague scheme of collectivization, according to which the least capable and most backward peasants were to be formed quickly into the most advanced kind of productive organization. Practically speaking, this was preposterous. The Communists wanted the peasants to produce more and to sell more, but as soon as a peasant began to take on more work and to use more land, the Party proclaimed him a "middle" or "rich" peasant and began to look upon him as an enemy whom all "poor" peasants should denounce. In fact, of course, this quasi-ritualistic rhetoric had significance only in the high circles of government, and its prevalence there only demonstrated that the Communist leaders had no agrarian program of their own nor any organization to carry one out.[34] Nevertheless, they kept up a remarkable flow of promises and directives, putting their hopes in the more or less sound principle that if positive action is utterly impossible for a government, its need to resort to rhetoric is all the greater. As Lenin once said (to Iakovlev) in a *pobedonostsevian* mood: "It will not do to brush aside revolutionary fantasies and the revolutionary enthusiam that goes with them. There is often more authentic realism in them than in the deliberate calculations of the 'practical men.' "[35]

A good example of the Bolsheviks' free-wheeling rhetoric in the civil war period is their "action" in 1918–1919 to take care of the considerable number of people who were leaving the cities to obtain food in the countryside. These moving crowds of refugees posed a major threat to city and country alike, and they had to be dealt with quickly. A report from Moscow guberniia indicates that the Bolsheviks there rose to the occasion as well as could be expected by offering the refugees land from the former state domains and private estates. The trouble with this solution was that the local peasants in each area had already seized the best fields for themselves, leaving only second-rate farmland for the refugees. All the Bolsheviks could do, therefore, was to throw together settlements of city folk on strange land that was usually of poor quality and leave them there without tools, seed, or work animals, in the midst of long-established villages that were doubtless hostile to the interlopers. In short, they set up DP camps, and very ill-supplied ones at that.[36] What did the Bolsheviks call them? State farms (sovkhozy),

[34] R. Wesson, *Soviet Communes* (New Brunswick, N.J.: Rutgers University Press, 1963), pp. 64–78, describes the genuine enthusiasm of a number of Old Believer sects in the 1920's for the *kommuna*, i.e., the most extreme form of collective farm (see below, n. 60); but aside from this small minority among the members of the collective farms, I have seen no reliable indication of any interest among the peasants in the collectives as such.

[35] This is Iakovlev's paraphrasing of what Lenin said in conversation with him in the early 1920's. See *Za kolkhozy* (Moscow, 1929), p. 123.

[36] *Sbornik zakonopolozhenii i rasporiazhenii po zemleustroistvu* (Moscow, 1927), pp. 142–143.

manned by the toiling poor; supposedly the most modern form of agrarian organization ever devised by man, where new agricultural methods would soon transform the land into gardens that would command the admiration of the surrounding villages. Thus did rhetoric transform a desperate expedient into thriving centers of agricultural development capable of leading the whole country forward.[37]

Confronted with this kind of thinking, which was realistic enough under the circumstances, the agricultural specialists seem to have attached themselves to the Bolsheviks by adopting the absurd but tactically useful dogma that collectivization according to the Bolshevik ideal would raise agricultural productivity. This dogma achieved formal expression in the decree of February 14, 1919, which gave the specialists in the NKZ control over the collectivization movement and at the same time set forth regulations for land settlement (see above, n. 21). From then on, the specialists' measures for land settlement and agronomic aid, designed primarily to raise productivity, could be advertised as collectivization or "progress toward collectivization." Opposition to land settlement, on the other hand, could be denounced as a deterrent to collectivization or "not true, Leninist collectivization."[38]

Specialists could adopt the Communist rhetoric without apprehension. It was utterly irrelevant to the problems of agricultural production and it had no concrete meaning for the peasants themselves. As Lenin said in a letter of 1921–1922, criticizing the Party's "theses" concerning its aims in the villages:

> We must state the matter in a completely different way, not repeating the worn out slogan–word "cooperate," but describing concretely what our experience with cooperation has been and how we can help its development. If this material is not available . . . then the decisions of the congress should include a demand to collect it and work it over from a practical point of view rather than an academic one. . . . It has not been proven that things are better in the collectives. It won't do to disturb the peasants with false komsomol-swaggering.[39]

Given the irrelevance of the Bolshevik rhetoric, the specialists could mouth it when they had to, and even believe it in a general way, and still operate in the countryside solely in the interests of practical agrarian reform. There grew up, then, an "alliance of rhetoric" between the specialists and the Party activists: an arrangement in which both sides tacitly agreed on the terminology they would use to refer to what was going on but continued to follow their own respective thought patterns in intellectual isolation. The

[37] Knipovich, pp. 10–14.
[38] See, e.g., Iakovlev, *Nasha*, pp. 106–110; Knipovich, p. 24.
[39] Quoted in Iakovlev, *Nasha*, p. 3.

Bolsheviks were spared the necessity of giving up their slogans about the peasantry, and the agrarian reformers could remain indifferent to all problems and considerations save those that emerged from their own statistical investigations.

This is not to say that there was no interaction between the Communist regime and the agricultural specialists during the 1920's; but until the second half of 1929, this interaction did not produce any serious effect on the thinking of the specialists or on the reforms that were actually being carried out in the countryside. On the other hand, during the early 1920's the specialists' devotion to land consolidation was continuously insinuated into the Bolshevik slogans. A law of October 9, 1925, from the Council of People's Commissars of the USSR went so far as to order rural authorities "to take measures to consolidate the strips of land as much as possible, setting up individually held, consolidated fields [*otruby*] wherever it does not seem possible to introduce some cooperative form of land use."[40] At the Fifteenth Party Congress in December, 1927, no less a figure than V. Molotov solemnly repeated the specialists' maxim that the complex interstripping of peasant land was "unsupportable" and that no social or economic improvement would be possible so long as it remained the predominant form of land use.[41]

Perhaps the greatest *coup de rhétorique* the specialists achieved was the temporary change they introduced in the meaning of the term *kulak*. In the mid-1920's, the government's official statements began to proclaim that land settlement would save the peasant villages from the domination of *kulaki* and that therefore anyone who opposed land settlement was likely to be a *kulak*.[42] This notion is particularly significant in view of the fact that the Bolsheviks had formerly believed that land settlement favored the wealthy. Lenin had said so.[43] Converting the Communists to a new slogan precisely opposed to one of Lenin's dictums less than ten years after the revolution was no small achievement—especially when the dictum contained a substantial measure of truth. M. Ia. Fenomenov, one of the most discerning observers of the Russian peasantry in the 1920's, maintained that it was, in general, the wealthier peasants who were more likely to favor consolidation projects in practice;[44] and in tsarist times scholars and administrators who gave the matter any thought generally assumed that land reform would bring more benefits to the wealthy than to the poor. Actually, there is no statistical evidence for

[40] The law ·is in *Sbornik*, p. 35.
[41] Quoted in Lewin, p. 29.
[42] See, e.g., *Sprav. zem.*, p. 7.
[43] Lenin's standard claim was that only the desperately poor and the exploiting rich consolidated their lands. See, e.g., a work of 1913 in *Collected Works* (38 vols., Moscow, 1964), XIX, 189–196.
[44] See his *Sovremennaia derevnia*, I, 71.

either tsarist or Soviet periods demonstrating any simple, *convincing* correlation between the wealth of a peasant and his attitude toward land
settlement. There were rich peasants who opposed it. Peasants with large
numbers of animals generally wanted to maintain common ownership of the
meadowlands, and those who had already consolidated their land into integral plots were inclined to oppose any new, villagewide consolidation that
would redivide the fields they had begun to cultivate on their own. In any
event, whatever the real relationship between a peasant's wealth and his attitude toward land settlement may have been, it had nothing to do with the
conversion of the Communists to the view that a *kulak* was one who *opposed*
land settlement. The significance of the conversion is simply that it marked
the apogee of the Communist-specialist alliance of rhetoric.

V

The most noteworthy outcome of the alliance of rhetoric was that it allowed
the specialists to work on agrarian reform according to their own inclinations
throughout the 1920's. As was noted above, the alliance received its first legislative expression in February, 1919. At that time, the NKZ took over responsibility for collectivization, and on this basis it acquired local agencies
of sorts and began to hire agricultural specialists.[45] In December, 1920, the
government ordered the army to release agricultural specialists, and the NKZ
openly undertook to set up a unified plan for agricultural reform on the basis
of "the experience of past years."[46] This was the beginning of "socialist" land
settlement, a term that made what was probably its first appearance in the
decree of February 14, 1919 (see above, n. 21).

For the tsarist government, the stated purpose of land settlement had been
to consolidate peasant strips into independent farm households on single, integral plots that the head of the household would own as his personal (*lich-
naia*) property. In the 1920's, on the other hand, public slogans demanded
that all land reform measures that did not actually collectivize peasant
holdings should at least prepare the way for the organizing of "poor" and
"middle" peasants into collective farms.[47] Rhetoric notwithstanding, the concrete measures to which socialist land settlement referred did not differ appreciably from those of tsarist land settlement. Boundary adjustment that

[45] Knipovich, pp. 11–12, 38–41.
[46] *Ibid.*
[47] Tsarist programs of land settlement were set forth in Article 1 of the law of
May 29, 1911. See A. A. Znosko-Borovskii (ed.), *Polozhenie o zemleustroistve* (St.
Petersburg, 1912), pp. 2–3. A resolution of the Fifteenth Party Congress of December,
1927, expressed the Communist idea. It is printed in *Sprav. zem.*, pp. 5–18.

led toward the forming of integral household plots was very similar in essence to that which prepared the way for the collectivization of a village's land into a single enterprise. P. N. Pershin, who worked on land settlement in both periods, noted only one difference that he thought significant. The tsarist government, he said, tried to forbid its agents to undertake "partial consolidations," i.e., reductions in the number of thin strips in a village field that made individual lots larger but still left each village field divided into several parts. By contrast, the Soviet regime allowed this. Pershin, writing in 1928, made much of how doctrinaire the tsarist government had been and how good the Soviet regime was for letting the peasants follow their own path of development, but it all came down to a small point.[48] In the 1920's, specialists who formed separate consolidated farms for each peasant family could call their operation a mere replacement of many small strips with a few lots that were larger and wider. Indeed, they could even call it collectivization,[49] just as in tsarist times they could change the strips to square plots and call it consolidation.[50] The specialists were always masters at doing what they and the peasants wanted to do while calling it what the government in power wished.

The tsarist roots of socialist land settlement are clearly discernible in the formal legislation of the 1920's.[51] An instruction of March 13, 1922, from the NKZ proclaimed the need for land settlement and gave some guidelines for carrying it out, but it had to advise the surveyors to follow old tsarist government regulations until the Soviet administration could prepare its own.[52] In fact, the Soviet administration did not prepare a comprehensive set of regulations until December, 1928. Specific enactments came out from time to time before then. The NKZ circular of April 20, 1923, gave a list of the types of socialist land settlement,[53] and the decree of October 9, 1925, from the Council of People's Commissars of the USSR tried to set up some coherent relationship between collectivization and land settlement.[54] Separate rules,

---

[48] His criticisms are in his *Zemel'noe ustroistvo*, pp. 84–89. Pershin objected only to the tsarist government, not to the reform programs. His faith in the general course that the Stolypin reform followed is clear (e.g., p. iii). Since 1930, of course, his writings have adhered strictly to the Soviet line.

[49] Iakovlev, *Nasha*, p. 54.

[50] Pershin, *Zemel'noe ustroistvo*, pp. 101–102. An order from Moscow guberniia of May 4, 1927, describes the realignment of the peasant fields from strips into square lots, and the desired result tallies precisely with what the tsarist specialists called partial consolidation. See Yaney, "Concept of Stolypin Land Reform," pp. 289–291; and *Sbornik*, pp. 173–174.

[51] Bochkov gives a survey of the legislation on land settlement in the early 1920's (pp. 129–150). For a selection of the laws themselves, see *Sbornik*, pp. 11–115.

[52] *Sbornik*, p. 57.

[53] *Ibid.*, p. 87.

[54] *Ibid.*, p. 35.

however, did not constitute a new concept of land reform. The types of land settlement described in the 1923 decree were essentially the same as those the tsarist government had been carrying out, and the 1925 decree represented a departure from collectivization, not from land settlement. As noted above, it authorized the specialists to form individual, consolidated plots in villages where the peasants preferred them to collectivization. The Party Instruction of October 20, 1927, admitted that Soviet law contained no guide for land settlement work and recommended, as the best set of rules available, a project code of land settlement procedures that had been drawn up in the Ukrainian SSR by P. N. Pershin, an ex-tsarist servitor. Pershin's project represented no serious departure from tsarist programs and regulations.[55]

While socialist land settlement was thriving under the pretext that it was furthering the cause of collectivization, the specialists were letting the existing sovkhozy and kolkhozy flounder along on their own. According to one official report from early 1929, land settlement operations carried out on kolkhoz and sovkhoz land in the RSFSR by the end of 1928 had covered a total of 9.1 million hectares,[56] which compares very poorly to the 152.6 million hectares that supposedly represent the total area affected by land settlement in the RSFSR during the same period. The specialists' inclination to ignore the collectivized area appears all the more pronounced if it is kept in mind that most of the land settlement work that was done in it was carried out in 1928. Of the 9.1 million hectares of collectivized land on which land settlement was carried out to the end of 1928, 4.4 million were on kolkhoz land, and of this only 1.4 million were completed in the years prior to 1928.[57] It is true that kolkhozy and sovkhozy covered only a small area in toto. The most passionate devotion to collectivization would not have allowed the specialists to cover more ground than was there. In fact, however, the specialists did not cover all the collectivized area. As of late 1927, less than half of the kolkhoz area and only 77 percent of sovkhoz land had benefited from their ministrations,[58] and even at the end of 1928—November 1, to be exact— the specialists had touched only 75 percent of kolkhoz land.[59] All these figures are probably grossly inaccurate, but the proportional relation between them furnishes a reasonably reliable indication of what was really going on. It was not in anyone's interest to distort the figures to emphasize the specialists' neglect of collectives.

Before 1928, many collective farms were simply groups of peasants who

---

[55] The project is in *Sprav. zem.*, pp. 45–53.
[56] *Sten. ot.*, p. 492.
[57] *Ibid.*, p. 335.
[58] *Ibid.*, p. 253; *Sprav. zem.*, p. 26.
[59] *Sten. ot.*, p. 485.

called themselves artels or TOZs but did nothing to change their methods of land use or land distribution.[60] Apparently interested only in the financial aid for which peasants who claimed to be forming collectives were eligible, they continued to live in their villages and to hold their lands in separate strips along with their uncollectivized brethren, living just as they always had in practice but giving lip service to the government's slogans.[61] Those kolkhozy and sovkhozy that did undergo land settlement were most often in fact divided into integral farms that were cultivated separately by each household. Concerning the sovkhozy, a reference work for agricultural specialists published in 1928 noted that land settlement on these state farms should not consist of "the cutting away of separate plots from the sovkhoz land for 'rational' land use by individual peasants *as has been done up to this time.*" Instead, sovkhoz lands should be consolidated into a single area to be farmed as a unit.[62] Judging from this, land settlement on the sovkhozy before 1928 very often meant little more than the formation of individually held, integral farms.[63] As for kolkhozy, Iakovlev noted in 1924 that the artels he observed had all taken form from the peasants' desire for consolidation of their strips into integral, individual lots;[64] and in January, 1929, a high-level NKZ official (Rozit) observed that most of the tiny kolkhozy that had been formed in 1928 were really *otruby,* i.e., individually held, integral farms.[65] There is evidence to support his assertion. Official figures for 1926 indicate that 55.5 percent of the artel land and 33 percent of the TOZ land was collectivized,[66] but, as Lewin has demonstrated, such general tabulations were practically worthless.[67] Somewhat more reliable are sample data taken from a

[60] Collective farms (kolkhozy) were of three general types: the *kommuna,* artel, and TOZ (*tovarishchestvo sovmestnoi obrabotki zemli*). In the *kommuna,* all the land, tools, and animals of the members were held collectively, whereas in the artel and the TOZ, prior to 1929, the relative amounts of property held collectively and individually could vary widely. The state farms (sovkhozy) were yet another affair. They were in theory state-managed farm enterprises that hired peasants to work as laborers. In practice, however, they varied widely. Some were bona fide factory-type enterprises. I am indebted to Professor Otto Schiller for the information that, before 1928, a number of rather large state farms were operated by foreign firms at a profit. Professor Schiller himself managed one in the Kuban in the period 1924–1928 on behalf of the Krupp Company in Germany. The fact remains, however, that many of the Russian-managed sovkhozy were little more than village farms much like the kolkhozy. There were a few of them in 1920 with areas as small as ten hectares (Knipovich, p. 13).

[61] Lewin, pp. 102, 242–244.

[62] *Sprav. zem.,* p. 29 (italics mine).

[63] *Materialy po perspektivnomu planu razvitiia sel'skogo i lesnogo khoziaistva, 1928/29–1932/33* (Parts I and II, Moscow, 1929), I, 63–64. Concerning the general nature of the sovkhozy, see above, n. 60.

[64] Iakovlev, *Nasha,* p. 54.

[65] *Sten. ot.,* p. 393.

[66] Wesson, p. 140.

[67] Lewin, pp. 98–99.

field survey of October, 1927, which show that, although the *kommuny* were collectivizing all of their *sown* land, the artels only collectivized 13.5 percent and the TOZs, 2.9 percent.[68] Doubtless, much of the difference between the percentages derived from the sample data and those from the official tabulations can be accounted for by subtracting the collectivized forests and meadowland, most of which the peasants already held in common in their traditional villages, from the total collectivized area. It is also probable, however, that the figures tabulated from official reports were simply exaggerated. In any case, it is clear that "collectivization" before 1928 went forward not only without much land settlement but also without much collectivization.

The pressure that the Party exerted in 1928–1929 to speed up and to "improve" collectivization[69] served only to intensify the campaign for land settlement. The Party called for larger artels and *kommuny*,[70] but the specialists concentrated more than ever on the formation of small TOZs.[71] Instead of increasing, the percentage of the land belonging to the members of the collectives that was actually owned by the collective farms and worked collectively declined somewhat in 1928.[72] The percentage of this land that was consolidated, however, rose sharply. Three-fourths of the land belonging to members of collectives was *consolidated* by the end of 1928;[73] yet something less than 10 to 20 percent of the sown land in TOZs and artels was actually worked collectively. The deduction is inescapable that most of the consolidated *sown* land in the collective farms was held and worked as individually held plots. In 1928–1929, the specialists were simply forming clusters of individual, consolidated farms, or *otruby*, and calling them kolkhozy.

The nature of these consolidated farms must have varied widely, but in a typical collectivization the members of a collective would continue to live together with the nonmembers in the old village cluster of houses, while their strips in each of the village fields would be combined into one lot. The "collective," then, would consist of a number of plots, one in each of the village's fields. Each field would contain at one end the strips of the uncollectivized villagers and at the other, the collectivized lot. In the collectivized lot the members of the collective were supposed to eliminate the strips and work all the land together as a team, and when they actually did this, they were in

---

[68] *Materialy po perspektivnomu planu,* I, 84.
[69] Moshkov, pp. 41–42.
[70] *Ibid.*
[71] According to Lewin, pp. 378–381, the emphasis on small TOZs continued at least until October, 1929. Moshkov, p. 42, asserts that the TOZs formed in 1928–1929 were larger on the average than those formed earlier, but his source is a publication of the early 1930's and therefore not reliable.
[72] *Sten. ot.,* p. 482.
[73] *Ibid.,* p. 341.

fact a collective farm of sorts.[74] Alternatively, however, each member of the collective could take one or more of the lots and farm them individually, and, indeed, the figures presented above indicate that this was probably the usual arrangement throughout the 1920's. Prior to forced collectivization, then, kolkhozy were generally akin to what the reformers of the tsarist regime had called a village divided into *otrub* or partially *otrub* farms.

It should be added, finally, that many kolkhozy actually formed in 1928 were of such small size as to represent little more than large families. *Average* sown area of TOZs formed in 1928 was 27.5 hectares; that of artels, 43.7 hectares; and that of *kommuny*, 69.3 hectares.[75] *Kommuny*, comprising about 13 percent of all collective farms in early 1929,[76] seem to have been the only collectives that actually lent themselves to the development of socialized agriculture. Official statistics often claimed high crop yields from them in the 1920's, but they are probably bogus. The *kommuny* were made up almost entirely of poor peasants without stock, and as of 1928 over 97 percent of them paid wages according to the number of workers in each family rather than the amount of work done,[77] a clear indication that they were still following primitive village traditions and were not effectively organized for production. On the whole, the kolkhozy of 1929 consisted of small groups of peasants—rarely more than a half-dozen families—who were consolidating their private strips into private lots.

Thus the collectivization boondoggle. There is no evidence apart from standard Communist denunciations of bourgeois specialists to indicate that the specialists of 1928–1929 were consciously conspiring among themselves to hoodwink the Communists or to seize power. The only explanation for their conduct that makes sense to me is simply that it stemmed from attitudes toward the peasants that individual specialists acquired as they did their jobs. Each specialist perpetrated frauds more or less consciously on specific occasions, usually in order to carry out practical projects for improving agriculture that were acceptable to the peasants but not to the government. By and large, the specialists seem to have believed sincerely and even fanatically that their work was actually bringing the Communist regime the support it desired. Land reform would increase agricultural productivity, and this would solve the government's problems.

It would also be incorrect to see the specialists' actions as mistakes or de-

[74] This process is described and illustrated in Bochkov, pp. 172–173.

[75] *Materialy po perspektivnomu planu*, I, 81. Bochkov, p. 158, reports that the average size of the collective farms in 1921–1925 in the RSFSR had been 154 hectares.

[76] *Sten. ot.*, p. 33.

[77] *Materialy po perspektivnomu planu*, I, 85.

partures from some imagined true path, or to conclude that because the alliance of rhetoric was absurd from a strictly logical point of view it must have been senseless or irresponsible. If the Communists had little more than rhetoric and an army to hold the country together in the early years of the Soviet regime, and if they realized in early 1921 that the army could not do the job, then an alliance of rhetoric was the only device they had that would allow them to pull the disparate elements of the state organization together.[78] Agricultural specialists were not the only ones to accept such an alliance with the Soviet government, nor were they the only ones to face the absolutely uncompromising choice between government under the Bolsheviks and no government at all. M. J. Larsons, a Russian banker before the revolution and a servitor of the Soviet government until 1923, when he left Russia, wrote the following description of the general attitude of specialists of all kinds who chose to serve the Soviet government:

> . . . there is a great number of experts in Soviet Russia who are . . . pronounced anti-communists, but who are nevertheless working assiduously and honestly to the best of their knowledge and their conscience. They are just serving their country . . . although this regime is either indifferent or hateful to them. They will be the first to leave the ship of State, once it is on the rocks. . . . On the other hand there are very many experts in Soviet Russia with tendencies to the Left, typical intellectuals who are not thinking "communistically," but who, nevertheless, do their duty faithfully and conscientiously, because of the two alternatives—tsardom or Soviet regime—they consciously prefer the latter. . . . They enter the service of the Soviet Government quite consciously, [and] are working with conviction for the reconstruction of the country.[79]

Surely, it would be fatuous to describe such men as essentially treacherous, ridiculous, or mistaken.

VI

The alliance of rhetoric was an understandable development and could even be viewed as a triumph of political organization, but it did not resolve the contradictions between agrarian reform and Soviet state. The cornerstone of the alliance was the Communist Party's practical indifference to rural so-

---

[78] The Soviet regime's utter inability to exert any kind of managerial control over industry or agriculture in the early 1920's is described exhaustively in R. W. Davies, *The Development of the Soviet Budgetary System* (Cambridge: Cambridge University Press, 1958), pp. 6–130.

[79] M. J. Larsons, *An Expert in the Service of the Soviet* (London: Ernest Benn, 1929), pp. 172–173.

ciety (see above, ns. 24, 26, and 27), and this in turn rested on the ability of rural Russia to furnish enough grain to satisfy the government's needs. In early 1928, when the grain supply to the cities began to fail noticeably,[80] it marked the beginning of the end of the alliance. Communist indifference to the countryside quickly changed to anxious concern and grain procurement campaigns. The cornerstone of the alliance of rhetoric crumbled rapidly, just as the agrarian reform it had fostered was reaching significant dimensions. The evidence does not show any intention or even realization on the part of the Communists that active grain procurement should or would lead to a clash with the specialists.[81] The campaigns began in January, 1928, and it was not until late 1929, almost two years later, that the clash came. The question remains, then: How did the alliance of rhetoric dissolve?

The background to the grain shortage that developed in the cities in 1928–1929 has been discussed in many scholarly works in great detail.[82] Suffice it to say here that it proceeded from the Party's attempts from 1925 on to build up Russia's industrial plant as rapidly as possible under central government direction without benefit of foreign investment or borrowing. I. Deutscher and A. Nove have suggested that the series of decisions and experiments that went into the formation of this policy were not necessarily the best possible ones, but that they were by no means uniformly unintelligent, given the circumstances the regime had to face.[83] Intelligently or unintelligently, the fact is that the government undertook the risk of producing serious economic dislocation in 1925–1926, without making any provision for the possible untoward consequences. Large-scale investment in heavy industry seems to have set off an inflationary trend, which the government tried to offset in 1926–1928 by purchasing ever larger quantities of grain at artificially low prices, and this caused the peasants to cut down on the amount of grain they brought to market.[84] Grain export fell to practically nothing by 1928,[85] and as the cities began to feel the shortage there were strikes among the workers, protesting the high price of grain in private markets.[86] By

[80] Lewin, pp. 260–261.

[81] *Ibid.*, pp. 245–250, 393.

[82] The general nature of the problems of Russian economic development is outlined in A. Baykov, "The Economic Development of Russia," *Economic History Review*, VII (December, 1954), 137–149.

[83] See I. Deutscher, *The Prophet Unarmed* (London: Oxford University Press, 1959), pp. 223–246; and A. Nove, *Economic Rationality and Soviet Politics* (New York: Praeger, 1964), pp. 20–25.

[84] Moshkov, p. 29. Jerzy Karcz has argued very convincingly that the government's attempt to lower grain prices in 1926–1927 was profoundly inept. It marked the first in a series of blunders that led to forced collectivization. See his "Thoughts on the Grain Problem," *Soviet Studies*, XVIII, no. 4 (April, 1967), 399–430.

[85] Moshkov, p. 52.

[86] Lewin, pp. 341, 393–395.

the end of 1927, then, an urban grain shortage of significant proportions was at hand. The Party, however, does not seem to have realized it until early 1928. Lewin tells us that the discussions in the Fifteenth Party Congress in December, 1927, reflect no awareness that some new policy might be necessary in the countryside.[87] Thus, on the eve of its food procurement campaign, the Party does not seem to have known (or to have been willing to discuss) what effects its industrial policies had produced in the villages. When the grain shortage did become noticeable, the Party had no plan for coping with it. In short, the growth of the Soviet government's industrial policy in 1925–1930 (and its effects) did not proceed from a plan. It was more like a series of reactions to the unforeseen consequences of its own actions, with each reaction producing a yet more desperate situation.[88]

The same generalization applies to the evolution of the food procurement campaign. Active procurement of grain by forced seizure began at the end of December, 1927, following the Fifteenth Party Congress. The congress had not called for forced procurement,[89] but, according to Lewin, reports of a bad harvest came in from some grain-producing areas in December, 1927, and these indicated that the grain supply problem would shortly become crucial.[90] The full significance of the oncoming grain shortage became apparent to the Communist leaders in February, 1928, and it was then that Stalin embarked on massive seizures in Siberia, taking up once again the wartime practice of sending gangs of the urban "loyal" into the countryside to confiscate *kulak* grain hoards.[91]

Stalin's campaigns got enough grain to satisfy immediate needs in early 1928, but in the months that followed, the peasants responded—as they had in the time of war communism—by planting less grain and/or hiding what they harvested.[92] In 1929, the food shortage in the towns again grew worse, and rationing had to be introduced in all of them.[93] In the countryside, the forced procurement programs expanded in scope and intensity. By late summer, more than 100,000 of the urban loyal were out in the villages hounding the peasants for grain.[94] New decrees regarding grain confiscation allowed the agents very broad powers, mainly by using the metaphor *kulak* to mean anyone with grain in storage.[95]

[87] *Ibid.*, pp. 177–190. See also Moshkov, pp. 32–33.
[88] Lewin, p. 223; Karcz, pp. 421–427.
[89] Moshkov, pp. 32–33.
[90] Lewin, pp. 193–197.
[91] *Ibid.*, pp. 199–207, describes Stalin's Siberian campaign of early 1928.
[92] Moshkov, pp. 31–35.
[93] *Ibid.*, p. 52.
[94] Lewin, pp. 343–349, and Moshkov, pp. 66–69, describe the forced seizures of 1929.
[95] Moshkov cites the law of June 28, 1929, as an example. It allowed village soviets

By mid-1929, the state was forcing the peasants to sell grain to it according to quotas assigned to each household by local soviets, an arrangement quite similar to what had once been called war communism.[96] In the short run, this was effective. The 1929 harvest was slightly smaller than that of 1928 (71.7 billion kilograms in 1929 as compared to 73.3 billion in 1928);[97] yet 16 million tons of grain came into the government's distribution system in 1929, as opposed to only 11 million in 1928.[98] Nevertheless, it gradually became clear that forced procurement by itself would not be enough. Despite the fact that the grain supply was adequate by the end of 1929, the threat of peasant resistance now loomed larger than ever. In the RSFSR, 702 instances of rural violence were reported for 1928, and 1,002 for the first nine months of 1929. Three hundred of the government's rural agents lost their lives in 1927–1929.[99] More ominous than scattered violence was the threat of a large-scale decrease in sown area. Reports from the countryside in late 1929 indicated that if the peasants were left to themselves in the spring of 1930, they would sow much less than they had in the previous year.[100] Moshkov indicates that this was when the Party had to decide whether to give up its forced programs and withdraw from the countryside, as it had in 1921, or form a permanent organization in the villages that would see not only to the procurement of grain but also to its planting, growing, and harvesting.[101]

The government's first attempt to exert any direct influence on the peasants to increase their sown area came in early 1928. No one had had any experience at this sort of thing, and so the first moves consisted of nothing more than vague orders to the local soviets that they should agitate among the peasants. A few local leaders tried to gather the peasants together and persuade them to sign agreements to sow more land, but this seems to have produced no positive result.[102] In the ensuing year, however, an elaborate program of *kontraktatsiia* developed. At first, *kontraktatsiia* had the appearance of a measure of agricultural improvement. Some peasants signed agreements to sow certain fields and use new methods and also to sell a certain portion of the harvest to the government at a fixed price. In return, the

---

(in the elections for which the *kulaki* could not participate) to assign grain delivery quotas to separate households as they wished and to punish any failures to meet the quotas. Thus, the soviets could act either on their own or under compulsion from government agents to take grain from whoever had it (pp. 63–65).

[96] *Ibid.*, p. 65.
[97] *Ibid.*, pp. 19–20.
[98] Lewin, pp. 366–367.
[99] *Ibid.*, pp. 219–221, 349–350.
[100] Moshkov, pp. 75–81; Lewin, pp. 394–395.
[101] Moshkov, pp. 65–67.
[102] Lewin, pp. 239–240.

government undertook to advance seeds, tools, and/or credit to the peasants. None of this came to anything because the government failed to make the promised advances,[103] but in 1929, the use of contracts persisted and expanded as a means simply to force the peasants to sow enough grain to meet the government's demands as well as their own needs.[104]

By itself, *kontraktatsiia* did not turn out to be an effective way to force the peasants to increase their crop land. If force continued to be the basic means to get grain to the cities, then force would also have to be used to get the seed into the ground. At about this time it occurred to the Communist leaders that the collective farm might serve as an effective machinery for forcing the peasants not merely to deliver grain but also to plant, cultivate, and harvest it. In December, 1929, the Party called for a rapid intensification of the collectivization campaign and this soon turned into the campaign of forced collectivization.[105] At this point, collectivization abruptly ceased to be a boondoggle and became instead an elaborate method of forced grain procurement.

Considered solely as a method of imposing forced quotas of grain production and delivery, there can be no doubt that forming collectives was a sound idea. The agricultural administrators of the German occupation forces in 1941–1943 noted that the collective farm was an admirable means to organize forced production and procurement of grain, and they tried to keep them in operation in most of the territory they occupied.[106] In December of 1929, however, the decision to use collectivization as a means to attack the peasantry brought the Communists into open conflict with the specialists. Collectivization, after all, had been their affair, and until 1929, collectivization had been in fact an agrarian reform movement that explicitly rejected force as a means to secure the peasants' cooperation.

Thus, the confrontation in 1929. The specialists had influence in the countryside, but they could not and would not accomplish the state's purposes. This was no mere dissident group, to be denounced at a congress or dismissed in disgrace. True, the specialists' points of view could be and were rejected when their advocates ventured to express them. Bukharin, for example, was shouted down in a meeting of the Party Central Committee

---

103 *Ibid.*, pp. 240–241.
104 *Ibid.*, pp. 360–361.
105 M. L. Bogdenko, "K istorii nachal'nogo etapa sploshnoi kollektivizatsii sel'skogo khoziaistva SSSR," *Voprosy istorii*, no. 5 (May, 1963), pp. 20–25; and M. A. Vyltsan *et al.*, "Nekotorye problemy istorii kollektivizatsii v SSSR," *ibid.*, no. 3 (March, 1965), pp. 3–25.
106 O. Schiller, *Ziele und Ergebnisse der Agrarordnung in den besetzten Ostgebieten* (Berlin: Reichsnährstandsverlag, 1943), p. 3.

that took place in November, 1928, when he claimed that the Party's use of force was destroying the peasants' incentive to produce and leading to the "degradation" of agriculture. According to Moshkov, Bukharin got these ideas from the *spetsialisty-agrarniki*.[107] In early 1929, Bukharin, still unbowed, wrote: "We shall conquer on the basis of scientific economic management or we shan't conquer at all,"[108] but by then his fight with Stalin had become an open affair, and his days of power were numbered. Muzzling Bukharin was one thing, however, and dispensing with the specialists was quite another. The specialists were a functioning link in the machinery of state—the only operational contact between government and peasants. So long as forced procurement was the Party's only aim in the countryside, operational contact with the peasants was not a necessity. Any thug from the city could be sent to search for grain hoards. But how could the Party hope to supervise planting, cultivating, and harvesting in any effective way exclusively through urban agents? Were not the specialists indispensable? On the face of it, it would seem that discharging the specialists en masse on the grounds that they would not collectivize properly made about as much sense as dismissing all the officers and men in the army because they could not fight properly. Yet, on the other hand, the Party had no way of coping with the specialists. Their manner of opposing the Party made them impervious to open debate or negotiation. Lacking any formal organization, the specialists could not have negotiated as a group even if they had wanted to. They had been agreeing with and echoing Communist rhetoric for over a decade, and in 1929, many of them, notably Iakovlev, were continuing to agree with every new absurdity that the Party expressed, while in the countryside, in the midst of all the search-and-seizure gangs and the growing hostility of Party activists, they were going right on with land reform at a faster rate than ever before, as if there had never been a Communist revolution. What, then, were the Communist grain procurers to do with the specialists?

VII

The forced collectivization campaign embodied the unequivocal decision that the specialists were to be dispensed with. They were not attacked directly in any official way. No law explicitly banished them from the countryside or forbade them to continue working. What happened, rather, was that a

[107] Moshkov, pp. 38–39.
[108] Lewin, p. 300.

series of decrees produced the cumulative effect of depriving their positions of any significance and making land reform according to their lights impossible.

The first official step was the order of January 7, 1930, which changed the land settlement process so radically as to make it unrecognizable. It directed that all land reform projects in the individual sector—i.e., the great majority of them—be abandoned abruptly and all effort concentrated on the collectives. Existing land settlement procedures and technical requirements were to be disregarded. Indeed, the only element of land reform that remained was an extremely simple injunction that "all boundary lines separating the land allotments of the members of the artel are to be eliminated and all fields are to be combined in a single land mass."[109] The basic rule governing the rearrangement of the fields was that the process would have to be completed before spring planting. Not only was the technique of land settlement extremely simplified but also the administrative processes by which it was carried out. A project for forming a collective required only the approval of its president-to-be, an agricultural specialist, and the raion executive committee (*ispolkom*). *No authority higher than the raion* had to know anything about the projects, which meant, in effect, that local specialists could not protest the projects to the NKZ.[110]

Given the simplification of the requirements for land settlement and the pressure from the Party on all branches of the government to get on with collectivization, the local specialist's vote on land settlement projects could not have retained any significance. To make the situation even more clear, an order of January 18, 1930, explicitly stripped the specialists of the direct executive authority (*rukovodstvo*) they had been exercising over land reform since about 1925 and put it in the hands of local executive committees.[111]

Actually, the laws of 1924–1925 had only implied that the specialists were to *rukovodit'* land settlement projects. The order of the Council of People's Commissars of the USSR of December 1, 1924, and that of the Central Executive Committee of the USSR of May 5, 1925, put land settlement in the hands of collegial commissions made up of the local executive committees, specialists, and elected representatives from the villages, much as the 1930 laws were to do.[112] The implication of the orders from the central government, however, seems to have been made explicit in those from the local agencies. An order of April 30, 1925, from the Moscow guberniia

[109] Statute on artels of 1930, printed in *Spravochnik po kolkhoznomu stroitel'stvu* (Leningrad, 1931), p. 146.
[110] *Ibid.*, pp. 146–147.
[111] The circular of March 6, 1930, which was based on the order of January 18, is in *ibid.*, pp. 145–146.
[112] The orders are in *Sbornik*, pp. 19–29.

administration specified that the executive committees were only "to supervise" (*nabliudat'*), whereas the specialists were "to carry out" (*rukovodit'*),[113] and in early 1928, a project law to govern land settlement, approved by the Central Executive Committee of the USSR, expressly ascribed *rukovodstvo* of the projects to the agricultural specialists.[114] At last, in December, 1928, this project became law, and the tendency to turn land settlement over to the specialists reached its full development.[115] The orders of January 7 and 18, 1930, then, embodied a sudden and drastic change of policy. Local specialists were abruptly stripped of their functional roles, cut off from their own central organization—the NKZ—and left with no part to play in the countryside except that of rubber stamps. It seems that many of them either quit or were discharged.[116]

Who did carry out forced collectivization? The first significant step the Party took to develop some sort of rural organization of activists was a combination purge and recruiting campaign in the rural areas, carried out in 1929–1930, that was intended to get the "careerists" out of the rural Party cells and to enroll more of the "poor toilers" from city and country.[117] The effect of the purge, however, was to drum out many members of peasant origin and to replace them mostly with members drawn from the cities.[118]

This was a beginning, but it was not enough to set up a new administration in the countryside capable of carrying out a crash program of collectivization. It will be recalled that the carrying out of so simple a process as the grain procurement campaign of late 1929 required 100,000 activists from the city. In 1930, the total number of activists, machine repairmen, and what have you who went to the villages reached 180,000, and many of these stayed on for several months.[119] It is impossible to say how much of this urban crowd worked on collectivization. Division of labor was not an important element in rural organization in 1930, and squadrons sent out to do one job often ended up doing another. One report complained that the

---

[113] *Ibid.*, p. 151.

[114] V. P. Miliutin, *Novyi zakon o zemleustroistve i zemlepol'zovanii* (Moscow, 1928), p. 59.

[115] The law is printed in *Izvestiia*, December 16, 1928, pp. 4–5.

[116] Bochkov, p. 194, says that in 1930–1934, many specialists concluded that there was no more for them to do in the countryside. He also says, p. 216, that in 1939, only 3 percent of the operating agricultural specialists had had any higher education. In January, 1928, 14 percent had had higher education (*Sprav. zem.*, p. 225).

[117] A. Kh. Mitrofanov, *Itogi chistki partii* (Moscow, 1930), p. 4.

[118] *Ibid.*, pp. 48, 55–58, 63. Of the total Party membership, 10.4 percent were expelled during the purge, but in the rural areas, 16.9 percent were expelled. Somewhat more new members were taken in than were expelled, and the vast majority of them were workers or officials. Yet Party membership in the collective farms doubled—not conclusive evidence, but it is indicative.

[119] Moshkov, pp. 84–86.

specially selected teams sent by the Party to carry out its purge were drafted into sowing and collectivization campaigns by local authorities and never did get around to purging anyone.[120]

In the early months of 1930, many of the urban loyal were engaged in forced sowing, i.e., procuring seed wherever they could find it and driving the peasants into the fields to plant it. Their method seems to have been to descend on villages in mobs and to go from house to house, taking whatever seed they found. Moshkov reports a typical event in the seed procurement campaign wherein 200 activists came to a village in the North Caucasus and spent a day and a night going from house to house "to persuade" the villagers to hand over their stores. Decisive measures of this sort on a large scale made the seed campaign quantitatively successful. The sown area in 1930 reached a record high. Moshkov also informs us, however, that many peasants had to slaughter their animals because they had no grain left to feed them,[121] and Shuvaev, writing about Voronezh guberniia, notes that much of the sowing carried out in 1930–1931 to suit the demands of the urban activists was carried out on waste and meadow land.[122] The sharp drop in productivity per unit area in 1931–1934 suggests that the forced sowing of 1930 and 1931 not only wasted seed on unproductive land but also disrupted crop rotation for years to come.[123]

The most significant activity of 1930, however, was not the purging of Party cells or forced planting, but forced collectivization itself. Forced collectivization entered its massive stage in November, 1929, when the Plenum of the Party Central Committee decided to send 25,000 industrial workers to the villages in the grain-producing areas.[124] These were to carry out (*rukovodit'*) collectivization in such a way as to complete the process before spring planting in 1930.[125] They were to travel to the villages with their families at government expense, and so long as they remained active, they were to continue to receive their salaries from the enterprises at which they had been employed. An order from the Council of People's Commissars of September 4, 1930, called upon enterprises to go on paying the salaries of their workers

[120] Mitrofanov, p. 12.
[121] Moshkov, pp. 77–81.
[122] K. M. Shuvaev, *Staraia i novaia derevnia* (Moscow, 1937), p. 71.
[123] Even the grossly exaggerated Soviet figures of the early 1930's show a drop in the harvest after 1930 at the same time the sown area increased (Moshkov, pp. 110–112, 223–230). Much of the record harvest of 1930—if there was one—may well have come from land that should have been left fallow. Bochkov speaks rather vaguely of crop rotation being very disorganized throughout the 1930's and he states repeatedly that land settlement remained a vital need up to World War II (pp. 190–193, 198–199, 213–218).
[124] For the areas within the grain-producing regions in which "sploshnaia kollektivizatsiia" was carried forward in early 1930, see Bogdenko, pp. 20–25.
[125] *Sprav. kolkh.*, pp. 74–76.

in the villages yet another year.[126] Moshkov tells us that 19,600 of the
"25,000" came to the villages in early 1930, and that their number subsequently increased to 35,000.[127] Apparently, this was not enough. On February 1, 1930, the army announced that it would send 100,000 volunteers,
selected for their "political literacy," to the villages of the grain-producing
regions to *rukovodit'* the formation of kolkhozy,[128] and an order of February
16, 1930, called for 7,200 members of urban soviets to volunteer for a
year's service as *rukovoditeli* in the villages.[129] None of these orders said
anything about the technical qualifications of the volunteers or the manner
in which they would be employed. For the central government it sufficed to
say that they were to be experienced organizers and "politically literate,"
that they were to go to the villages, and that they were to *rukovodit'*.[130]

The crash campaigns for sowing, procurement, and collectivization continued for well over a year in the grain-producing regions.[131] The last forced
sowing by an officially proclaimed campaign came in the spring of 1931,
and collectivization and grain procurement ceased to be called campaigns
only after 1932. The last rural purge connected with these campaigns came
in 1933, when Party politotdely were set up in the Machine Tractor Stations
to conduct yet another sweeping attack on what remained of rural administration. Only in 1934 did a much-purged NKZ begin to resume a measure
of control over agriculture through normal administrative methods.[132]

To sum up, forced collectivization was, among other things, a process
whereby the central government unleashed a mob of somewhat less than
200,000 urban workers and soldiers on the villages in the grain-producing regions with de facto power to do anything they could organize themselves to
do. Ostensibly, they were to form the peasants into productive units; actually, their only enforceable orders were to get grain. It is highly doubtful that
any uniform policy was followed. It is even questionable that in all cases the
boundaries between the little strips of village land were really plowed
under.[133] In short, there was no systematic control to assure that the government's new emissaries would show any respect either for the peasants' rights

[126] *Ibid.*, pp. 84–85.
[127] Moshkov, p. 85.
[128] *Sprav. kolkh.*, p. 91.
[129] *Ibid.*, pp. 85–86.
[130] *Ibid.*, pp. 74–75, 84–85, 91.
[131] Moshkov, pp. 83–220, describes the various campaigns.
[132] R. F. Miller, "The Politotdel: A Lesson from the Past," *Slavic Review*, XXV,
no. 3 (September, 1966), 475–496.
[133] Shuvaev, pp. 70–76, noted in 1937 that the fields of two ostensibly collectivized
villages in Voronezh were still divided into the old strips (the result, he says, of the
efforts of Trotskyite-Bukharinist saboteurs, together with Japanese and German spies).
Bochkov refers to continuing difficulties with land settlement in the 1930's (see
above, n. 123).

or for the government's orders. Only one thing is clear: the countryside did deliver an adequate amount of grain to the towns in 1930 and in the years thereafter. What actually happened to the land, however, was known only to those who were on it, and to this day no scholar has described in any systematic way what forced collectivization really did to the villages.[134]

VIII

Stalin's decision to force collectivization as a means to insure regular grain delivery to the cities was brutal and extremely harmful to the rural social order. It should be kept in mind, however, that the arbitrary violence of the early 1930's did not spring so much from the orders of this or that Party leader as from the nature of the process itself. The choice facing the Party leaders in 1929 was not merely between one policy and another: What are our aims? What regulations should we impose? How should we define the powers of the government's agents? The practical alternatives were much further apart: land reform by a bureaucracy of specialists, or invasion by a mob of "loyal" ignoramuses. The choice of late 1929 was between these two, *and there was no middle ground.*

The reason there was no middle ground was that the agricultural specialists were both a movement and a bureaucratic administration, and the Soviet government could not attack the movement without also destroying its own administrative system. With the elimination of the specialists, the Party destroyed the only bureaucratic machinery the Soviet government had in rural Russia, thereby completely severing itself from the peasantry. The potpourri of rural Party cells, village soviets, and raion executive committees could neither carry out orders, nor enforce regulations, nor even furnish the central government with reliable information. There were, of course, NKVD agents and a variety of special inspectors and amateur informants, but they did not get to the villages very often, and when they did they rarely found any reliable basis for judging who was acting properly and who was not. By what standard were they to decide? In any case, the secret agents could do no more than remark on what had already happened, and their personal, unstandardized reports, though valuable in the absence of any systematic administration, could no more sustain an effective flow of information than had those of Nicholas I's Third Section a century before.[135]

---

[134] M. L. Bogdenko and I. E. Zelenin in "Osnovye problemy istorii kollektivizatsii sel'skogo khoziaistva v sovremennoi sovetskoi istoricheskoi literature," *Ist. sov. krest'.*, pp. 191–222, said in 1963 that historians have not yet attempted to study "the internal development of the kolkhozy and the sovkhozy" (p. 197). The peasant farm "lies outside the field of vision of the historian" (p. 210).

[135] On the NKVD and other nonsystematic sources of information, see M. Fainsod,

In late 1929, then, Stalin had not only to change his policy; he had to abandon what there was of administration and social structure in rural Russia and to build up a new organization from scratch, one that could begin *immediately* to force the peasants to plant seed and deliver harvests on the government's terms. The specific measures the Party leaders wanted carried out in the countryside were of relatively little significance next to the simple fact that no trained men or any organization or institution were available to carry them out. Under the circumstances, it is not relevant to speak of "mistakes" marring an otherwise sound procedure in 1928–1933, as Soviet scholars are fond of doing. If one admits that some sort of force was necessary in order to get grain to the cities, then it will not do to complain that there was too much of it or that it was not directed properly. *The government had to get rid of the specialists*, and this meant that it had to give up all hope of controlling or directing what happened in the countryside.

The specialists were not pushed aside because they had failed the government. On the contrary, they had served the Soviet government well in the countryside. For 23 years, they had been working not only to increase agricultural productivity but also to introduce the basic elements of rational law and administration to peasant society. Despite extensive rural violence, wars, famines, and political collapses, they had succeeded and were succeeding to a remarkable degree. Such was the strength of their movement and its roots in rural society that, in 1928–1929, their programs were going forward with increasing vigor despite the explicit opposition of the government as a whole. In 1929, however, the Party leaders decided that the need of the state was not to develop peasant society but to make war upon it, and this meant that all the service the movement had rendered to state and society became suddenly anachronistic. The very success of the specialists and the Communists in working together for agricultural development made it impossible for them to face the problem of grain procurement without breaking apart abruptly, each side feeling itself betrayed by the other.

IX

It is not my purpose to set forth anything so ambitious as a reinterpretation of the causes of forced collectivization, but it is appropriate to point to certain elements in Soviet government in the 1920's that the experience of the agricultural specialists brings out. It has been noted that, during the civil war, the Communists came to rely heavily on rhetoric as a substitute for ac-

Smolensk under Soviet Rule (Cambridge, Mass.: Harvard University Press, 1958), pp. 73–74, 84–86, 153–172, 378–408.

tions that seemed necessary but could not be carried out, and it has been further suggested that in the circumstances of civil war this was sound statesmanship. Confrontation between prerevolutionary rural administration and Party agitators produced a union that I have called an alliance of rhetoric, a device that brought together Party agitators who could not run anything and specialist-administrators who could manage programs but could not assume the responsibilities of political authority. Notwithstanding the advantages of an alliance between these two very disparate elements and the government's desperate need for it, it had its weaknesses, not the least of which was that it hindered the systematic flow of information. Administrators who had to play at agitation were not necessarily dishonest, but in general their confidence in one another often depended more on the agreement of their rhetoric than in the validity of the information they communicated to one another. This being a fact of life in the 1920's, administrators and specialists all too often suppressed valid information simply in order to preserve the confidence that their colleagues placed in them. Information that contradicted the rhetoric might very well be interpreted as a personal attack, and therefore administrators and specialists often suppressed what they knew, to a point where they came to expect one another to suppress information in the common interest. Under the conditions imposed by the alliance of rhetoric, all information, all debate, and all scholarly study were suspect. Thus the alliance made very difficult that systematic accumulation of statistics and scientific formulation of plans upon which the Soviet government was so desperately trying to base itself.

The weaknesses in the alliance of rhetoric suggest something about the social structure within which all those who were involved in governing the Soviet Union in the 1920's had to work and to identify themselves. There was such a social structure, as there is in any administration, and judgments about the behavior of individual Party leaders have too often failed to take it into account. It seems to me quite wrong to assume that the men who accepted the conditions of the alliance and worked as best they could within its atmosphere of abiding mistrust were *ipso facto* ignoble. Likewise, it will not do to assume that anyone who strove to impose order and direction upon the tangle of structures and movements that went to make up Soviet government was *ipso facto* a would-be tyrant lusting for power. Stalin, who ultimately did unite his colleagues and impose order on the government, was by no means the only man in the Soviet administration who identified his followers by their acceptance of his rhetoric, nor was he the only one to imagine conspiracies against himself when he heard his slogans questioned. Party leaders, administrators, and specialists all lived in a paranoiac climate thrust upon them by the cruel paradoxes posed by early Soviet history. The traditional scholarly propensity to attribute policy excesses and blunders in Soviet administration to personality disorders of the main actors (e.g., Stalin, Molotov, Kaganovich) is not a particularly fruitful approach to the study of collectivization or of the other major policy decisions of this historical period. Indeed, if the role of personality is to be assessed, it would seem much more to the point to ask what manner of man would have been able to hold Russia together at all in a time like 1928–1933.

2 : From Stalin to Brezhnev: Soviet Agricultural Policy in Historical Perspective

Jerzy F. Karcz

The task of writing a broad survey of Soviet agricultural policy is facilitated by detailed, careful studies by many of our colleagues and by the earlier work of such outstanding authorities as Jasny and Timoshenko, which provide in many instances the necessary background material for the painting of a broad panorama. My debt to them is thus acknowledged at the outset, but it will be worth our while to note what I still regard as an outstanding limitation on writers about to embark on sweeping generalizations. This limitation arises from significant differences in focus and concentration of attention on the part of writers dealing with the post-Stalin period as opposed to those who concerned themselves with agriculture in the early and the mature period of the personality cult. Many studies of Soviet society after 1953 benefited from the great advantages of careful estimates of Soviet national income prepared by Abram Bergson and his associates at the RAND Corporation, as well as by continuing study of the characteristic features of the Soviet command economy. Significant insights were also gained by concurrent interest in and greater understanding of developing societies as such, while the relatively large amount of statistical information provided by Soviet sources has by now been carefully sifted and evaluated by trained western economists in a manner unique in the history of economic analysis and of economic historiography.

By contrast, our knowledge of developments in the Soviet countryside during the relatively longer, equally interesting, and—in some respects—more crucial period of the 1920's, thirties, and forties is not, in general, based on background studies of identical quality. This is by no means the fault of those who worked on (and for the most part during) that period.

As is well known, the volume of statistical information dealing with agricultural developments after the collectivization drive was very considerably reduced and many of the available data were to a considerable extent "doctored" to suit the needs of the Soviet regime and its leaders. Thus, much effort undertaken by a highly qualified but numerically small body of experts had to be devoted to the construction of meaningful statistical series and to the clarification of many mysteries and inconsistencies of contemporaneous Soviet literature. The writers of that period also labored under the handicap of significant gaps in their understanding of the actual trends and of the functioning of Soviet economy as a whole, and they were understandably more concerned with the provision of a broader and more generalized account of Soviet rural life. Under the circumstances, it is not an exaggeration to say that rural and agricultural developments of that period still supply a relatively unexplored field of scientific research for historians and social scientists.[1]

I

A second look at and a careful review of many currently held beliefs and opinions appear to be in order for the period preceding the great industrialization drive and the collectivization of Soviet agriculture. That this is so for economists is patently indicated by the recent outstanding study of Moshe Lewin.[2] One of the fundamental conclusions that emerges from his research on the Soviet peasantry in the twenties is the fact that the Great Industrialization Debate as well as the various measures of Soviet economic policy implemented at that time (in the village as well as elsewhere) took place in an environment characterized by extreme scarcity of hard-core information and the relative abundance of conflicting and contradictory data that could easily be (and to a large extent were) used to bolster a political argument. This, I believe, is a fact of central importance for our understanding of this period and all those who ignore it proceed at their own peril. It is perhaps here that the practitioners of my own discipline, preoccupied as we are with many important and equally interesting problems, can render yeoman's service to

[1] This can be said even though N. Jasny's *The Socialized Agriculture of the USSR* (Stanford, Calif.: Stanford University Press, 1949) withstood remarkably well the acid test of time and further research. Jasny would have agreed with my plea for further research not only because the available data are steadily though slowly increasing but also because the focus of our research has shifted somewhat.
[2] M. Lewin, *La paysannerie et le pouvoir soviétique, 1929–1930* (Paris: Mouton and Co., 1967). An excellent English translation under the title *Russian Peasants and Soviet Power* (Evanston, Ill.: Northwestern University Press, 1968) is now available.

historians of all denominations by studying the twenties with all the care and professional expertise that is now employed in the study of the sixties.

The collectivization of Soviet agriculture is indeed the watershed in the history of Soviet rural society and a starting point for any review of Soviet agricultural policies in the last 40 years. We know that Stalin's decisions on this issue resulted in one of the greatest—if not the greatest—economic and social upheavals of this century. By one method of measurement, the associated losses of livestock in 1928–1933 came to almost 27 percent of the Soviet capital stock in 1928.[3] "Several million households, up to a total of 10 million persons or more must have been deported, of whom a great many must have perished." The total deaths due to the great Soviet famine of 1932–1934—a direct consequence of collectivization—may never be precisely established, but a figure of some 5 million appears to fit well with demographic data.[4] Directly and indirectly, Stalin's recourse to this course of action affected the pattern of Soviet industrialization, the kind of economic system which still prevails today, and the standards of living of his and the succeeding generations.

It is therefore of some interest to underline some of the points that deal with the background of these decisions. The resolve to proceed in this manner is correctly linked with what Lewin calls "the accursed problem" of the relation of the Soviet regime to the peasantry, particularly in the context of the forthcoming industrialization program. The "accursed" nature of the problem was viewed by those who then faced it in the Soviet Union (as well as by many outside observers) in the form of a dilemma.[5] The projected pace of the industrialization drive and the significant contributions that the agricultural sector was to make to this drive appeared to clash head-on with the objective requirement for rising agricultural production, particularly that of grain.

Of crucial importance in connection with the desired pace of development was the condition of the Soviet capital stock. It was widely believed—partly as a result of eloquently stated arguments by Preobrazhenskii in his *New Economics*—that the danger of the actual physical collapse of the existing industrial capital was very great in the middle twenties and that it could

---

[3] Richard Moorsteen and Raymond P. Powell, *The Soviet Capital Stock* (Homewood, Ill.: Richard D. Irwin, Inc., 1966), pp. 339–341.

[4] Lewin, p. 508, is the source for the direct quotation. The losses due to famine are placed anywhere from 1 to 15 million (the higher figures include losses due to associated diseases). The estimate of 5 million is made by Dana G. Dalrymple, "The Soviet Famine of 1932–34," *Soviet Studies*, XV, no. 3 (January, 1964), 261.

[5] There were, of course, many dilemmas in this context—including the problem of the appropriate agricultural policy toward the poor peasant in the context of reconstruction needs of the early 1920's.

only be averted by a massive wave of replacement investment that might simultaneously be used to modernize and renovate the existing capital assets. This belief indeed appears to have resulted in a shift of Bukharin's views on the matter of industrialization.[6]

It has now been shown by David Granick that the actual—as opposed to the perceived—need for a massive injection of new investment into the economic stream was not as compelling as was assumed at the time. The rate of physical retirement of existing assets in two important industries—metal fabricating and textiles—during the early thirties is found to have been very low.[7] Granick carefully refrains from generalizing the results of the findings based on a limited sample. Additional evidence on this subject probably exists in other technical journals and newspapers of the period where it might be discovered by further studies of individual Soviet industries— only a few of which have so far been undertaken by western scholars.[8]

If Granick's results can be generalized, however, it would be appropriate to conclude that the arguments in the debate and the decisions which followed (including the one by Stalin on collectivization) were based on a truly monumental error of judgment and a mistaken view of reality. Until we know more about this, the probability that this was indeed the case remains significant.

If Soviet views on the condition of the industrial sector may have been erroneous, the image they held of the agricultural sector of their economy was apparently distorted to a much greater extent. There was then (and there still is) a good deal of confusion with respect to farm output data for the twenties. For the years preceding World War I, this confusion is by now compounded: as is well known, output data for 1909–1913 or 1913 were revised several times in the USSR and no purpose would be served by covering again the ground explored by others.[9] Less well known are revisions of output data for the twenties, undertaken both during that period and in the thirties. As a result, it was difficult to discover then (and it may be even more difficult to do so now) what were the actual trends in such crucial

[6] Cf. Alexander Erlich, *The Soviet Industrialization Debate, 1924–1928* (Cambridge, Mass.: Harvard University Press, 1960), Chapter IV.
[7] David Granick, *Soviet Metal-Fabricating and Economic Development* (Madison: University of Wisconsin Press, 1967), pp. 135–136. The entire Chapter 4 is relevant in this context.
[8] So far, we only have the Ph.D. dissertation of Abraham S. Becker (textiles), that of John P. Hardt (electric power), and the book by M. Gardner Clark, *The Economics of Soviet Steel* (Cambridge, Mass.: Harvard University Press, 1956). Clark does not deal with this problem.
[9] See Jasny, *Socialized Agriculture*, Appendix Notes G and J, and Arkadius Kahan, "Soviet Statistics of Agricultural Output," in Roy D. Laird (ed.), *Soviet Agricultural and Peasant Affairs* (Lawrence: University of Kansas Press, 1963), pp. 134–160 and comment by Luba Richter.

variables as the per capita output of grains. We list below the various figures that can be obtained for the period 1909–1913 (assuming as is generally done that the average harvest was roughly 85 percent of that of 1913) and we compare it with a figure for per capita grain output in 1925/26–1927/28 (average, kilograms/head).[10]

	1909–1913	1925/26–1927/28
Gosplan estimate of 1925	681	
Ivantsov's revision of the twenties	590	
Gosplan estimate of 1928	496	
TsSU estimate, published in 1960	471	
Official estimate, published in the twenties		517
Official estimate, as revised in the thirties		503

In percentage terms, we thus have either an increase of 4.2 percent, or no increase to speak of, or a decline ranging from 12.4 to 24.1 percent. One can sympathize with those who are forced to "plan without data" and with those who are forced to make fundamental decisions on the basis of such plans. But it is also essential that the extent of their ignorance be more widely acknowledged and that we withhold final judgment on the real facts until we know more about them.

There was a similar confusion with respect to the equally crucial data on trends in grain marketing during the twenties, compounded by either outright falsification or failure to understand the nature of a statistical calculation.[11] Again, the fact that there *was* this kind of confusion is of great importance for our own understanding of the period. Matters did not end there. Much has been written about the stratification of Soviet peasantry in the period following the revolution, but here, too, some myths persist to this day. The famous data on the increase of the number of peasant households (a matter of great significance for the decisions we now deal with) were used among others by Stalin, who talked about the rise from 16 to 25 million households. Since it now appears that in 1916, the number of peasant households in the 1939 territory was already 21 million,[12] the increase is of the order of 25 rather than 56 percent. It is equally relevant for the problems at hand (though the significance of this fact varies with the nature of the problem) that 4 million of these households had no land at all. The depar-

[10] Grain output figures for 1925/26–1927/28 are from Soviet sources quoted in my "Thoughts on the Grain Problem," *Soviet Studies*, XVIII, no. 4 (April, 1967), 408. Soviet figures for 1909–1913 are taken from 1913 data in Jasny, *Socialized Agriculture*, p. 726, and Kahan, p. 137. Population for 1909–1913 is taken as 138.2 million.

[11] Karcz, "Thoughts on the Grain Problem," p. 401.

[12] V. P. Danilov, *Sozdanie material'no-tekhnicheskikh predposylok kollektivizatsii sel'skogo khoziaistva SSSR* (Moscow, 1957), p. 26.

ture of these potential recruits for the developing industry would have had only minor significance on future trends in agricultural production.[13]

All these uncertainties are of capital importance for the understanding of the decision to collectivize and for the nature of the alleged basic dilemma referred to above.

Even without further research, however, one tentative conclusion may safely be formulated: there is a significant probability that the major *economic* dilemma that we referred to earlier was not one that *had* to be resolved by collectivization and the associated compulsory procurement of farm products or by the abandonment of a sensible and fruitful industrialization drive. In other words, the dilemma may have been more apparent than real, while the real state of affairs in the industrialization context was amenable to other, less drastic solutions which might well have avoided the great, delayed, and persistent costs of collectivization which we will examine later.

Economists interested in problems of economic development (particularly in the socialist countries) have by now formulated a concept of the so-called Soviet industrialization strategy. In one of its more extreme formulations, the entire agricultural sector, as well as all the industrial inputs required for its functioning, are considered as a giant input into the industrialization process, where not only bread (to paraphrase Bergson) but also all that is needed to make bread become intermediate products. The output of industry is thus viewed as a single objective maximized by the planners.

Models of this sort have their uses, and the analysis of Soviet economic growth over a longer period does indeed provide interesting partial answers that are relevant to the usefulness of, as well as the pitfalls associated with, the working of such a model. But its use in historical explanations may lead to great dangers of the *post hoc ergo propter hoc* variety. Similarly, the importance of certain economic arguments in the context of decision-making may contribute to the understanding of that process, but the availability of sound economic arguments does not, in itself, establish the compelling or the inevitable—let alone, necessary—nature of a given course of action.

The researches of Moshe Lewin show clearly that the decision to collectivize agriculture was very largely a function of the so-called grain problem, which culminated in the grain procurement crisis of 1928 (I ignore here the political aspects of the situation). It was indeed at this time that the short-run usefulness of compulsory methods of collection (employed once before under war communism) was rediscovered by Stalin. Lewin's and my own work also show that this crisis was induced by certain economic policies of

[13] Rudolf Schlesinger, "On the Scope and Necessity of Error," *Soviet Studies,* XVII, no. 3 (January, 1966), 354.

the Soviet government, beginning with the decline in government grain prices for the 1926/27 harvest.[14] In the light of these findings, it is paradoxical that all the arguments that are still used to bolster the proposition that collectivization was inevitable must ultimately be couched in terms of the necessity to acquire grain.

As indicated earlier, there is considerable doubt on the magnitude of the decline in the per capita output of grains between the prewar period (1909–1913) and the last years of the New Economic Policy. Enough information has recently been released on the magnitude of the grain output during the entire period 1925–1940 to reveal a state of affairs that differs vastly from claims made earlier: without exception, the figures available now are even lower than the estimates made by Jasny some 20 years ago. The total and per capita output of grains was as follows:[15]

	Million Tons	Kilograms/Head
1925/26–1927/28 average	72.7 – 76.0	503 – 517
1928 – 1932 average	73.6	473
1931 – 1933 average	69.2	428
1933 – 1937 average	72.9	427
1934 – 1936 average	66.2	410
1936 – 1940 average	79.4	473
1938 – 1940 average	77.9	456

It is therefore difficult to speak of collectivization as a solution for the grain production problem, the existence of which cannot be viewed in separation from the effect of many government policies.

It is, of course, true that collectivization and the related grain procurement policies increased the (gross) marketed output by nearly 20 percent between 1925–1927 and 1928–1932 (average). Less widely recognized is the fact that the *entire* increase in total gross marketings of grain between 1928 and 1932 (or 1928 and 1933 for that matter)—which is greater than 20 percent, because of the decline in marketings in 1928—can be accounted for by the decrease in livestock herds that accompanied collectivization. The underlying calculation uses 1927/28 livestock feeding norms for grain. In-

[14] Lewin, and Karcz, "Thoughts on the Grain Problem."
[15] Data for 1925/26–1927/28 are from Karcz, "Thoughts on the Grain Problem," p. 408. Other output data are from I. E. Zelenin, "Kolkhoznoe stroitel'stvo v SSSR v 1931–1932 gg.," *Istoriia SSSR*, no. 6 (1960), p. 35, and "Kolkhozy i sel'skoe khoziaistvo SSSR v 1933–1935," *ibid.*, no. 5 (1964), p. 14. The output for 1936 fits well with the reported figure of yields of 5.6 quintals per hectare in M. A. Vyltsan, *Ukreplenie material'no-tekhnicheskoi bazy kolkhoznogo stroia vo vtoroi piatiletke (1933–1937 gg.)* (Moscow, 1959), p. 122. The figures for 1938 and 1939 are after Vyltsan, "Kolkhoznyi stroi nakanune Velikoi Otechestvennoi voiny," *Istoriia SSSR*, no. 1 (1962), p. 43, and are quite likely to be too high (cf. *Sovetskie archivy*, no. 4 (1967), p. 62).

deed, in this important initial period of industrialization collectivization appears to have contributed to the rise in marketings not so much because it introduced a particularly efficient instrument of grain collection in the shape of the collective farm (see below) but primarily because the manner in which it was implemented resulted in the great (some 50 percent) decline in the number of animals consuming grain.

But it can be argued that it was not so much the rise in marketings as that of state procurements, and the resulting flow of grain into the granaries of the state, that was crucial in the present context, particularly with respect to the availability of grain for exports but also for rising internal consumption.

The available Soviet data on the marketings, procurements, and dispositions of grain for the period of the first Five-Year Plan are shown in Table 1. Leaving aside the question of exports for the moment, it does not seem likely that rising internal requirements (influenced, as they were, by a very drastic increase in the number of urban consumers, which was in turn a function of the violent upheaval in the countryside and of the enforced pace of industrialization) would have created any significant problems. Allocations to internal civilian consumption in Table 1 include grain destined for rural population in deficit grain areas that were then expanding the production of technical crops and reducing or abandoning local cultivation of grain.

Total gross grain marketings of 1925/26–1928/29, in spite of the declining terms of trade for grain in state procurement, were of the order of 15.6 million tons. The decline in net marketings after 1926/27 was due not so much to the less favorable weather as to the mistaken, "colossally stupid" (to paraphrase Molotov) government price policies. It is reasonable to believe that problems of internal consumption would have become significant only beginning with 1931/32. By this time, alternative policies leading to the increase in grain production—such as replacement of wooden by steel plows, or an orderly expansion of the state farm sector—might well have provided the necessary cushion.

We thus come to the export problem and its importance in terms of procurements and dispositions by a government anxious to acquire foreign exchange and imported machinery. Total grain exports under the first Five-Year Plan came to approximately 12.7 million tons, or to some 2.5 million tons of grain on an annual basis.[16] Before World War I, grain exports of

[16] According to Iu. A. Moshkov, *Zernovaia problema v gody sploshnoi kollektivizatsii* (Moscow, 1966), insert following the last page of the book, the total of exports for 1928 through 1932 came to 12,641,000 tons. These are presumably calendar years, yet Moshkov lists a figure of 2.2 million tons for exports of 1932, while we know (see sources to Table 1) that the corresponding figure came to 1.8 million tons. Conceivably, Moshkov's figure refers to grain earmarked for exports.

Table 1 : *Grain procurements and dispositions, USSR, 1925/26–1932/33.*

	1925/26	1926/27	1927/28	1928/29	1929/30	1930/31	1931/32	1932/33
					(MILLION TONS)			
1. Gross marketings[a]	15.5	16.2	16.1	15.7	19.5	22.6	23.7	19.4
2. Net marketings[b]	9.4	10.3	8.3	8.3	10.2	17.9	18.8	13.7
3. State procurements[c]	n.a.	11.6	11.0	10.8	16.1	22.2	22.7	18.9
4. Including centralized[d]	8.4	10.6	10.1	9.7	16.1	22.2	22.7	18.9
5. Total dispositions	8.5	10.4	10.8	9.8	13.9	20.5	23.0	19.4
6. Total internal dispositions	6.3	7.9	10.4	9.7	12.6	14.7	18.5	17.6
7. Internal civilian dispositions	5.6	7.3	9.7	9.2	11.8	13.8	17.6	[16.6]
8. Armed forces and internal security	.6	[.6]	[.6]	.6	[.8]	[.9]	.9	[1.0]
9. Exports	2.2	2.5	.4	.1	1.3	5.8	4.5	1.8

[a] Gross marketings are defined as all off-farm sales other than those within agriculture as such. See Karcz, "Thoughts on the Grain Problem," p. 403, and Barsov, p. 69.

[b] Net marketings are defined as the so-called *sal'do sela* (net balance of the village) or by deducting from gross marketings the amount subsequently repurchased by the agricultural population or by farms through retail trade or through government allocations. See *ibid.*

[c] Including the milling tax in kind and decentralized procurements. The magnitude of the latter in 1926/27 and 1927/28 is given by the difference between rows 6 and 7. Alternative figures for decentralized procurements are available as follows: 1927/28, 905,300 tons; 1928/-29, 637,100 tons. Cf. *Ekonomicheskoe obozrenie*, no. 4 (1929), p. 196. It is assumed that there were no decentralized procurements from 1929/30 onwards.

[d] Including the milling tax in kind in its entirety.

SOURCES: For data on marketings, see Karcz, "Thoughts on the Grain Problem," p. 408 (and the Soviet sources cited on pp. 431–433) and Barsov, pp. 70–71.

For 1931/32, see Moshkov, p. 133. The figure for exports is the total available for the so-called "Fund of the Committee for Procurements of the Council for Labor and Defense" which conducted all export operations (*ibid.*, p. 132). The figure for exports for 1931/32 is given as 4,806,000 short tons by Volin, *Survey of Soviet Russian Agriculture*, p. 180. Volin cites *Entsiklopediia Sovetskogo eksporta* (Berlin, 1928) as one of his sources for earlier years.

For other years, see Karcz, "Thoughts on the Grain Problem," pp. 408, 431–432. It is now possible to estimate with reasonable accuracy the armed forces' consumption of grains for the entire period as a result of the publication of Moshkov's data. The figures for 1932/33 are estimates based in part on trends shown by Moshkov's grain balance (insert after the last page of his book) and on the data for exports in 1932 and 1933 (calendar years). These come from Zelenin (1964) as 1.8 million tons for 1932 and 1.7 million tons for 1933. Cf. Zelenin's p. 20, note. The figure for 1932 procurements comes from Gosudarstvennaia Planovaia Komissiia pri Sovete Narodnykh Komissarov SSSR, *Vtoroi piatiletnii plan razvitiia narodnogo khoziaistva SSSR* (Moscow, 1934), II, 528. A figure of 19.0 million tons is given in TsSU, *Strana Sovetov za 50 let* (Moscow, 1967), p. 122.

tsarist Russia amounted to some 10 million tons annually; in 1925/26 they came to 2.2 million tons and rose to 2.5 million tons in 1926/27. Thus, the somewhat higher annual totals required for the first Five-Year Plan *as a whole* do not appear to have been impossible to achieve by Soviet agriculture of the twenties, given appropriate technological and price policies designed for this purpose. This is especially true if we recall that any industrialization program would have been taking a certain number of mouths from the countryside and that (given the available data on grain consumption in 1926/27) each man, woman, and child would have reduced his annual consumption of grain products by 55 kilograms when going to the city.

Let us assume that grain yields on the existing grain acreage would have been rising annually by 1.25 percent since 1926/27 and that the marketed share of grain (which came to 21–22 percent in 1925–1927) would have remained at the level of 22 percent in 1928 and 1929, rising to 23 percent in 1930 and 1931 and to 24 percent in 1932. Over the period of five years, fluctuations in weather may be assumed to cancel out. On that account alone, total market output (consisting virtually of state procurements since 1930) would have come to 90.3 million tons over the period 1928–1932. If, in addition, we allow only for one-half of the increase in grain acreage that did actually occur in the form of orderly expansion of state farms supplied with proper equipment (instead of the *shturmovshchina* that did occur),[17] with yields at the unchanging 1925–1927 level and a marketed share of 40 percent for these farms, total hypothetical grain marketings (procurements) would rise to the level of 95 million tons. This is exactly the amount marketed, largely through compulsory procurement, over the five years of the first plan.

Large quantities of grain procured in 1929–1932 appear to have been lost in storage or in the course of procurement. For example, in 1929 and 1932, the *annual* loss came to more than a million tons on a volume of procurements of 16 and 22 million tons respectively. These figures do not include losses and waste incurred in distribution from centralized stocks to processing industries and the trade network. Total loss in procurement and centralized storage alone under the first plan came to about 4 million tons (per capita grain consumption in 1924–1927 came to .23 tons in the village and .18 tons in the city).[18]

For agricultural years (July through June), Lazar Volin, *A Survey of Soviet Russian Agriculture* (Washington, D.C.: U.S. Department of Agriculture, 1951), shows a total of about 13.5 million short tons. I do not wish to initiate a sterile controversy, and the figure used in the text is deliberately somewhat higher than these data indicate.

[17] By 1931, food supply of some state farms producing grain had to come from state resources. Cf. Moshkov, p. 133. All in all, 275,000 tons of food grains were allotted to all state farms for food supplies of workers.

[18] Table 1 shows that by July 1, 1931, grain stocks should have come to 4.6

A substantial part of the losses in 1929 and 1930 was probably due to shortage of storage facilities at a time of rapid increase in procurements (60 and 25 percent respectively). This, too, is a factor that should be kept in mind in the present context.

So far, we did ignore the bunched, actual time pattern of Soviet grain exports under the first plan. This is because our concern here is with problems of development policy over a period of time rather than with the explanation of what did actually happen. I have not yet seen an argument advanced in the present context which states that the actual pattern and timing of grain exports in 1928–1932 was in some sense optimal or "objectively necessary" for the success of the plan. This is, of course, the crux of the matter. While we know too little about these things, we do know that the pattern of imports was affected by collectivization itself; hence, any argument to the effect that what happened must have necessarily happened when it happened is open to the objection of circular reasoning. In addition, enough is now known about the first plan, the vast amount of capital frozen in unfinished construction, and the creation of very significant excess capacity (including—oddly enough—the agricultural machinery industry where this capacity was not used fully until 1936)[19] to suggest that a different pattern and timing of investment, construction, exports, and imports might well have achieved substantially the same results in terms of final output without serious prejudice to future development.

II

It is indeed sobering to view the collectivization of agriculture in the light of our earlier discussion. But the stark fact remains that the extremely ambitious industrialization program (so aptly referred to by Jasny as the source of bacchanalian planning) and the collectivization of agriculture did take place. Once implemented, both policies were viewed by Stalin and other directors of the system as goals in their own right, the abandonment of which was clearly regarded as incompatible with the continuation of the regime as constituted at that time.

It is possible to view the early period of socialized agriculture in the USSR as that dominated by Stalin's policies of "collecting the agricultural

---

million tons in addition to stocks on hand on July 1, 1929, which did not exceed 0.5 million tons; see Moshkov, p. 52, and Karcz, "Thoughts on the Grain Problem," p. 412. Actually, stocks on July 1, 1931, came only to 2.1 million tons, according to Moshkov, p. 133.

[19] Granick, pp. 66, 293.

surplus," and the perfection of the institutional and organizational framework oriented toward that purpose. Indeed, I have myself elaborated an organizational model that seeks to identify the key mechanisms and relationships of "command farming," or agriculture oriented toward that purpose.[20] Models of this sort are quite useful as shorthand expressions of complex relationships. But they may unwittingly contribute to the impression that command farming in the USSR arose as part of a larger strategy of economic development. In reality a closer historical analysis suggests that command farming ultimately emerged as the end product of a series of somewhat disjointed attempts to deal with a problem at a time without much thought given to the probable and significant consequences of a measure or a series of measures. (That the end result turns out to be consistent with a particular goal or a series of goals does not necessarily mean that that goal was actually pursued at any time). Indeed, this explanation is quite consistent with the clearly visible seesaw pattern that characterizes much of the Soviet agricultural policy in this—as well as in the later—period.

One of the earliest examples of this pattern is provided by Stalin's famous "Dizziness with Success" letter. We now know that the letter represented a major departure from official Party policy, based on a variant of collectivization decision elaborated by Stalin and Ia. A. Iakovlev. While we do not know exactly the contents of the document adopted at the Presidium meeting of January 3, 1930, we have been told that the views of those who favored collectivization of small tools and smaller livestock did ultimately prevail. While farms organized at that time were primarily of the artel rather than the commune variety, we also know that that type of artel was closer to the commune than to the artel described in the 1935 charter.[21] Consequently, the Party line in the area of remaining private property and the so-called "deviations" from the altered policy contributed gravely to the slaughter of livestock. This was not an unmixed blessing from the standpoint of increasing the marketed share of grain. But the resulting loss of manure (only 7 to 36 percent of quantities considered as a bare minimum were applied in the early thirties) affected significantly the disappointing trends in yields and total grain output during the same period. The loss of manure was felt significantly on a different plane as well. For here lies the origin of Villiams' *travopol'e,* an extraordinary enlistment of pseudoscience into the service of the Stalinist solution of agricultural problems. It is by no

[20] Jerzy F. Karcz, "An Organizational Model of Command Farming," in Morris Bornstein (ed.), *Comparative Economic Systems,* rev. ed. (Homewood, Ill.: Richard D. Irwin, Inc., 1969), pp. 278–299.

[21] M. A. Vyltsan, N. A. Ivnitskii, and Iu. A. Poliakov, "Nekotorye problemy istorii kollektivizatsii v SSSR," *Voprosy istorii,* no. 3 (1965), pp. 11–13.

means clear whether the campaign in itself was as harmful as Khrushchev later pretended that it was: although Villiams' insistence on true grass was not the best alternative for raising yields, the campaign might have contributed to more rapid introductions in rotations. A careful student of the subject suggests that its greatest negative impact was "the resulting distortion of . . . investment in higher education and research."[22] Thus, Lysenkoism is in a sense an indirect intellectual descendant of the livestock losses in 1929–1933, as is perhaps the neglect of the cadaster and proper soil mapping.

Another and a related aspect deals with the correction of the so-called abuses of lower Party apparatus (who were apparently totally dismayed by Stalin's sudden about-face in March, 1930) in the process of collectivization as such. A great deal of hope was at first placed on the so-called contractual delivery system as a prime method of grain procurement in the years 1929–1932. Indeed, it is no exaggeration to say that the method of contractual deliveries was viewed by some writers (including Gatovskii) as one of the forms of exchange relationships conducive to the introduction of rigidly centralized, absolute command economy, dominated by direct exchange, where money might play only a passive role, designed to facilitate accounting.[23]

It is also well known that the government (which could never hope to fulfill its own obligations under the contracts) very frequently resorted to imposition of supplementary procurement plans. This undermined the legal nature of the procurement target and of the contract itself, created an important credibility gap in the relationship of the collective farm to the state, and set the stage for future practices of this sort that were to plague the Soviet farms for years. In spite of these supplementary targets, however, the early collective farm, bolstered by *kontraktatsiia*, did not prove to be an effective instrument of collection of farm products, particularly of grains. Indeed, collectivization as such now appears to have been a much less effective supplier of the fuel necessary for the process of growth than we have grown accustomed to believe.

Trends in the hitherto obscured period, 1928–1932, were recently elucidated in a very important article by A. A. Barsov.[24] Some of his most

[22] David Joravsky, "Ideology and Progress in Crop Rotation," in Jerzy F. Karcz (ed.), *Soviet and East European Agriculture* (Berkeley and Los Angeles: University of California Press, 1967), p. 168. The entire paragraph is based on Professor Joravsky's findings.

[23] Cf. Karcz, "Organizational Model of Command Farming," p. 283.

[24] A. A. Barsov, "Sel'skoe khoziaistvo i istochniki sotsialisticheskogo nakopleniia v gody pervoi piatiletki (1928–1932)," *Istoriia SSSR*, no. 3 (1968). I became acquainted with this article on the very eve of the deadline for press, and am grateful to the editor for allowing me to make the necessary changes at the eleventh hour.

Table 2 : *Market output of agriculture and purchases of industrial goods by agricultural population, 1928–1932.*[a]

	1928	1929	1930	1931	1932
	(MILLION RUBLES)				
A. At 1913 world market prices:					
Value of "market output" of agriculture[b]	3,312	3,727	4,237	4,360	3,376
Value of industrial goods purchased by agriculture, including investment goods[c]	1,463	1,787	1,971	1,908	1,767
"Deductions, not compensated for"	1,849	1,941	2,266	2,452	1,609
B. At 1928–1929 Soviet prices:[d]					
Value of gross market output, 18 product groups[e]	3,764	4,216	4,432	4,562	3,692
Value of industrial consumer goods, purchased by agricultural population[f]	3,351	4,080	4,396	3,706	3,331
Value of industrial goods, including investment goods purchased by agriculture	3,951	4,804	5,322	5,153	4,768

[a] When making comparisons between the value of market output and the value of *all* industrial goods including investment goods sold to "agriculture," the reader should bear in mind that a part of the marketed output during part of this period represented disinvestment (in livestock).

[b] The definition is peculiar. Grain is entered according to the net concept of marketings, while other products are entered according to the gross concept of marketings.

[c] Excluding repurchase of grain products by agriculture.

[d] 1928/29 farm prices for marketings, and 1928 average prices of purchase on all markets.

[e] Grains, sunflower seeds, flax seeds, hemp seeds, raw cotton, flax fiber, hemp fiber, sugar beets, tobacco, makhorka, potatoes, vegetables, meat, milk, eggs, hides, and wool. These should account for more than 95 percent of the value of market output.

[f] In state and cooperative retail trade and on the uncontrolled market.

SOURCE: Barsov (cf. Table 1), pp. 70, 75, 78. We do not compute the residual representing "deductions, not compensated for" in part B, because the prices used are not of the same year and because the coverage of market output is not complete. The reader will bear in mind in any case that the calculations do not include incomes of the agricultural population from nonagricultural activity or from transfer payments.

important data are presented, in a rearranged form, in Tables 2 and 3. These figures also provide most of the raw material for an extensive reinterpretation of the *economic* rationale of the decision to collectivize, but this important task may best be performed in a separate publication. Barsov's data, however, confirm Professor Bergson's view that the peasants contributed much less (and the workers correspondingly more) to Soviet capital formation than has been supposed. In fact, Barsov computes the share of agriculture in what he calls "centralized state revenues" devoted to non-

Table 3 : *Price and parity indices and barter terms of trade, 1928–1932.*

	1928	1929	1930	1931	1932
1. Volume of industrial consumer goods sold to agricultural population	100.0	122.4	131.2	110.6	99.4[a]
2. Market output of agriculture	100.0	109.5	127.9	131.6	101.9
3. Barter terms of trade (row 1 ÷ row 2)	100.0	111.8	102.6	84.0	97.5
4. Index of agricultural producer prices in all marketings	100.0	117.2	180.0	198.8	313.5
5. Index of prices of all industrial goods purchased by agriculture, including investment goods	100.0	98.8	109.1	167.7	240.8
6. Parity index A (row 4 ÷ row 5)[b]	100.0	118.6	165.0	118.5	130.2
7. Index of state (planned) procurement prices of farm products	100.0	100.6	115.7	118.6	109.3
8. Index of state retail prices of industrial consumer goods[c]	100.0	98.6	107.4	180.1	284.5
9. Parity index B (row 7 ÷ row 8)	100.0	102.0	107.7	65.9	38.4
10. Index of retail prices of industrial consumer goods on uncontrolled market[d]	100.0	139.3	218.2	392.8	845.7
11. Parity index C (row 7 ÷ row 10)	100.0	72.0	53.0	30.0	13.0
12. Index of prices of farm products on the uncontrolled market	100.0	233.2	525.3	814.6	3,005.7
13. Parity index D (row 12 ÷ row 8)	100.0	236.5	489.1	452.3	1,056.5

a This is mistakenly shown as 100 in Barsov's Table 4. The figure was corrected on the basis of ruble data he also lists on p. 75.
b See n. a to Table 2 for reservations on interpretation.
c Thirty-five products, 1927/28 = 100.
d The volume of sales on this market declined from 360 million rubles in 1928, to 236 million in 1929, to 142 million in 1930; it then rose to 266 million in 1931 and declined to 96 million rubles in 1932.
SOURCE: Barsov, pp. 74, 75, 77. I have calculated the parity indices and barter terms of trade.

agricultural capital formation and the maintenance of nonproductive activity. His figures are as follows (percentage of total centralized state revenue, so defined):

1928	64.3
1929	41.5
1930	35.7
1931	30.9
1932	20.4

In constant ruble value, the 1932 figure is considerably lower than its 1928 counterpart.[25] Thus, Bergson's findings, based on data for 1937, also hold true for the very early period of massive industrialization. In effect, the damage done to agriculture within the first three years of the industrialization drive was so severe that it affected adversely its ability to contribute significantly to further economic development. These policies, which exerted such a detrimental impact on future productivity trends, also led to the emergence of astronomical quasi rents for favorably located producers who were able to sell on the uncontrolled (if not always the legal) market. It is for this reason that the parity index A shown in Table 3 is included there only for the sake of completeness. Its indiscriminate use tends to confuse the issue and to conceal the extent of human misery and suffering. Trends indicated by the alternative parity indices B, C, and D are much more illuminating, even though they describe accurately only the situations faced by selected groups of producers.

By 1931/32, the agricultural sector was slowly grinding to a halt in the performance of its developmental and nondevelopmental functions. As Tables 2 and 3 indicate, this was true even though Stalin appears to have launched an early version of his own "New Course" during the year. In part, this was the result of some special circumstances. A special, campaignlike wave of supplementary procurement took place in March, 1932, as a result of a military threat in Manchuria. For 1931/32, grain procurements from collective farms reached the total of 40 percent of collective farm harvest— a factor that contributed gravely to the great Soviet famine of 1932–1934, and to the substantial outflow of households from collective farms located in grain-producing areas. The situation must have been serious enough for the government to enact a whole series of measures in the spring of the year. These included the lowering of grain procurement quotas, the legalization of the collective farm market trade, and yet another condemnation of com-

[25] *Ibid.*, p. 80. On pp. 81–82 Barsov makes explicit his conclusion that the main burden of the "heroic effort" of socialist industrialization lay on the shoulders of the working class. For Bergson's view see Abram Bergson, *The Real National Income of Soviet Russia Since 1928* (Cambridge, Mass.: Harvard University Press, 1961), p. 257.

pulsory collectivization of livestock. In spite of an increase in the degree of collectivization and a small increase in the size of the grain harvest, grain procurements in 1932/33 fell by nearly 4 million tons.

In 1932 alone, collective farm market prices rose by a factor of 3.5; they reached their peak in the first quarter of 1933. This coincides well with the accounts of the famine and its aggravation in the winter and spring of 1933. If conditions were difficult in the city, they may well have been worse in the countryside. Only three out of five collective farm households had household plots, and this was also true of cattle ownership. Less than one-third owned sheep or goats and only one household in six raised pigs. Grain distributions of that time provided an ordinary household with about enough grain to feed 2.2 adults at rations corresponding roughly to 1926/27 per capita consumption of grain products (when substantially more protein and calories in general were available from other sources). Even this was an average with an unusually wide dispersion. Fully 43.5 percent of collective farms distributed less grain than indicated by our figures. There is some indication that the situation may have been due to some unusual stockpiling and/or nearly total exhaustion of all existing stocks (including seed reserves) at the local farm level.[26] Even Stalin himself was forced to admit in January, 1933, that state and collective farms were "weak, not yet [fully] formed economic units which are passing through approximately the same period in their organization as did our industrial plants in 1921–22. It is evident that the majority of them cannot be profitable [*rentabel'nye*]. But they will become profitable in the course of 2–3 years. . . ."[27]

The year 1932/33 was one of more general crisis in the economy: in January, 1933, output of coal, coke, steel, rolled steel, and petroleum as well as iron ore and pig iron fell below their corresponding totals for 1932. "The monthly output figures continued to run behind those of 1932 for a few months after January 1, 1933."[28] For 1932, on the other hand, the gross national product estimates of Moorsteen and Powell show the only decline on record since 1928. Given the nature of the measurements, it seems safe to conclude that the condition of the economy was grave indeed and the political impact was even greater. The émigré sources which suggest that

[26] On the famine, see Dalrymple, pp. 252–253. For other data see Zelenin (1960), p. 38, and Zelenin (1964), p. 21. According to the available data, the share of grain uses *other* than state procurement and distribution to members was unusually large in 1932—over 50 percent. This share was reduced beginning with 1933. Just what did happen in 1932 is not clear at all.

[27] As quoted in V. Rezvina and G. Dobugodlo, "K itogam raspredeleniia dokhodov 1933 g. v kolkhozakh," *Sotsialisticheskaia rekonstruktsiia sel'skogo khoziaistva*, no. 9 (1934), p. 44.

[28] N. Jasny, *Soviet Industrialization, 1928–1952* (Chicago: University of Chicago Press, 1961), pp. 116–117.

the matter of Stalin's replacement was seriously considered at the time may well be close to the truth.

It is in this context that many of the mechanisms of command farming assumed the form which was to remain virtually unchanged until well beyond the death of Stalin. The first of these was a reorganization of the procurement system in 1932–1933. The famous compulsory deliveries made their appearance in December, 1932, and were soon followed by MTS payments in kind and state purchases. Together with the collective farm market, the procurement reforms of 1932–1933 represent the formalization of the multiple price system. On the face of it, the two-price system in state procurement could be viewed as a clever adjustment to the realities of the situation that clearly required an increase in the volume of procurement, and as a disguised attempt to raise the average price of some products. Procurements did, in effect, increase (with purchases accounting for a considerable proportion of procurements—20 percent of potatoes in 1937), seemingly to the short-run advantage of all concerned.

Long-run effects were of a different nature. Enough is now known about the operation of the two-price system in procurements to indicate that farm prices in socialist countries are not totally devoid of an allocational effect, especially in those instances where the substitution of one product for another is feasible. Thus, we know of cases when rye, grown in mountain areas, was replaced by much less yielding wheat, simply because all wheat could be sold at the higher purchase price. To an unknown but probably a significant extent, the structure of production was thus seriously affected. The fact that farm prices of food products remained—by and large—unchanged after 1932 only intensified the allocational impact of procurement prices. For the *real* purchase price was considerably higher than the nominal price, since a guaranteed supply of industrial consumer goods—that could not be obtained in regular trade channels—was guaranteed to the sellers.[29] Since those farms which could sell were largely to be found among the richer, more productive units, the system of two prices amounted to a hidden subsidy to the more productive farms.

The introduction of MTS payments in kind also seemed to facilitate collection of grain in a manner that was ostensibly free of the connotation associated with compulsory deliveries at what are now called symbolic prices. Since the size of the payment varied directly with the yield, MTS payments in kind were also affected by the introduction of the infamous biological yield. It is now apparent from glimpses of archival materials that the esti-

---

[29] Jerzy F. Karcz, *Soviet Agricultural Marketings and Prices, 1928–1954* (Santa Monica, Calif.: RAND Corp., 1957), p. 90. The retail value of industrial products sold to sellers in this manner was up to three times the value of grain sold. Cf. Zelenin (1964), p. 19.

mates of this yield, performed by a special state commission, were greatly resented at the local level by many officials, including at least one republican Party secretary. This was, of course, to be expected, but pressures to raise the marketed share and to "pull up grain production to the level of Five Year Plan targets" proved stronger, and biological yield continued to be used until 1952.[30]

The impact of MTSs as centers of machinery was by no means uniform. The station may be viewed as a reasonable device for concentrating scarce capital equipment and achieving a better utilization of this equipment. As an economic unit, however, it was not often an efficient enterprise. In the early war years (and on many other peacetime occasions) MTSs were often accused of maximizing the output of "accounting hectares of work done," with little regard for the consequences. Originally, they tended to supply the largest volume of services in areas where the animal power was at its lowest level relative to sowings. It is by no means clear that they always helped their customers to achieve higher yields.[31] The two problems are closely related and have often been described as stemming from the presence of two managers on the same unit of land. This would account for Venzher's suggestion to abolish the stations as early as 1937 and for the frequent practice of assigning a tractor brigade to a single collective farm for the duration of a year. It is, of course, essential to remember that the MTS also performed a variety of political and indoctrination functions of extraordinary importance to the government.

Equally important in the long run was the official recognition of the household plot, or of the extremely hybrid nature of collectivized agriculture in the USSR. This has been made clear with respect to the more recent period by Karl-E. Wädekin. The virtual symbiosis of the two sectors which he identifies for the fifties and the sixties was even more true of the thirties.[32]

In 1937, when conditions in the socialized sector were very good indeed, privately operated plots provided 52.1 percent of the total output of potatoes and vegetables and 56.6 percent of that of fruit. For animal products, the corresponding percentages were: milk, 71.4; meat, 70.9; hides, 70.4; wool, 43. On the other hand, less than 1 percent of the total output of grain was produced on private plots. There is little wonder, therefore, that the "collective farmer looked at the collective farm only as a supplier of grain,"

---

[30] *Ibid.*, p. 13.

[31] Vyltsan, *Ukreplenie*, pp. 123–124, 130. In 1935, grain yields in farms *not* served by MTSs were 8.5 percent higher than in farms so served.

[32] Karl-E. Wädekin, *Privatproduzenten in der sowjetischen Landwirtschaft* (Cologne: Wissenschaft und Politik, 1967). An expanded English version is to be published shortly by the University of California.

a formulation that we owe to Ia. A. Iakovlev, then Commissar of Agriculture of the USSR.[33]

It could hardly have been otherwise. During the thirties, income from free market sales provided up to 75–86 percent of joint cash income of farmers from market sales and kolkhoz cash distributions, and the private plot was virtually the only source of supply of peasant families for potatoes, vegetables, and animal products. Then, as well as today, much of the plot output was possible only because of increased supplies of grain and other feed from the socialized sector. Grain distributions rose markedly after 1933 (cf. p. 52). In the middle and late thirties, allowing for harvest fluctuations, farms distributed enough grain to feed some 4.1 persons per household at the 1926–1927 rates of personal consumption in the village.[34] Such figures make no allowance for the grain fed to livestock on the plot, but even they tend to exaggerate the level of living standards in relation to the twenties. In 1934–1935, about one-third of households received enough grain from the farm to maintain less than three persons per household (in comparable terms). In 1939, some 700,000 (out of a total of 19.3 million) households received no grain at all, and distribution to several million others must have been exceedingly small. In 1940, 6.8 percent of collective farms distributed no grain at all as income in kind, while another 42.2 percent issued only less than one kilogram per labor-day worked. During the same year, one-eighth of the farms paid no cash for labor-days worked, while 54.8 percent paid less than 0.60 rubles (of the 1940, old variety). A surviving Ukrainian ditty of that period illustrates well the reality of village life for many:

> Tato, mama v kolkhozi
> Diti holi na morozi
> Ni korovy ni svini
> Tilkie Stalin na scini.[35]

The improvement that did occur after 1933 and the abolition of rationing in 1935 must be interpreted in the light of the enforced changes in the diet

[33] Vyltsan, Ivnitskii, and Poliakov, p. 24.

[34] Cf. Nancy Nimitz, *Farm Employment in the Soviet Union, 1928–1963* (Santa Monica, Calif.: RAND Corp., 1965), pp. 93, 112, and Warren Eason, *The Agricultural Labor Force and Population in the USSR, 1926–1941* (Santa Monica, Calif.: RAND Corp., 1954), p. 122, for the underlying data.

[35] Cf. Zelenin (1964), p. 21; Vyltsan, "Kolkhoznyi stroi nakanune," p. 47. Very rough calculations for 1939 indicate that the top 30,000 farms (12.3 percent) accounted for at least 30.9 percent—and probably for considerably more—of all grain distributed to collective farm households in the USSR as a whole. The data for 1940 come from V. B. Ostrovskii, *Kolkhoznoe krest'ianstvo SSSR* (Saratov, 1967), pp. 58–59. The Ukrainian ditty is taken from the memoirs of L. Jurewicz in *Zeszyty historyczne,* no. 15 (1963), p. 158.

and of the famine of 1932–1934, which seems to have been particularly severe in rural areas in 1933. This is a subject which is still scrupulously avoided by Soviet historians of that period, but a factor of first importance in understanding trends in output utilization and food supplies.

If the village could not have survived without the private sector, neither could have the city. In 1935 and 1937, procurements of vegetables were roughly at the level of collective farm market sales, and the household plots of workers and employees provided much of the personal consumption of these and many other products. The volume of market sales of some products, expressed as a percentage of state procurements (to which the private sector also made a substantial contribution) was as follows:[36]

	1935	1937
Meat	40	63
Milk	33	28
Potatoes	23	31
Grains	5	6

The hybrid nature of socialized agriculture, resulting from this interdependence, was of profound significance for the attitudes in the Soviet countryside, as well as for prospects of further improvement of the economic performance of Soviet agriculture. Certain Soviet historians now admit that it was a forlorn hope to seek a correct relation between the private and the socialized sector during that period (this was formally the official line) in conditions when private interest and indeed the survival instinct pulled the farmer toward the private plot.[37]

Two-sector agricultures are quite common in nonsocialist environments; indeed, the agriculture of the United States is characterized by the co existence of a commercial and a subsistence sector.[38] The contribution that the latter group makes—and did make in the past—to the economic development of the country is quite substantial. But this is seldom a contribution in product terms, except to the extent necessary to maintain personal consumption of the low-income farm families in that sector. In the Soviet case, of course, both sectors contributed products to state procurements with the result that the standard of living on weaker farms was less than it could have been had productivity been greater on their more productive counterparts, while improvements in productivity on the latter were (often artificially) restricted by lack of machinery and other off-farm inputs, allotted to

[36] For collective farm market data, see Vyltsan, "Obshchestvenno-ekonomicheskii stroi kolkhoznoi derevni v 1933–1940 gg.," *Istoriia SSSR*, no. 2 (1966), p. 59.

[37] *Ibid.*, p. 48.

[38] Cf. W. F. Owen, "The Double Developmental Squeeze on Agriculture," *American Economic Review*, LVI, no. 1 (March, 1966), 43–70.

the weaker counterparts in order to maintain production at levels that still allowed for some contribution to state procurement. Certain other characteristics of command farming can also be traced to the direct or indirect impact of measures taken earlier, largely in response to the apparent exigencies of the moment. Thus, the emphasis placed on government procurement was heavily reflected in practices of agricultural planning. To a large extent, it is possible to say that agricultural planning as such had been abandoned with the advent of collectivization and the underlying stress on procurement, which absorbed most of the planning effort and contributed heavily to the low level of specialization among Soviet farms.[39] In those instances where this was not necessarily the case, as was true of the implementation of certain cropping systems, there is evidence of ample distortion of such schemes precisely under the pressure for greater procurement, while insufficient time had been allowed for the introduction of suggested patterns (particularly in the light of all the turbulence associated with collectivization).[40] Similarly, an army of plenipotentiaries of various denominations (occasionally referred to derisively as *upal namochennyi*) affected many decisions of agricultural administrators and farm managers, whose authority was limited severely by the prevalent planning practices.

In terms of agricultural production and productivity, the results are well known. The prewar period may indeed be viewed as a lost decade. Total output approached—but did not surpass—the level of 1928, in spite of an increase in sown area, a somewhat greater labor input, and an apparent recovery in the total capital stock. Consequently, productivity indices for this period show a decline ranging from 3 to 24 percent, depending upon the nature of calculation and treatment of the labor input.[41] That this was the case should be no surprise in view of the low level and the distorted structure of incentives, of changes in the structure of agricultural capital which no longer corresponded to the pattern of production, and of severe limitations on decision-making and agricultural planning in the broadest sense of the words.

The system of command farming that arose as a result of successive adjustments to a series of threatening crises or crisislike situations was highly unstable. Its very impact on production and productivity made farming less and less able to respond in a flexible manner to rising demands placed upon it by the continued policy of industrialization.

[39] In part because of administrative interference, in part as a result of "safety factor" planning by procurement officials.

[40] Joravsky, pp. 160–163.

[41] D. Gale Johnson, "Agricultural Production," in Abram Bergson and Simon Kuznets (eds.), *Economic Trends in the Soviet Union* (Cambridge, Mass.: Harvard University Press, 1963), p. 216, and Jerzy F. Karcz, "Soviet Agriculture: A Balance Sheet," *Studies on the Soviet Union*, no. 4 (1967), pp. 113–114.

Judging by trends in procurements alone, the system of command farming appeared to function better and better after 1932. Yet, output increased little under the third Five-Year Plan, and there were many other signs of the working of certain disfunctional effects to produce another series of measures designed to deal with the resulting problems. Most of these measures were introduced within a period of about nine months beginning with December, 1938, when an increase in allocations to indivisible funds was recommended by the Party. There followed the decree ordering the census and reduction in size of household plots, the related establishment of minimum labor-day inputs by collective farmers, and finally the shift in procurement procedures dealing with the establishment of compulsory delivery quotas for livestock (extended within the year to virtually all products subject to delivery in this form). In addition, a whole series of measures dealing with improvement in the structure of collective farm incentives and premiums based on productivity was also introduced in the late thirties.

The bunching of these measures within a relatively short time indicates considerable concern with developments in the collective farm sector. As it happens, this is one of the areas in which Soviet and western research fails to provide enough data for reasonable final conclusions. We do have some all-union averages on trends in employment on collective farms and the number of members who worked for relatively short periods of time on the socialized sector, or who did no work at all on collectivized fields. There are also some scattered and arbitrarily selected data of the same sort on individual areas or oblasti. We do know that the reduction of the size of plots affected 41 percent of all collective farm households and that in some areas (Orel, Penza, Smolensk, Kursk, and Kalinin oblasti, and in the Maritime krai) the share rose to 75–86 percent. We also know (through a memorandum of the deputy chairman of Gosplan, dated April 24, 1940) that a considerable part of the confiscated and highly productive land (the burden of the reduction fell on orchards and gardens rather than on areas in field crops) was not brought back into production; in some areas, such as the Stalingrad oblast', "some" collective farm households were left entirely without plots at first, while many others received reduced allotments of a size well below that stipulated in the Model Charter. But there is little by way of information on the relation of, e.g., extralegal enlargement of plots to incomes received from the collective farm as such, though we do know, in general, that plots tended to be larger where income from the farm was low. Little is also known on the types of migration that were then taking place. But it can be said that the campaign to train tractor drivers was a virtual failure, since their total number hardly changed from 1937 to 1939.[42]

[42] All data on the impact of the plot reductions in 1939 are from Ostrovskii, pp.

We know little of the relation of the improvement in incentives to income levels by region. In addition, developments of this period were clearly affected by the atmosphere of the approaching war, but there is some reason to believe that this is too often used as a convenient explanation for many unrelated phenomena.

In spite of these problems, some general considerations may be offered tentatively. There are many indications that this entire program consisted once more of a series of individual measures that were not altogether consistent with each other. Thus, while the increase in the allocations to investment funds (1938) may be consistent with the rising requirements for livestock structures made necessary by the projected expansion of collectivized herds (1939), it is nevertheless difficult to believe that a construction program of this kind could or should have been attempted on the eve of an expected war. Nor is the improvement in the structure of incentives consistent with the projected rise in socialized livestock herds, or with measures designed to restrict the size of the household plot—the major source of collective farmer income in that period. The program to expand socialized livestock operations is also difficult to explain given the reduction in machinery allocations to the agricultural sector that began in 1937. Whether or not the reduction was due to retooling for military production, or whether it only reflected yet another impact of the Great Purge, is another point that must be elucidated.

The third Five-Year Plan projected a 50 percent increase in the production of crops, a 91 percent increase in the output of animal products, and only an 11 percent increase in the production of grains. Simultaneously however, the famous *travopol'e* was being introduced, with the result that grain sowings declined significantly in the major grain areas. It was apparently easy to enforce *travopol'e* on state farms—and their share in state procurement declined disproportionately to the decline in total procurement. If the *travopol'e* was expected to reduce the size of labor inputs, the imposition of minimum labor quotas is also difficult to explain, especially since at that time (as well as in 1936), the proportion of nonable-bodied in the agricultural population was nearly the same as that of the able-bodied.[43] Finally, the introduction of *travopol'e* itself is an astonishing measure, given the existence of the real or imagined external threat (we should add that

---

69–72. The information on trends in the available personnel of tractor drivers and *mekhanizatory* is from Arkadius Kahan in Carl Eicher and Lawrence Witt (eds.), *Agriculture in Economic Development* (New York: McGraw-Hill, 1964), p. 257. Virtually all those trained between January 1, 1938, and December 31, 1939 (268,000 individuals) appear to have left the farms for other occupations.

[43] Iu. V. Arutiunian, *Sovetskoe krest'ianstvo v gody Velikoi Otechestvennoi voiny* (Moscow, 1963), p. 316.

according to Joravsky's researches, a substantial variety of crop patterns did actually qualify as *travopol'nye*, so that the actual damage may well have been smaller than one might at first believe).[44]

There are thus enough questions about the measures introduced in 1938–1940 to allow a hypothesis that here, once again, we deal with *ad hoc* measures designed to redress particular situations in the short run—without adequate consideration of the future. For if the concern was due to the disappointing pattern of yields and productivity, then it is difficult to imagine what the consequences would have been in the long run, if war had not intervened. At this stage, too, there appear to have been many alternative ways of handling the difficulties and improving the overall functioning of the hybrid agricultural system. It is difficult to argue that nothing else could have been done, as long as we know as little as we actually do about the possibilities of increasing taxes (including deliveries) from slightly enlarged plots. Wartime experience does suggest, however, that this potential was far greater than the Soviet leaders had thought.

III

Soviet agriculture and the Soviet rural society were catapulted into the war shortly after the implementation of these changes that only accentuated the disfunctional features of command farming. Wartime developments cannot be discussed in full detail, but we should first stress the unbelievable resilience, patriotism, and persistence of the Soviet rural population in the face of great adversity. This was ultimately the result of enemy action, but was more directly attributable to the necessity of maintaining output with greatly reduced inputs of both labor and capital. In spite of these reductions, it proved possible to maintain the 1940 grain area (in the unoccupied territory) until about 1943. But yields and output declined considerably, until in 1945, grain production amounted to less than half that of 1940.[45]

Government procurement remained a first-priority objective. By 1943, deliveries and sales to the state rose to roughly 44 percent of output—they came to 41 percent on the eve of war. Distribution to members, however, was cut to a level of 40 to 60 percent of the last prewar years. Amounts allotted for distribution in kind came to 200 kilograms per capita in 1940, a figure nearly 13 percent below personal consumption rates of 1926/27. A very drastic decline set in subsequently, until only 70 kilograms were available for distribution (though not necessarily distributed) in 1945. All

---

[44] Joravsky, p. 165.
[45] Arutiunian, p. 164.

this led to a renewed, and so easily understandable, tendency to encroach upon collective farm fields, as private plots became the main source of subsistence for the families of farmers. The tendency was to attack with great—though probably misplaced—vigor, since "more often than not" the acreage involved was insignificant in relation to total holdings of the farm or that part of it which could be worked with the available labor. It is an open question whether yields would have been greater if these relatively small amounts had been left in private hands.[46]

A rapid rise in collective farm market prices and a curious delay in the revision of rates of agricultural taxation resulted in a sizable increase in collective farm cash earnings, a large part of which was subsequently wiped out in the 1947 currency reform. It is significant that, in spite of the very great difficulties with feed supplies, individual livestock holders were able in the last three years of the war to rebuild considerably their cattle holdings. By 1945, these were roughly at the level of 92–94 percent of prewar, though holdings of pigs came only to 36–42 percent of 1940.[47]

Of the entire Soviet period, the early postwar years are the least adequately analyzed in western professional literature. This is probably one of the greatest gaps in our knowledge of Soviet agricultural policy and of developments in the countryside. Nor have Soviet historians and economists, with access to archival material, treated the period 1946–1952 with the same degree of relative (though incomplete) frankness that now characterizes some of the writing on collectivization and the thirties.[48]

This is unfortunate, because it is possible that agricultural policy was also one of the fields in which a clash of views (if not of wills) did take place at that time. After all, this is the period of the curious appearance of the Council on Kolkhoz Affairs, the organization of which followed an official decree condemning many administrative abuses of the collective farm charter as well as the illegal appropriations of socialized land. It was also the period of the three-year livestock plan and of what must have been the *zveno* and the *agrogorod* controversy in the highest policy-making circles. It is tempting to relate this to Kaser's view of Voznesenskii's policies, but such attempts do not lead us very far in the absence of additional evidence.[49] In any event,

[46] *Ibid.*, p. 344.

[47] *Ibid.*, pp. 342–343.

[48] An exception is I. M. Volkov's "Kolkhoznaia derevnia v pervyi poslevoennyi god," *Voprosy istorii*, no. 1 (1966), pp. 15–32. Volkov stresses (and deplores) the use of administrative methods, but he incorrectly identifies their origin in wartime practices. Failure to raise prices and to increase the level of incentives is briefly explained by constraints on available resources.

[49] According to Kaser, Voznesenskii was a forerunner of the current market-oriented school of Soviet economists. See M. Kaser, *Comecon*, 2nd ed. (London: Oxford University Press, 1967), pp. 21–25, 32–35. Additional evidence may well be needed to resolve that point. In any case, efforts to tie Voznesenskii's fortune to harsh

none of the fundamental mechanisms of command farming were ultimately significantly affected and the years 1946–1952 must be viewed on the whole as one of the harshest periods of surplus collection.

As always, trends in grain output and procurements were significant. Stalin appears to have ended the war with grain stocks of approximately 10 million tons, while output (in 1945) was less than half of the prewar. A further decline occurred in draught-stricken 1946. But the ratio of procurements to output remained well above prewar and the accumulation of stocks continued in spite of disappointing trends in output. By 1952, stocks rose to some 33 million tons, or roughly the level of annual procurements.[50]

On the one hand, the Party paid lip service to the peasantry by introducing legislation aimed at the increase of privately held livestock (February, 1947). On the other hand, shortages of feed and increases in the rates of the agricultural tax made private livestock production unattractive. Between 1945 and 1948, the total proceeds of the agricultural tax rose by 75 percent: the increase in these proceeds during the year 1948 alone came to 51.8 percent. By the end of 1952, the number of cows in the private sector was 31 percent below that of 1940 and 21 percent below the level of 1945. On January 1, 1953, pig holdings in private hands were nearly half as large as they had been in 1940 (this was a quarter below the level of 1945). About half of the collective farm households had no cows and less than a third kept pigs. In 1952, average monthly earnings of a collective farmer came to 13 rubles as opposed to the average monthly wage of some 67 rubles for the economy as a whole. In 1948 and in 1950, the private plot provided the collective farm household with 54.5 and 45.3 percent of its total cash income respectively.[51]

Largely as a result of these trends, gross farm output, which came close to its prewar level in 1949, stagnated for the next three years around that level, in spite of substantial investment which absorbed about 16 percent

---

policies in agriculture are not very successful. The consolidation of collective farms and the liquidation of *zvenos* did take place after his arrest in March, 1949. But the big increase in agricultural taxes took place in 1948; see A. G. Zverev, *Natsional'nyi dokhod i finansy v SSSR* (Moscow, 1961), p. 232. Moreover, the share of grain procurement in grain output declines slightly beginning with 1950.

[50] Nancy Nimitz, *Soviet Government Grain Procurements, Distributions and Stocks, 1940, 1945–1963* (Santa Monica, Calif.: RAND Corp., 1964), Table 2. The Soviet statistical agencies have by now published detailed figures on output and procurements for all the years since 1945 in *Narodnoe khoziaistvo SSSR v 1967* (Moscow, 1968), pp. 326–327, 336.

[51] Ostrovskii, pp. 77–78. See also Nimitz, *Farm Employment*, pp. 93–105; Tsentral'noe Statisticheskoe Upravlenie pri Sovete Ministrov SSSR, *Chislennost' skota v SSSR* (Moscow, 1957), pp. 137, 144, 151, 164; and Jerzy F. Karcz, "Seven Years on the Farm: Retrospect and Prospects," in U.S. Congress, Joint Economic Committee, *New Directions in the Soviet Economy*, Part II-B (Washington, D.C.: Government Printing Office, 1966), p. 399.

of total capital expenditures by the state, cooperatives, and collective farms. The speed with which Stalin's successors began to introduce changes in agricultural policy after the dictator's death suggests strongly that they viewed the agricultural situation with great concern and perhaps apprehension.[52]

IV

In contrast to earlier periods, analytical literature on trends in agricultural policy after 1953 is by now quite voluminous.[53] There is thus little need for a comprehensive description, and I will only emphasize the general characteristics.

Trends in agricultural policy in the years since 1953 reveal that many factors responsible for the emergence of command farming under Stalin continued to operate after his death as well. Thus, the rapid rate of economic growth and the related rise in money incomes in the nonagricultural sector, together with the high income elasticity of demand for food, implied a steadily rising demand for farm products on the part of the state. The extent to which this demand rose was further influenced by the desire of the leadership to improve the composition of the citizens' diet and by the continuing exports of grain, this time primarily to other socialist countries in Eastern Europe. Thus, it must have been difficult for the planners to reduce the importance attached to a high and rising volume of marketings.

On the other hand, a lasting improvement in the performance of the agricultural sector required a number of institutional reforms designed to increase the efficiency of agricultural production through the provision of greater and more effective producer incentives and decentralization in

[52] Dr. Karl-E. Wädekin, in his as yet unpublished study of policy toward the private sector, shows that restrictions existing on private livestock holdings (or the burden of taxation) were probably informally relaxed soon after the death of Stalin. In effect, the private sector met its livestock goals for October, 1954 (established in September, 1953), by October 1, 1953. The study will be included in the English translation of his book referred to in n. 32.

[53] See Jerzy F. Karcz and V. P. Timoshenko, "Soviet Agricultural Policy, 1953–1962," *Food Research Institute Studies,* IV, no. 2 (May, 1964); F. A. Durgin, Jr., "Monetization and Policy in Soviet Agriculture Since 1952," *Soviet Studies,* XV, no. 4 (April, 1964); Nancy Nimitz, "The Lean Years," *Problems of Communism,* XIV, no. 3 (May–June, 1965); Jerzy F. Karcz, "The New Soviet Agricultural Program," *Soviet Studies,* XVII, no. 2 (October, 1965); Douglas Diamond, "Trends in Output, Inputs and Factor Productivity in Soviet Agriculture," in U.S. Congress, *New Directions in the Soviet Economy*; Keith Bush, "Agricultural Reforms Since Khrushchev," *ibid.*; Roger A. Clarke, "Soviet Agricultural Reforms Since Khrushchev," *Soviet Studies,* XX, no. 2 (October, 1968); Karl-E. Wädekin, "Manpower in Soviet Agriculture: Some Post-Khrushchev Developments and Problems," *ibid.,* no. 3 (January, 1969).

decision-making, as well as increased supplies of off-farm inputs to agriculture from other sectors of the economy. In short, the task called for some fundamental changes in the nature of command farming. The extent to which these measures would be successful depended on the one hand on the external constraints on allocation of resources (which would affect the supply of off-farm inputs and investment funds), and on the other upon the degree to which the agricultural sector would respond to institutional reform. The complex interrelationships between the private and the socialized sectors and the existence of numerous feedback effects associated with command farming seemed to emphasize the necessity to proceed cautiously, and preferably by using bundles of well-integrated or at least consistent policy measures.

It is in this connection that it is important to recall that the priority given by Soviet leadership to the expansion of the socialized—as opposed to the private—sector was then (and still is) a policy objective in its own right. Given the levels of productivity in the socialized sector in the early fifties and the existence of the feedback effects just referred to, measures granting priority to the development of this sector, rather than agriculture as a whole, could not always be consistent with the broader goals of raising the efficiency of Soviet agriculture.

It is within this framework that we should consider the trends in agricultural policy after 1953—a much more complex course of action than a simple attempt to decompress command farming through modernization. The substantial amount of decompression that did occur under Malenkov and Khrushchev was not so much the logical result of a consistent master plan as that of a series of more or less related measures. Most of these were individually useful and some of them were absolutely necessary for the task of modernization, but their combined impact fell short of its potential precisely because of inconsistencies in policy goals or between individual policy measures.

Considerable improvement occurred in incentives during the period 1953–1958 through increases in procurement prices by a factor of three, a reduction in the total value of the agricultural tax imposed on the private producer (by more than one-half in 1953 and 1954), and a reduction in delivery quotas. In consequence, average real earnings of collective farmers from their farms doubled in five years. Simultaneously, the supply of off-farm inputs was also considerably increased.

Two other shortcomings of command farming—excessive centralization in decision-making and institutional obstacles to rational calculation—were somewhat alleviated by the reform in planning procedures (1955) and by the emphasis placed on cost consciousness and the need to calculate. While all these reforms were taking place, acreage under crops expanded by 40 million hectares (or 23 percent) under the New Lands program. Under the combined impact of these measures, output rose by 43–50 percent and major gains were recorded in factor productivity.[54]

Yet, not all the adopted policy measures were consistent with the goal of decompression and rationalization. While imposition of gross output targets was formally abolished, Khrushchev and many lesser administrators pressed for the expansion of corn acreage and production; this and other similar pressures were effective.[55] Substitution of money wages for income in kind—pressed since 1956—did not always increase the scope of choice for the recipient, who was often unable to convert cash into the type of inputs (feed) he desired.

These difficulties were aggravated in the early years of the Seven-Year Plan when agriculture lost much of its earlier priority, when machinery supplies and credit allocations declined, and when the terms of trade shifted against farming at a time when rapid increases in socialized herds were promoted and a full-swing campaign occurred against the private plot. In such circumstances, little improvement could be gained even from otherwise sensible reforms—such as the abolition of the MTS—as long as procurement targets kept rising and when strict retirement norms for machinery restricted the autonomy of local decision-making further. Administrative lines of authority became entangled in the webs of frequent reforms. Farmer earnings fell in 1959 and 1960, partly as a result of the campaign against the private stock. Migration from the village intensified, output began to stagnate, capital-output ratios rose drastically, and joint factor productivity declined. Some improvements in incentives and the financial position of farms did occur after 1960, but no decisive changes in policy were introduced until after the ouster of Khrushchev in October, 1964.[56]

Actually, it was only after Khrushchev's dismissal that a major and (so far) sustained effort at decompression of command farming was made in the Soviet Union. Though some *ad hoc* measures were implemented in November–December, 1964, to deal with important emergencies, a reasonably consistent package of policy measures designed to raise efficiency *and* output was introduced in March, 1965 (and later elaborated primarily

[54] For details see Karcz and Timoshenko, and Nimitz, *Farm Employment*, p. 97. The lower range of the output increase refers to net output as estimated by Johnson, p. 211, and to the period 1956–1958 (average) since 1950. The upper limit refers to the increase from 1950–1952 to 1956–1958 and to gross output. See also Lazar Volin's "Khrushchev and the Soviet Agricultural Scene," in Karcz, *Soviet and East European Agriculture*, pp. 4–5.

[55] Gross output targets were replaced by procurement targets which did influence the structure of production to a very significant extent.

[56] For details see Nimitz, "The Lean Years," and Karcz, "Seven Years on the Farm."

during the spring of 1966).[57] The new program consisted of raised procurement prices (by and large designed to eliminate most farming operations conducted at a loss until then), cancellation of a major part of collective farm debt, provision of greater credits, and a substantial change in the nature of the collective farm income tax. Simultaneously, an ambitious investment program, which included a state component that was to double in five years, was also announced together with plans for major programs of irrigation and land improvement. Deliveries of machinery and fertilizer to agriculture were to be raised significantly; it appears that plans for the supply of machinery aimed at a 1970 inventory that would be roughly adequate for what Khrushchev once called "the timely performance of farming operations"—a factor of major importance given the climate.

The resulting improvement in the financial position of the farms was to be reflected, to a disproportionately higher extent, in higher earnings of farmers from the socialized sector. Under the provisions of the Five-Year Plan for 1966–1970, incomes of collective farmers were to rise by 38 percent, or nearly twice as much as incomes of workers and employees and considerably more rapidly than gross cash revenue of collective farms. This promised to narrow the gap between urban and rural earnings and, in the countryside, between those of collective farmers and state farm workers. The increase in incentives, accompanied by removal of restrictions on the private sector, was clearly designed to deal with the persisting problem of the labor supply.

One of the more significant aspects of the new program was the announced intention to reduce the pressure on farms by establishing fixed procurement quotas for the duration of the Five-Year Plan (in general, this pledge appears to have been kept).[58] Much greater operational autonomy was granted to directors of the—by now—800 state farms which operate within the framework of a new and much improved system of success indicators (one of which is profit). The new climate, in spite of certain discordant notes referred to below, has contributed significantly to the performance of the agricultural sector.

So far this has been quite impressive, particularly because the government did ultimately decide to reduce some supplies of inputs allotted to agriculture in 1965–1966. For example, state investment in agriculture is now running at a level 20 percent below the original plans,[59] and some of the cuts appear to have been made in 1968. Similarly, machinery deliveries of tractors, trucks, and many other items are running so far behind the delivery rates implied in the original goals that these goals will not be met.

[57] See the articles on this period by Bush, Clarke, and Karcz cited in n. 53.
[58] *Sel'skaia zhizn'*, December 21 and 27, and *Pravda*, December 8, 1967.
[59] Brezhnev's speech in *Pravda*, October 31, 1968.

Thus, once more agriculture has found itself at the shorter end of a tug of war related to resource allocation. But in spite of this, gross output increased in 1966–1968 at the average rate of 3.5 percent per annum, and many of the older inefficient practices (such as the enforced maintenance of large livestock herds regardless of trends in feed supplies) have been eliminated or at least attenuated. It is quite likely that the main reason for this good performance lies in the beneficial impact of increased farm earnings: these rose by 30 percent in three years, and are quite likely to meet the professed goal.

Precisely because the impact of reduced investments and machinery allocations is likely to be observed with a lag, it does seem best to reserve judgment at this point on the overall progress of decompression of command farming in the Soviet Union and the likely form of future agricultural policy. So far, nothing has happened that would preclude the return to more exacting, harsher methods of administration and management that applied in the past.[60] And periods of expansion have—so far—been often followed in the USSR by those of stagnation.

V

Policies are customarily evaluated in terms of their goals. In the case of Soviet agricultural policy during the last 40 years, policy goals and objectives have been inseparably linked with those of economic growth. This is because the decision to collectivize, which in one way or another has exerted a critical influence over agricultural developments ever since, was itself related to the decision to implement a program of rapid and unbalanced industrialization.

I analyzed the performance of Soviet agriculture in a developmental context employing the framework supplied by Bruce F. Johnston and John W. Mellor on a recent occasion.[61] Not surprisingly, the conclusions reached at that time were that Soviet agriculture did indeed perform its developmental functions, especially during the thirties, adequately but only in the sense of maintaining what Grossman calls the balance of the economy. On some occasions, however, that balance was very seriously threatened (particularly in 1932–1933—see pp. 51–52). Undoubtedly, the greatest contribution was that of releasing manpower to nonagricultural occupations, which has been called by Kuznets a part of the factor contribution.

[60] Especially after the publication of a relatively conservative (in relation to expectations, that is) new draft charter for collective farms. See *Pravda,* April 24, 1969.

[61] See Karcz, "Soviet Agriculture." Agriculture contributes by increasing the supply of food, raw materials, foreign exchanges (through export earnings), manpower, and savings.

This much is, of course, indisputable. Whether or not Stalin and his colleagues did envisage all consequences of their course of action of 1929–1930 is—in one sense—beside the point. They did act as if the agricultural sector was expendable and seemed to have pulled back only from the very brink of disaster. But from another standpoint, the question of the impact of their policies on the agricultural sector itself is very important indeed. As we argued above, one of the main costs of collectivization was its detrimental influence on output and productivity trends during the prewar decade.[62] It was precisely then that a greater product contribution by the agricultural sector could have relieved very substantially the burdens placed by rapid industrialization on the welfare of the country's citizens. Moreover, if the function of supplying labor was discharged effectively (or perhaps excessively so), total factor contribution during that period could have been increased if large claims were not made by agriculture on the country's scarce capital resources. Thus, the contribution made by agriculture to Soviet economic development of the thirties may well have brought the same effect and yet be different in the mix of its individual components.

This has not been the only cost, since other costs of the policies pursued from Stalin to Brezhnev are related to the emergence and the persistence of command farming. The institutions and attitudes generated by the latter have proved to be quite difficult to eradicate, not only in the USSR but also in other socialist countries of Eastern Europe. These factors, including the distortion of incentives, of patterns of decision-making, and hence also of specialization and production, as well as trends in the supply of labor, were developed in various efforts to increase the short-run contribution of agriculture to economic development, and they must therefore be viewed as part and parcel of what is often called "the Soviet development strategy."[63] For a long time, the impact of all these factors on productivity has been adverse though in a different degree and has contributed heavily to further claims made by agriculture on investable capital resources.[64]

[62] This is also a major argument in Charles K. Wilber, "The Role of Agriculture in Soviet Economic Development," *Land Economics*, XLV, no. 1 (February, 1969), 94. Wilber's calculations ignore the fact that virtually all the growth of output occurred only after 1953 (*ibid.*, Tables I and II).

[63] Wilber does not appear to grasp this important relationship. His discussion of incentives correctly identifies the root of the difficulty in the system of triple prices rather than in ownership as such. Yet, confiscatory low prices were an instrument of forced saving and the accompanying delivery quotas an instrument of surplus collection. Both were directly related to the rate of growth sought. There would have been no command farming in the absence of rapid industrialization. This, of course, does not imply that incentives must be distorted in any collective farm anywhere.

[64] Incremental output-capital ratios, computed by Lisichkin, turn out to have been as follows: 0.98 for 1951–1955; 0.87 for 1956–1960; 0.08 for 1961–1965 (*Novyi mir*, no. 12 (1967), p. 235).

It might then be useful to follow Granick and view changes in economic organization as investments (or disinvestments) in the nation's invisible capital, which contribute (with a positive or a negative sign) to the rate of economic growth just as do investments in human capital.[65] In this sense, the emergence and the consequences of command farming due to its impact on efficiency must be viewed as long-run social costs of Stalin's basic decisions on the rate and nature of industrialization and of those on agricultural organization deemed necessary to implement the former. (Economic growth is, of course, a social benefit in the long run as well as in the short.)

We are thus ultimately faced with the problem of evaluating the so-called Soviet development strategy, "which is often viewed as the purchase of growth by 'successfully' deferring some agricultural problems to the future," when—as has been recently alleged—these problems are "easier to solve at a [higher] stage of development."[66] Obviously, systematic appraisal of this issue transcends the boundaries of this paper largely because policies must also be judged in terms of the available alternatives. But a few general remarks on this issue ought to be made in closing.

First, the problem of identifying a policy objective that is relevant in this context is not as simple as might at first appear. "Rapid industrialization" or "a rapid rate of industrial growth" is not precise enough for the purpose at hand. Conceivably, Stalin's colleagues and Stalin himself may well have been satisfied with a somewhat lower growth rate than those high rates that were actually achieved in the thirties and in the postwar period. Alternatively, a different time pattern of growth rates as well as of investments might well have been equally acceptable as long as certain other constraints were met. One of these may well have been the achievement of a given level of output and/or capacity at a certain point of time.

Second, some of these time patterns of investments to which Stalin may well have been indifferent, in relation to the one actually achieved, could be realized in practice either by a greater degree of mobilization of resources, or by a more efficient use of resources already employed, or by some combination of the two. As is well known, Soviet achievements in the field of growth under Stalin were primarily the result of a drastic, if not ruthless, mobilization of resources, while gains in efficiency played only a minor role. Thus, the means as well as the ends of policy in this period appear to be considerably less tractable than might at first appear.

When both factors are taken into consideration, it seems best to view them in a framework appropriate for a general equilibrium analysis, where the value of one variable depends on those of others. In this particular con-

[65] Granick, pp. 132–133, 266.

[66] Both quotations are from Wilber, p. 92. His expression "successfully" is contrasted with an alleged "failure" of Soviet agriculture.

text, as long as one is not forced to follow the actual pattern of events (and this is a proper framework for discussion of a policy or a "developmental strategy"), a slight shift in goals may well have made different means quite acceptable and palatable. All too often it is rigidly assumed that climatic[67] or historical limitations in the USSR were such that any top Party decision maker in 1928–1929 could either do what Stalin did (and achieve roughly the same results) or perish, figuratively or literally. To me, such an approach recalls the engineering bias in economics.

So far, we have been dealing only with the economic factors related to the appraisal of Soviet agricultural policy. On these grounds alone, there appear to be sufficient grounds for a reappraisal of the frequently held economic rationale of collectivization (and hence also of the agricultural policy as such).

Such a reappraisal will note that all agricultures contribute to the economic development of their respective countries and that this is not only true of the Soviet Union. It should thus ultimately be possible to make fruitful comparisons between various models of agricultural transformation in the course of economic development. In the meantime, we should bear in mind that the crucial decisions on agricultural policy (and particularly those of 1928–1929) were influenced heavily by political and ideological factors. A balanced judgment on agricultural policy cannot ignore ideological preferences or the struggle for power any more than it can ignore the persisting costs of command farming.

[67] Thus, e.g., much is made by Wilber of soil and climatic limitations, and of an estimate made in 1957 to the effect that Soviet grain yields are "at reasonable levels." Yet, from 1955–1957 (average) to 1966–1968 (average), grain yields in the USSR rose by 48.3 percent, with most of the increase occurring after Khrushchev's dismissal. Should we allow a discount for 1966–1968 yields (15 percent), the increase would still come to 25.8 percent.

PART II

Rural Administration, Law, and Farm Management

3 : Continuity and Change in the Administration of Soviet Agriculture Since Stalin[1]

Robert F. Miller

"Comrades! The Soviet land is in the flower of its strength and is confidently marching forward on the road to Communism. A most important component of the program of communist construction is the practical resolution of the task of creating in our country . . . an abundance of agricultural products" (Khrushchev at the September Plenum of the Central Committee in 1953).[2]

With such phrases Khrushchev signalled the beginning of his campaign to revitalize Soviet agriculture. For the first time since the launching of the mass collectivization drive agriculture was to receive attention as an important economic sector in its own right. Although in the ensuing years there would be substantial backsliding in particular areas, there can be no doubt that the changes in orientation and substantive policy toward the village marked a definite turning point in Soviet agriculture. This paper will consider some of the major administrative aspects of these post-Stalin developments, particularly as they were manifested at the local level in the varying patterns of interaction of Party, governmental, and economic organs.

It is almost a truism in modern administrative theory that administration

---

[1] This paper is based on materials included in my book, *"One Hundred Thousand Tractors": The MTS and the Development of Controls in Soviet Agriculture*, published in the Russian Research Center Series of the Harvard University Press in 1970. I am greatly indebted to the Russian Research Center for generous material and moral support at various stages of the project.
[2] N. S. Khrushchev, *Stroitel'stvo kommunizma v SSSR i razvitie sel'skogo khoziaistva* (Moscow, 1962), I, 84.

is an integral part of the policy process. Administrative practices are capable of radically altering the substance and intent of policies. The Soviet system is no more immune that others to this general political phenomenon.

I have suggested in another place[3] the difficulties in any single-factor approach to the study of Soviet policy-making. A full analysis should consider at least the following four factors or explanatory variables: ideology; the continuing Darwinian competition for power at the upper levels of the political system; the personal style of leadership of the top Soviet ruler(s); and objective situational or substantive requirements. As in most political systems it is usually the last of these factors, the situational requirements, that is decisive in any given Soviet policy decision. What is unique in the Soviet decision-making process, however, is the extent to which the other three variables intervene in the shaping of the final decisions. Indeed, considerations of ideology, elite power competition, or personal leadership style may so strongly condition the perceptions of, or responses to, situational requirements that the effects of the latter on policy may be seriously distorted or even negated entirely. Thus, for ideological or political reasons some problems may never be processed for solution at all, while others may be handled in a quite unexpected manner.

These four factors are also relevant to the administrative side of the policy process. The historical tendency of the system toward frequent administrative reorganizations, for example, may be at least partially accounted for by the ideological principle of a necessary correspondence between political structure and stage of economic development. There is a strong built-in assumption that at every stage of economic development there exists a proper mix not only of policies but also of the political and administrative institutions for carrying them out.[4] The preservation of the MTS system by Stalin in 1952 and its eventual liquidation by Khrushchev in 1958 were explained, at least overtly, in precisely such terms.

The impact of the ongoing power struggle on Soviet administrative processes and structures has long been recognized. Both in Stalin's day and since, political considerations have often been important factors in the reorganizations of the agricultural bureaucracy. Explanations for the delayed reorganization of 1939 and the accelerated reorganization of 1961, for example, would be less than complete without an account of the high-level political conflicts involved.[5]

---

[3] Miller, *"One Hundred Thousand Tractors,"* Conclusion.

[4] See, for example, D. M. Gvishiani, *Sotsiologiia biznesa: kriticheskii ocherk amerikanskoi teorii menedzhmenta* (Moscow, 1962), p. 44.

[5] These events are discussed in Chapter V and the Epilogue of Miller, *"One Hundred Thousand Tractors."* For an excellent treatment of the struggles surrounding the 1961 events see Sidney I. Ploss, *Conflict and Decision-Making in Soviet Russia:*

The least tangible of the explanatory variables is personal style. Despite the many continuities in structure and practice of Soviet agricultural administration, even from precollectivization days, there have clearly been differences in atmosphere and emphasis under successive rulers. Thus, it is possible to speak meaningfully of a Stalinist, a Khrushchevian, and a post-Khrushchevian style of agricultural administration. These stylistic differences have had a considerable influence on the manner in which situational requirements have been perceived and acted upon.

In contrast to the other three variables, the situational factor is usually the easiest to pinpoint. As used in this paper, this variable encompasses the shape and nature of administrative structures and processes as well as the substantive agricultural policies with which they are found to be associated. That is, problems of staffing new institutions, jurisdictional disputes, and the overlapping of administrative functions may be considered situational requirements in the administrative dimension of policy-making.

The student of Soviet politics and administration is invariably struck by the repetitive, almost cyclical pattern of administrative reorganizations. Over the years there has evolved a more or less limited range of structural responses to particular types of problems. Although the choice of a particular structural solution is usually prompted by situational requirements, other factors, such as style, may exert important conditioning influences, as Khrushchev's numerous organizational experiments demonstrate. However, Khrushchev's experiences also show how difficult it is to break established organizational patterns and how narrow the range of structural options really is. The determined efforts of the Brezhnev-Kosygin regime to return to the basic Stalinist format of agricultural administration (but not the substantive policies) further illustrate these limitations, although they may also be taken to illustrate the broad range of functions which may be performed by any given set of structures.

I

Before proceeding with an analysis of specific post-Stalin administrative changes, it will be helpful to describe in some detail the basic administrative patterns of Party and governmental involvement in agricultural administration as they evolved over the years. The role of local Party officials, particularly raion Party secretaries, in agricultural management can hardly be exaggerated. Soviet organizational theorists never tire of asserting the exist-

---

A Case Study of Agricultural Policy, 1953–1963 (Princeton, N.J.: Princeton University Press, 1965), p. 176, and *passim*.

ence of clear lines of separation between Party, governmental, and economic organs in the management of agricultural affairs. Party officials are supposed to be concerned only with overall guidance or "leadership" (*rukovodstvo*), while the governmental and economic officials are supposed to handle the functions of management and administration (*upravlenie*) per se.[6] In actual practice, however, the only realistic way to view the Soviet administrative system is as an integral pattern of functions, with Party, governmental, and managerial roles completely intertwined.[7] The resulting picture is often one of extreme confusion of roles, although this confusion is more apparent than real.

In a broad sense the confusing overlap of functions can be traced to the spurious distinction that is made between policy and administration in Soviet administrative theory. But there are more specific situational explanations. Historically, Soviet leaders have been far more concerned with short-run agricultural production and procurement results than in long-run administrative order, at least to the present time. There has been a strong tendency for local Party officials, the persons held most directly accountable for these results, to involve themselves directly in administrative and managerial affairs during crucial periods of the crop cycle, thus usurping the functions of nominally responsible government and economic officials.

This is not to say that the formal theoretical division of labor is entirely a dead letter. It has always had a certain normative influence. Soviet leaders have generally been aware that episodic interference by raikom bosses is disruptive of long-run administrative efficiency, that it undermines the morale and effectiveness of local managerial and technical personnel. Moreover, Party leadership itself is assumed to entail a certain type of expertise and *modus operandi* which may be impaired by overinvolvement in administrative details.[8] The "proper style" of Party leadership is ideally supposed to consist mainly in the use of such standard techniques as the ideological and political tempering of responsible administrative and production officials, the mobilization of primary Party organizations for the application of pressure at strategic points of administration and production, and the carrying out of periodic checks on the fulfillment of Party and government tasks. The assumption is that this type of indirect leadership will keep local administrators and specialists on their toes, thereby enhancing their effectiveness and securing their conformity to the policies of Party and government

---

[6] See, for example, L. Slepov, *O stile v partiinoi rabote* (Moscow, 1953), p. 30.
[7] For an interesting example of the application of this approach to industry, see Jerry F. Hough, "The Soviet Concept of the Relationship between the Lower Party Organs and the State Administration," *Slavic Review*, XXIV, no. 2 (June, 1965), 215–240.
[8] Slepov, p. 30.

leaders. In short, the ideal of correct Party leadership is strong guidance and influence rather than direct control: getting the responsible bureaucrats and managers to act in the desired fashion with a minimum of outside interference.

The discrepancies between this ideal and actual practice have usually been quite striking. The traditional ideological biases and the developmental priorities of the Soviet system have made a career in agricultural administration relatively unattractive to the ambitious and talented. Although the situation has improved somewhat in recent years, there have accordingly been persistent shortages of competent specialists in local agricultural organs and farms. This problem has undoubtedly been aggravated by the aforementioned tendency of raikom officials to undermine the work of the specialists by interfering in their business. Yet the pressures under which they operate virtually compel the *raikomovtsy* to interfere in this way. The fact that raikom secretaries are held personally accountable for physical results makes them reluctant to rely very heavily on the mediocre personnel of administrative agencies and farms in times of stress, such as annual planting and harvest campaigns. For when the chips are down, as raikom officials have always known, errors of omission are likely to be more severely punished than errors of commission. The resulting vicious circle of crisis management has been extremely difficult to break.

Nevertheless, there are crises and crises. Over the years there have evolved two distinct patterns, or modes, of Party leadership at the local level: one for more or less normal periods, the other for particularly grave crises. I have called these patterns the "raikom mode" and the "politotdel mode" respectively.[9] Under the raikom mode the forms and processes of indirect Party leadership are maintained at least part of the time. Agriculture, being only one of the concerns of raikom secretaries (albeit usually the most important one), is left much of the time under the supervision of lesser-ranking persons of the raikom apparatus. The content of Party work during these relatively quiescent periods generally approximates the norm of indirect Party control. The heads and instructors of the organizational and the *agitprop* departments of the raikom carry on the traditional Party missions of training and distribution of cadres, strengthening the PPO of the villages and farms, etc. Thus, for approximately half the year raikom practice is fairly consistent with the ideal of division of labor among Party, governmental, and economic institutions and with the ideal model of indirect control.

It is during the height of the agricultural season that this division of labor

[9] Miller, *"One Hundred Thousand Tractors,"* Chapter VI. I have discussed these patterns also in "The Politotdel: A Lesson from the Past," *Slavic Review*, XXV, no. 3 (September, 1966), 475–496.

often tends to break down. At such times the raikom seems to shift gears, transforming itself (that is, its leading core of *apparatchiki*) into a managerial organ of a particularly forceful type, with raion agriculture as its enterprise. Deluged with demands by their Party superiors for reports on plan or campaign target fulfillment, raikom secretaries immerse themselves in the most detailed questions of production. Regular patterns of authority are often disrupted, as responsible officials from all walks of life in the raion centers—raikom instructors, agricultural officials, journalists, and even school principals—are dispatched by the secretaries as raikom plenipotentiaries to individual farms, where they are expected to apply unceasing pressure for the attainment of the campaign's goals.

These violent swings between direct and indirect raikom control have been likened in the Soviet vernacular to a hospital fever chart. There is a general awareness that such *likhoradka* (fever) is not a healthy condition, that violent fluctuations in the intensity of Party leadership are deleterious to administrative efficiency and even to long-term agricultural growth itself. At the same time, given the regime's traditional preoccupation with short-term production goals, the method has been fairly effective; and its successful practitioners have reaped their rewards in promotions and honors, official protestations to the contrary notwithstanding. Indeed, the fact that such distinctly different patterns of leadership are possible under the raikom mode shows that it is an amazingly flexible structural arrangement.

Nevertheless, during periods of extremely grave tensions the regime found it to be not flexible or effective enough. In such periods there developed an essentially different mode, the "politotdel mode" of Party control in agricultural production. (It has been used in other sectors as well, for example, the military and the transportation system.) Under this mode the regular territorial Party organs, the raikomy, are by-passed, and control over Party forces in a given area is given to special, production-oriented Party organs attached to the key production or administrative institutions in the area. These organs are expected to apply continuing political pressure in production affairs in the most direct manner.[10] Until 1958, the natural point of attachment for these organs was the Machine Tractor Station system. On the one occasion when they were required after 1958, they were situated in the dominant local administrative agencies: namely, the Territorial-Production Administrations of 1962–1964.

The various historical shifts from one mode to another offer numerous opportunities to study the interaction of the several factors involved in Soviet administrative decision-making. Shifts to the politotdel mode, in particular, have demonstrated the importance of stylistic and political factors.

---

[10] *Ibid.*, pp. 475–476.

Thus, the initial resort to the politotdel mode in late 1932 was as much the result of the personal stylistic preferences of Stalin and his leading agricultural henchman of the time, Lazar Kaganovich, as it was of the deterioration of the situation in the villages. There had been ample evidence of deterioration long before the end of 1932. Most other politicians confronted with this situation, including Stalin's erstwhile opponents in the Politburo, would have in all likelihood opted for a relaxation of controls. Stalin chose to intensify them with the politotdely as his chief instruments.

The subsequent decision to return to the raikom mode and to regularize agricultural administration was also influenced greatly by nonsituational factors. The excesses of politotdel rule manifest by the end of 1933 served to deepen the existing cleavage with provincial Party secretaries, most of whom were ordinarily loyal Stalinists. Whatever their personal preferences, Stalin and Kaganovich were unable to ignore the mounting groundswell of demands for a return to a more normal pattern of rule in the countryside.[11]

The remaining years before World War II saw a prolonged effort to regularize the institutions and procedures of the agricultural system. Against the background of intensifying political and secret police controls throughout Soviet society, genuine efforts were made to rationalize the structure of the agricultural bureaucracy and to maintain the specificity of functions between its main local agencies, the MTS and the raion land department (*raizo*). The role of raikom secretaries remained important in the local administrative setup, but the formal restraints of the raikom mode were essentially preserved.

The Great Patriotic War witnessed a return to the politotdel mode in agriculture as well as in other sectors of society. With the turning of the tide of battle in early 1943, there was a shift back to the raikom mode, which remained in effect for the remainder of Stalin's life. However, the level of raikom involvement in agricultural management remained unusually high throughout the immediate postwar period. Little attention was given to the rehabilitation of regular agricultural organs, which had functioned only fitfully during the war, until the beginning of 1947. The February Plenum of that year was specifically devoted to the revitalization of the machinery of agricultural administration. Particular attention was given to the MTS and the *raizo* as the key instruments of local control. Although there was much talk of a re-emphasis on the indirect methods of raikom leadership at the time, the old, episodic "campaign style" of Party guidance in fact remained a central feature of the village scene, as Ovechkin's sketches so vividly illustrate.[12]

---

[11] *Ibid.*, pp. 489–491.
[12] Valentin Ovechkin, *Izbrannye proizvedeniia v dvukh tomakh* (Moscow, 1963), esp. vol. II, *Raionnye budni*.

Thus, by the time of Stalin's death agricultural policy and administration had settled into a drearily stereotyped pattern. Fundamental challenges to the system, such as the Venzher and Sanina proposals to liquidate the MTS and to strengthen the kolkhozy, were rejected with alarm as incompatible with the very idea of socialized agriculture. As the Stalin era drew to a close, an atmosphere of stagnation pervaded the agricultural scene.

II

Whatever the magnitude of Khrushchev's ultimate achievements—and at least for the first five years of his reign they were quite impressive—his rule in agriculture could hardly be called dull and stagnant. His experimental style was particularly noteworthy in the area of administration. Despite the surface appearance of self-confident pragmatism, his was a style characterized by many paradoxes and ambivalences. On the one hand, Khrushchev obviously shared the old Bolshevik faith in organization as an omnipotent problem-solving device. On the other hand, the frequency and intensity of his reorganizational measures suggest that he had surprisingly little respect for the formal lines of authority and structural differentiation upon which modern principles of management are based, even in Soviet theory. To a great extent he reversed the Stalinist priority of political control over economic efficiency, introducing a broad program of economic incentives to perform indirectly much of the regulatory work which the old Stalinist command system had done directly with so much stress and strain. Yet he certainly did not diminish the leading role of the Party apparatus with respect to economic questions. On the contrary, he raised the long-term economic responsibilities of local Party bosses to perhaps the highest level in Soviet history. To be sure, his continued reliance on the Party had important political motives. The Party apparatus provided his main power base in the struggle with his opponents in the Presidium, and the allotment of leading positions to Party *apparatchiki* in his various industrial and agricultural reforms was undoubtedly a form of political patronage. Beyond this, he was clearly wedded to the idea that Party secretaries *should by right* occupy the leading positions in the management of the country. However, he qualified this enhancement of Party responsibilities with the requirement that Party leadership be based on managerial and technical competence, rather than on mere political authority. It was an assignment that the *apparatchiki* were not always capable of fulfilling.

Two key desiderata in Khrushchev's approach to agricultural administration were "closeness to production" and "responsibility." He felt that the proper testing grounds of Party leadership under the new dispensation were

the "front lines of production." The raikom mode and the processes associated with it did not, in his view, provide sufficient continuity of attention
to agriculture; and the raikomy were too far removed physically from the
seat of production to make truly competent leadership possible. Moreover,
the traditional system of overlapping jurisdictions which Stalin had used to
keep tabs on the bureaucrats tended, in his words, "to depersonalize" (*obez-
lichivat'*) responsibility for performance.[13]

The essence of Khrushchev's approach to organizational problems was,
therefore, to pinpoint responsibility by making specific institutions, such
as the MTS, and specific individuals, such as the raikom secretary, highly
visible in the conduct of agricultural affairs. One of his main goals was to
make it no longer possible for leading officials to hide behind a smokescreen
of shared or blurred responsibilities.

1953–1957

In his speech to the September Plenum of 1953, Khrushchev made clear
the crisis in Soviet agriculture. The series of organizational changes he proposed was in keeping with his diagnosis. However, the addition of a program
of significant economic incentives to the traditional practice of tightening up
political and administrative controls in such circumstances foreshadowed a
distinctly new style of crisis management.

The agricultural bureaucracy had long been a particular *bête noire* of
Khrushchev. He had often in the past ridiculed its desk-bound rigidity and
its inability to cope with difficult new tasks. One of his initial steps at the
upper levels of the bureaucracy was to move administration closer to
production by shifting operational command from the USSR Ministry of
Agriculture in Moscow to the several republican ministries. Under the reorganization of December 9, 1953, the central ministry was thus transformed
into essentially a general staff agency for overall coordination of agricultural
activity and for the performance of technical, supervisory, and house-
keeping functions in support of the republican ministries.[14] An important indicator of the new setup was the transfer of the accounts of the MTS system
to the republican budgets.[15] The specialized operational *glavki* of the All-
Union Ministry in Moscow were replaced by a system of field inspectors

[13] Khrushchev, *Stroitel'stvo kommunizma*, I, 79, for example.
[14] Order (*prikaz*) of the Ministry of Agriculture of the USSR, no. 1029, December
9, 1953, "Struktura ministerstva sel'skogo khoziaistva SSSR," *Kolkhoznoe zemledelie*
(house organ of the ministry), December 17, 1953.
[15] A. A. Ruskol and N. G. Salishcheva, *Pravovoe polozhenie mashinno-traktornoi
stantsii i kharakter ee dogovornykh otnoshenii s kolkhozami* (Moscow, 1956), pp.
17–18, 20.

under a Chief Administration of Production-Territorial Inspection, which was to maintain links with the various levels of the bureaucracy. In 1955, this system of inspectors was extended to the provincial level, where specialized departments in the agricultural organs were replaced by inspectorates.[16] Thus, at the local levels, too, formal structural units were broken up in order to push administrative personnel into the field.

It was at the basic raion level that the thrust of the new organization scheme is most clearly seen. In a fundamental attack on the old system, Khrushchev completely abolished the lowest level of the agricultural bureaucracy, the *raizo*, and transferred most of its functions with respect to kolkhozy, such as production planning and agronomic and zootechnical supervision, to the MTS.[17] (Certain other responsibilities, mostly of a formal nature, such as the registration of plans and contracts, were transferred to the *raiispolkom*.) Since the earliest days of the collective farm system there had been a persistent rivalry between the *raizo* and the MTS over jurisdiction in the kolkhozy. In this competition, power, as a rule, tended to gravitate naturally to the MTS as an operating agency with considerable direct leverage in the vital production affairs of the kolkhozy. Thus, from time to time the authority of the *raizo* had to be reaffirmed by the intervention of the top leaders, who were apparently genuinely committed to the principle of maintaining at least a modicum of separation between operations and administration.[18] Khrushchev, on the other hand, with his extreme production orientation and his antipathy for bureaucracy, saw little value in maintaining this "superfluous" bureaucratic link. (He would apply the same principle—that key production organs be given maximum responsibility for all aspects of agricultural operations—to the procurement function, which he also concentrated in the MTS in 1956.)[19]

Thus, the MTS system, the symbol *par excellence* of state control over production, was made the focus of Khrushchev's initial campaign to bring leadership "closer to production." The kolkhoz amalgamation campaign inaugurated by Khrushchev in 1950 had significantly increased the leverage of the average station by reducing substantially the number of kolkhoz units with which it had to deal.[20] Now much of Khrushchev's early effort went into bringing the actual capabilities of the MTSs into line with their presumed

[16] V. Safonov, "Struktura novaia, a metody starye," *Partiinaia zhizn'*, no. 6 (March, 1956), pp. 56, 58.

[17] See, for example, I. F. Pokrovskii, *MTS—opornyi punkt gosudarstvennogo rukovodstva kolkhozami* (Moscow, 1954), p. 186.

[18] The story of the rivalry between the MTS and the *raizo* is treated in Chapter V of Miller, "*One Hundred Thousand Tractors*."

[19] *KPSS v rezoliutsiiakh . . .* (Moscow, 1960), Part IV, p. 174.

[20] The average number of kolkhozy served by one MTS declined from 32 in 1949 to 11 by the end of 1952.

potential capabilities. An important part of this effort was the strengthening of MTS personnel resources. As a starter, all seasonal tractor drivers and other skilled machinery operators were put on the full-time payroll of the stations.[21] In addition, almost all of the former agronomic and animal husbandry specialists of the *raizo*, many specialists from the upper reaches of the agricultural bureaucracy, as well as most kolkhoz specialists were made permanent staff members of the MTS.[22] These MTS specialists were then attached to individual kolkhozy of the MTS zones to provide close coordination and direction of field operations.

The capstone of the new system of local administration was a radically altered format of Party control. It was tantamount to a return to the politotdel mode, with local Party leadership of production concentrated at the command points of production, the MTSs. Although the politotdel structure itself, with its hybrid combination of Party and governmental authority,[23] was not re-established, many of the basic structural, jurisdictional, and procedural characteristics were very similar. This is not surprising, since Khrushchev was clearly seeking the type of continuous, intensive Party involvement in agricultural management previously associated with the politotdel.

The new arrangement was generally consistent with Khrushchev's policy of moving responsible officials from their desks to the fields, which we have noted with respect to the agricultural bureaucracy. The raikom was, thus, to a great extent decentralized. Its agricultural *otdel* was completely abolished; and so-called "instructor groups" of three or four instructors, headed by resident raikom secretaries, were established in each MTS zone in the raion.[24] In theory each instructor was to be permanently attached to one or two kolkhozy and was expected to live in one of them. The instructors were thereby in a position to exert continuous pressure on the farms and to mobilize local Party members for maximum effectiveness in production. The "zonal" raikom secretaries, in addition to performing similar functions in the MTS, were charged with close, on-the-spot coordination of all Party efforts in the zone for the maximization of production. The first secretary (and usually also the second secretary) remained in the raion center to exercise general supervision of the "zonal" groups and to carry on the usual Party organizational and ideological work.[25]

In principle, the new arrangement provided a significant intensification of

---

[21] Khrushchev, *Stroitel'stvo kommunizma*, I, 229.
[22] I. S. Kuvshinov, *MTS—reshaiushchaia sila kolkhoznogo proizvodstva* (Moscow, 1955), p. 13; see also Khrushchev, *Stroitel'stvo kommunizma*, I, 65, 425.
[23] Miller, "The Politotdel," p. 479.
[24] *KPSS v rezoliutsiiakh . . .*, Part III, p. 652.
[25] *Ibid.*

Party influence over production. Indeed, there had already been a substantial advance toward the physical prerequisites for such an intensification by virtue of the increased Party coverage of kolkhozy the merger campaign had made possible. By September, 1953, the proportion of kolkhozy with primary Party organizations had surpassed 80 percent, as compared with well under 50 percent before the mergers.[26] For the first time in Soviet history rural Party forces were becoming at least potentially useful instruments in support of regime policies.

In practice the performance of the new MTS-based administrative system did not live up to expectations. Crop production did increase substantially, thanks mainly to higher prices paid to kolkhozy and to huge investments in the virgin lands program. But the contributions of the new administrative system and the MTS itself to these achievements were of dubious value. In fact, the longer the MTS operated under the new conditions of "visibility," the more evident its weaknesses and the more questionable the very concept of the MTS became. The ideological support the MTS had accumulated, which had served to shield it from serious attack during Stalin's reign, rapidly dissipated in the more pragmatic atmosphere of the Khrushchev era.

Growing disillusionment with the MTS was expressed in a piecemeal dismantling of the complex edifice of MTS controls over the kolkhozy. One of the earliest targets of Khrushchev's ire was the system of agronomic and zootechnical supervision provided by MTS staff specialists in the kolkhozy. Ignoring the traditionally sad plight of specialists in the kolkhoz, Khrushchev attributed their ineffectiveness under the new conditions to the fact that they were on the MTS payroll and thus not "materially interested" in the performance of the kolkhozy.[27] Accordingly, in August, 1955, most MTS specialists were transferred to complete dependence on the kolkhozy.[28] (Actually, they were given a grace period of up to three years, during which time they would receive supplementary wage payments from the state.)

Another serious problem was utilization of the greatly expanded permanent labor force of the MTS. During idle winter months it was virtually impossible to keep this million-plus army of machinery operators productively employed.[29] If before the vast majority of them were the responsibility of

[26] Khrushchev, *Stroitel'stvo kommunizma*, I, 8, 72 (my calculations).
[27] *Ibid.*, II, 122.
[28] Decree of the Central Committee, CPSU, and the Council of Ministers, USSR, of August 20, 1955, "O merakh po dal'neishemu uluchsheniiu agronomicheskogo i zootekhnicheskogo obsluzhivaniia kolkhozov," in B. A. Boldyrev (ed.), *Sbornik zakonodatel'nykh i vedomstvennykh aktov po sel'skomu khoziaistvu* (Moscow, 1957), I, 182–187.
[29] See, for example, V. G. Venzher, "O razvitii i ukreplenii ekonomicheskikh sviazei MTS i kolkhozov," *Voprosy ekonomiki*, no. 3 (March, 1954), pp. 47–55.

their home kolkhozy, now they were wards of the state. There was just not enough repair and construction work to keep them all employed. Thus, by 1955, there had already begun to appear suggestions for doing away with a large proportion of them by training some in multiple skills, or at least by shifting some of the wage burden back to the kolkhoz.[30]

This was just one aspect of the larger problem of MTS costs, which was beginning to attract high-level attention soon after the introduction of the reforms. Although the MTS, through *naturoplata* receipts, was a major source of state grain procurements, and although it performed a broad range of valuable administrative functions for the state ostensibly free of charge, there was increasing concern over the real costs of MTS services as early as 1954. Up to that time—since early 1938, that is—no one had really attempted to run a cost-benefit analysis on the MTS, largely because of its ideologically sacrosanct position. In 1954, Khrushchev himself took up the cudgel, and at the Twentieth Party Congress in 1956, over considerable conservative opposition, announced the beginning of a program of "gradual" transfer of the MTS to *khozraschet*.[31]

In addition to the questions of MTS efficiency there were disturbing signs of trouble with the reorganization of the raikom, the heart of the new administrative arrangements. The entire scheme had been predicated on the availability of sufficient numbers of relatively well-trained cadres. The criteria for selection of zonal instructors had been weighted more heavily toward technical agricultural expertise than was normally the case for raikom instructors.[32] The number of secretaries and instructors required under Khrushchev's specifications—one secretary for each MTS and one instructor for every one or two kolkhozy in the MTS zone—was in any case considerable. My rough calculations, on the basis of the total number of MTSs and kolkhozy in September, 1953, give a combined total requirement of approximately 55,000 persons.[33] Given the selection criteria, this was nearly an impossible demand. And in fact it appears that the total number of officials in the zonal groups—secretaries and instructors—never exceeded 30,000 at any time.[34]

Besides the scarcity of the requisite personnel, the reorganization en-

[30] Decree of the Central Committee, CPSU, and the Council of Ministers, USSR, of August 23, 1956, "Ob oplate traktoristov i drugikh mekhanizatorskikh kadrov MTS," in Boldyrev, I, 382–384.
[31] *KPSS v rezoliutsiiakh . . .*, Part IV, p. 174.
[32] See, for example, the article by E. Stroitelev, "Sovershenstvovat' metody partiinogo rukovodstva," in *Partiinaia rabota v MTS* (Moscow, 1954), p. 33; also, Khrushchev's statements to this effect at the February-March Plenum (1954), Khrushchev, *Stroitel'stvo kommunizma*, I, 279.
[33] *Ibid.*, pp. 8, 79 (8,950 zonal secretaries plus five times that for instructors).
[34] *Ibid.*, p. 490.

countered serious attitudinal and political problems from its inception. Judging from contemporary local press reports, the raikom secretaries, at least, did not respond to the challenge to go out to the command posts of production with any great alacrity. Given the often primitive conditions of the MTSs, it is perhaps understandable that many of them did not wish to move themselves and their families from the relative comfort of the raion centers.[35] Some apparently never did establish themselves permanently in the MTSs and continued to commute from the raion centers every day— sometimes at distances of 25 to 30 kilometers, under Russian road conditions![36] Khrushchev himself expressed annoyance at the slow pace of implementing the new program. At the February-March (1954) Plenum of the Central Committee he complained, "Many raikom secretaries visit the machine-tractor stations and the kolkhozy only on the fly, as rare guests. They go there, hold a conference, and run home to the raion center."[37]

Some zonal secretaries may have realized, if Khrushchev did not, that exile to a remote MTS might mean a significant loss of prestige and authority, for which the formal designation as raikom secretary could not fully compensate. To a certain extent the authority of the raikom official is a function of his physical propinquity to or contact with the holders of power in the raion center. The validity of this proposition was confirmed by a noted tendency of many raikom first secretaries to ignore the zonal secretaries in the conduct of regular raikom business. V. Churaev, a prominent Central Committee organization specialist, complained in 1956 that zonal secretaries were often not even invited to conferences of the raikom apparatus.[38] Under the circumstances it is not surprising that the turnover of zonal secretaries was fairly high.[39]

Many of the difficulties experienced in the organization and operations of the zonal raikom setup had a political basis. There was an aura of impermanence about the entire scheme, reflecting the insecure status of Khrushchev's own political position. On several occasions he referred to "some comrades"—unnamed, presumably in high Central Committee circles—

[35] See, for example, "Blizhe k zhizni, k sel'sko-khoziaistvennomu proizvodstvu" (lead editorial), *Kommunist* (Saratov daily), January 19, 1954; and "Likvidirovat' obezlichku v rukovodstve kolkhozami i MTS" (lead editorial), *Gor'kovskaia Pravda* (Gor'kii daily), January 26, 1954.

[36] S. D. Khitrov, speech at Eighth Oblast' Party Conference in Voronezh, *Kommuna* (Voronezh daily), February 11, 1954.

[37] Khrushchev, *Stroitel'stvo kommunizma*, I, 277–278.

[38] V. Churaev, "Rukovodstvo khoziaistvom Rossiiskoi federatsii i voprosy partiino-organizatsionnoi raboty," *Kommunist,* no. 7 (May, 1956), p. 22.

[39] Thirty-five percent of the zonal secretaries were replaced in the RSFSR in 1955, according to Churaev, p. 21. Turnover in some areas was considerably higher, for example, in Novosibirskaia oblast' and Khmel'nitskaia oblast'.

who were questioning the viability of the zonal format.[40] Nevertheless, Khrushchev was able to maintain it until November of 1957, when he had already made up his mind to do away with the MTS altogether.[41] In the meantime, the striking decline in the prominence given to the work of the zonal groups in the provincial press during the last year and a half of their existence suggests that they were no longer considered to be a major force for political and administrative control in the village. As had been the case in earlier experiments with the politotdel mode, local Party officials eventually settled into a routine of secondary economic detail work, which greatly impaired their effectiveness as special Party leadership organs.[42]

In retrospect, the zonal raikom setup proved to be one of the least successful of the series of experiments with local Party leadership in agriculture. Its failure was a reflection of the inability of the MTSs to measure up to expectations as centers of administration and control in the countryside. This inability in turn underlined the basically atavistic character of Khrushchev's efforts to cope with the growing problems of agricultural modernization by a system of *reduced* administrative specialization. In his own unique way Khrushchev would eventually try to deal with this problem.

In any case, by 1956 or 1957 he seems to have come to the conclusion, mainly for economic reasons that need not be considered here, that the future of Soviet agriculture lay with kolkhozy (and sovkhozy) as integral production units. The era of the MTS had finally come to a close.[43]

1958–1960

The elimination of the MTS left a huge gap in the structure of Soviet agricultural administration. Much of Khrushchev's effort in agricultural policy and administration in the ensuing years was devoted to filling it. One of the immediate causes of the gap was the inordinate haste with which the MTS was liquidated. By the end of 1958 fewer than 10 percent of the stations in existence at the beginning of the year were still operating.[44]

[40] For example, at the Twentieth Party Congress; see Khrushchev, *Stroitel'stvo kommunizma*, II, 219.

[41] Decree of the Central Committee, CPSU, September 19, 1957, "Ob izmenenii struktury sel'skikh raikomov partii," in *Spravochnik partiinogo rabotnika*, 2nd ed. (Moscow, 1960), pp. 545–546.

[42] For example, "Boevaia zadacha sel'skikh raikomov" (lead editorial), *Partiinaia zhizn'*, no. 5 (March, 1957), p. 8.

[43] For a discussion of the reasons for the liquidation of the MTS, see Chapter XIII of Miller, "*One Hundred Thousand Tractors.*" The high-level political implications are treated in Ploss.

[44] I. S. Malyshev (gen. ed.), *Sel'skoe khoziaistvo SSSR, statisticheskii sbornik* (Moscow, 1960), p. 41.

The reasons for this haste need not detain us long here. Sidney Ploss has documented the existence of a strong conservative opposition to the elimination of the MTS.[45] Having decided that the MTS must go—primarily on economic grounds—Khrushchev, fearing that the normal sluggishness of the bureaucracy would give his opponents a chance to marshal their forces, rushed the liquidation process to completion. Thus, political as well as stylistic and situational factors appear to have figured in the rapid implementation of the "reorganization" policy, as it was euphemistically called.

From a political standpoint the strategy may well have been correct. The rapid sale and transfer of MTS operational capabilities left little enough room for second thoughts or half measures. From an economic and technical standpoint the wisdom was less clear, however.

Among the most immediate problems were the institution of some form of state control over the maintenance and utilization of farm machinery and the stimulation of technological innovation in the kolkhozy. The ideological conceptions which had supported the existence of the MTS system for so many years made the Soviet leaders particularly sensitive to these very real problems. The long-term solution by "sovkhozization" was given an extra fillip by the demise of the MTS, particularly the rapidity with which it was accomplished. Conversions of kolkhozy to sovkhozy proceeded at a very high rate during the first two post-MTS years until considerations of cost and the intrusion of political issues caused Khrushchev to de-emphasize "sovkhozization" as a major policy.[46] The more immediate solution, through the system of Repair-Technical Stations (RTS), was even less fruitful. These stations, which were based on the repair facilities of the MTS, were given responsibility for the repair of kolkhoz machinery and the sale of new machines and implements—all on a strictly cash basis. Given the state of kolkhoz repair capabilities and the shortage of trained technical personnel in the countryside, something like the RTS was essential. Yet within a year of the abolition of the MTS, Khrushchev, ostensibly bowing to a wave of criticism of RTS operations and the alleged demands of certain strong kolkhozy, had begun to encourage the liquidation of the RTS too.[47]

Underlying these various shifts in specific areas of agricultural policy was a fundamental reappraisal of the role of the kolkhoz. During the period

[45] Ploss, pp. 106–107.

[46] See the speech by Polianskii in *Plenum Tsentral'nogo Komiteta Kommunisticheskoi partii Sovetskogo Soiuza, 10–18 ianvaria 1961 g.: Stenograficheskii otchet* (Moscow, 1961), p. 32. For other indications of the official view, see the section "Perepiska s chitateliami" (unsigned), *Kommunist*, no. 8 (May, 1961), pp. 113–114.

[47] See his speech in *Plenum Tsentral'nogo Komiteta Kommunisticheskoi partii Sovetskogo Soiuza, 15–19 dekabria 1958 g.: Stenograficheskii otchet* (Moscow, 1959), p. 60.

Khrushchev appears to have gone through what might be described as a rebirth of faith in the kolkhoz. He had "rediscovered" the kolkhoz as far back as 1956, when he had begun to take note of its growing potential as a source of agricultural investment and local initiative. Certainly one of the main reasons for his sudden decision that the MTS was expendable was his new-found faith in the capabilities of the kolkhozy. The "sovkhozization" campaign can be viewed as only a partial exception to this attitude, since it was directed mainly at the deadwood of the kolkhoz system.

A particularly interesting manifestation of the change in attitude toward the kolkhoz was the toleration, if not active encouragement, during the nationwide discussions of the MTS liquidation, of numerous proposals to expand the organizational framework of the kolkhoz system. Some of the proposals envisioned the re-establishment of the *Kolkhoztsentr* system of the late twenties and early thirties, that is, a substantially autonomous cooperative movement with secondary, tertiary, and national administrative links. This new organization was to be responsible for the administration of all aspects of kolkhoz production, supplies, and a number of other functions customarily performed by state organs. A beginning had already been made during the middle fifties with the establishment of inter-kolkhoz construction enterprises. Khrushchev now lent his support to the creation of inter-kolkhoz repair stations to take over the RTSs.[48]

By the end of 1959, however, Khrushchev began to have second thoughts about the project. Either on his own or under pressure from his colleagues —the latter seems more likely—he had come to the conclusion that such a potentially powerful organized agricultural interest group might be dangerously resistant to Party manipulation. Thus, he found it necessary to declare at the December (1959) Plenum that the re-creation of a *kolkhoztsentr* was "evidently" out of the question.[49] He did, however, encourage the formation of functional inter-kolkhoz enterprises at the local level. This cautious policy has been continued by Khrushchev's successors, and today there are numerous inter-kolkhoz construction, cattle-breeding, cattle-feeding, electric power, and other enterprises. Some of them, like *Mezhkolkhozstroi*,[50] have fairly elaborate oblast' and republican offices with tie-ins to the regular governmental and economic agencies; but as yet there are no major multifunctional associations in the kolkhoz sector.

[48] Khrushchev, *Stroitel'stvo kommunizma*, III, 397.

[49] *Plenum Tsentral'nogo Komiteta Kommunisticheskoi partii Sovetskogo Soiuza, 22–25 dekabria 1959 g.: Stenograficheskii otchet* (Moscow, 1960), p. 409.

[50] See, for example, K. Burilkov, "Zabota o kolkhoznykh stroikakh," *Sel'skaia zhizn'*, May 6, 1965; also, N. Leshchenko and N. Khelemendik, " 'Mezhkolkhozstroi' zhdet priznaniia," *ibid.*, December 24, 1963.

The spirit of new beginnings and of critical reappraisal engendered by the MTS decision was carried over into the area of formal agricultural administration. The sequence of reorganizations and structural innovations involving the MTS, begun in late 1953, assumed the proportions of a veritable parade once the pivotal structure of the MTS was eliminated. In seeking to replace the functions of the MTS, Khrushchev generally tried to avoid the traditional practices of formal bureaucratic "layering" by keeping administrative and political controls as flexible and nonspecific as possible. Thus, he reacted very negatively to suggestions presented during the nationwide discussions on the MTS for a return to the *raizo* as the basic unit of local administration. Instead, he placed the responsibility for most aspects of production administration in the hands of a new raion inspectorate for agriculture, with primary links to the *raiispolkom*, rather than to the regular agricultural apparatus. To emphasize this local connection the chief of the inspectorate was made *ex officio* deputy chairman of the *raiispolkom*; and important local functional agencies, such as seed-control and agrochemical laboratories, were attached to the inspectorates and financed out of the raion budget.[51] (Formerly, when they had been attached to the MTS, they had been financed out of the national and then the republican budgets.) A loose form of consultative coordination of kolkhoz activities in the raion was to be effected by a "production-technical council" under the *raiispolkom*, chaired by the chief of the inspectorate and comprising representatives of the farms and interested raion agencies, such as the raion planning commission. Experience with similar coordinating councils in the past suggests that its operational impact was not likely to be great.

The relative looseness of this administrative arrangement implied that the major responsibility for general direction and coordination of production activities would fall once again on the raikom. As Howard Swearer has pointed out, however, the raikom was poorly equipped to handle these responsibilities during this period.[52] In scrapping the zonal raikom secretary arrangement in the late fall of 1957, Khrushchev had restored the traditional territorial raikom format. However, he had not reinstated the agricultural *otdel*. There were now three secretaries and two *otdely*, organizational and *agitprop*. The eight to ten instructors of the *orgotdel* were expected to concern themselves with agricultural matters in addition to their regular Party

[51] Decree of the Central Committee, CPSU, and the Council of Ministers, USSR, of April 18, 1958, "O dal'neishem razvitii kolkhoznogo stroia i reorganizatsii mashinnotraktornykh stantsii," in N. D. Kazantsev (ed.), *Istoriia kolkhoznogo prava, sbornik zakonodatel'nykh materialov SSSR i RSFSR, 1917–1958 gg.* (2 vols., Moscow, 1959), II, 479.

[52] Howard Swearer, "Agricultural Administration under Khrushchev," in Roy D. Laird (ed.), *Soviet Agricultural and Peasant Affairs* (Lawrence: University of Kansas Press, 1963), pp. 25–26.

organizational responsibilities.[53] Had the scenario called for a return to the ideal model of indirect raikom control, this arrangement might have been satisfactory. But since Khrushchev clearly intended the raikom to remain heavily involved in agricultural production affairs, the burdens on local Party leaders were bound to be excessive.

At the same time, there were certain developments in Party organization in the village during the period which may have compensated for the structural weaknesses of the raikom to some extent. Thanks to the influx of former MTS personnel, the continuing farm mergers, and intensified recruitment, Party coverage in the kolkhozy had steadily increased. By mid-1960, virtually every kolkhoz had a PPO, with a fairly respectable average membership of 28 persons. More than 10 percent of the kolkhozy in the country had PPOs with more than 50 members.[54] In January, 1959, the Central Committee issued a potentially very important decree authorizing the establishment of Party committees, with the rights of raikomy in certain questions, in all kolkhozy with PPOs of more than 50 Party members and in sovkhozy with more than 100 members. Party units in kolkhoz brigades and other subsidiary production groups were made subordinate to the committees with the rights of regular PPOs. The Party committees thus became intermediate organs between the raikom and the Party members in the "front lines of production" in a manner similar to the abortive "sub-raikomy" of 1934.[55] Theoretically, this setup greatly increased the leverage of raikom instructors in their task of mobilizing the kolkhoz labor force for current production goals. However, as of mid-July, 1960, only 4,130 kolkhozy (about 8 percent) and 1,046 sovkhozy (about 15 percent) qualified for the establishment of Party committees.[56] These low percentages and the traditionally low-level salience of kolkhoz Party organizations in the raikom control pattern lead one to question just how much the increasing strength of Party coverage in the village could really compensate for the structural weaknesses of the raikom.

It may not have been entirely coincidental that the years 1959 and 1960 witnessed a serious decline in "socialist discipline" in the countryside. Whether this was a consequence of the weaknesses of the raikom, excessive reliance on the good faith of kolkhoz management, the impossible financial and production burdens placed on the agricultural system by Khrushchev

[53] M. Polekhin and F. Iakovlev, "O nekotorykh voprosakh organizatsionnopartiinoi raboty," *Partiinaia zhizn'*, no. 13 (July, 1960), p. 12.
[54] "Kak raikom nachinaet rabotat' posle perestroiki svoego apparata" (unsigned), *ibid.*, no. 2 (January, 1958), p. 40.
[55] Polekhin and Iakovlev, p. 12.
[56] Decree of the Central Committee, CPSU, of January 26, 1959, "O sozdanii partkomov v krupnykh partorganizatsiiakh kolkhozov i sovkhozov," in *Spravochnik partiinogo rabotnika*, 2nd ed., pp. 574–575.

in his rush to "overtake and surpass" the United States—or any combination of these and other factors—is, of course, impossible to tell with any degree of certainty. The Soviet press and Khrushchev's speeches were full of complaints of falsification of production statistics, of fraudulent livestock operations, and of improper crop planning.[57] The inevitable reaction was a tightening of the flaccid machinery of agricultural controls. The post-MTS honeymoon was coming to an end.

1961

Nineteen sixty-one was a year of transition and movement in agricultural administration, although at the time it was not at all clear what the ultimate direction of this movement would be. A number of important organizational changes were made along lines of tightened control. But the spirit of experimentation and improvisation continued. Rather than following the traditional prescriptions for administrative centralization in periods of tightening controls by strengthening the lines of authority within the Ministry of Agriculture, Khrushchev sought to create a number of independent, nationwide functional agencies that were more likely to be susceptible to his personal control from the top. The prevailing aura of impermanence was heightened by some serious behind-the-scenes infighting and the settling of political scores.

The tightening-up process began with an extensive purge of provincial Party secretaries. Fainsod notes that between October, 1960, and October, 1961, almost 50 percent of the obkom and kraikom first secretaries were replaced or transferred.[58] Although some strictly political issues were involved in these shifts, it was clear that agricultural issues—opposition to agricultural policies or the failure to implement them successfully—were also important.

By February, 1961, Khrushchev felt strong enough to push through his pet project of smashing the agricultural bureaucracy and at the same time destroying the power base of a person who had increasingly become a thorn in his side, Minister of Agriculture V. V. Matskevich. Under the reorganization of February 21, the central ministry was completely deprived of operational responsibilities and recast in the role of a research and education

---

[57] See Khrushchev's memorandum to the Presidium of October 29, 1960, in Khrushchev, *Stroitel'stvo kommunizma*, IV, 182; also, his remarks in *Plenum . . . 10–18 ianvaria 1961*, p. 592.
[58] Merle Fainsod, *How Russia Is Ruled*, rev. ed. (Cambridge, Mass.: Harvard University Press, 1963), p. 226.

agency.[59] Significantly, the personnel of the ministry, much to their dismay and discomfort, were transferred en masse to experimental farms and research facilities outside of Moscow. In another blow at specialized administration, the recently created raion agricultural inspectorates were totally abolished.

At the same time, however, an important step was taken to recentralize control over the repair and sale of farm machinery by the creation of a separate new hierarchy of "Farm Machinery Associations," headed by an All-Union Farm Machinery Association, "Soiuzsel'khoztekhnika."[60] In a reversal of the trend away from centralized, state-owned machinery repair enterprises, Khrushchev ordered the transfer to the new agency and its local raion offices of all remaining RTSs. The specialized operational stations, such as the Land-Reclamation Stations (MMS) and the Pasture Improvement and Livestock Stations (LMS, LZhS), which had survived the liquidation of the MTS, were also placed under its local offices.

To compensate for the gap in local governmental supervision of kolkhoz operations left by the abolition of the "unproductive" raion agricultural inspectorates, Khrushchev introduced an idea he had been pushing since the middle fifties: to bring the procurement organs directly into the production process to insure that production planning and operations conformed to state requirements. Accordingly, on February 26, 1961, he established a new State Committee of Procurements, with republican, oblast', and raion branches, under the USSR Council of Ministers. The "state inspectorate for procurements" under this setup was made responsible not only for procurements but also for the supervision of kolkhoz production operations throughout the year, relying for coercive sanctions on the authority of the raikom and the raiispolkom.[61]

This new attempt to perform the functions of agricultural administration without a formal administrative apparatus was no more successful than

[59] Decree of the Central Committee, CPSU, and the Council of Ministers, USSR, of February 21, 1961, "O reorganizatsii Ministerstva sel'skogo khoziaistva SSSR," *Spravochnik partiinogo rabotnika,* 3rd ed. (Moscow, 1961), pp. 342–352.

[60] Decree of the Central Committee, CPSU, and the Council of Ministers, USSR, of February 21, 1961, "Ob obrazovanii Vsesoiuznogo ob"edineniia Soveta Ministrov SSSR po prodazhe sel'skokhoziaistvennoi tekhniki, zapasnykh chastei, mineral'nykh udobrenii i drugikh material'no-tekhnicheskikh sredstv, organizatsii remontai ispol'zovaniia mashin v kolkhozakh i sovkhozakh ('Soiuzsel'khoztekhnika')," in *ibid.,* pp. 353–355. For Khrushchev's about-face on repair facilities, see *Plenum . . . 10–18 ianvaria 1961 g.,* p. 543.

[61] Decree of the Central Committee, CPSU, and the Council of Ministers, USSR, of February 26, 1961, "O perestroike i uluchshenii organizatsii gosudarstvennykh zakupok sel'skokhoziaistvennykh produktov," *Spravochnik partiinogo rabotnika,* 3rd ed., pp. 358–366, esp. p. 362.

similar efforts in the past. However well situated the procurement organs might have been in theory to supervise the various stages of production, in practice it was difficult to get them to employ their full authority in nonprocurement matters. Moreover, under this setup important areas of kolkhoz activity were left almost completely neglected. Thus, such vital matters as kolkhoz finances and the introduction of new agronomic techniques, which had formerly been under the purview of the raion agricultural inspectorates, were left in abeyance.[62] Virtually all of these "residuals" of administration implicitly devolved upon the raikom. And as we have seen above, the raikom during this period was ill-equipped and too understaffed to perform these various supervisory functions adequately. Sooner or later the demands of functional specificity would have to be recognized.

1962–1964

Recognition came, after a fashion, in the two-stage reorganization of March and November, 1962. This reorganization did mark a re-establishment of a more formal division of functions in the agricultural control machinery, but it still bore the imprint of Khrushchev's persistent antispecific biases and his obsessive rejection of past structural patterns in the quest for an elusive "philosopher's stone" of organizational perfection.

The main thrust of the reorganization was to emphasize still further the responsibility of Party officials for agricultural production and procurements. Structurally, it featured a combination of strong line-type administrative organs with special supervisory Party committees at each level. At the apex of the system, Party and governmental authority was completely fused in an All-Union Agricultural Committee, headed by a first deputy chairman of the USSR Council of Ministers. Significantly, its incumbent was a high-ranking career *apparatchik* from Khrushchev's personal entourage, N. G. Ignatov, who had recently been dropped from the Party Presidium in one of the continuing power trade-offs of the period.[63] The committee included also the head of the agricultural *otdel* of the Central Committee for union republics, the Minister of Agriculture, the chairman of the Farm Machinery Association, and the deputy chairman of Gosplan for agriculture. The All-Union Committee had its close counterparts at the republican, oblast', and krai levels, headed by the respective first secretaries

[62] L. Merdik, "Zagotoviteli ili organizatory proizvodstva?" *Sel'skaia zhizn'*, February 4, 1962.

[63] Theodore Shabad, "Top Farm Agency Named by Soviet," *New York Times*, April 30, 1962.

of the Party committees at each level. These committees were responsible for policy guidance and continuing supervision of all agricultural affairs in their territories.

Day-to-day technical aspects of agricultural administration were entrusted to a new system of administrative organs, beginning at the republican level. Following Khrushchev's 1961 policy, these organs combined production and procurement functions. There were republican "Ministries of Production and Procurement of Agricultural Product," with counterpart administrations (*upravleniia*) at the oblast' and krai levels.[64]

As was the case with most of Khrushchev's reforms, the most radical and vital changes were at the lowest levels of administration. The heart of the 1962 reorganization was the so-called Territorial Kolkhoz-Sovkhoz or Sovkhoz-Kolkhoz (depending on the predominant type of farm in a given area) Production Administrations. Nine hundred sixty of these TPAs were formed in the 3,421 rural raions in existence at the beginning of 1962.[65] They were directly subordinate to the provincial organs of production and procurement. Their operating staffs included a chief of the TPA and a group of "inspector-organizers," usually agronomists or zootechnicians, each of whom was assigned to a fixed number of kolkhozy or sovkhozy (from three to six farms, as a rule). The individual inspector-organizer was responsible for the full range of production-related activities, including planning, accounting, and the introduction of modern farming techniques, as well as regular field operations. An interesting aspect of this local arrangement was its standardized approach to both kolkhozy and sovkhozy. In the beginning some interpreted this feature as an official encouragement for the "convergence" of the two types of farms—a contemporary euphemism for sovkhozization.[66] Whether or not this was Khrushchev's ultimate intention is an intriguing question; in any case, the argument was rarely heard subsequently.

Perhaps the most striking feature of the 1962 reorganization was its provisions for Party involvement in administration. Basically it represented a return to the politotdel mode of Party control. Indeed, in establishing Party committees in the TPAs, Khrushchev expressly cited the MTS politotdel.[67] He reinforced this impression on the eve of the radical restructuring of the provincial Party apparatus in a memorandum to the Presidium, when he

[64] An organization chart of the 1962 structure in the RSFSR is presented in Fainsod, p. 567.
[65] The number of TPAs was subsequently increased. By October, 1964, the original total of 960 had almost doubled.
[66] See, for example, the unsigned editorial "Novyi etap v razvitii sel'skogo khoziaistva," *Sovetskaia Rossiia*, March 20, 1962.
[67] *Plenum Tsentral'nogo Komiteta Kommunisticheskoi partii Sovetskogo Soiuza, 5–9 marta 1962 g.: Stenograficheskii otchet* (Moscow, 1962), p. 75.

declared, "We must establish production as the basis of Party leadership. . . ."[68]

The Party committees of the TPAs were headed by strong "Party organizers," listed on the *nomenklatura* of the obkom, kraikom, or republican central committee. Each "partorg" had a staff of "inspector–Party organizers" (IPOs), each of whom, like their counterparts on the TPA staff, was assigned to a definite number of kolkhoz or sovkhoz PPOs (usually five to seven).[69] The duties of the Party committee staffs were in many ways similar to those of the old MTS politotdel: namely, to keep a "Party eye" on production and related operations of the farms.

Under the March arrangement the raikom temporarily continued to exist, although it was clearly a "fifth wheel" in the administrative structure because of disparities in territorial coverage. As had been the case with the MTS politotdely in 1933 and 1941, the new organs immediately came into conflict with the raikomy. By June, Khrushchev had already concluded that the raion itself as an administrative unit was superfluous.[70] Accordingly, in November he abolished the raion link, along with the raikom, and transferred the remaining functions of the latter to the Party committees of the TPAs. Thus, by the end of 1962 the production-oriented TPA had become the basic unit of governmental and Party control in the countryside. As such, it became a vital component of the drastically reorganized system of Party and state organs established at the November Plenum, when, under the rubric of the "production principle," the entire political and administrative apparatus at the provincial level was split into independent industrial and agricultural hierarchies.

The 1962 reorganizations represented a major political gamble for Khrushchev. The bifurcation of the crucial provincial Party link is an especially good example of the complex interaction of political, stylistic, and situational factors in administrative policy-making. Unfortunately, space does not permit a consideration of the kremlinological implications of the reorganization. Azrael has pointed out quite cogently, in my opinion, that the reorganization was calculated to undermine the positions of the powerful obkom secretaries, upon whom Khrushchev had begun to feel entirely too dependent.[71] This interpretation does not take sufficiently into account, however, Khrushchev's long-standing personal commitment to the enhancement of

---

[68] Khrushchev, *Stroitel'stvo kommunizma*, VII, 174.

[69] See, for example, I. Moroz, "Apparat partkoma za rabotoi," *Partiinaia zhizn'*, no. 7 (April, 1964), p. 37.

[70] N. S. Khrushchev, "Vsemerno ukrepliat' proizvodstvennye kolkhozno-sovkhoznye upravleniia," *Pravda*, June 30, 1962.

[71] Jeremy R. Azrael, *Managerial Power and Soviet Politics* (Cambridge, Mass.: Harvard University Press, 1966), pp. 145–147.

the functional relevance of Party leadership in the economy. Khrushchev, perhaps better than any of his opponents, seems to have understood the long-term dangers for the maintenance of Party control posed by nonspecific, "general" forms of Party leadership in an age of increasing specialization and technical expertise—precisely the dangers suggested by Professor Brzezinski in his well-known article in *Problems of Communism*.[72] The 1962 reorganization can be viewed among other things, therefore, as a genuine attempt to guarantee the continuing relevance of Party leadership by forcing Party leaders to attend to substantive matters.

Unfortunately for Khrushchev, the problem itself may well have been insoluble. The structural solution he offered, at any rate, proved to be inadequate for the size of the task he had set for it. If it accomplished anything, it was to illustrate the limitations of structural manipulation as a technique for solving substantive problems. In this respect his opponents were probably right. For in a very short time virtually the entire catalogue of past difficulties reappeared. Staffing problems once again proved to be a major obstacle to the full implementation of the reorganization. Despite optimistic estimates of the number of trained specialists available for assignment, it proved difficult to recruit the necessary complement of inspector-organizers for the TPAs.[73] And of those actually recruited there were many complaints about their poor training and lack of operational skills. In the area of Party controls, the Party leaders in the TPAs, just as had been the case with their predecessors in the MTS politotdely, soon began to be accused of over-involvement in production matters and of "supplanting" the administrative and technical personnel of the TPAs and farms.[74] Perhaps the crowning insult, however, was the accusation that the TPAs were rapidly reverting to the bureaucratic practices of the *raizo*.[75]

By the summer of 1964, Khrushchev was evidently somewhat disillusioned with the results of the reorganization. There were reports that he was contemplating still another reorganization of the agricultural machinery.[76] Before a new paroxysm of reorganizations could begin, he was, mercifully, overthrown.

[72] Zbigniew Brzezinski, "The Soviet Political System: Transformation or Degeneration?" *Problems of Communism* (January–February, 1966), pp. 1–15.

[73] See, for example, "Konkretnost', delovitost'" (lead editorial), *Pravda*, May 27, 1964; "Znanie dela—osnova rukovodstva" (lead editorial), *ibid.*, August 25, 1964.

[74] See, for example, N. Osadchenko, "Ne k litsu belotserkovtsam," *Pravda Ukrainy*, July 16, 1963; "Edinstvo slova i dela" (lead editorial), *Partiinaia zhizn'*, no. 17 (September, 1963), pp. 4–5; I. Pronin, "Tsentral'naia figura apparata partkoma," *ibid.*, no. 12 (June, 1964), p. 35.

[75] V. Khalmanov, "Proizvodstvennoe upravlenie ili raizo?" *Sel'skaia zhizn'*, November 27, 1963.

[76] Theodore Shabad, "Soviet Premier Scores Secrecy," *New York Times*, August 11, 1964.

III

From the standpoint of originality and high drama, Khrushchev as chief agricultural administrator has been a hard act to follow. But Soviet leaders, alas, have other concerns besides the entertainment of Western analysts. Brezhnev and his colleagues have been very self-conscious in seeking to avoid the turmoil and instability of their predecessor's reign, which they have studiously tried to portray as an aberration. Indeed, they have bent over backward to restore the forms (although not the policies) of the pre-Khrushchevian system of agricultural administration. On the whole, they have succeeded in creating an atmosphere of stable routine which, judging from the remarkable absence of leadership turnover, must be congenial to agricultural bureaucrats.

Within six months of Khrushchev's departure the essential features of the traditional raikom mode of Party controls had been restored. At the November (1964) Plenum the divided structure of oblast' and krai Party organs, based on the "production principle," was replaced by the normal unified structure associated with the traditional "production-territorial principle." The Party committees of the TPAs were also abolished and replaced once again by regular territorial raikomy.[77] In this latter connection, it has repeatedly been emphasized that the less direct norms of Party involvement associated with what we have called the ideal model of raikom control were expected to predominate.[78] It is perhaps significant in this respect that the agricultural *otdel* was not re-established.

It is also interesting to note in connection with the stress on a new look for the raikom that the size of the rural Party complement had increased steadily in the intervening years. By March, 1965, the average kolkhoz PPO contained 40 Party members, and the average sovkhoz PPO 78 members.[79] Thus, the physical conditions for the ideal model were improving substantially. Whether or not this improvement will have much operational significance only time will tell. The historical pattern of raikom neglect of the kolkhoz PPO in operational matters is certainly a good reason for skepticism. On the other hand, the relatively low-key approach to production and procurement matters of the post-Khrushchev regime—really the *sine qua non*

[77] See the detailed description of the reorganization in "Vernost' leninskim organizatsionnym printsipam" (lead editorial), *Pravda,* November 18, 1964.

[78] For example, "V interesakh dela" (lead editorial), *Partiinaia zhizn',* no. 23 (December, 1964), p. 7, where the "incompetent interference" of Party officials in agricultural affairs during the 1962–1964 period is condemned in particularly strong language.

[79] "Sel'skii raikom partii" (lead editorial), *ibid.,* no. 6 (March, 1965), p. 5.

of an effective system of indirect control—seems to have been maintained with a good deal of determination.

The restorationist movement has deeply affected the formal agricultural administrative apparatus as well. The USSR Ministry of Agriculture was fully reinstated early in 1965, and Matskevich was called back to head it. The All-Union Ministry, the republican ministries, and the oblast' and krai agricultural administrations were all reorganized along traditional lines, basically following the old production-branch format. Thus, there are now separate *glavki* for grain crops, technical crops, potatoes and vegetables, veterinary services, mechanization and electrification, etc.[80] As usual the most radical changes involved the lowest levels of administration. The TPAs were replaced by new raion agricultural administrations, which are similar in structure and functions to the old *raizo*, with the significant exception that they are independent of the *raiispolkomy*. The 1,800-odd TPAs in the country at the time of Khrushchev's ouster were converted to 2,434 rural raions (the number has since grown to about 2,800), thus retaining some of the consolidation effects of Khrushchev's reforms, although even this contribution is in the process of being overridden.[81]

A cursory glance at Soviet agricultural administration since Khrushchev, as reflected in Soviet publications, might suggest that little has really changed. There are the same exhortations for increased output, for more competent Party leadership, for a greater role for the agricultural specialist, etc. Indeed, the conscious effort to return to past structural patterns of Party and governmental control might even suggest a reversion to the harsh practices of the Stalin era. This clearly has not happened. For the conservative tendencies in organization have not extended to the crucial area of agricultural policy. As in industry, the new leaders seem to be much more attuned to the need for a consistently applied system of material incentives.

The details of the new policy of stable, generally attainable goals for agriculture will be discussed by others. Here I would point only to certain important stylistic changes in the approach to agricultural problems. Although Khrushchev made a number of important first steps toward a more pragmatic, problem-solving strategy, he was far too impatient by temperament to apply this approach consistently. He never really gave the new institutions and combinations he created a chance to prove themselves. Objective problems and circumstances were never given due consideration in

[80] V. V. Matskevich, "Na uroven' novykh zadach," *Sel'skaia zhizn'*, June 24, 1965.
[81] Brezhnev's speech in *Plenum Tsentral'nogo Komiteta Kommunisticheskoi partii Sovetskogo Soiuza, 24–26 marta 1965 g.: Stenograficheskii otchet* (Moscow, 1965), p. 5. There has since been a continuing increase in the number of rural raions. As of July 1, 1967, there were already 2,746 rural raikomy, indicating a slightly larger number of rural raions than this. "KPSS v tsifrakh," *Kommunist*, no. 15 (October, 1967), p. 101.

the rush to attain the grandiose goals he set for agriculture. One of the really basic achievements of his successors has been to extend to agriculture the approach that has long been applied in industry: a generous consideration for the fundamental requirements of science, technology, and managerial expertise. If Khrushchev's successors are less colorful, they are apparently better prepared to consider concrete issues with dispassion. A good example, perhaps, has been their attitude on the private plots.

This is not to say that the new policies have not encountered opposition. Although the importance of the political factor in decision-making is apparently less acute than during Khrushchev's feverish incumbency, there has been some infighting at fairly high levels over the maintenance of the March (1965) agricultural investment targets. Polianskii mentioned in October, 1967, that he and Brezhnev had been fighting a running battle—not entirely successfully—with certain elements in the planning and financial bureaucracy (undoubtedly supported by high-ranking Party officials) over agricultural investments.[82] Judging from Brezhnev's speech at the October (1968) Plenum and the subsequent Central Committee decree, the struggle has been won, at least for the moment, and the present policies will be allowed to continue.[83] Thus, there is no prospect for a return in the foreseeable future to the old command system of Party and governmental controls at the local level.

At the same time it is wise to keep in mind that the continuation of the current relatively relaxed procurement policies and administrative arrangements is entirely dependent, as in the past, on physical success. A series of poor harvests, a sudden upsurge in official demand for agricultural products, or a drastic shift of resources away from agriculture could conceivably lead to unbearable pressures for a return to the command system of administration. The experiences of the Khrushchev era do not offer grounds for general complacency about the stability of present trends.

IV

The history of Soviet agriculture since Stalin illustrates the complexity of the factors involved even in such seemingly cut-and-dried areas as administration. The loose four-variable paradigm presented in the introduction, although not weighted for relative explanatory significance in Soviet deci-

[82] D. Polianskii, "O roli soiuza rabochikh i krest'ian v pereustroistve sovremennoi derevni," *Kommunist*, no. 15 (October, 1967), p. 24.

[83] See the decree of the Central Committee, CPSU, of October 31. 1968, "O khode vypolneniia reshenii XXIII c"ezda i plenumov TsK KPSS po voprosam sel'skogo khoziaistva," *Pravda*, November 1, 1968.

sion-making, does help to attune one to the main variables and to suggest the ways in which they may be expected to interact.

One of the factors underscored by the present analysis, but usually ignored by political scientists, is that of individual leadership style. In an "apparat-state" like the USSR the norms of an impartial civil service, characteristic of modern western political systems, generally do not apply. Moreover, the top leadership figures themselves are likely to have spent a good part of their adult lives in so-called organizational work and to have a good deal of interest in it—more so, relatively, than their western counterparts. Thus, strong leaders like Stalin and Khrushchev are apt to have a considerable influence on administration as well as policy and to leave the imprint of their styles on administrative structure and behavior. The extreme proclivity for structural experimentation during Khrushchev's incumbency was obviously a manifestation of his personal leadership style—a style that was probably informed to a great extent by the early Bolshevik ideological faith in the efficacy of organization as the key to solving substantive problems.

The influence of political considerations in Soviet policy and administration has been well established. Soviet leaders have often resorted to reorganization as a means of strengthening their power positions and disposing of opponents. In recent years it has become fashionable to treat the political struggle as the single most important factor in the operation of the Soviet system. The salience of political factors in decision-making under Khrushchev would seem to provide a good deal of support for such a conclusion. Whether political opposition was an independent variable, however, or merely a reaction to the imperiousness of his style and/or the radical content of his policies, is really the important question. Political scientists, and not only Sovietologists, are all too prone to underrate the importance of substantive policy considerations in explaining the workings of political systems.

For underlying the overall pattern of Khrushchev's policy actions was an extremely compelling set of substantive situational problems. Foremost among them, perhaps, was the shortage of physical resources for carrying his original reform programs to completion. There can be little doubt that resource scarcity and the threat it posed for the success of his whole program—and his position—were major factors in his ceaseless search for administrative shortcuts and manipulations. Many of his measures had a Ponzi-like quality. And his frantic quest for an ideal administrative solution reflected the desperation of a gambler down on his luck.

Perhaps the most important lesson of the Khrushchev era—a lesson which has apparently been well learned by his successors—is the correlation between functional specificity and administrative efficiency. A high degree of functional differentiation, combined with suitable adaptability and flexibility, has been recognized in contemporary political science and organization literature as a hallmark of political modernization.[84] Khrushchev's insistence on direct Party involvement of a most patent sort in managerial and technical matters was certainly anachronistic. His successors have taken a number of steps to remedy the situation, generally by returning to the norms of the indirect raikom mode of Party control in agriculture and the re-creation of substantially autonomous administrative and managerial institutions, although the degree of independence is, of course, only relative. Whether this new policy of political restraint and stability can be maintained is an interesting question, which will ultimately be determined by a combination of situational, political, ideological, and perhaps even stylistic factors. For the long-term implications of the "modernizing model" of administration with respect to the general principle of Party control over the economy may well become a matter of concern to present or future Party leaders.

[84] See, for example, Samuel P. Huntington, "Political Development and Political Decay," *World Politics*, XVII (April, 1965), 386–430. Huntington asserts that functional adaptability is more important than specificity, a point with which Khrushchev certainly agreed. His failure can be taken as an indication either that the Party is an obsolescent political institution—a premature conclusion in my opinion—or that Huntington's formulation needs considerable tightening and/or qualification.

4 : The Changing Nature of the Kolkhoz Chairman

Jerry F. Hough

One of the most persistent problems of the Soviet countryside has been the difficulty of attracting qualified personnel to the kolkhoz and of retaining them. The young people—particularly graduates of the seven-year or secondary schools—have often left for the city; those trained in the city—even agronomists—have often shown great reluctance to accept employment on the farm. In significant part, the countryside has been caught in a vicious circle. Conditions have been poor, therefore qualified personnel have not wanted to come or stay, and therefore it has been difficult to improve conditions.

The flight from the countryside has been intensified by a number of social-political-economic factors, many of which are discussed in other papers in this book. This paper focuses on one relatively neglected factor, the personnel policy followed by the Soviet leadership in its selection of kolkhoz chairmen and regional agricultural and Party officials. It explores the changes in personnel policy over the last four decades, drawing material not only from secondary Soviet sources but also from an examination of over 310 published biographies of kolkhoz chairmen. This study illuminates some of the difficulties caused by the criteria often used for personnel selection, and it suggests that these criteria have frequently fostered the flight of management talent from the countryside. It also examines the policy changes which seem to have been directed to the correction of this problem.

I

The November, 1929, Plenum of the Central Committee, which signalled the beginning of the mass collectivization drive, called for the "decisive promotion of workers as organizers and leaders of kolkhozy," and it launched a mass program of recruiting workers for supervisory work in the countryside. The first group of these men—the famous "25,000ers" was overwhelmingly composed of rank-and-file workers with long production experience (89 percent of the group were said to be of this background).[1] Of the 25,000ers, 70 percent were Party members and 9 percent were members of the Komsomol.[2] The 25,000ers were but the forerunner of a much larger movement of city workers into the countryside. Between 1928 and 1938, over 250,000 such men were appointed to permanent kolkhoz posts.[3] Not all of these workers became chairmen, but the chairmen of the first years of mass collectivization came in very large part from men of this background. In the words of Bienstock, Schwarz, and Yugow, "kolkhoz administrative staffs were composed chiefly of persons alien to rural life and without knowledge of local conditions or of the people among whom they had to work."[4] In these circumstances the relationship between chairman and kolkhozniki must have been quite strained.

After the initial collectivization drive, the turnover among the kolkhozy chairmen was extremely high. A survey conducted in 24 republics, territories, and oblasti showed that 36 percent of the chairmen were changed in 1933 alone.[5] At the end of 1934, one-third of the chairmen had one to two years tenure, 30 percent a tenure of two to five years, and the rest presumably had held their jobs for less than a year.[6] By 1937, only 9 percent of these officials had held their post for five years or more—that is, since the days of the early industrialization drive.[7] (Of the 1937 chairmen, 46 percent had held their positions for less than a year.)

As the original worker-chairmen were removed, they were often replaced by men of a quite different background. As Bienstock, Schwarz, and Yugow report, no comprehensive studies of the social origins of kolkhoz chairmen were published toward the end of the prewar period, but official statistics on the percentage of Party members among chairmen are quite suggestive.

[1] S. Trapeznikov, *Istoricheskii opyt KPSS v sotsialisticheskom preobrazovanii sel'-skogo khoziaistva* (Moscow, 1959), p. 149.

[2] I. Pronin, "Podgotovka kvalifitsirovannykh kadrov v sel'skom khoziaistve SSSR," *Ekonomika sel'skogo khoziaistva*, no. 6 (1967), p. 22. In Trapeznikov, p. 149, it is stated that 75 percent of the 25,000ers were members of the Party.

[3] Gregory Bienstock, Solomon M. Schwarz, and Aaron Yugow, *Management in Russian Industry and Agriculture* (Ithaca, N.Y.: Cornell University Press, 1948), p. 179.

[4] *Ibid.*, pp. 179–180.

[5] M. A. Vyltsan, "Pod"em kolkhoznogo proizvodstva vo vtoroi piatiletke (1933–1937)," *Voprosy istorii*, no. 9 (1958), p. 6.

[6] I. E. Zelenin, "Kolkhozy i sel'skoe khoziaistvo SSSR v 1933–1935 gg.," *Istoriia SSSR*, no. 5 (September–October, 1964), p. 6.

[7] Bienstock, Schwarz, and Yugow, p. 181.

The proportion of Communists among the collective farm chairmen fell from 46 percent in the early 1930's, to 30 percent in 1936, to 19 percent in 1938.[8] Education attainments of the new chairmen were quite low: in 1939, only 8 percent had as much as incomplete secondary education, two-thirds had elementary education, and the rest were essentially semiliterate.[9] In one raion studied in detail at this time, 76 percent of the chairmen came from the villages of their kolkhozy, and 7 percent from neighboring villages. Only one-fifth had been city workers or hired farmhands.[10]

Biographies have been found of 50 persons who became kolkhoz chairmen in the period 1929–1940 and survived into the 1950's.[11] A breakdown of the origins of this group is similar to that found in the raion mentioned in the preceding paragraph. Among these 50 chairmen, there is a sharp difference between those who first came to their posts before 1932 and those who were named in that year or later. Of the 14 persons who became kolkhoz chairmen from 1929 through 1931, only one seems to have come from the local countryside. Seven had been long-time workers immediately prior to their appointment, six had been low-level political or soviet officials (three of them had been workers only a few years earlier). On the other hand, only two of the 36 who became chairmen in the period 1932–1940 had come to their posts from a worker's job. Twenty-three had been promoted from within the kolkhoz.[12] Another six had been chairman or secretary of

---

[8] *Ibid.*

[9] *Pravda,* March 7, 1940, quoted in *ibid.*, p. 182. The 1959 census combined the categories of kolkhoz chairman and deputy chairman. It indicated that only 2.3 percent of these officials had incomplete secondary education or better. *Itogi vsesoiuznoi perepisi naseleniia 1959 goda SSSR* (Moscow, 1962), p. 181.

[10] Bienstock, Schwarz, and Yugow, p. 182.

[11] The chairmen who survived into the fifties and sixties and who were prominent enough to be elected to the Supreme Soviet or to have their obituaries printed in the press are, of course, the most successful of the kolkhoz chairmen. One cannot be certain how similar their backgrounds are to those of the less successful chairmen. However, as shall be seen, the backgrounds of the chairmen in our sample do differ, depending upon the period in which they first became chairmen, and, as in this case, these differences usually correspond fairly closely to the statistical information available. Perhaps the centralized nature of Soviet personnel selection, coupled with the usual Soviet practice of conducting business through the use of "campaigns," greatly increases the likelihood that a nonrandom sample will produce background profiles which are more representative than would otherwise be the case. We cannot be certain about the reliability of other inferences drawn from the sample, but it is frequently quite suggestive. At a minimum the biographical data illustrate phenomena which are documented in the secondary sources.

[12] Soviet biographies usually do not distinguish between a chairman selected from within the kolkhoz and one who comes from a lower position in another kolkhoz. Thus here, as elsewhere in the paper, the category "from within the kolkhoz" really means "from within some kolkhoz." In some cases in the 1930's, the precise year of a man's selection as chairman is not given in the biography, but had to be determined by interpolation.

the village soviet, but now they were primarily persons with an agricultural rather than an industrial background. Less than one-quarter were Party members at the time that they became chairmen.

Bienstock, Schwarz, and Yugow concluded that the new chairman constituted "a definite type of 'responsible worker' ": "He has come to recognize that he is a part of the government, a carrier of Soviet policy."[13] Yet, while the kolkhoz chairman of the late 1930's clearly was responsible to the government and the Party—and removable by the local Party raikom—the biographies of these men suggest that they usually were more of the "us" than of the "them" in the countryside. It is likely that most were perceived primarily as the representatives of their kolkhozy, trying to act as buffers between the kolkhozniki and the outsiders (the "them") centered in the MTS and the raion center. In the words of a 1968 newspaper editorial, "He was an intelligent, not very literate peasant, who knew, however, how to count centners and rubles. [The peasants] respected him for his business sense; they invited him to weddings and christenings; they rebuked him at meetings, at the same time feeling sorry for him as they would a father burdened with great cares."[14]

The pattern of kolkhoz chairman selection of the late 1930's continued into the early wartime period. Sixty to 70 percent of kolkhoz chairmen and brigadiers were called into the army in the first year of the war, and many others were drafted later.[15] Their replacements often were women and older men from the villages, particularly in areas under German occupation or threatened with it. Some 68 percent of the new chairmen in the first year of the war came from within the kolkhoz, and the proportion of women among them rose from 2.6 percent in 1940 to 14.2 percent at the end of 1943.[16]

As the war drew to a close—and perhaps even earlier in the important agricultural areas far from the front—a new type of kolkhoz chairman came to the fore. The wartime chairmen were removed in great numbers. (In 1946, 41 percent of the chairmen had a tenure of less than one year.)[17] Their replacements were usually men returning from the army, and they had a relationship with the peasants quite different from that of their prewar predecessors: "[The postwar chairman] brought from the war strictness

13 Bienstock, Schwarz, and Yugow, pp. 182–183.
14 *Sovetskaia Rossiia,* February 6, 1968, p. 1.
15 Iu. V. Arutiunian, *Sovetskoe krest'ianstvo v gody Velikoi Otechestvennoi voiny* (Moscow, 1963), p. 95.
16 *Ibid.,* pp. 97–99. In regions under German occupation or near the front, 27.2 percent of the chairmen were women at the end of 1943; in other regions, only 8.9 percent of the chairmen were women (*ibid.,* pp. 99–100).
17 I. M. Volkov, "Kolkhoznaia derevnia v pervyi poslevoennyi god," *Voprosy istorii,* no. 1 (January, 1966), p. 19.

and discipline. He decided to overcome the savage devastation with a desperate attack, as he had recently taken enemy entrenchments. His ears sometimes became deaf to the innumerable human complaints and requests which he could in no way satisfy. The word 'give' became the most frequent in his lexicon."[18]

However, it was not simply army experience which distinguished the new chairmen from those of the late 1930's. Part of the difference stemmed from the pressures under which they worked. As Khrushchev graphically emphasized in 1953 and 1954, postwar governmental demands on kolkhozy were overbearing,[19] and those on their chairmen were scarcely less so. In the words of one historian of the post-Khrushchev period, "the practice of bringing the chairmen to judicial responsibility without sufficient justification became fairly widespread."[20] With few resources at his disposal to motivate kolkhoznik response, the postwar chairman had little alternative other than to "become deaf to the innumerable human complaints and requests which he could in no way satisfy."

Indeed, judging from the available biographical data, an ability to apply pressure may have been one of the major criteria used in the selection of kolkhoz chairmen in the early postwar period. Biographies have been found of 47 chairmen who first assumed their posts in the years 1945–1949, and they suggest that (perhaps outside of the Baltic states) the regime increasingly returned to the practice of bringing these officials to the kolkhoz from the outside.[21] Even excluding those peasants who became chairmen after a number of years in the army, over 55 percent of the chairmen in the sample came from outside the kolkhoz. Another 10 percent were promoted from within, but in reality they were outsiders who had been sent to the farms only a few years before. A Soviet scholarly study of the countryside in 1946 indicates that this practice was widespread. Its author asserts that "many of these leaders, having come to head kolkhozy, did not even become members of kolkhozy." At the end of 1946, he states, there were 238 such chairmen in Ivanovo oblast', 273 in Kalinin oblast', 332 in Vladimir oblast', and 211 in Moscow oblast'.[22]

One of the usual characteristics of the new kolkhoz chairman was membership in the Party (T. H. Rigby estimates that approximately 40 percent

[18] *Sovetskaia Rossiia,* February 6, 1968, p. 1.
[19] See particularly his speech to the Central Committee in September, 1953, and his memorandum to the Party Presidium in January, 1954. N. S. Khrushchev, *Stroitel'stvo kommunizma v SSSR i razvitie sel'skogo khoziaistva* (Moscow, 1962), I, 7–100.
[20] Volkov, p. 29.
[21] Of the seven chairmen of kolkhozy in the Baltic states, five appear to have been local peasants.
[22] Volkov, p. 29.

of the chairmen were Party members in 1948),[23] but their general educational level remained low. In late 1945, only 0.3 percent of the chairmen in the USSR had received higher education, 3.5 percent had obtained secondary education, 90.7 percent elementary education, and 5.5 percent were semiliterate.[24] The available biographies suggest, however, that an "ability to count centners and rubles" remained an important criterion of selection. Of the 40 chairmen outside the Baltic states, 20 percent had held accounting-financial positions, 15 percent had been teachers, 15 percent had worked in the trade network (usually the rural co-ops), and over 20 percent had been chairmen or secretaries of village soviets.

The biographies of the chairmen of this period—even those of the successful chairmen who retained their posts into the late 1950's and the 1960's —are frequently quite unimpressive. One, who became chairman at the age of 30, for example, had become the head of a library at the age of 18 and then a senior Pioneer leader in a secondary school. After seven years in the navy, he was successively the head of a club in a factory, deputy chairman of a raion consumers' cooperative organization, and chairman of a village soviet.[25] Even the biography of a graduate of the Timiriazev Agricultural Academy might be undistinguished: senior agronomist of the oblast' land department, head of the oblast' land department, director of an MTS, senior agronomist of a raion agriculture department, then kolkhoz chairman.[26] These men obviously had proved equal to their job or they would not have been selected as deputies to the Supreme Soviet over a decade later. Nevertheless, to the extent that these types of background were typical for kolkhoz chairmen of this period, there is little reason to be surprised at the high rate of turnover of chairmen which continued to be reported.

II

It is customary to point to 1955—the year of the famous "30,000er" movement—as a crucial turning point in the history of the kolkhoz chairman. In reality, however, the 30,000er movement really represented the continuation of a program which was begun after Khrushchev entered the Central Committee secretariat in 1949 and which was intensified after he became First Secretary in 1953.

Khrushchev's intervention in national agricultural policy dates from the

[23] T. H. Rigby, *Communist Party Membership in the USSR, 1917–1967* (Princeton, N.J.: Princeton University Press, 1968), p. 434.
[24] Volkov, p. 19.
[25] *Deputaty Verkhovnogo Soveta SSSR, sed'moi sozyv* (Moscow, 1966), p. 311.
[26] *Deputaty Verkhovnogo Soveta SSSR, piatyi sozyv* (Moscow, 1959), p. 435.

initiation in 1950 of the policy of amalgamating the nation's kolkhozy—a policy which contributed to the reduction of the number of kolkhozy from 250,000 in 1949, to 124,000 in 1950, to 69,000 in 1958, and to 36,000 in 1965. It was this event which was a crucial watershed in the history of the kolkhoz chairman. The increase in the size of the farm meant in itself the final break with the prewar policy of a kolkhoz chairman from and of the local peasants. The chairman of a large farm inevitably became a remote figure, particularly to the peasants in the more distant settlements.[27] Moreover, in practice, as will be seen, the new chairmen of the amalgamated kolkhozy increasingly were named to their posts from the outside.

After the amalgamation, the level of education of the majority of kolkhoz chairmen continued to be low. As late as July 1, 1953, 52 percent had only an elementary education, and 11 percent were "in essence, semiliterate people."[28] However, among the new kolkhoz chairmen could be found men with a level of education almost unknown in earlier years. By July 1, 1953, over 16,000 chairmen (18 percent of the total) had higher and secondary specialized education—2.6 percent a higher education and 15.4 percent a secondary specialized one.[29] By the time of the call for 30,000 volunteers to head lagging kolkhozy in March, 1955, this figure had risen to 29.3 percent of the chairmen.[30] The proportion of these men with agricultural higher or secondary specialized education is not indicated, but it has been reported that of the men who were named kolkhoz chairmen in 1951 and 1952, 12,000 were agricultural specialists.[31]

There are no comprehensive data available on the work experience of the more educated officials coming to head kolkhozy in these years. In 1953, however, Khrushchev had spoken of the need for "first of all, good organizers," and he had asserted that "in the present conditions one of the most important forms for strengthening further the union of workers and peasants is [the sending] of personnel of the socialist city to the kolkhoz countryside."[32] It seems clear that personnel selection was guided by this line of thinking. Biographies are available of 82 persons who first became kolkhoz chairmen from 1950 through 1954, and they indicate that only 13 were promoted from within the kolkhoz—and six of them were women who

[27] See Alec Nove, "Peasants and Officials," in Jerzy F. Karcz (ed.), *Soviet and East European Agriculture* (Berkeley and Los Angeles: University of California Press, 1967), pp. 62–63.
[28] A. N. Karamelev, "Dvizhenie tridtsatitysiachnikov i ukreplenie kolkhozov," *Voprosy istorii KPSS*, no. 1 (1962), p. 116.
[29] Khrushchev, I, 73; *Sel'skoe khoziaistvo SSSR, statisticheskii sbornik* (Moscow, 1960), p. 474.
[30] Karamelev, p. 125.
[31] *Ibid.*, p. 115.
[32] Khrushchev, I, 75.

became chairmen in what probably was a short 1953 campaign to promote local women to this post.[33] A policy of selecting outsiders as chairmen is also suggested in the fact that the percentage of Party members among chairmen rose rapidly in these years, reaching 79.6 percent by July 1, 1953, and 90.5 percent by April 1, 1956.[34]

The new chairmen of 1950–1954 came from a variety of lines of work. A number had backgrounds similar to the new chairmen of the late 1940's: one was a raion inspector of statistics, another a school principal, another a chairman of a raion consumers' co-op, another a chairman of a rural soviet with a most diverse and dubious career.[35] However, an increasing number had years of experience in governmental and/or Party supervision of agriculture. Of the 38 outsider-chairmen in the sample who were first named to their posts in 1953 and 1954, 79 percent had such a background. Immediately prior to their appointment as chairmen, ten had been in the oblast' and raion agricultural organs (often as head of the abolished raion agriculture department), two had been administrative officials in the MTS system, and three had been chairmen of a village soviet. Five had come from the Party raikom, five from Party work in the MTS (usually as deputy director for political work), and five from leading work in the raion soviets. Many had the type of combined agricultural-soviet-Party experience which has been typical of rural raion officials throughout the postwar period. One, for example, had come out of the navy in 1946 to become head of the raion division of Gosbank, secretary of the Party raikom, head of the raion agriculture department, and then deputy chairman of the *raiispolkom* before becoming kolkhoz chairman in 1954.[36] Complaints later appeared that "some" Party and soviet organs sent to the kolkhozy men who had been unsuccessful in the raion center, but for the first time a number of kolkhozy came to be headed by men with substantial administrative experience which was directly relevant to their new jobs.

In 1955, the leadership demanded the intensification of the policy of sending outsiders to kolkhozy. In an open appeal (*obrashchenie*) "to all Party, soviet, trade union, and Komsomol organizations, to workers, engineering-technical personnel, and white collar workers of the Soviet Union," the Cen-

---

[33] Of the 82 persons in the sample who became chairmen in this period, 11 are women. One of the women was named chairman in each of the years 1950, 1951, and 1954, and eight of them in 1953. Six of the eight 1953 women chairmen were promoted from within the kolkhoz, one was a section agronomist of an MTS (and likely was attached to the kolkhoz), and one was a chairman of a village soviet who had been a kolkhoz brigadier several years earlier.

[34] *Sel'skoe khoziaistvo SSSR*, p. 474.

[35] See, for example, the biographies in *Deputaty . . . piatyi sozyv*, pp. 116 and 123, and in *Deputaty . . . sed'moi sozyv*, pp. 261 and 373.

[36] *Deputaty . . . sed'moi sozyv*, p. 90.

tral Committee and the Council of Ministers called for sending 30,000 "progressive and highly-qualified people of the socialist city for permanent work as kolkhoz chairmen."[37] To stimulate the flow of volunteers, the leadership offered very generous monthly payments to supplement the regular salaries which were paid out of kolkhoz income; to train these men, it set up three-week courses in all republican and oblast' centers and then placed the new chairmen for two months in advanced farms in the regions to which they were being sent.[38] Over 100,000 persons volunteered to serve as 30,000ers, and 20,416 were accepted and sent to the farms in 1955. In 1956 and early 1957, 5,508 more were sent. Another 6,154 chairmen, who had already been sent to kolkhozy in 1954 and early 1955, were retroactively given the privileges of a 30,000er, bringing the total number of this group to 32,078.[39]

A Soviet scholarly study of the 30,000ers reports that of the 18,000 sent to the kolkhozy of the RSFSR, the Ukraine, Belorussia, and Kazakhstan in 1955, around 55 percent had higher or specialized secondary education.[40] Unfortunately, this study presents a detailed analysis of the background of the 30,000ers in only two western regions—the republic of Belorussia and the oblast' of Smolensk—and then only of those sent in 1955. In these two areas there was a wide variation in the background of the officials chosen (see Table 1).

Table 1 : *Background of the 30,000ers.*

Institution of Prior Employment	Belorussia[a]	Smolensk
	(PERCENT)	
Party organs	29	13
Soviets	10	54
Agricultural organs	8	4
Industrial enterprises[b]	29[c]	24
Other organizations	21	5

[a] The figures for Belorussia do not add up to 100 percent in the source.
[b] In the Belorussian case, this category was actually labelled "economic organizations and industrial enterprises" and presumably included MTS officials.
[c] The economic and industrial employees in Belorussia were distributed in the following manner: workers, 13; foremen, 25; engineering-technical personnel, 48; shop heads, 32; enterprise leaders, 31.
SOURCE: Karamelev, pp. 119–120.

[37] *Direktivy KPSS i sovetskogo pravitel'stva po khoziaistvennym voprosam* (Moscow, 1958), IV, 372.
[38] The first year at his post the 30,000er was given 1,500 extra rubles a month, 1,200 extra rubles a month the second year, and 1,000 rubles a month the third year. See the Central Committee–Council of Ministers decision "About measures for further strengthening the kolkhozy with supervisory personnel" in *ibid.*, pp. 392–398.
[39] Karamelev, pp. 118, 121.
[40] *Ibid.*, p. 119.

Judging from the 30 biographies available of persons who became kolkhoz chairmen in 1955, the 30,000ers with industrial backgrounds did not make particularly successful kolkhoz chairmen. In fact, none of the 30 men came directly from such a background. Rather, 30 percent had come from Party organs (usually the rural raikomy), 24 percent from soviets, 23 percent from the MTSs, 7 percent from other agricultural organizations, 13 percent from other institutions, and 3 percent from within the kolkhoz. (Of course, if a large majority of the workers and officials of "economic organizations and industrial enterprises" in Belorussia and Smolensk were actually employed in the MTSs, then the statistics of the sample correspond fairly well to those cited in Table 1.) Of the former Party and soviet officials among the 30 000ers in the sample, over half (and perhaps as many as three-quarters) were involved in large part in the supervision of agriculture. (It is perhaps interesting to note, however, that a third of the 30 chairmen had had teaching experience sometime in their careers, compared with less than 10 percent in the 1950–1954 group.)

After 1956, the statistics on the percentage of kolkhoz chairmen with higher and secondary specialized education give the impression of a continuation of the policy of sending more specialists to head the kolkhozy. The proportion of chairmen with higher and secondary specialized education (*not* all with agricultural education, it should be emphasized)[41] rose from 29.3 percent in April, 1955, to 37.1 percent in April, 1956, then remained basically unchanged for two years, and afterwards rose to 50.4 percent in 1959, 58.4 percent in 1961, and 69.6 percent in April, 1966.[42] Yet these statistics are somewhat misleading, for the number of kolkhozy was reduced radically in this period—from 85,000 in 1956, to 55,000 in 1959, to 36,000 at the end of 1965.[43] As a result, the actual number of chairmen with higher and secondary specialized education dropped from 31,450 in 1956 to 25,700 in 1958 and (with the exception of a short-term rise in 1959) remained more or less at that level into the mid-1960's.[44]

In practice, the turnover of kolkhoz chairmen in the second half of the 1950's was much lower than it had been in the first half of the decade. According to a 1960 statistical handbook, on July 1, 1953, 23.8 percent of kolkhoz chairmen had held their positions for less than a year,[45] but in

---

[41] See p. 114.

[42] Karamelev, p. 125; *Sel'skoe khoziaistvo SSSR*, p. 474; *Ekonomika sel'skogo khoziaistva*, no. 10 (October, 1961), p. 11; *Narodnoe khoziaistvo SSSR v 1965 g.* (Moscow, 1966), p. 440.

[43] *Sel'skoe khoziaistvo SSSR*, p. 50; *Narodnoe khoziaistvo . . . 1965,* p. 405.

[44] These figures were calculated on the basis of the statistical sources cited in ns. 42 and 43.

[45] *Sel'skoe khoziaistvo SSSR*, p. 474.

September, 1953, Khrushchev put this figure at one-third.[46] The high rate of turnover continued with the initiation of the 30,000er movement, and on April 1, 1956, the proportion of chairmen with less than one year tenure stood at 29.7 percent.[47] However, Khrushchev had insisted that the 30,000-ers accept permanent appointments in the kolkhozy, and a large number did remain in their posts for some time. Over 25,000 of the 30,000ers were still kolkhoz chairmen on June 1, 1958—three-quarters having been there for at least two years and half of them for at least three years.[48] The proportion of kolkhoz chairmen with under one year tenure fell to 17 percent in 1957 and 1958 and to 4.6 percent by April 1, 1959.[49] The proportion of chairmen with three or more years' tenure rose from 36.4 percent in 1956 to 56.5 percent in 1959.[50] Only RSFSR figures have been found for April 1, 1960, but they are almost identical with the 1959 USSR figures: 4.8 percent with tenure of under a year, 39.9 percent with one to three years, and 55.3 percent with three years or more.[51]

While kolkhoz chairmen were changed in the late 1950's, the overall turnover statistics indicate that poor kolkhoz performance was often handled not by appointing a new chairman but by amalgamating the kolkhoz with a more successful one or by changing it into a sovkhoz. (In the period 1956–1964 the number of households per kolkhoz rose 43 percent, the number of sovkhozy from 5,098 to 10,078.)[52] For this reason the number of kolkhoz chairmen removed was considerably higher than the number of new chairmen appointed. If a poor kolkhoz was merged with another, it presumably came under a more successful manager; if it was transformed into a sovkhoz, it was almost certain to be placed under a director with higher or secondary specialized education.[53]

The men who did become kolkhoz chairmen for the first time in the last half of the 1950's seem quite similar to those who were selected in the first half of the decade. As has already been mentioned, the 30,000er movement

[46] Khrushchev, I, 73.
[47] *Sel'skoe khoziaistvo SSSR*, p. 474.
[48] Karamelev, p. 125.
[49] *Sel'skoe khoziaistvo SSSR*, p. 474.
[50] *Ibid.*
[51] V. O. Morozov, "Iz istorii razvitiia sel'skogo khoziaistva RSFSR (1953–1958)," *Istoriia SSSR,* no. 4 (July–August, 1961), p. 35.
[52] *Sel'skoe khoziaistvo SSSR*, pp. 42, 158–159; *Narodnoe khoziaistvo . . . 1964,* pp. 390, 399.
[53] The percentage of sovkhoz officials with higher and secondary specialized education was consistently much higher than in the kolkhozy throughout the postwar period, and it only increased as the number of sovkhozy rose. By 1965, 91.8 percent of the directors had such education. See *ibid.*, p. 426, for the education level not only of the directors but of other sovkhoz officials as well.

actually continued into early 1957 (with various oblast' officials being prodded by 19 additional Central Committee–Council of Ministers decisions),[54] and the abolition of the MTS in 1958 (and then of the RTS) resulted in the movement of more higher administrative personnel into the kolkhoz. In the fall of 1959, when Party journals were again emphasizing the need for "strengthening the leadership of the kolkhozy" (and when the number of chairmen with higher and secondary specialized education actually did rise),[55] the reports about the new chairmen had a familiar ring to them. In Belorussia, for example, there were 235 new kolkhoz chairmen, 39 of whom had been raikom secretaries, 27 *raiispolkom* chairmen and deputy chairmen, 49 heads and chief specialists of the raion agriculture inspectorates, and many of the rest undoubtedly MTS-RTS officials.[56] The available biographies of new kolkhoz chairmen of this period reveal a similar pattern. As before, the small contingent of women chairmen had primarily been promoted from within the kolkhoz,[57] but of the 47 men who first became kolkhoz chairmen in the period 1956–1960, 74 percent came from the outside.

The amalgamation of kolkhozy and the personnel policy of the 1950's combined to insure that by the end of the decade kolkhozy were normally headed by men with considerable administrative experience (much of it usually in agriculture). Moreover, these changes created the conditions necessary for a development long desired by the leadership—a management-employee relationship much closer to that found in industry.

The administrative situation created in the kolkhoz sector by the personnel policy of the 1950's was, however, different from that in industry in one crucial respect. The engineer who had dreams of becoming a plant manager or even an industrial minister knew that the path to these posts usually began with lower-level work within the enterprise. To a young man, the offer of a lower administrative job within a plant presented at least the potential of a bright future. The ambitious agronomist, on the other hand, was in a different position. Given the personnel policy of the 1950's, his hopes of becoming kolkhoz chairman rested on finding a staff job in the MTS or the raion-level agricultural organs and rising to an administrative post there. If he accepted a lower-level administrative post within the kolkhoz, existing personnel practice gave him little chance of being promoted to the chairmanship. (Indeed, few of the men for whom biographies are available moved from an agronomical post in a kolkhoz to higher positions above the kolkhoz chairman level.)

[54] Karamelev, p. 121.
[55] See p. 112 of this chapter.
[56] *Partiinaia zhizn'*, no. 19 (October, 1959), p. 13.
[57] Of the eight women who became kolkhoz chairmen in the period 1956–1960, six came from within the kolkhoz.

The leadership further increased the problem of attracting qualified people to the kolkhoz by keeping the post of kolkhoz chairman largely out of the normal lines of promotion to higher Party, soviet, and agricultural positions. In December, 1959—a time when successful 30,000ers might well have been thinking of the possibility of promotion—Khrushchev reported that S. N. Fak, a kolkhoz chairman in Orel oblast' since 1954, had indeed been named first secretary of the Party raikom. However, his kolkhozniki were unhappy at the prospect of losing a very capable chairman, and they wrote a letter to the Central Committee and "comrade Khrushchev personally," petitioning that Fak be left in his post. In this letter the kolkhozniki asserted, "We think that the Orel Party obkom acted incorrectly. Surely couldn't a man be found in the oblast', in the apparatus of the Party obkom, to be secretary of the Dmitrov raikom? It seems to us that it's easier to find a man to be raikom secretary than to find a kolkhoz chairman who loves his work and dedicates himself to it as much as comrade Fak."[58]

To "agitation in the hall and applause," Khrushchev praised the analysis. He continued, "I want to ask the secretary of the Orel obkom, comrade V. S. Markov, who is an experienced Party official, how it turned out that the obkom did not understand what the kolkhozniki understand well."[59] He then concluded his discussion of the incident in the most categorical terms: "Comrades! It is unconditionally necessary to satisfy the request of the kolkhozniki and to leave comrade Fak at the post of kolkhoz chairman."[60]

This incident has frequently been cited in western literature as a prime example of the type of public gesture a dictator uses to increase his public support, and undoubtedly this factor does much to explain the length and form of the First Secretary's response. However, behind the folksy language was a very real personnel policy, one followed not only in the late 1950's but throughout the postwar period. Whatever may have been the fate of kolkhoz chairmen leaving office, few were promoted to important Party and governmental posts in the provinces. Full biographies have been found of 195 persons who were first secretary of a rural raikom sometime during the postwar period, 410 persons who were obkom first secretary in this period, 204 who were oblispolkom chairman, and 122 who were republican minister of agriculture, republican deputy minister of agriculture, or head of an oblast' agriculture administration.[61] Of the raikom first secretaries, less than 5 percent had held the post of kolkhoz chairman before their selection as raikom leader, compared with 4 percent of the oblispolkom chairmen, less

---

[58] Khrushchev, IV, 93–94.
[59] *Ibid.*, p. 94.
[60] *Ibid.*, p. 95.
[61] There is some overlap in these figures, for a man who had been raikom first secretary before becoming obkom first secretary would be included in both categories.

than 2 percent of the high agricultural officials, and 1 percent of the obkom first secretaries.

Many of the officials for whom we have biographies did have substantial experience in lower agricultural administration—but in the MTS and sovkhozy rather than in kolkhozy. Some 33 percent of the high agricultural officials had been director (or in some cases chief agronomist) of an MTS or a sovkhoz, while 21 percent of the oblispolkom chairmen had been an administrative or political leader in one of these two institutions. About 16 percent of the raikom first secretaries had been director of an MTS or sovkhoz, 5 percent had been chief political officer at one of these institutions, and at least an additional 7 percent had held high posts in oblast' or raion agriculture administrations.[62]

The personnel policies followed with respect to kolkhoz chairmen can hardly have promoted the movement of those with drive and ambition into the post of kolkhoz chairman, let alone into the junior managerial and staff posts on the farms. One would not want to attribute the difficulties in recruiting agronomists to the kolkhozy, or the failure of the number of specialists in the kolkhozy to rise in the last five years of the Khrushchev period, solely —or even primarily—to the regime's personnel policy.[63] Surely much can be explained by the economic and social consequences of the stagnation of agricultural production in these years. But it would be incorrect, I think, to discount the impact of personnel policy, particularly for ambitious men with the drive which the leadership was most eager to bring to the countryside.

III

The kolkhoz chairmen of the 1960's—especially of the late 1960's—are much more difficult to discuss than their predecessors. Less statistical evidence has been published, fewer scholarly articles have been written on the subject, and fewer speeches on agriculture have been given by the General Secretary.

It is reasonably clear, however, that the early 1960's were marked by an increase in the turnover rate for kolkhoz chairmen. As the results of the harvests became unsatisfactory in this period, the 30,000ers discovered that the regime's call for men for "permanent work" in the countryside carried no guarantee with it. (And, with the special bonuses to the 30,000ers expiring at about the time that kolkhoz income came under pressure, many

[62] In addition, a number of raikom secretaries are said to have engaged in unspecified "soviet work." In many cases this may have included a stint as head of the agriculture department or deputy chairman of the *raiispolkom* for agriculture.

[63] For the statistics, see *Narodnoe khoziaistvo . . . 1964*, p. 421.

of these men may have been quite eager to return to the city.) Khrushchev
signalled the change in policy in February, 1961, when, after several years
of relative silence on the subject, he returned to a familiar theme: "If we
want . . . to receive a high harvest from the fields, it is necessary to clean
the fields of weeds. . . . There are such weeds even among the people who
have made their way into the midst of the leaders of kolkhoz and sovkhoz
production."[64] A certain number of "weeds" were, in fact, pulled. In the
Ukraine, where there were just under 10,000 kolkhozy, 1,500 Communists
were "directed" to the post of kolkhoz chairman by the end of the summer of
1961, and the language of the speech reporting this fact leaves open the possibility that more had been promoted from within the kolkhoz.[65] In Bash-
kiria in the summer of 1962, it was reported that 24 percent of kolkhoz
chairmen had a tenure of under one year and another 33 percent had a tenure of from one to three years.[66]

With the increasing turnover of chairmen came several changes in the
background of the men who occupied this position. In the first place, the
percentage of chairmen with higher or specialized secondary *agricultural*
education rose very sharply, at least by the second half of the 1960's. Before
this time, reports on the education of kolkhoz chairmen limited themselves
almost exclusively to the category "higher and secondary specialized education," thereby including graduates of Party schools, pedagogical institutes,
and so forth. In the second half of the decade, officials found it worthwhile
to refer specifically to agricultural education, and some of the statistics
are quite impressive. For example, in Stavropol' krai, 75 percent of kolkhoz
chairmen and sovkhoz directors were said to have higher and secondary
education in 1958 (not even secondary specialized education, it should be
noted); in 1967, 85 percent of these men had higher and secondary agricultural education.[67] In 1958, it was reported without criticism that 260 of 500
kolkhoz chairmen in Dnepropetrovsk oblast' had higher and secondary education; by 1968, over 90 percent of kolkhoz chairmen and sovkhoz directors
in the oblast' were agricultural specialists.[68]

A second change in the 1960's has been an apparent reversal of Khrushchev's policy of selecting kolkhoz chairmen in large part from among "the
best organizers of the socialist town." Party officials now state that "practice shows that leaders of the farms and the chief specialists at times make
mistakes in their actions solely because they had not previously passed

[64] Khrushchev, V, 92.
[65] *Pravda Ukrainy*, September 29, 1961, p. 6.
[66] *Partiinaia zhizn'*, no. 13 (July, 1962), p. 22. Quoted in Howard R. Swearer,
"Agricultural Administration under Khrushchev," in Roy D. Laird (ed.), *Soviet
Agricultural and Peasant Affairs* (Lawrence: University of Kansas Press, 1963), p. 22.
[67] *Partiinaia zhizn'*, no. 14 (July, 1958), p. 16; *ibid.*, no. 7 (April, 1967), p. 41.
[68] *Ibid.*, no. 12 (June, 1958), p. 35; *ibid.*, no. 13 (July, 1968), p. 23.

through the lower steps of supervisory work."[69] (The author of these lines emphasized the importance of chairmen having had the experience of being a brigadier.) In the past, Party officials now reported, "we often turned to the oblast' organizations for help in selecting candidates for the post of kolkhoz chairman or sovkhoz director";[70] at the present time they claim to be selecting local people, largely from within the local farms. When raikom secretaries cite examples of outsiders being brought in to improve a lagging farm, they most often refer to lower officials in nearby successful farms:

A year and a half ago the raikom recommended to the kolkhozniki [of "Zaria Kommunizma"] that they elect Nikolai Petrovich Shpilevyi as chairman. Prior to this he had worked as chief accountant in the advanced kolkhoz named Lenin and had adopted much of the style and methods of leadership of its chairman, Hero of Socialist Labor, M. K. Dudchenko. He has higher economic education. For a long time we [the Party raikom] kept an eye on him and studied him at work. We became convinced that he deeply understood the economy of his farm and possessed organizational ability. . . .

Having taken N. P. Shpilevyi into the reserve for promotion, the raikom periodically began to use him to fulfill different assignments: to present reports to seminars for kolkhoz chairmen and sovkhoz directors, to participate in the preparation of questions for examination by the raikom bureau and plenary sessions. And finally the time arrived when we considered it possible to promote him to independent work.[71]

While there clearly has been a change in emphasis in the enunciated criteria for selecting kolkhoz chairmen, it has not been possible to determine the frequency with which chairmen are, in fact, now selected from below. No comprehensive statistics have been found on this subject, and there are available only nine biographies of persons who first became kolkhoz chairmen since 1961. It is perhaps significant, however, that six of the nine chairmen had five to ten years of lower staff or administrative experience within a kolkhoz (usually, it seems, the one in which they became chairman) and that a seventh chairman had risen within a local sovkhoz before being given leadership of a kolkhoz. Ranging in age from 29 to 42 when they first became chairmen, the nine joined the Party only in their late twenties or early thirties (the age at which industrial managers have long become Party members).

Not only is there a possibility that the biographies of the kolkhoz chairmen are increasingly coming to resemble those of Soviet plant managers, but the official descriptions of their role also sound more familiar to a student of

[69] *Ibid.*, no. 6 (March, 1968), p. 40.
[70] *Pravda*, February 12, 1969, p. 2.
[71] *Partiinaia zhizn'*, no. 11 (June, 1966), p. 40.

Soviet industrial management: "It is not simply kolkhozniki who surround the chairman now but also specialists of different branches. Even if he has finished two institutes, he still will not be able to understand all the details of complicated contemporary production. . . . Together with the chairman stand excellent assistants: the agronomist is the fully-empowered boss of the fields and plants; the zootechnician is the head of the farms and cattle yards; the engineer or the mechanic is a specialist on the machines and mechanisms."[72]

While the Party leadership seems to be trying to apply the model of Soviet industrial management to the kolkhozy, it is too soon to know if the kolkhoz chairmanship is destined to become the key step toward higher agricultural, governmental, and Party positions that plant managership has been in industry. It will require the biographical data of the 1970's to answer this question. Those who would predict this development may, however, be heartened by the biography of one deputy to the USSR Supreme Soviet selected in 1966—Semen K. Grossu of Moldavia. Grossu was born in 1934 and graduated from the Kishinev Agricultural Institute in 1959. He was appointed chief agronomist of a kolkhoz and then joined the Party in 1961. Sometime in the early 1960's he became kolkhoz chairman, and in 1965 at the age of 31 he was named head of the Suvorov raion agricultural administration.[73] One might well imagine Grossu (or some counterpart) becoming raikom first secretary toward the end of the decade, a lower official of the secretariat of the Moldavian Central Committee or a deputy minister of agriculture in the mid-seventies, and so forth.

Yet, in at least one key respect, the administrative situation which seems to be evolving in the countryside inevitably is radically different from that found in large-scale industry. In industry there is only one territorial link between the plant manager and the USSR ministry, and in much of heavy industry (particularly in plants in the RSFSR) there is none. A man can become plant manager in his late forties or early fifties, remain in this post for some five years, and still hope for promotion into the ministry. In agriculture, on the other hand, there are three territorial links between the kolkhoz chairman (or the sovkhoz director) and the USSR ministry—the raion agricultural administration, the oblast' agricultural administration (at least in the larger republics), and the republican ministry of agriculture. To have a successful career in agricultural administration, therefore, a man needs to be promoted above the kolkhoz level at a relatively early age—not necessarily at the age of 31, as was Grossu, but surely by 35 or 40 at the latest.

The crucial question for agricultural personnel policy is: Should the

---

[72] *Sovetskaia Rossiia*, February 6, 1968, p. 1.
[73] *Deputaty . . . sed'moi sozyv*, p. 122.

large, highly mechanized farm which is being developed in the Soviet Union be managed primarily by men in their late twenties and early thirties? Or, if it usually is managed by men in their forties and fifties, will the leadership be able to attract to the kolkhoz and sovkhoz sufficient numbers of men with the necessary drive and ambition?

I suspect that the answers to these two questions represent a very serious dilemma for Soviet agricultural administration. It is a dilemma which may be soluble only by a fairly radical change in the planning-administrative system—specifically by coming to rely upon price mechanisms to control the farm manager to the point that the need for large agricultural administrative structures at intermediate territorial levels will disappear. In such circumstances, the "distance" between the farm manager and the USSR ministry would be short enough to permit managers to be recruited from men in early middle age who still have hope of significant career advancement. Of course, if the independence of the farm manager became sufficiently great, the post might well come to be regarded as the culmination of a career, not a step at the lower levels of a hierarchy. If such a system were adopted, it would provide an extremely interesting test for the proposition that very large-scale operations are as compatible with efficiency in agriculture as in industry.

5 : Structural Change and the Quality of Soviet Collective Farm Management, 1952–1966

Robert C. Stuart

During and after the Khrushchev era there have been significant adjustments in the basic structure of the Soviet collective farm and its operational features. Amalgamation has increased the size of the kolkhoz and of its component production brigades, enhancing the importance of the latter as a decision-making unit. Both the decision-making framework and the rules of the game have changed under the impact of monetization.[1] The range of structural and operational adjustments has been diverse and beyond the limits of the present paper. Here we focus upon the changing structure of the kolkhoz and upon the qualitative improvement of management.

Structural and functional changes in the kolkhoz and its production brigades have necessitated attempts to improve managerial quality in conjunction with monetization. We argue, however, that, at least for the immediate future, the benefits of these reforms may be limited because of (1) the tendency for dysfunctional consequences of structural change to offset improved managerial inputs, (2) inadequate attention to the improvement of managerial quality at the brigade level commensurate with its enhanced decision-making functions, and (3) the marked neglect of training relevant to the economic aspects of decision-making.

[1] For an excellent discussion of some of the problems of this period, see Frank A. Durgin, Jr., "Monetization and Policy in Soviet Agriculture Since 1952," *Soviet Studies*, XV, no. 4 (April, 1964), 375–407. For a more extended treatment, see Robert C. Stuart, "Managerial Decision-Making in Soviet Collective Agriculture, 1952–1963" (Ph.D. dissertation, University of Wisconsin, 1969).

I

Since the early 1950's, the typical kolkhoz has grown significantly in land area.[2] In 1950, there were approximately 121,400 agricultural artels, with sown area per artel averaging 1,062 hectares.[3] By the year 1964, there were 37,600 such artels with sown area averaging 3,280 hectares each.[4] This amalgamation campaign, which began earlier and continued throughout the 1950's (at varying rates both spatially and temporally), was also accompanied by conversions of kolkhozy into sovkhozy and, in some cases, by withdrawals of land from the agricultural sector.[5] Although adequate data are difficult to obtain, the nature of these changes for the period 1957–1963 is summarized in Table 1. It might be noted that while the number of kolkhozy declined in all regions (although at varying rates of change), the sown area of the collective sector did increase in some regions, notably the central Black Earth zone and the Turkmen Republic.[6]

The amalgamation process has had an impact upon the kolkhoz more significant than mere increase in size. In particular, the period under consideration has been characterized by expansion of brigade size and alteration of the functional characteristics of the brigade as a basic production unit.[7] Let us examine the nature of these changes.

To consider the changing nature of the production brigade, it is helpful to distinguish between *simple amalgamation* and *complex amalgamation*. In the former case, the number of kolkhozy declines while the sown area of each brigade and the number of brigades, in total, remain as before. It is a simple regional combination of existing kolkhozy to form larger kolkhozy. In simple amalgamation, the brigade, as a production unit, would remain essentially unchanged, although the number of brigades per kolkhoz increases and, from the viewpoint of the kolkhoz manager, only the prob-

[2] We initially consider land area as a measure of kolkhoz "size" and later examine the expansion of other inputs.

[3] *Narodnoe khoziaistvo . . . 1964*, pp. 245, 272–273.

[4] *Ibid.*

[5] While many aspects of structural change are relevant to an understanding of Soviet agricultural development, the amalgamation process is of greatest immediate interest for examination of decision-making procedures *within* the kolkhoz.

[6] One possible explanation might be recent emphasis upon reclamation of bog and marsh lands.

[7] Thus one can argue that a brigade of increased size, in terms of the inputs that it commands, and increased importance, in terms of the decisions made at the brigade level and the decision-making tools that are utilized (for example, machinery and equipment at the brigade level and the introduction of *khozraschet* at this level), is a fundamentally different type of organization than that prevailing in the past.

Table 1 : *USSR state and collective farms, organizational changes, 1957–1963.*

	1957	1958	1959	1960	1961	1962	1963
Decline—kolkhozy	6,486	8,854	14,245	9,455	3,487	761	1,156
Increase—sovkhozy	807	97	494	879	906	289	606
Newly organized—kolkhozy	109	30	26	—	7	7	4
Dismantled—kolkhozy	1,031	368	101	163	504	317	343
Amalgamated—kolkhozy	1,866	8,010	12,271	4,550	1,092	683	1,037
Converted—kolkhozy	5,730	1,256	2,074	5,068	2,906	402	271

SOURCES: *Narodnoe khoziaistvo . . . 1962*, pp. 330, 352; *Narodnoe khoziaistvo . . . 1965*, p. 257; *Sel'skoe khoziaistvo*, pp. 43, 51; V. G. Venzher, *Ispol'zovanie zakona stoimosti v kolkhoznom proizvodstve*, 2nd ed. rev. (Moscow, 1965), p. 113. These figures should be taken as orders of magnitude only. For example, in a given year, several kolkhozy may be newly formed but later amalgamated or even converted.

lem of administering the affairs of the brigades may become more complicated.

In the alternate pattern, complex amalgamation, sown area expands per kolkhoz and per brigade at approximately the same rate. Hence the number of brigades per kolkhoz would remain the same, and the resources at the command of the brigade manager as well as of the kolkhoz manager will have expanded.[8] Given that the permanency of the production brigade is a relatively recent phenomenon (roughly post-1955), and also recognizing data limitations, we may test for the existence of the two patterns in the relatively limited period 1957–1961.[9]

From the data assembled in Table 2, it is apparent that the amalgamation process has been predominantly *complex*, at least for the period 1957–1961. In 1957, there were on the average 5.43 production brigades per kolkhoz, and the figure grew to only 5.73 by the year 1961.[10] As might be expected, regional patterns of amalgamation have differed, in some cases significantly, from the norm of complex amalgamation. In Kazakhstan, for example, conversion of kolkhozy to sovkhozy has been the paramount direction of change. In Belorussia there was a relatively small change but, for the period

[8] By resources we mean, broadly speaking, land, labor, and capital. It would be necessary to demonstrate, of course, that the typical brigade manager of the present day exerts significantly increased control over both these inputs and the nature and level of brigade output.

[9] Recognizing in some cases rather sharp spatial and temporal differentials, we would nevertheless argue that the changes during the period 1957–1961 can be taken as broadly representative of the basic pattern of structural change in the post-1952 period.

[10] Computed from *Narodnoe khoziaistvo . . . 1958*, p. 494; *Narodnoe khoziaistvo . . . 1961*, pp. 440–441; I. I. Sigov, *Razdelenie truda v sel'skom khoziaistve pri perekhode k kommunizmu* (Moscow, 1963), p. 139; G. I. Shmelev, *Raspredelenie i ispol'zovanie truda v kolkhozakh* (Moscow, 1964), p. 55.

Table 2 : *Selected indicators of structural change of collective farms, USSR, 1957–1961 (1957 = 100).*

	1958	1959	1960	1961
Number of kolkhozy	88	70	57	53
Number of brigades[a]	86	75	62	56
Sown area of kolkhozy[b]	99	98	93	84
Man-day labor input[c]	97	97	88	81
Capital investment[d]	129	160	144	143

[a] The number of brigades refers to production brigades of all types. By 1957, the majority of production brigades were permanent in nature, thus eliminating the possibility of double counting.

[b] Sown area refers to the socialized sector only, all crops.

[c] The labor input is measured in millions of man-days and refers to all collective farm members earning labor-days in the socialized sector of the kolkhoz, including those participating in the tractor brigades of the Machine Tractor Stations. For details of the estimating procedure, see Nimitz, pp. 6–15.

[d] Capital investment is the official Soviet series in 1956 ruble prices. Investment in animal herds and capital repair is not included. Also, expenditure by kolkhozy for the purchase of machinery and equipment from the MTS is not included. Kolkhozy devoted to the production of fish products are excluded.

SOURCES: *Narodnoe khoziaistvo . . . 1960*, pp. 500–501; *Narodnoe khoziaistvo . . . 1961*, pp. 316, 440–441, 537–538; Nancy Nimitz, *Farm Employment in the Soviet Union, 1928–1963* (Santa Monica, Calif.: RAND Corp., 1965), p. 7; *Sel'skoe khoziaistvo*, pp. 51, 56–57; Shmelev, p. 55; Sigov, p. 139.

1959–1960, the net result of both conversions and amalgamations appears to have expanded the size of the brigade vis-à-vis the kolkhoz.[11]

With only limited exceptions (for example, Lithuania, 1960–1961), the size of the brigade has not grown relative to the size of the kolkhoz. In absolute terms, though, both have grown significantly with respect to sown area and capital investment expenditures (the latter with significant temporal fluctuations). However, the labor force has declined at about the same rate as the decline in the number of kolkhozy.[12]

[11] In the post-1956 period, there was a campaign, especially in western Belorussia, to move peasants from homestead to collective farm settlements and thus reduce the dispersion of the population. Certain financial and other benefits were promised to the participants. In part, the goal was a concentrated population to reduce the cost of providing services and also to bring the labor force closer to the place of work. See, for example, V. Kamensky, "Better Organization in Resettlement from Farmsteads," *Sovetskaia Belorussia*, June 25, 1957, p. 3, translated and reprinted in *Current Digest of the Soviet Press*, IX, no. 27 (August 14, 1957), 24–25.

[12] In some cases (Lithuania) the decline of the labor force and number of kolkhozy has been almost identical, while for other regions, the former has generally declined somewhat more slowly than the latter. The general pattern of our indices (labor force declining and capital investment increasing) is an understandable pattern of input substitution that we would expect in the agricultural sector during the development process. In the present case, however, the rather similar behavior of the indices for number of kolkhozy and labor force may provide a partial and dynamic explanation for the amalgamation process. If we assume that for a given region (for

Thus far we have assumed that brigades are homogeneous units, comparable over time and among kolkhozy. Such is not the case. The nature of the production brigade has changed significantly since the early 1950's. In particular, if we classify according to the date at which the brigade was constituted and to the nature of the tasks performed by the given brigade, certain trends become apparent. First, there has been a marked tendency to move away from the temporary brigade (for example, seasonal). Second, there has been a tendency to abandon the specialized production brigade (for example, performing a single task either on a temporary or permanent basis) for permanent complex brigades.[13]

In recent years, brigades have been classified as complex, branch, or specialized. The *complex* brigade is largely a product of the amalgamation process. It is frequently formed on the base of a formerly independent kolkhoz. The complex brigade is permanent in nature and brings together a wide range of inputs and outputs under one administrative roof. Complex brigades have become increasingly important in recent years. With the abolition of the MTS in 1958, they have ordinarily become tractor–complex brigades, since machinery and equipment have been transferred to the brigade level.

By 1957, complex brigades accounted for 14 percent of all production brigades and increased to 34 percent by 1962.[14] Between 1958 and 1960, the average number of collective farm members per complex brigade grew from 105 to 135.[15] Also, the number of collective farm members engaged in complex brigades, as a proportion of those engaged in all brigades, rose from 25 percent in 1958 to 39 percent in 1960.[16] In some instances the complex brigade has come to resemble closely the department (*otdelenie*), which is the organizational form utilized in the sovkhoz, and it has been so labelled. This pattern has prevailed in the south and southwest.

It might be noted that the development of the complex brigade has been most prevalent where agricultural production is least specialized. Thus,

---

example, Kazakhstan) the size distribution (in terms of labor force per kolkhoz) has little variability and, further, that Soviet leaders feel they know what optimal size is for that particular region (again on the basis of labor force per kolkhoz), amalgamation might be viewed as a mechanism for the maintenance of this optimal size. Given the importance of the labor force and the problems associated with labor planning in the kolkhoz, such a view might be sustained.

[13] This pattern is in line with the oft-stated Soviet goal of "improving" the kolkhoz as an organizational form—that is, "raising" it to the level of the sovkhoz, the latter being seen as organizationally superior.

[14] K. P. Obolenskii, G. G. Kotov, and G. K. Rusakov (eds.), *Voprosy ratsional'noi organizatsii i ekonomiki sel'skokhoziaistvennogo proizvodstva* (Moscow, 1964), pp. 218–219.

[15] Computed from Sigov, pp. 138–139.

[16] *Ibid.*

while 34 percent of all production brigades in the USSR in 1962 were complex, only 2.3 percent in Central Asia were of this type, and the figures for Kalinin, Smolensk, and Kirov oblasti were respectively 75.8 percent, 78.1 percent, and 90.0 percent.[17] Significant regional size differentials also prevail. For 1961, the average complex brigade in the northwest region of the USSR occupied 264 hectares of plowland, as opposed to approximately 3,000 hectares in Kazakhstan.[18] The complex brigade is viewed officially as an advanced organizational form. The average size of the complex brigade varies regionally in a pattern comparable to size variations among the parent kolkhozy. Finally, it might be noted that there has been a tendency for the size of the complex brigade to expand as machinery and equipment are added to form tractor–complex brigades. The pattern of complex brigade development for 1957–1961 is presented in Table 3, and the general pattern of brigade development is given in Table 4.

The various types of *branch* and *specialized* brigades remain in wide though declining usage (Table 4). There is considerable regional size vari-

Table 3 : *The development of complex and tractor–complex brigades, USSR, 1957–1961.*

	1957	1958	1959	1960	1961
Total brigades (all types)	416,033	357,666	314,049	256,991	232,365
Complex brigades	59,010	67,909	77,012	73,925	68,190
Tractor–complex brigades[a]	n.a.	11,940	16,892	18,189	n.a.

[a] The tractor–complex brigade is a complex brigade that is mechanized in the sense that machinery and equipment are held at the brigade level. This is basically an outgrowth of the abolition of the MTS in 1958.

SOURCE: Data for the years 1957–1960 from Sigov, p. 139. Data for the year 1961 from Shmelev, p. 55.

Table 4 : *Brigade structure of kolkhozy of the USSR, 1957–1961.*

	1957	1958	1959	1960	1961
Total brigades	416,033	357,666	314,049	256,991	232,365
Field brigades	213,495	183,980	139,090	105,353	97,583
Tractor brigades	94,201	55,423	50,123	37,114	33,266
Tractor–field brigades	5,562	12,614	15,178	14,507	11,721
Vegetable brigades	26,043	21,870	17,329	14,370	12,838
Fruit brigades	10,515	9,546	9,153	10,460	8,767
Other brigades	7,207	6,324	6,164	1,262	—

SOURCE: Data for the years 1957–1960 from Sigov, p. 139. Data for the year 1961 from Shmelev, p. 55.

[17] Obolenskii, Kotov, and Rusakov, pp. 218–219.
[18] *Ibid.*, p. 230.

ation, as there is for complex brigades.[19] Between 1958 and 1960, field brigades, as a proportion of all types of brigades, declined from 51.4 percent to 41.0 percent, and the number of kolkhoz members engaged in these brigades declined from 60.3 percent to 45.5 percent as a proportion of those engaged in all brigades.[20] Thus, as the number of field brigades decreased, the number of kolkhoz members assigned to them also declined, the net result being a small absolute change in average field-brigade size, from 94 kolkhoz members (1958) to 89 (1960).[21] This may be compared with the early 1950's when field brigades normally averaged 80–100 peasants in the south and 60–80 in regions other than the Black Earth.[22] The share of tractor brigades in all brigades has declined, while tractor–field brigades have increased relatively. However, both types together represented only 20 percent of all brigades in 1960, and at that time engaged only 9.6 percent of the labor force engaged in all brigades.[23] Finally, there has been little alteration of vegetable brigades in terms of total number and/or personnel involved and only a slight shift in the importance of orchard brigades.[24]

II

Along with these changes in the number, size, structure, and functions of collective farms and their component production brigades, the decision-making process at both kolkhoz and brigade levels has been undergoing significant adjustments, including the expansion of the *khozraschet* system and the introduction of necessary decision-making tools, most notably cost accounting.[25] If these changes are to yield positive returns, the quality of managerial personnel must also be improved.

[19] Thus for the year 1961, field brigades varied in hectares of plowland from roughly 194 in the northwest part of the RSFSR to over 2,700 in the northern Caucasus; tractor–field brigades varied from 163 hectares in Central Asia to almost 2,500 hectares in the Volga region of the RSFSR; vegetable brigades varied from 24 hectares in the Volga-Viatka region of the RSFSR to almost 200 hectares in Kazakhstan; and, finally, orchard brigades varied from approximately 21 hectares in western Siberia to almost 150 hectares in the Ukraine and Moldavia. For details, see *ibid*.

[20] Sigov, p. 139.

[21] Computed from *ibid*.

[22] For a very useful discussion of the amalgamation process in the early 1950's, see R. E. F. Smith, "The Amalgamation of Collective Farms: Some Technical Aspects," *Soviet Studies*, VI, no. 1 (July, 1954), 16–32.

[23] Sigov, p. 139.

[24] Orchard brigades as a portion of all production brigades grew from 2.7 percent (1958) to 4.1 percent (1961), while for the same period the labor force engaged in orchard brigades as a portion of the total labor force engaged in all brigades grew from 1.5 percent to 4.2 percent (see *ibid*.).

[25] For a discussion of these adjustments, see the sources cited in n. 1.

For the most part, Soviet collective farm chairmen are males from 30 to 50 years of age. Regional age variations are not significant, although chairmen do tend to be somewhat younger in the Baltic region. The minor role played by women in top managerial positions is indicated in Table 5.[26] Women who do reach upper-level positions tend, like their male counterparts, to be between 30 and 50 years old.

With regard to middle- and lower-level management (brigade, *ferma*, link, etc.), the 1959 census data suggest that as one moves downward in the managerial hierarchy, the role of women increases markedly, though with significant regional variability, and there is greater emphasis upon youth.[27] This pattern suggests limited upward mobility for female managerial personnel. The relevant data are summarized in Table 6.

Membership in the Communist Party, though somewhat less significant in earlier years, has come to be a prerequisite for managerial placement, though there are some regional differences as indicated in Table 7.

To the extent that the managerial function in collective farms is changing and that such changes are officially recognized, one would expect the process of managerial selection, training, and promotion to reflect appropriately the changing requirements. This has not necessarily been the case, as we shall see.

Managerial recruitment procedure has never been fully explained, but it has apparently alternated between centralized mass recruitment campaigns and decentralized selection primarily through Party channels. Although there has been only one instance of mass recruitment of chairmen in recent years, the campaign replaced approximately 25 percent of collective farm chairmen and accordingly bears further investigation.[28]

The recruitment campaign of 1955 was a sequel to that of 1951–1952, the general aim of both being improvement in the quality of top managerial personnel. While the campaign of 1951–1952 placed 12,000 agricultural specialists at the head of collective farms, the 1955 campaign emphasized

[26] Soviet writers have themselves suggested that there is a bias against women and that the strength of this bias is in direct proportion to the importance of the managerial position. There are, of course, reasons other than pure sex discrimination that can in part account for the very low participation of women in managerial positions. See, for example, Shmelev, pp. 119–127.

[27] The emphasis upon youth at lower managerial levels is understandable. However, the extent to which women, for example, have over a period of time played an important role at lower levels but a minuscule role at upper levels indicates a very limited degree of mobility (upward). Likewise, on the basis of age, the typical age of a kolkhoz manager vis-à-vis a lower-level manager indicates very slow upward mobility.

[28] In this section we rely heavily upon a most informative article by A. N. Karamelev, "Dvizhenie tridtsatitysiachnikov i ukreplenie kolkhozov," *Voprosy istorii KPSS*, no. 1 (1962), pp. 115–126.

Table 5 : *Proportion of female kolkhoz chairmen, selected regions, 1953–1961.*

	July 1, 1953	March 1, 1954	1955c	1956	1957	1958	1959	1960	1961
USSR	2.8%			1.5%b	1.3%a				
RSFSR	.3a						1.7%	1.7%	2.1%
Irkutsk oblast'							.2	.2	
Kirov oblast'				1.6					
Saratov oblast'							1.1	1.2	
Bashkir ASSR	.4						.3	.3	.3
Moldavia	2.8	2.0%	1.6%	1.3	1.3	1.3%	.9	.9	1.1
Kirgizia	1.4	1.2	.9	1.0		1.3	.9	.9	1.1
Lithuania	1.8		1.6	1.7	1.7	1.7			
Azerbaidzhan						2.1			

a End of the year. b December 1, 1956. c For 1955 and subsequent years, all data as of April 1.

SOURCES: *Narodnoe khoziaistvo RSFSR . . . 1958*, p. 326; *Narodnoe khoziaistvo RSFSR . . . 1959*, p. 366; *Narodnoe khoziaistvo RSFSR . . . 1960*, p. 345; *SSSR v tsifrakh* (1958), p. 232; *Dostizheniia Sovetskogo Azerbaidzhana za 40 let v tsifrakh*, p. 134; *Narodnoe khoziaistvo Bashkirskoi SSR*, p. 213; *Narodnoe khoziaistvo Irkutskoi oblasti*, p. 141; *Narodnoe khoziaistvo Kirovskoi oblasti*, p. 94; *Narodnoe khoziaistvo Kirgizskoi SSR*, p. 109; *20 let Sovetskoi Litvy*, p. 215; *Narodnoe khoziaistvo Moldavskoi . . . 1962*, p. 198; *Narodnoe khoziaistvo Saratovskoi oblasti . . . 1960*, p. 175.

Table 6 : *Proportion of female middle-level managers, 1959 (kolkhozy only).*

	Field Brigadier	Husbandry Brigadier	Ferma Leader	Link Leader
USSR	8.3%	12.7%	15.0%	87.3%
RSFSR	12.7	18.2	20.1	88.3
Ukraine	4.3	7.1	9.3	96.4
Belorussia	2.4	14.5	13.0	95.7
Uzbekistan	2.8	1.9	2.8	14.0
Kazakhstan	4.0	5.6	6.4	58.5
Georgia	2.6	3.2	7.5	30.9
Azerbaidzhan	1.8	2.5	6.6	63.0
Lithuania	1.9	17.3	17.9	32.3
Moldavia	1.9	5.9	8.5	40.0
Latvia	6.4	71.4	54.0	10.2
Kirgizia	2.1	6.7	5.4	51.6
Tadzhikistan	4.0	—	3.7	10.6
Armenia	3.0	3.9	2.4	58.0
Turkmenistan	4.4	—	11.3	21.3
Estonia	15.7	73.4	67.4	n.a.

SOURCE: *Itogi*, all volumes.

Table 7 : *Proportion of collective farm chairmen who are members of the Communist Party.*

	1950	July 1, 1952	1953a	1956	1957	1958	1959	1960
USSR		79.4%	79.6%	90.5%	91.2%	92.6%	93.5%	95.3%
RSFSR							94.0	
	(1946)	(1951)						
Ukraine	40.2%	74.2		83.3	95.7	94.4	97.1	
Belorussia							96.5	
Uzbekistan							93.1	
Kazakhstan							95.4	
Georgia							93.8	
Azerbaidzhan							92.6	
Lithuania	9.2	48.5	72.1	73.0	70.6	72.6	72.6	
Moldavia							96.0	
Latvia							81.3	
Kirgizia							98.1	
Tadzhikistan							96.9	
Armenia							99.7	
Turkmenistan							92.7	
Estonia							76.0	

a For 1953 and subsequent years, all data as of April 1.

SOURCES: *Narodnoe khoziaistvo . . . 1959*, p. 452; *Sel'skoe khoziaistvo*, p. 475; M. P. Panchenko, *Vidtvorennia suspil'nogo produktu v kolgospakh* (Kiev, 1963), p. 121; *20 let Sovetskoi Litvy*, p. 215.

Table 8 : *Characteristics of newly recruited collective farm chairmen, Smolensk oblast', 1955.*

Total number recruited in 1955	362
With higher education	25%
With incomplete higher and	
secondary education	40%
Communist Party members	93%
Background of newly recruited chairmen:	
Leading Party workers	45
Komsomol	3
Soviets	197
Workers from agricultural organs	14
Industrial enterprises	87
Other organs	16

SOURCE: Karamelev, p. 119.

Table 9 : *Previous position of workers of industrial enterprises recruited as new collective farm chairmen in Belorussia during 1955.*

Total number of new chairmen recruited	
from industrial enterprises	149
Workers	13
Foremen	25
Engineering and technical workers	48
Superintendent of a shop	32
Head of an enterprise	31

SOURCE: Karamelev, p. 120.

a broader set of characteristics: (1) education, though not necessarily in an agricultural specialty, (2) demonstrated leadership capability, and (3) Party membership.[29] Some evidence on the backgrounds of these new chairmen is presented in Tables 8 and 9.

Ultimately, 32,078 new collective farm chairmen were designated as members of the "30,000er" group, and, according to Soviet reports, applications for these farm positions exceeded the actual number of positions available.[30] If the quality of managerial personnel can be measured by level of educational achievement, the campaign of 1955 was a success.[31] Among

[29] While Soviet leaders (especially Khrushchev) have continually tended to attribute agricultural shortcomings to poor management, they seem to deny the existence of any special managerial talent. Thus the "desired" characteristics of such an input can be gleaned only by examination, after the fact, of recruitment patterns.

[30] Karamelev, p. 119.

[31] While we might reasonably assume that many of these new managers were placed on "poor" farms, nevertheless, the financial inducements (namely ruble supplements of 1,500, 1,200, and 1,000 in the first through third years respectively) must have been quite attractive, especially given the relatively poor earnings position of the typical kolkhoz manager at this time—both absolutely and vis-à-vis the peasants.

18,000 new recruits in the RSFSR, Ukraine, Belorussia, and Kazakhstan, approximately 55 percent had higher education of some sort, while the comparable figure for all kolkhoz chairmen at the time (1955) was approximately 29 percent.[32] Throughout the period under study, the formal educational attainment of top managerial personnel has improved significantly, though with some regional variation (Table 10).

The recruitment campaign of 1955 had a significant impact upon the composition of top managerial personnel, but this procedure, as far as we know, has not been repeated subsequently. Accordingly, we must examine the more typical recruitment procedure.

In theory, the collective farm chairman and the members of the management board (*pravlenie*) are elected by a general meeting of kolkhoz membership. Although a new chairman is normally brought before a general meeting (or meeting of representatives through the brigade structure), rejection is most uncommon. More fundamental is the selection of the candidate.

The raion administration (under which kolkhozy and sovkhozy presently fall) maintains a personnel file (*nomenklatura*) composed of the names of those individuals who are considered suitable for chairmanship.[33] The list is most likely composed of the names of those persons whose good performance has made them known to upper-level Party officials. Undoubtedly education and Party status are important, but even more important is the previous work record of the individual. There seems to be a good deal of weight placed upon the completion of a successful period in a lower-level administrative post where, presumably, potential leadership capabilities have been tested. After initial selection by the raion administration, the candidate's name will be presented to the local Party committee at the raion center. Finally, the candidate will be recommended to the collective farm and "elected" at the general meeting.[34]

The new farm chairman has a good deal of say in the selection of members of the kolkhoz management board. The farm's agricultural specialists will ordinarily be members of it, as well as the secretary of the kolkhoz Party organization and, possibly, representatives from the middle-level management team.

If the recruitment procedures practiced in recent years have served to upgrade the formal qualifications of top managerial personnel, such has not been the case at lower levels. The level of educational attainment at the

[32] Karamelev, p. 119; *Narodnoe khoziaistvo . . . 1958*, p. 531.
[33] Based upon interviews conducted by the writer with officials in Krasnodarskii krai during August of 1966.
[34] There are cases where a Party nominee will be rejected by the meeting, although such cases are apparently rare.

Table 10 : *Proportion of collective farm chairmen with complete higher and secondary specialized education.*

	1946	1950	1951[a]	1952[b]	1953	1955	1956	1959	1963	1966
USSR				15.1%	18.0%	29.3%	37.1%	50.4%	63.3%	69.6%
RSFSR	8.6%		14.9%		16.0			45.0	56.8	63.7
Ukraine							35.7	62.3	73.1	78.5
Belorussia					13.6			51.4	63.6	70.1
Uzbekistan								52.3	73.3	77.6
Kazakhstan								63.1	77.9	77.6
Georgia								55.6	68.7	69.9
Azerbaidzhan		3.8%						65.0	61.3	72.9
Lithuania					5.5	14.6	22.0	38.2	52.5	57.8
Moldavia					32.3	39.8	48.6	73.8	83.7	90.2
Latvia								52.6	64.1	70.9
Kirgizia				11.5	15.8	18.2	30.4	31.7	85.4	74.6
Tadzhikistan								39.8	61.4	60.2
Armenia								62.1	73.9	76.2
Turkmenistan								50.9	59.9	74.5
Estonia								40.2	54.7	59.6

[a] Data prior to 1951 as of July 1.   [b] Data from 1952 as of April 1.

SOURCES: *Narodnoe khoziaistvo . . . 1961*, p. 466; *Narodnoe khoziaistvo . . . 1962*, p. 373; *Narodnoe khoziaistvo . . . 1965*, p. 440; *Narodnoe khoziaistvo RSFSR . . . 1962*, p. 355; *Narodnoe khoziaistvo Kirgizskoi SSR . . . 1957*, p. 109; *Narodnoe khoziaistvo Moldavskoi SSR . . . 1962*, p. 198; *Sel'skoe khoziaistvo*, pp. 474–475; *20 let Sovetskoi Litvy*, p. 215; *Dostizheniia Sovetskoi Belorussii za 40 let*, p. 87; Panchenko, p. 121.

brigade and *ferma* levels remains low. Furthermore, Soviet statistics usually report those having higher and/or secondary education as a single category, but the proportion of this group with higher education is typically small. As of April, 1959, only 5.1 percent of brigadiers of production brigades and 5.6 percent of *ferma* leaders had higher and/or secondary specialized education.[35] By April, 1966, the proportion had grown to 10.4 percent and 10.9 percent for brigadiers and *ferma* leaders respectively.[36] Regional differentials remain significant. In April, 1966, the proportion of brigadiers of production brigades with higher and/or secondary specialized education ranged from a low of 3.8 percent in Tadzhikistan to a high of 32 percent in Estonia.[37] The range for *ferma* leaders similarly extends from a low of 5.6 percent in the RSFSR to a high of 33.7 percent in Georgia.[38]

It is an interesting comment upon Soviet priorities to note that the educational achievement of agricultural specialists is significantly higher than that of the middle- or upper-level managerial personnel. For the years 1959 and 1966, for the USSR as a whole, more than 90 percent of all zootechnicians and agronomists had received higher and/or secondary specialized education, and regional differentials among specialists are small.[39] In 1966, the proportion of agronomists with higher and/or secondary specialized education varied from a low of 77.6 percent in Tadzhikistan (which is markedly lower than most other republics) to a high of 97.8 percent in Latvia.[40]

Unfortunately, most Soviet statistical series do not report the type of education obtained by managerial personnel. In the top management category, those with higher education are probably agricultural specialists (agronomists, zootechnicians, etc.), though, as we have pointed out, relatively few top managers have attained higher education. Nicholas DeWitt has pointed out that of 91,070 professionals (higher education) engaged in Soviet agriculture in December, 1959, some 18,153 were engineers, 66,936 were agricultural specialists, and the remaining 7,981 represented various unclassified specialities.[41] Some useful general insights are provided by data from the Kirgiz Republic assembled in Table 11.

Generally, the attainment of secondary specialized education is predominant. Also, the relative preference for those with an agricultural education in the early 1950's has been reversed in recent years. The shift can be

[35] *Narodnoe khoziaistvo . . . 1962*, p. 373; *Narodnoe khoziaistvo . . . 1965*, p. 440; *Sel'skoe khoziaistvo*, pp. 470–471.

[36] *Ibid.*

[37] *Ibid.*

[38] *Narodnoe khoziaistvo . . . 1965*, p. 440; *Sel'skoe khoziaistvo*, pp. 472–473.

[39] *Ibid.*

[40] *Ibid.*

[41] For a discussion of terminology and data, see Nicholas DeWitt, *Education and Professional Employment in the U.S.S.R.* (Washington, D.C.: U.S. Government Printing Office, 1961), pp. 28–33, 519.

Table 11 : *Level and type of education of collective farm chairmen of the Kirgiz Republic, selected years.*

	1953[a]	1955[b]	1956	1958	1959	1960	1961
Proportion of all chairmen with higher and secondary specialized education	15.8%	18.2%	30.4%	33.2%	31.7%	45.0%	54.7%
Higher education	1.7	1.6	3.1	3.9	7.0	12.1	15.5
Agronomists, zootechnicians, and veterinary doctors	1.0	1.0	1.2	1.7	n.a.	n.a.	n.a.
Other specialists	0.7	0.6	1.9	2.2	n.a.	n.a.	n.a.
Secondary specialized education	14.1	16.6	27.3	29.3	24.7	32.9	39.2
Agronomists, zootechnicians, and veterinary doctors	8.7	12.4	12.7	11.2	n.a.	n.a.	n.a.
Other specialists	5.4	4.2	14.6	18.1	n.a.	n.a.	n.a.

[a] July 1. [b] For 1955 and subsequent years, all data as of April 1.
SOURCE: *Narodnoe khoziaistvo Kirgizskoi SSR . . . 1960*, p. 140.

explained on several possible grounds, three of which are particularly important. First, the thrust of Soviet policy (amply demonstrated by the campaign of 1955) has been to place in managerial positions those who are educated—above all, those who are intelligent in a general sense and have demonstrated a degree of leadership capability and an ability to interact successfully with others, quite apart from specific formal training. Second, the tendency in recent years has been to attach agricultural specialists to the collective farm proper (rather than to the MTS or raion administration). With competent staff specialists playing an active role in management of the farm (both as advisors to management and as members of the management board), one would anticipate a diminished need for specialized technical training on the part of managerial personnel. Third, there has been emphasis in recent years upon general training for lower-level personnel, for the seasonality of agricultural production makes the specialist with a "wide profile" desirable.

To the extent that structural change and monetization have altered the character of decision-making within the collective farm, requiring careful cost-profit calculations, one would anticipate an increased emphasis upon economic training commensurate with the needs of decision makers in this new atmosphere. This has not been the case, as can be seen in Table 12. As recently as 1960, 47.4 percent of all accounting workers on collective farms had no formal accounting training whatever.[42] Although only 2.1 percent of accounting heads had no accounting training, 77.4 percent of accountants at the brigade and *ferma* level had no training.[43] In recent years there has been considerable discussion of the need for improved and expanded training in accounting and economics, apparently in response to the monetization process and the introduction of *khozraschet* at the brigade level. There is no evidence to suggest that any significant improvement has been forthcoming. Much of the training of a bookkeeper apparently centers upon routine matters relating to the completion of planning documents. Further, the services of an economist (e.g., for a planning department) have been available only on a very small number of well-established farms.

According to the Soviet economist V. P. Rozhin, collective farms have fared poorly in obtaining trained economists. In 1959, in Krasnodarskii krai (one of the best and most advanced agricultural regions in the Soviet Union), Rozhin points out that on the average per kolkhoz there were 13.4 agronomists, zootechnicians, veterinarians, and engineers with higher and/or secondary specialized education.[44] At the same time, there was one econo-

[42] V. P. Rozhin, *Nekotorye voprosy pod"ema ekonomiki slabykh kolkhozov* (Moscow, 1961), p. 52.
[43] *Ibid.*
[44] *Ibid.*, p. 55.

Table 12 : *Educational level of accountants, bookkeepers, and recorders on Soviet collective farms, January 1, 1960.*

Working in Kolkhozy	Accountants (head of kolkhoz accounting)	Accountants (bookkeepers in office)	Bookkeepers and Recorders (brigade and ferma)	All Accounting Workers in Kolkhoz[a]
Complete higher education	0.5%	0.2%	0.1%	0.2%
Complete secondary specialized education	10.5	7.5	1.9	5.5
Graduates of:				
Agricultural schools for kolkhoz accountants	35.4	23.4	4.2	16.8
All-Union extension accounting courses	29.4	13.4	3.3	11.5
Short-term courses for bookkeepers	22.1	23.0	13.1	18.6
Total	97.7	67.5	22.6	52.5
Without bookkeeping training	2.1	32.5	77.4	47.4

[a] Not including bookkeeper-adjustors.
SOURCE: Rozhin, p. 52.

mist-planner (with similar educational achievement) for every third kolkhoz.[45] The situation had been improved by 1965, to approximately one economist-planner for each collective farm in the Krasnodar region.[46] Nevertheless, in spite of continual pressure in the Soviet press, economics remains a much neglected subject for rural personnel.

III

Structural change has fundamentally altered the kolkhoz and has recast the production brigade in a mold reminiscent of the individual kolkhoz of the past. The post of kolkhoz manager has increasingly become an administrative position focusing upon coordination, a function previously performed primarily at the raion level.[47] At the same time, the role of the brigade manager has been enhanced.

[45] *Ibid.*
[46] *Ibid.*
[47] To make any judgment regarding the degree of centralization or decentralization, one would have to examine the decision-making role of the manager at all levels within the kolkhoz. If the kolkhoz manager has retained a measure of authority and re-

To the extent that the monetization process has altered the nature of decision-making procedures within the kolkhoz, one would expect to see the recruitment of a new type of managerial team—above all, one trained to utilize new decision-making tools and to operate within a new framework.[48] Such changes would seem to be necessary at the kolkhoz and especially the brigade levels.

Although the measurement of managerial quality and inferences about decision-making quality are necessarily rather crude, it is apparent that the changing organizational structure of the kolkhoz in combination with the redefinition of managerial roles and the prerequisites for functioning in those roles will be important factors in the future operation of the kolkhoz. For top-level managerial personnel, where quality improvement has been most notable, recruitment policy and educational and training policy have been contributing factors. However, with the enhanced importance of lower level managerial and technical personnel, it is surpising that the recruitment procedure, which after all is a state and Party affair, has not been more responsive to the "needs" of the kolkhozy. Finally, the paucity of training in accounting methods in particular, and economics in general, would seem to be wholly contradictory to the trends of structural and functional change, thus in part limiting the benefits to be realized from these adjustments.

---

sponsibility similar to that held prior to the present amalgamation and monetization campaigns, one could argue that there has been, in fact, a degree of centralization.

[48] The attractiveness of the position of kolkhoz manager is difficult to establish. However, the writer would argue that in recent years, while formal promotional possibilities within the system do not appear to have been a significant inducement, nevertheless, it must be recognized that (1) amalgamation has been, in a sense, a form of promotion for those who remained as managers of the new larger farms, (2) money rewards of kolkhoz managers both absolutely and vis-à-vis peasant earnings have probably increased substantially, and (3) there are substantial nonmonetary benefits accruing to the position of kolkhoz manager. For a formal argument of this position, see Stuart.

6 : The Law of Farm-Farmer Relations

Peter B. Maggs

I

The Collective and State Farms

The arable and grazing land in the Soviet Union is divided among primary producing organizations of two main types: collective farms and state farms. Recent years have seen the increase in the size of farms (by the consolidation of smaller farms) to the point where the typical farm is now a large-scale economic undertaking. The average collective farm has 2,800 hectares of cultivated land, almost a million rubles in buildings and equipment, and over a thousand head of livestock.[1] One farm may include a number of villages and hundreds of farm families. The typical state farm is four times as large as the average collective farm, but usually has inferior land which is farmed less intensively.[2] The large size of the farms may provide economies of scale in production; whether or not it does so in fact is a question for the economist. The large size undoubtedly creates complex problems of organization and administration; many of these are dealt with by the elaborate legal system regulating farm-farmer relations.

The history of collective and state farm law has been told adequately elsewhere,[3] and a few words will suffice to remind the reader of the main lines of development. Ever since their establishment, the state farms have

[1] *Izvestiia*, April 25, 1969, p. 1.
[2] P. A. Skipetrov, *Obobshchestvlenie truda i sotsialisticheskaia sobstvennost'* (Moscow, 1968), p. 220.
[3] State farms: G. A. Aksenenok, *Pravovoe polozhenie sovkhozov v SSSR* (Moscow, 1960). Collective farms: A. M. Kalandadze, "Kolkhoznoe pravo," in *Sorok let sovetskogo prava* (Leningrad, 1957), I, 426–474, II, 435–483; A. Bilinsky, "Aktuelle Rechtsprobleme der Kolchosen," *Jahrbuch für Ostrecht*, VIII, no. 1 (1967), 21–80.

139

been state enterprises—government corporations—farming large areas of land in accordance with national economic plans, paying regular wages to their workers, and, with some exceptions, conducting their affairs on a pattern similar to that of Soviet state industrial enterprises. The collective farms were in form, and to a significant extent in substance, peasant cooperatives.[4] As originally created, collective farms had three basic legal attributes reflecting their nature as cooperative rather than as state enterprises: ownership by members of shares in the property of the cooperative; decision-making by a general meeting of the members; and distribution of the proceeds of collective activity in accordance with the share of work performed. The collectivization process was violently resisted by a large proportion of the peasantry and has never been completed; each household on the collective farm retains a plot of land for private farming.

Ever since collectivization in the 1930's, there has been a gradual erosion of the features which distinguished collective farms from state farms, and a substantial number of collective farms have actually been converted into state farms. The 1961 Program of the Communist Party promised to continue this process, providing "the economic flourishing of the collective farm system will create the conditions for a gradual convergence, and eventually a merging, of collective farm property ownership and public ownership into a uniform communist ownership."[5] The legal changes involved in this process have gone relatively smoothly, since they have generally involved improvements in the economic position of the collective farm peasantry.

Changes have also taken place with regard to the rights of collective farmers to their small uncollectivized private plots. Legal measures adopted under Stalin encouraged such private production to meet wartime emergency needs. Khrushchev, on the other hand, had legislation enacted sharply curtailing the size and use of such private plots, measures unpopular with the peasantry. While Khrushchev's successors promptly repealed this legislation, they have not restored the plots to their former dimensions.

In a major agricultural policy speech delivered on March 24, 1965, L. I. Brezhnev, speaking of collective and state farming, stated, "It must be assumed that these two types of social farming will exist and develop for a long time to come. *At the present stage our duty is not to accelerate the transformation of one form into another, but in every way to assist the development and flourishing of both types of social farming.*"[6] Despite this statement, the present leadership has moved rapidly in the internal reform of col-

[4] Bilinsky, "Aktuelle Rechtsprobleme."

[5] *XXII c"ezd KPSS, stenograficheskii otchet* (Moscow, 1962), III, 285.

[6] Report by L. I. Brezhnev at Plenary Session of the Central Committee of the CPSU, March 24, 1965, *Izvestiia*, March 27, 1965, p. 1.

lective farm organization. The most basic principles of the collective farm system have been reaffirmed in the Fundamental Principle of Land Legislation adopted in 1968,[7] and in the new model collective farm charter published in 1969.[8] The leadership has kept faithfully the promise implied in this statement, that there will be no further encroachments upon the permitted area of private farming. The reforms in the collective sector have been made relatively painlessly, because each reform has been accompanied by a substantial transfusion of funds to the farms.

The Law of Farm-Farmer Relations

The phrase "farm-farmer relations" is not a standard term of Soviet legal terminology, but is merely adopted for convenience to designate the portion of Soviet agricultural law chosen for separate treatment here. A full study of Soviet agricultural law would have to include an extensive analysis of the system of planning, contractual, tax, administrative, and property law measures whereby the activity of the farms is directed and coordinated with the rest of the economy. It would also include an analysis of the relation and relative importance of Party apparatus and the legal system in directing farm activity. This paper, however, will be limited to a discussion of the law governing the relations within each farm, relations to which the parties include the farms, their managers, their members and employees, and their families. Needless to say, this approach must inevitably give an incomplete picture, for the shape of the internal relations of the farm is often determined by its external relations.

The sources of the law of farm-farmer relations are varied. The primary features and many of the details of internal legal relations are provided by legislation at the USSR and republic levels.[9] Many secondary rules and regulations are promulgated by farm management itself. With respect to collective farms, a special situation prevails. Basic legal relations have been determined by the charter adopted by each collective farm on the basis of a "model charter" promulgated in 1935.[10] Many provisions of this charter became obsolete, and a draft of a new model charter[11] was published in April, 1969. The new model charter was adopted at a Congress of Collective Farmers held in November, 1969, in Moscow.[12] A second peculiarity of the legisla-

[7] *Vedomosti Verkhovnogo Soveta SSSR*, no. 51 (1968), item 485; English translation in *Current Digest of the Soviet Press*, XXI, no. 1 (January 22, 1969), 14–20.

[8] *Izvestiia*, November 28, 1969, pp. 1–3.

[9] Aksenenok, pp. 7–29; N. D. Kazantsev (ed.), *Kolkhoznoe pravo* (Moscow, 1962), pp. 63–105.

[10] *Sobranie zakonov SSSR*, no. 11 (1935), item 82.

[11] *Izvestiia*, April 24, 1969, pp. 1–2.

[12] *Ibid.*, November 28, 1969, pp. 1–3.

tion affecting collective farms is that much of it is in the form of "recommendations."[13] This form serves two purposes. First, it pays lip service to the theoretically self-governing cooperative nature of collective farm administration. Second, it may provide some latitude for adjustment to local conditions by the farms in their implementation of the recommendations.

There are various channels for the settlement of legal disputes between farms and farmers. In general, as will be discussed below, in the past, members of collective farms have been quite restricted in the opportunity to obtain court protection of their rights as compared to members of state farms. Recently, however, there has been a trend toward broadening the opportunities for judicial protection.

II

The Difference between Employment and Membership

In legal theory, the basic difference between the position of the collective farmer and the state enterprise worker is that the relation of the former to his farm is that of member to cooperative, while the relation of the latter to his enterprise is that of employee to employer. It should be obvious that the difference between the two types of relationships determines only the legal form and not the content of the relations involved; one cannot deduce anything from the form about the actual rules of hiring, firing, discipline, and compensation. On the other hand, the legal form has not been without influence in the development of these relations; one who understands the legal form can better comprehend and predict the development of farm institutions. The remaining sections of this paper will be concerned mainly with this question of the relation of farm to farmer as it is developing.

Employment and Acquisition of Membership

On state farms, as in other state enterprises, the basic method for the establishment of employment relations is the conclusion of a labor agreement between the employer and the prospective employee. On collective farms, on the other hand, the basic method of establishing a work relationship is acceptance into membership. In general, there is no competition for employment, no "civil service" regulations operating on either collective or state farm systems.

[13] P. E. Nedbailo, *Primenenie sovetskikh pravovykh norm* (Moscow, 1960), pp. 84–90.

For the purpose of comparison of legal treatment, prospective employees may be divided into a number of categories: young entrants into the labor force; farmers transferring from other employment; specialists; and managerial personnel.

Under Soviet laws regulating child labor, young people officially enter the labor force upon reaching their sixteenth birthday. A young person in a farm family is generally employed or accepted into membership by the farm where he lives when he becomes 16 years old. Such young people joining "by inheritance" constitute the overwhelming majority of entrants into the farm labor force. The internal regulations of collective farms generally provide for the automatic enrollment of children of members upon their sixteenth birthday, and provide for formal confirmation of the admission at the next regular meeting of the collective farm membership or its representatives.[14] On state farms, children reaching 16 may apply for employment in the regular manner. While instances of refusal to accept into collective farm membership have been reported,[15] such cases are probably infrequent, given the shortage of young agricultural laborers. Likewise children of employees are probably almost always granted their requests for employment on state farms. No judicial remedy would be available to young people refused employment. They could appeal to the administrative organization superior to the state farm refusing them employment, or to the executive committee of the district of the collective farm refusing them membership, or they could complain through nonlegal channels such as the Party or the press.

A second category of new members or employees is composed of persons who have previously been employed elsewhere. Typically, these are persons who quit agricultural work to move to the city and now wish to return to farming. Others, because of marriage or family connections, may wish to transfer from one farm to another. The collective farm management, and perhaps the mass of farm membership, exercise some real discretion in deciding whether or not to admit applicants in these categories.[16] Applicants refused admission have a legal right to appeal to the district executive committee, which may order reconsideration, but one Soviet commentator states that this right is not implemented in practice.[17] On state farms applications from persons in this second category would be considered by the same procedures as all other applications for employment.

A third category of new members or employees is found on newly estab-

---

[14] Kazantsev, pp. 112–113.
[15] *Ibid.*
[16] G. E. Bystrov, "Volevoe soderzhanie pravovykh aktov kollegial'nykh organov upravleniia kolkhozov," *Pravovedenie*, no. 5 (1968), pp. 69–77.
[17] *Ibid.*

lished farms in the more remote areas of the USSR. These are persons recruited under procedures similar to those used in Soviet industry.[18]

Recruitment of specialists follows different lines. The two main sources of new technical and managerial personnel are the assignment of persons finishing educational institutions and the training of members and employees under farm sponsorship. Students in Soviet higher education institutions generally receive a state scholarship, in exchange for which they come under a legal obligation to work at an assigned job for three years after graduation.[19] Most graduates of agricultural education institutions are assigned to state farms, with collective farms getting a much smaller number than their economic significance would warrant.[20] This imbalance has led to complaints by a number of Soviet commentators, who have correctly pointed out the economic irrationality of failing to provide collective farms with skilled personnel.[21] Reforms may be expected in this area, either along the lines of giving collective farms a better position in the assignment process, or by an increase in the total number of agricultural graduates to supply the needs of the collective farms. An alternative method of obtaining specialists, practiced by both state and collective farms, is the training of farm personnel by agricultural education institutions under a contractual arrangement. This method typically involves two contracts: one between the farm and the school to pay tuition costs and one between the farm and the student, whereby the farm pays his room and board in exchange for his promise to return to the farm at the end of his education.[22] The contractual arrangement has proved inadequate, however, in many instances, for a large percentage of trainees fail to return to the farm.[23] The farm's theoretical remedy in such a case, to sue for the return of the money expended on room and board, is often illusory, for even if it wins its case, the ex-student has no cash to pay the judgment.[24] Of course the workers' state has no debtors' prisons with which the defaulting trainee could be threatened. Soviet legal commentators

[18] See U.S. Department of Labor, Bureau of Labor Statistics, *Labor Law and Practice in the U.S.S.R.* (Washington, D.C.: G.P.O., 1964), p. 38; V. S. Andreev and P. A. Gureev, *Organizovanyi nabor rabochikh v SSSR* (Moscow, 1960).

[19] U.S. Department of Labor, p. 39. Also important is the selection and assignment of executive personnel by the Communist Party (*ibid.*, p. 40).

[20] V. S. Kuz'michev, "Planomernoe vosproizvodstvo rabochei sily—vazhnoe uslovie razvitiia sel'skogo khoziaistva," in S. F. Demidova *et al.* (eds.), *Nekotorye voprosy upravleniia sel'skokhoziaistvennym proizvodstvom* (Moscow, 1967), pp. 214–244.

[21] *Ibid.*

[22] A. B. Godes, A. V. Davidov, and A. M. Kalandadze, *Iuridicheskoe obsluzhivanie kolkhozov i sovkhozov* (Moscow, 1965), pp. 94–95.

[23] *Ibid.*; Ts. A. Stepanian and V. S. Semenov (eds.), *Klassy, sotsial'nye sloi i gruppy v SSSR* (Moscow, 1968), pp. 118–125; Kuz'michev; G. I. Zinchenko and M. K. Minin, *Ekonomicheskoe stimulirovanie i nauchnaia organizatsiia sel'skokhoziaistvennogo truda* (Moscow, 1968), pp. 77–92.

[24] Godes, Davidov, and Kalandadze.

have suggested various approaches for putting more teeth in the contract, and some of these suggestions may well be adopted.[25]

Once an important source of specialists was the transfer of personnel of Machine Tractor Stations to the collective farms during the 1950's.[26]

Termination of Membership, Discharge, and Resignation

A state farm worker, like any worker at a state enterprise, may voluntarily quit at any time. He may also be discharged for violation of labor discipline or may be retired for old age or disability.[27] A Soviet writer lists five typical reasons for the termination of collective farm membership: movement to permanent employment at a state enterprise; movement to another collective farm; movement to another location; expulsion from the collective farm; and death.[28]

The most common reason for voluntary termination of membership or employment is a decision by the farmer to take a job in an urban area. The state farm employee is free to resign to do so. The collective farm employee theoretically should have the permission of the collective farm membership to leave; however, there is no effective legal sanction for failure to obtain this permission. When a member or employee leaves a farm permanently, the land assigned to his family for personal farming may be reduced in area or eliminated.[29] The same may be done in the case of a member leaving temporarily, unless there are special circumstances, such as study, military service, or holding an elective office.[30] Since the land allotment is in essence a "fringe benefit" of farm employment, it is natural to expect that it would no longer be given to a family that has no members working on the farm.

A number of farms cooperate with state labor recruitment agencies in channeling farmers to outside jobs.[31]

One legal problem encountered by persons wishing to move from the farm to the city is the internal passport scheme. Passports are not routinely issued to all farmers, and a farm manager is not legally required to provide the documents which a farmer needs to apply for an internal passport, without which he may not reside legally in an urban area.[32] From Soviet statistics,

[25] See the sources cited in n. 23.
[26] Kazantsev, p. 113.
[27] U.S. Department of Labor, pp. 42–43.
[28] Kazantsev, pp. 129–136.
[29] *Ibid.*, pp. 478–482.
[30] *Ibid.*
[31] Andreev and Gureev.
[32] Bilinsky, "Aktuelle Rechtsprobleme," p. 34; *Polozhenie o pasportakh*, approved by a decree of the Council of Ministers of the USSR of October 21, 1953, "Ispolnitel'nyi

it is clear that the vast majority of young people on farms do obtain internal passports and do move to urban areas.[33] However, absent legal restriction, the number leaving might be still larger. A real problem encountered by the young farmer attracted to big city life is that, in addition to a passport, he must have a residence permit (*propiska*), and these are extremely difficult to obtain for the major cities of the European part of the Soviet Union (they are easy to obtain in small towns and in other areas where the government is encouraging settlement).[34] One further possibility is for the farmer deliberately to violate the passport and/or residence permit laws. Millions of people do this each year, particularly with respect to residence permits, and most of them get away with it, though penalties can be severe for those caught repeatedly.[35]

In addition to the large numbers who voluntarily quit farm work, a small number of persons are discharged or expelled from the farms for violation of labor discipline. The legal procedures involved will be discussed in the section of this paper dealing with labor relations.

Retirement will be discussed in the section of the paper on compensation and benefits. Retirement of a collective farmer does not terminate his membership, but retirement of a state farmer does terminate his employment.[36] On both state and collective farms retirees are allowed to keep a plot of land for private farming.[37]

III

Labor Organization

Labor organization and discipline on collective farms are governed by "rules of internal order" promulgated by each farm on the basis of model rules. State farms have rules of internal labor order similar to those promulgated at other state enterprises. The rules, for both collective and state farms, state the work obligation of the farmers, govern the care of equip-

---

komitet Moskovskogo gorodskogo Soveta deputatov trudiashchikhsia," in *O sobliudenii obshchestvennogo poriadka i pravil blagoustroistva v Moskve* (Moscow, 1958), pp. 406–416.

[33] See the revealing statistical studies in Stepanian and Semenov, pp. 118–125.

[34] A. Bilinsky, "Das innere Ressort in der UdSSR," *Jahrbuch für Ostrecht*, VII, no. 2 (1966), 150ff.

[35] Soviet citizens who should know have told this author and others that 20–30 percent of the population of some major cities do not have their residence permits in order. Under Article 198 of the RSFSR criminal code, repeated offenders may be sentenced to up to one year of deprivation of freedom.

[36] Kazantsev, pp. 106–136.

[37] *Ibid.*, pp. 478–482; Aksenenok, pp. 168–174.

ment, and provide details of organizational division, bonus standards, penalties, labor safety, vacations, and private farming allotments.[38]

Recently there has been considerable discussion in the Soviet Union, particularly with regard to collective farms, of ways in which the labor organization system could be reformed to increase individual responsibility and incentive. Many economists have argued that considerable organizational flexibility is needed in view of the great variety of types of farming operations that are being conducted in the USSR and the need for further experiments to determine the optimum forms of organization and compensation.[39] The draft of the new model charter for collective farms, in what is perhaps its most important article, would provide this flexibility: "Art. 26. The forms of organization of production and labor—plots, farms, brigades, links and other production subdivisions—shall be established and applied by the collective farm depending upon the concrete conditions of the farming operation and the level of mechanization, specialization and production technology. . . ." At the same time, economists have generally agreed that, particularly since the amalgamation of the farms, the success of some smaller unit than the farm as a whole should be used as a basic determinant of compensation. Some have even recommended the assignment of land and machinery to individual farmers and farm families; others urge the use of links or small brigades as the basic unit to which land and equipment would be assigned, while others would use large brigades, roughly equivalent in size to collective farms before the amalgamation.[40] Article 26 of the new charter would provide flexibility, though it would appear to rule out the capitalistic-sounding proposal of assigning land and equipment to individual farmers: "Plots of land, tractors, machinery and stocks, draft animals and livestock, the necessary building and other means of production shall be attached to production subdivisions." Economists have also agreed that each production subdivision should be operated on the basis of "internal economic accountability," and this proposal also has been incorporated in the draft charter. "Internal economic accountability" (*vnutrikhoziaistvennyi raschet*) is a Soviet legal term deserving some explanation. V. V. Laptev, the leading Soviet authority on legal regulation of economic activity, defines four main features as character-

---

[38] U.S. Department of Labor, p. 43; Bilinsky, "Aktuelle Rechtsprobleme," pp. 69–70.

[39] V. Bagdagiulian, *O stimulakh i rukovodstve sel'skokhoziaistvennogo proizvodstva* (Erevan, 1967), pp. 42–49; A. M. Emel'ianov (ed.), *Khozraschet i stimulirovanie v sel'skom khoziaistve* (Moscow, 1968), pp. 208–226; I. V. Nizovtsev (gen. ed.), *Vnutrikhoziaistvennyi raschet i material'nye stimuly v kolkhozakh i sovkhozakh Gor'kovskoi oblasti* (Gorky, 1967), pp. 249–266; A. M. Kalandadze, "Pravovoe obespechenie material'noi zainteresovannosti v kolkhozakh," in N. S. Alekseev and D. A. Kerimov (eds.), *Aktual'nye problemy sovetskogo gosudarstva i prava v period stroitel'stva kommunizma* (Leningrad, 1967), pp. 392–427; Zinchenko and Minin, pp. 98–99.

[40] See the sources in n. 39, particularly Bagdagiulian, pp. 42–49, and Kalandadze, "Pravovoe obespechenie," p. 405.

istic of economic accountability within an industrial enterprise[41] (the same characteristics would apply, by analogy, to a state or collective farm).[42] The first of these is operative independence—the production subdivision should have a substantial and legally defined area of discretion in fulfilling tasks planned for it by the enterprise administration. The second is independent means of production—the production subdivision should have specific means of production assigned to it on a long-term basis. The third is a system of sanctions to insure economic accountability—the production subdivision should be required to make suitable compensation where its failures cause difficulties for other parts of the enterprise. The fourth is a system of material incentives—appropriate rewards should be given for success in fulfilling the tasks set for it. Laptev gives less emphasis to another important aspect of internal accountability, that of expecting each production subdivision to produce goods and services whose total value will cover the cost of operating the subdivision. While this principle has long been accepted in Soviet industry, its application was impossible in Soviet agriculture as long as procurement prices were unreasonably low.

Discipline

Disciplinary penalties and procedures differ considerably between state and collective farms. The state farm manager may use the variety of formal sanctions found in the system of Soviet industrial labor discipline. The main sanctions available to the collective farm administrator are of an informal nature. On paper, at least, the state farm worker has substantially greater legal guarantees against unfair application of disciplinary sanctions.

On the state farm, disciplinary penalties include various degrees of warning and reprimand, temporary transfer to lower-paid labor, and discharge. Discharge may be only on one of the grounds specified in the labor code, such as absenteeism or incompetence, and only by the procedures specified by Soviet labor legislation, which prohibits discharge without consent of the trade union.[43] A discharged state farm worker may sue in court for reinstatement to his job, and may win reinstatement if he proves he was wrongfully discharged.[44] Similar suits by discharged workers in Soviet industry are frequently successful;[45] however, no information as to the results of

[41] V. V. Laptev, *Vnutrikhoziaistvennye otnosheniia na promyshlennom predpriiatii; pravovaia organizatiia* (Moscow, 1965), pp. 118–149.
[42] Emel'ianov; Nizovtsev.
[43] U.S. Department of Labor, pp. 33–35.
[44] *Ibid.*
[45] While statistics are not published, this is the general impression gained by the author and other American specialists in Soviet law from conversations with Soviet lawyers and judges.

reinstatement proceedings brought by state farm workers has come to the attention of this author.

Collective farm administrators may impose the following formal penalties upon members, as provided in Article 35 of the new charter: censure, reprimand, severe reprimand, transfer to lower-paid work, and warning of possible expulsion.[46] The collective farmer is thus brought into a position relatively equal to that of the state farmer. Before the new charter was adopted, he could also be subjected to fines and layoffs, which are specifically forbidden by Soviet labor law as applied to state farms.[47]

In the area of expulsion, the powers of the collective farm administration are also greater than those of state farm managers. A member of the collective farm may be expelled by a vote of a majority of those present at a meeting of the membership. Appeal procedures are like those with respect to admission, with the appellant retaining membership until confirmation of the decision to exclude.[48] In contrast to the discharged state farm worker, the expelled collective farmer has no right to judicial review.

In addition to formal penalties, the collective farm chairman has a variety of informal penalties at his disposal. The average collective farmer depends for a large portion of his income on his privately owned livestock and on the plot allocated to him for private farming. However, he is dependent upon the farm administration to obtain the transport, fodder, seed, fertilizer, draft animals, etc. that he needs. Thus the administration is in a position to cause the farmer heavy financial loss merely by not cooperating in his private farming operations. In addition, the private plot itself may be reduced in size or replaced by one on inferior land, without the farmer having any recourse in court.

Civil Liability

The position of the collective farm worker prior to the new charter was somewhat worse than that of the state farm worker as far as potential civil liability to the farm. The collective farmer could be forced to pay up to the full value of damage caused by his negligence, while the state farm worker's liability was limited to one-third of one month's pay for any individual mishap caused by his negligence.[49] Article 13 of the new charter applies the

[46] Bilinsky, "Aktuelle Rechtsprobleme," p. 71.
[47] *Ibid.*
[48] Kazantsev, pp. 129–136.
[49] Vsesoiuznyi nauchno-issledovatel'skii institut sovetskogo zakonodatel'stva, *Kommentarii k zakonodatel'stvu o trude* (Moscow, 1966), pp. 283–287; A. K. R. Kiralfy, "Employers' and Employees' Civil Liability in Soviet Law for Industrial Accidents," *International and Comparative Law Quarterly*, XIV (July, 1965), 969.

same limit to the collective farmer's liability. There is, however, an important exception, liability for injury to livestock, where both collective and state farm workers are subject to full liability for negligent injury, and to liability at the rate of one and one-half times the value of the livestock for theft.[50] Existing procedures on both state and collective farms allow for checking off sums due for damages from amounts due for pay without a formal court hearing.[51]

Criminal Liability

Soviet criminal law contains a number of provisions that play an important role in the conduct of farm labor and management. Citations here are to the criminal code employed in the RSFSR;[52] provisions in other republics are quite similar. Probably the most common crime on the farm is the theft of farm property; such theft is severely punishable, with no distinction made between state and collective farm property, under Articles 89 through 97 of the criminal code. Article 98 provides punishment for intentional destruction of state and collective property, while Article 99 provides punishment for certain cases of negligent damage. Article 99–1 provides punishment for criminally wrongful use of agricultural equipment. It was added to the code to help ameliorate what has apparently been a continuous and severe problem, the rapid physical deterioration of agricultural machinery.

Article 152–1, which punishes distortion of reports of plan fulfillment, was added to the code following a number of instances evidencing a nationwide problem of falsification of agricultural production reports.

Private enterprise is generally forbidden in the USSR except for a few specifically licensed activities. Certain types of farm labor contracts have fallen afoul of this prohibition, which is enforced under Articles 153 and 154 of the code. Khrushchev's policy of subsidizing bread for the cities, while restricting sales of fodder to owners of livestock, led to the passage of Article 154–1, forbidding the feeding of bread to cattle. Distilling alcoholic beverages, a popular pastime on Soviet as on American farms, is prohibited by Article 158.

Specifically applicable to farms are Article 160 on violation of veterinary

---

[50] *Kommentarii*, pp. 292–325.
[51] Kiralfy; Article 13 of the new charter would limit the amount which could be checked off to one-third of one month's pay.
[52] *Ugolovnyi kodeks RSFSR*. There are many Russian editions. For an excellent English translation with an extensive introduction, see H. J. Berman (with James W. Spindler, co-trans.), *Soviet Criminal Law and Procedure: The RSFSR Codes* (Cambridge, Mass.: Harvard University Press, 1966).

health regulations and Article 161 on violation of plant disease restrictions. Article 199, forbidding squatting, also might apply to the farms.

Farm managers could be punished under Articles 170–172, dealing with abuse, excess, and neglect of authority, particularly for abuse with mercenary motives.

IV

Forms of Compensation

Compensation to farm workers has taken a number of forms. These include current and deferred monetary payments, payments in crops, allocation of land for private farming, and granting of grazing rights on farmland. In recent years the trend has been toward monetary payments. Under Khrushchev there was a tendency to restrict the allocation of land for private farming; however, the restrictions imposed then have now been eliminated.

Until recently, the most significant difference in the position of a collective farm employee on the one hand, and the employee of a state farm or other state enterprise on the other, was in the area of compensation for work performed. Here the cooperative nature of the collective farm, which in many other respects was a legal fiction, had real significance. For the total fund for compensation to collective farmers was the net income of the farm from its operations, less a prescribed proportion set aside for investment. This fund was divided among the farmers in accordance with work done, in a manner which will be described below. There was no lower limit on compensation, but the upper limit was equivalent to the wages which would be paid for the same work at a state farm.[53] During the early 1960's, a number of collective farms became remunerative so consistently that they were able to pay regular wages on the state scale to workers as an advance against expected income.[54] This change was the first in a series of steps which culminated in the institution of a regular wage system for collective farms essentially similar to that in use for state farms.

Until the late 1960's, the basic measure of work on a collective farm was the labor-day, while the state farms operated on a piecework wage system. The labor-day was not a day worked but rather an arbitrary unit of measure designed to equate work in occupations involving different amounts of skill and output.[55] Before 1956, the content of a labor-day was regulated by

[53] Kalandadze, "Pravovoe obespechenie."
[54] I. F. Kaz'min, "Novoe zakonodatel'stvo ob oplate truda kolkhoznikov," *Uchenye zapiski VNIISZ*, no. 12 (1968), pp. 87–100.
[55] Kalandadze, "Pravovoe obespechenie."

federal decree. A 1956 decree authorized collective farms to set for themselves the work norms constituting labor-days.[56] The decree was based on
the theory that rapid technical progress in agriculture required flexibility
in setting and raising work norms. Work norms set by the collective farms
were subject to approval by the district executive committee and were
expected to follow certain guidelines, so the new freedom was by no means
unlimited.[57]

The labor-day served two functions. It was a measure both of work required and of compensation for work done. Typically, each collective
farmer was required to work a certain minimum of labor-days on the collective portion of the farm during specified calendar periods. The purpose
of this regulation was to prevent slighting collective lands in the interests of
personal plots.[58] This system was criticized in that it allowed highly skilled
and productive workers to fulfill their obligation to the collective with
relatively few days spent working on the collective, while the unskilled had
to work many days to accumulate the required number of labor-days.[59] As a
result of this criticism, and perhaps because of the shortage of skilled labor
for work on the common land, the work obligation of skilled and unskilled
laborers has been equalized and is now expressed in terms of the number
of actual days worked during a given calendar period.[60]

The second use of labor-days was for determination of shares in the
annual surplus of the collective after all deductions for taxes, nonlabor expenses, and investment funds. Each member shared in proportion to the
number of labor-days he had earned. This system has now been replaced
by the piecework wage system described below.

The Wage System

The most striking change in the law regulating internal farm relations
has been the complete overhaul of the collective farm wage system, to bring
wage levels and payment schemes much more in line with those on state
farms.[61] This major reform would appear to have a number of basic goals.
The short-range goal is to obtain better results from farm labor by offering
better incentives. The medium-range goal is to keep at least a minimum

[56] *Izvestiia*, March 10, 1956.
[57] Kaz'min.
[58] V. Gsovski, *Soviet Civil Law* (Ann Arbor: University of Michigan Press, 1948),
I, 747.
[59] Kalandadze, "Pravovoe obespechenie."
[60] *Ibid.*
[61] Kaz'min; the legislation is collected in A. S. Pankratov (ed.), *Zakonodatel'stvo o
proizvodstve, zagotovkakh i zakupkakh sel'khozproduktov* (Moscow, 1967), pp. 263–388.

number of well-qualified agricultural workers in the collective farm system, and perhaps to encourage an increase in the general skill level. The long-range goal is the preparation of conditions for the replacement of the collective farm system by a new system which could be labeled "communist."

The reform of the collective farm compensation system was made possible by another reform, one beyond the scope of this paper, namely, the reform of the state agricultural planning and procurement system to provide greater incentives and higher cash incomes for collective farms as entities.[62] The following discussion will deal with the mechanisms by which this higher income is being transformed into incentives for the individual collective farmers.

The basic characteristic of the payment system during the first decades of collective farm operation was its true cooperative nature (unlike other aspects of the collective farm charter which were legal fictions from the beginning). Leaving aside for the moment the procedures whereby various members' proportional shares were determined, the important fact was that the sum (whether in money or in kind) available for compensation was basically the remainder of the income of the collective farm after all expenses and other obligations were paid. This method of determination of compensation meant that the pay of collective farmers differed in two respects from that of persons on state farms. First, farms whose superior geographic locations were not made the subject of full disguised rent payments to the state, in the form of sufficiently lower purchase prices, were able to pay a higher average compensation to their members.[63] Second, while the inadequate prices paid to state farms for food meant a burden not on the workers but on the treasury, which had to subsidize state farms since the workers continued to receive their wages, for the collective farms the situation was different. To the extent that prices were low or subsidies inadequate, the burden fell on the members, for the result was that the surplus available for distribution was correspondingly low.[64]

The key change in the collective farm wage reforms has been the incorporation of compensation of members into the general Soviet system of planned wages. In other words, planning authorities are now required to calculate wages as an expense of the collective farm and to plan for farm income sufficient to cover this expense.[65] The cooperative nature of the collective farm, to the extent that it still exists, is thus reflected only in the system of distribution of supplementary pay and bonuses.

[62] See Chapter 2.
[63] N. M. Manaserian, *Differentsial'naia renta i rentabel'nost' kolkhozov* (Erevan, 1967).
[64] Emel'ianov, p. 241.
[65] Kaz'min.

The old labor-day system was abolished during the latter part of the 1960's and was replaced by a piecework system like that used on Soviet state farms and in industry.

Jobs are divided into various categories depending upon the skills required to perform them, with daily pay norms set for each category. (This approach differs somewhat from that in Soviet industry, where workers qualify for certain skill categories and are paid the rates for those categories.) The daily pay norm is multiplied by the number of days worked in a year and the total is then divided by the number of units of output to be obtained. The farm member is then paid a wage equal to the amount produced multiplied by the rate set for each unit of production.[66]

Let us take an example of rates from the RSFSR legislation and simplify it somewhat:[67] the basic pay rate recommended for piecework of the fifth skill category (e.g., operating milking machines) of animal care is 2 rubles 73 kopecks per day. A piecework rate is set at 1 ruble 36.5 kopecks per hundred kilograms of milk, so that if the cows assigned to an individual milkmaid produce, as expected, 200 kilograms per day, she will receive 2 rubles 73 kopecks per day.

Farmers are paid in advance 60–70 percent of the wage norm. The advance is not forfeited no matter how poor the performance. However, payment of the remainder due depends upon calculation of actual performance and is by no means guaranteed.

Legally allowed flexibility for the collective farm in the wage-setting process comes in two ways. First, legislation on the wage system is in the form of recommendations, leaving room for local flexibility.[68] In the second place, piece rates can be manipulated by setting high or low norms. Even if the letter and the spirit of the regulations are obeyed, the average compensation on collective farms will fall well below that on state farms, because of the relative lack of skilled workers on collective farms.

Supplementary pay had an important role under the old collective farm compensation system. Since the compensation of farm members was based on residual income, final compensation could not be determined until residual income was determined. In practice, advances or guaranteed payments were made during the year, and the rest of compensation due was paid after the end of the year once the results of the year's operation were known. A number of Soviet commentators have argued that supplementary pay will no longer be needed once the transformation to a regular wage system is complete, but others have questioned this assumption.[69] In fact, supple-

[66] Pankratov, pp. 267ff.
[67] *Ibid.*, p. 276.
[68] Nedbailo.
[69] Kalandadze, "Pravovoe obespechenie."

mentary pay has continued to be used as a means of encouraging production of crops in short supply.[70]

In Soviet industry and on Soviet state farms, it has long been the practice to pay bonuses to management personnel who succeed in performing or exceeding the planned tasks set for them. Similar bonus payments have been made in the past on collective farms. As part of the reform of the collective farm compensation scheme, legislation has been passed to reform the bonus payment system on collective farms and to bring it in line with that on state farms.

Deferred compensation in the form of pensions had always existed on both state and collective farms; however, before 1965, only state farms were included in the general social insurance scheme, while collective farms paid pensions in accordance with their abilities, usually in far smaller amounts than state farms. Starting on January 1, 1965, the collective farms were incorporated into the general state pension scheme, though the benefit schedule for collective farmers is still not as generous as that for industrial workers.[71]

In addition to their regular employees and members, both state and collective farms frequently employ individuals to perform certain services on a temporary basis under a negotiated contractual arrangement. These contracts are often looked upon with suspicion by law enforcement authorities, who suspect them to be a cover for illegal private business activity, and considerable litigation has resulted from them.[72]

An important form of compensation is the allocation of land for private farming to families on state farms and to households on collective farms.[73] Under Khrushchev, attempts were made to reduce the size of all such allocations and to introduce a system of arbitrary penalties of reduced allocations for farmers who failed to work a sufficient amount of time on the collective land.[74] His successors have relied much more on monetary incentives than on threats to encourage work on the common land.

The rights of farmers, particularly of collective farmers, to legal relief in case of disputes over compensation are quite limited. Generally, suit can be brought only to recover sums listed as due the farmer in the farm's account books, but not paid. Disputes over the correctness of calculations of compensation due and over the size of land allocations are settled administratively by the district executive committee or through Party or other informal

[70] Kaz'min.
[71] V. N. Mikhalkevich (ed.), *Kommentarii k zakonodatel'stvu o pensiiakh i posobiiakh kolkhoznikam* (Moscow, 1967).
[72] Godes, Davidov, and Kalandadze, pp. 96–97.
[73] Kalandadze, "Pravovoe obespechenie."
[74] Kazantsev, pp. 478–482.

channels.[75] Such channels might be expected to be more inclined to favor farm administrators than the courts would be. A number of Soviet commentators have proposed substantially broadening the areas in which judicial relief would be available.

V

The history of Soviet agricultural law reveals a pattern composed of a static period, interruption by a short period of sharp change, the retroactive legal codification of these changes, followed by another static period, and so on. The suddenness of changes has been reflected in the persistence of institutions of preceding periods as legal fictions into later periods.[76] Thus, for instance, the stability of the 1920's after the introduction of the NEP was interrupted by the violent changes of collectivization, and the resulting legal relations were retroactively codified in the model charter of 1935, which embodied the legal fiction of voluntary collectivization. A new model charter has now been adopted. This charter codifies many changes which have taken place in collective farm relationships since Stalin's death and makes a number of minor changes aimed at equalizing the status of the collective and state farmer. Some of its articles appear to be designed to do more, to revitalize the collective farm, as a legal form capable of serving the many different types of agricultural organization most suited to the varied lands, climates, and peoples of the USSR. The next decade will tell whether the conservative or the creative elements of the charter prevail.

[75] G. G. Kharatishvili, "Nekotorye ustavnye prava i obiazannosti chlenov kolkhozov," *Pravovedenie*, no. 4 (1968), pp. 97–101.

[76] On the legal fiction in general, see L. Fuller, "Legal Fictions" (Parts 1–3), *Illinois Law Review*, XXV (1930–1931), 363ff., 513ff., 865ff.

PART III

Recent Trends in the Rural Economy

7 : The Nonagricultural Rural Sector

Karl-Eugen Wädekin

It is common knowledge that expansion, absolutely and relatively, of the nonagricultural sector of the rural society and economy is typical of modern European development. During earlier stages of urbanization crafts and trade tended to be drawn into the towns and cities, but modern agricultural technology, rising rural consumer demand, and modern transportation facilities, which make commuting to cities possible, have modified this pattern. Although the urban economy and society still expand the most, the nonagricultural rural sector also expands in a shrinking rural society. Soviet Russia is no exception to this rule, but the process is only beginning.

The concentration of crafts and trade in urban communities was under way in Russia long before the Bolshevik revolution. Collectivization and subsequent Soviet agricultural policies provided an additional impetus by decimating the rural population during collectivization, by draining off afterwards much of the remaining rural labor surplus, by almost exterminating the traditional small crafts in the countryside, especially after World War II,[1] and by assigning to the villages solely the task of feeding the rapidly growing urban population. As late as the Nineteenth Party Congress, in October of 1952, Malenkov spoke out against the nonagricultural economic activities of kolkhozy—surely not without Stalin's blessing. Clearly, the considerable increase in the nonagricultural population between 1950 and the beginning of 1953 (see Table 1) occurred despite the dictator's will. Thus, until recently, there prevailed in practice the view that the Soviet countryside was to be as exclusively as possible an agricultural production area.[2]

---

[1] On the fate of *kustari* and *domashnii promysel,* see K.-E. Wädekin, "Handwerke, Baugewerbe und materielle Dienstleistungen in sowjetischen Dörfern," *Sowjetstudien,* no. 25 (1969), pp. 38–73.

[2] G. Aksenenok, "Nazrevshie problemy pravovogo regulirovaniia sel'skogo khoziaistva," *Kommunist,* no. 18 (1968), p. 73.

During the last 15 years things have changed greatly. In the eyes even of Soviet authors, growth of the nonagricultural share of the rural population has become one of the "main tendencies of change in the rural social structure."[3] However, before elaborating on this type of change and showing some of its recent aspects and effects, it is appropriate to formulate the socioeconomic categories under which this expanding portion of the Soviet rural population may be subsumed. One immediately comes to the heart of the matter in attempting to present what overall figures and estimates can be gleaned from Soviet sources, for Soviet statisticians do not publish the pertinent figures in a direct way and do not even collect some data that would be useful. Although Soviet scholars seem recently to have become aware of a fundamental difference between the rural population in general and the agricultural population in particular,[4] comprehensive data of this sort are not to be found in Soviet sources even today.

One thing must always be kept in mind: the kolkhoz has never been merely an agricultural or production unit in the strict sense of the word. It has rather been an all-comprehending, compulsory living sphere of a particular rural community (or several communities).[5] It has always exercised—more or less, depending upon the given period—functions of local public administration (the *sel'skii sovet*), and in this capacity it has also comprised the nonagricultural producers of the village(s) it includes. However, those who are permanent employees of a state enterprise or consumers' cooperative, or (until 1960) who were members of a cooperative of small craftsmen (*kustari*), or who have remained "individual peasants" have generally, but not totally, been excepted from its power orbit. The case is similar, though not exactly the same, for the sovkhoz.

Moreover, the immense size of today's kolkhozy and state farms raises special problems in distinguishing agricultural and nonagricultural employment. For example, it seems reasonable to consider a man who repairs tractors within and for an agricultural production unit as employed in agriculture. But what if he is working in a central village of 1,000–2,000 or more inhabitants and for a kolkhoz or sovkhoz with dozens of tractors, combine-

---

[3] A. Sukharev, "Osnovnye tendentsii izmeneniia sotsial'noi struktury derevni v protsesse stroitel'stva kommunizma v SSSR," in *Izmeneniia sotsial'noi struktury sovetskogo krest'ianstva* (Minsk, 1965), p. 7; cf. recently, on the Soviet Far East, the similar but less emphatic statement by R. Ivanova, "Tekhnicheskoe perevooruzhenie sel'skogo khoziaistva i problemy trudovykh resursov," *Voprosy ekonomiki*, no. 4 (1969), p. 132.
[4] See the review in *Voprosy filosofii*, no. 12 (1968), p. 131, of a book by P. P. Maslov, *Sotsiologiia i statistika* (Moscow, 1967); this author's talks with members of the Economic Institute of the Academy of Sciences in Moscow in 1967 showed the same awareness, though it was stated then that data of that kind are being collected (in what way and what details?) but not published.
[5] See G. Ipsen, "Arbeitskraft und Arbeitsvermögen," in *Osteuropa-Handbuch: Sowjetunion—Das Wirtschaftssystem* (Cologne: Böhlau, 1965), p. 55.

harvesters, and other machinery? Clearly, in any Western European village his repair shop would be a separate entity and the workers would be considered nonagricultural. Similar cases are those of a chief engineer of a large sovkhoz or of people wholly employed in a kolkhoz construction brigade or in subsidiary production (*podsobnyi promysel*).

It is also worth mentioning in advance that, by Soviet definition, a kolkhoz or sovkhoz may not only be situated, partly or entirely, within urban limits, but may even be classified as an "urban-type community," despite being wholly or predominantly an agricultural enterprise. This is so because an "urban settlement" is defined (although the numbers vary by union republic) by the size of its population and by type of employment, with the latter expressed in terms of "workers" and "employees," as opposed to "kolkhozniki."[6] Thus a sovkhoz village of a certain size may well be classified as a "workers' settlement" or "urban-type settlement" (*rabochii poselok, poselok gorodskogo tipa*).[7] This goes a long way, though not all the way, toward an explanation of why, in the 1959 census, 15 percent of agricultural workers and employees were classified as living in "urban settlements," as opposed to only 4 percent of agriculturally employed kolkhozniki.[8]

I

In attempting primarily to provide a statistical framework, this presentation will be confined to the last 15 or 20 years. Evidence available for the decade before 1955 is scarce, and it is moreover distorted by the fact that, until 1950–1952, not all peasants of the newly annexed territories had as yet been driven into kolkhozy. The prewar years are beyond this author's immediate research.

Leaving aside the problem of fishermen, hunters, and the forest industries as components of the "rural economy,"[9] one can, in deductive fashion, discern the following main categories of nonagricultural labor in rural areas:

1. Commuters living in rural areas and
   a. working permanently or principally in urban places,
   b. working temporarily (even if principally) in urban places, but still considered kolkhoz members.

[6] See B. S. Khorev, *Gorodskie poseleniia SSSR* (Moscow, 1968), pp. 19–21; B. V. Erofeev, "Razvitie poniatiia gorodskikh zemel' v sovetskom zakonodatel'stve," *Sovetskoe gosudarstvo i pravo*, no. 7 (1968), pp. 106ff.

[7] Khorev, *Gorodskie poseleniia*, p. 19.

[8] *Itogi Vsesoiuznoi perepisi naseleniia 1959 goda: SSSR (svodnyi tom)* (Moscow, 1962), Table 33.

[9] See W. W. Eason, *The Agricultural Labor Force and Population in the USSR, 1926–1941* (Santa Monica, Calif.: RAND Corp., 1954), pp. 5, 53.

2. Workers and employees (including kolkhoz members) of rural non-agricultural enterprises turning out material products both
   a. separately from kolkhozy and state farms and
   b. within kolkhozy and state farms.
3. Workers and employees (including kolkhoz members) in rural non-agricultural service enterprises or organizations operating both
   a. separately from kolkhozy and state farms and
   b. within kolkhozy and state farms.
4. Rural craftsmen who are
   a. in individual production (essentially the negligible number of *nekooperirovanye kustari*; the illegal or half-legal *chastniki* who are either beyond working age or who formally have employment in the public sector),[10]
   b. members of a kolkhoz or state farm workers.

Admittedly these categories are crude, schematic, and open to a number of questions (e.g., How to define principal employment? What activity within a kolkhoz may be called nonagricultural?), but they must do for our purpose, for they are already almost too fine for the kind of data available in Soviet sources. The main difficulty is that these are categories of labor and not socio-economic classifications of families. "Mixed households" (*smeshannye dvory*) are a widespread phenomenon in the present-day kolkhoz[11] and probably in state farms as well. One such household may, for instance, include a man who works as a teacher or for a nearby state enterprise, a wife who is a kolkhoz clerk (only in rare cases will a teacher's wife work as a simple kolkhoznitsa) and a son who is a kolkhoz *mekhanizator* or *brigadir*. So long as workers or employees participate in the economic sphere of the kolkhoz household, either by their own labor or financially, they may be considered household members,[12] although they are not kolkhozniki from the standpoint of labor statistics. However, Soviet statistics must be used in the form in which they are made available, and only then can one attempt to extract additional information from them or to find a common denominator. Fortunately, there will be, as a rule, only one male wage earner in a family (or one female of working age if there is no male), and his (her) employment will determine the socio-economic status of the family.

Probably the only means by which the number of the nonagricultural

[10] See Wädekin, "Handwerke," pp. 41–42, 68–73.

[11] For sources see K.-E. Wädekin, "Nicht-agrarische Beschäftigte in sowjetischen Dörfern," *Osteuropa-Wirtschaft*, no. 3 (1968), pp. 191–192; see also F. Abramov, "Vokrug da okolo," *Neva*, no. 1 (1963), p. 121.

[12] A. G. Pervushin and N. A. Sinitsyn, "Esli vy rabotnik sel'skogo khoziaistva," in *Molodezh'!—Tvoi prava i obiazannosti* (Moscow, 1968), pp. 163–164.

rural population (not labor) may be determined is to deduct the agricultural population from the total rural population, and then to make certain adjustments. Although this can be done only by ignoring the mixed household, this procedure yields estimates with which one can work. (A number of unavoidable uncertainties are explained in the appendix: the resulting figures are far from exact, but it is believed that they show the overall magnitudes and trend.)

Table 1 : *The rural population of the USSR (millions, beginning of year).*

1. Year	2. Total Rural Population	3. Rural Kolkhoz and State Farm Population	4. Other Rural Population (millions)	4. Other Rural Population (percent)[a]
1939[b]	114.4	77	37–38	32–33%
1950	109.1	79–80[c]	29–30	27
1953	107.8	76.0	32	29–30
1955	108.1	79.0	29.1	27
1956	109.7	79.6	30.1	27.5
1959	108.8	72.5	36.3	33
1961	107.9	72.5	35.4	33
1963	108.1	72.0	36.1	33
1964	107.9	71.9	36.0	33
1965	107.6	73.7	33.9	31.5
1966	107.1	73.0	34.1	32
1967	106.4	72.1	34.3	32

[a] Column 4 ÷ column 2 × 100.
[b] Prewar territory.
[c] Including an estimated 400,000 individual peasant households (families); compare the cattle and sown area for these and "other groups" in *Sel'skoe khoziaistvo SSSR*, pp. 128, 266.

SOURCES AND DERIVATIONS: Total rural population from *Narodnoe khoziaistvo . . . 1967*, p. 7. Figures for 1939 kolkhoz population calculated from *Itogi*, Tables 1 and 28 (urban kolkhoz population crudely estimated as ca. 2 million); state farm population for 1939 from Eason, p. 40, adjusted by adding an estimated number of employees for 1937 in *Trud v SSSR*, p. 126. For other years kolkhoz and state farm population derived by adding columns 3 and 4 of Table 3 in the appendix to this paper, with the exception of 1950 and 1953, which are estimates on the basis of employment figures (as given by Nancy Nimitz, *Farm Employment in the Soviet Union, 1928–1963* (Santa Monica, Calif.: RAND Corp., 1965), p. 112, and by *Narodnoe khoziaistvo . . . 1960*, p. 521, and *Narodnoe khoziaistvo . . . 1963*, p. 363) in relation to later employment and population figures. The remaining population (column 4) is derived as a residual.

The decrease in the kolkhoz and state farm population (mostly agricultural) was rather slow over the period covered by Table 1, excepting 1956–1959, because the more rapid decrease in kolkhoz population was in part offset by the increase in sovkhoz population. However, on the one hand, this is also a result of opposing regional developments: some southern and southeastern regions showed an increase while there was a more rapid decrease in the rest of the country. On the other hand, aggregate figures do not disclose the rising average age and rapidly diminishing proportion of able-bodied in the agricultural population,[13] which must also be true for those sovkhozy that have recently been converted from kolkhozy. Although in 1959, according to Mashenkov, the proportion of males in the age range 16–59 and of females in the age range 16–54 was 51.2 percent of the rural kolkhoz population[14] (and perhaps very slightly more if urban kolkhozniki had been included), it was only 36–37 percent in 1965 (or 20.23 million persons).[15] On the whole, therefore, the age structure of the agricultural population is such that at present and for the near future a more rapid decrease is to be expected—a diminution more rapid than decreasing labor requirements would allow for—except again for some southern and southeastern regions.[16]

For the residual rural population (composed mostly of nonagricultural population) the most striking features displayed in Table 1 are the rapid increase in the four-year period 1956–1959 and the subsequent stagnation. Apart from the fact that this stagnation is somewhat misleading, as will be shown below, due to the expansion of the nonagricultural subsector of kolkhozy and state farms, these trend changes merit a closer examination. There are three postwar periods in which the residual rural population decreased: 1953–1955, 1959–1961, and 1964–1965. The decrease in 1959–1961 is merely formal, for 3.4 million people were reclassified as "urban" during these two years by administrative conversion of their settlements to urban-type.[17] Naturally enough, this statistic must have included, in addition to a certain number of newly created sovkhoz settlements (see above), mainly settlements with an above average nonagricultural component, which would reduce the ratio of nonagricultural to agricultural population in rural settlements. The decreases in the nonagricultural rural population for 1953–

[13] This has been demonstrated recently by this author in "Manpower in Soviet Agriculture," *Soviet Studies*, XX, no. 3 (January, 1969), 286ff.

[14] V. F. Mashenkov, *Ispol'zovanie trudovykh resursov v sel'skoi mestnosti* (Moscow, 1965), p. 17.

[15] G. V. D'iachkov, *Obshchestvennoe i lichnoe v kolkhozakh* (Moscow, 1968), p. 115 (Table 36).

[16] Wädekin, "Manpower," pp. 290–291 and *passim*; cf. V. Smirnov, "Dvizhenie i ispol'zovanie trudovykh resursov sela (po Nechernozemnoi zone RSFSR)," *Ekonomicheskie nauki*, no. 5 (1969), pp. 40–47.

[17] In 1959–1964, 4.4 million, according to N. P. Golubkova, "Pereraspredelenie rabochei sily iz sel'skogo khoziaistva . . .," in G. S. Grigorian (ed.), *Problemy proizvoditel'nosti truda i narodnogo potrebleniia v period razvernutogo stroitel'stva kommunizma* (Moscow, 1965), p. 13, of which one million were in 1961–1964, according to I. S. Paskhaver, *Sel'skoe khoziaistvo SSSR v pokazateliakh statistiki* (Moscow, 1968), p. 19.

1954 and 1964–1965 were accompanied by an atypical increase in the kolkhoz population, a result, it is believed, of essentially political changes, i.e., of the easing up on kolkhozy and especially on the private sector following Stalin's death and Khrushchev's ouster respectively. Most probably, these events induced a number of people to return to agricultural jobs or, rather, to remain in them. In each instance, after a short-lived reversal of the trend, the nonagricultural component resumed its previous course of growth. The same is true after 1961, when a more normal rate of conversion of rural to urban settlements was observed.

It will be shown at a later point that not all of the kolkhoz and state farm population should be considered agricultural, but the first question to be answered is whether or not the whole of the residual rural population is truly nonagricultural.

With certain reservations, the personnel of land improvement stations of *Soiuzsel'khoztekhnika* may be called agricultural labor not subsumed under the kolkhoz and state farm population given in Table 1. Their numbers have increased in recent years and, for 1966, may be estimated at some 250,000 persons.[18] Including dependents, the total is possibly half a million people.

A certain part of the residual population in Table 1 (column 4) must be composed of administrative and advisory agricultural personnel in district centers of nonurban status and of scientific agricultural institutions in rural areas (but most of which are classified as sovkhozy or subsidiary state farms anyway), and thus they may be considered agricultural labor (with their dependents) outside kolkhozy and state farms. Surely they number less than 100,000 employed persons. More important and rather difficult is the problem of those employed in the administration of agricultural procurement and material-technical supply. To the author's knowledge, Soviet sources have never disclosed any figures for these categories, except those given by Khrushchev in 1955, when he gave a figure of some 900,000 for the agricultural procurement organizations alone, which he wanted to have reduced by one-half.[19] Assuming that he succeeded only to a certain extent in reducing these personnel, and adding the organizations of agricultural material-technical supply, we may estimate this part of the labor force at some 900,000 by the time of the census.[20] All of this means that there are some 2.5 million of

[18] From the numbers of stations and their machinery; see V. Kozlov and V. Iambaev in *Sel'skaia zhizn'*, September 22, 1966, p. 2.

[19] N. S. Khrushchev, *Stroitel'stvo kommunizma v SSSR i razvitie sel'skogo khoziaistva* (Moscow, 1962), II, 19, 53.

[20] Including trade shops, canteens, etc., there were 1.54 million in the countryside by January 15, 1959 (see *Itogi,* Table 33). Of these, in 1965, some 600,000 were employed in shops, canteens, restaurants, etc., as can be calculated from the number of such places (*Narodnoe khoziaistvo . . . 1965,* p. 654) and the average number of persons employed in each, as given by V. A. Morozov, *Trudoden', den'gi i torgovlia na sele* (Moscow, 1965), p. 243.

the agricultural population outside kolkhozy and state farms. Whether they all may really be called agricultural population is questionable, for most of them compare with trade and marketing organizations in western countries. However, in order to be on the safe side, so considering them reduces the size of the residual (nonagricultural) population given in Table 1 accordingly.

II

It is difficult to imagine what other component of the residual rural population may be considered agricultural. Thus the remaining nonagricultural population is mainly, though not wholly, composed of the (a) part of each category given in the classification above. Roughly one-fourth of the nonagricultural rural sector's employed population works in cultural and educational institutions, another fourth works in industry, and one-fourth more in construction.[21]

Practically the whole of the rural population, and part of the urban, are engaged in private agricultural production in one degree or another, overwhelmingly for their own consumption. It may be safely surmised that numbers of wives and other family members, able-bodied or not, are principally engaged in private agricultural production, along with household work in most cases. Nevertheless, there should be very few cases in which this activity is the main source of income for those families in which the man or other main earner is permanently employed in a nonagricultural job. And rural households with no money earner are, as a rule, kolkhoz households. (For kolkhoz households, private agricultural production may not so rarely be the main source of income even today. But where adult members of the kolkhoz household are employed nonagriculturally within the kolkhoz, their income from such employment is, as a rule, above average and thus higher than from private production.) Thus the influence of the private sector on the socio-economic characteristics of rural nonagricultural families may be neglected.

According to the 1959 census (applied, however, to settlement classifications as of January 1, 1961), 10.1 million members of the rural population were living in nonagricultural settlements (of which 331,600 were in those of forestry and the wood industry) situated almost exclusively in the RSFSR, with 35 percent in settlements of 100–500 persons and another 34 percent in settlements of 500–2,000 inhabitants.[22] These people may safely be con-

[21] Estimates are founded on calculations for 1959 and 1962, as given in Wädekin, "Nicht-agrarische Beschäftigte," pp. 187–189.

[22] *Itogi*, and *Itogi Vsesoiuznoi perepisi naseleniia 1959: RSFSR* (Moscow, 1962), Tables 9.

sidered almost exclusively members of the nonagricultural rural population, belonging to all four categories enumerated above, but under the (a) headings. Of course, most of them must have been private agricultural producers with land plots and private livestock holdings, but this does not place them in the agricultural category.

The kolkhoz and state farm rural population of Table 1 includes a number of employed persons and their dependents who are in fact either not employed or only partially employed in agricultural activities. These may be categorized under the (b) headings of the classification given above.

The easiest to define in a statistical sense are those employed in nonagricultural branches within kolkhozy and state farms (sections 2b, 3b, and 4b of our classification). Soviet labor statistics enumerating "cadres in agriculture" on an average annual basis (i.e., labor in agricultural enterprises) show separately those who are employed in agriculture proper.[23] The remainder must be obtained as a residual, and it also includes members of fishery kolkhozy and, probably, some professional kolkhoz hunters. Assuming that enlisted supplementary agricultural labor (*privlechennye litsa*) is, with few exceptions, employed in agriculture proper, the total of nonagricultural labor within kolkhozy and sovkhozy, in millions on an average annual basis, for each year is:[24]

1950	3.0	1964	2.5
1955	3.3	1965	2.4
1959	3.6	1966	2.5
1960	3.4	1967	2.8

To these totals must be added people working in the agricultural sector but in nonagricultural professions. The census of January 15, 1959, put the combined total at 5.26 million,[25] of which 2.6 million were kolkhozniki (see below). Assuming that this is equivalent to an average annual total for 1959 of 5.0 million and that it includes the 3.6 million given for 1959 immediately above, there remain some 1.5–2.0 million people employed in nonagricultural professions within agricultural enterprises (including all agricultural organizations and institutions) as yet not accounted for.

The number of those who are employed in cultural-welfare activities and in capital repairs of buildings and structures in state farms is already excluded in the Soviet statistical data, and thus implicitly they are already

[23] For example, *Narodnoe khoziaistvo ... 1967*, p. 491.
[24] For 1967: *Narodnoe khoziaistvo ... 1967*, p. 491; for 1959: *Narodnoe khoziaistvo ... 1961*, p. 461 (assuming that the number of *privlechennye litsa* was 0.5 million, as in 1955 and 1960); for all other years: *Trud v SSSR* (Moscow, 1968), pp. 124–125.
[25] Obtained by deducting the number of those in agricultural professions (*Itogi*, Table 44) from the total in agriculture (*ibid.*, Table 33).

included in our derivation of the residual rural population in Table 1, column 4. Excluding seasonal workers as well, but not supplementary agricultural labor enlisted from the outside (*privlechennye litsa*) which cannot be separated out of the published figures, the share of state farm labor not engaged in agriculture proper still amounts to 8–9 percent in each year during recent years, and it was an even higher proportion prior to 1960, before the mass conversions of kolkhozy into sovkhozy.[26] The bulk of these are composed of the permanent workers of maintenance shops and of the subsidiary and service branches of state farms. In sovkhozy alone this group totalled 489,315 on August 2, 1965 (plus only 32,000 not in permanent employment).[27] The corresponding number for other state farms cannot have surpassed by any wide margin 50,000 persons, since the total labor force in state farms other than sovkhozy was only one-tenth that of all state farms.[28] In addition, there was some 0.3–0.5 million other nonagricultural labor included in the annual average figures for the state farm sector.[29] Of these, there are 90,000 minor service and custodial personnel (*mladshii obsluzhivaiushchii personal i rabotniki okhrany*) and 215,000 employees other than the higher agricultural technical employees.[30] An unknown number of people working in nonagricultural professions within the administrative framework of state farm agriculture should be also added (see below, the parallel category for kolkhozy).

In order to arrive at totals comparable to those for the rural population, which exclude state farms located within urban boundaries, an estimated 15 percent (see appendix) must be deducted from these figures.

The overall trend shows an increase in nonagricultural labor on state farms in absolute terms, but the relative increase was very slow after the 1961 setback.[31] But since those employed in cultural-welfare activities and

[26] *Trud v SSSR*, pp. 124–126; *Narodnoe khoziaistvo . . . 1967*, p. 491.

[27] *Trud v SSSR*, p. 232.

[28] *Ibid.*, pp. 126–127.

[29] Assuming that of the total of 500,000 *privlechennye litsa* in 1965 in agricultural work, no less than 200,000 and no more than 400,000 worked on state farms. Deducting these as well as the seasonal workers from the annual average labor force in state farm agriculture, one arrives at an annual average of 6.55–6.75 million, as opposed to an annual average of 7.55 million of all state farm labor, excluding seasonal and *privlechennye* workers (see *ibid.*, pp. 125–126). The difference is 0.8–1.0 million, among whom are the above mentioned 489,315 plus about 50,000 in repair shops and subsidiary and service enterprises of the state farms.

[30] *Ibid.*, p. 126. "Mladshii obsluzhivaiushchii personal" is defined by *Statisticheskii slovar'* (Moscow, 1965), p. 317, as: "litsa zanimaiushchie dolzhnosti po ukhodu za pomeshcheniiami predpriiatiia (uborshchiki, istopniki, dvorniki, garderobshchiki i t. p. rabotniki)."

[31] *Ibid.*, pp. 124–125. The conversion of kolkhozy, especially in 1959–1961, introduced millions of the kolkhoz population into the sovkhoz sector and thus blurred the socio-economic characteristics of the latter.

in capital repairs of buildings and structures in state farms are not included in the statistical data, this is only half the story as far as life in state farm settlements is concerned. Otherwise it may be assumed, with the mounting building activities and the recent policy of improving the cultural and material services in the countryside, that the numerical expansion of the nonagricultural sector within state farm villages would appear greater. Even so, the aggregate figure for this sector, including nonagricultural professions in state farms, is believed to have been well beyond one million in 1965.

A similar breakdown is not available for kolkhoz labor statistics, except for the 1959 census. In that year there were 32.3 million employed kolkhozniki, of which 31.7 million were in agriculture, including kolkhozy within urban boundaries and excluding persons serving with or drafted into the armed forces.[32] Of the total, 28.7 million were listed as having agricultural employment involving physical labor,[33] and an estimated 400,000 were in agriculture at all[35] which yields a total of 3.2 million persons. The proportion kolkhozniki in nonagricultural employment in kolkhoz agricultural production, to which must be added the 557,000 kolkhozniki not employed in agriculture at all,[35] which yields a total of 3.2 million persons. The proportion implied by these figures for nonagricultural kolkhoz employment (one-tenth) is too low since it applies to all working kolkhozniki, thus including those employed only part of the year. In fact, almost all of the 14.5 million unskilled female kolkhozniki employed in physical labor in 1959[36] cannot be regarded as permanent workers. This adjustment reduces the number of permanently employed kolkhozniki in 1959 to some 18 or 19 million. On the other hand, the nonagriculturally employed kolkhozniki are mostly permanent labor force, which—from what else is known about kolkhoz labor organization—is implied by the fact that only 500,000 of these were females in 1959.[37] Thus, the 3.2 million kolkhozniki in nonagricultural employment and outside agriculture in 1959 must be considered as equivalent to a very little less than 3 million on an average annual basis, as opposed to 18–19

[32] *Itogi,* Table 33.

[33] *Ibid.,* Tables 45 and 46.

[34] Of those, 267,000 had medium or higher education; see *Sel'skoe khoziaistvo SSSR* (Moscow, 1960), p. 467, to which an estimated 130,000 in such professions without an adequate education, the so-called *praktiki,* are added.

[35] *Itogi,* Table 33, arrived at by deduction. Of these, 85,000 were employed in education, science, arts, and health, but the bulk, 439,000, in industry, building, transport, and post (*sviaz'*). Probably most of the 439,000 were in building, among them the semilegal "shabashniki," whose number is unknown but cannot be negligible (for details on "shabashniki," see Wädekin, "Handwerke," pp. 63ff.

[36] *Itogi,* Table 46.

[37] Same sources and estimates as for figures including males. The "shabashniki," practically all males, do not work year-round, it is true, but during the season they work so much overtime that they may be considered principally employed in this activity; cf. Wädekin, "Handwerke," pp. 66–67.

million permanent kolkhoz laborers of all kinds, i.e., some 15 to 17 percent. Of these, 0.55 million (in 1959) were employed in maintenance shops and subsidiary enterprises and 0.7 million in construction and capital repair activities. (In 1962, there were only 0.5 million in each group.)[38]

No similarly detailed data are available for later years, but, in a rough way, the trend can be discerned with the help of otherwise noncomparable figures. On an average annual basis, and neglecting supplementary labor enlisted from the outside (which are negligible in kolkhozy), some 10 percent of kolkhoz labor were not employed in agriculture prior to 1961, and for 1962–1966, the percentage was 7 percent (to which must be added those who held nonagricultural professions in agricultural production).[39] In 1967, this figure rose again absolutely and relatively.[40]

It has been shown elsewhere[41] that this reduction in nonagricultural workers in kolkhozy was partly a consequence of state policy directed against kolkhoz subsidiary production. But it was also partly caused by the expansion of nonagricultural activities by inter-kolkhoz enterprises (especially construction). Column 4 of Table 1 includes the expansion of employment of these enterprises. The conversion of kolkhozy into sovkhozy also played a role. Thus there was no real numerical reduction in nonagricultural employment in kolkhoz villages in 1962–1966, whereas the expansion in 1967 was a real one, caused by the reversal of state policy with respect to subsidiary production and by the expansion of construction activities on kolkhozy (and in inter-kolkhoz enterprises as well).[42]

Therefore, it may be safely assumed that there are among the rural kolkhoz and state farm population some 3.5 to 3.8 million people either in nonagricultural employment or not employed at all in agricultural branches. (Several hundred thousand of those as of 1959 in kolkhozy must be subtracted for more recent years since their kolkhozy have been converted to sovkhozy, and they appear in state farm statistics for 1965.) Including dependents, but taking rough account for the able-bodied family members fully employed agriculturally, this means that some 7 to 8 million of the kolkhoz and state farm population for 1959 (see Table 1) are essentially

[38] *Ibid.*, p. 49.
[39] *Trud v SSSR*, pp. 124–125.
[40] *Narodnoe khoziaistvo* . . . *1967*, p. 491.
[41] Wädekin, "Handwerke," pp. 47ff.
[42] For comparative production figures of subsidiary nonagricultural kolkhoz and sovkhoz operations in 1964 and 1967, and also for some retarding factors, see A. Pronin, "Razvitie podsobnykh predpriiatii i promyslov v kolkhozakh i sovkhozakh," *Ekonomika sel'skogo khoziaistva*, no. 4 (1969), p. 48. Compare the figures for kolkhoz incomes other than agricultural in the Mari ASSR, which went up rapidly in 1955–1960 (from 3.0 to 4.7 million rubles), then down to 3.3 million in 1965, and again rose to 4.0 million in 1967, in *Mariiskaia ASSR v tsifrakh* (Ioshkar-Ola, 1967), p. 136.

nonagricultural and ought to be added to the nonagricultural population from the sociological standpoint. Given the overall trend, this figure is believed to have been somewhat less in the mid-1950's and above 8 million by 1967. A very tricky question is posed by commuters to urban places (section 1 of our classification). The Soviet Central Statistical Administration registers around 3 million persons living in villages but working in urban areas,[43] but Soviet authors reproducing this figure hint that a much higher one is possible—no less than 10 million, including urban-urban and urban-rural commuters.[44] An estimate of some 5 million rural-urban commuters would probably be of the right order for recent years. For Moscow and its environs a figure of 1.2 million (for all kinds of commuters) was lately given, for Gor'kii 75,000, for Khar'kov 125,000.[45] In the case of rural districts around Khar'kov, 44.1 percent of the economically active rural population in the zone nearest to Khar'kov commuted to the city in 1959, in a second, more remote zone the respective percentage was 26.5, and in a third zone it was still 12.7 percent. In all three zones combined, rural inhabitants formed about one-third of all commuters.[46] Almost one-fifth of all persons employed (and 24 percent of the workers) in Khar'kov lived outside the urban community, and since 1955 their number has grown much faster than the population of Khar'kov.[47] Admittedly, the bulk (73.5 percent) of all Khar'kov commuters (106,500 in 1959) came from urban settlements near the city,[48] but, as shown above, the rest (28,200) formed a rather substantial proportion of the rural population around Khar'kov.

Commuting—the Soviet term is *maiatnikovaia migratsiia*—received almost no attention until 1965.[49] Today its importance is generally recognized

[43] This fits in with indirect evidence from S. L. Seniavskii, *Rost rabochego klassa SSSR* (Moscow, 1966), pp. 28–29, which yields a figure of around 9.5 million workers and employees (excluding agriculture and forestry) in rural areas in 1962 (see also Wädekin, "Nicht-agrarische Beshäftigte," pp. 187–188) whereas the census results show 13.6 million residing in rural areas (*Itogi*, Table 33). Taking into account that Seniavskii's are annual average figures and therefore have to be somewhat lower than the census figures, the difference might well indicate the number of rural-urban commuters.

[44] D. I. Valentei, "Nauka o narodonaselenii," *Ekonomicheskaia gazeta*, no. 42 (1968), p. 20.

[45] E. I. Ruzavina, "Migratsiia rabochei sily pri sotsializme," *Vestnik moskovskogo universiteta, seriia VII: Ekonomika*, no. 4 (1968), p. 27.

[46] M. V. Kurman and I. V. Lebedinskii, *Naselenie bol'shogo sotsialisticheskogo goroda* (Moscow, 1968), p. 90, Table 41.

[47] *Ibid.*, pp. 87, 93; on the long-term increasing importance of commuters to Khar'kov, see *ibid.*, p. 71.

[48] *Ibid.*, p. 89.

[49] It was given only two short sentences in *Statisticheskii slovar'*, p. 317, and the second of these said that it was being investigated mainly in big cities and their suburbs. But recently it was stated that this phenomenon shows up preponderantly

by Soviet scholars, but "research on commuting is at present made difficult by the lack of statistical material."[50] In our context the question is complicated by the fact that it is not known how many commuters are subsumed under kolkhoz population (members of kolkhoz households, but working—temporarily or permanently—outside) and how many are not. Excluding students, 3 percent of the kolkhoz population (including urban kolkhozy) were working in as well as outside the kolkhoz on a temporary basis. Until 1962, probably another 2 million worked solely outside kolkhozy.[51] Proportionally this is greater than the proportion of kolkhoz labor not employed, or not principally employed, in agriculture in the thirties.[52] By 1965, the total (excluding here kolkhozniki working in other kolkhozy or cooperatives) was 2.7 million, of which 1.45 million did not work in their own kolkhozy at all.[53] Probably the majority of such kolkhozniki work in urban areas, but this is only an informed guess. It may be assumed, but it is by no means certain, that those still working temporarily in kolkhozy are counted in the kolkhoz population and the others excluded.

Nothing is said in Soviet sources about commuters from state farm villages, but the derivation of the figures given in Table 3 (see appendix) excludes them from the state farm population.

III

Thus the rural agricultural kolkhoz population (Table 1) must be reduced for 1967 by probably 2 to 4 million commuters (including their dependents), thus bringing it to something around 40 million. Correspondingly, the nonagricultural population—excluding about 3 million for land improvement stations, delivery apparatus, etc. (see above)—would reach around 42 to 43 million. In other words: *The current Soviet rural population is about three-fifths agricultural, with something more than one-fifth in state farms and other state organizations and somewhat less than two-fifths in kolkhozy, and the remaining two-fifths are nonagricultural, including some kolkhoz and state farm population.* These figures quantify a phenomenon which must be viewed against a broader background.

---

around the medium towns (Valentei, p. 20), and, in 1967, investigations were mainly directed to the medium and small towns; see B. Khorev, "Konkretnye sotsial'no-demograficheskie obsledovaniia v 1967 g.," *Ekonomicheskie nauki*, no. 7 (1968), pp. 110–111.

[50] T. Ter-Izrael'ian, "Nauchnaia konferentsiia po problemam narodonaseleniia Zakavkaz'ia," *Vestnik statistiki*, no. 3 (1969), p. 78. Yet for the 1970 census a special questionnaire on commuters was prepared.

[51] Wädekin, "Nicht-agrarische Beschäftigte," pp. 195–196.

[52] Eason, p. 55.

[53] D'iachkov, p. 115 (Table 36).

The expansion of the nonagricultural population and economy in the Soviet countryside is not only an intrusion of nonagricultural branches of the economy into the villages, nor is it merely an increase in the size (if not the number) of nonagricultural settlements. It is going on within kolkhozy and sovkhozy as well, and it is caused by the increasing demand for nonagricultural services within agriculture, by the recently favored expansion within kolkhozy and sovkhozy of food-processing, building and packaging materials, and other industries for agriculture,[54] by the need to employ the rural masses during the long winter season, and by the rapidly growing demand for agricultural specialists with secondary and higher education. Recent Soviet publications are filled with discussions of these problems.[55]

But there are also obstacles to the development of rural industries, especially shortages of material and equipment.[56] The demand for agricultural specialists is far from being satisfied.[57] Although the number of specialists and also of the so-called mechanizers is increasing, it is not doing so rapidly enough. In order to bring more skilled labor of this sort into the villages it is necessary to expand and improve the material and nonmaterial services in these areas, which in turn makes it imperative to provide more and better service personnel in the villages, at least in the central ones.[58] The number of 36,000 new jobs in rural (including nonurban district centers) retail shops of the RSFSR alone during 1966–1968, and the intention to create 23,000 more in 1969–1970,[59] are impressive. But, as the same authoritative source (the president of *Rospotrebsoiuz*) goes on to say, this is not the end, and it is not sufficient for the rising demand. The Soviet press is full of reports on the inadequate quantity and quality of rural services.[60]

Recent Soviet plans for village reconstruction, though still influenced by ideological preferences, reflect these objective necessities.[61] Not only capital equipment and building materials form a bottle-neck in the implementation of these plans, but also the scarcity of construction labor in rural districts.

[54] See the decree of the Council of Ministers of the USSR of September 30, 1966, "O meropriiatiiakh po dal'neishemu razvitiiu mestnoi promyshlennosti i khudozhestvennykh promyslov," *Resheniia partii i pravitel'stva po khoziaistvennym voprosam*, VI (Moscow, 1968), 248–254.

[55] For example, A. Koriagin, "Vosproizvodstvo rabochei sily v derevne," *Ekonomika sel'skogo khoziaistva*, no. 12 (1968).

[56] See, among others, I. Sokolov in *Sel'skaia zhizn'*, March 30, 1969, p. 2.

[57] For details see Wädekin, "Manpower."

[58] See E. V. Deniskina, "Svoeobrazie otraslei neproizvodstvennoi sfery na sele," *Vestnik moskovskogo universiteta, seriia VII: Ekonomika*, no. 6 (1966), pp. 34–35.

[59] M. Denisov in *Sel'skaia zhizn'*, March 11, 1969, p. 2.

[60] See lately I. Butenko in *Sel'skaia zhizn'*, March 30, 1969, p. 3; P. Pavlov in *Izvestiia*, October 23, 1968; and V. Koroleva, "Tovarishch Servis," *Neman* (October, 1968), the latter two as cited in *Radio Svoboda*, Munich, TsIO 61/69.

[61] For an account of these recent developments, see K.-E. Wädekin, "The Countryside," *Problems of Communism*, XVIII, no. 3 (May-June, 1969), 12–20.

As one official of a building trust recently put it: "It is difficult to build in the villages. There is no labor, and the fluctuation in cadres is great."[62]

The rapid modernization and mechanization of agriculture itself, which is indispensable in view of catastrophically decreasing available labor resources over wide parts of the country, is also a factor pushing forward the expansion of nonagricultural services and production destined to serve the agricultural sector. In view of these technical, economic, social, and demographic necessities, the expansion of the nonagricultural rural sector, as it has gone on since 1953, cannot be considered excessive. Past negligence has to be made up. The persistent lag of rural building industry and organizations behind plans is a glaring example.[63]

These processes, together with a certain expansion of rural nonagricultural production not directly connected with agricultural needs, naturally make themselves felt in greater degree in the large villages of several thousand inhabitants. Arutiunian has analyzed one such large kolkhoz village in the southern Ukraine where, of 5,158 inhabitants in 1963, only 51 percent were kolkhoz members, the others being workers (mostly in a nearby lime and brick factory) and employees (mostly in administration, cultural and educational institutions, trade, and material services with their families).[64] Villages of this size (5,000 or more inhabitants) are—with the exception of Moscow oblast' and a very loosely knit belt stretching from the middle Volga to Krasnoiarsk—almost exclusively situated in the south of the Soviet Union (Moldavian SSR, central and southeastern Ukraine, Rostov and Krasnodar provinces, the central Black Earth region, the Central Asian oases, and a small area around Lake Khanka in the Far East).[65] The case appears to be similar for villages of 2,000–5,000 inhabitants.[66] In these regions, most of which are agriculturally overpopulated and in some parts of which the rural population is still increasing, industrialization and the expansion of the nonagricultural rural sector should not be difficult to carry out. But it is precisely the other regions, with their rural labor deficit and out-migration and their dying rural crafts, which most need such development. Unfortunately, this general observation cannot be fully substantiated due to the lack of information, particularly regional statistics.

Already in prerevolutionary times the Russian (and other) village was not purely agricultural. Seasonal labor migration to nonagricultural jobs

[62] V. Evsiukov in *Sel'skaia zhizn'*, March 27, 1969, p. 2.
[63] See recently the leading article in *Sel'skaia zhizn'*, January 24, 1969.
[64] Iu. V. Arutiunian, "Sotsial'naia struktura sel'skogo naseleniia," *Voprosy filosofii*, no. 5 (1966), pp. 51–61.
[65] See map in Khorev, *Gorodskie poseleniia*, between pp. 224 and 225.
[66] This is, though not very clearly, to be seen in *Itogi*, Table 9, and *Itogi, RSFSR*, Table 10.

was a widespread phenomenon.[67] Even during the thirties this continued to be so,[68] and nonagricultural activity has expanded during the last 15 years. This should not be overlooked in any research on Soviet rural life. But the place of the former small and traditional crafts is being taken by socialized industry and trade, and previously almost nonexistent cultural and educational services are being added. The way the Soviet leadership wants this process to develop is expressed in the slogan of "agrarian-industrial associations" (*agrarno-promyshlenie ob"edineniia*). Although heralded in the Party program of 1961, this development involves more than a question of ideology, whatever form it takes. It is critically necessary in view of the rising demands placed on agricultural production, which must be fulfilled with rapidly shrinking labor resources. The expansion of rural nonagricultural activities is the only way to achieve a lasting recovery of Soviet agriculture and rural society. After a period of stagnation the process has recently received a new impetus, and it will in all probability continue in the future. Moreover, the impending rapid shrinkage of the agricultural population will enhance the relative significance of the nonagricultural rural population as well.

APPENDIX

To arrive at figures for the nonagricultural rural population, one must first find figures for the agricultural component and deduct the latter from the total rural population. This is rendered difficult because Soviet statistics do not present such figures directly and because the figures presented (percentage of kolkhoz population and annual average agricultural labor) include also urban territories with agricultural enterprises and organizations.

The kolkhoz population seems to be most easily derived, because statistical volumes give its percentage share in the total Soviet population. Even the urban part of this population is known approximately (see below). But the statistical handbooks do not explain whether the percentage figure applies to the end or to the beginning of the corresponding year, or whether it is a mid-year or annual average figure.

DePauw assumes, without explicitly saying so or giving any reasons,

[67] On this fact and its continuity up to the present, see S. P. Dunn and E. Dunn, *The Peasants of Central Russia* (New York: Holt, Rinehart and Winston, 1967), pp. 9–11, 15, 81–85.
[68] See the numbers of absent kolkhoz population and of those working in "cultural-living services" of the kolkhozy in Eason, pp. 17, 54; compare the examples given by E. Dorosh, "Ivan Fedoseevich ukhodit na pensiiu," *Novyi mir*, no. 1 (1969), p. 12, and no. 2 (1969), p. 39.

that the percentage figures apply to the end of the year, and his assumption is supported by the fact that two reputable Soviet authors seem to do likewise.[69] On the other hand, Soviet statistical volumes always treat the census percentage figures of January 17, 1939, and of January 15, 1959, as applying to 1939 and 1959 and not to the end of 1938 and 1958, which would have been the right thing to do if the current figures were meant as end-of-year. For 1937, too, Eason found that the percentage very probably applies to the beginning of the year.[70] Morozov seems to have the beginning of 1964 in mind when he speaks of "c. 56 million,"[71] which makes sense only if he relates the percentage figure of 1964 to the population figure as of January 1 of that same year. Amvrosov's figure of 52 million rural kolkhozniki (see below) would imply the incredibly high number of 4.8 or 5 million urban kolkhozniki, if an end-of-year calculation (see Table 2) were right. Thus, there is indirect evidence *pro* as well as *contra* DePauw's assumption, and therefore three rows of figures will be calculated in order to find out which fits best into what is otherwise known of the numerical development of kolkhoz population over time.

According to the second column, the decrease in the kolkhoz population was most rapid between the beginning of 1959 and the beginning of 1962 (i.e., end of 1961); during 1962 the decrease was relatively slow. This conforms to the fact that the conversion of kolkhozy into sovkhozy was most widespread in 1959–1961 and ebbed at the beginning of 1962.[72] But, according to the other two columns, the *sovkhozizatsiia* wave would have reached its peak in 1962, and it would not have ebbed before the end of that year, which does not conform with the known facts about conversions. Similarly, the second column shows a rapid decrease in the kolkhoz population during 1965. This fits in with the rather high pace of *sovkhozizatsiia* in that same year (as well as in 1964, when the kolkhoz population was increasing enough to offset the draining of personnel), which ebbed in 1966.[73] But the fourth, and in less degree the third, column would have the recent *sovkhozizatsiia* drive in 1966, which is contrary to known facts. For these reasons, the fourth (DePauw's) and the third columns are rejected. The second is used for further calculations and estimates.

[69] J. W. DePauw, *Measures of Agricultural Employment in the USSR: 1950–1966* (Washington, D.C.: U.S. Department of Commerce, 1968), p. 20, Table 3; Arutiunian, p. 54 (in table: 57.9 million for 1963); D'iachkov, p. 6 (55.3 million for 1966).
[70] Eason, p. 172.
[71] Morozov, p. 150.
[72] See labor figures below, Table 3, and K.-E. Wädekin, "Die Expansion des Sovchoz-Sektors in der sowjetischen Landwirtschaft," *Osteuropa-Wirtschaft*, no. 1 (1968), pp. 9, 21–22; Wädekin, *Die sowjetischen Staatsgüter* (Wiesbaden: Otto Harrassowitz, 1969), pp. 39ff.
[73] See figures below, Table 3, and Wädekin, *Die sowjetischen Staatsgüter*, pp. 49–53.

Table 2 : *The kolkhoz population of the Soviet Union, 1955–1967.*

| | Share of Total Soviet Population | MILLIONS OF KOLKHOZNIKI, IF FIRST COLUMN FIGURE IS ASSUMED TO REFER TO: | | |
Year	on Kolkhozy	beginning of year	middle of year	end of year
1955	41.2%[a]	76.1	76.7	77.5
1956	40.0[a]	76.6	77.2	77.9
1959	31.4	65.55	—	—
1961	28.0	60.5	61.0	61.5
1962	26.3	57.8	58.6	58.7
1963	25.6	57.1	57.6	57.9
1964	24.8	56.1	56.5	56.8
1965	24.6	56.4	56.7	57.0
1966	23.6	54.6	55.0	55.3
1967	22.63	53.0	53.3	53.5

[a] Percentage figure includes cooperative artisans and members of their families. These can be estimated as 4.0 million in 1955 and 2.6 million in 1956, following DePauw. These figures are deducted from the calculated absolute figures of kolkhoz population. The percentage accordingly would be 39.2 in 1955 and 38.7 in 1956 instead of 41.2 and 40.0.

SOURCES: Absolute and percentage figures for 1959 from *Itogi*, Table 27. All total population figures from *Narodnoe khoziaistvo . . . 1967*, p. 7. Percentage figures for 1955: *Narodnoe khoziaistvo*, p. 19; for 1956: *SSSR v tsifrakh* (Moscow, 1958), p. 9; for 1961–1965, *Narodnoe khoziaistvo* for each year, as follows: 1961, p. 27; 1962, p. 14; 1963, p. 28; 1964, p. 33; 1965, p. 42; for 1966: *SSSR v tsifrakh* (Moscow, 1966), p. 12; for 1967: *Narodnoe khoziaistvo . . . 1967*, p. 35. All other figures calculated as explained above.

The kolkhoz population has to be reduced by the number of kolkhozniki residing in urban areas. There were 3.25 million urban kolkhozniki at the 1959 census,[74] and for 1966 we have Amvrosov's statement that there were 52 million rural kolkhozniki[75] (very probably for the beginning of the year). This leaves a remainder of 2.6 million for urban areas. The latter figure, which is less in comparison to 1959, is plausible, because near towns and cities an especially large number of kolkhozy were converted into sovkhozy. Therefore, a rounded figure of 3 million urban kolkhozniki will be deducted for all years up to 1962, after which it will be gradually reduced to 2.6 million.

For sovkhozy and other state farms there are no population figures, but there are labor data. Recently, these data were subdivided into permanent workers, seasonal workers, and employees; a seasonal breakdown[76] is also given. That makes it possible to deduct the number of annual average sea-

[74] *Itogi*, Table 27.
[75] A. Amvrosov in *Izvestiia*, August 11, 1967.
[76] *Trud v SSSR*, pp. 126–129.

sonal workers from total labor. The result is presented in the first column of Table 3. Since the 1959 census results show 15 percent of agricultural workers and employees residing in urban areas,[77] a deduction of 15 percent is made for all years. Moreover, hypothetical figures for the beginning of the year are interpolated from neighboring annual averages, thereby deducting, for seasonal variations of permanent workers' numbers, 10 percent in 1955–1962, 5 percent in 1965 and following years, and, by interpolation, 8 percent for 1963 and 6 percent for 1964.[78] The resulting figures are those of the second column (Table 3).

It is believed that in those households where one member was a permanent worker or employee of the state farm, it was in most cases a male family member, and that only a few households had a second member permanently working on a state farm.[79] On the other hand, households in which no member was permanently working on a state farm also must have been very few. Therefore, the number of permanent workers and employees as of January is believed to have been almost equal to the number of households (families) in sovkhozy and other rural state farms. Since, for rural workers and employees, the average family size in 1959 was 3.9 persons, and since about 10 percent of single persons must be taken into account,[80] the number of permanent workers and employees is multiplied by 3.5 to arrive at the size of the state farm population. As family size has been declining in recent times (but probably more so in kolkhozy), this factor is reduced to 3.45 for the years 1961–1963, and to 3.4 since then. The result is given in the third column of Table 3. The number of rural kolkhozniki (fourth column) is derived as explained above.

The assumptions and derived estimates, as explained above, contain quite a number of uncertainties, but the author cannot think of a better way to obtain the desired statistics. Therefore, the figures given in Table 3 are believed to be the best "guesstimates" possible at present.

[77] *Itogi*, Table 33.

[78] See *Trud v SSSR*, pp. 128–129.

[79] On January 15, 1959, there were 5.9 million workers in agriculture (other than kolkhozniki and employees, but including all agricultural organizations and institutions, not only state farms). Only 2.5 million of them were females, but among these more than half—1.3 million—constituted the female majority of the 2.1 million physical workers in agricultural activities without special skills, and of whom only 780,000 were males (*Itogi*, Tables 33, 45, 46). The unskilled agricultural laborer is, as a rule, not permanently employed. It follows that of the permanent workers in state-owned agriculture, only 1.1 million or less were females, and at least 2.7 million (more than 70 percent) were males. Of the annual average numbers of sovkhoz and other state farm workers and employees even less were female—8 percent in 1958 (*Vestnik statistiki*, no. 1 (1967), p. 87) and 9 percent in 1960 and 1967 (*ibid.*, no. 1 (1969), p. 87).

[80] *Itogi*, Tables 63 and 64.

Table 3 : *Agricultural (kolkhoz, sovkhoz, and other state farm) rural population of the Soviet Union, 1955–1967.*

Year	Permanent Labor of Sovkhoz and Other State Farms[a] (thousands, annual average)	Of Which Rural at Beginning of Year (thousands, estimate)	State Farm Population[b] (millions, estimate)	Rural Kolkhoz Population at Beginning of Year (millions, estimate)[c]
1955	2,147	1,570	5.5	73.5
1956	2,225	1,660	5.8	73.8
1957	3,102	2,070	7.2	——
1958	3,738	2,600	9.1	——
1959	4,029	2,920	10.2	62.3
1960	5,191	3,500	12.2	——
1961	6,174	4,350	15.0	57.5
1962	6,607	4,880	16.8	54.8
1963	6,783	5,150	17.7	54.3
1964	6,951	5,450	18.5	53.4
1965	7,549	5,850	19.9	53.8
1966	7,759	6,180	21.0	52.0
1967	7,780	6,370	21.7	50.4

[a] Excluding those employed in the cultural-welfare services and in capital repairs of buildings and structures.
[b] Including dependents.
[c] Except for 1959 and 1966.

8 : Recruitment and the Quality of the Soviet Agricultural Labor Force

Norton T. Dodge

Development of any part of an economy is the result of the interaction of the several factors of production. These must complement one another properly for the efficient operation and growth of any given sector. For example, within the limits of a certain technology, the failure of labor or management to make effective use of the other factors, land and capital, due to the inadequate quantity, poor quality, or improper application of labor or management, will adversely affect static efficiency as well as the development process. Similarly, failure of management to develop new technology and, with the aid of adequately trained labor, to introduce it promptly and effectively will also retard development. Thus, human as well as material resources are critical in the development process.

Among the many problems plaguing the agricultural sector of the Soviet economy is the poor quality of its human resources. In this paper we shall look first at various qualitative factors adversely affecting the agricultural labor force, such as the age-sex imbalance and low level of educational attainment, and then examine some of the resulting intransigent and perplexing problems. Fortunately, the frequently dramatized problem of keeping Soviet boys "down on the farm" has recently been the subject of serious sociological research. Therefore, in the light of these new studies, we may examine the prospects for restoring a more efficient age-sex-educational mix in the agricultural labor force through the recruitment and retention of larger numbers of young men.

This paper is a by-product of research supported by the Office of Economic and Manpower Studies of the National Science Foundation and done in collaboration with Murray Yanowitch and Murray Feshbach. The author is responsible for any shortcomings in the present work.

I. SEX COMPOSITION

For a decade following the revolution all but a very small proportion of the Soviet working population was engaged in agriculture. Planting, cultivating, and harvesting were as much a part of a woman's life as a man's. According to the 1926 census, approximately nine-tenths of the women and four-fifths of the men in the labor force were working in agriculture. In 1959, after three decades of increasing industrialization, only 55 percent of the working women and 43 percent of the working men were occupied in agriculture.[1]

The shift from primarily agricultural employment to a rough balance between agricultural and nonagricultural employment reflected, of course, the transformation of the Soviet Union from a largely backward, agrarian economy to a comparatively highly developed and complex economy—still possessing, however, a large, relatively backward agricultural sector insulated in many ways from modern industrial life.

Soviet agricultural employees may be grouped into four basic categories. At the time of the 1959 census the largest category (31.7 million) was made up of persons who were members of, and contributed most of their labor to, collective farms. A second group (6.6 million) were workers and employees engaged primarily in work on state farms. A third group (9.8 million) reported themselves engaged primarily in private subsidiary farming and worked private garden plots for their own use and the local market.[2] The fourth category of agricultural workers, individual peasants, had almost passed out of existence.

From a parity with men in 1926, women's share in agricultural employment has increased significantly to some 60 percent. In 1959, of the three significant categories of agricultural workers, women composed 57 percent of all collective farmers, 41 percent of all workers and employees on state farms, and 91 percent of all workers in private subsidiary agriculture.[3] The work of these women is often heavy and otherwise physically demanding. Indeed, women perform most of the "physical" work in Soviet agriculture.

---

[1] *Itogi Vsesoiuznoi perepisi naseleniia 1959 goda: SSSR* (Moscow, 1962), Tables 30 and 33, pp. 96–97, 104–105. As imperfect and dated as are census data, they are our only source of age-sex information and must be used.

[2] *Ibid.*, p. 168; *Zhenshchiny i deti v SSSR* (Moscow, 1961), pp. 114–119; *Zhenshchiny i deti v SSSR* (Moscow, 1963), pp. 94–99.

[3] Norton T. Dodge and Murray Feshbach, "The Role of Woman in Soviet Agriculture," in Jerzy F. Karcz (ed.), *Soviet and East European Agriculture* (Berkeley and Los Angeles: University of California Press, 1967), p. 266.

On Collective Farms

The relative contribution of men and women to collective farm labor can be measured in terms of (1) the proportion of men and women; (2) the proportion of labor-days (*trudodni*) earned by men and by women; or (3) the proportion of man-days worked by men and by women.

The proportion of women among able-bodied farmers working on collective farms rose to a peak of 76 percent during World War II and declined to 57 percent in 1959, several points higher than in the mid-1930's.[4]

In applying the labor-day measure, we must remember that the labor-day is not only a measure of time worked but a composite yardstick that reflects the type and quality of work performed as well. A tractor or combine driver, for example, earns more labor-days per shift than an unskilled worker in a field brigade.[5] In appraising the contribution of women to collective farm work, the proportion of labor-days earned reflects, therefore, not only the quantitative but also the qualitative aspects of their contribution. On the whole, women perform the less skilled tasks. Indeed, most women collective farmers—17.4 million, or 97 percent in 1959—are engaged in physical labor.[6] Of these, 14.5 million, or 83 percent, were employed then in non-specialized and unskilled work, as opposed to 66 percent of the men (see Table 1). Therefore, men typically average more labor-days per man-day than women. The situation in the Ukraine in 1957 can be considered fairly representative for the Soviet Union as a whole: able-bodied males received on the average 1.9 labor-days for every man-day while women received only 1.7.[7]

The different demands on the two sexes are reflected in the minimum number of days of work required in a year. Without exception the number of days required of women is smaller than that required of men, and a sizable proportion of the women do not earn the obligatory minimum because their energies are concentrated more on the home and private garden plots.

In addition, the seasonality of work by men and women differs significantly and affects adversely the contribution by women. Of the two major branches of collective farm activity—crop growing and animal husbandry—

[4] *Ibid.*, p. 270.

[5] B. I. Braginskii, *Proizvoditel'nost' truda v sel'skom khoziaistve: metodika uchet i planirovanie* (Moscow, 1962), p. 194. The situation in the Ukraine in 1957 can be considered fairly typical: able-bodied males received on the average 1.91 labor-days for every man-day while women received only 1.68. As a rule, the coefficient for men is higher because they do more complicated and harder work.

[6] *Itogi,* Tables 23, 46, pp. 104–105, 160.

[7] I. S. Paskhaver, *Balans trudovykh resursov kolkhozov* (Kiev, 1961), p. 74.

Table 1 : *Percentage of women among collective and state farmers engaged in predominantly physical labor, by occupation, USSR, January 15, 1959.*

Occupation	Collective Farmers	State Farm and Other Workers
Administrative and supervisory personnel:		
Heads of livestock and poultry subfarms	15.0%	25.2%
Brigadiers of field brigades	8.3	12.9
Brigadiers of livestock brigades	12.8	18.0
Other brigadiers	5.2	9.3
Skilled workers and junior supervisory personnel:		
Bookkeepers	18.6	27.5
Tractor and combine drivers	0.8	0.7
Implement handlers and workers on agricultural machinery	1.4	5.1
Field-team leaders	87.3	85.5
Specialized agricultural workers:		
Workers in plant breeding and feed production	71.3	67.3
Cattle farm workers	60.4	47.0
Milking personnel	98.8	99.1
Stablemen and grooms	7.1	11.6
Swineherds	90.6	93.0
Herdsmen, drovers, shepherds	17.5	22.0
Other livestock workers	21.0	52.0
Poultry workers	93.4	94.3
Beekeepers	15.2	23.5
Orchard and vineyard workers	41.1	62.0
Vegetable and melon growers	80.6	78.2
Irrigators	10.8	18.5
Nonspecialized agricultural workers	66.0	63.4
Total employed in physical labor	60.1	44.6

SOURCE: *Itogi*, pp. 159–160.

the former is highly seasonal but the latter requires constant attendance throughout the year. According to the 1959 census, women comprised 51 percent of the animal husbandry workers.[8] However, the share of all collective farm women employed in animal husbandry in 1959 was small (12.8 percent).[9] Therefore, the overwhelming proportion of collective farm women

[8] *Itogi*, Tables 45, 46, pp. 159–160. G. Shmelev and V. Lazenkov, "Ispol'zovanie zhenskogo truda v kolkhozakh," *Ekonomika sel'skogo khoziaistva*, no. 10 (1962), p. 30, point out that most, and especially the milkmaids and poultry workers, are girls and young women with children of preschool age.

[9] *Itogi*, Tables 45, 46, pp. 159–160. N. I. Shishkin (ed.), *Trudovye resursy SSSR* (Moscow, 1961), p. 99, n. 8, gives the following percentages: 1956, 11.7 percent; 1958, 12.1 percent; 1959, 12.6 percent.

(87.2 percent) were employed in highly seasonal field work—the planting, cultivating, and harvesting of crops—where they made up 66 percent of all workers.[10]

It is not surprising, therefore, that data from Rostov oblast' show wide variations in the course of the year in the rates of female participation in collective farm work. In 1959, fewer than 57 percent of the women employed in July worked during the four winter months.[11] During these slack periods women devote more time to their private plots and to care of their children and other household duties. Such irregular participation by women, while perhaps desirable to the women themselves and their families, has tended to keep them from developing the special knowledge and skills required for the more attractive and remunerative kinds of agricultural work.

Both the smaller labor-day coefficient for women and the fewer man-days worked have the result that women, on the average, contribute less work measured in labor-days than men. In determining the importance to the economy of female participation in the agricultural labor force, an allowance must be made for this fact.

On State Farms

The second group of agricultural workers comprises those on state farms and in other state agricultural enterprises. These workers and employees, numbering 6.6 million in 1959, have the same employment status as those in industry and other nonagricultural branches of the economy.

The proportion of women among state farm and related workers—41 percent—is smaller than among collective farmers. Like women collective farmers, women working on state farms are primarily assigned to the less skilled jobs. Of the 2.7 million women employed in this sector in 1959, almost 2.3 million, or 92 percent, were reported to be engaged in "primarily physical" labor.[12] Approximately three-fifths of these were nonspecialized workers who made up 63.4 percent of the total employment of both men and women in this category. The percentage of women in the different agricultural occupations varies widely, but the pattern is similar to that for collective farmers (see Table 1).

[10] *Itogi*, Tables 45, 46, pp. 159–160. Shiskhin, p. 99, gives the following percentages: 1956, 79.8 percent; 1958, 78.8 percent; 1959, 78.2 percent.
[11] Shmelev and Lazenkov, p. 29. For earlier and similar figures see B. Babynin, "Trudovye resursy kolkhozov i ikh ispol'zovanie," *Problemy ekonomiki*, no. 2 (1940), p. 71.
[12] Dodge and Feshbach, p. 280.

In the Private Subsidiary Economy

The third group of agricultural workers includes those who are engaged primarily in the private subsidiary sector—the major remnant of private enterprise in the Soviet Union. In 1959, almost 10 million persons reported work on private plots as their principal occupation. Although occupying only 3.7 percent of the sown area in 1959, these plots accounted for a substantial share of total agricultural output, particularly of certain key products such as potatoes (64 percent), meat (41 percent), milk (47 percent), and eggs (81 percent).

The plots are cultivated primarily by members of collective farm families. They accounted for 58 percent of the total number of workers reported primarily employed in this sector in the 1959 census. Families of state farm workers and of other workers and employees are estimated to have contributed 30 and 12 percent respectively. When employment is converted to man-year equivalents so that labor inputs from all sources—part-time and full-time—are taken into account, the contribution of collective farmers working on private plots in their spare time, together with their families, is estimated to have been 71 percent of total inputs in the subsidiary economy.[13]

Women account for the great majority of persons working primarily in the private subsidiary economy. In 1959, almost 9 million women made up 91 percent of the workers of both sexes. Among the able-bodied age groups, the share of women was even larger (96 percent), since men in these age groups usually are engaged full-time in the socialized sector. The share of women among over- and underage workers was slightly smaller (86 percent).[14]

Among Administrators and Specialists

The proportion of women among specialized, managerial, and administrative personnel in the Soviet economy as a whole has increased from 31 percent in 1941 to 50 percent in 1957. Although gains were made in every field, the proportion varies widely from one branch of the economy to an-

[13] M. Weitzman, M. Feshbach, and L. Kulchycka, "Employment in the USSR," in U.S. Congress, Joint Economic Committee, *Dimensions of Soviet Economic Power* (Washington, D.C.: Government Printing Office, 1962), p. 662.
[14] Dodge and Feshbach, p. 279.

other. The highest percentages are in public health institutions (88 percent) and educational-cultural services (66 percent). Much lower are the proportions in industry (31 percent), transportation and communications (28 percent), and construction (22 percent). However, agriculture, our particular concern, has the lowest proportion (21 percent) among the major branches of the economy.[15]

Women are rarely found at the highest managerial levels in agriculture. There are few female chairmen of collective farms or directors of state farms or other state agricultural enterprises (see Table 2).[16] Only during World War II did the proportion of women in these posts become significant, rising from 2.6 percent at the end of 1940 to 14.2 percent at the end of 1943.[17]

Table 2 : *Administrators and specialists on collective and state farms, by occupation and sex, December 1, 1956.*

	MEN AND WOMEN		WOMEN		
	Number (thousands)	*Percentage Distribution*	*Number (thousands)*	*Percentage Distribution*	*Percent Women*
Collective farm chairmen and directors of state farms	89.9	15.8	[1.7]	[1.4]	[1.9]
Agronomists	106.2	18.7	42.5	55.7	40
Animal husbandry technicians	69.1	12.2	30.4	24.5	44
Veterinarians, veterinary feldshers, veterinary technicians	73.9	13.0	13.3	11.1	18
Unspecified	227.5	40.1	[31.1]	26.3	[10]
Total	566.7	100.0	119.0	100.0	21

SOURCE: Dodge and Feshbach, p. 281.

With demobilization, government policy encouraged experienced officers to return to their home villages to serve as chairmen. Consolidation of collective farms in the 1950's and 1960's also caused a further shrinkage of

---

[15] *Ibid.*, pp. 280–281.

[16] The role of women in agricultural management is discussed in detail in Robert Stuart's contribution to this volume (see Chapter 7). See especially his Tables 5 and 6. See also *Sel'skaia zhizn'*, February 14, 1969.

[17] Iu. V. Arutiunian, *Sovetskoe krest'ianstvo v gody Velikoi Otechestvennoi voiny* (Moscow, 1963), p. 289. The proportion of women chairmen of collective farms and women directors of state farms has varied considerably among the different republics. It is usually much lower in more backward areas, such as Transcaucasia and Central Asia.

opportunities for women since a man was more likely to emerge as chairman when several farms were combined. By the end of 1956, fewer than 2 percent of all chairmen and directors were women. Today the situation is similar: 2 percent of the chairmen and 1 percent of the directors are women.

Such a limited number of women at the top of the administrative pyramid has not gone unnoticed. At a regional farm conference in Kiev in 1961, Khrushchev stated: "We all know what an enormous role women play in all the sectors in the building of communism. But for some reason there are few women in this hall. Just take a pair of binoculars and have a look around. What is the reason for this? It will be said that it is mainly administrative workers who are present here. It turns out that it is the men who do the administrating and the women who do the work."[18] In spite of such official concern, the number of women working in administrative positions remains small at the present time.

Women do, however, make up a large percentage of the agricultural specialists on state and collective farms (see Table 2), and the growth in the number of women professionals with a secondary specialized or higher education in agriculture has been rapid. Among agronomists they accounted for 40 percent of the total; among livestock specialists, 44 percent; and among veterinarians and technicians, 18 percent. These three occupational groups accounted for almost 75 percent of the women employed as agricultural managerial and specialized personnel.

Some insight into the future of women as agricultural specialists can be gained by looking at the proportions of women being trained in agricultural fields. Assistant agronomists, breeding technicians, mechanics, veterinary aides, bookkeepers, and others are trained for employment in agriculture by specialized secondary educational institutions. These occupations are not particularly popular occupations for girls (see Table 3) but nevertheless, in 1959, more than 100,000 girls were estimated to have been enrolled in agricultural *tekhnikumy*, making up more than a third of the enrollment.[19]

In higher education where agronomists, zootechnicians, veterinarians, and related specialists are trained, agriculture is the least popular field for women (see Table 3). An extensive sampling of "candidate" degrees (roughly comparable to our Ph.D. degree) in selected years (see Table 4) shows, however, that the proportion of women completing degrees in agriculture and veterinary medicine has been close to the average for all fields and also close to the proportion of female undergraduates enrolled in agriculture.

However, the percentage of women earning Soviet doctoral degrees in

[18] *Izvestiia,* December 26, 1961.
[19] See Nicholas DeWitt, *Education and Professional Employment in the USSR* (Washington, D.C.: National Science Foundation, 1961), p. 179. DeWitt estimates that total enrollment in agricultural *tekhnikumy* in 1959 was 300,000.

Table 3 : *Percentage of women in student enrollment in specialized secondary and higher educational institutions, USSR, selected years.*

| | SPECIALIZED SECONDARY EDUCATIONAL INSTITUTIONS | | HIGHER EDUCATIONAL INSTITUTIONS | |
| | Total Enrollment | Enrollment in Agricultural Fields | Total Enrollment | Enrollment in Agricultural Fields |
Year				
1927	37.6%	15.4%	28.5%	17.4%
1930	38.8	31.0	28.3	25.4
1935	43.0	30.2	39.5	30.2
1940	54.6	37.0	58.0	46.1
1945	67.1	66.0	77.0	79.0
1950	43.6	41.0	53.1	39.3
1955	54.8	43.0	52.3	39.3
1960	47.0	38.0	43.0	27.0
1965	50.0	36.0	44.0	26.0
1967	52.0	35.0	46.0	27.0
1968	54.0	36.0	47.0	27.0

SOURCE: Dodge and Feshbach, Table 11, p. 291; *Narodnoe khoziaistvo . . . 1965*, p. 700; *Narodnoe khoziaistvo . . . 1967*, p. 802; and *Narodnoe khoziaistvo . . . 1968*, p. 693.

Table 4 : *Estimated percentage of women recipients of candidate and doctoral degrees, agricultural and veterinary fields, USSR, selected years.*

Degree and Field of Study	1936–1937	1941–1942	1956–1958	1959–1961	1962–1964
Candidate degree:					
All fields	20.5%	n.a.	32.8%	30.0%	27.9%
Agricultural and veterinary fields	19.5	n.a.	36.1	33.1	28.6
Doctoral degree:					
All fields	9.6	5.5%	14.8	17.7	21.2
Agricultural and veterinary fields	n.a.	2.7	12.5	11.1	13.0

SOURCE: Dodge, pp. 137–138.

agriculture is much smaller (13.0 percent), in comparison both with other fields (21.2 percent) and with the percentage receiving candidate degrees (28.6 percent). Certainly the smaller proportion of women at the highest educational level accounts in part for the smaller proportion of women occupying the more responsible and highly specialized jobs in agriculture. In view of these figures, particularly those for higher education, it seems likely that the proportion of women among agricultural specialists will decline with the passage of time. The proportion of women enrolled in agricultural specialties in specialized secondary educational institutions (36 percent) and higher educational institutions (27 percent) has been lower in recent years, as Table 3 indicates, than the proportion of employed women specialists with a secondary specialized education (46 percent) and with a higher education (40 percent).[20]

In summary, Soviet women compose a disproportionately large share of the less skilled workers in agriculture and a disproportionately small share of the professional and high-level administrative workers. However, their role at all levels, particularly the highest, is unusually important in comparison with other advanced societies. Such a heavy dependence on women, particularly on such large numbers of unskilled women with no real career commitment or training, is far from ideal and poses serious problems for the future development of Soviet agriculture.

II. AGE STRUCTURE

That older persons remain in agriculture while the younger move into industry and other rapidly expanding sectors is a phenomenon often observed in economic development. The feature distinguishing the Soviet case is the disproportionate number of women among the large number of older agricultural workers. Since the effects of World War II[21] cut across all sectors of the population and the economy, the age structure for each sex occupied in agriculture, as opposed to the sex structure, does not differ markedly from the rest of the economy, as is evident from an examination of the following two figures.

Figure 1, which contrasts the age distribution in 1959 of males employed in "physical" occupations in agriculture with the distribution in other sectors of the economy, shows that the proportion of males in the 50 years and older age group is much larger for physical workers in agriculture than in the rest of the economy (22.4 percent versus 14.0 percent). In the 20 to 49 year age group the situation is reversed, and the proportion of non-agricultural workers in physical occupations is higher (78.0 percent versus 62.0 percent). However, in the youngest age group—those under 20—it drops and the proportion of agricultural workers is again substantially larger

[20] *Strana Sovetov za 50 let* (Moscow, 1967), p. 238, and *Zhenshchiny i deti v SSSR* (Moscow, 1969), pp. 98, 100.
[21] Substantial losses in the male population were suffered earlier in World War I, the civil war, collectivization, and the purges, all in addition to the tremendous losses suffered in World War II.

190 : *The Soviet Rural Community*

Figure 1 : *Age distribution of males engaged in agricultural and nonagricultural "physical" occupations, USSR, January 15, 1959.*[a]

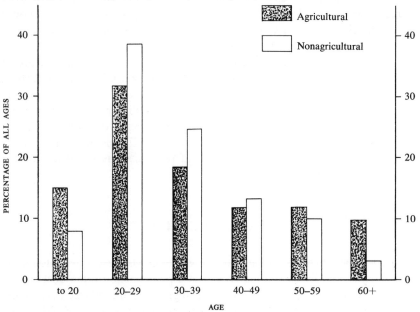

[a] Excluding private subsidiary agriculture.
SOURCE: Dodge and Feshbach, p. 298, and *Itogi*, pp. 136, 143, 162–163, 168.

(15.6 percent versus 9.8 percent). Thus, there is a larger proportion of both very young and very old male workers in agriculture than in the rest of the economy.

The disparity between the age distribution of women working in agriculture and in other sectors of the economy is particularly marked in the older age groups. Figure 2 shows that in 1959 the proportion of those engaged in "physical" agricultural work who are 50 years of age or older is almost double that of the proportion employed in the rest of the economy (20.5 percent versus 10.9 percent). The proportion of agricultural women in the 30 to 39 year age group also is slightly larger (20.8 percent versus 19.4 percent). But the proportion of those who are under 20 years of age is slightly smaller (10.8 percent versus 11.7 percent).

Figure 3, comparing the 1959 age distribution of males and females engaged in "physical" agricultural work, shows dramatically how heavily agriculture depends on older women. If we single out the 30 to 59 age groups, we find that 59 percent of the women but only 44 percent of the men are included in these age groups. Women in these age groups numbered 11.7 million, while men numbered only 6.2 million. Accordingly, men made up

Figure 2 : *Age distribution of females engaged in agricultural and nonagricultural "physical" occupations, USSR, January 15, 1959.*[a]

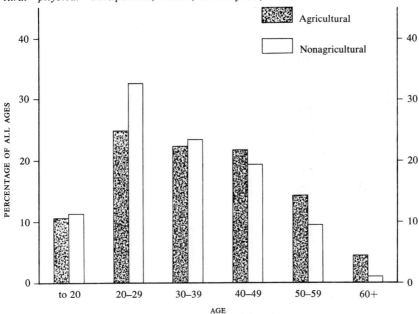

a Excluding private subsidiary agriculture.

SOURCE: Dodge and Feshbach, p. 298, and *Itogi*, pp. 136, 143, 162–163, 168.

only 34.5 percent while women accounted for 65.5 percent of the physical workers in agriculture in these key age groups.

The 1959 age distribution in the private subsidiary sector of agriculture is even more unbalanced. A very high proportion of persons employed in the private subsidiary sector is in the overage group (60 years and more for men and 55 and over for women). Among women of all ages who consider working in this sector to be their principal occupation, the majority are over 45 years of age, and 46 percent are in the overage group. Typical of these women would be a grandmother who leaves the socialized labor force to take care of her grandchildren plus the family garden plot while her daughter or daughter-in-law works in the socialized sector. Among the much smaller number of males working in this sector, the percentage in the overage group is much larger than for women, amounting to more than three-quarters of the total. These are primarily men who have retired and who can devote much of their time to their private plots.

These data make clear that the age distribution of Soviet agricultural employment, like the sex ratio, is far from ideal. The proportion of the elderly for both sexes is excessively high. In addition, while the proportion

Figure 3 : *Age distribution of males and females engaged in "physical" occupations in agriculture, USSR, January 15, 1959.*[a]

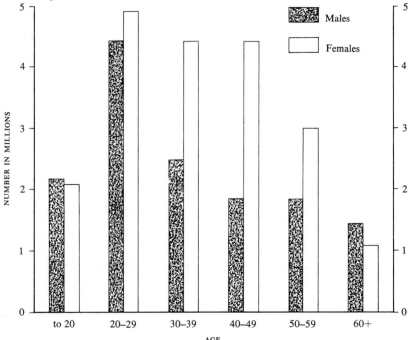

[a] Excluding private subsidiary agriculture.
SOURCE: Dodge and Feshbach, p. 269.

of males employed in the younger than 20 group is unusually high, the proportion in the prime working ages of 20 to 50 years of age is unusually low. In combination, the resulting age-sex structure cannot help but affect adversely the efficiency of the agricultural labor force.

III. EDUCATIONAL ATTAINMENT

Literacy and education play an essential part in the transformation of peasant-agricultural into urban-industrial nations.[22] In this process the training of the agricultural population may seem quite secondary. However, if agriculture is to support rather than hinder industrial development, particularly after the underutilization of the agricultural population has been largely eliminated, shifts of labor out of agriculture into industry or other sectors

[22] See Neil J. Smelser and Seymour Martin Lipset, "Social Structure, Mobility and Development," in Smelser and Lipset (eds.), *Social Structure and Mobility in Economic Development* (Chicago: Aldine, 1966), esp. pp. 29–42.

must be accompanied by an increased productivity of those who remain behind. This may be difficult to achieve, even with increased inputs of capital, because a relatively high level of training and skills is necessary to introduce and to apply effectively advanced agricultural technology and modern methods of production. The problem is particularly acute if those who leave agriculture, as is so often the case, tend to be the most energetic and best educated of the younger workers.

In the Soviet Union, as in all parts of the world, urban-rural differences in educational attainment are large. When differences among major socio-economic groups—members of employee, worker, and collective farm families—are examined, even larger differences are spotlighted. If differences in age and sex are considered as well, the gulf between the extreme groups becomes very wide indeed.[23] These differences reflect, of course, the emphasis of the Soviet regime on raising educational levels in those occupational fields and age groups considered critical to economic growth and its neglect of agriculture, particularly the training and education of the older elements of the agricultural population and especially older women.

In spite of the advances between the 1939 and 1959 censuses (see Table 5) in narrowing the gap between the urban and rural groups in the USSR, the level of educational attainment in agriculture, as represented by collective farmers, remains low. Four-fifths of the women and some three-quarters of the men still have no more than an incomplete seven-year education. Collective farm women, despite rapid advances in their education, remain educationally the most backward of the major socio-economic groups. In 1959, one-half of the women working on collective farms had less than a four-year education (see Table 6). Women employed on state farms were only slightly better off—two-fifths had less than a four-year education. The proportion of men lacking a four-year education on collective and state farms was one-third and one-quarter respectively. In agricultural administration only about one-sixth of the men and women had completed a higher education, and only about one-third had a specialized secondary or higher education. It is of particular interest that the educational level of women in administration is generally higher than that of men, reflecting, no doubt, differences in the routes by which men and women have risen to administrative jobs, men tending more frequently to come up through the ranks without the help of formal education.

The educational level of persons occupied in agriculture varies greatly with age as well as sex (see Table 7). Among women collective farmers at the time of the 1959 census, from 70 percent in the 40–44 age group to

[23] For a detailed presentation and discussion of the 1959 census data on this subject, see Norton T. Dodge, *Women in the Soviet Economy* (Baltimore: Johns Hopkins Press, 1966), Chapter 8 and Appendix VI.

Table 5 : *Workers, employees, and collective farmers with higher and secondary education, by type of residence, USSR, 1939, 1959.*[a]

Residence Group and Sex	TOTAL		WORKERS		EMPLOYEES		COLLECTIVE FARMERS	
	1939	1959	1939	1959	1939	1959	1939	1959
	(NUMBER PER THOUSAND OF TOTAL POPULATION IN A GIVEN GROUP)							
Urban population	242	564	96	424	555	898	50	241
Male	235	537	122	430	496	872	63	287
Female	255	597	54	413	641	918	26	193
Rural population	63	316	60	311	454	879	17	226
Male	81	337	73	320	394	828	24	260
Female	42	294	27	296	632	927	10	198

[a] Including those with incomplete secondary education for all groups and both years.

SOURCE: *Itogi*, p. 116.

Table 6 : *Educational levels of persons employed in agriculture, by branch and sex, USSR, January 15, 1959.*

	COMPLETED HIGHER EDUCATION		SPECIALIZED SECONDARY AND INCOMPLETE HIGHER EDUCATION		GENERAL SECONDARY AND INCOMPLETE SECONDARY EDUCATION		ELEMENTARY AND INCOMPLETE SEVEN-YEAR EDUCATION		LESS THAN FOUR-YEAR EDUCATION	
	Male	Female	Male	Female	Male	Female	Male	Female	Male	Female
	(PERSONS PER THOUSAND EMPLOYED)									
All agriculture	5	2	20	9	258	198	415	310	302	481
State farms	10	5	29	16	265	233	436	332	260	414
Collective farms	2	1	14	6	249	192	411	308	324	493
Repair-Technical Stations (RTS) and related stations	17	32	50	110	417	406	435	228	81	224
Administration of agriculture (trusts, offices, etc.)	148	177	171	216	311	361	282	123	88	123

SOURCE: *Itogi*, pp. 125, 127.

Table 7 : *Educational level of collective farmers and their families, by age and sex, 1959.*[a]

Age	HIGHER, INCOMPLETE HIGHER, AND SPECIALIZED SECONDARY EDUCATION		GENERAL SECONDARY EDUCATION		INCOMPLETE SECONDARY AND SEVEN-YEAR EDUCATION		INCOMPLETE SEVEN-YEAR AND ELEMENTARY EDUCATION		LESS THAN FOUR-YEAR EDUCATION	
	Male	Female	Male	Female	Male	Female	Male	Female	Male	Female
All ages	10	4	24	14	148	112	285	209	533	661
10 and over	13	5	33	18	203	139	390	260	361	588
10–19	1	2	42	43	312	335	402	375	243	245
20–24	30	26	118	76	386	367	398	372	68	159
25–29	20	11	22	12	201	171	598	515	159	291
30–34	25	10	18	13	266	232	530	497	161	248
35–39	32	9	28	14	252	160	465	424	223	393
40–44	28	5	17	4	131	43	465	245	359	703
45–49	15	2	8	1	49	10	347	118	581	869
50–54	8	1	5	1	27	6	291	104	669	888
55–59	5	—	5	1	20	5	271	82	699	912
60–64	3	—	4	1	14	4	234	61	745	944
65–69	2	—	3	—	11	3	202	49	782	948
70 and over	1	—	2	—	7	2	134	29	856	969

[a] Figures represent the number of persons per thousand.
SOURCE: *Itogi*, pp. 113–114. The last two columns are calculated as residuals.

nearly 100 percent of those 70 and over had less than a four-year education. At the same time, only about a quarter of those under 30 had less than a four-year education. Men approached the 70 percent level at age 50, ten years later than women, while among most of those under 35 substantially less than a quarter had less than a four-year education.

For those with a specialized secondary or higher education, the age distribution was similar. No women in the older age groups had this level of education. Those who did were concentrated in the 20 to 40 year age groups. Similarly, few older men had a specialized secondary or higher education. Those who had achieved it were largely concentrated in the age groups between 20 and 50, and their proportions were several times those of women. An exception is found, however, in the 20–24 age group. Here, the proportion of women (26 per thousand) is very close to that of men (30 per thousand) and the proportions of both, but particularly of women, were well above those in most other age groups.

From these figures for collective farmers, we can see that with the passage of time and the disappearance of the oldest generation the educational level of persons in agriculture will rise substantially. The crucial question, however, is not whether the level of educational attainment will improve but whether it will improve rapidly enough to permit an effective use of the new technology and improved methods which must be introduced to achieve the agricultural productivity desired in the years ahead. On this point Karl-Eugen Wädekin remarks that "a rising capital input will remain largely ineffectual, if there is a shortage of skilled labor which can handle the modern equipment effectively" and then quotes V. P. Rodionov's statement that "the increase in the level of technical equipment of agricultural production is frequently impeded by the fact that kolkhoz personnel include insufficient young workers with a high level of general knowledge."[24]

An increase in the level of education significant enough to meet these new needs will require two developments: increased educational opportunities for rural youths, and the attraction to or retention in agricultural occupations of the more educated youths. In the light of present social conditions in Russia and especially the social forces at work in rural areas, it may be difficult to accomplish either of these objectives.

An indication of the obstacles confronting rural youth in pursuit of an education is given by a Novosibirsk study (Table 8) which contains an unusually detailed breakdown of occupational backgrounds of parents and permits a comparison of the fates of urban and rural school graduates.[25]

---

[24] Karl-Eugen Wädekin, "Manpower in Soviet Agriculture: Some Post-Khrushchev Developments and Problems," *Soviet Studies,* XX, no. 3 (January, 1969), 293.

[25] V. N. Shubkin, "Molodezh vstupaet v zhizn'," *Voprosy filosofii,* no. 5 (1965), p. 65.

The differential access to full-time, postsecondary education of these two groups is especially striking. Only 10 percent of collective and state farm children who graduated from secondary school wished and were able to continue full-time schooling. The children of urban specialists and industrial workers were considerably more motivated and more fortunate, with 82 and 61 percent respectively being accepted at specialized secondary or higher educational institutions.

The relatively unfavorable position of children from rural backgrounds, regardless of the specific occupations of their parents, also emerges in the greater success experienced by children of industrial workers compared to rural specialists' children in continuing full-time education beyond the general secondary school. While differential opportunities are clearly in evidence for children of urban specialists and nonspecialists, they are less pronounced than the general urban-rural differential. Even those urban groups which rank relatively low in opportunities to pursue advanced education in Novosibirsk (children of personnel in service and trade occupations and workers in transportation) do not compare unfavorably with rural specialists' children.

The Novosibirsk and other studies show that the social class composition of students in higher educational institutions departs significantly from that of the population as a whole and of students in earlier grades. The social origins of daytime students entering higher education in Sverdlovsk in 1965 confirms such a departure (Table 9), but reveals something much less obvious as well.[26] The Sverdlovsk data show significant differences between the class composition of students at the university and at the technical institutes. While the share of children of workers and collective farmers in both types of institutions is clearly below the share of each group in the population—workers, 70 percent; collective farm peasants, 8 percent— there is a substantial difference between the proportions of worker and peasant enrollment at these two types of institution.[27]

In 1965, the largest single group of students at the Urals State University came from specialists' families (39 percent). Specialist parents together with white-collar employees accounted for 58 percent of the first-year students. Workers' children accounted for approximately one-quarter of the daytime entering class. There was also a sizable miscellaneous group (17 percent) of children of pensioners, invalids, and those with undetermined

[26] Daytime students accounted for 44 percent of higher educational institution admissions in 1965 and 56 percent of graduates; see *Narodnoe khoziaistvo . . . 1965*, pp. 694, 696.

[27] M. N. Rutkevich, *Zhiznennye plany molodezhi* (Sverdlovsk, 1966), p. 222. See also his "Sotsial'nye istochniki popolneniia Sovetskoi intelligentsii," *Voprosy filosofii*, no. 6 (1967), pp. 15–23, in *Current Digest of the Soviet Press*, September 20, 1967, pp. 14–17.

Table 8 : *Plans of graduating students of Novosibirsk oblast' secondary schools and their actual status following graduation, by occupational background of parents, 1963.*[a]

Occupational Background of Parents[b]	PLANS OF GRADUATING STUDENTS			ACTUAL STATUS OF GRADUATES		
	Work	Combining Work and Study	Full-Time Study	Work	Combining Work and Study	Full-Time Study
Specialists, urban	2%	5%	93%	15%	3%	82%
Specialists, rural	11	13	76	42	—	58
Workers in industry and construction	11	6	83	36	3	61
Workers in transportation and communication	—	18	82	55	—	45
Agricultural personnel, nonspecialists	10	14	76	90	—	10
Trade and service personnel	9	15	76	38	3	59
Others	12	38	50	63	12	25
Total	7	10	83	37	2	61

[a] These figures are based on a 10 percent sample of graduates of secondary schools of Novosibirsk oblast' in 1963.
[b] Where both parents were living, this was determined by the occupation of the father.
SOURCE: Shubkin, "Molodezh vstupaet v zhizn'," p. 65.

occupations. The number of young people of peasant origin was strikingly low—1 percent of the total.[28]

Table 9 : *Composition of first-year daytime students at higher educational institutions, by occupational category of parents, Sverdlovsk, 1965.*

| | COMPOSITION OF STUDENT BODY | |
Occupational Category of Parents	Urals State University	Technical Institutes[a]
Workers	24.4%	44.9%
Employees and specialists	57.7	50.0
Specialists	38.5	n.a.
Employees	19.2	n.a.
Collective farmers	1.0	4.8
Others[b]	17.2	—
Total	100.3[c]	99.7[c]

[a] These include the Sverdlovsk polytechnical, mining, railroad, lumber, and medical institutes. The term "technical institute" normally does not include medical institutes, but it has been impossible to separate the data for the latter from the totals shown here.

[b] Pensioners, invalids, and cases in which occupation was not determined.

[c] Failure of components to add up to 100 is due to approximations in figures cited in the source below.

SOURCE: Rutkevich, *Zhiznennye plany molodezhi*, pp. 226, 228.

The situation is far different at the institutes. Of the five institutes examined, four taught engineering and the fifth taught medicine. The more proletarian nature of their student body is unmistakable. Workers' children represented a sizable minority of first-year students, some 45 percent of the total and, together with children of collective farmers, accounted for one-half of the entering classes. If medical school students, 64 percent of whom were children of specialists and white collar employees, are excluded, the contrast between working class representation at the university and institutes is even more pronounced. Most important, the share of sons and daughters of collective farmers is almost 5 percent of the student body of the institutes, five times higher than at the Urals State University.

Perhaps of greater concern to the Soviet leadership is the small representation of peasant youth even in higher agricultural educational institutions. In 1961, only one-third of the students admitted to higher agricultural institutions were of peasant origin. In their valuable study of the Russian peasantry, Ethel and Stephen Dunn report that the Moscow Land-Use Engineering Institute admitted only 27 people from villages as against 248

[28] The proportion of worker and peasant children was higher in the late 1950's and early 1960's as a result of the preferential admission of those with work experience, but when this policy was modified in 1965, their share fell close to the 20–25 percent that had prevailed earlier in the 1950's.

from cities. They remark that "this compounds the difficulty of maintaining adequate personnel on the land since, as some Soviet writers themselves point out, city people can hardly be expected to exile themselves voluntarily to provinces."[29] The city-dwellers are attracted to agricultural studies because competition for admission is less intense. A degree in any field is preferable to none at all, and admission to any higher educational institution postpones and may even obviate military service. Furthermore, many endeavor to change to another institution and field once their studies have begun.[30]

Although the percentage of rural people with specialized secondary or higher education remains small, substantial gains have been made in the educational status of agricultural personnel in responsible positions. The percentage of kolkhoz chairmen with higher education increased from 21.1 in 1953 to 63.8 in 1958, and of chief agronomists from 36.8 to 71.4 during the same period.[31] An increase was also recorded in the percentage of heads of repair workshops with higher or specialized secondary education, although the 1953 and 1958 figures are both somewhat lower than for kolkhoz chairmen.

IV. PROBLEMS OF RECRUITMENT AND RETENTION

The problem of the drift from the countryside, particularly of the youngest and most able elements of the population, is a serious one which preoccupies many Soviet sociologists and economists as well as economic planners. As we have seen, various aspects of this problem have been dealt with in Soviet publications. The difficulties, however, are most eloquently reflected in Soviet literature.[32] We shall look at some examples before turning to the more systematic studies by scholars. Bukhovskii puts the problem very simply in a story about a regional center.[33] "The old people are retiring and the young struggle to get to town." In the same vein, a woman in V. Savchenko's story, "Pis'mo," notes: "Everybody is attracted to the cities. In the peasantry, she muses, only old people and women are left . . . and after we die nobody will be left."[34] Fedor Abramov sums up the problem very

[29] Stephen P. Dunn and Ethel Dunn, *The Peasants of Central Russia* (New York: Holt, Rinehart and Winston, 1967), p. 88.

[30] I. Salnikov, "Nazrevshie voprosy podgotovki sel'skokhoziaistvennykh kadrov," *Kommunist*, no. 4 (1968), pp. 53–59.

[31] Dunn and Dunn, p. 89.

[32] See A. G. Gaev, "The Kolkhoz and the Kolkhoz Worker in Soviet Literature," in Roy D. Laird and Edward L. Crowley (eds.), *Soviet Agriculture: The Permanent Crisis* (New York: Praeger, 1965), pp. 20–26. The following examples are drawn primarily from Gaev.

[33] K. Bukhovskii, "Tri pis'ma iz kolkhoza," *Oktiabr'*, no. 12 (1966), p. 136.

[34] V. Savchenko, "Pis'mo," *Novyi mir*, no. 4 (1966), p. 118.

pointedly in the thoughts of his collective farm chairman in *Vokrug da okolo*:[35]

> The elderly kolhoz [*sic*] women on whose shoulders had rested all the hardships of the postwar confusion had now faded away: the hands of one were deformed by rheumatism; another had developed a hernia, a third—some other ailment. Yes, and how could you achieve a sharp increase in farm output with these half-literate women; all they knew was how to pitch hay, in the ancient way, for the cattle. So you had to round up the senior schoolgirls and keep them at it for weeks and months on end. If a girl herself was willing, her mother would be up in arms. What? Have my daughter raking manure? Was it for this that the old man and me broke our backs so she could get an education.[36]

Thus, the Soviet writers bear out vividly Wädekin's assertion, "It is not the outflow of labour itself which is the problem, but the way in which it happened and still happens under Soviet conditions."[37] As Wädekin elaborates, "The outflow from agriculture applies almost exclusively to the working section of the [agricultural] population, especially its younger part; almost two-thirds of the net balance of migrants to the towns are in the age group 15–29."[38] Data on population movement provided by Anokhina and Shmeleva[39] for Kalinin oblast' support this statement. Between 75 and 80 percent of the persons moving away permanently from kolkhozy were 35 years of age or younger. The increasing difficulty of keeping young people on the farm, particularly those who have special skills or training and whose presence would be the most valuable, has certainly become one of the most disturbing phenomena in the Soviet rural scene.

Literature puts it more interestingly. The dedicated chairman of a kolkhoz in Elena Nikulina's story, "Duplyanka," expresses the problem: "At night Opanas Marveyevich Peredery slept badly. He would lie on his back for hours, hardly breathing, but sleep would not come. He was overcome by thoughts of his son, who could find no work to his liking, and of the collective farm. . . . 'But all of us here are farmers by trade,' he thought. 'The earth is our calling. Miners and metallurgists pass on their trade to their children. Why is my son the only one to turn up his nose at the land? Why does a young girl like Vera ridicule the work of a kolkhoznik?' "[40]

The drift from the land is so much the norm that any reversal of the

---

[35] Fedor Abramov, *Vokrug da okolo*. An English translation is available: *The New Life* (New York: Grove Press, 1963).

[36] *Ibid.*, pp. 25–26.

[37] Wädekin, p. 287.

[38] *Ibid.*, p. 289.

[39] L. A. Anokhina and M. N. Shmeleva, *Kul'tura i byt kolkhoznikov Kalininskoi oblasti* (Moscow, 1964), pp. 63–67.

[40] Elena Nikulina, "Duplyanka," *Nash sovremennik*, no. 6 (1963).

trend attracts special attention. A story by A. Kuznetsov entitled "At Home,"[41] which appeared at the beginning of 1964, opens with the return to her native village of a girl who has completed her secondary education in the city. She applies to the kolkhoz chairman for a job. The rarity of her case, that of an educated young person wishing to work on the land, is illustrated by the following dialogue:

> "What has brought you to the country?" [the chairman] asked in a suspicious, unfriendly tone. "There are no young men here, we need them ourselves."
> "That's not why I've come . . . ," Galya flared up.
> "What for then?"
> "Nothing."
> "Mmm, well. To get some service in? Or have you done something you shouldn't have?"
> "I haven't done anything. I simply used to live here."[42]

Similar insights are provided by Alexander Solzhenitsyn in *The First Circle*.[43] He writes of a girl from the country working for an advanced degree at the University of Moscow: "It was true that in their Machinery and Tractor station there was an agronomist. He kept writing Dasha and asking her to marry him. But she was about to get her degree and the whole village would say, 'What did the girl study for—to marry an agronomist? Any woman field-gang leader on the farm would have been just as good for him.' "[44] Solzhenitsyn then goes on to describe the difficulty of being fully accepted among the free-wheeling urban intelligentsia if one has come from a peasant background: "On the other hand, Dasha felt that even as a Candidate of Sciences she still could not set foot in the society she wanted to be a part of; she was not light-minded or carefree enough. . . ."[45] We must assume, however, that Dasha, like most, did not return to the village despite her insecurities in the urban-intellectual world.

Prewar Studies by Inkeles and Others

As background to the present situation, the findings of Alex Inkeles and Raymond Bauer[46] regarding pre–World War II stratification, mobility, and career aspirations are most instructive. The unattractiveness of careers in

[41] A. Kuznetsov, "Doma," *Novyi mir*, no. 1 (1964).
[42] *Ibid.*, p. 4.
[43] Alexander Solzhenitsyn, *The First Circle* (New York: Harper and Row, 1968).
[44] *Ibid.*, p. 271.
[45] *Ibid.*
[46] Alex Inkeles and Raymond A. Bauer, *The Soviet Citizen* (Cambridge, Mass.: Harvard University Press, 1959).

agriculture in the 1930's was clear from the responses of the displaced persons interviewed in the preparation of their study. Inkeles and Bauer noted:

> . . . it almost never occurred to the children of the intelligentsia or even the ordinary white collar level that a job as a peasant or even a worker was worth thinking about, whereas more than two-fifths of the workers and almost two-thirds of the peasant boys chose such manual jobs. Even here, however, it is interesting to note the avoidance of work as a collective farmer. Almost four times as many boys from peasant families wanted to become workers as were willing to stay on as collective farm peasants. Young women show the same class pattern, but they actually exceed their brothers in preference for the better jobs.[47]

The anti-agriculture attitudes of the 1930's are elaborated further in Table 10.

Table 10 : *Occupational aspirations of males under 21 in 1940, by social origin.*

	SOCIAL ORIGIN OF RESPONDENT			
Occupation		*Semiprofessional*		
Aspired to	*Professional*	*and White-collar*	*Worker*	*Peasant*
Arts	20%	18%	10%	4%
Applied science	38	42	26	6
Medicine	20	20	9	4
Military[a]	5	4	4	2
Other professional	10	7	4	6
Semiprofessional				
and white-collar	2	2	4	15
Worker	5	7	40	50
Farmer	0	0	3	13
Total number				
of respondents	40	45	77	68

[a] Includes army, navy, aviation, and merchant marine.
SOURCE: Inkeles and Bauer, p. 89.

Such aspirations make it clear that for most young people ambition far exceeded opportunity. Indeed, Inkeles and Bauer found that while more than half the sons of workers aspired to jobs above the semiprofessional level, only 14 percent could expect to achieve that end. Although sons of peasants set their occupational sights lower, 22 percent aiming at positions above the semiprofessional level, only 8 percent could expect to achieve their goal. Of the 50 percent who aspired to the position of worker, some 44 percent could expect to achieve this more limited aim.[48]

[47] *Ibid.*, p. 88.
[48] *Ibid.*, p. 81.

Not surprisingly, Inkeles and Bauer found that the desire for a career is greatest among young people. They found that "going from those over fifty to those under thirty the index for the intelligentsia jobs rose steadily from 1.80 among those over fifty to 2.26 amongst the youngest."[49] By contrast, the index for farmer occupations fell drastically from 2.43 for those over 50 to a mere 0.26 for those under 30. Thus, among those in the younger age groups, intelligentsia-type jobs tended to be "over chosen" and farm jobs "under chosen," another indication of youthful reluctance to stay on the farms.[50]

Inkeles and Bauer also compared the proportions in various age groups of those who desired a career and felt that they had an opportunity to achieve one, and of those with the desire but no sense of opportunity. They found that the ratio of satisfied to frustrated in the younger intelligentsia was 1.61 to 1, whereas among the peasantry the situation was reversed, with the satisfied being outnumbered by the frustrated 3.38 to 1. This study clearly indicates that the peasants believed that the likelihood of attaining a career was slight.[51]

In another study of refugee ratings of occupations, Inkeles and Rossi found that the occupations of rank-and-file collective farmer, farm brigade leader, and collective farm chairman were consistently at or near the bottom of the list. Their rankings, from various standpoints, among 13 occupations are given in Table 11.

Among all occupations, that of collective farmer came in a poor last. The job of farm brigade leader scored higher than party secretary for the response category "general desirability," but when ratings in all five response categories are combined, the position of brigade leader drops below that of party secretary, placing all three agricultural occupations at the bottom of the composite rankings.

Recent Studies by Soviet Sociologists

More recent studies by Soviet sociologists such as V. N. Shubkin, M. N. Rutkevich, I. M. Nazimov, and L. A. Margolin tend to confirm the findings of Inkeles and his associates for the prewar period.[52] In an important Shub-

49 Their measure is a ratio based on the percentage of an age group desiring to be in an occupation divided by the percentage actually in an occupation.
50 Inkeles and Bauer, p. 95.
51 *Ibid.*, pp. 96–97.
52 See Murray Yanowitch and Norton T. Dodge, "Social Class and Education: Soviet Findings and Reactions," *Comparative Education Review,* XII, no. 3 (October, 1968), 248–267 for a discussion of some of these studies. See also Murray Feshbach, "Manpower in the USSR: A Survey of Recent Trends and Prospects," in *New Directions in the Soviet Economy* (Washington, D.C.: G.P.O., 1966), p. 726.

Table 11 : *Ranking of occupations of collective farm chairman and rank-and-file collective farmer among 13 occupations.*

Occupation	General Desirability	Material Position	RANKING Personal Satisfaction	Safety (Political)	Popular Regard	Composite
Farm brigade leader	10th	10th	11th	5th and 6th	11th	11th
Collective farm chairman	12th	4th	9th	10th and 11th	13th	12th
Rank-and-file collective farmer	13th	13th	13th	2nd and 3rd	7th	13th

SOURCE: Alex Inkeles with Peter H. Rossi, "Multidimensional Ratings of Occupations," *Sociometry* (September, 1957), Table 1. The last column results from summing the first five given in the article.

kin study,[53] the unpopularity of agricultural occupations, although not limited to urban youth, was more clearly evident among urban than rural students. Thus, the two principal agricultural occupations, field crop worker and livestock raiser, were included among the ten lowest ranked occupations by urban respondents but not by rural. Among the latter, however, their rankings—49 and 52 respectively out of 74 occupations—reflected the general distaste for agricultural occupations.

The Soviet predicament which these figures illustrate is vividly demonstrated by the results of a study of the future plans and intentions of 430 secondary school graduates in Smolensk oblast'.[54] Of these, 27 planned to remain and work on their kolkhozy; 56 planned to attend an agricultural technical school or higher educational institution, presumably returning to work in some skilled capacity in agriculture; 31 intended to seek jobs in industry; 102 wanted to enter a higher technical institution in some field other than agriculture; 124 were planning professional training (engineering, medicine, teaching, and so on); 90 intended to continue their education, but had not yet decided on a field. Thus only 83 persons—less than 20 percent—intended to devote themselves to agriculture. Even if one adds the 48 graduates who chose nonagricultural professions but intended to return to the village as physicans, teachers, or engineers and a portion of the 90 who have not yet chosen their profession, a clear majority planned to go to the city.

Studies of the occupational plans of rural secondary school students in the Sverdlovsk and Moscow regions also reveal that the overwhelming majority aspire to nonagricultural occupations. The number expressing a preference for a career in agricultural occupations was very small.[55]

Moscow region, 8th–10th grades, 1964–1965	5.4%
Moscow region, 8th–10th grades, 1966–1967	7.2
Sverdlovsk region, 8th grade, 1964–1965	7.0
Sverdlovsk region, 11th grade, 1964–1965	13.0

These figures, though undoubtedly higher than those which studies of urban youngsters would reveal, underscore the widespread unpopularity of a career in agriculture regardless of socio-economic background.

There are, however, some important differences between rural and urban

[53] V. N. Shubkin, "Opyt ispol'zovaniia kolichestvennykh metodov v konkretnom sotsiologicheskom issledovanii voprosov trudoustroistva i vybora professii," in A. G. Aganbegian (ed.), *Kolichestvennye metody v sotsiologicheskikh issledovaniiakh* (Novosibirsk, 1964), pp. 152–267.

[54] *Izvestiia*, November 22, 1964, cited in Dunn and Dunn, pp. 87–88.

[55] R. N. Kniazeve, "Proforientatsiia v sel'skoi shkole," *Shkola i proizvodstvo*, no. 7 (1968), p. 27; Rutkevich, *Zhiznennye*, pp. 35, 196.

youngsters in the types of nonagricultural occupations preferred by each group. We have already seen that the career plans of urban secondary school students are focused predominantly on intelligentsia occupations, with workers' jobs being attractive to only a small minority. For these youngsters, an intelligentsia career represents the next step beyond their parents' occupational status (when these are workers), or simply the maintenance of the career status already attained by their parents. Among rural school children, however, the achievement of an industrial worker's status marks a significant move up the occupational ladder and away from the rural environment. Hence, a distinctly larger proportion of rural than of urban school children express a readiness to enter the occupation of industrial worker.[56] For them, popularity of intelligentsia occupations as a group coexists with relatively low esteem for certain individual occupations. A rural intelligentsia occupation like agronomy was less "attractive" than a broad range of workers' occupations.[57] The relatively low standing of such a rural intelligentsia occupation must reflect not only a general distaste for agricultural work but also the association of such work with the primitive and culturally limited life of the countryside.

Rural students also rated chemical industry workers higher than "scientists" in biology, philology, and economics. There are several possible explanations for the limited popularity of these intelligentsia occupations. For rural respondents, the work of "scientists" such as philologists and philosophers is remote and esoteric. Futhermore, the occupational aspirations of rural students are strongly focused on the more tangible worker and engineering occupations. Hence, with one exception, all "scientific" occupations were ranked lower (within the whole group of 74 occupations) by rural than by urban respondents. Among the latter, however, and perhaps among some of the former as well, the low standing of the social sciences, philosophy, and biology may reflect an awareness of the reputed low quality of much of the intellectual work in these areas.[58]

Although no Soviet studies appear to have been published of occupational ratings by adults similar to the Novosibirsk study of secondary school students, Soviet sociologists have studied adult attitudes by asking parents to name the occupation which they would like their children to enter. The most revealing of these studies was conducted in the city of Nizhnii Tagil

[56] N. I. Krylov, "O namereniiakh starshikh shkol'nikov v otnoshenii budushchei professii," *Izvestiia Akademii pedagogicheskikh nauk RSFSR*, no. 123 (1962), pp. 28–29; Shubkin, pp. 177–178; Rutkevich, *Zhiznennye*, p. 161.

[57] The following industrial workers' occupations were rated higher than the agronomists' by all respondents combined: lathe operators, electricians, electric and gas welders, miners, steel founders, chemical workers, weavers, and spinners.

[58] Such an awareness could readily have stemmed from the respondents' exposure to school courses and teachers of these subjects.

in 1964.[59] Of the 316 parents of students graduating from secondary school, about 75 percent expressed a preference for intelligentsia occupations for their children. Fewer than one-fifth of the parents regarded a worker's occupation as the most desirable for their children.[60] As might be expected, employment in agriculture was a fate which very few parents (less than 5 percent of the sample) wished for their children. Thus, at least in broad outline, there is a pronounced similarity in the attitudes of Nizhnii Tagil adults and Novosibirsk students toward the major occupational groupings.

The special value of the Nizhnii Tagil study is the evidence it offers of the influence of social class differences on parents' occupational preferences for their children. What the contrasting patterns of occupational preferences suggest is that social classes differ somewhat in the channels through which they hope to see their offspring attain intelligentsia status. An industrial worker is more likely than a professional person to associate the achievement of such status for his children with their becoming engineers rather than scientists or teachers in higher education. Even employment in agriculture or trade may appear to some industrial workers as an opportunity for their children to enter specialists' occupations.

Another study conducted in Sverdlovsk oblast' in 1964 reveals rural adult attitudes toward specifically agricultural occupations and suggests that there is a nearly universal disdain for agricultural work among rural as well as urban adults.[61] The author of the study complains that "parents incline their children primarily towards obtaining a specialty unrelated to agriculture."[62] Only 9.4 percent of the 8th graders and 14.3 percent of the 11th graders who were queried reported that their parents advised them to seek future employment in agriculture. The advice of relatives and friends, many of whom had moved to the city, was to leave the countryside. Only 8 percent of the students were advised to remain and to seek careers in agriculture. It seems clear that if any elements of a "traditional society" persist in the Soviet countryside, strong family pressure on children to remain in rural occupations is not among them.

Proposed Remedies

In developing countries, movement away from the land is the normal pattern and Soviet planners and scholars are fully aware of this. Ianov, for

[59] L. A. Margolin, "Svoboda vybora professii kak uslovie i forma proiavleniia svobody lichnosti," *Nauchnye doklady vysshei shkoly, filosofskie nauki,* no. 2 (1966), pp. 34–42.
[60] *Ibid.,* p. 38.
[61] Rutkevich, *Zhiznennye,* pp. 159–176.
[62] *Ibid.,* p. 167.

example, has pointed out that throughout history the village has fed the city not only bread and milk but also strong, healthy, and talented young men and women.[63] However, it is the intensity and character of the migration at the present time which so disturbs the Soviets. Time and again Soviet planners have thought that the flow to the cities, in its undesirable aspects, would be stopped by new agricultural policies, but this has been wishful thinking, expressing hopes rather than reality. In a recent article A. Leont'ev states, "In fact, the problem of population movement from the village to the city assumes increasingly greater urgency with each passing year."[64]

The primary motivations for leaving the countryside are dissatisfaction with the standard of living there and the lack of cultural opportunities (clubhouses, movies, theaters, concerts, sports facilities, etc.) and interesting companions. Paradoxically, better schools in rural areas are a force working toward greater movement out of agriculture and into the cities. Improved education not only increases the capabilities of rural youth but also creates aspirations beyond the farm.

Because of the attraction of urban life for young people, a cure for the age-sex-education imbalance in agriculture is not within easy reach. Indeed, success would probably require the investment of billions of rubles in the rural infrastructure, the costly strengthening of rural incentives, and a major reshaping of the organization and administration of agricultural production. Such extensive changes might take decades to implement even if vigorously pursued. Indeed, no remedy for the age-sex-education imbalance in Soviet agricultural employment can effect a quick cure. Improvement of necessity must be spread over several generations since the recruitment and retention of needed youth, particularly trained young men, can only have a small incremental effect year by year on the character and quality of the labor force. Attracting or retaining more young people in agriculture will, of course, be difficult to accomplish since the attitudes and aspirations as well as the actions of Soviet youth, both past and present, indicate a profound lack of interest in, if not an actual aversion to, remaining "down on the farm."

Some attempts to improve conditions have been made by the Soviet regime, although they are largely of an indecisive or tentative nature. For example, there has been much discussion about bringing rural conditions more in accord with urban. The most ambitious proposal was, of course, the development of *agrogorodi* in the early 1950's. Also, incentives on collective farms were improved following Stalin's death, albeit inadequately and imperfectly. Thus far, however, the regime has not been prepared to

[63] Cited in A. Leont'ev, "Migratsiia 'selo-gorod': sostoianie i perspektivy," *Voprosy ekonomiki* (March, 1969), pp. 154–155.

[64] *Ibid.*, p. 153.

commit the resources required for an effective use of incentives as a means of stopping the migration to the cities. The third area of reform—organization and administration—has seen many shifts in programs and emphasis, but basic structural or organizational changes have not yet been effected.

Some recent proposals for organizational changes are of interest, especially Alexander Ianov's suggestion that the intelligentsia be given more stake in the development of agriculture. In fact, a lead editorial, "The Intellectual Lives in the Village," published in *Pravda* (March 17, 1968) suggests that Ianov's proposal has struck a sympathetic chord with certain of the Soviet leadership. Ianov was troubled that secondary school graduates "almost entirely leave the villages" and fail to return "even when they become agricultural specialists," but try somehow or other to remain in the cities.[65] "As a result," Ianov pointed out, "over 90 percent of the intermediate leadership staff, the direct leaders of production in our kolkhozy, is made up of people with an elementary education." In an experiment in Kostroma oblast', in order to insure that young people not leave kolkhozy, a minimum wage was guaranteed which was higher than that earned by older and more experienced workers doing the same job. Ianov, however, argues that what made the secondary school graduates leave for the cities was not just the lack of material goods in the country, but the archaic organizational structure of the kolkhozy, which did not provide any "scope for the application of all their intellectual and creative forces. And these forces rebel."

The remedy proposed by Ianov has been discussed in the Soviet press for several years and experiments to prove its usefulness have been going on in many places. He proposed that a system of mechanized teams (*zveno*) should replace the system of production brigades which work according to established norms. These teams would be allotted a certain area of kolkhoz land, given agricultural machines to till the land, and thus become its real "masters," operating on a cost-accounting basis (*khozraschet*). But Ianov went even further than most advocates of these mechanized teams. He suggested that in order to make the teams fully successful, the very administrative structure of the kolkhoz should be changed. There would have to be a "democratization of rural society," as he called it.

Although Ianov did not spell out his intentions, he made it clear that in this process of democratization the role of the kolkhoz chairman would be reduced to that of leader of the village community, and the leaders of the mechanized teams would become fully independent organizers of farm production, working without orders from above. Ianov emphasized that such a form of organization "addressed to the independence, initiative and

[65] A. Ianov, "Kostromskoi eksperiment," *Literaturnaia gazeta*, December 27, 1967.

spirit of production of participants," to "creators" and not to "robots," would appeal to the young intelligentsia and would induce the modern, gifted, and intelligent kolkhoz youths to stay in the villages to become leaders and organizers of production.

Quite a different approach to the problem of keeping trained youth in agriculture was proposed by I. Salnikov.[66] He agreed that there exists a great shortage of qualified specialists at the intermediate leadership level of kolkhozy (brigadiers, chiefs of dairy farms, etc.), but proposed rather orthodox—one might say Stalinist—methods to overcome this shortage.

Salnikov first observed that the supply of specialists to kolkhozy and sovkhozy depends upon two factors: the number of cadres trained and their "fixation [*zakreplenie*] at the place of work." After pleading for a revision upward of present plans for the training of farm specialists, he proposed a "contract plan" for keeping trained personnel on the farms. Since such a substantial percentage of trained agriculturalists never return to the land, he argued, "Apparently, it will be necessary to recruit for the agricultural VUZY and technical schools primarily on passes [*putevka*] from the kolkhozy, sovkhozy, and other agricultural organizations, which will pay out scholarships to their future specialists. On this basis there must arise determined contractual relations between the enterprise and the specialist, by means of which the latter will be obliged to return to work on the farm for a determined period of time."[67]

As Christian Duevel has pointed out, the solutions offered by Ianov and Salnikov are worlds apart.[68] Ianov would like to attract and hold trained rural youths by giving them real opportunities for creative and independent work at the intermediate levels of kolkhoz management. Salnikov would solve the problem by "fixing" the young specialists in the village by decree, very much in the tradition of serfdom.

How the regime will resolve this problem, indeed whether it ever will, cannot be foreseen. We can be certain, however, that if this problem remains unresolved, so will the basic ills of Soviet agriculture.

V

Any significant improvement in the distorted age-sex-education structure of the agricultural labor force through the recruitment and retention of more trained young people will require a major effort and commitment by

66 Salnikov, pp. 53–59.
67 *Ibid.*, pp. 55–56, quoted by Christian Duevel, "Two Ways to Activate the Soviet Rural Intelligentsia," *Radio Liberty Dispatch*, April 8, 1968, p. 5.
68 *Ibid.*

the regime. To date, despite the widespread discussion of the necessity to attract youth to the farms and to keep them there, particularly trained specialists, the regime has been unwilling to make the necessary commitments to (1) improve adequately the material and cultural environment of rural areas and (2) provide the lattitude and incentives necessary to make agricultural work attractive. Unless the quality of agricultural labor is substantially improved by these means, the introduction of more demanding but more efficient modern methods and advanced techniques of agricultural production will be retarded and often ineffectual. Failure to develop a younger, better-trained, more enthusiastic agricultural labor force will continue to limit the possibility of major improvements in agricultural output and efficiency for some decades to come. This, in turn, will mean that the shortcomings of agriculture will continue to retard the overall growth of the Soviet economy.

9 : The Revolution in Soviet Farm Household Income, 1953-1967

David W. Bronson and Constance B. Krueger

From 1953, the year of Stalin's death, through 1967, the total income of the agricultural population from farm wages and private plot activity more than doubled, while the number of farm workers declined by approximately 10 percent (see Appendix Table 1).[1] Total nonfarm wages increased slightly more than agricultural incomes in this period, but about half of the rise was attributable to a 76 percent increase in nonfarm employment. The substantially larger rise in income per worker in agriculture resulted predominantly from the revolutionary increases in total wage payments to Soviet farm families for work performed in the socialized sector.[2] Such

[1] The concepts of agricultural and industrial incomes and employment in this study do not conform strictly to the definitions used in standard classifications of economic activities in income and production studies; see, for example, United Nations, *International Standard Classification of all Economic Activities*, Statistical Papers, Series M, no. 4, rev. 1 (New York, 1958). In this study the income of the agricultural population includes (1) the wages of collective farmers from the socialized sector and the value of net production from their private plots and (2) the wages of workers on state farms and subsidiary agricultural enterprises and the value of net production from their private plots. Thus the definitions used in this paper are not strictly according to economic sectors but according to socio-economic groups defined by the USSR Central Statistical Administration.

The "socialized sector" refers to all farm activity except private plot activity. Agriculture is the only sector in the Soviet economy in which a significant share of output is derived from private enterprise. Each household the head of which is occupied in work on a collective farm or in a state enterprise is permitted to produce some farm commodities from a small area of land or a small holding of livestock for its own use or to sell. In addition, some pensioners and a small number of able-bodied persons have plots but do not hold jobs in the socialized sector.

[2] Total wage payments include (1) for wage and salary workers employed on state farms and in subsidiary agricultural enterprises: regular wage payments including money and in-kind payments valued at state retail prices based on hourly and standard

payments increased nearly three-fold from 1953 to 1967, while private plot income rose by only one-quarter.

The drastic change in rural wages is of interest on three counts. First, it represents a reversal of the policy of suppressing labor and other costs in agriculture in order to finance industrial development. Second, it provides the opportunity to answer some long-standing questions such as the magnitude of urban-rural income differentials, the trend in agricultural wages, and the size of aggregate peasant incomes. Third, it tests the hypothesis advanced by some that the key to the problem in agriculture is to raise wage rates enough that persons living on farms will increase their participation in the socialized sector.[3]

I

Western scholars long have been interested in the nature of official income policy toward Soviet farmers, but the lack of data has stymied efforts to test alternative hypotheses. Those brave enough to write about peasant wages were forced to rely on bits and pieces of information from Soviet secondary sources, often dealing with gleanings from a relatively small body of data, such as facts obtained from case studies of individual farms.[4] Soviet reticence, however, began to ease in 1965 with the publication of data for selected years on average monthly wages for wage and salary workers by sector of the economy.[5] Subsequent statistical abstracts have filled in the data for most years since 1955. Finally in 1968, the USSR for the first time published official data for several years on total and average man-day wage payments made to collective farmers for work performed in the socialized sector.[6] Although far from complete, these data answer some questions and are useful as benchmarks from which estimates for other years can be interpolated.

Still missing from the income picture, however, are official data on income from private plot activity. In 1967, roughly one-half of family income of

---

piece rates, wage supplements such as payments for longevity and service in remote areas, bonuses, other payments such as additional pay to brigadiers for organizing the work of brigades and allowances for holiday pay, and sick leave and (2) for collective farm members: money and in-kind payments for work performed in the socialized sector.

[3] See, for example, Nancy Nimitz, *Agriculture under Khrushchev: The Lean Years* (Santa Monica, Calif.: RAND Corp., March, 1965), p. 2.

[4] Alec Nove, "Incentives for Peasants and Administrators," in Roy D. Laird (ed.), *Soviet Agricultural and Peasant Affairs* (Lawrence: University of Kansas Press, 1963), pp. 51–68.

[5] *Narodnoe khoziaistvo ... 1964*, p. 555.

[6] *Narodnoe khoziaistvo ... 1967*, p. 466.

collective farmers and somewhat less for families working at state agricultural enterprises[7] was accounted for by the "private" sector, comprising family holdings of one and a half acres or less, with one or two head of livestock. Although increasing information on the contribution of private activity to the total income of farm households is coming to light in secondary Soviet sources, lack of reliable data makes it impossible to measure precisely total incomes accruing to Soviet households from private plot activity.

After briefly describing some of the economic factors that led to the revolutionary increases in farm wages after 1953, this paper presents estimates of the magnitude of the rise in overall income of farm households as well as the size and trends of incomes from the major sectors of agriculture—collective farms, state farms, and private activity. Details on the sources and methodology used in deriving the estimates are presented in notes to the appendix tables. Urban-rural wage differentials are compared and the sources of the increased incomes of farmers are reviewed. Finally, some tentative conclusions are presented on the impact of higher incomes on patterns of rural work and life.

II

The Soviet Union has never explained fully the underlying motivation for adopting the measures responsible for the upsurge in rural wages after 1953. Apparently, the revolution in farm wages represents an attempt to resolve the chronic problems of obtaining sufficient agricultural production and achieving greater efficiency by emphasizing incentives rather than coercion to motivate rural labor.

In 1953, Stalin's heirs were confronted with an agricultural sector that had been stagnating since 1948 and was producing at about the same level as in 1940.[8] In 1953, moreover, the agricultural sector barely met the basic food requirements of the population and was able to supply only a small fraction of the rising urban demand to substitute quality foods (animal products, fruits, and vegetables) for starchy staples (grain products and potatoes). In short, the new leadership had reason to promote simultaneously a rapid acceleration in growth of overall farm output, a major change in the composition of output, and an increase in the efficiency of agricultural production so that resources could be released to other sectors of the econ-

---

[7] Includes for the entire period, state farms and subsidiary state agricultural enterprises and, in addition, for the period 1950–1958, Machine Tractor Stations and their successors, the Repair-Technical Stations.

[8] Ia. B. Lapkes, *Tekhnicheskii progress i proizvoditel'nost' truda v sel'skom khoziaistve* (Moscow, 1968), p. 125.

omy. Indeed, as Khrushchev stated in 1953, ". . . the problems of building communism cannot be successfully solved without the advance of agriculture."[9]

The new leadership decided to spur gains in output by recourse to an arsenal of conventional weapons: massive investments in new plant and equipment, a major expansion in cultivated acreage, increased use of soil additives and other agricultural chemicals, introduction of new varieties, improvement of cropping practices, and so on. For the most part, the program of expanding output rapidly was to be undertaken within the framework of the existing institutional arrangements for organizing and managing the large socialized farm enterprises. Because of ideological constraints, official policy could not permit a major expansion of the private sector. And, because the socialized sector was to be relied upon as the primary source of additional output, the average collective or state farm worker would have to be induced to put forth a greater effort if a prohibitive increase in the size of the agricultural labor force was to be avoided. This followed from the official view that, in general, the low reward per day of activity, relative to the much higher return for a day's work on the private plot or in nonfarm employment, had a depressing effect on the quality and quantity of work contributed to the socialized sector. Hence, there was a presumption that a major boost in the average reward for work on the collective and state farms would spark a major reduction in labor input per unit of output. Such a reduction was all the more important given the planned emphasis on output in such labor-intensive activities as livestock and vegetable production.

Because the revolution in farm wages is only one of many major changes that have occurred in agriculture since 1953, the impact of wage changes on production and employment cannot be measured with precision. As suggested above, higher wages were designed to attack specific problems such as the relatively low average number of man-days worked in the socialized sector and the inability to attract and retain professional and skilled labor. The degree to which these problems have been eliminated or persist today indicates, in part, the efficacy of the new wage policy.

III

Sources of the Higher Incomes

Many interrelated factors are responsible for the dramatic rise in incomes of the agricultural population. Wage drift associated with rising labor pro-

[9] N. S. Khrushchev, *Stroitel'stvo kommunizma v SSSR i razvitie sel'skogo khoziaistva* (Moscow, 1962), I, 77.

ductivity undoubtedly accounts for part of the rise in income of farm households. Official Soviet statistics claim that labor productivity on state farms[10] increased about 80 percent during 1953–1967,[11] while average annual wages more than doubled. On the collective farms during the same period, labor productivity more than doubled and average annual wages almost tripled. These increases in wages clearly exceed the amounts called for by Soviet wage doctrine (approximately a 1 percent increase in wages for every 2 percent increase in labor productivity).[12] On the basis of this doctrine, only about 40 percent of the rise in the average wage of state farm workers and approximately one-fifth of the rise for collective farmers can be attributed to gains in productivity.

The shift by the post-Stalin leadership to a policy of providing rewards in excess of productivity gains in agriculture, in order to stimulate higher production, accounts for the largest share of the advance in rural incomes. The low pay levels on collective and state farms in the early 1950's had also reflected deliberate government policy. In the case of collective farms, restricted wage payments were the result of financial stringency caused by low prices, high taxes, and limited credit. The low pay on state farms was the result of the low priority of agriculture compared to industry and construction. In order to implement the new wage policy, the new regime effected a number of fiscal and price measures that insured the ability of farms to expand wage funds. These included (1) conversion of a considerable number of collective farms with low wage structures into higher-paying state farms; (2) increases in procurement prices and tax and debt relief which boosted revenues of the remaining collective farms; (3) changes in state farm wage laws substantially increasing wage rates; (4) introduction of a "floor" for collective farm wages, which mitigated the status of the collective farmer as a residual claimant to farm income and greatly reduced the wide year-to-year fluctuations in peasant income; and (5) introduction of fringe benefits in the form of a state-administered and subsidized social insurance program for collective farm members.

Conversion of collective farms to state farms began in the mid-1950's on the grounds that state farms represent a "higher order of socialism," that they produce at lower cost than collective farms, and that conversion would be the best way to help financially distressed collective farms. During

[10] State farms are engaged primarily, but not exclusively, in agricultural production. They are also engaged in auxiliary activities such as peat production, wood processing, production of construction materials, and the processing of agricultural products. On the average, each farm carries on approximately three "outside" activities employing about 5 percent of the farm work force. About 90 percent of the output of outside activities is used on the farm.

[11] *Narodnoe khoziaistvo . . . 1958*, p. 526; *Narodnoe khoziaistvo . . . 1967*, p. 123.

[12] *Sotsialisticheskii trud*, no. 4 (1962), p. 12.

1959–1963, the peak of the conversion program, some 10,721 collective farms, or one-fifth of all collective farms, were transferred to state farm status.[13] Two and one-half million workers lived on these farms,[14] for the most part on the bottom rung of the economic ladder. The average annual wage of able-bodied workers on all collective farms in the early 1960's was about one-half the wage level of workers on state farms. The wage differential for farms that were subsequently converted was even greater since these were the most backward and economically the weakest. Thus conversion not only raised sharply the earnings of transferred farmers, but it also raised the average pay level of all collective farms by eliminating those in the lowest category.

Until the late 1950's, collective farms were under a dual system of delivery quotas—nominal procurement prices for much of farm output and a relatively high, fixed price for the remaining product. The system left farms with little money to pay members and consequently offered little incentive to members to work. After 1952, average prices received by farms for their products rose sharply as compulsory delivery quotas were reduced, allowing farms to sell a larger share of their product at higher prices. Also, both compulsory and "voluntary" delivery prices were increased by the state. In 1958, the dual system of pricing was replaced by a single price for both plan and above-plan deliveries. In 1965, a multiple pricing scheme was again initiated for several major products with above-plan deliveries procured at prices as much as 50 percent higher than prices for plan deliveries.[15] As indicated in Table 1, the average price for all farm products increased more than three-fold between 1952 and 1966. The average prices

Table 1 : *Index of average prices paid by the state to collective farms and individual producers for agricultural products, selected years, 1952–1966 (1952 = 100).*

	1953	*1955*	*1958*	*1960*	*1963*	*1966*
All products	154	209	296	299	355	412
Grain	236	553	695	717	848	1,113
Cattle	385	585	1,175	1,243	1,573	2,103
Technical crops	115	117	143	139	164	169

SOURCE: Stoliarov, p. 121.

[13] V. G. Venzher, *Ispol'zovanie zakona stoimosti v kolkhoznom proizvodstve* (Moscow, 1965), p. 113.
[14] S. L. Seniavskii, *Rost rabochego klassa SSSR (1951–1965 gg.)* (Moscow, 1966), p. 55.
[15] For a discussion of these reforms, see S. G. Stoliarov, *O tsenakh i tsenoobrazovanii v SSSR* (Moscow, 1969), pp. 13–21.

paid for grain and livestock more than doubled during 1952–1953, and by 1966 had increased ten-fold and twenty-fold respectively. These price measures facilitated the growth of collective farm revenues from 4.3 billion rubles in 1952 to 23.1 billion in 1966. Other measures that served to improve the financial condition of farms in the 1960's included reduction of taxes, adding almost half a billion rubles annually to retained farm revenues; expansion of farm credits from 4.7 billion rubles in 1964 to over 7 billion in 1965 and the easing of credit terms; cancellation of some farm debt;[16] and authorization of long-term loans to finance pay for farm administrators and machine operators at state farm wage rates.

The government has also increased agricultural subsidies allocated directly from the state budget. Allocations from the state budget have been made to subsidize state farms to the degree that revenues have been insufficient to meet rising labor costs. In addition, a state-administered social insurance program, similar to that long in existence for state enterprise wage and salary workers, was initiated for collective farmers in 1965. Under the funding arrangements designed to cover the cost of the social insurance program, collective farms contribute 4 percent of their annual revenues to a centralized social insurance fund, and 400 million rubles annually have been allocated from the state budget.[17]

Until the mid-1960's, the expansion of wages on collective farms was dependent on increasing the amount of residual income remaining after all other obligations (e.g., production costs and taxes) had been met. The residual income was then divided among the members. A decree adopted in May, 1966, "recommended" that, beginning July 1, 1966, collective farms replace the traditional system of irregular and uncertain wage payments with a system of "guaranteed" payments.[18] Under the new arrangements, pay scales on collective farms were to be identical with state farm pay rates, except for those collective farms where pay already exceeded the state schedule. To finance the program, farms (which theretofore were unable to use borrowed funds for wage payments) were now instructed to borrow when existing funds were inadequate to cover scheduled wage payments, and state banks were ordered to grant such loans during 1967–1970. By December, 1968, 97 percent of all collective farms were reported operating on the new system.[19]

For workers in state agriculture, increases in wage rates required legisla-

[16] Keith Bush, "Agricultural Reforms Since Khrushchev," in U.S. Congress, Joint Economic Committee, *New Directions in the Soviet Economy*, Part II-B (Washington, D.C.: G.P.O., 1966), pp. 451–472.

[17] *Narodnoe khoziaistvo . . . 1967*, p. 886.

[18] *Pravda*, May 18, 1966, p. 2.

[19] *Ekonomicheskaia gazeta*, no. 2 (1969), p. 26.

tive acts. Two major reforms in 1961 and 1965 boosted basic wage scales and improved bonus provisions on state farms. As a result, the average wage of state farm workers increased by 14 percent in 1962 alone, and at an average annual rate of more than 6.5 percent during 1961–1967 (twice the rate of nonfarm workers).

Larger bonuses, both in absolute amount and as a percentage of total pay, have also contributed to higher wages on state farms during the 1960's. Average annual bonus payments per state farm worker increased from 7 rubles, or 1 percent of annual earnings, in 1960, to 97 rubles, or 11 percent of pay, in 1965 (see Table 2). The increase is due to more liberal bonus

Table 2 : *Bonus payments to state farm workers.*

Year	Average Annual Bonus per State Farm Worker (rubles)	Bonus as Percent of Average Annual Wage
1960	7	1.1
1961	3	0.5
1962	5	0.6
1963	9	1.1
1964	67	7.9
1965	97	10.9

SOURCES: 1960–1962: L. N. Kassirov and V. A. Morozov, *Khoziaistvennyi raschet v kolkhozakh i sovkhozakh* (Moscow, 1965), p. 375; 1963–1965: *Ekonomika sel'skogo khoziaistva*, no. 12 (1966), p. 43.

arrangements and to the abolition of some restrictive measures rather than to improved productivity. Since 1965, new bonus arrangements, including bonuses for raising certain crops such as sugar beets, probably have continued the trend of increasing the importance of bonuses in relation to total pay.

Magnitude and Composition of Income Gains

Both the rate of growth and the changes in the sources and composition of aggregate farm household income are noteworthy. The sum of farm wages and private plot income of the total farm population grew from 18.6 billion rubles in 1953 to 38.3 billion rubles in 1967, or at an average annual rate of nearly 5.3 percent (see Appendix Table 1). Wage payments alone rose from 6.3 billion rubles in 1953 to 23.0 billion in 1967, or at an average annual rate of 9.7 percent. Year-to-year growth of farm wages, however, has been erratic, following not trends in agricultural production but, rather, policy decisions of the central authorities. In 1958, for example, total farm wages were 1.7 percent less than the preceding year, despite the fact that 1958 was the best year in the 1950's for total agricultural production. Indeed, during 1956–1960, aggregate farm wages stagnated. The most rapid growth in total farm wages occurred immediately following the accession to power of new regimes. During the two-year period 1954–1955, farm wages increased by 70 percent. The ascendance of Brezhnev and Kosygin in 1964 was followed by a 26 percent rise in wages in 1965–1966. It should be noted, however, that much of the gain in 1965–1966 resulted from reforms that were initiated by Khrushchev and carried out by Brezhnev and Kosygin.

A major feature of the changes in the sources and composition of farm income has been the differing rates of growth among the major sectors within agriculture. Average wages per worker on collective farms grew rapidly, while the wages of workers in state agriculture grew at a modest rate (see Appendix Table 2), and incomes from private plots changed the least over time. Monetization of incomes is another major change that has occurred since 1953. The share of income in kind has declined sharply, and money wages, a relatively minor form of payment for work in the socialized sector of collective farms in 1953, became the dominant form of payment in the early 1960's.

Trends in Income of Collective Farm Families

Collective farm families derive income from three sources: (1) wages and benefits in the form of money and in-kind payments for work in the socialized sector of collective farms, (2) consumption or sale of products raised on private plots attached to each household, and (3) wages and benefits from the state.[20] The composition and size of incomes of collective farm families have been transformed radically since 1953. Despite a decline of almost one-quarter in the number of collective farm households, total income of collective farm families increased approximately 69 percent between 1953 and 1967.[21] As shown in Table 3, the growth was due largely to a two-fold increase in wage payments to members for work in the socialized sector. As a result, the share of income of collective farm families originating from work in the socialized sector rose from less than one-third in 1953 to more than one-half in 1967. The structure of wages from the socialized sector during 1953–1967 has undergone significant transformation also. A

[20] I. Iu. Pisarev (ed.), *Metodologicheskie voprosy izucheniia urovnia zhizni trudiashchikhsia* (Moscow, 1962), p. 52.

[21] Except for the population census conducted in 1959, the Soviets have not published data on the total number of persons living on collective farms. The number of households on collective farms, which is published, is believed to reflect the trend in the collective farm population.

Table 3 : *Incomes of members of collective farms from farm wages and private plot activity, selected years, 1953–1967 (1953 = 100).* [a]

	1953	1958	1960	1963	1965	1967
Income of collective farm members from						
farm wages and private plot activity	100	135	125	132	155	169
Wages from the socialized sector	100	177	164	198	261	311
Private plot income	100	118	109	105	113	112
			Source of Income			
Income of collective farm members from						
farm wages and private plot activity	100%	100%	100%	100%	100%	100%
Wages from socialized sector	29	38	38	43	48	53
Private plot income	71	62	62	57	52	47

[a] For sources and methodology, see Appendix Table 1.

policy of monetization of collective farm wages has caused the value of in-kind payments to decline from 2.6 billion rubles in 1953 to 1.1 billion in 1967, while money wages grew from 1.8 billion rubles to 12.6 billion (see Appendix Table 1).

Until the mid-1960's, meager pensions and welfare payments were made to collective farm members from the so-called "social consumption funds" established by the farms from their net revenues. Only part of the funds was transferred directly to individuals; the remainder was spent on child care facilities, cultural institutions, homes for farm chairman, and education. Data on trends, magnitude, and distribution of the funds are very fragmentary and come from secondary Soviet sources. One source indicates that during the early 1950's pension and welfare payments by collective farms were virtually nonexistent.[22] Another author states that in 1953 kolkhozy allo-cated 66 million rubles to social consumption funds.[23] Perhaps half of this went directly to the peasants. By 1961, the size of social consumption funds had reportedly grown to 470 million rubles,[24] and a different source states that in 1961, 55.7 percent (about 262 million rubles) of the funds were expended in the form of transfer payments to individuals.[25] Thus, in the early 1960's, transfer payments by collective farms were adding approxi-mately 1 percent to peasant incomes.

By 1965, the need for farms to aid their members directly was largely eliminated by the introduction of a state-administered social insurance pro-gram. In that year, transfer payments by collective farms amounted to only 29 million rubles.[26] Because the data are so scarce and the amounts involved are so small, transfer payments to peasants by collective farms have not been included in our estimates of the earnings of the collective farm population. This is not believed to affect significantly the size or trends of total peasant income, but, to the degree that such transfer payments have occurred, the estimates of total income are understated.

The second major source of income is from the consumption or sale of goods raised on private plots. Data on plot income are gathered by the Central Statistical Administration through the use of monthly budget surveys conducted among 26,000 collective farm families scattered throughout the

[22] M. Z. Bora (ed.), *Real'nye dokhody i zhiznennyi uroven' trudiashchikhsia* (Minsk, 1966), p. 138.
[23] M. B. Markovich, *Statisticheskie pokazateli obshchestvennykh fondov potreble-niia* (Moscow, 1964), p. 27.
[24] *Ekonomicheskie nauki*, no. 6 (1969), p. 38.
[25] N. S. Lagutin, *Problemy sblizheniia urovnia zhizni rabochikh i kolkhoznikov* (Moscow, 1965), p. 68.
[26] G. V. D'iachkov, *Obshchestvennoe i lichnoe v kolkhozakh* (Moscow, 1968), p. 165.

Soviet Union.[27] These data have never been published officially, and until recently only scattered references, such as the share of private plot income in the total income of collective farm families, appeared in secondary sources.[28] In 1968, however, a Soviet book revealed for the first time the ruble values of average income of collective farm households from private plot activity.[29] Our estimates of total plot income are derived by multiplying the average plot income per family by the number of collective farm families (adjusted from an end-of-year to a mid-year basis) reported annually in the statistical yearbook.

Evaluation of the income data originating from the budget survey is hindered by ambiguity concerning survey procedures. Plot income is defined by the survey as total value of production of the plot minus production expenses. The part of private plot product that is sold is valued at the prices actually realized. The part that is consumed by the household is valued at the average price at which such products are actually sold by collective farms and individual farmers.[30] It is not known what checks are made to determine that the 26,000 families in the sample are representative of all collective farm families. Although there is evidence that Soviet authorities believe the surveys are reliable, several Soviet texts attack the representativeness of the survey.[31] Lacking information that would permit refinements, we have tentatively accepted the estimates of plot incomes as derived by official budget surveys.

Total income from private plots is estimated to have grown only from 11.0 billion rubles in 1953 to 12.3 billion in 1967, an annual rate of less than 1 percent. Because of the rapid increase in wages from the socialized sector, the share of income originating from private plots declined from approximately 71 percent of the total in 1953 to 47 percent in 1967.

Finally, some collective farm family income originates in state social insurance payments to family members and in wage payments to members hired by state enterprises either on a temporary or permanent basis. Unfortunately, data have not been published on such "outside" income. However, state insurance payments to collective farmers probably were insignificant

---

[27] For a thorough description of the sample budget survey, see John W. DePauw, *The Soviet Statistical System: The Continuous Sample Budget Survey*, International Population Reports Series P–95, no. 62 (Washington, D.C.: U.S. Department of Commerce, 1965).

[28] For example, V. F. Maier, *Dokhody naseleniia i rost blagasostoianiia naroda* (Moscow, 1968), p. 108.

[29] D'iachkov, p. 68.

[30] N. I. Buzliakov, *Metody planirovaniia povysheniia urovnia zhizni* (Moscow, 1969), p. 86.

[31] *Ibid.*, p. 168; N. M. Rimashevskaia, *Ekonomicheskii analiz dokhodov rabochikh i sluzhashchikh* (Moscow, 1965), pp. 59–62; *Voprosy ekonomiki*, no. 5 (1967), p. 48.

as a source of income before 1965. We were able to estimate that, in 1966, roughly 2 billion rubles were paid to collective farmers for work in the state sector.[32] In the early 1960's, about 2 million persons living on collective farms were permanently employed in state enterprises, and probably the number has not changed drastically since then.[33] Thus, it is felt that the bulk of these wage payments are going to persons residing in collective farm households but working in state enterprises and listed on state payrolls. Income derived from such activity, however, may be better treated as non-agricultural. Lack of data and questions about the propriety of including such income, even if data were available, have caused us to exclude estimates of income from outside sources from the estimates of total income of collective farmers.

Trends in State Farm Workers' Income

The estimation of total income of persons living on state farms tends to be less complicated than the incomes of collective farm families. Wage payments are the predominant source of income and originate only in the state sector. In-kind payments by state farms constitute a relatively minor source of income, and the share of income originating from private plot activity is considerably less than on collective farms. And, unlike the case of collective farm households, state farm households receive transfer payments from only one source.

Total wage payments to workers in state agricultural enterprises grew from just under 2 billion rubles in 1953 to 9.3 billion rubles in 1967. For the period as a whole, about one-half the wage increase can be attributed to growing employment in the state agricultural sector and about one-half to higher average wages. Between 1953 and 1960, however, approximately two-thirds of the gain came from growth in employment and only one-third from higher wages. During 1960–1967 the trend was reversed: about two-thirds of the growth resulted from higher wages, with one-third from growth in employment.

The growth in average wages occurred as a result of a number of wage reforms rather than from upgrading labor force skills on state farms. Indeed, unskilled and semiskilled field workers have been beneficiaries of the largest wage gains (see Table 4). Since 1956, increases in daily wage rates for unskilled field workers ranged from 40 to nearly 200 percent, depending on

---

[32] I. D. Laptev and S. I. Semin (eds.), *Rentabel'nost' i rasshirennoe vosproizvodstvo v sel'skom khoziaistve* (Moscow, 1968), p. 123.

[33] Murray Feshbach, "Manpower in the USSR: A Survey of Recent Trends and Prospects," in U.S. Congress, Part III, p. 760.

Table 4 :   *Average monthly wages of state farm workers, selected years, 1950–1966 (1950 = 100).*

	1955	1960	1963	1966
All workers on state farms	122	141	176	209
Technical workers	126	134	146	176
Unskilled and semiskilled workers	124	145	181	215
Clerical and administrative workers	123	127	156	165

SOURCE: *Trud v SSSR*, p. 145.

type of work and locality of farm.[34] In part, pay raises for unskilled workers were brought about by legal changes raising the minimum wage for wage and salary workers from 27 rubles a month in 1957, to 40 rubles in 1965, to 60 rubles beginning in 1968.[35] Farm managers and highly skilled workers such as agronomists and other technicians have gained least in higher salary rates. Since 1957, monthly salary rates of farm managers have increased only 17–20 percent. Yet, between 1955 and 1967, overall growth in the average wage of state farm workers amounted to about 80 percent, or an average of more than 5 percent increase per year. In no other sector of the economy have workers enjoyed such a rapid increase in average wages (see Table 5). Nevertheless, in 1967, state agriculture ranked eighth out of 12 sectors in average wage level—a notable improvement over its last-rank status in 1955.

Private plots are a second significant source of income for persons living on state farms. The limited data at hand indicate that the share of state farm family income originating from private plots was 28 percent in 1960 and 20 percent in 1966.[36] Official data pertaining to private plot income of state farm workers are based on sample budget surveys. However, the information published is even more meager than comparable information for collective farms. Estimates of private plot income for years for which no data are available are, therefore, necessarily crude (see Appendix Table 1). For the years between 1960 and 1966, the estimates are derived by interpolation; arbitrary assumptions are made for earlier years. According to these estimates, plot income increased 131 percent between 1953 and 1967, or at about the same rate as the growth of employment in state agriculture.

Transfer payments are a more important source of income to wage and salary workers than to collective farmers. One source reports that transfer

[34] S. V. Kal'chenko *et al.* (eds.), *Spravochnaia kniga direktora sovkhoza* (Moscow, 1956), I, 122; *Ekonomicheskaia gazeta*, no. 51 (1967), p. 30.
[35] Maier, pp. 141–142, 146.
[36] *Voprosy ekonomiki*, no. 11 (1968), p. 47.

Table 5 : *Sectors of the economy, by percent increase in average monthly wage, 1956–1967.*

Sector	1967 Wages as a Percent of 1955 Wages
State agriculture	180.5
Construction	159.2
Health	158.2
Trade, public dining, material-technical supply	157.7
Housing, communal economy	150.3
Transportation	149.4
Average for All Sectors	*144.1*
Industry	142.7
Administration	141.3
Communication	140.3
Education	137.3
Credit and insurance	132.9
Science	118.7

SOURCE: *Trud v SSSR*, pp. 138–139.

payments added 6 percent (year not specified, but apparently in the early 1960's) to the money income of the average wage and salary worker family.[37] Presumably transfer payments to families of state farm workers would not differ significantly from the average for all state sectors.

Trends in Urban-Rural Wage Differentials

The revolution in agricultural wages has narrowed substantially the differentials in average "direct" wages among able-bodied collective farm workers, state farm workers, and workers in industry (see Table 6).[38] The

[37] Rimashevskaia, p. 24.

[38] Remuneration for work performed is composed of several elements. First, there is the direct wage or salary, including bonuses that an enterprise remits to its workers individually. This element of remuneration is relatively easy to measure and is the data on wage payments published by many countries, including the USSR. Second, there is a package of benefits that M. P. Fogarty has labeled the "indirect wage," which generally is a growing share of total incomes of workers. In this category Fogarty includes (1) free-time benefits, paid holidays, and shorter working days or weeks; (2) services incidental to employment such as severance pay; and (3) "income-disposal benefits (spending the workers' income for him)," including canteens, industrial health, clubs, sport fields, factory-run resorts, family allowances, sick pay, and retirement pensions. See M. P. Fogarty, "Portrait of a Pay Structure," in J. L. Meij (ed.), *Internal Wage-Structure* (Amsterdam: North-Holland Publishing Co., 1963), pp. 72–73.

In the case of the Soviet Union, private plot income could be viewed as an "indirect wage." These benefits are largely unquantifiable, but they do add to the balance of advantage of a particular job. How far they should be reckoned part of the pay

Table 6 : Comparison of average annual and daily wages of workers in industry and agriculture, selected years, 1953–1967.[a]

	1953	1958	1960	1963	1964	1965	1966	1967
Average annual wages:[b]								
Industry	100.0	100.0	100.0	100.0	100.0	100.0	100.0	100.0
State farms	53.9	61.0	59.0	68.2	70.2	72.1	74.7	74.9
Collective farms[c]	17.9	28.6	25.2	31.8	36.9	42.3	46.6	48.1
Average wages per day worked:[b]								
Industry	100.0	100.0	100.0	100.0	100.0	100.0	100.0	100.0
State farms	63.1	67.9	65.9	78.3	81.2	83.5	86.7	86.9
Collective farms[c]	24.6	40.0	34.1	43.0	50.1	57.5	63.3	65.7

[a] For sources and methodology, see Appendix Table 2.
[b] Includes only wages in money and in kind (valued at state retail prices) from job, and excludes outside income such as pensions and private plot income.
[c] Able-bodied workers only (men 16–59 years, women 16–54 years).

effect of "indirect wages" on total incomes cannot be measured satisfactorily, but the evidence at hand suggests that over the period as a whole, indirect benefits received by industrial workers were substantially greater than those received by farm workers and that this gap widened significantly. The sharp rise in direct wages on farms relative to industry, however, offset this difference, and the differential in total incomes has probably narrowed between farm and industrial workers.

Direct Wages

In terms of average annual wages, collective farmers earned in 1953 less than one-fifth of the amount earned by the average industrial worker, while a worker on a state farm earned slightly more than one-half as much as a worker in industry. By 1967, collective farmers were earning about one-half of the industrial wage, while state farmers earned three-fourths as much as the worker in industry. Such comparisons, however, do not reflect differences that exist in the actual amount of time spent on the job by workers in the various sectors of the economy.

Data on average hourly wages are needed to eliminate variations in time spent on the job and thus to obtain a truer picture of wage differentials. Unfortunately, these data are not available for the USSR. However, some information exists on differences by sector in the average number of days worked per year. Comparing average wages by sector on this basis alters the differential picture somewhat.[39] According to official data for 1960, state farm workers were employed about 5 percent more days a year than industrial workers (280 days, compared with 267 days). Soviet statistical methods, however, invalidate this comparison. The Soviet practice of including the number of man-days worked in state agriculture by seasonal and part-time workers, while excluding these workers from the work population on which the average is based, inflates the average annual number of man-days worked on state farms.[40] Scattered references report that the average num-

---

workers receive is uncertain since personal preferences lead to an unequal usage among workers eligible to receive them.

[39] In industry and on state farms, a work-day is a standard number of daily work hours, and the Central Statistical Administration requires enterprises to submit detailed records on hours worked. For collective farms, however, no such statistics are available. Until 1959, records were not even kept on the number of days workers appeared for work in the socialized sector. Since 1959, man-day records have been submitted, but there is no standard length of man-day. Soviet sources indicate that in some cases a person working as little as one hour is credited with an entire man-day. Although the data are not comparable, they indicate roughly the substantial differences in actual time worked on collective farms and in enterprises in the state sectors.

[40] Nancy Nimitz, *Farm Employment in the Soviet Union, 1928–1963* (Santa Monica, Calif.: RAND Corp., November, 1965), pp. 138–140.

ber of man-days actually worked per state farm worker was 235–245 per year during 1955–1959, or about 90 percent as many days as the industrial worker.[41] We feel that these figures are analogous to those published for industry, and therefore we have used the data for 1955 and 1959 to construct estimates for the other years in the series (see Appendix Table 2). The average able-bodied collective farmer, in comparison, worked only three-quarters as many days as the industrial worker.

The earnings differential between farm workers and industrial workers thus appears to be narrowed even further when measured on a days-worked instead of an annual basis. However, a factor not reflected in this computation is the reduction in the length of the scheduled work week for state workers from 48 to 46 hours in 1956 and to 41 hours by the end of 1960. Thus, since 1956 there has been a 15 percent reduction in the average length of the work-day for state workers, but there is no indication that a corresponding change has occurred for collective farm workers, who are not covered by Soviet labor law.[42]

Indirect Wages

Although indirect wages cannot be quantified, their inclusion in a measure of wage differentials would probably narrow the gulf between urban and rural incomes. Until the introduction of a universal social insurance program in 1965, the only significant indirect wage available to collective farm workers came from their maintenance of private plots. Income from the plot gave these workers a measure of protection against the vicissitudes of earnings from the socialized sector. State farm workers are similarly entitled to private plots, but more severe legal restrictions (plot size on state farms cannot normally exceed 0.15 hectare, compared to 0.5 hectare on collective farms)[43] and more attractive alternative income opportunities diminish the importance of plots as a source of income for state workers.

From 1953 until 1965 the social insurance program covering all state workers was a factor contributing to the relative advantage enjoyed by state workers over collective farmers. State workers were also entitled to paid maternity leave and to accident and sick pay. In addition, retirement, survivors', and disability pensions were paid to former state workers and their families, adding to both income and security. With the exception of chair-

[41] N. I. Shishkin (ed.), *Trudovye resursy SSSR* (Moscow, 1961), p. 105.

[42] Because of the seasonal nature of agricultural work, Soviet labor law permits the length of the work-day on state farms to exceed the scheduled hours during periods of peak activity. Shortened work-days are substituted for scheduled work periods during slack periods to adjust total hours worked annually to the scheduled norm.

[43] V. E. Grigorovskii and M. A. Alekseev, *Lichnoe podsobnoe khoziaistvo kolkhoznikov, rabochikh i sluzhashchikh v SSSR* (Leningrad, 1968), p. 54.

men and certain technical workers who qualified for benefits under the program for state workers, collective farmers were not covered by any state welfare program until 1965. Before that time the establishment of pension programs on collective farms had been optional and entirely at the expense of the individual farm. As a result, many collective farms had no program at all and those with programs usually failed to match the benefits received by workers at state enterprises.

Even after a state-administered social insurance program for collective farmers was instated in 1965, benefits were smaller and eligibility requirements more stringent than under the program for state workers. Nevertheless, collective farmers benefited significantly. The number of collective farm pensioners rose from 2.6 to 6.9 million,[44] and the average size of pensions increased from approximately 6 rubles a month to about 15 rubles a month.[45] Thus more than one billion rubles were added to the money income of collective farm families during 1965. In 1968, the pensionable age for collective farmers was reduced by five years, putting them on an equal footing with state employees. As noted above, the lack of welfare measures for collective farmers before 1965 sharply widened the apparent income gap between collective farm workers and state workers. The introduction of social insurance benefits for collective farm workers in 1965 caused this income gap to narrow much more than the direct wage comparison would indicate.

Other forms of indirect wages are enjoyed almost exclusively by workers in state enterprises, including state farms. These include eight holidays with pay a year and a paid vacation after eleven months of employment; collective farmers receive no pay for holidays or vacation. In 1964, the average length of paid vacation for industrial workers was 18.8 days and for workers on state farms, 13.8 days.[46] By all accounts, amenities such as clubs, libraries, and sports facilities are more plentiful in industry than on state farms and are least available on collective farms. Such factors contribute to the gulf between the urban and rural levels of living and make the retention and recruitment of labor for farm jobs more difficult.

IV

The Soviet wage system is designed to perform two important functions in the labor market. First, through a differentiated wage structure, it facilitates the allocation of labor by encouraging the requisite flow of workers into each of several branches of the economy. Second, through piece rates and bonus

[44] *Sotsialisticheskii trud*, no. 2 (1967), p. 15.
[45] *Sotsial'noe obespechenie*, no. 12 (1964), p. 2.
[46] *Trud v SSSR* (Moscow, 1968), p. 241.

arrangements, the wage system provides incentive by rewarding effort and penalizing shirkers. Problems in allocating labor and providing incentives in agriculture were severe in 1953, and the subsequent wage reforms were aimed at providing solutions for those problems. Although available data do not permit definitive evaluation of the efficacy of the wage reforms with respect to agriculture, certain conclusions may be drawn with reference to some of the changes in agriculture since 1953.

By relaxing coercion and improving incentives, Stalin's heirs have tried to break a supposed vicious cycle—low wages, low productivity, low levels of output, low wages—and in this way to increase production, to lower costs, and to release labor for work in other sectors of the economy. Soviet leaders must be disappointed with the results to date. Productivity in agriculture has not risen sufficiently to permit a substantial transfer of labor from agriculture to other sectors of the economy. While labor productivity in Soviet industry rose by 144 percent during 1954–1967,[47] the Soviet index of labor productivity in the socialized sector of collective farms rose by 118 percent and increased by only 81 percent on state farms.[48] According to official estimates, average annual employment in the socialized sector of agriculture declined by only 7 percent between 1953 and 1967. Western estimates of the total agricultural labor force, including persons who worked exclusively on private plots, indicate a 9 percent drop during this 14-year period.[49]

Since 1953, the average number of man-days worked by able-bodied workers in the socialized sector of collective farms has remained around 200 per year, about two-thirds the amount the state deems available. Moreover, the proportion of able-bodied collective farmers abstaining entirely from work in the socialized sector has been growing, nearly doubling between 1950 and 1965. In the latter year about 8 percent of able-bodied collective farmers did not work in the socialized sector even one day during the year.[50] The average annual number of man-days worked by state farm workers apparently has changed little since the early 1950's. One of the acknowledged goals of the policy of increasing wages for work in the socialized sector of agriculture since 1953 has been to break the peasants' dependence on private plots for income. Several Soviet sources, reporting on different years, indicate that collective farmers have spent approximately one-third of their working hours at plot activities.[51] By assuming that all

[47] *Narodnoe khoziaistvo . . . 1967*, pp. 120–121.
[48] *Narodnoe khoziaistvo . . . 1958*, p. 526; *Narodnoe khoziaistvo . . . 1967*, p. 123.
[49] Ritchie H. Reed, *Estimates and Projections of the Labor Force and Civilian Employment in the USSR: 1950–1975*, International Population Reports Series P–91, no. 15 (Washington, D.C.: U.S. Department of Commerce, 1967), p. 15.
[50] *Ekonomika sel'skogo khoziaistva*, no. 12 (1966), p. 77; *Voprosy ekonomiki*, no. 11 (1966), p. 28.
[51] *Voprosy ekonomiki*, no. 5 (1967), p. 51; Nimitz, *Farm Employment*, p. 85.

work time is spent either on the plot or in socialized agriculture and that these two sectors are the source of all household income, we estimate, very roughly, earnings per day of plot activity by using the estimates of income from plot activity (Appendix Table 1) and of wages and man-days worked in socialized agriculture (Appendix Tables 1 and 2). The comparison of

Table 7 : *Comparison of average pay per day in socialized agriculture and private plots of collective farms, selected years, 1953–1967.*

Year	Average Pay per Day's Work in Socialized Agriculture (rubles)[a]	Average Pay per Day's Work on Private Plots (rubles)[b]	Average Pay per Day in Socialized Agriculture as a Percent of Average Pay per Day on Plots
1953	0.82	4.11	20
1958	1.56	5.21	30
1959	1.40	4.37	32
1960	1.40	4.67	30
1961	1.61	4.64	35
1962	1.82	5.25	35
1963	1.92	5.13	37
1964	2.27	5.64	40
1965	2.68	5.79	46
1966	3.05	5.87	52
1967	3.32	5.97	56

[a] Appendix Table 2.
[b] By dividing the total wage bill from the socialized sector of collective farms (Appendix Table 1) by the average pay per man-day from the socialized sector of collective farms (Appendix Table 2), a total number of man-days worked in the socialized sector was derived. Total man-days worked in the socialized sector were assumed to be equal to 66.7 percent of all man-days worked in the socialized sector and on private plots. For each year the total number of man-days worked in the socialized sector was divided by 66.7 to get a total man-days series. Total man-days minus man-days worked in socialized sector equals man-days worked on private plots. For each year plot income (Appendix Table 1) was divided by the derived man-days series for the private plot to derive plot income per man-day.

daily earnings in the two sectors indicates (Table 7) that a day's earnings from work on the private plot in 1967 was 80 percent greater than the average daily wage in the socialized sector, despite the three-fold increase posted for the latter since 1953. The continued existence of a large differential in the average return per work-day in favor of the private sector surely must be frustrating to official efforts to bring about a shift of labor application from the plot to the socialized sector.

Even during the harvest period, when labor demand is at a peak and farm management exerts its greatest pressure to get everyone including the young and the aged into the fields, the manpower of collective farm households spends a larger share of time working on private plots than during other periods of the year, according to available evidence. In Novosibirsk oblast' in 1964, for example, all participants from collective farm households on the average spent 35 percent of available work time during the harvest period working on their plots, which compares with slightly more than 25 percent for the year as a whole (see Table 8). Similar.patterns were reported in Grodno oblast' (Belorussia) and Krasnodar krai (RSFSR) during 1960–1961,[52] suggesting that the Novosibirsk experience is not atypical.

Table 8 : *Distribution of work time of collective farmers in Novosibirsk oblast', by age and sex, 1964.*[a]

| | DISTRIBUTION OF WORK TIME | | | |
| | FOR THE YEAR AS A WHOLE | | FOR THE HARVEST PERIOD | |
	In Collective Farm Activity	*On Plots*	*In Collective Farm Activity*	*On Plots*
Total for all categories of collective farmers	73.3%	26.7%	65.0%	35.0%
Able-bodied	77.9	22.1	71.2	28.8
Males (age 16 to 59)	90.5	9.5	88.6	11.4
Females (age 16 to 54)	65.4	34.6	54.9	45.1
Over-aged; disabled	37.4	62.6	35.0	65.0
Juveniles (up to and including 16)	49.4	50.6	15.5	84.5

[a] The year 1964 was a "normal" agricultural year for Novosibirsk oblast'. That is, there is no evidence of conditions (e.g., crop failure in the collective farms due to drought) that would have given collective farmers an expectation of an abnormally low return per work-day in collective farm activity.

SOURCE: Churakov and Suvorova, p. 110.

Higher rural incomes were also expected to assist in overcoming another dimension of the labor problem in agriculture—the low quality of manpower on farms. This problem has been characterized by the generally low educational attainment of the rural population, the inability to attract and retain technical and skilled manpower, and the reliance on women, youth, and the aged for physical work. Even without a wage reform, some improvement in the quality of labor would be expected over time as the rural population benefits from universal education and longer schooling. Higher farm wages were expected to accelerate this trend and to diminish the other qualitative problems by putting agriculture into a more competitive position in the labor market.

The problem of low educational attainment exacerbates Soviet efforts to

[52] V. F. Mashenkov, *Ispol'zovanie trudovykh resursov sel'skoi mestnosti* (Moscow, 1965), pp. 131–132.

administer agriculture like industry, i.e., through the medium of large-scale enterprises with formal planning of production and detailed systems of records and reports. Thus, unlike agricultural operations in many other countries, Soviet agriculture requires a highly skilled administrative elite in order to function smoothly. Yet the general educational level in agriculture lags far behind that in the rest of the economy. The problem is particularly acute on collective farms where, in 1967, only one out of three workers had more than eight years of education. In contrast, three out of five industrial production workers (excluding administrative staffs and clerical and technical workers) had more than eight years schooling.[53]

The results of efforts to increase the number of machine operators have been especially vexing. Between 1950 and 1967, some 11.7 million machine operators (including 8 million tractor drivers) were trained for work in agriculture.[54] About half of these machine operators received their training during the 1960's when substantially higher wages were in effect. At the end of the period, however, there were only 1.9 million more machine operators in agriculture than at the beginning—3.3 million in 1967, compared with 1.4 million in 1950.[55] A more dramatic indicator of the regime's failure to solve the shortage of skilled labor on the farms is the ratio of operators per machine. In order to operate on a multishift basis during the critical periods of planting and harvesting activity, an average of 1.8 to 2.3 operators are needed per machine.[56] So far authorities have been fighting a losing battle, with the number of machines growing faster than the number of operators. In 1950, there were 1.47 operators for each tractor and combine. The ratio declined to 1.12 in 1960 and to 1.05 in 1965. In the latter year, the shortage of tractor drivers restricted 80 percent of all tractors to one-shift operation.[57]

In farming, as in other sectors of the economy where physical labor predominates, the proportion of work done by able-bodied males is another indicator of the quality of labor inputs. Farm managers, given a choice, would be expected to choose men over women workers. With wages going up more rapidly in agriculture than in other sectors of the economy, it could be expected that males would transfer to the higher-paying agricultural jobs, and women would be forced to take jobs in other sectors of the economy or at lower-paying work on farms. Soviet data indicate only a slight tendency of this sort. The proportion of men in the work force on state farms in-

[53] *Narodnoe khoziaistvo . . . 1967*, p. 34.
[54] *Ibid.*, p. 667; *Trud v SSSR*, pp. 310–311.
[55] *Trud v SSSR*, p. 129.
[56] S. F. Demidov *et al.* (eds.), *Nekotorye voprosy upravlenia sel'skokhoziaistvennym proizvodstvom* (Moscow, 1967), p. 223.
[57] *Ibid.*, p. 224.

creased from 51 percent in 1950 to 56 percent in 1966.[58] In contrast, the proportion of men in the industrial labor force declined from 54 percent to 53 percent during this period. The proportion of total man-days worked by able-bodied males in the socialized sector on collective farms rose from 40 percent in 1950 to 46 percent in 1965.[59] This shift occurred despite the fact that during this period the average annual number of man-days worked per able-bodied male declined by 8 percent while man-days worked per female increased by 8 percent.[60] On both state and collective farms, however, the relative shift to a greater use of male labor occurred during 1950–1958. Since then the proportion of man-days worked by males on collective farms has remained constant and the proportion of males on state farms has declined.[61]

V

The precise degree and exact causes of the apparent failure of the wage reform to bring about a significant rise of labor productivity in agriculture cannot be specified. It may be useful, however, to note three factors that have contributed to this failure, even though it is not possible to assess their relative weights.

First, the fact that the return per day from private plot agriculture still exceeds that obtainable in the socialized sector of collective farms results in the continued input to private plots of a large share of total work time available on collective farms. A conflict between private plot and collective work apparently is not significant on state farms because private plots are smaller and work rules for state workers limit free time.

Second, the failure to translate rural income gains into comparable real increases in the rural level of living has also tended to dampen the effectiveness of the wage reforms. The increased incomes in agriculture are designed, in part, to compensate for the poor work conditions—the work is seasonal and often must be accomplished under adverse conditions, far from the amenities of the city. By raising the level of rural wages, Soviet authorities have sought to overcome the reluctance of young workers to remain on the farm and to reduce the turnover of skilled workers sent to farms. The supply of goods and services to rural residents has not, however, kept pace with rising incomes. As a result, the actual level of living in the countryside re-

[58] *Trud v SSSR*, p. 76.
[59] V. Ia. Churakov and L. I. Suvorova, *Ispol'zovanie trudovykh resursov v kolkhozakh i sovkhozakh* (Moscow, 1967), p. 43.
[60] *Ibid.*, p. 48.
[61] *Narodnoe khoziaistvo . . . 1958*, p. 664; *Narodnoe khoziaistvo . . . 1967*, p. 654.

mains significantly below the level in the city, and the amount of money held in savings accounts in state banks by the rural population has spiraled upward. The sum held in these accounts for rural depositors grew from 206 million rubles in 1950 to 6 billion rubles in 1966, and the average size of deposit per account during this period increased from 52 rubles to 370 rubles.[62] Despite this increase, the wealth seems to be unevenly shared. In 1967, fewer than one in five rural residents had savings accounts, compared with more than one in three for urban residents.[63]

Third, the wage structure in agriculture has failed to reflect clearly the established goals. To be effective as an instrument for improving the allocation of resources, a wage system must directly associate rewards and penalties with attainment of goals; and rewards must be adequate to motivate workers. Soviet and western observers are in nearly unanimous agreement that neither of these success criteria has been met in Soviet agriculture.[64] Moreover, the myriad changes in wage laws since 1953 have not significantly altered the structure of the wage system, but have only added to the confusion.

As an incentive system, the pre-1962 wage and bonus system for state farm workers failed largely because of its complexity and capriciousness. Workers were paid not by occupation but by job performed; moreover, they could not be secure about the nature and duration of the jobs they would be performing, and they were thus uncertain about prospective earnings. Inequities in the grading of jobs added complexity and capriciousness because workers came to recognize certain work as "advantageous" and other work as "disadvantageous." The wage rates for some jobs were higher than for others of equal or greater importance and difficulty. For example, there was a 31 percent wage differential between harrowing and plowing, despite the fact that there was little difference in the skill levels required. As a result, brigade leaders had to contend with machine operators vying for the highest-paying jobs and workers ignoring or rushing through low-paying jobs to get to the better-paying ones.[65] Moreover, the same job on neighboring farms was often paid at different rates because of inequities in norm-setting.

[62] *Vestnik statistiki*, no. 1 (1967), p. 18.

[63] *Narodnoe khoziaistvo . . . 1967*, pp. 7, 699. The savings spiral could be motivated by many factors including the establishment of "nest eggs," saving for expensive durable goods, or the inability to spend money because of a shortage of goods and services. Because of the low levels of living in the countryside in the past, it seems doubtful that savings are the result of a satiation of demand. Furthermore, Soviet newspaper accounts attest to the inability of authorities to supply rural areas with goods and services sufficient to meet demands.

[64] D. Gale Johnson, "Soviet Agriculture," *Bulletin of the Atomic Scientists* (January, 1964), pp. 10–11.

[65] *Voprosy ekonomiki*, no. 9 (1966), pp. 46–47.

The overhaul of the state farm wage system, a part of the overall wage reform carried out between 1956 and 1961, presented an opportunity to correct many of the shortcomings of the wage and bonus system, but the changes that became effective in 1962 left the wage system as complex as ever. Currently the base wage of tractor drivers is made up of 27 elements, and there are approximately 100 types of supplementary payments.[66]

It is clear from published accounts that, in addition to the inherent structural weaknesses of the various pay schemes, failure fully to implement the rules has further limited the efficacy of the wage system. A typical complaint concerning the current state of affairs in the payment of machine operators is illustrative: "Many sovkhozy are not making full use of measures for material incentive that have been established by the government. Machine operators do not receive additional payments for raising crops or increased wages for crop harvesting in the established amounts. Machine operators are not being certified in class, nor are increased wage increments paid them for higher class rating."[67]

The shortcomings of the wage system for state farm workers appear minor when compared to the situation that has prevailed on collective farms. Lacking the cohesion of a centrally established and administered wage system, the method of payment to workers on collective farms has been based until recently on two principles that have tended to nullify the incentive aspects of wage increases implemented since 1953. First, until 1967, collective farm workers were residual claimants, receiving as pay at the end of the year only a share of whatever sum of rubles and product was left over after all other farm expenditures were deducted. At best the worker had only a vague idea of what his labor in the socialized sector was worth. Second, failure to reward extra effort directly further reduced the already tenuous connection between effort and reward. Since the additional revenue to the farms produced by an additional unit of effort was divided among all workers, an individual who put forth an extra effort shared his reward with his fellow workers.[68] The following statement, which succinctly identifies the central problem of the farm wage system, recently appeared in *Zhurnalist*: "People want simply and readily understandable forms of labor relations and wages. Actually, the rank-in-file kolkhoz or sovkhoz worker has no clear idea of how his wages are computed. Receiving his income on the basis of a 'norm' and a multitude of increments, he can scarcely establish any logical connection between what he does and what he receives."[69]

[66] *Sel'skaia zhizn'*, December 27, 1968, p. 2.
[67] *Ekonomicheskaia gazeta*, no. 34 (1966), p. 22.
[68] For a discussion of these factors, see Johnson.
[69] *Zhurnalist* (May, 1969), pp. 16–17.

APPENDIX

This appendix consists of three tables:

1. Total income of the agricultural population from farm wages and private plot activity, 1953–1967.

2. Average wages and days worked in industry, state agricultural enterprises, and collective farms, 1953–1967.

3. Income and expenditures of collective farms, 1950, 1952–1961.

The notes to each table include the sources and methodology used in deriving the data. When available, official data are used. For the remainder, it was necessary to use Soviet data appearing in various sources and, in some cases, to derive independent estimates.

Appendix Table 1 : *Total income of the agricultural population from farm wages and private plot activity, 1953–1967 (current rubles, billions).*

	1953	1954	1955	1956	1957	1958	1959	1960	1961	1962	1963	1964	1965	1966	1967
Total income of the agricultural population from farm wages and private plot activity[a]	18.6	n.a.	n.a.	n.a.	n.a.	26.6	25.2	26.0	26.6	29.4	29.5	32.3	34.8	36.8	38.3
a. Income of collective farm members and administrative-technical staff[b]	15.4	n.a.	n.a.	n.a.	n.a.	20.8	19.7	19.2	18.8	20.5	20.3	22.4	23.9	25.1	26.0
(1) Wages from the socialized sector[c]	4.4	5.6	7.3	8.3	7.9	7.8	7.7	7.2	7.7	8.4	8.7	10.0	11.5	12.8	13.7
(a) Money[d]	1.8	2.6	3.1	4.3	4.5	5.2	4.9	4.9	6.0	6.6	7.0	7.9	9.1	10.9	12.6
(b) In kind (valued in money)[e]	2.6	3.0	4.2	4.0	3.4	2.6	2.8	2.3	1.7	1.8	1.7	2.1	2.4	1.9	1.1
(2) Private plot income[f]	11.0	n.a.	n.a.	n.a.	n.a.	13.0	12.0	12.0	11.1	12.1	11.6	12.4	12.4	12.3	12.3
b. Income of state agricultural wage and salary workers[g]	3.2	n.a.	n.a.	n.a.	n.a.	5.8	5.5	6.8	7.8	8.9	9.2	9.9	10.9	11.7	12.3
(1) Wages[h]	1.9	n.a.	3.4	3.5	4.0	3.9	3.7	4.5	5.4	6.4	6.6	7.2	8.1	8.8	9.3
(2) Private plot income[i]	1.3	n.a.	n.a.	n.a.	n.a.	1.9	1.8	2.3	2.4	2.5	2.6	2.7	2.8	2.9	3.0

NOTES TO APPENDIX TABLE 1

a Derived for each year as the sum of income of collective farm members and administrative-technical staff (line a) plus income of state agricultural wage and salary workers (line b).

b Derived for each year as the sum of the two subitems.

c This series records pay in both money and products (the latter valued in state retail prices of the year) for work by collective farm members and by administrative-technical personnel in all areas of collective farm activity—in basic production, services, subsidiary enterprises, capital investment, and capital repair. Included are basic pay and bonuses, the latter including both regular supplements to pay such as vacation pay, aid to temporarily disabled members, maternity leave for women, supplements for skill levels, longevity, and the like, and supplements paid in connection with the final success of the agricultural year. Details of coverage are found in the following sources: *Narodnoe khoziaistvo . . . 1967*, p. 936; N. M. Studenkova, *Metodika ischisleniia sebestoimosti produktsii v kolkhozakh i sovkhozakh* (Moscow, 1965), p. 13; E. Kirillov, *Finansirovanie i kreditovanie sel'skogo khoziaistva* (Moscow, 1963), p. 136; E. Kirillov, *Finansirovanie i kreditovanie sel'skogo khoziaistva* (Moscow, 1968), pp. 145, 146, 151.

Estimates are derived as follows:

1953–1957: Estimated for each year on the basis of money pay and the share that money pay represented of total pay. For money pay, see line a(1) (a) of this table. Share data are presented in L. V. Zaverniaeva (ed.), *Osnovy ekonomiki sotsialisticheskogo sel'skogo khoziaistva* (Moscow, 1963), p. 226. The share for 1957 presented in the source has been increased somewhat (from 55 to 57 percent) with cognizance of the increase in the number of collective farms which calculated pay on the basis of man-days rather than on the basis of labor-day units of work.

1958–1962: V. G. Venzher, *Kolkhoznyi stroi na sovremennom etape* (Moscow, 1966), p. 80.

1963: Derived as a residual, the difference between the income of collective farm members from both pay for collective farm labor activity and the value of benefits from collectives' socialized fund of consumption, and the value of these benefits from the socialized fund of consumption only. These data are presented in *Ekonomika sel'skogo khoziaistva*, no. 4 (1967), p. 72.

1964: Derived from the statement that total pay to collective farmers for collective farm labor increased 14.9 percent in 1965 over the 1964 level (A. I. Arkhipov, *Plan, sbyt i initsiativa sel'skokhoziaistvennykh predpriiatii* (Moscow, 1967), p. 4. Official Soviet data for 1965 (see below) were used in the calculation here.

1965–1967: *Narodnoe khoziaistvo . . . 1967*, p. 466.

[d] 1953–1961: Derived for each year as the sum of money pay from current operating funds plus money pay from investment funds. These two series are derived in Appendix Table 3. See Appendix Table 3, line (6) for money pay from current operating funds, and see n. r of Appendix Table 3 for money pay from investment funds.

1962: Estimated at 78 percent of total pay (money and in kind), the share for 1961.

1963, 1965–1967: Estimated on the basis of statements regarding the share which money pay represented of total pay (money and in kind). For 1963, see V. A. Morozov, *Trudoden', den'gi i torgovlia na sele* (Moscow, 1965), pp. 139, 141; for 1965–1966, see *Ekonomicheskaia gazeta*, no. 40 (1968), p. 7 of insert; for 1967, see *Ekonomika sel'skogo khoziaistva*, no. 1 (1969), p. 10.

1964: Derived from the statement that collective farmers' money pay for collective farm labor increased 15.2 percent in 1965 over the 1964 level (Arkhipov, p. 4).

[e] Derived for each year as a residual, the difference between total pay (money and in kind) and money pay only.

[f] Derived for each year with the exception of 1967 (for which the 1966 level of plot income is assumed) as the product of Soviet sample family budget survey data regarding the average income of a collective farm family from its private plot times the mid-year number of collective farm households. Sample family budget survey statistics on the average income of a collective farm family from its plot are available as follows.

1958–1964: D'iachkov, p. 68.

1953: Derived on the basis of the statement that the collective farm family's average income from the private plot increased in 1964 by 39 percent over the 1953 level (*ibid.*, p. 69).

1965: Derived on the basis of the collective farm family's average total income (*ibid.*, p. 162), and the share represented by income from the plot (*ibid.*, p. 69).

1966: Derived on the basis of the statement that the average income of a collective farm family from its pay for work in the socialized sector exceeded its income from the plot by only 4 percent in 1966 (Laptev and Semin, p. 123). (For the computation here, the 1966 average income of a collective farm family from its pay for work in the socialized sector was derived as the quotient of dividing the total collective farm pay bill of 12.8 billion rubles (*Narodnoe khoziaistvo . . . 1967*, p. 466) by the mid-year number of collective farm households.)

For each year, n, the mid-year number of collective farm households was derived as the average of the number of households end-year n and the number of households end-year $n-1$. End-year data on the number of collective farm households are available as follows.

1952: *Narodnoe khoziaistvo . . . 1960*, p. 492.

1953, 1957: *Sel'skoe khoziaistvo SSSR*, p. 50.

1958–1962: *Narodnoe khoziaistvo . . . 1962*, p. 330.

1963: *Narodnoe khoziaistvo . . . 1963*, p. 341.

1964: *Narodnoe khoziaistvo . . . 1965*, p. 405.

1965, 1966: *Narodnoe khoziaistvo . . . 1967*, p. 466.

[g] 1953, 1958–1959, 1967: Estimated for each year on the basis of wages of state agricultural wage and salary workers, and the share that wages are estimated to have represented of income from both wages and private plots. For wages, see line b(1). Shares are approximated on the basis of shares established for 1960 and for 1966 in n. i. Thus, wages are estimated to have represented in 1953 three-fifths of the income of state agricultural wage and salary workers from both wages and private plots (a slight reduction from the 1960 level); two-thirds in 1958 and in 1959 (the 1960 level); and three-fourths in 1967 (the 1966 level).

1960–1966: Derived as the sum of income from wages and income from private plots.

[h] Derived for each year as the product of the annual average employment in state agriculture times the average annual wage in state agriculture. State agricultural employment is defined here to include all wage and salary workers working in Soviet agriculture with the *exception* of those wage and salary workers who are, in fact, hired personnel of collective farms. The average annual wage in state agriculture is assumed to be equal to the average annual wage of wage and salary workers employed in state farms and in subsidiary state agricultural enterprises.

The annual average number of wage and salary workers employed in state agriculture is derived as follows.

1955, 1960–1966: Derived for each year as the sum of the annual average number of wage and salary workers in state farms and subsidiary agricultural enterprises, in MTSs and RTSs (where applicable), and in service areas of agriculture and in veterinary science (*Trud v SSSR*, pp. 24–25).

1953, 1956–1959, 1967: Derived for each year as a residual, the difference between (a) the total annual average number of wage and salary workers in Soviet agriculture and (b) the number of wage and salary workers working in collective farms as hired personnel. Data regarding item (a), the total annual average number of wage and salary workers employed in Soviet agriculture, are available for 1953 and 1956–1957 in *Narodnoe khoziaistvo . . . 1958*, pp. 658–659; for 1958–1959 in *Narodnoe khoziaistvo . . . 1960*, p. 636; and for 1967 in *Narodnoe khoziaistvo . . . 1967*, p. 648. The annual average number of wage and salary workers working in collective farms as hired personnel, item (b), is estimated for 1953 and 1956–1967 at 100,000 annually, in fact, the level for 1950 and for 1955; for 1958–1959 at 120,000 annually, approximately the level for 1960; and for 1967 at 200,000, the number available from preliminary data for the year (*Trud v SSSR*, pp. 24–26).

Average monthly wage data for wage and salary workers employed in state farms and in state subsidiary agricultural enterprises were adjusted to an annual basis. Sources are as follows:

1953, 1956: Computed by applying to official data for 1960 (below) an index, 1953–1963, of state farm wages presented in Z. A. Samedzade, *Proizvoditel'nost' truda v sovkhozakh* (Baku, 1966), p. 112.

1955, 1960–1966: *Trud v SSSR*, pp. 138–139.

1957, 1959: International Labour Office, *Year Book of Labour Statistics— 1967* (Geneva, 1967), p. 622.

1958: *Narodnoe khoziaistvo . . . 1964*, p. 555.

1967: *Narodnoe khoziaistvo . . . 1967*, p. 648.

[i] Data on income of state agricultural wage and salary workers from their private plots are obtained, as are similar data for collective farm members, by means of sample family budget surveys conducted by the Central Statistical Administration. Information collected in the surveys of state agricultural worker families is even more meagerly revealed and discussed in Soviet texts than is that collected from collective farm member families. Thus, estimates presented in Appendix Table 1 are necessarily crude and are built upon estimates which can be derived for 1960 and for 1966.

Estimates are derived as follows:

1960, 1966: Derived for each year as a residual, the difference between estimated total income from wages, state benefits, and private plots, and estimated income from wages and state benefits only. First, income from wages and state benefits is estimated on the basis of income from wages (line b(1) of table) and the assumption that wages represent at least 75 percent of wages plus state benefits—in fact, the relationship for all wage and salary workers in the national economy (*Narodnoe khoziaistvo . . . 1967*, p. 657). Second, income from wages, state benefits, and private plots is derived on the basis of these derived estimates of income from wages and state benefits only, and the share that wage and benefits income represented of total income of a state farm family from wages, benefits, and private plots—in 1960, 72 percent and in 1966, 80 percent (*Voprosy ekonomiki*, no. 11 (1968), p. 47).

Thus, in 1960, of total income from wages and private plots, wages represented 67 percent and plots 33 percent; in 1966 wages constituted 75 percent and plots 25 percent.

In summary:		BILLION RUBLES	
		1960	*1966*
	Total income of state agricultural wage and salary workers from wages, benefits, and private plots	8.3	14.6
less	Income from wages and state benefits	6.0	11.7
	Wages	(4.5)	(8.8)
	State benefits	(1.5)	(2.9)
equals	Income of private plots	2.3	2.9

1953, 1958–1959, 1967: Derived for each year as a residual, the difference between income of state agricultural wage and salary workers from both wages and private plots, and income from wages only.

1961–1965: Interpolated between estimates for 1960 and 1966.

Appendix Table 2 : *Average wages and days worked in industry, state agricultural enterprises, and collective farms, 1953–1967.**

	1953	1954	1955	1956	1957	1958	1959	1960	1961	1962	1963	1964	1965	1966	1967
a. Average annual wages, current rubles															
(1) Industry[a]	917	926	940	958	1,006	1,045	1,074	1,096	1,134	1,159	1,181	1,206	1,240	1,282	1,344
(2) State farms and subsidiary state agricultural enterprises[b]	494	n.a.	559	588	600	637	654	647	696	793	805	847	894	958	1,007
(3) Collective farms[†c]	164	197	246	259	263	299	284	276	310	363	376	445	525	598	647
b. Average number of days worked															
(1) Industry[d]	275	274	273	272	267	268	266	267	264	263	264	266	266	266	266
(2) State farms and subsidiary state agricultural enterprises[e]	235	n.a.	235	235	240	240	245	240	235	235	230	230	230	230	230
(3) Collective farms[f]	200	203	200	186	188	192	203	197	193	199	196	196	196	196	195
c. Average wages per day worked, current rubles															
(1) Industry[g]	3.33	3.38	3.44	3.52	3.77	3.90	4.04	4.10	4.30	4.41	4.47	4.53	4.66	4.82	5.05
(2) State farms and subsidiary state agricultural enterprises[h]	2.10	n.a.	2.38	2.50	2.50	2.65	2.67	2.70	2.96	3.37	3.50	3.68	3.89	4.18	4.39
(3) Collective farms[†i]	0.82	0.97	1.23	1.39	1.40	1.56	1.40	1.40	1.61	1.82	1.92	2.27	2.68	3.05	3.32

* All data for agriculture (as for industry) refer only to work and earnings in the *socialized sector*. Excluded is all income from private plots. Data on collective farms are further restricted (for comparability with industry and state agriculture) to work and earnings of able-bodied workers only (males 16 to 59 years, females 16 to 54 years).
† Includes money and in-kind payments (valued at state retail prices of the year).

NOTES TO APPENDIX TABLE 2

[a] Official data regarding the average wage of wage and salary workers in industry are available for all the years except 1953, 1954, 1956, 1957, and 1959. Estimates for these years can be calculated by applying data regarding percent changes to years for which official data are available. Sources are as follows:

1953: *Pravda*, April 27, 1954.

1954: L. S. Bliakhman, *Proizvoditel'nost' i oplata truda v period razvernutogo stroitel'stva kommunizma* (Leningrad, 1964), pp. 151–152.

1955, 1960–1966: *Trud v SSSR*, pp. 138–139.

1956–1957: D. N. Karpukhin, *Sootnoshenie rosta proizvoditel'nosti truda i zarabotnoi platy* (Moscow, 1963), p. 108.

1958: *Narodnoe khoziaistvo . . . 1964*, p. 555.

1959: Estimated on the assumption that the average wage of wage and salary workers of industry increased over the 1958 level by the same percentage as did wages of industrial wage workers only (International Labor Office, p. 517).

[b] 1953, 1956: Computed by applying to official data for 1960 an index, 1953–1963, of state farm wages presented in Samedzade, p. 112.

1955, 1960–1966: *Trud v SSSR*, pp. 138–139.

1957, 1959: International Labor Office, p. 622.

1958: *Narodnoe khoziaistvo . . . 1964*, p. 555.

1967: *Narodnoe khoziaistvo . . . 1967*, p. 648.

[c] 1953–1965: Derived by applying an index of annual wages for work in the socialized sector by able-bodied collective farm workers (T. I. Zaslavskaia, *Raspredelenie po trudu v kolkhozakh* (Moscow, 1966), p. 38; *Ekonomika sel'skogo khoziaistva*, no. 3 (1967), p. 20) to an estimated wage for 1960. The 1960 estimate is derived as the product of the average number of man-days worked per able-bodied collective farmer in 1960 (E. S. Karnaukhova (ed.), *Puti povysheniia proizvoditel'nosti truda v sel'skom khoziaistve SSSR* (Moscow, 1964), p. 64) times the average pay per man-day in 1960 (see line c(3), this table).

1966–1967: Derived for each year as the product of the average number of man-days worked per able-bodied collective farmer, line b(3), times the average pay per man-day, line c(3).

[d] Official data based on enterprise reports of time actually worked by industrial production workers are assumed applicable for all workers of industry.

1953: Assumed at the 1952 level. For 1952, see *Narodnoe khoziaistvo . . . 1962*, p. 131.

1954: Arbitrarily assumed between the levels for 1952 and 1955.

1955–1957: Shishkin, p. 69.

1958–1962: *Narodnoe khoziaistvo . . . 1962*, p. 131.

1963–1964: *Narodnoe khoziaistvo . . . 1964*, p. 138.

1965: *Narodnoe khoziaistvo . . . 1967*, p. 209.

1966–1967: Arbitrarily assumed at the 1965 level.

e 1955, 1959: Shishkin, p. 105.

1953, 1956–1958, 1960–1965, 1967: Arbitrarily assumed.

1966: Calculated from Laptev and Semin, p. 102.

f 1953–1959, 1961–1965: Derived for each year as the quotient of the average annual wage of able-bodied collective farm workers, line a(3), divided by the average wage per day worked, line c(3).

1960: Karnaukhova, p. 64.

1966: Assumed at the 1965 level.

1967: *Vestnik statistiki*, no. 8 (1969), p. 18.

g Derived for each year as the quotient of the average annual wage, line a(1), divided by the annual average number of days worked, line b(1).

h Derived for each year as the quotient of the average annual wage, line a(2), divided by the annual average number of days worked, line b(2).

i 1953–1957: Derived by applying an index of the average pay per man-day (Zaslavskaia, p. 38) to the average pay per man-day in 1958 (see 1958, below).

1958–1964: Cited by Suslov to "Materialy k vsesoiuznomu nauchnomu soveshchaniiu po problemam ekonomicheskogo stimulirovaniia intensifikatsii sel'skokhoziaistvennogo proizvodstva," MGU, 1966, Part I, p. 31, in I. F. Suslov (ed.), *Effektivnost' sel'skokhoziaistvennogo proizvodstva* (Moscow, 1967), p. 211.

1965–1967: *Narodnoe khoziaistvo . . . 1967*, p. 466.

Appendix Table 3 : *Income and expenditures of collective farms, 1950, 1952–1961 (current rubles, billions).*

	1950	1952	1953	1954	1955	1956	1957	1958	1959	1960	1961
a. Money income[a]	3.42	4.28	4.96	6.33	7.56	9.46	9.52	13.20	13.68	13.34	13.57
b. Money expenditures[b]	3.42	4.28	4.96	6.33	7.56	9.46	9.52	13.20	13.68	13.34	13.57
(1) Obligatory payments to the state[c]	0.47	0.69	0.75	0.76	0.89	1.06	1.13	1.31	1.53	1.57	1.27
(a) Income tax[d]	0.25	0.42	n.a.	n.a.	0.63	0.75	0.85	1.03	1.24	1.21	0.93
(b) Insurance premiums[e]	0.12	0.17	n.a.	n.a.	0.16	0.21	0.18	0.18	0.20	0.28	0.28
(c) Indirect taxes and collections[f]	0.10	0.10	0.10	0.10	0.10	0.10	0.10	0.10	0.09	0.08	0.06
(2) Repayment of long-term loans[g]	0.12	0.12	0.15	0.17	0.21	←—— not applicable ——→					
(3) Deductions from income[h]	0.59	0.93	1.09	1.40	1.69	2.19	2.10	3.67	4.02	3.82	3.71
(a) For replenishment of indivisible funds[i]	0.55	0.74	0.87	1.12	1.32	1.67	1.68	3.04	3.33	3.20	3.20
(b) For replenishment of working funds[j]	0	0.13	0.15	0.19	0.23	0.34	0.22	0.40	0.33	0.29	0.10
(c) For replenishment of special funds[k]	0.04	0.06	0.07	0.09	0.14	0.18	0.20	0.23	0.36	0.33	0.41
(i) Fund of aid and pensions[l]	0	0	0	0.01	0.04	0.04	0.04	0.06	0.11	0.15	0.18
(ii) Fund for cultural-welfare needs[m]	0.04	0.06	0.07	0.08	0.10	0.14	0.16	0.17	0.25	0.17	0.21
(iii) Fund for construction of houses for members[n]	←—— not applicable ——→									0.01	0.02
(4) Production expenditures[o]	1.03	1.05	1.17	1.35	1.63	1.93	1.89	3.15	3.33	3.22	2.80
(5) Administrative-economic expenditures[p]	0.03	0.04	0.05	0.06	0.08	0.10	0.10	0.13	0.14	0.13	0.14
(6) Labor payments (from current operating funds)*[q]	1.18	1.45	1.75	2.59	3.06	4.18	4.30	4.94	4.66	4.60	5.65

* In addition, since the beginning of 1956, labor payments have also been made to members from investment funds. See n. q for explanation. These payments are estimated for 1956 at 0.16 billion rubles; 1957, 0.19; 1958, 0.21; 1960, 0.34; 1961, 0.35.[r]

NOTES TO APPENDIX TABLE 3

[a] 1950, 1953, 1955–1957: *Narodnoe khoziaistvo ... 1958*, p. 498.
1952, 1958–1961: *Narodnoe khoziaistvo ... 1962*, p. 342.
1954: N. Kisman and I. Slavnyi, *Sovetskie finansy v piatoi piatiletke* (Moscow, 1956), p. 61.

[b] In financial accounts of collective farms, money expenditures for the year equal total money income for the year (N. I. Kovrov, *Finansovoe khoziaistvo kolkhozov i sovkhozov* (Moscow, 1964), p. 65).

[c] 1950, 1959–1961: Derived for each year as the sum of the three subitems.
1952–1953, 1955–1958: Estimated on the basis of statements regarding the share which obligatory payments made to the government by collective farms constituted of the collectives' total money income: for 1952–1953 and 1956, see S. I. Neden and M. I. Nesmiia (eds.), *Voprosy sebestoimosti i rentabel'nosti v kolkhozakh* (Moscow, 1959), p. 35; for 1955, see *Finansy SSSR*, no. 10 (1957), p. 34; for 1957–1958, see *Den'gi i kredit*, no. 9 (1959), p. 8.
1954: Derived from the statement that obligatory payments by collective farms in 1956 were 39 percent greater than in 1954 (Neden and Nesmiia, p. 23).

[d] 1950, 1955–1960: G. F. Dundukov (ed.), *Gosudarstvennyi biudzhet SSSR i biudzhety soiuznykh respublik* (Moscow, 1962), p. 8.
1952: N. Laptev (ed.), *Finansy i sotsialisticheskoe stroitel'stvo* (Moscow, 1957), p. 66.
1961: G. V. Darkov (ed.), *Gosudarstvennyi biudzhet SSSR i biudzhety soiuznykh respublik* (Moscow, 1966), p. 11.

[e] 1950: Derived by applying to collective farms' obligatory and voluntary property insurance coverage of 19.68 billion rubles in 1950 (Laptev, p. 356), an estimated premium rate of 1.2 percent. This is the rate for 1955 and for 1956 established on the basis of premium payments for 1955 and for 1956, as estimated in this table, and collectives' total coverage under both types of insurance, 14.39 billion rubles in 1955 and 16.70 billion rubles in 1956 (*ibid.*). This technique of estimation is considered acceptable for two reasons: (1) there were no known changes in rates between 1950 and 1956, and (2) the percentage distribution of total coverage between obligatory and voluntary insurance remained unchanged with 83–84 percent under obligatory and the remaining 16–17 percent under voluntary coverage (*ibid.*). The second point is important because voluntary rates are much higher than obligatory rates.
1952, 1955–1958: Derived for each year as a residual, the difference between total obligatory payments of collectives and the sum of their payments of income taxes and indirect taxes and collections.
1959: Derived as a residual, the difference between collective farms' total payments for all types of property insurance of 0.767 billion rubles for 1956–1959 (*Finansy SSSR*, no. 1 (1965), p. 52) and their total payments for 1956–1958 as estimated in this table.
1960–1961: Collective farms' total payments for all types of property insur-

ance amounted to 1.3665 billion rubles for 1960–1963 (*ibid.*). This total can be spread over the four years with little precision. The revaluation of assets in 1958 and 1959, an apparent delay or postponement of the increased insurance costs incurred with the acquisition of machinery and other property in the MTS reorganization of 1958–1959, and an adjustment in some insurance rates charged collective farms in 1960 prohibit the application of a single rate to total coverage data which are available for 1958–1961 in A. G. Zverev, *Natsional'nyi dokhod i finansy SSSR* (Moscow, 1961), pp. 255–256.

For 1960, the entry is derived as the year's residual entry of the table, since for this classic year the general size of each entry in collective farms' accounts is known, and for most items the exact number is known.

Similarly for 1961: each entry, with the exceptions of insurance payments and deductions from income for replenishment of working capital, is known. For this year the residual was split arbitrarily with cognizance of special problems in the working capital entry as detailed below (see n. j).

ᶠ Included here are "miscellaneous collections." Texts identify these as being mostly fees on collective farm market sales. The remainder is probably fines of various kinds and penalties for underfulfilling plans, especially livestock plans (N. I. Khmelev, *Finansovoe khoziaistvo kolkhozov* (Moscow, 1946), pp. 91–92; D. M. Iarkov, *Finansirovanie i kreditovanie sel'skokhoziaistvennykh predpriiatii* (Moscow, 1957), p. 215). With the major revision in collective farms' accounts in 1960, texts now list these collections in "all-economic expenditures" rather than in "taxes, insurance, and collections." For this table their listing as obligatory payments is continued, however.

Estimates are presented below, and for each year the sum of the two line items is entered in the table above.

	1950	1952–1958 Annually	1959	1960	1961
	(MILLION RUBLES)				
Collective farm market fees	50	70	68	65	40
Other collections	50	30	25	20	20
Total	100	100	90	80	60

While the above estimates of fines and penalties are purely notional, fees charged on collective farm markets are approximated as follows:

1950, 1955–1961: Derived for each year as a residual, the difference between estimated market fees paid by all sellers and those paid by farm households (as sellers) only. Total market fees paid by all sellers are approximated on the basis of republic budget revenue from these fees (Dundukov, p. 68; Darkov, p. 70), and the share of total fees deducted to the republic budget—an estimated 80 percent for 1950 and 40 percent for 1955–1961. (The higher share for 1950 cannot be documented but is indicated from a study of the market turnover series and the budget series for revenue from market fees. The lower share is included in D. A. Allakhverdian and N. N. Liubimov, *Finansy SSSR* (Moscow, 1958), p. 231.) Fees paid by farm household sellers in collective farm markets are estimated at an annual level of 50 million rubles based on (1) the prevalent journal statements regarding the number of collective farmers to be found daily in the markets—"700,000 collective farmers, a non–productive expenditure of more than 250 million man-days in a year" (*Voprosy ekonomiki*, no. 2 (1962), p. 59), and (2) the daily fee rates (D. V. Burmistrov (ed.), *Spravochnik nalogovogo rabotnika* (Moscow, 1954), pp. 190–191; M. P. Zakharov (ed.), *Biudzhet i biudzhetnye komissii mestnykh sovetov* (Moscow, 1965), p. 135). Fees levied on sellers in collective farm markets vary from ten kopeks to one ruble based on the type of space used to conduct sales. A flat rate of 20 kopeks was assumed here on the basis that collective farmers would sell for the most part from the ground and hand rather than from wagons or trucks.

1952–1954: Arbitrarily estimated at the level derived for 1955–1958.

[g] Through the end of 1955, repayment of long-term loans was met from current money income and beginning in 1956, from investment funds (*Planovoe khoziaistvo*, no. 3 (1957), pp. 27–28). Thus, for this table the entry appears as a separate line only for years 1950–1955.

1950: Estimated at the 1952 level.

1952–1953: Approximated from data in *Vestnik statistiki*, no. 2 (1960), p. 91, by the following technique:

long-term loans outstanding end-year n
plus long-term extensions in year $n + 1$
minus long-term loans outstanding end-year $n + 1$
equals implied repayments in year $n + 1$

This technique, however, does not record interest payments and would count any long-term debts written off (cancelled without payment) by the government in the course of a year as repayments. This policy of financial aid to collective farms which was a part of the government's program of assisting weak and inefficient collective farms in the early sixties after abolition of the MTSs is not known to have been applied in the early fifties.

1954–1955: S. Koriunov, *Nedelimye fondy i kapital'nye vlozheniia kolkhozov* (Moscow, 1960), p. 23.

[h] Derived for each year as the sum of the three subitems.

[i] 1950, 1955: *Narodnoe khoziaistvo . . . 1958*, p. 494.

1952–1953, 1956–1959: *Narodnoe khoziaistvo . . . 1959*, p. 423.

1954: Koriunov, p. 23.

1960–1961: *Narodnoe khoziaistvo . . . 1962*, p. 330.

[j] 1950: Prior to 1952, collective farms set aside no monetary working funds for the next year's needs. Seasonal needs in the first half of the new year were covered by short-term loans from the state. In-kind funds of seed and fodder were maintained, however. Beginning in 1952, at the recommendation of the government, collective farms set aside "carry-over funds" of both purchased materials for production and demand deposits to meet the production needs of the early part of the new year (V. N. Semenov, *Rol' finansov v ukreplenii ekonomiki kolkhozov* (Moscow, 1967), p. 192).

1952, 1954–1955: Estimated for each year at 3 percent of total money income, the share for 1953 and approximately the share for 1956.

1953, 1956–1960: Estimated on the basis of statements regarding the share which deductions from monetary income for replenishment of working funds constituted of collective farms' total money income; for 1953, see Neden and Nesmiia, p. 36; for 1956–1960, see G. P. Kosiachenko (ed.), *Denezhnye dokhody kolkhozov i differentsial'naia renta* (Moscow, 1963), p. 136.

1961: Arbitrarily estimated at 0.1 billion rubles. This allowance, though out of line with deductions in preceding years, appears not so unlikely when consideration is given the accounting system changes of 1960 which authorized the use of investment funds as well as current money income as a source of replenishing working funds. This funding change is explained in R. V. Alekseeva and A. P. Voronin, *Nakoplenie i razvitie kolkhoznoi sobstvennosti* (Moscow, 1963), pp. 97–98. Subsequent texts on the financial accounting system of collective farms substantiated this explanation (Kovrov, p. 74; Kirillov (1963), p. 144).

ᵏ 1950, 1952: Estimated for each year at 1.3 percent of money income, the share for 1953.

1953, 1959: Markovich, p. 27.

1954–1958: Derived as the sum of the subitems.

1960: Kosiachenko, p. 220.

1961: Estimated on the basis of the statement that the deduction from monetary income for replenishment of special funds constituted 3 percent of collective farms' money income (Alekseeva and Voronin, p. 88).

¹ The fund of aid and pension insurance furnishes money for pensions for the aged and invalids, allowances for temporary illnesses and maternity leaves, holidays, ticket purchases, and the like. These pensions are not to be confused with the pension coverage extended to collective farm members, beginning in 1965, under a central union fund of social insurance. From late 1964, the latter item appears as a separate entry in collective farms' accounts.

1950, 1952–1953: In the fifties, the aid fund consisted mostly of in-kind funds of feed and fodder for the use of members. There was no system of monetary pensions. No deductions from money income into the fund are assumed to have been made.

1954: An allowance of 10 million rubles is made with consideration of the 1953 increase in procurement prices for agricultural products which perhaps at last allowed collective farms the luxury of extending or planning for monetary aid and benefits for their members.

1955, 1957–1958: Calculated from A. V. Rumiantseva, *Obshchestvennye fondy kolkhozov* (Moscow, 1960), p. 34. Here it has been assumed that Rumiantseva has misread her line entries in that the number she presents as collective farms' money deductions into all socialized funds of consumption is, in fact, their money deduction into only the first section of this account, namely, the aid and pension fund. The assumption is supported by her text and the size of the numbers.

1956: Assumed equal to the level of 1955 and 1957.

1959: Derived as a residual, the difference between total deductions for replenishment of special funds and the deduction for replenishment of the fund for cultural-welfare needs only.

1960: Kosiachenko, p. 220.

1961: Estimated on the assumption that deductions to the aid and pension fund represented 45 percent of total deductions to all special funds, as was the case in 1960.

ᵐ From the fund for cultural-welfare needs are financed the current operating and maintenance expenditures of collective farms for nurseries, schools, libraries, clubs, radio stations, the purchase of books and magazines, and education of cadres. Capital investment in the above facilities is financed from investment funds and not from the cultural-welfare fund.

1950, 1952–1953: The whole of deductions from money income for replenishment of special funds is assumed to have been for cultural-welfare needs. The derivation of the estimates for these four years is explained in n. k above.

1954–1955: Estimated for each year at 1.3 percent of money income, the share for 1953.

1956: *Ekonomika sel'skogo khoziaistva*, no. 7 (1957), p. 37.

1957–1960: Estimated on the basis of statements regarding the share which deductions from monetary income for replenishment of the special fund for cultural-welfare needs constituted of collective farms' total money income (Kosiachenko, p. 136). The entry for 1960 is also explicitly given (*ibid.*, p. 220).

1961: Estimated on the assumption that deductions from money income for replenishment of the fund for cultural-welfare needs represented 51 percent of total deductions to all special funds, as was the case in 1960.

ⁿ This fund is assumed to have been introduced in 1960 when numerous changes in the system of collective farms' accounts were incorporated. It is listed in Alekseeva and Voronin, p. 88.

1960: Derived from official data presented in Kosiachenko, pp. 136, 220.

1961: Estimated on the assumption that deductions to the fund represented 4 percent of total deductions to all special funds, as was the case for 1960.

ᵒ Production expenditures record monetary expenditures for (1) pay of work and current production services performed for collective farms by MTSs, RTSs, or *Soiuzsel'khoztekhnika*; (2) pay of hired labor—noncollective farm members who are hired for current repair of buildings, machines, equipment, and agricultural inventory; for work in subsidiary enterprises of collectives, and for agricultural labor at harvest time; and (3) purchases of materials for current operations—mineral fertilizer, fuel and oil, herbicides and insecticides, seed, fodder, electricity, raw materials for subsidiary enterprises run by the collectives, small inventory such as pitchforks, and current repair of buildings, tractors, agricultural machinery, transport means, and equipment. Production expenditures do not record expenditures of seed, feed, and other materials produced and used by the collective farms.

1950: Estimated at 30 percent of money expenditures, the share reported for 1951 (*Voprosy ekonomiki*, no. 1 (1952), p. 41).

1952: Estimated on the basis of the statement that production expenses amounted to 24.6 percent of money income (Neden and Nesmiia, p. 37).

1953–1955: Estimated on the basis of the 1952 entry here and an index of production expenditures for 1952–1956 (*ibid.*, p. 52).

1956: Since the text accompanying the above cited index stated that production expenditures increased from 1952 to 1956 "by almost 86 percent," the 1956 index number of 186 was not used here. Instead, the 1956 entry was estimated on the basis of the statement that production expenditures amounted to 20.4 percent of money income in 1956 (*ibid.*, p. 37). This number is more in line with an estimate of 1.88 billion rubles which can be calculated from another source in which a listing of production expenses is presented together with the share that this subtotal represents of total production expenses of the year (Alekseeva and Voronin, p. 200).

1957: Estimated on the basis of the statement that production expenses amounted to 19.9 percent of money income (P. S. Buianov *et al.* (eds.), *Razvitie obshchestvennogo khoziaistva kolkhozov* (Moscow, 1960), p. 166).

1958–1960: Estimated for each year on the basis of short-term credit extended by Gosbank to collective farms for production expenses, and the share that this credit represented of collectives' total production expenditures. For credit extensions for 1958 and 1960, see A. Nadezhdina (ed.), *Gosudarstvennyi bank SSSR k XXII s"ezdu KPSS* (Moscow, 1961), p. 61. For 1959, see Alekseeva and Voronin, p. 83. For shares, 1958–1960, see *Den'gi i kredit*, no. 7 (1961), p. 33.

1961: Kosiachenko, p. 25.

ᵖ Recorded here are two categories of expenses—all-economic or all-farm (*obshchekhoziaistvennye*) and administrative-governmental (*administrativno-upravlencheskie*). Accounting texts usually define the two categories as a whole, but from a study of several definitions (especially that presented in Kovrov, p. 62) the following itemization has been compiled. Included in all-economic expenditures are expenditures for maintenance of offices and storage facilities, current repair of these facilities and their equipment, and for small inventory; expenditures for current repair of roads, bridges, means of communication; insurance and amortization of general use and cultural-welfare structures (schools, clubs, and the like); miscellaneous collections, such as fees in collective farm market trade, fines, penalties, duties, interest on loans. (For this table miscellaneous collections are counted as obligatory payments to the state.)

Included in administrative-governmental expenditures are expenditures for stationery, postal charges, telegraph, telephone, lights, heat, travel allowances, maintenance of light automobiles for administrative officials, and money pay of the chairman, accountant, and other hired specialists.

Having included in administrative-economic expenditures the latter item— pay of the chairman and others—the accounting texts then promptly list it as a *separate* expenditure item in the ubiquitous table regarding "money income and its distribution." If wages are counted within administrative economic expenditures, certainly no more than base wages are counted, for all supplementary pay and pay from accrued work units are counted in the members' pay entry in collective farm accounts (Kirillov (1968), pp. 145–147).

As calculated for this table, the entry for administrative-economic expenditures is defined as excluding any pay to chairmen, specialists, and other administrative people. Instead, the pay of these people is counted in the table's final line item.

No decipherable data regarding administrative-economic expenditures are available. Estimates for this table are calculated for each year at one percent of collective farms' money income, in line with the collective farm statute which authorizes no more than 2 percent of annual money income for these expenses (Iarkov, p. 216).

q The labor payments entry records collective farms' money payments for the labor of members and staff. Until the abolition of MTSs in 1958, labor-day payments to MTS tractor brigades were also included in this entry, an expenditure of 55 million rubles in 1954 and of 87 million rubles in 1955 (N. Liapin *et al.* (eds.), *Sbornik statei po ekonomicheskim voprosam* (Moscow, 1957), p. 157). Included in the entry are members' base pay and supplemental pay (bonuses, vacation pay, supplements for skill levels, longevity, and the like) and supplemental pay of administrative-technical personnel as well (Kirillov (1968), p. 145). As derived for this table, the entry is calculated to include both base and supplemental pay of members and administrative-technical personnel.

Through the end of 1955, the entry counts pay for both current production labor and capital investment–capital repair labor of members. From the beginning of 1956 through the end of 1959, the coverage excludes the money pay of members engaged in certain capital investment activities, namely, construction of livestock shelters and other structures and the planting and preparation of perennial plantings, such as orchards and forests. These labor payments were financed from investment funds (*Ekonomika sel'skogo khoziaistva*, no. 1 (1960), p. 24).

Beginning in 1960, the entry is assumed to record only pay for current production labor and to exclude *all* pay for labor in capital investment–capital repair activities. (No statute authorizing the use of investment funds for the payment of members' labor in all investment activities can be cited. It is thought, however, that the extensive 1960 changes in collective farms' financial account system (see Alekseeva and Voronin, pp. 98–99) must have included such authorization, answering in part the repeated criticism in Soviet economic literature of the split financing and the nonsensical inclusions and exclusions of the former scheme. Indeed, texts on collective farms' financial accounts now show these labor payments to be covered by investment rather than current operating funds (Kovrov, p. 65; Kirillov (1963), p. 141). Estimates of these investment funds used to finance labor payments are derived in n. r below.

Estimates for labor payments financed from current operating funds are derived as follows:

1950, 1952–1960: Derived for each year as the table's residual entry, the difference between total money outlay and the sum of expenditures for obligatory payments to the state, repayment of long-term loans (where applicable), deductions from income, production expenses, and administrative-economic expenditures. It is to be noted that these residuals are almost identical with estimates of 1.84 billion rubles for 1953, 5.00 for 1958, 4.68 for 1959, and 4.60 for 1960, which can be derived for the line item on the basis of advances of procurement organizations to collective farms and the share which the part of these advances earmarked for labor payments (an automatic 50 percent of total advances; *Ekonomika sel'skogo khoziaistva*, no. 5 (1963), pp. 19–20) constituted of the general fund for money pay of labor. For advances data for 1953, 1958, and 1960, see Nadezhdina, pp. 61, 71; for 1959, see L. N. Kassirov, *Oborotnye sredstva kolkhozov* (Moscow, 1962), p. 90. For share data, all years, see Nadezhdina, p. 72.

1961: *Ekonomika sel'skogo khoziaistva*, no. 11 (1962), p. 9. The number is assumed to exclude labor payments from investment funds.

ᵣ 1950, 1952–1955: As explained in n. q, investment accounts were not used as a source of funds for paying members for their labor in capital investment–capital repairs activities prior to the beginning of 1956.

1956–1958: Koriunov, p. 23.

1959: Estimated on the assumption that investment funds used to finance labor payments to members increased over the 1958 level by 17 percent as did, in fact, expenditures for the two applicable items of investment—construction and plantings (Kh. E. Potapov and N. G. Ovchinnikov (eds.), *Povyshenie urovnia razvitiia kolkhoznogo proizvodstva* (Moscow, 1961), p. 91).

1960–1961: As explained in n. q, beginning in 1960 all money payments to members for their labor in investment–capital repair activities are assumed to have been financed from investment funds. For each year these labor payments are approximated roughly at 15 percent of collective farms' expenditures for construction of buildings and shelters, plantings, irrigation and melioration, construction of roads and bridges, manufacture of inventory for the farms' own use, and capital repair (Alekseeva and Voronin, p. 105).

10 : Progress on Mechanization in Soviet Agriculture

Folke Dovring

Soviet agriculture in recent years has become richly endowed with mechanical means of operation. How richly is sometimes overlooked by western observers unaware of comparative data from other countries and impressed with the apparent shortage of essential inputs in Soviet agriculture. To show how this latter state of affairs derives from inefficient use of machines and other inputs rather than from any shortage of supply in the quantitative sense, some comparisons with other countries will be necessary; for obvious reasons, the United States will serve as principal case for such comparison.

I

Let us start with a quick overview of the whole investment and farm expense situation to get a general frame within which to characterize the mechanization issue. Because of the special sources available for 1959, that year will be treated as a benchmark and will receive somewhat more attention than individual preceding and subsequent years.

Investment in Soviet agriculture is given in official statistics as shown in Tables 1 and 2. Agriculture's share in net material product has been somewhat more than one-fifth through the years since the late 1950's. Its share in gross productive fixed capital formation has been somewhat smaller (as is normal in most countries), varying between 15 and 20 percent of total gross productive fixed investment since, at least, the mid-fifties. More significant is the share which fixed investment in agriculture is of the national product, since most of the investments draw on the other sectors (see Table

Table 1 : *USSR, national income and investment (billions of rubles, current prices).*

| | NET MATERIAL PRODUCT | | | GROSS PRODUCTIVE FIXED CAPITAL FORMATION | | |
Year	Total	Agriculture	Other	Total	Agriculture	Agriculture as Percent of Total
1955	98.5			19.6	3.8	19.4
1956	106.2			22.4	4.0	17.9
1957	112.8			25.3	4.2	16.6
1958	127.7	30.8	96.9	29.4	4.7	16.0
1959	136.2	28.9	107.3	33.3	5.0	15.0
1960	145.0	29.7	115.3	35.9	5.2	14.5
1961	152.9	32.1	120.8	37.5	5.7	15.2
1962	164.6	37.0	127.6	39.3	6.3	16.0
1963	168.8	34.7	134.1	41.3	6.9	16.7
1964	181.3	39.0	142.3	45.0	8.2	18.2
1965	193.5	43.6	149.9	48.7	8.7	17.9
1966	207.4	50.3	157.1	52.4	9.5	18.1
1967	225.5	50.7	174.8	56.7	10.2	18.0
1968	243.1	52.0	171.1	61.3	11.4	18.6

SOURCES: *Yearbook of National Accounts Statistics* (New York: United Nations, 1966), pp. 598 ff.; for 1965, 1966, 1967, and 1968: *Narodnoe khoziaistvo . . . 1968*, pp. 523, 525, 570.

Table 2 : *USSR, fixed productive capital formation in agriculture (millions of rubles, comparable prices).*

Year	Total	Buildings and Installations	Orchards, Vineyards, and Other Permanent Plantations	Tractors, Means of Transportation, Agricultural Machines, Implements, and Inventory Not Included Above
1959	5,124	2,966	143	2,015
1960	5,209	3,309	159	1,741
1961	5,733	3,610	208	1,915
1962	6,358	3,988	208	2,162
1963	7,025	4,288	233	2,504
1964	8,301	5,022	227	3,052
1965	8,708	5,459	254	3,249
1966	9,521	6,179	321	3,342
1967	10,197	6,616	349	3,581
1968	11,435	7,435	370	4,000

SOURCES: *Narodnoe khoziaistvo . . . 1965*, p. 537; *1967*, p. 624; and *1968*, p. 526. On machine costs: Ezhevskii, pp. 46–56.

Note that the last column may include some of the repair costs, part of which are entered into the second quadrant of the input-output tables and thus among capital formation, according to M. Eidel'man, "Kak otrazhaetsia v mezhotraslevom balanse kapital'nyi remont oborudovaniia," *Vestnik statistiki*, no. 4 (1968), pp. 51–54.

2).[1] This share has varied between 4 and 4.5 percent. This proportion is in itself startlingly high and has few parallels elsewhere in the world. It becomes even more so when added to the share which annual production expenditures draw from the nonagricultural sectors.

Expenditures for current external production inputs in Soviet agriculture are nowhere shown in routine tabulations. Some data can be inferred from the input-output tables of 1959 and 1966, and tentative ones for 1962 and 1964.[2] Removing from the specifications the items coming from agriculture itself (intra-industry turnover) and those from the light industries (as containing sizable quantities of agricultural products being returned to agriculture), the following numbers are found (billions of rubles, current prices):

1959	6.8 or 7.3 (two alternative tabulations)
1962	7.8
1964	8.9
1966	9.0

These data are on the low side, because all of the light and food industries were excluded. The totals break down as somewhat less than half in heavy industry, with the balance in transport and trade in 1959 and 1962, and the reverse proportions in 1964 and 1966. When these data on current production expenditures are combined with those for fixed capital formation shown in Table 2, it becomes clear that external inputs into Soviet agriculture were of the magnitude of 11–12 billion rubles in 1959, 13–14 billion in 1962,

[1] Comparison of time series data will show that increase of livestock inventory accounts for a minor part only of capital accumulation in recent years; see for instance *Strana Sovetov za 50 let* (Moscow, 1967), pp. 35, 37, indicating no great change in this item since 1955.

[2] Summary versions of the 1959 and 1962 tables (in money terms) are published in A. N. Efimov and L. Ia. Berri (eds.), *Metody planirovaniia mezhotraslevykh proportsii* (Moscow, 1965), pp. 96ff., 114. The first quadrant (the interindustry flow table) of the 1959 table is published in considerable detail in *Narodnoe khoziaistvo . . . 1960* (in money terms), pp. 101–143, with some analytical results, pp. 144–151, and in *Narodnoe khoziaistvo . . . 1961* (in terms of direct labor), pp. 77–117, with certain analyses on pp. 118–119. A summary version of the first quadrant (with somewhat more detail than in the full table summary mentioned above) is printed in Efimov and Berri, pp. 100–101, and also in G. I. Grebtsov *et al.*, *Osnovy razrabotky mezhotraslevogo balansa*, ed. A. Aganbegian (Moscow, 1962), pp. 40–41. (This summary table has the advantage of horizontal and vertical totals for the quadrant.) Summary data from the 1966 table are in *Vestnik statistiki*, no. 11 (1968), pp. 89–96; details of the first quadrant are in *Narodnoe khoziaistvo . . . 1967*, pp. 64–111, and some analytical results, *ibid.*, pp. 112–117. The tentative 1964 table is published in V. Belkin, V. Ivanter, and N. Konstantinov, "Planovaia model' proizvodstva i realizatsiia obshchestvennogo produkta i natsional'nogo dokhoda," *Voprosy ekonomiki*, no. 5 (1968), pp. 58–69 (table on p. 60). A. Ezhevskii, "Sistema material'no-tekhnicheskogo obespecheniia sel'skogo khoziaistva," *Ekonomika sel'skogo khoziaistva*, no. 4 (1968), pp. 46–56, indicates some physical quantities of materials: rolled steel for repairs and collective farm construction, about a million tons a year in recent years; cement for collective farm construction, about 5 million tons yearly.

and 16–17 billion in 1964 and 1966, or between 8 and 9 percent of the total net material product in all four years.

Such a rate of contribution from the nonagricultural sectors is exceptionally high. As was shown recently, 3 percent of GDP is normal for external inputs into agriculture, and this rather independently of time, place, and level of income.[3]

If the ruble amounts, and the official exchange rate, are taken at face value, then these amounts are of about the same absolute magnitude as in the United States in the same years, for the same input items. In the United States, however, variable external inputs, at $10–$11 billion, prevail over capital costs which came to over $4 billion in the years mentioned. The contrast in direct labor supply in the two countries underlines the unusual magnitude of Soviet farm expenses.

These results can be further illustrated by comparing the amounts of labor used to generate the external inputs. Calculations based on the 1959 input-output tables indicate that the 6.8–7.3 billion rubles' worth of current production inputs generated outside agriculture represent the use of 3.9 million work-years of nonagricultural labor.[4] For the fixed investment, no corresponding figure can be shown. Short of anything more conclusive, the 5 billion rubles' worth of fixed investment in agriculture in 1959 may be assumed to have absorbed 2–3 million work-years.[5] Thus at least 6–7 million work-years, or more than one-tenth of the nonagricultural work force, have contributed to agriculture in 1959. Considering the nature of these accounts, which include only "material product," it is significant that the whole number of *rabochie i sluzhashchie* in the 1959 census, employed in productive work other than agriculture, amounted to about 42 million (both sexes).

---

[3] A. Simantov, "The Dynamics of Growth and Agriculture," *Zeitschrift für Nationalökonomie*, XXVII, no. 3 (1967), 328–351.

[4] L. Komina, "Voprosy metodologii opredeleniia polnykh trudovykh zatrat," *Vestnik statistiki*, no. 6 (1967), pp. 42–50; labor-use table on p. 47, assuming that 33 million work-years are 88.2 percent of total labor input, with 10.4 percent for external annual inputs and 1.4 percent for amortization. In a previous publication, "Soviet Farm Mechanization in Perspective," *Slavic Review*, XXV, no. 2 (June, 1966), I had (p. 290, n. 11) assessed the current production inputs to have required "between 2.5 and 3 million man years" which still did not include investment costs. The data quoted from Komina show that this estimate was very much on the low side, but the source quoted (*Narodnoe khoziaistvo . . . 1961*, p. 118) did not allow very precise interpretations. The estimates borrowed from Komina break down as 2 million in industry (of which 1⅓ in heavy and ⅔ in light industry), 1.4 million in trade and allied services, and less than .5 million in transportation, all of which is compatible with the data in *Narodnoe khoziaistvo . . . 1961*.

[5] The amount given for "amortization" in Komina's article is much too low to represent true annual capital costs, as will become evident from the rates at which machines are scrapped (see below). The tentative table for 1964 (see n. 2 above) already gives amortization in agriculture as 3.1 billion rubles, or more than twice the amount proposed for 1959.

The corresponding use of "indirect labor" in United States agriculture amounts to about 2 million man-years in recent years, and only 1.5 million in the 1920's;[6] it is unlikely ever to have exceeded these magnitudes in the remote past.

Changes in the indirect labor inputs in Soviet agriculture cannot be traced with any confidence. The magnitude is likely to have been abnormally large at least through the 1950's and up to the present.

These magnitudes come into further perspective from the supply of direct farm labor. The input of labor into Soviet agriculture (except the private sector) is given in Table 3, from official sources.[7] It is noteworthy that total labor in agriculture did not decline much during 1961–1967. Other sources tell us that total labor input into agriculture, including the private sector, amounted to 33 million work-years in 1959, 32 million in 1960, and 31 million in 1963.[8] The figure of 31 million is again given for 1966 and 1967.[9] Thus there has been very little change in labor input, either in the socialist or the private sector, during the early half of the 1960's, a period of spectacular buildup of investments.

It is true that the age structure of this agricultural work force is abnormal, so that a considerable reduction may be expected soon. The geographic incidence is likely to be very uneven, due to higher birthrates among non-Russian peoples.

At the same time that the total agricultural work force hardly declined during the 1960's, the "mechanizator cadres," which had risen from 1.4

[6] F. Dovring, *Productivity of Labor in Agricultural Production*, Agricultural Experiment Station Bulletin 726 (Urbana: University of Illinois College of Agriculture, 1967), pp. 12–13; details are in W. F. Gossling, "A New Economic Model of Structural Change in United States Agriculture and Supporting Industries" (Ph.D. dissertation, University of Illinois, 1964), pp. 250–251.

[7] Different and consistently higher estimates of labor input into Soviet agriculture have recently been published by John W. DePauw, *Measures of Agricultural Employment in the USSR: 1950–1966*, International Population Reports Series P-95, no. 65 (Washington, D.C.: U.S. Department of Commerce, October, 1968), with summary figures under several alternative estimates, p. 5. For the collective farms, labor force is shown as substantially larger than annual average employment, the concept quoted in our Table 3. Also the state and the private sectors are shown with larger quantities than according to the source in Table 3 and *Narodnoe khoziaistvo . . . 1967*, p. 491. It is not necessary to discuss these differences here; the essential point is that these calculations show only a moderate decline in the farm work force or labor input during the 1950's, and no significant change at all during the early and mid-1960's.

[8] See Dovring, "Soviet Farm Mechanization," p. 288.

[9] *Strana Sovetov za 50 let*, pp. 162–163 (same source as for Table 3), and *Narodnoe khoziaistvo . . . 1967*, p. 494. For the same year, a different source indicates the agricultural labor force (including individual household plot workers) as 31 percent of the total (A. Ul'ianova, "Trud v SSSR," *Vestnik statistiki*, no. 11 (1967), pp. 3–12; percent representations, p. 5), which indicates a total labor force in the vicinity of 100 million; this again may agree roughly with *Narodnoe khoziaistvo . . . 1965*, pp. 556, 558.

Table 3 : *Number of workers employed in kolkhozy, sovkhozy, and auxiliary agricultural enterprises (average for each year; million persons).*

	1950	1960	1961	1962	1963	1964	1965	1966	1967	1968
Total employed	30.7	29.0	28.1	27.7	27.3	27.3	28.0	27.9	27.7	27.5
Kolkhozy[a]	27.6	22.3	20.7	20.0	19.4	19.2	18.9	18.6	18.4	18.1
Sovkhozy, etc.	2.4	6.3	7.4	7.7	7.9	8.1	9.1	9.3	9.3	9.4
MTS	.7	.4	—	—	—	—	—	—	—	—
In addition: outside workers	.2	.5	.5	.4	.4	.4	.5	.5	.5	.5
Total workers employed in agriculture[b]	27.9	26.1	25.5	25.2	24.9	25.2	25.6	25.4	24.7	24.6
Kolkhozy	25.1	20.1	18.7	18.1	17.6	17.7	17.6	17.3	16.7	—
Sovkhozy, etc.	2.2	5.8	6.8	7.1	7.3	7.5	8.0	8.1	8.0	—
MTS	.6	.2	—	—	—	—	—	—	—	—

[a] In the collective part of the kolkhozy; average of 12 monthly employment figures, regardless of age and of number of days worked during the month.

[b] Including work by outside workers in agriculture, but excluding work by kolkhoz and sovkhoz workers outside agriculture.

SOURCES: *Strana Sovetov za 50 let,* pp. 162–163; *Narodnoe khoziaistvo . . . 1967,* p. 491, and *1968,* p. 446.

million in 1940 and 1950 to 2.6 million in 1960, rose further to 3.2 million in 1966 and 3.3 million in 1967 and 1968.[10] This is much less than the con-current training of new cadres would indicate,[11] but is still a substantial increase in skilled workers. The number of specialists with higher- or medium-level training working on kolkhozy and sovkhozy also increased, totalling over 400,000 in 1966.[12] Thus the average quality of the work force should have risen; it is interesting to note that the mechanizators alone now come close to equalling the total agricultural work force in the United States. These data underline the conclusion drawn from those on indirect labor: that Soviet agriculture in the 1960's has obtained hardly any productivity increases other than those stemming from higher unit yields of crops and livestock and the resulting rise in total output.[13]

II

The accumulation of three principal groups of power machines is shown in Tables 4, 5, and 6. The increase in tractors and trucks is steady but slow; in combine harvesters, there actually was a small net decline in some years. The most striking feature in all three tables is the high rate of scrapping. In almost all years in all three tables, net increase represents but a minor fraction of new supplies, and scrapping thus corresponds to the equivalent of the bulk of the new acquisitions, indicating a high rate of depreciation. This contradicts the small allowances for amortization in the input-output tables. If the scrappings are summed cumulatively from the bottom, in all three tables seven to eight years of scrapping will add up to the inventory of seven to eight years ago.

The contrast with the United States is also striking. Here the fleets on hand are two to three times larger, but the rates of scrapping (in relation to the totals) are half or less of those in the USSR, and cumulative summing from the bottom will take about 20 years to reach the inventory size of a past year.

[10] *Strana Sovetov za 50 let,* p. 163. There are slightly different figures in, e.g., S. Mel'nik, "Razvitie mekhanizatsii sel'skogo khoziaistva za 50 let sovetskoi vlasti," *Tekhnika v sel'skom khoziaistve,* no. 11 (1967), p. 3.

[11] *Strana Sovetov za 50 let,* p. 241.

[12] *Ibid.,* p. 232.

[13] This conclusion is implicitly (and maybe inadvertently) borne out by data in T. L. Basiuk, "Sotsialism preobrazil sel'skoe khoziaistvo," *Ekonomicheskie nauki,* no. 11 (1967), pp. 53–61; his Table 7, p. 60, shows average labor expenditure per centner of output, in "person-days," separately for kolkhozy and sovkhozy, in 1960 and 1965, for ten important commodities, and the changes are, on the whole, so modest that they reflect principally physical yield increases, leaving virtually no improvement in the efficiency of direct (on-farm) labor despite the very large strides in mechanization during these years.

Table 4 : *USSR, tractors in agriculture (natural units, in thousands).*

Year	1 Existing at End of Year	2 Net Increase during Year	3 Supplied to Agriculture during Year	4 Scrapping = Col. 3 − Col. 2
1950	595	—	92	—
1953	744	—	76	—
1954	795	51	—	—
1955	844	49	123	74
1956	870	26	140	114
1957	924	54	148	94
1958	1,001	77	158	81
1959	1,054	53	144	91
1960	1,122	68	157	89
1961	1,212	90	185	95
1962	1,329	117	206	89
1963	1,442	113	239	126
1964	1,539	97	223	126
1965	1,613	74	240	166
1966	1,660	47	276	229
1967	1,739	79	287	208
1968	1,821	82	290	208

SOURCE: *Narodnoe khoziaistvo* gives years and other sources.

In regard to tractors, new supplies to agriculture in the USSR reached the level of the United States[14] in 1960 and have been consistently higher since then; in recent years even the absolute numbers scrapped per year in the USSR have caught up with the United States.[15]

In combine harvesters, the position is even more extreme. Even though the fleet in the United States is nearly twice as large as in the Soviet Union, it is now declining slightly and scrappings of some 30,000 to 60,000 a year are matched by somewhat smaller annual shipments, both of which are considerably smaller than in the USSR during the years represented in Table 5.

For trucks only the total number on farms can be compared, which is about three times as many in the United States as in the USSR, but separate

[14] These references are exclusive of garden tractors in the United States.

[15] Cf. V. Antoshkevich, "Sroki sluzhby mashin i amortizatsiia v sel'skom khoziaistve," *Voprosy ekonomiki,* no. 11 (1965), pp. 64–74, with depreciation scales on p. 67; after ten years, only 4 percent of the machines survive (p. 68); optimum depreciation, pp. 72ff. Official depreciation scales established in 1963 allowed a tractor to live six to eight years (different lengths for different models), other machines seven years, according to M. I. Siniukov, "Voprosy ratsional'nogo ispol'zovaniia i vosproizvodstva sel'skokhoziaistvennoi tekhniki," *Izvestiia Timiriazevskoi sel'skokhoziaistvennoi akademii,* no. 6 (1966), pp. 200–208; Table 4 (p. 206) shows 15.5 percent of the tractors to be older than eight years, 4.9 percent of the combines, and 48.7 percent of the trucks (data as of the end of 1965).

Table 5 : *USSR, grain combines (thousands).*

Year	*1* *Existing at* *End of Year*	*2* *Net Increase* *during Year*	*3* *Supplied to* *Agriculture* *during Year*	*4* *Scrapping =* *Col. 3 − Col. 2*
1950	211	—	—	—
1952	292	—	—	—
1953	318	26	—	—
1954	338	20	—	—
1955	338	—	46	46
1956	375	37	80	43
1957	483	108	134	26
1958	502	19	65	46
1959	494	−8	53	61
1960	497	3	57	54
1961	498	1	70	69
1962	520	22	79	57
1963	517	−3	80	83
1964	513	−4	79	83
1965	520	7	79	72
1966	531	11	86	75
1967	553	22	96	74
1968	581	28	98	70

SOURCE: *Narodnoe khoziaistvo* gives years and other sources.

Table 6 : *USSR, trucks in agriculture (thousands).*

Year	*1* *Existing at* *End of Year*	*2* *Net Increase* *during Year*	*3* *Supplied to* *Agriculture* *during Year*	*4* *Scrapping =* *Col. 3 − Col. 2*
1953	424	—	69	—
1955	544	—	111	—
1956	631	87	114	27
1957	660	29	125	96
1958	700	40	102	62
1959	729	29	76	47
1960	778	49	66	17
1961	796	18	70	52
1962	875	79	83	4
1963	922	47	69	22
1964	954	32	63	31
1965	982	28	70	42
1966	1,017	35	106	71
1967	1,054	37	108	71
1968	1,097	43	114	71

SOURCE: *Narodnoe khoziaistvo* gives years and other sources.

figures for shipments to farms do not appear to be available in the United States, and hence scrappings cannot be inferred either.

The facts are thus that the USSR has a much smaller fleet of power machines in agriculture than the United States, but the Soviet machines are worn out much faster. It is easy to explain this as wasteful and incompetent use of machines, but such an explanation cannot be quantified; hence it cannot be assured that it is the whole or even the main explanation. A more logical one, and one that is likely to cover a large part of the situation, is in more intensive use of each machine: this is often said to be one of the advantages of large-scale socialist agriculture over the small-scale family-size farms in a country like the United States.

One indication of the intensity of use is in the consumption of petroleum fuels. In 1959, the input-output tables indicate over a billion rubles' worth of petroleum products used as inputs in agriculture. This points to a magnitude between 20 and 25 million tons.[16] This is, in fact, not far from the same magnitude as in the United States in the same year.[17] The Soviet oil industries more than doubled their output since 1959 (see n. 16), and consumption of liquid fuels on farms has increased further and is now of a magnitude similar to that in the United States. In early 1968, a writer discussing the whole fuel situation in the USSR states that agriculture uses up a large part of all liquid fuels—about 41 percent of the diesel oil and about 26 percent of the gasoline. When these data are combined with Campbell's calculations for petroleum fuel consumption in recent years, it appears that agriculture took about 14 to 15 percent of all domestic consumption of petroleum fuels in the USSR.[18]

The magnitudes involved do indeed indicate much larger annual use of each machine than in the United States. Use of machines is indicated by

[16] In 1959, USSR production of crude oil was about 130 million tons; export of crude oil and refined petroleum products amounted to about 25 million tons, leaving 105 million tons between domestic productive and consumptive uses. Specification in the input-output tables gives agriculture 27 percent of the productive uses, which must have been the bulk of total domestic uses. Cf. n. 18 below. In 1967, crude oil output was 286 million tons (*Strana Sovetov za 50 let,* p. 68; cf. *Petroleum Times,* July 5, 1968, p. 988, which gives 288.9 million). Output in 1968 thus should be at or above 300 million tons.

[17] The U.S. census of agriculture in 1959 shows gross expenditures for motor fuel on farms (farm business share) as $1,554 million which, at 16 cents per gallon, comes to approximately 24 million tons of gasoline. The 1964 census shows a total motor fuel expenditure (same definition as in 1959) of $1,787 million; at 15 cents a gallon, this comes to just under 30 million tons of gasoline (in 1964, gasoline accounted for two-thirds of U.S. farm motor fuel expenditures).

[18] S. Litvak, "Toplivno-energeticheskii balans SSSR i effektivnost' izpol'zovaniia energoresursov v narodnom khoziaistve," *Vestnik statistiki,* no. 1 (1968), pp. 32–41. And at nearly the same time, N. Gusev (deputy chairman of the Gosplan), writing authoritatively in *Ekonomika sel'skogo khoziaistva,* no. 12 (1967), says (p. 8) that agriculture consumes 36 percent of the diesel fuel and 28 percent of the gasoline,

Table 7a : *Mechanization of basic agricultural work in crop production on sovkhozy and kolkhozy (in percent of the total for the work operation indicated).*

	1940	1945	1950	1960	1964	1965	1966
Plowing for spring crops	69	66	84	100	100	100	100
Grain sowing	61	39	75	100	100	100	100
Sugar beet sowing	93	75	92	100	100	100	100
Cotton sowing	81	71	92	100	100	100	100
Potato planting	4	0.8	6	58	69	73	78
Inter-row cultivation:							
Sugar beets	—	—	—	86	85	87	87
Potatoes	—	—	—	72	83	86	90
Combine harvesting:							
Grains, including corn	47	27	53	92	97	97	99
Sugar beets	—	—	2	54	58	67	74
Cotton harvesting	—	—	—	11	19	22	29
Potato digging	2	0.4	3	34	48	54	58
Haying	12	8	24	68	76	79	81

SOURCE: *Strana Sovetov za 50 let*, pp. 158–159.

Table 7b : *Mechanization of work in animal husbandry–fermy in the kolkhozy and sovkhozy in 1966 (in percentages of the number of animals of each kind).*

	Kolkhozy and Sovkhozy	Kolkhozy	Sovkhozy
Milking cows	31	23	43
Mechanized water supply:			
On cattle farms	59	61	56
On swine farms	75	74	77
Mechanized shearing of			
sheep (electric machines)	87	80	94

SOURCE: *Strana Sovetov za 50 let*, p. 159.

the use of fuel, unless the motors are very much less efficient, which is not likely. Combining this with the high rates of scrapping, we conclude that annual tractor-mileage and combine-mileage in the USSR are likely to be similar to those in the United States; on trucks, a similar conclusion would be premature.

The buildup of mechanical means of traction did not lead to as rapid a decline in work animals as some observers might have expected. Even work oxen were a significant resource in the early 1950's and had not quite disappeared at the end of the decade. More important is that horses in agriculture, which had numbered 38 million in 1916, were still more than half that number in 1940, and, after the losses of the war, were again built up to 15 million in 1953; more recent data indicate a slow decline from 11 million in 1960 to 8 million in 1966. A few calculations indicate that the share of horses in total tractive power on farms was almost 25 percent in 1940 and on the order of 2–3 percent in the early 1960's; the basis for such calculations remains unclear, however, especially since animal power is present 365 days a year whether used or not, while mechanical power also depends on use rate and fuel consumption.[19]

How comprehensively agricultural operations are mechanized in the USSR is difficult to assess. Official sources usually give only selected data which may entail selection bias, let alone other possible errors. Tables 7a

---

which is too high and must be cut down in 1968: "v tselom po strane kazhdyi protsent ekonomii goriuchego sostavit bolee 300 tys. t."—indicating over 30 million tons used in agriculture (the figure is much too small to refer to all uses in the country). The high rate of fuel consumption may have inspired the new interest in electrical traction; see the article by Listov and Shchurov, quoted in n. 29 below. R. W. Campbell, *The Economics of Soviet Oil and Gas* (Baltimore: Johns Hopkins Press, 1968), p. 164 (Table 26), gives structural data on USSR domestic consumption. The 1966 input-output tables (see n. 2 above) show petroleum products used by agriculture as worth 1,287 million rubles, or 25 percent of all productive uses (289 million, or 22 percent, in animal husbandry, the rest in crop production).

[19] The possibility of larger mileage per machine, and hence a shorter life span per

Table 7c : *Level of mechanization, selected tasks in animal husbandry, July 1, 1968.*

	Water Supply	Feed Distribution	Manure Removal	Milking of Cows
Cattle	62	25	37	37
Hogs	75	31	36	—
Poultry	100	55	56	—

SOURCE: N. Tabala, "Chto sderzhivaet mekhanizatsiia rabot v zhivotnovodstve," in *Tekhnika v sel'skom khoziaistve*, no. 11 (1968), pp. 12–14 (these data from Table 1, p. 12).

and 7b show a rather optimistic picture which was released recently in a jubilee publication. Table 7c, drawn from a recent self-critical article, includes some of the less favorable aspects and shows only small progress in 1966–1968. Nearly the same level and pace of increase are reflected in some recent articles dealing with the same crop enterprises as in Table 7a.[20] One of these also indicates an efficiency level in grain mechanization (in the northern Caucasus) which is not far from what is achieved in the grain belts of North America.[21]

These data are specific to certain enterprises. A somewhat more comprehensive collection of figures on crop operations is shown in Table 8. Here, no group of operations is shown as 100 percent mechanized at the time of writing, but several are so indicated in the "perspective."

With such large mileage per machine and with the high level of fuel consumption, one would expect mechanization to have become more comprehensive than is the case. Current plans indicate still larger numbers of machines within the next few years, and at the same time there is a widespread complaint that existing machines are not sufficiently used. This complaint comes forward both in a very authoritative textbook[22] and in a spate of journal articles.[23]

---

machine, is in contrast to draft animals where annual capacity and life span cannot be manipulated in any comparable degree. Calculations based on the equality of one horse to 7.5 tractor HP, shown in E. Schinke, *Die Mechanisierung landwirtschaftlicher Arbeiten in der Sowjetunion* (Wiesbaden: Harrassowitz, 1967), p. 29, appear to avoid this difficulty of comparing animal and mechanical tractive power. Evidently the comparison comes out differently also according to the seasonality of the year's work flow, which in large parts of the USSR is quite different from Western Europe.

[20] A. Kononenko, "Kompleksnaia mekhanizatsiia vozdelyvaniia zernovykh kul'tur," *Ekonomika sel'skogo khoziaistva*, no. 6 (1968), pp. 108–115 (with data from 1928, 1932, 1937, 1958, and 1965 on p. 109).

[21] *Ibid.*, p. 110.

[22] According to T. L. Basiuk, *Organizatsiia sotsialisticheskogo sel'skokhoziaistvennogo proizvodstva*, rev. ed. (Moscow, 1965), p. 83, tractors of kolkhozy and sovkhozy are utilized only one-third of the year, and transportation jobs need more mechanization, especially since the loading and unloading of merchandise is mainly manual.

[23] Thus, according to V. Grachev, "Povyshenie effektivnosti izpol'zovaniia mashin-

Table 8 : *Levels of mechanization, selected operations, 1960–1965 and "perspective."*

Operation	PERCENT MECHANIZATION IN			
	1960	1963	1965	Perspective
Preparation of soil	42	55	65	100
Application of fertilizer	17	25	30	100
Watering	14	19	24	100
Chemical plant protection	50	60	62	100
Cultivation and harvest of grains, pulses, and oilseeds	48	64	67	97
Cultivation and harvest of corn (grain and silage)	36	58	70	100
Cultivation and harvest of sugar beets	53	74	90	100
Cultivation and harvest of cotton	53	65	74	100
Cultivation and harvest of potatoes	25	48	57	100
Cultivation and harvest of vegetables	4	6	7	30
Cultivation and harvest of fiber crops	27	37	46	90
Care of orchards and vineyards	6	9	11	45
Haying	58	70	77	100
Animal husbandry	32	43	48	80
Loading and unloading jobs	50	68	78	100

SOURCE: O. Konovalov, "Osnovnye napravleniia razvitiia sel'skokhoziaistvennogo mashinostroeniia," *Voprosy ekonomiki*, no. 5 (1965), pp. 3–14 (these data on p. 7).

The simple view which equates machine productivity with mileage of annual use is not the only one heard in the debate, however. Another complaint of long standing regards the efficiency of the machines as such.[24]

---

no-traktornogo parka v sel'skom khoziaistve," *Voprosy ekonomiki*, no. 7 (1966), pp. 41–49, the number of days' use is higher now on the kolkhozy than previously on the MTSs, but not yet sufficiently. The same concept of "productivity of a machine" (i.e., number of days' use per year) comes back in articles in *Ekonomika sel'skogo khoziaistva*, no. 2 (1966), pp. 48–54 (A. Zalevskii) and no. 9 (1967), pp. 78–83 (S. Fraer), and also in *Vestnik statistiki*, no. 2 (1968) (I. Butorin) and *Tekhnika v sel'skom khoziaistve*, no. 3 (1968), pp. 1–4 (A. Kononenko).

[24] Thus, for instance, S. Orlov, "Pochemu veliki prostoi mashin," *Kolkhozno-sovkhoznoe proizvodstvo*, no. 6 (1965), pp. 22–24, complains of low performance per tractor, and A. Pokinchereda, "Problema analiza ispol'zovaniia mashinno-traktornogo parka v kolkhozakh," *Vestnik statistiki*, no. 3 (1968), pp. 3–13, concludes (p. 13) that contemporary tractors are fairly expensive machines—more efficient ones should be produced. Symptomatic also is the set of tables on tractor use (machine days per year per tractor) in *Vestnik statistiki*, no. 6 (1968), pp. 89–95.

This leads to what is now the central problem of Soviet agricultural mechanization: its high costs. To make mechanization really comprehensive, the plan for 1966–1970 envisaged a total capital outlay in agriculture (for the five years) of 70 billion rubles, of which 41 billion were for government outlay, or about twice the amounts for 1961–1965.[25] Outright warnings against high capital costs in agriculture have begun to come in the journals. One article purports to show that for each ruble of productive capital (*osnovnye proizvodstvennye fondy*) the value of agricultural production was 2.32 rubles in 1940, 2.22 in 1950, 1.35 in 1960, and only 1 ruble in 1964; in other words, the output-to-capital ratio is falling sharply.[26] The same problem is also treated elsewhere with a different definition.[27] Some of the writers who insist on more utilization of each machine admit that output grows slower than capital.[28]

Even this incipient recognition of the necessity to economize with inputs fails to identify the core of the problem, which is in the rate of return to all factors of production. Using each machine more hours per year is really the solution of a scarcity economy (as in the past of the USSR), not that of a mature industrial economy (such as the present Soviet economy has the means to be). Such intensive use of each machine leads, among other things, to more rapid depreciation and higher repair costs as well as to higher fuel consumption, and the exhortation to use machines more intensively may encourage uneconomic use (e.g., for small jobs which are better done with simpler means). Making the machine fleets larger and using each machine fewer hours per year (as in the United States) will, in fact, make sense, because the larger capital overhead will be compensated by the gains in timeliness of operation and in flexibility of organization, as well as by the lower depreciation scales; and for these reasons, the planned expansion in the number of machines is right after all, in principle. The fall in output-to-capital ratio (or, the rise in capital/output ratio) would not necessarily be of concern if capital were substituting for labor on a large scale. If such were the case, a rising capital/output ratio would (up to a point) be normal.

It is the failure of Soviet agriculture sharply to reduce its employment of direct (on-farm) labor which makes the rising capital intensity so star-

[25] A. Il'ichev, "Usilenie roli promyshlennosti v razvitii sel'skogo khoziaistva," in *Ekonomicheskie nauki* (Nauchnye doklady vysshei shkoly—Ministerstvo vysshego i srednego spetsial'nogo obrazovaniia SSSR), no. 4 (1966), pp. 9–18.

[26] Iu. Kiruchkin and L. Maksimova, "Industrializatsiia sel'skogo khoziaistva," *Ekonomicheskie nauki,* no. 5 (1966), pp. 50–57 (data quoted on p. 51).

[27] P. Klemyshev, "O fondoemkosti produktsii v sel'skom khoziaistve," *Voprosy ekonomiki,* no. 6 (1966), pp. 82–91 (esp. p. 85).

[28] Grachev, p. 41.

tling. Even the reduction in labor force which is to be expected as a consequence of aging will not suffice to bring it down to numbers in reasonable
proportion to externally generated factors. Concurrently, there may have
been a failure of Soviet society to absorb agriculture's surplus labor in
other occupations, but whether this is the primary reason for the situation
is at best open to doubt. It may very well be that agriculture's own over-
complicated organizational structure tends to retain excess labor and thus
to frustrate the economic effects which mechanization ordinarily should
have brought about.

III

The tendency toward overcapitalization (in relation to labor) of Soviet
agriculture is but one facet of the wider problem of a centrally planned
economy where economic criteria for the use of capital have long been lacking. In a nutshell, the problem is this: It does not help to keep a high rate
of savings if the use of capital is inefficient; the result will be the same as
that of a lower rate of savings plus a higher degree of efficiency in the use of
capital. *A fortiori*, then, if efficiency in the use of capital is actually *declining*, as it well may have been for some time in the Soviet economy in general
and apparently very much so in agriculture, then the rate of savings would
have to *go up* in order to maintain a steady rate of growth in the system. It
could thus be possible to operate a system where production as a whole
goes up and up, but more and more of it is reinvested, leaving surprisingly
little for people to consume (to say nothing of the quality problems, which
we have not touched upon here). The dilemma of a centrally planned economy becoming increasingly capital-intensive explains the tendency to back-
track more and more toward presocialist concepts in economic logic and
accounting.

The criteria of profit rate, rent, and depreciation charges have been introduced so recently in the USSR that their effect on the use of capital in
agriculture is as yet not widely felt.[29] The success or failure of bringing these

[29] It is characteristic that all the unsolved problems of making the present and
immediately prospective mechanization work efficiently have not deterred speculation
on *automation* in agriculture; thus, such articles as P. M. Vasilenko and I. I. Vasilenko,
"Avtomatizatsiia—dvizhushchaia sila tekhnicheskogo progressa," *Mekhanizatsiia i elek-
trifikatsiia sotsialisticheskogo sel'skogo khoziaistva,* no. 6 (1967), pp. 2–6 (mainly
"pep talk"), and S. P. Gel'fenbein *et al.,* "Traktornyi agregat kak ob"ekt avtomatizatsii,"
ibid., no. 12 (1967), pp. 22–26, proposing the unmanned tractor ("agri-robot"), partly
on the basis of experiments abroad. Another sign that the organizational sources of
inefficiency are not duly appreciated is in the new proposals for *electrical traction* as
a partial remedy to high fuel costs; for example, according to P. I. Listov and S. V.
Shchurov, "Nekotorye voprosy energetiki sel'skogo khoziaistva," *ibid.,* no. 7 (1968),

economic reforms to bear on agricultural mechanization will decide whether Soviet agriculture is going to become one of the system's progressive sectors or one of its increasingly embarrassing drains on resources.

pp. 1–6, this system was used to some extent in the late 1940's, then abandoned as uneconomical; now the authors purport to show competitiveness against liquid fuels, without anticipating the effect of better economizing with liquid fuels.

11 : Financing the Modernization of Kolkhozy

James R. Millar

Several years ago *Pravda* ran a series of rather enthusiastic articles on the application of hydroponic techniques to Soviet agriculture. Pictures accompanying these articles displayed efficient-looking, white-smocked young women tending plants that were being raised in metal drawers lining the walls of a modern building. It was a true agro-factory. Doubtless the appeal hydroponics apparently has for the Soviet agricultural expert derives in large part from the fact that temperature, sunlight, and nutrients are all subject to precise control, especially since the Soviet Union is characterized by such diverse and relatively unfavorable soil and climatic conditions. However, a careful scrutiny of both the articles and the accompanying photographs revealed another attractive feature: nowhere was a peasant to be found. Hydroponics represents, then, "the ultimate" as a solution to the agricultural problems that have persisted under both Russian and Soviet political regimes, for its widespread introduction would eliminate dependence both upon unpredictable and unfavorable natural conditions and upon an unreliable and backward peasantry. As the refrain of a once popular song goes, "Who could ask for anything more?"

Unfortunately, of course, even if the widespread application of hydroponic techniques were technically feasible, it would be extremely capital-intensive and therefore prohibitively expensive, at least for the foreseeable future. However, as the "ultimate" solution to Soviet agricultural problems, hydroponic culture might serve as a standard with which to appraise the reforms that have been undertaken in Soviet agriculture since Stalin's death. There is general agreement among western students of Soviet agriculture that considerable progress has been made toward the modernization of the agricultural sector in terms of this kind of standard, although all also agree that much remains to be done. But progress has undoubtedly been made toward increasing and modernizing the capital stock in agriculture, and progress has been made toward the creation of a competent, reliable, and disciplined agricultural work force.

In examining the Soviet agricultural experience, we sometimes tend to neglect the fact that the pursuit of these two critical objectives requires the pecuniarization of the agricultural sector. Economic history is unequivocal about this, however. Industrialization and modernization simply do not occur except in conjunction with the process of pecuniarization. Increased capital investment in agriculture requires increased access to the Soviet main money circuit, which alone permits access to capital goods produced in other sectors of the Soviet economy. (The "main money circuit" is here defined to include product and service, transfer, and financial transactions among the various final sectors of the Soviet economy, e.g., the household, state budgets, enterprise capital account sectors.) Similarly, the creation of a competent and reliable agricultural work force requires, among other things, access to the fruits of Soviet industrial progress. In other words, modernization of the agricultural sector must be financed in the strict sense of that word, for the Soviet economy is a money economy. Professor Grossman has written somewhere that in the Soviet economy, as elsewhere, money is power. We can be somewhat more explicit about in what that power consists. The power of money in a pecuniary society like the Soviet one is the access it provides to the sources as well as to the fruits of industrialization. This paper focuses upon the way in which the increased access of the kolkhoz sector to the Soviet main money circuit has been financed since 1953 and upon the problems and peculiarities that have characterized this process.

Before turning to the analysis proper, it is necessary to say a few words about the peculiar institutional structure of the kolkhoz sector and the significance of these institutional features for price and financial policy in this sector of the Soviet economy. A few additional words are necessary concerning the nature of the reforms that have been introduced since Stalin's death.

I

The kolkhoz has been and remains today a peculiar institution in the Soviet economy. For the sake of brevity, let me merely list the distinct features of the kolkhoz sector that are significant for this study.

1. It is a self-governing producer cooperative, although not free from state interference on many levels.

2. The kolkhoz holds its land rent-free in perpetuity from the state.

3. Members collectively "own" the fixed and working capital of the

kolkhoz, but no member may alienate any portion of the "indivisible fund" of fixed and working capital should he withdraw from the collective. What is more, a fixed share of current income must be transferred to the indivisible fund each year.

4. Until 1958, the greater part of the stock of agricultural equipment utilized on kolkhozy was owned by the MTS, which hired out its services to kolkhozy for in-kind payments (*naturoplata*).

5. The kolkhoz does not have access to interest-free capital grants from the state budget. Thus, fixed capital investment must be financed out of inside funds or through long-term borrowing from Gosbank.

6. Similarly, the kolkhoz is not eligible for subsidies or subject to profit withdrawals from or to the state budget.

7. It is subject, however, to a tax of approximately 12 percent, which was levied upon income gross of wage distributions until March, 1965, and on net income only since that time.[1]

8. Kolkhoz members' earnings represent a residual share in farm income, which is paid out partly in kind and partly in cash. The introduction of a guaranteed annual wage in July, 1966,[2] modifies this feature should farm earnings not suffice to cover the guaranteed minimum annual wage bill. Otherwise, total earnings of farm members still represent a residual share in farm income.

9. Since July, 1966, the kolkhoz has been permitted to finance a portion of advances on wage and income distributions to members with short-term credit provided by Gosbank.

10. The collective farm market (CFM) is directly competitive with state agricultural procurement agencies both for the output of the kolkhoz proper and for the time and energy of kolkhoz members, since prices on the CFM may make work on one's private plot more attractive than work on the collective.

These ten features, taken together, distinguish the kolkhoz from state enterprises in general (although, rather ironically, recent changes in both the kolkhoz and the state enterprise sectors have tended to reduce somewhat the differences between them), and they have significant implications for state price and financial policy in the kolkhoz sector. In contrast to the determination of wholesale prices elsewhere in the Soviet economy, the determination of average realized agricultural procurement prices directly affects the funds available for transfer to capital account and for distribution to members contributing to farm production. And to the extent that capital account expenditures must be financed with inside funds, these two uses of funds are directly competitive. Moreover, the distribution of

[1] *Pravda*, March 27, 1965, p. 5.
[2] *Ibid.*, May 18, 1966, p. 2.

income between rural and urban workers is also affected by agricultural procurement price formation.

The kolkhoz sector is, therefore, an *independent cost-bearing sector*, which means that the state budget need not share in its economic fortunes (and especially in its misfortunes). This characteristic of kolkhozy has served in the past to insure that the kolkhoz and its members would bear both the costs of year-to-year fluctuations in agricultural output and the discrimination the state apparatus has practiced against the sector as a whole. The kolkhoz and its members have been able to shift a portion of these costs to the urban household sector through the collective farm market, and other ways have existed for them to evade state discrimination in some degree, which has led the state repeatedly to the use of mandatory delivery obligations and other coercive measures. But these measures only emphasize the peculiar importance of prices, markets, and financial policy in this sector of the Soviet economy. In short, the distinctive features of the kolkhoz sector have made the ramifications of price-fixing and the consequences of credit policy wider, more complex, and of greater economic import than elsewhere in the central management of Soviet productive enterprises.

II

Before turning to an examination and analysis of the sources and uses of funds statements for the kolkhoz sector, it will be useful to review briefly the nature of the changes and reforms that have been introduced in the state's policy toward the kolkhoz sector and the way in which the peculiar character of the kolkhoz sector has been affected by these policy changes.

Considerable evidence can be found to support the hypothesis that Stalin chose a rather convenient time to depart from the Soviet scene. Nowhere is this more obvious than in the severe contradiction that had developed between agricultural policy on the one hand and what appears to have been an attempt to improve the real income of wage workers and salaried officials on the other. According to Soviet official data, prices on consumer goods retailed through the state network were reduced by 50 percent in a series of steps between the end of 1947 and April of 1952, with prices on food products falling by a disproportionate 67 percent. Another price reduction, which was presumably already in the works when Stalin died, took place in April, 1953.[3] During the same period, 1947–1952, average realized procurement prices on food-field and animal husbandry products, which

---

[3] *Narodnoe khoziaistvo . . . 1956*, p. 211.

were in 1947 already below the 1940 level, were reduced substantially.[4]

Moreover, again according to Soviet official figures, average gross agricultural output per capita for 1950–1953 was 6 percent less than the average for 1926–1929 and only 4 percent greater than the average for 1938–1940.[5] Given that food products composed 60 percent or more of the average Soviet consumer budget and that the income elasticity of demand for these goods was substantial, Stalin's policies toward the urban-worker household and the agricultural sectors were clearly contradictory. And there is considerable evidence of excess demand for food products between 1947 and 1953.[6] Obviously, a policy purporting to favor consumers while at the same time increasing an already severe degree of discrimination against the main producers of primary consumer goods was bound, sooner or later, to come to grief, and it was clearly somewhat late in the day when Stalin died.

Stalin's heirs went into action immediately on the agricultural front. Although the most reasonable course on economic grounds might have been to raise (and adjust) both retail and agricultural procurement prices on food products, they chose instead to stabilize retail prices while increasing average realized procurement prices, thus absorbing the difference with the turnover tax margin.[7] With minor exceptions this policy was followed until 1962, when the first major increase in food product prices was announced.[8] Favorable changes in tax rates on the kolkhoz and private plot sectors were similarly absorbed by the state budget.

Just how deliberate this radical change in agricultural policy was is debatable. To the distant observer, viewing the turns and twists that characterized decision-making in the decade or so following Stalin's death, agricultural policy appears to have grown more like Topsy than according to plan and expectation. Nonetheless, two distinct patterns emerge. The period 1953–1957 appears as one in which an attempt was made to make Stalin's old system workable. No major institutional changes were introduced. Instead, the tax burden was lightened somewhat, the terms of trade were improved, personal income from work on the collective was increased, the relatively greater discrimination against food-field and animal husbandry product producers was eased, and arbitrary administrative practices were curtailed. Policy is characterized in this period, therefore, by an

[4] A. N. Malafeev, *Istoriia tsenoobrazovaniia v SSSR / 1917–1963* (Moscow, 1964), pp. 267, 270, 286, 295.

[5] Iu. V. Arutiunian, "Osobennosti i znachenie novogo etapa razvitiia sel'skogo khoziaistva SSSR," in *Istoriia sovetskogo krest'ianstva i kolkhoznogo stroitel'stva v SSSR* (Moscow, 1963), p. 409.

[6] See, for example, Malafeev, pp. 265–266.

[7] *Ibid.*, pp. 410–411, 412–413; *Sel'skoe khoziaistvo SSSR* (Moscow, 1960), p. 117.

[8] Malafeev, pp. 299–300.

attempt to substitute material incentives for coercive administrative procedures and to call forth rather than to oblige the production and delivery
of agricultural products, although the movement in this direction was hesitant, parsimonious, and in some instances contradictory. The overall effect
was, however, to enhance the role of prices, markets, pecuniary incentives,
and financial channels for the kolkhoz sector.

In 1958, the old procurement system was overturned with the abolition
of the MTS, the elimination of the four-channel, multiple-price procurement
system, and the curtailment of in-kind transactions between state agencies
and the kolkhoz. Again the net effect was to enhance the significance of
markets, prices, pecuniary incentives, and financial channels, although the
way in which these reforms were carried out produced a short-term reversal of the progress that had been made to that time.

The reforms that have been introduced since Khrushchev's fall from
power have followed the overall pattern and direction established under his
hegemony.

III

Let us turn at this point to see how the various reforms and changes in state
policy show up in the sources and uses of funds statements for the kolkhoz
sector for 1952–1962. We shall consider only a few main sources and uses
of funds. In the first section that follows, ordinary, or nonfinancial, sources
of funds are examined. The second section is devoted to two main ordinary,
or nonfinancial, uses of funds, and in a third section net financial sources
and uses of funds are considered. In the final section these separate components are put together in order to describe the general behavior of the
kolkhoz sector.

The empirical foundation of the analysis that follows is a compilation
of sources and uses of funds statements for the kolkhoz sector for the
years 1949–1962 inclusive. Basically, a sources and uses of funds statement
records all product and service, transfer, and financial transactions engaged
in by the sector during a specified period of time, e.g., one year. The statement tells us, then, where the money came from that financed the various
uses the sector made of funds during the year, and it tells us where the
money went as well. Obviously, policy changes that affect realized input
or output prices, the level of net transfer payments, or the conditions under
which money may be obtained or returned and advanced through financial
channels produce impacts that can be read in the sources and uses of funds
statement. Of course, the accounts do not record in-kind transactions unless
these have been given a pecuniary evaluation, and the flows composing

these statements are current rather than constant ruble measures. Thus a sources and uses of funds statement does not provide a comprehensive picture of the sector's economic behavior. But it is ideal for an examination of the way economic activity is financed and, if supplemented with other measures, it provides a useful and informative framework with which to analyze and evaluate a wide range of economic policy measures.

The limitations imposed by time and by the demands of exposition require that the presentation be based upon a consolidation of the separate capital and current account statements, with some resulting loss of detail. On the other hand, data limitations restrict the analysis to annual sources and uses of funds statements, which means that little can be said about financing within-the-year differences in the time shapes of receipts and disbursements of the kolkhoz sector.

Ordinary Sources of Funds

Between 1952 and 1962 total operating money proceeds of the kolkhoz sector rose from 4.28 to 15.24 billion rubles, or more than three-fold (all figures are given in "new" (1960) rubles). Almost the whole of this 11 billion–ruble increase in money proceeds is attributable to the increase in the sector's receipts from sales and deliveries to state and cooperative procurement agencies, which increased five-fold during this period. Thus, the relative significance of receipts from sales and deliveries to state and co-operative procurement agencies in total nonfinancial proceeds was substantially enhanced during this period, accounting for about 82 percent in 1962, as opposed to approximately 57 percent in 1952.

The greater part of the five-fold increase in money proceeds from state and cooperative agencies reflects a rising level of average realized prices paid on procurements rather than an increase in the physical volume of procurements, although the latter did increase substantially. According to the Soviet official index, the average realized procurement price level rose more than three-fold between 1952 and 1962.[9] This price level increase is itself a product of several factors. First, procurement prices (as opposed to realized prices) were advanced on many farm products at various times during this period, with relatively greater price increases being allocated to food-field and animal husbandry products. Second, prior to 1958, a considerable part of the rise in average realized prices is attributable to favorable changes in the proportions flowing through the four main channels of the multiple-price procurement system, i.e., a shift toward the higher price

[9] *Ibid.,* pp. 412–413.

channels. Third, abolition of the MTS and of the obligatory delivery channel in 1958 provided a substantial boost to the average realized price level,
for products previously procured through in-kind payments for MTS services and at very low prices through the obligatory delivery channel now
flowed through the more favorable *zakupka* channel.

Overall improvement in the level of average realized procurement prices
reflects a diminution in price discrimination against the kolkhoz sector as
a whole. The radical change in relative prices represents a relative diminution in discrimination within the sector against food-field and animal husbandry products. Thus, the reforms introduced have provided the sector
as a whole and the food product and animal husbandry subsectors in particular with increased access to the Soviet main money circuit, an increased
access very largely financed by an inflation in average realized procurement
prices.

A rough measure of the extent to which the inflation of realized procurement prices accounted for the increased nonfinancial proceeds of the kolkhoz sector between 1952 and 1962 is ascertainable. There are two ways
in which this gain from inflation may be conceived. Both methods rely upon
deflating receipts from sales and deliveries to state and cooperative procurement agencies and taking the differences between the constant ruble,
physical volume series and the current ruble evaluation as the measure of
the gain from inflation. However, on the one hand, we may conceive of
the gain from inflation as a cumulative measure from a fixed base year, e.g.,
1952. The cumulative gain from inflation is, then, a measure of the difference between current receipts from sales and deliveries to the state and what
these receipts would have been had 1952 realized prices prevailed throughout. On the other hand, we may measure the incremental gain from inflation
in each year over the previous year's average realized price level by moving
the base year forward each year. The cumulative gain from inflation,
therefore, tells us something about the cumulative impact of price and
price-related reforms over any given period, while the incremental gain
from inflation tells us something about the impact of reforms in particular
years.

Taking the cumulative gain from inflation first (see Chart 1), the gain
is 2.4 billion rubles in 1954, 2.9 in 1955, and approximately 4.5 in 1956
and 1957. The cumulative gain from inflation jumps above 7 billion rubles
in 1958 and remains somewhat above that level until 1962, when it stands
somewhat above 9 billion rubles. In other words, the kolkhoz sector had at
its disposal, in 1962, approximately 9 billion rubles attributable to price
and price-related reforms carried out between 1952 and 1962. This gives
one some idea of the magnitude of the reform impact over this period.

The incremental gain from inflation (see Chart 2) exceeds 1 billion rubles

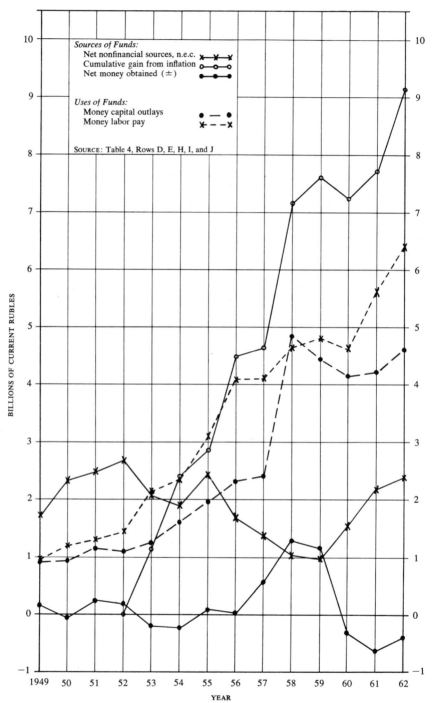

Chart 1 : *Summary sources and uses of funds statements, 1949–1962, and the cumulative gain from inflation, kolkhoz sector.*

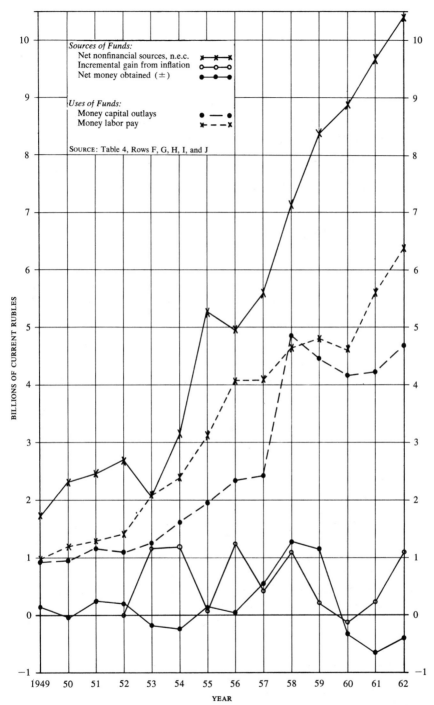

Chart 2 : *Summary sources and uses of funds statements, 1949–1962, and the incremental gain from inflation, kolkhoz sector.*

in five of the 11 years under consideration: 1953, 1954, 1956, 1958, and 1962. With the exception of the .4 billion–ruble gain in 1957, gains for the remaining years are negligible. The incremental gain from inflation gives us some idea of the year-to-year impact of changes in the terms of trade for the kolkhoz sector.

Although these two measures probably overstate the kolkhoz sector's gains from favorable changes in its terms of trade, I doubt if the overstatement is very great. In any event, as we shall see, with only one significant exception, increases in nonfinancial uses of funds have been financed almost exclusively by favorable changes in the sector's terms of trade.

Ordinary Uses of Funds

Let us turn now to nonfinancial uses of funds from 1952 to 1962 (see Chart 1 or 2). We shall consider only two main uses of funds: money pay distributions to kolkhozniki and money expenditures on capital account. Money pay to kolkhozniki rose from 1.4 billion rubles in 1952 to 6.4 billion rubles in 1962, approximately five-fold.[10] Money pay increased in 1952–1962, therefore, more rapidly than total money proceeds and more or less proportionally to the increase in receipts from sales and deliveries to state and cooperative agencies. The increase in total money pay reflects in substantial degree the substitution of money pay for in-kind distributions to farm members. In 1952, money pay composed 25 percent of total pay, and in 1962, 68 percent.[11] Total payments to kolkhoz members, therefore, almost doubled between 1952 and 1962.

Money expenditure on capital account doubled between 1952 and 1957, rising from 1.1 to 2.4 billion rubles, and it doubled again in 1958 in connection with the acquisition of the MTS physical assets, rising to 4.9 billion rubles in this year. Thereafter, money expenditure on capital account fell somewhat but remained in excess of a 4 billion–ruble annual rate.

A year-by-year comparison (see Chart 1 or 2) of money pay disbursements and money capital account expenditure shows quite clearly that, although both series move in the same direction, these two uses are directly competitive for nonfinancial sources of funds. From 1952 through 1956, increased nonfinancial sources of funds were distributed disproportionally to money pay. In 1958, money capital account expenditure more than

[10] Nancy Nimitz, *Farm Employment in the Soviet Union, 1928–1963* (Santa Monica, Calif.: RAND Corp., November, 1965), p. 96.

[11] F. A. Durgin, Jr., "Monetization and Policy in Soviet Agriculture Since 1952," *Soviet Studies*, XV, no. 4 (April, 1964), 397; T. I. Zaslavskaia, *Raspredelenie po trudu v kolkhozakh* (Moscow, 1966), p. 167.

regained its pre-reform relative position. However, in subsequent years money pay again rose disproportionately. Thus, apart from the involuntary increase in capital account money expenditure associated with the acquisition of the MTS. the kolkhoz sector tended during the period under observation to distribute increased nonfinancial proceeds disproportionately in favor of money pay.

Net Financing through Financial Channels (Net Money Obtained)

Now let us turn to an examination of net funds obtained or returned and advanced by the kolkhoz sector through financial channels. As opposed to nonfinancial sources and uses of funds, it is customary to treat financial flows on a net basis. The kolkhoz sector has access through normal procedures to three types of financial liability: short-term borrowing, long-term borrowing, and trade credit, e.g., advances on deliveries from procurement agencies. A fourth type of liability was provided to help finance the acquisition of the physical assets of the MTS system: deferred payment to the state budget. Trade credit apparently is not significant on a year-to-year basis and little data are available anyway, so this item is ignored in what follows. The main form of financial asset available to the kolkhoz is its cash balance, which is the sum of two demand deposit balances: deposits on current account and deposits on capital account. Net money obtained or advanced and returned by the kolkhoz sector through financial channels is determined as the algebraic sum of year-to-year changes in these components of its loanfund balance. For simplicity of exposition the net flow of funds to or from the kolkhoz sector through financial channels will be labelled "net money obtained," which may be positive or negative ($\pm$).

Conceptually, apart from the statistical discrepancy, net money obtained through financial channels is the balancing item in the sources and uses of funds statement. If ordinary uses of funds exceed ordinary sources, the difference must be financed through financial channels, and conversely. Thus, if net money obtained is positive, the other sectors of the Soviet economy, taken together, have advanced funds to the kolkhoz sector. If net money obtained is negative, the kolkhoz sector, by advancing or returning funds through financial channels, is financing ordinary expenditures elsewhere in the Soviet economy.

Net money obtained on consolidated account (i.e., a consolidation of current and capital accounts, see Chart 1 or 2) was positive in the two years preceding the initiation of reforms. However, during the next two years, 1953 and 1954, the kolkhoz sector returned and advanced funds through financial channels to the tune of about a quarter of a billion rubles each year. Net money obtained in the two subsequent years, 1955 and 1956, was positive but negligible. However, net money obtained was significantly positive in each of the three following years, amounting to half a billion rubles in 1957 and to about a billion rubles in 1958 and in 1959. The positive sign of net money obtained in 1957 was largely due to a state-sponsored campaign for the acquisition of private livestock. The MTS transaction and the resulting increased level of money operating expenses were responsible for the net inflow of funds through financial channels in 1958 and 1959. And during the following three years, 1960–1962, the kolkhoz sector advanced and returned funds through financial channels at a rate close to half a billion rubles per year, which was in part a result of the very rapid liquidation of deferred payments extended by the state budget on the MTS transaction and in part due to the rebuilding of cash balances depleted in consequence of the MTS transaction.

Thus, with one major exception, financial channels did not provide significant funds in support of the modernization of the kolkhoz sector. The exception is itself ambiguous in this respect, for the MTS transaction is an exception in more ways than one. In the first place, purchase of the physical assets of the MTS was obligatory, and to the extent that it was not financed out of inside funds, financing was provided by the state budget in the form of deferred payment and not through established financial channels.[12] Undoubtedly, this procedure was made necessary by the fact that most kolkhozy would not have been able to qualify for long-term credit under established procedures. The MTS transaction is an exception in another sense as well, for it did not represent a net addition to the capital stock available to kolkhozy for productive operations, although some gain in efficiency may have resulted from the elimination of dual management and conflicts of interest between the MTS system and kolkhozy.

Moreover, although the provision of financing in the form of deferred payments did partly offset the impact of the MTS transaction on other, more productive, uses of funds in 1958, the rapidity with which these obligations were liquidated and the need to replenish cash balances depleted by the transaction had a severe negative impact upon money pay (and total pay as well) to kolkhozniki and upon money expenditures on capital account from 1959 to 1961. Thus the strain imposed upon the financial position of kolkhozy halted temporarily the progress that had been made toward pecuniarization of the sector, toward improvement in incentives to work on the collective, and toward net capital formation. If the long-term consequences of the MTS transaction were favorable, the short-term

[12] M. G. Vainer (ed.), *Effektivnost' kapital'nykh vlozhenii v sel'skoe khoziaistvo* (Moscow, 1963), pp. 200–201.

effects were seriously unfavorable and to all indications needlessly so. Nonetheless, the kolkhoz sector weathered the storm, if some farms did not, and the earlier, more favorable pattern was re-established by 1962.

A consideration of net money obtained by the kolkhoz sector during the period 1952–1962 indicates, therefore, that financing through financial channels played an equivocal role in the modernization of the sector. The implication is that state financial policy failed to support, and in some instances undercut, the major institutional and price reforms that were carried out in the kolkhoz sector.

The Behavior of the Kolkhoz Sector, 1952–1962

The evidence provided by sources and uses of funds statements indicates that the kolkhoz sector tends, in the absence of administrative pressure, to respond somewhat passively to changes in money income, despite being the only producing sector with access to long-term financing. By "passively responding" to income changes, I refer to the fact that changes in the sector's ordinary expenditures tend to follow rather than to lead its income changes. Although borrowing on capital account tends to provide a net source of funds, net money advanced or returned on current account has tended to offset this inflow. Disregarding the MTS transaction, the pecuniarization and improvement in money and total earnings and the increased money expenditures on capital account were financed almost exclusively by increased average realized procurement prices. And the increased money income provided in this way was to some extent offset by a net financial flow away from the kolkhoz sector in five of the 11 years under consideration. The tendency is, then, for the sector to save more than it invests, a rather curious finding.

IV

There are a number of possible explanations for the rather conservative investment behavior of the kolkhoz sector. These possible determinants of kolkhoz behavior fall into two main categories: (1) those connected with the expected remunerativeness and the availability of capital goods and (2) those related to the availability of loanfunds and the composition of the sector's loanfund balances. A case can be made, I believe, for either category, but I shall concentrate on the latter since little attention has been devoted to it. Moreover, I am prepared to maintain that state financial policy has been sufficient to explain the passive behavior of the kolkhoz sector, whatever the case for the other category.

I shall be very brief and merely outline the main determinants of the conservative financial behavior indicated by the sources and uses of funds statements for the kolkhoz sector for the years 1952–1962.

First, until July, 1966, kolkhozy were not permitted to finance distribution to members through short-term borrowing.[13] One consequence of this "goods only" policy was a tendency for kolkhozy to hold relatively large cash balances on current account over the winter months, a practice accentuated by central administrative pressure on kolkhozy to pay a portion of monthly or quarterly advances to working members in cash. Moreover, until 1959, a ceiling on the total of outstanding short-term debt was set by the sum of the sector's cash balances on current account.[14] The aim of this restriction was, no doubt, to prevent net money obtained on current account from rising above zero for the sector as a whole, but the effect was to insure that net money obtained would be negative since the time shapes of receipts and disbursements were relatively homogeneous for the various kolkhozy. The effect was, then, to make short-term credit unavailable when it was most needed and available when least necessary.

Second, the requirement that a fixed proportion of money proceeds be transferred to capital account, coupled with the bunching of receipts in the autumn months, has tended to create a relatively large cash balance on capital account, since capital expenditures and accumulation follow different time patterns. Third, the terms and conditions for long-term borrowing by kolkhozy have made it advisable to maintain relatively large cash reserves, for it is not possible to refinance outstanding debt and failure to make principal and interest payments on outstanding debt precludes further borrowing.[15]

These factors have made it advisable and desirable for the kolkhoz to hold sizable cash balances. Thus, holdings of financial assets tend to rise with the level of money income and to offset increments to the sector's financial liabilities.

A fourth and fundamental determinant of conservative kolkhoz finan-

---

[13] *Pravda*, May 18, 1966, p. 2.

[14] Descriptions of short-term credit policy may be found in: E. A. Kirillov, *Finansy kolkhozov* (Moscow, 1962), pp. 34–35; M. K. Shermenev (ed.), *Finansy i kreditovanie sel'skokhoziaistvennykh predpriiatii* (Moscow, 1963), Chapter VI; I. D. Laptev et al. (eds.), *Obshchestvennye fondy kolkhozov* (Moscow, 1961), pp. 187–189.

[15] For a description of the terms and conditions for long-term borrowing, see Shermenev, pp. 280–290, and D. S. Moliakov (ed.), *Finansirovanie narodnogo khoziaistva* (Moscow, 1962), pp. 145–149. For the Party directive outlining the 1961 financial reform for the kolkhoz sector, see K. I. Orliankin (ed.), *Sbornik reshenii po sel'skomu khoziaistvu* (Moscow, 1963), pp. 78–114.

cial behavior is to be found in what appears to be a distinct distaste on the part of Soviet economists, bankers, and administrators for debt instruments as means to finance capital investment expenditures. The differential rent discussions, for example, which I have analyzed elsewhere,[16] indicate a strong preference for financing capital investment from inside funds, a preference which apparently is founded in the misconception that financial accumulation must *precede* investment. This preference for inside fund financing is seen in the neglect of financial instruments in general in the Soviet economy, except on a short-term basis, and in the conservative and stringent conditions under which long-term loans are available to kolkhozy. An important consequence of this distaste for debt is also seen in the fact that kolkhoz access to long-term borrowing is essentially a function of the current-year success of the kolkhoz rather than the expectation of remunerative investment. For unless the current year is relatively good, the kolkhoz will find it difficult to raise additional funds through financial channels.

All things considered, a tentative conclusion may be drawn at this point. State financial policy and practice have been very conservative, sufficiently conservative to preclude the use of financial channels to finance modernization of the kolkhoz sector in any significant degree. This has thrown the burden upon price policy, thus further complicating the already complex problems of price formation presented by the peculiar nature of the kolkhoz sector. The repeated extensions on existing long-term debt, the tendency to forgive rather than to refinance kolkhoz debt, the manner in which the MTS was financed, and the recent favorable change in the conditions for short-term borrowing all substantiate this conclusion.

[16] James R. Millar, "Price and Income Formation in the Soviet Collective-Farm Sector Since 1953" (Ph.D. dissertation, Cornell University, 1965), Chapters IV and V.

Table 1 : *Current account sources and uses of funds, kolkhoz sector, 1949–196*

	Sources of Funds	1949	1950	1951	1952	1953	1!
A.	Deliveries and sales to state and cooperative agencies	—	2.150	—	2.450	3.240	4.
B.	Sales in collective farm trade	—	0.920	—	1.460	1.360	1.
C.	Sales of subsidiary enterprises and income, n.e.c.[a]	—	0.350	—	0.370	0.360	0.
D.	Total operating sources	2.770	3.420	3.860	4.280	4.960	6.
E.	Insurance benefits (crop and working capital)	—	—	—	—	0.055	
F.	Total nonfinancial sources	2.770	3.420	3.860	4.280	5.015	6.
G.	Net funds obtained through financial channels	0	0	0.114	0.131	0	
H.	Total sources of funds (rounded)	2.770	3.420	3.970	4.410	5.020	6.
	Uses of Funds						
I.	Income tax payments	0.240	0.254	0.380	0.420	0.400	0.
J.	Insurance premiums and transfers, n.e.c.	0.060	0.070	0.080	0.270	0.350	0.
K.	Total payments to the state	0.300	0.324	0.460	0.690	0.750	0.
L.	Money expenditure on productive needs	0.840	1.030	1.160	1.050	1.150	1
M.	Operating outlays, n.e.c.	0.030	0.040	0.040	0.050	0.050	0
N.	Total outlays on production-related needs	0.870	1.070	1.200	1.100	1.200	1
O.	Money labor payments	0.930	1.185	1.290	1.410	2.110	2
P.	Money transfer to capital account	0.446	0.550	0.621	0.740	0.867	1
Q.	Retirement of long-term debt (to capital account)	0.080	0.060	0.127	0.120	0.147	0
R.	Money transfer to working capital account	—	—	—	—	0.150	0
S.	Money transfer to cultural-welfare fund	0.060	—	—	0.090	—	
T.	Money transfer to aid and pension funds	0	0	0	0	0	0
U.	Total transfers above	0.586	0.610	0.748	0.950	1.164	1
V.	Total nonfinancial uses of funds	2.686	3.189	3.698	4.150	5.224	6
W.	Net current account funds advanced or returned through financial channels	0.065	0.174	0	0	0.192	0
X.	Total uses of funds above (rounded)	2.750	3.360	3.700	4.150	5.420	6
Y.	Discrepancy: uses of funds not accounted for	0.020	0.060	0.270	0.260	−0.400	−0

[a] n.e.c.: not elsewhere classified.
[b] Subsequently subsumed under indivisible fund transfer (Row P).

1955	1956	1957	1958	1959	1960	1961	1962	Source or Operation	
5.480	7.470	7.410	10.850	11.380	10.880	11.520	13.140		A.
1.570	1.390	1.360	1.550	1.480	1.500	1.190	1.230		B.
0.510	0.600	0.750	0.800	0.830	0.960	0.860	0.870		C.
7.560	9.460	9.520	13.200	13.690	13.340	13.570	15.240	A+B+C	D.
—	—	—	0.115	—	0.270	—	—		E.
7.560	9.460	9.520	13.315	13.690	13.610	13.570	15.240	D+E	F.
0	0	0.267	0	0.914	0.061	0	0	Table 3, Row E	G.
7.560	9.460	9.790	13.320	14.600	13.670	13.570	15.240	F+G	H.
0.625	0.752	0.849	1.031	1.238	1.207	0.887	1.000		I.
0.265	0.308	0.284	0.317	0.268	0.290	0.290	0.290	K−I	J.
0.890	1.060	1.133	1.348	1.506	1.497	1.177	1.290	I+J	K.
0.630	1.930	2.085	3.155	3.349	3.560	2.795	2.795		L.
0.080	0.100	0.238	0.449	0.210	0.130	0.485	0.485	N−L	M.
0.710	2.030	2.323	3.604	3.559	3.690	3.280	3.280	L+M	N.
0.100	4.060	4.065	4.673	4.792	4.633	5.610	6.390		O.
0.322	1.673	1.682	3.042	3.334	3.196	3.203	3.430	Table 2, Row C	P.
0.205[b]								Table 2, Row A	Q.
—	0.341	0.219	0.396	0.329	0.293	—	—		R.
—	0.142	0.162	0.172	0.246	0.173	—	—		S.
0.040	0.040	0.040	0.060	0.110	0.150	0.180	0.180		T.
0.567	2.196	2.103	3.610	4.019	3.812	3.383	3.610	P+Q+R+S+T	U.
0.267	9.346	9.624	13.235	13.813	13.632	13.440	14.570	K+N+O+U	V.
0.067	0.191	0	0.217	0	0	0.543	0.530	Table 3, Row E	W.
0.330	9.540	9.620	13.450	13.810	13.630	13.980	15.100	V+W	X.
0.230	−0.080	0.170	−0.130	0.790	0.040	−0.410	0.140	H−X	Y.

Table 2 : *Capital account sources and uses of funds, kolkhoz sector, 1949–1962*

	Sources of Funds	1949	1950	1951	1952	1953	19
A.	Transfer to retire long-term liabilities	0.080	0.060	0.127	0.120	0.147	0.1
B.	Money pay transfer for f.a.c.[a]	—	—	—	—	—	0.1
C.	Indivisible fund transfer	0.446	0.550	0.621	0.740	0.867	1.1
D.	Total transfers from current account	0.526	0.610	0.748	0.860	1.014	1.
E.	Direct money receipts on capital account	0.179	0.284	0.280	0.280	0.289	0.1
F.	Total nonfinancial sources	0.705	0.894	1.028	1.140	1.303	1.6
G.	Net funds obtained through financial channels	0.213	0.140	0.135	0.083	0.014	0.
H.	Total sources	0.918	1.034	1.163	1.223	1.317	1.
	Uses of Funds						
I.	Money capital expenditures, n.e.c.	—	0.512	0.608	0.686	0.875	1.
J.	Money capital repair expenditures	—	0.120	0.125	0.136	0.165	0.
K.	Acquisition of working and productive cattle	—	0.322	0.405	0.267	0.209	0.
L.	Total money capital outlays	0.914	0.955	1.138	1.089	1.249	1.
M.	Funds advanced or returned through financial channels	0	0	0	0	0	
N.	Total uses of funds	0.914	0.955	1.138	1.089	1.249	1.
O.	Discrepancy	0.004	0.079	0.025	0.134	0.068	0.

[a] f.a.c.: force account construction.
[b] Series subsumed in indivisible fund transfer subsequently.

Table 3 : *Loanfund financing, kolkhoz sector (current rubles, millions).*

	Current Account	1948	1949	1950	1951	1952	1
	Loanfunds receivable, December 31						
A.	Deposit balance	145.6	210.6	384.5	336.6	271.3	5
B.	Increment loanfunds receivable	—	65.0	173.9	−47.9	−65.3	2
	Loanfunds payable, December 31						
C.	Short-term debt	—	—	42.8	108.4	174.0	2
D.	Increment loanfunds payable	—	—	—	65.6	65.6	
E.	Net funds obtained, current account	—	−65.0	−173.9	113.5	130.9	−1
	Capital Account						
	Loanfunds receivable, December 31						
F.	Deposit balance	237.4	213.9	285.1	346.0	409.0	5
G.	Increment loanfunds receivable	—	−23.5	101.8	61.0	61.0	1
	Loanfunds payable, December 31						
H.	Long-term debt	225.9	415.5	657.5	853.3	997.3	1,1
I.	Increment long-term debt	—	189.6	242.0	195.8	144.0	1
J.	Deferred liability, MTS purchase	—	—	—	—	—	
K.	Increment deferred liability	—	—	—	—	—	
L.	Net funds obtained, capital account	—	213.1	140.2	134.8	83.0	
	Consolidated Account						
M.	Net funds obtained, consolidated account	—	148.1	−33.7	248.3	213.9	−1

[a] Adjusted to reflect the change in trade receivables for these years (*Obshchestvennye fo*

rrent rubles, billions).

1955	1956	1957	1958	1959	1960	1961	1962	Source or Operation	
0.205[b]									A.
0.161	0.072	0.058	0.077[b]						B.
1.322	1.673	1.682	3.042	3.334	3.196	3.203	3.430		C.
1.688	1.745	1.740	3.119	3.334	3.196	3.203	3.430	A+B+C	D.
0.244	0.273	0.284	0.322	0.600	0.958	0.964	1.020		E.
1.932	2.018	2.024	3.441	3.934	4.154	4.167	4.450	D+E	F.
0.149	0.221	0.282	1.476	0.259	0	0	0.130	Table 3, Row L	G.
2.081	2.239	2.306	4.917	4.193	4.154	4.167	4.580	F+G	H.
1.528	1.725	1.687	3.966	2.780	2.441	2.566	2.894		I.
0.216	0.247	0.262	0.381	0.683	0.703	0.657	0.630		J.
0.201	0.335	0.437	0.503	0.662	1.025	0.994	1.127		K.
1.945	2.307	2.385	4.850	4.446	4.167	4.218	4.651	I+J+K	L.
0	0	0	0	0	0.372	0.108	0		M.
1.945	2.307	2.385	4.850	4.446	4.539	4.326	4.651	L+M	N.
0.136	−0.068	−0.079	0.67	−0.253	−0.385	−0.159	−0.071	H−N	O.

1954	1955	1956	1957	1958	1959	1960	1961	1962	Source or Operation	
95.7	985.5	1,189.8	1,022.1	1,170.2	697.2	600.8	1,122.0	1,716.1		A.
92.5	89.8	204.3	−167.7	218.8[a]	−586.6[a]	−96.4	521.2	594.1	Increment A	B.
36.9	260.0	273.2	372.8	374.6	701.7	666.0	644.0	708.0		C.
23.1	23.1	13.2	99.4	01.8	327.1	−35.7	−22.0	64.0	Increment C	D.
59.4	−66.7	−191.1	267.1	−217.0	913.7	60.7	−543.0	−530.2	D−B	E.
14.0	698.1	776.8	625.6	465.7	324.9	279.3	474.0	689.6		F.
84.0	84.0	78.8	−151.2	−159.9	−140.8	−45.9	195.0	215.6	Increment F	G.
43.7	1,576.2	1,876.1	2,007.1	2,173.0	2,355.9	2,378.3	2,645.6	3,101.6		H.
0.6	232.5	299.8	131.0	165.9	182.9	22.4	267.3	456.0	Increment H	I.
—	—	—	0.0	1,150.0	1,085.0	645.0	465.0	355.0		J.
—	—	—	—	1,150.0	−65.0	−440.0	−180.0	−110.0	Increment J	K.
6.6	148.5	221.0	282.2	1,475.8	258.7	−371.7	−107.7	130.4	I+K−G	L.
2.8	81.8	29.9	549.3	1,258.8	1,172.4	−311.0	−650.7	−399.8	E+L	M.

236).

Table 4 : *Financing kolkhoz development (current rubles, billions).*

		1949	1950	1951	1952	1953	19
A.	Combined nonfinancial sources of funds[a]	3.480	4.310	4.890	5.420	6.310	7.
B.	Nonfinancial uses of funds, n.e.c.[b]	1.760	2.000	2.410	2.740	3.100	3.
C.	Consolidated nonfinancial sources, n.e.c.	1.720	2.310	2.480	2.680	3.200	4.
D.	Estimated cumulative gain from inflation (1952 = 100)	—	—	—	—	1.140	2.
E.	Net nonfinancial sources, n.e.c. (I)	1.720	2.310	2.480	2.680	2.060	1.
F.	Estimated incremental gain from inflation	—	—	—	—	1.140	1.
G.	Net nonfinancial sources, n.e.c. (II)	1.720	2.310	2.480	2.680	2.060	3.
H.	Money labor payments[a]	0.930	1.190	1.290	1.410	2.110	2.
I.	Money nonfinancial capital outlays[a]	0.910	0.960	1.140	1.090	1.250	1.
J.	Net money obtained through financial channels[a]	0.150	−0.030	0.250	0.210	−0.180	−0.
K.	Discrepancy[a]	0.030	0.130	0.300	0.390	−0.340	0.

[a] Figures have been rounded.
[b] I.e., exclusive of money labor payments.

NOTES AND SOURCES FOR TABLE 1

For full citations, see Sources at the end of this appendix.

Rows A, B, and C
    1950, 1953, 1956–1959: *Sel'skoe khoziaistvo*, pp. 64, 56.
    1952, 1960–1962: *Narodnoe khoziaistvo . . . 1962*, p. 342.
    1954: Abriutina, p. 119.
    1955: *Narodnoe khoziaistvo . . . 1960*, p. 496.

Row D
    1949: Computed from Venzher, *Kolkhoznyi*, Table 10, p. 66.
    1951: Hoeffding and Nimitz, p. 35 and footnotes (a) and (b), p. 36.
    1954: *Narodnoe khoziaistvo . . . 1956*, p. 140.

Row E
    1953: Zverev, p. 256, and Koriunov, p. 15.
    1958, 1960: Derived from Zverev, pp. 255–256, and Vainer, p. 197.

Row G
    See Table 3.

Row I
    1949: Hoeffding and Nimitz, p. 35 and corresponding notes, pp. 36–38.
    1950, 1955–1960: *Gos. biudzhet*, p. 8.
    1951: Estimated as twice the portion of kolkhoz income tax payments allo-

1955	1956	1957	1958	1959	1960	1961	1962	*Source or Operation*	
9.490	11.480	11.540	16.760	17.620	17.760	17.740	19.690	Tables 1 and 2	A.
4.170	5.290	5.560	8.560	9.020	9.000	7.830	8.180	Table 1	B.
5.320	6.190	5.980	8.200	8.600	8.760	9.910	11.510	A−B	C.
2.860	4.490	4.630	7.180	7.610	7.240	7.730	9.160		D.
2.460	1.700	1.350	1.020	0.990	1.520	2.180	2.350	C−D	E.
0.060	1.240	0.420	1.080	0.220	−0.110	0.230	1.090		F.
5.260	4.950	5.560	7.120	8.380	8.870	9.680	10.420	C−F	G.
3.100	4.060	4.070	4.670	4.790	4.630	5.610	6.390	Table 1, Row O	H.
1.950	2.310	2.390	4.850	4.450	4.170	4.220	4.650	Table 2, Row L	I.
0.080	0.030	0.550	1.260	1.170	−0.310	−0.650	−0.400	Table 3, Row M	J.
0.350	−0.150	0.070	−0.060	0.530	−0.350	−0.570	0.070	(D+E)−(H+I) +J, or (F+G) −(H+I) +J	K.

cated to republic budgets, as was the case for 1950 and 1952. *Gos. biudzhety,* p. 13.

1952: *Finansy,* p. 66.

1953–1954: United Nations, IV, 34.

1961: Alekseeva and Voronin, p. 49.

1962: Venzher, *Kolkhoznyi,* p. 80.

Row J

1949–1951: Hoeffding and Nimitz, p. 35 and corresponding notes, pp. 36–38.

1957: Nimitz, *Soviet National Income,* pp. 98–99.

1958: Rozhin, p. 35.

Row K

1952–1954: Neden and Nesmiia, based upon percentages of money income given on pp. 23, 35.

1955: *Finansy SSSR,* no. 10 (1957), p. 34.

1956–1957: Nimitz, *Soviet National Income,* pp. 98–99.

1958: Rozhin, p. 35.

1959: *Obshchestvennye fondy,* p. 230.

Row L

1949: Hoeffding and Nimitz, p. 35 and corresponding notes on pp. 36–38.

1950: Estimated as 30 percent of money receipts, as was the case for 1951.

1951: Computed as 30 percent of money receipts. *Voprosy ekonomiki,* no. 1 (1952), p. 41.

1952: Neden and Nesmiia, p. 37, where it is given as 24.6 percent of money receipts.

1953–1954, 1956: Computed from absolute and percentage data given in Alekseeva and Voronin, p. 200.

1955: Interpolation, 1954 and 1956.

1957: Nimitz, *Soviet National Income*, pp. 98–99.

1958–1961: Nedelin *et al.*, pp. 24–25, 204.

1962: Same as 1961.

Row M

1949–1951: Hoeffding and Nimitz, p. 35 and accompanying notes, pp. 36–38.

1952: Bergson, p. 187.

1953–1956, 1960: As computed by Bronson and Krueger in Chapter 10, Appendix Table 3, of the present volume.

1957: Nimitz, *Soviet National Income*, pp. 98–99.

1958: Rozhin, p. 35.

1962: Same as 1961.

Row N

1959: *Obshchestvennye fondy*, p. 230.

1961: U. S. Department of Agriculture, p. 41.

Row O

1949, 1951: Hoeffding and Nimitz, p. 35 and accompanying notes on pp. 36–38.

1956–1957: Nimitz, *Soviet National Income*, pp. 98–99.

1958: Rozhin, p. 35.

1959: *Obshchestvennye fondy*, p. 230.

1950, 1954: Computed by multiplying the total number of *trudodni* earned in each year (*Narodnoe khoziaistvo . . . 1956*, p. 141) by the average money pay per *trudoden'* reported for each year (for 1950, see Venzher, *Voprosy*, p. 221) and estimated absolute figure for 1958, based on 1958 total money pay (for 1954, index given by Teriaeva, p. 107).

1952: Nimitz, *Farm Employment*, p. 96.

1953: *Partiinaia zhizn'*, no. 13 (1957), p. 27.

1955: *Istoriia*, p. 411.

1960: Derived by splicing indices of total money pay given by Konnik, p. 61, and *Finansy*, p. 172, and then utilizing the absolute figure for 1956 in this table.

1961: U.S. Department of Agriculture, p. 41.

1962: Nimitz, *Farm Employment*, p. 96.

Row R

1953: Neden and Nesmiia, p. 36, and money receipts for 1953.

1954: Alekseeva and Voronin, p. 83.

1956–1960: Nedelin *et al.*, p. 136, and money receipts, Row D, in this table.

Row S
 1949: Hoeffding and Nimitz, pp. 35, 36–38.
 1952: Bergson, p. 187.
 1956–1960: Nedelin *et al.*, p. 136, and Row D of this table.

Row T
 1949–1961: As derived by Bronson and Krueger in Chapter 10, Appendix Table 3, in the present volume.
 1962: Same as 1961.

Row U
 1957: Nimitz, *Soviet National Income*, pp. 98–99.
 1958: Rozhin, p. 35.

Row W
 See Table 3.

NOTES AND SOURCES FOR TABLE 2

For full citations, see Sources at the end of this appendix.

Row A
 1949–1953: Golev, pp. 35, 47.
 1954–1955: Koriunov, p. 23.

Row B
 1954–1958: Koriunov, p. 23.

Row C
 1949, 1951: Estimated respectively as 16 percent and 16.1 percent of total money receipts in these years.
 1950: *Sel'skoe khoziaistvo*, pp. 56–57.
 1952: *Narodnoe khoziaistvo . . . 1959*, p. 423.
 1953–1958: Koriunov, pp. 15, 23.
 1959–1961: Vainer, p. 197.
 1962: *Narodnoe khoziaistvo . . . 1962*, p. 330.

Row E
 1949–1950: Row F minus Row D.
 1951–1952: Interpolations.
 1953, 1958: Koriunov, p. 15.
 1954: Partial data, Koriunov, p. 28.
 1955–1956: The total for these two years is estimated from the annual average figure for 1955–1957, given by Alekseeva and Voronin, p. 91, and the known total for 1957 and the known subtotal for 1956 given on p. 69, and in Vainer, p. 197.
 1957–1961: Vainer, p. 197, and Koriunov, p. 15.

1962: Computed from Nedelin, pp. 46–47, and the indivisible fund transfer for 1962.

Row F

1949–1950: Computed from data on deposits to capital account in these years as a percent of total sources on capital account, Golev, p. 39, plus Row A of this table.

Row I

1950: Alekseeva and Voronin, p. 106, and total, Row L.

1951–1955: Golev, p. 51.

1956: *Gos. bank*, p. 61.

1957–1958: Koriunov, p. 43.

1960–1961: Alekseeva and Voronin, p. 105.

1962: Nedelin, p. 57.

1959: Determined by subtracting known figures for 1956–1958 and 1960 from aggregate for 1956–1960 given in *Gos. bank*, p. 61.

Row J

1950: Alekseeva and Voronin, p. 106, and total, Row L.

1951–1955: Golev, p. 51.

1953, 1957–1958: Koriunov, p. 43.

1956–1960: Vainer, p. 47.

1960–1961: Alekseeva and Voronin, p. 105.

1962: Nedelin, p. 57.

Row K

1950: Alekseeva and Voronin, p. 106, and total, Row L.

1951–1955: Golev, p. 51.

1956, 1960: *Gos. bank*, p 61.

1957–1958: Koriunov, p. 43.

1960–1961: Alekseeva and Voronin, p. 105.

1962: Nedelin, p. 57.

1959: *Gos. bank*, p. 61, total for 1956–1960 less other known years.

Row L

1949–1950: Estimated from data provided by Golev, pp. 35, 37, 40.

1959: Computed from Table 55 in Alekseeva and Voronin, p. 200.

NOTES AND SOURCES FOR TABLE 3

For full citations, see Sources at the end of this appendix.

Row A

1948–1955: Atlas, pp. 141, 218, 238, 281.

1956–1958: *Narodnoe khoziaistvo . . . 1958*, p. 913.

1959: *Narodnoe khoziaistvo . . . 1959*, p. 808.

1960–1962: Atlas *et al.*, p. 151.

Row B
1958–1959: Adjusted to reflect data on the change in trade receivables for 1958 and 1959 given in *Obshchestvennye fondy*, p. 236.

Row C
1950, 1953, 1956–1959: *Obshchestvennye fondy*, p. 188.
1952, 1960–1962: *Narodnoe khoziaistvo . . . 1962*, p. 639.
1955: Bachurin and Kondrashev, p. 299.
1951, 1954: Interpolations.

Row F
1950, 1953, 1956–1958: *Narodnoe khoziaistvo . . . 1958*, p. 914.
1955: Golev, p. 53.
1952: Derived from Koriunov, p. 30, and 1956 balance.
1959: *Narodnoe khoziaistvo . . . 1959*, p. 808.
1960–1962: Atlas *et al.*, p. 151.
1948–1949: Computed from data on deposits and withdrawals to this account for the years 1946–1950 (Golev, pp. 39, 40) and the balance for 1946 (p. 77), taking the 1947 20 percent currency reform reduction into account.
1951, 1954: Interpolations.

Row H
1950, 1953, 1955, 1956: Golev, p. 72.
1952, 1959–1962: *Narodnoe khoziaistvo . . . 1962*, p. 642.
1957–1958: *Narodnoe khoziaistvo . . . 1958*, p. 909.
1948–1949, 1951, 1954: Determined from long-term loan extension and retirement data and the known year-end balances for 1950, 1952, and 1955. Tsagolov, p. 174, and Golev, pp. 35, 47.

Row J
Year-end balances for deferred payments for MTS assets have been estimated as follows (current rubles, millions):

	1958	1959	1960	1961	1962	1963	1964
Extensions	1,150[a, b]	315[b]	0	260[c, e]	0	0	0
Retirements	0	380[g]	440[g]	440[g]	110[g]	110[g]	110[g]
Year-end balance	1,150	1,085	645[d]	465[d]	355	245	135[f]

[a] Koriunov, p. 83; Alekseeva and Voronin, p. 101.
[b] Vainer, pp. 200–201, and regular long-term loan extensions as given in *Narodnoe khoziaistvo . . . 1962*, p. 641.
[c] Usoskin, p. 309.
[d] *Gos. bank*, p. 73. The figure given for July 1, 1961, is 554 million rubles.
[e] *Gos. bank*, p. 64.
[f] D'iachenko *et al.*, p. 236, which indicates at least a 120 million–ruble balance on December 31, 1964.
[g] Retirement rates are arbitrarily determined to coincide with known final balances for July 1, 1961, and January 1, 1965, as follows:
(1) 1958 balance allotted over 3-year period;
(2) 1959 extension allotted over 5-year period;
(3) 1961 extension allotted over 5-year period.

NOTES AND SOURCES FOR TABLE 4

For full citations, see Sources at the end of this appendix.

Row A
Table 1, Row F, plus Table 2, Row F.

Row B
Table 1, Row V minus Row O, i.e., all current account nonfinancial uses other than money pay.

Row D
Estimated as the difference between the current-ruble value of deliveries and sales to state and cooperative agencies (Table 1, Row A) and the deflated, constant-ruble value of the same series (1952 = 100). The index of average state procurement prices is taken from Stoliarov, p. 121 (Table 17).

Row F
Estimated as for Row D, but by moving the base year of the price index forward for each year.

SOURCES CITED IN THE TABLES

Abriutina, M. S. *Sel'skoe khoziaistvo v sisteme balansa narodnogo khoziaistva.* Moscow, 1965.
Alekseeva, R. V., and A. P. Voronin. *Nakoplenie i razvitie kolkhoznoi sobstvennosti.* Moscow, 1963.
Atlas, M. *Razvitie gosudarstvennogo banka SSSR.* Moscow, 1958.
Atlas, M. S., *et al. Kreditno-denezhnaia sistema SSSR.* Moscow, 1967.
Bachurin, A. V., and D. D. Kondrashev (eds.). *Tovarno-denezhnye otnosheniia v period perekhoda k kommunizmu.* Moscow, 1963.
Bergson, Abram. *The Economics of Soviet Planning.* New Haven Conn.: Yale University Press, 1964.
D'iachenko, V. P., *et al. 50-let sovetskikh finansov.* Moscow, 1967.
Finansy i sotsialisticheskoe stroitel'stvo. Moscow, 1957.
Finansy SSSR, no. 10 (1957).
Golev, Ia. I. *Sel'skokhoziaistvennyi kredit v SSSR.* Moscow, 1958.
Gosudarstvennyi bank SSSR k XXII s''ezdu KPSS. Moscow, 1961.
Gosudarstvennyi biudzhet SSSR i biudzhety soiuznykh respublik, statisticheskii sbornik. Moscow, 1962.
Gosudarstvennye biudzhety soiuznykh respublik v piatoi piatiletke, statisticheskii sbornik. Moscow, 1957.
Hoeffding, O., and Nancy Nimitz. *Soviet National Income and Product, 1949–1955.* Santa Monica, Calif.: RAND Corp., April 6, 1959.

Istoriia sovetskogo krest'ianstva i kolkhoznogo stroitel'stva v SSSR. Moscow, 1963.

Konnik, I. I. *Den'gi v period stroitel'stva kommunisticheskogo obshchestva.* Moscow, 1966.

Koriunov, S. *Nedelimye fondy i kapital'nye vlozheniia kolkhozov.* Moscow, 1960.

Narodnoe khoziaistvo SSSR v 1956 godu. Moscow, 1957.

Narodnoe khoziaistvo SSSR v 1958 godu. Moscow, 1959.

Narodnoe khoziaistvo SSSR v 1959 godu. Moscow, 1960.

Narodnoe khoziaistvo SSSR v 1960 godu. Moscow, 1961.

Narodnoe khoziaistvo SSSR v 1962 godu. Moscow, 1963.

Nedelin, S. I. (ed.) *Organizatsiia finansov kolkhoza.* Moscow, 1964.

Nedelin, S. I., *et al. Denezhnye dokhody kolkhozov i differentsial'naia renta.* Moscow, 1963.

Neden, S. I., and M. I. Nesmiia (eds.). *Voprosy sebestoimosti i rentabel'nosti v kolkhozakh.* Moscow, 1959.

Nimitz, Nancy. *Farm Employment in the Soviet Union, 1928–1963.* Santa Monica, Calif.: RAND Corp., November, 1965.

―――. *Soviet National Income and Product, 1956–1958.* Santa Monica, Calif.: RAND Corp., June, 1962.

Obshchestvennye fondy kolkhozov i raspredelenie kolkhoznykh dokhodov. Moscow, 1961.

Partiinaia zhizn', no. 13 (1957).

Rozhin, V. P. *Nekotorye voprosy pod"ema ekonomiki slabykh kolkhozov.* Moscow, 1961.

Sel'skoe khoziaistvo SSSR, statisticheskii sbornik. Moscow, 1960.

Stoliarov, S. G. *O tsenakh i tsenoobrazovanii v SSSR.* Moscow, 1969.

Teriaeva, A. "Pod"em obshchestvennogo proizvodstva i sovershenstvovanie form oplaty truda v kolkhozakh." *Voprosy ekonomiki,* no. 1 (1959).

Tsagolov, N. A. (ed.) *Razvitie kolkhoznoi sobstvennosti v period razvernutogo stroitel'stva kommunizma.* Moscow, 1961.

United Nations. *Economic Survey of Europe in 1960.* Geneva: Secretariat of the Economic Commission for Europe, 1961.

U.S. Department of Agriculture. *Soviet Agriculture Today.* Foreign Agricultural Economic Report no. 131. Washington, D.C.: U.S. Government Printing Office, December, 1963.

Usoskin, M. M. *Organizatsiia i planirovanie kredita.* Moscow, 1961.

Vainer, M. G. (ed.) *Effektivnost' kapital'nykh vlozhenii v sel'skoe khoziaistvo.* Moscow, 1963.

Venzher, V. G. *Kolkhoznyi stroi na sovremennom etape.* Moscow, 1966.

―――. *Voprosy ispol'zovaniia zakona stoimosti v kolkhozakh.* Moscow, 1960.

Voprosy ekonomiki, no. 1 (1952).

Zverev, A. G. *Natsional'nyi dokhod i finansy SSSR.* Moscow, 1961.

PART IV

The Texture of
Rural Life

12 : The Peasants as a Social Class

Alexander Vucinich

Soviet law and ideology state explicitly that peasants occupy a lower social position than workers. Five complementary explanations are given for the relatively low status of the peasants as a distinct social class. The first explanation is ideological and received much more elaboration during the 1930's and 1940's than at the present time: the creators of the Marxist legacy were quite consistent in their emphasis on the proletariat—an urban creation—as the only social class capable of spearheading a revolutionary movement guided by Communist ideology. The second explanation is historical: the socialization of industry preceded the collectivization of agriculture and created the historical conditions for the emergence and advancement of agricultural socialism. The third explanation is psychological: in comparison with the worker, the peasant is regarded as more influenced by traditions incompatible with socialist norms. The fourth explanation is social: in the grand division of labor in society, a lower value is attached to agricultural work than to industrial work. The fifth explanation is economic: the peasant, unlike the worker, has not yet been fully incorporated into the socialist economic system inasmuch as he is partially engaged in private economy.[1]

Until the end of World War II, empirical study of the rural community— and of the peasants as a social class—was sporadic, unsystematic, and theoretically unsophisticated.[2] Since the war, the kolkhoz community has been studied on a large scale first by ethnographers and then by both ethnographers and sociologists. Ethnographers, led by the Institute of Ethnography, a research unit of the Soviet Academy of Sciences, have been

[1] Alexander Vucinich, "Soviet Ethnographic Studies of Cultural Change," *American Anthropologist*, LCII (1960), 867.

[2] Earlier sociological studies of the rural community are briefly surveyed in Iu. V. Arutiunian, "Iz istorii sotsiologicheskikh issledovanii sela," *Sotsial'nye issledovaniia* (Moscow, 1968), II, 197–210.

interested in the cultural transformation of the peasantry—primarily the diffusion of urban traits in the countryside. They have focused their attention on the emergence of a new way of life through a constant and deep-rooted conflict between modern urban culture and rural traditionalism. They have accumulated valuable material on kolkhoz institutions, rural tradition, and urbanization processes.

Sociologists, on the other hand, have shown a marked interest in an empirical—and quantitative—scrutiny of the dynamics of social stratification in the rural community. They approach the problem of stratification on two levels: they continue to elaborate the five-fold differentiation of workers and peasants as distinct classes, but they also study status differentiation within the peasant class. They deal as much with the dynamics of intraclass stratification as they do with interclass relations.

In examining the differences between the two basic classes of Soviet society, modern Soviet sociologists readily admit that they are hampered by the lack of a clear and generally accepted definition of the workers' class. Today there are three distinct interpretations of this class.[3] According to the ideological and legalistic interpretation, it includes all persons working in enterprises and agencies whose institutional base is in public property; it covers all employed persons not classified as collective farmers. The second interpretation limits the workers' class to persons engaged in production—but not in services—based on public property. It includes both the ordinary workers and the engineering and technical intelligentsia engaged in industrial production. The third interpretation defines the workers' class as a social formation made up exclusively of persons engaged in "physical" work in publicly owned enterprises and institutions. It excludes all persons engaged in "mental" work, who are divided into employees (nonspecialists) and intelligentsia (specialists). Taking a hint from Polish sociology, the more alert sociologists find the concept of the workers' class a rather ambivalent tool for a satisfactory study of the inner dynamics of Soviet society. They contend that even the most specific definition of the workers' class has too many variables and unstructured attributes to be useful as a heuristic tool in comparative social class analysis. For this reason serious Soviet writers do not engage in sweeping comparative analyses of the two classes, but resort to a more modest examination of manageable variables. In the analysis of the peasant class, they usually combine two approaches: a *legalistic* study of the changes in the organization of kolkhoz economy and a *sociological* comparison of urban and rural cultures. Both approaches concentrate on the gradual transformation of kolkhoz economy into an integral component of full socialism. Each requires closer scrutiny.

[3] M. P. Rutkevich, "Problemy izmeneniia sotsial'noi struktury sovetskogo obshchestva," *Filosofskie nauki,* no. 3 (1968), pp. 46–47.

I

The legalistic study concentrates on legally defined differences between the factory (as the typical institutional base of the workers) and the kolkhoz (as the typical institutional base of the peasants). The factory is built upon the foundations of "consistent" socialism: both its means of production and its products are national property. The kolkhoz is built upon the foundations of "inconsistent" socialism since some of its property is "cooperative" rather than "national" and since it allows for the existence of a subsidiary private agricultural economy. The legalistic analyses reveal a wealth of information showing that "production relations" in collective agriculture are gradually approaching the socialist consistency of "production relations" in industry; that is, the differences between public ownership of industry and cooperative ownership of kolkhozy have increasingly become more nominal than real. The current phase in the directed development of collective farming "is characterized by a gradual transformation of cooperative-kolkhoz property into general-national property and by the process of a gradual eradication of social differences between the workers' class and the peasants, the city and the village."[4]

The gradual expansion and consolidation of consistent socialism in the agricultural economy is best illustrated by recent changes in the "indivisible funds" of the kolkhozy and by the economic activities of new inter-kolkhoz associations and joint government-kolkhoz economic enterprises.

In the modern kolkhoz the basic form of collective ownership of the means of production is the so-called indivisible funds, which include not only farm machinery and other cooperative equipment but also kolkhoz-built schools, hospitals, and farm buildings. The kolkhoz has no authority to divide these funds among individual members or to reduce them in any way.[5] They are de facto general national property and, for all practical purposes, indistinguishable from industrial means of production. They—and this is the chief characteristic of consistent socialism—invite *direct* government control over the economic and cultural activities of collective farms. During the initial phase in the development of kolkhozy, the bulk of the operating means of production consisted of the shares invested by individual kolkhozniki who had the legal right, more nominal than real, to reclaim them if they decided to leave the collective farm. Today no kolkhoznik

[4] A. K. Kurylov, "Kolkhoz kak sotsial'nyi institut sovetskogo obshchestva," *Filosofskie nauki,* no. 4 (1967), p. 32.

[5] N. A. Aitov, "Izmeneniia sotsial'noi prirody i klassovykh osobennostei krest'ianstva," in *Sotsiologiia v SSSR* (Moscow, 1965), I, 369.

has a private investment in collective agriculture. The purchase of farm machinery from the MTSs marked a major step toward bringing the indivisible funds closer to the general national property. By purchasing MTS equipment, the kolkhozy did not acquire the right to dispose of it. They merely opened another important vista for direct government control over kolkhoz economy and, according to Soviet legal theory, direct government control is the surest index of consistent or advanced socialism. Soviet writers make it abundantly clear that the rapid growth of indivisible funds and their paramount role in collective farming have not as yet fully assured direct government control over kolkhoz activity. The expanding financial participation of the government in the construction of rural roads, industrial plants, and dwellings contributes substantially to the planned incorporation of collectivized agriculture into the state economic sector.

The massive coalescence of comparatively small kolkhozy into huge associations effected during the 1950's has been heralded by Soviet interpreters of the law as another important step toward equating the cooperative property of collective farms with the general national property of industry. One aim of this coalescence was to replace the social atomism of scattered and relatively isolated rural communities with politically integrated larger social units. As viewed by Soviet interpreters, large kolkhozy facilitate not only the process of socializing kolkhoz property but also the industrialization of agricultural work. Industrialization, in turn, means the introduction of both advanced machine technology and "industrial control" over agricultural production, i.e., strict, precise, and daily control over the work of each kolkhoznik. The amalgamation of kolkhozy has also helped strengthen government control over the kolkhoz economy and made it possible to concentrate the mechanisms of Party supervision and activities in the countryside.

The present kolkhoz—holding, on average, 6,700 acres of cultivated land—serves as a basis for the formation of inter-kolkhoz associations, a new organizational development in the countryside and a powerful mechanism through which the kolkhoz economy is brought closer to the economic sector based exclusively on public ownership of the means of production. Inter-kolkhoz associations enable neighboring collective farms to pool their resources for a more rational and efficient solution of specific problems related either to agricultural production or to essential rural services.[6] The most common inter-kolkhoz associations are engaged in local construction projects. They pool the resources of member kolkhozy for the joint construction of schools, hospitals, small power plants, local roads, and larger farm buildings. An inter-kolkhoz association may operate a joint poultry

[6] A. I. Volkov, *O mezhdukolkhoznykh organizatsiiakh* (Moscow, 1963), pp. 3–8.

farm, a hog-fattening station, a food-processing plant, a motor pool, or a seed repository. These agencies introduce a new form of industrial specialization into the rural community. In their administrative organization, production control, and financial activities they are virtually indistinguishable from urban industry. They help create the conditions for a future merging of kolkhozy and sovkhozy into uniform agricultural enterprises no different from urban industrial establishments.

Another relatively recent development in the rural community is government-kolkhoz agencies, organized for the purpose of the joint operation of specific economic enterprises such as larger rural power stations, small mines, and food-processing plants which cannot be operated by kolkhoz funds alone. By contributing to the year-round employment of the rural population, these agencies help consolidate consistent socialism in the villages.

The legalistically oriented interpreters of these organizational changes in the kolkhoz economy are correct in pointing out the gradual reduction of cooperative property and the corresponding growth of general national property. They are also correct in their claims that the kolkhoz is on its way out and will eventually be replaced by agricultural enterprises which, in all probability, will be a unique synthesis of kolkhozy and sovkhozy and will be state enterprises. Legalistic observers of the rural community agree that the gradual eradication of differences between peasants and workers is the same as the gradual elimination of peasants as a distinct component of Soviet society. Noting the various processes leading to the elimination of the peasant class, they place particular emphasis on the technological advances in farming which have created a surplus of manpower in kolkhozy and have sent armies of peasants into industry.

Today the peasantry, as defined by law and ideology, make up less than one-quarter of the total population. During the last ten years a massive reduction in the peasant class has been effected through an intensified transformation of kolkhozy into sovkhozy.[7] In a speech delivered on October 30, 1968, L. I. Brezhnev announced that from 1957 to 1967 the number of sovkhozy increased from 5,000 to 12,800 and that at the present time sovkhozy held 43 percent of the cultivated land in the USSR. Today, one-half of the rural inhabitants are classified as workers, and sovkhozniki make up the bulk of this group.

The building of rural industries has also contributed to the formation of a new segment of rural workers. Today it is common to find kolkhoz families in which some members are kolkhozniki and some are workers; they live

[7] M. P. Kim (ed.), *Istoriia sovetskogo krest'ianstva i kolkhoznogo stroitel'stva v SSSR* (Moscow, 1963), p. 370.

together but work in different sectors of the national economy, each representing a different phase in the evolution of socialism.[8] The kolkhozniki who become "workers" by their transfer to rural state enterprises cease to be "peasants" only in a legal sense; in their style of life and mentality they continue to be indistinguishable from the kolkhozniki. In a vast majority of cases the transfer to a state enterprise is not an improvement either in the standard of living or in the opportunities for professional advancement. It is merely part of a regrouping of the rural population for a bolder attack on the lingering cultural isolation of the peasantry.

II

Thus far we have concentrated on legalistic interpretations of the differences between workers and peasants as two legally defined social classes. These interpretations are anchored in the Marxian foundations of Soviet ideology: on the assumption that class identifications are determined by the relation of individuals and groups to the means of production. The workers form one class because they own no means of production and the peasants form another class because they own some means of production, either on a family basis (associated with the private plots) or on a cooperative basis (associated with the kolkhoz).

The emergence of "concrete" sociological investigations of rural life has produced a new view of the underlying principles of class differentiation in the Soviet Union. An increasing number of both sociologists and sociologically oriented journalists now recognize that the nature and dynamics of stratification in Soviet society can be studied most fruitfully within two complementary frameworks, the first concentrating on the differences between urban and rural communities in terms of general social welfare and cultural amenities and the second dealing with the differences in the standards of living of various general professional groupings. While the first framework is suitable for empirical studies of interclass differences, the second is useful for a study of intraclass differentiation. In the application of both frameworks, sociologists now concede that "social planning cannot be reduced to economic planning" and that "social relations cannot be reduced to the relations in production."[9] Social reality, with both "harmonious" and "contradictory" processes, is much more complex than the institutional base of Soviet economy.

[8] A. V. Losev *et al.* (eds.), *Sotsial'no-ekonomicheskie preobrazovaniia v Voronezhskoi derevne* (*1917–1967*) (Voronezh, 1967), pp. 194–195.

[9] A. G. Aganbegian (ed.), *Kolichestvennye metody v sotsiologicheskikh issledovaniiakh* (Moscow, 1966), p. 13.

The social differences between urban and rural communities in the Soviet Union have not been studied systematically and comprehensively. However, the academic and ideological literature abounds with scattered information and general observations which clearly show that much thought has been given to this problem of primary sociological significance. All studies of social stratification in the Soviet Union recognize that status achievement is defined by the state as the direct or indirect holder of national wealth. Every person works directly or indirectly for the state, and every person's status is determined to a large measure by two criteria: the rewards he receives from the state for his contributions in the social division of labor and the opportunities for professional advancement awarded to him by the state.

The basic differences between urban and rural communities are most graphically expressed in the differential benefits they receive from the state. The per capita income of persons engaged in kolkhoz work is approximately one-half the per capita income of unskilled urban workers. While one-half of the country's population lives in rural communities, they receive only one-third of the annual production of consumer goods. One-third of kolkhozy have no electricity. In individual regions the picture is even less favorable. For example, in 1960, only 50 percent of Uzbek kolkhozy had electricity.[10] Rural transportation and public health institutions are far below urban standards. In 1959, according to S. G. Strumilin, the housing of 100 million urban inhabitants covered a total of 781 million square meters of floor space; in the same year the housing of 107 million rural inhabitants covered a total of 430 million square meters of floor space.[11]

At a time when education provides the main avenue of social mobility, the plight of the rural school is a major national problem. In 1968, only 11 percent of Moscow University's freshmen came from rural communities. There are no precise data on the social origin of students on the national level. However, representative local and regional studies agree that, while two-thirds of all high school graduates from the families of urban intelligentsia enroll in the institutions of higher education, only one-third of high school graduates from the families of urban workers and employees and one-tenth from rural families extend their education beyond the secondary level. According to V. Kantorovich, "the road to intellectual professions has been made easier for the hereditary intelligentsia."[12]

---

[10] Kh. M. Mil'tykbaev, *Izmenenie sotsial'noi struktury obshchestva v period razvernutogo kommunisticheskogo stroitel'stva. (Na materialakh Uzbekistana)* (Tashkent, 1965), p. 73.

[11] P. K. Kurochkin (ed.), *Voprosy formirovaniia nauchno-ateisticheskikh vzgliadov* (Moscow, 1964), p. 70.

[12] V. Kantorovich, "Sotsiologiia i literatura," *Novyi mir*, no. 12 (1967), p. 127. See also N. A. Aitov, "Sotsial'nye aspekti polucheniia obrazovaniia v SSSR," in *Sotsial'nye issledovaniia*, II, 193; Rutkevich, "Problemy izmeneniia," p. 52; and, by the

314 : *The Soviet Rural Community*

Inadequate scholastic preparation is the main reason for the poor showing of rural students at the entrance examinations. A Moscow University registrar noted that graduates of rural high schools have developed a "psychological block" against entrance examinations and that many promising students shy away from them. It is now admitted that instruction in many rural schools is of inferior quality. Rural schools are short of space, and often a single teacher handles two, three, or four grades simultaneously. Rural teachers are inadequately trained and the schools lack auxiliary teaching materials. *Pravda* reported in January, 1968, that 40 percent of all schools in the Cheliabinsk region did not have a physics laboratory, and less than 20 percent had a chemistry laboratory. The influence of the family on the formation of favorable educational goals and habits is much weaker in the village than in the city. In many kolkhozy and sovkhozy, school children are assigned farm duties even though they may be below the minimum working age as defined by law.[13] As a result, these children lack sufficient time for both homework on school assignments and extracurricular reading. Special evening courses designed to prepare high school students for college entrance examinations exist only in the cities.

Education has opened the paths of vertical mobility but it has also placed the peasants in an unfavorable competitive position for social advancement. When Soviet writers talk about the massive transformation of peasants into workers during the last decade, they refer primarily to horizontal mobility. Looked at from the vantage point of the rural population, education helps make Soviet society open, but it also imposes drastic limitations on vertical mobility. The prevalent opinion among educational officials is that entrance standards should not be lowered, but, instead, positive steps should be undertaken to eliminate the differences in rural and urban education.

Education, according to Soviet ideologists, is the safest path to the progressive elimination of differences between physical and mental work. Optimistic faith in the triumphs of automation and cybernetization over all economic activities makes education the greatest national value and the major avenue to vertical social mobility.

However, there are some limitations on the role of education as the prime factor in social stratification and professional advancement. In the first place, a person benefits from his professional education only if he occupies a position in the social division of labor which corresponds to the level of his formal training. Education by itself is not a guarantee of upward mobility; it is of consequence only when it leads to appropriate employment. Today

---

same author, "Sotsial'nye istochniki popolneniia sovetskoi intelligentsii," *Voprosy filosofii,* no. 6 (1967), p. 19. (Rutkevich's analysis is hampered by inconsistencies in the definition of the workers' class.)

[13] *Pravda,* November 11, 1968.

one of the major problems in Soviet industry is the misemployment of specialists: for example, it is not unusual to find persons—mostly women—who work as ordinary workers even though they are engineers by training. In 1956–1960, one-third of all graduates of the L'vov Commercial and Economic Institute had no choice but to accept employment in fields below their competence.[14] This means that vertical social mobility is determined not only by the level of education but also by the availability of higher positions.

In the second place, several concrete sociological studies conducted in Moscow factories have shown that the overeducation of workers tends to make them less productive. Managers have learned that certain jobs are performed better by persons who graduated from eight-year schools than by persons who graduated from ten-year schools. The problem actually is not in overeducation per se, but in the attitude of persons who feel that their education has not received the social recognition it deserves. Since many graduates of ten-year schools seek industrial employment only after they have competed unsuccessfully for admission to institutions of higher education, they often have difficulty in adjusting to the routines of factory work. They are also likely to spend much time searching for more suitable employment or preparing themselves for new tries at college entrance examinations.

Professional mobility in the Soviet Union has become more rigid and limited for two reasons: first, there are more aspirants for higher education than there are openings in universities and schools of similar rank and, second, the country has more candidates for professional positions than it has vacancies. A sociological study conducted by a laboratory of the Department of Economics at Moscow University concludes that industry is not always ready to find employment for young persons with higher education and that the secondary schools graduate young men and women who are psychologically unprepared to join the ranks of industrial workers.[15]

The limitations of education as an instrument of professional advancement in the rural community are of a different order. The kolkhoz is a technological paradox: while it uses airplanes to spread insecticides over growing crops, it also relies for many operations on the same kinds of tools which were used a hundred years ago. Kolkhoz mechanics operate up-to-date farm machinery, but over 70 percent of the farmers live in the age of pre-industrial technology. Since technological underdevelopment ties a disproportionately large number of people to agricultural work, it makes part-time rural employment an instrument forestalling urban unemployment. It performs a socially useful role by synchronizing the economic

[14] *Ibid.*, April 20, 1968.
[15] *Literaturnaia gazeta*, no. 27 (July 3, 1968).

distribution of manpower with the political goal of providing employment for every person. Since it can guarantee employment to relatively small numbers of professionals in both manual and administrative work, it does not foster conditions favoring formal education beyond the elementary school.

The collective farm environment affects the success of rural inhabitants in three ways: it provides education of lower quality, it limits the educational aspirations of the rural population, and it makes education a primary means in the search for employment outside the rural community. At the present state of development of the Soviet economy, the huge mass of uneducated peasants is a necessary evil—the key to a demographic balance of Soviet economy. Soviet students of rural life do not try to conceal the cultural backwardness of the rural community and the comparatively low standards of rural existence. They consider the advancement of the economic and cultural standards in the countryside and the elimination of the peasant class as two sides of the same evolutionary process. In the meantime, the limitations on the role of education in the village as a mechanism of professional advancement stem from a deliberate effort of the central planning authorities to synchronize the training of professional manpower with current technological needs. The uneducated peasant is an index of the present-day rationality of the Soviet economy. Unplanned urban overeducation is matched by a planned rural undereducation. Both are sociologically significant indicators of the strains and stresses of a dynamic economy.

There is a pronounced difference in the attitude of Soviet ideologists and social scientists, on the one hand, and Soviet literary men, on the other, toward the kolkhoz village. The ideologists and the social scientists place the dynamics of the kolkhoz community in a dialectical framework: they engage simultaneously in a romantic exaltation of the cultural transformation of the peasant population and a prosaic portrayal of the trends leading to a full disappearance of the peasant as a social and economic category. They readily admit that the present-day social and economic organization of the kolkhoz is a historical product of temporary adaptation to the industrial underdevelopment of the country at the time of mass collectivization of agriculture. The kolkhoz is also viewed as a product of strategic concessions to the pre-industrial culture and psychology of rural Russia which placed great emphasis on the private ownership of agricultural land.[16]

Soviet literary men who have made village life a topic of their creative work are more prone to extol the virtues of peasant psychology than to

[16] A. F. Tarasov, *Razvitie kolkhoznoi sobstvennosti v obshchenarodnuiu* (Rostov, 1967), p. 361.

dissect the compounded social correlates of the rural economy. The "whole-ness" of human existence, the primordial enjoyment of man's proximity to nature, and the purity of primary social relations in which local customs blend with socialist norms are popular themes in novels depicting the life of the kolkhoz peasant. It is true that these novels have their tamed heroes and untamed villains, but their strength—when they have it—is in a quiet search for the blessings of rural tranquillity and the attributes of elemen-tary humanity. The more discerning critics judge these novels more by their subtle philosophies than by their categorizations of characters in terms of socialist realism. Many novelists and literary critics express nostalgia for the purity of rural existence, but none is willing to admit that modern civi-lization, anchored in science and technology, has made the peasant an anachronism.

A *Literaturnaia gazeta* critic openly lamented the one-way street implied by national dedication to gradual elimination of the cultural differences between the city and the village, which in practice means a gradual exten-sion of urban culture into every phase of rural life, a full "intellectualization of physical work," and a recognition of science and technology as the heart of modern culture. He was unhappy with the modern negation of reciprocity in the relations between urban and rural cultures and insisted on the possi-bility of the evolution of a more humanistic culture in which rural tradition would retain and cultivate its distinctiveness and add to a more harmoni-ous development of the personality.[17] A civilization, according to the same writer, which is dominated by the urban intelligentsia can be neither versa-tile nor harmonious. He admits, however, that writers who emphasize the distinctive vitality and evolution of rural culture may be engaged in "an idle conflict with the century." And he is reminded by his colleagues that the village monopoly on the "wholeness of life" is not a sociological axiom but a subjective hypothesis requiring both closer scrutiny and empirical verification.[18] In his criticism of the scientific-technical base of social mo-bility, he is more nostalgic than realistic, for the elimination of the peasant as a social category is a universal product of intensive industrialization rather than a unique goal of Soviet socialism.

At the present time, according to Soviet writers, the class structure of the Soviet Union is dominated by two opposing processes: the interclass integration and the intraclass differentiation.[19] Thus far the topic of inter-class integration has been the central theme of this paper. In Soviet litera-ture it has become customary to identify the process of interclass integration

[17] *Literaturnaia gazeta*, no. 52 (December 25, 1968).
[18] *Ibid.*, no. 9 (February 28, 1968).
[19] Iu. V. Arutiunian, *Opyt sotsiologicheskogo izucheniia sela* (Moscow, 1968), p. 47.

with the progressive elimination of socio-economic and cultural attributes which separate rural from urban communities. The process of urbanization is viewed as the key process leading to a more even distribution of cultural and economic goods in the two types of communities and, therefore, to an equalization of two major social classes: the workers and the peasants. All Soviet writers are inclined to view urbanization as a process of accelerated change.

A closer examination of the process of interclass integration shows that Soviet views on the gathering momentum of the process of urbanization apply only to the transformation of the peasant's legal status. The official statistical data show the momentous change in the Soviet class structure as defined by law and ideology: in 1939, the peasants made up 44.6 percent of the total population and in 1966, a little less than 25 percent. Since 1957, a vast majority of peasants who have changed their class identification have remained in the villages, working in various services, state industrial enterprises, and sovkhozy. While it is true that the new "workers" show some deviation from the peasant style of life, they continue to be an integral part of rural culture and are essentially indistinguishable from the peasant population. Legally, they are now workers; sociologically, they are still peasants. Soviet ethnographers have dealt extensively with the kolkhoz communities, but they have not produced a single study of the sovkhoz community. The reason for this omission is obvious: the urbanization of sovkhoz workers has not proceeded at an appreciably faster pace than the urbanization of kolkhoz peasants. Soviet law and ideology identify 25 percent of the total Soviet population as peasants; sociological research makes it clear that between 40 and 45 percent of the total population are peasants.

While the legal transformation of peasants into workers has accelerated, the social transformation has decelerated. The major reason for this is the decreasing accessibility of professional educational institutions to peasants. In recent years the rate of increase of public schools has been disproportionately large in comparison with the rate of increase of institutions of higher and professional education. The inevitable result of this disparity has been the accentuated competition for admittance to the universities and similar institutions—a competition in which peasants admittedly do poorly. This does not mean that Soviet society has become closed. It means that vertical mobility has become limited and that horizontal mobility has been the major instrument for the transformation of peasants into workers. Interclass integration, which has received much emphasis in Soviet writing, is more nominal than real. Peasant psychology changes much slower than the law.

III

Intraclass differentiation of peasantry is a new topic of sociological research in the Soviet Union. All writers agree that the comparatively slow development of agricultural technology is reflected in a correspondingly slow professional differentiation of kolkhozniki. The study of intraclass differentiation provides sociologists with a new vantage point in the analysis of the social dynamics of the rural community. The stratification of kolkhozniki is quite elementary, but it provides a previously untapped source of basic information on the life opportunities and standards of living of the peasant population. Current Soviet studies of rural social stratification are hampered by heavy ideological involvements, rather rudimentary research techniques, and the full absence of a theoretical articulation of microsociological research.

As a social class, the peasants are divided into four groups:[20]

Group A includes persons who occupy white-collar positions requiring professional training. Here belongs a wide range of managerial personnel from kolkhoz chairmen to the heads of work brigades. It also includes various agricultural experts, accountants, veterinarians, economic planners, and engineers.

Group B is made up of office employees whose positions do not require professional training.

Group C includes mechanical equipment operators and repairmen.

Group D consists of persons engaged in physical labor which—at the present level of development of agricultural technology—requires no special training. This group includes mostly the so-called *raznorabochie*, persons who are freely shifted from one type of unskilled physical labor to another. Since they form between 70 and 75 percent of all collective farmers in the Soviet Union, they are the most typical representatives of the kolkhoz population.[21] Their large numbers are the best index of the comparatively rudimentary professional differentiation of Soviet peasants.

[20] Iu. V. Arutiunian, "Podvizhnost' sotsial'noi struktury sela," *Vestnik Moskovskogo universiteta*, no. 3 (1966), pp. 16–17. See also Arutiunian, *Opyt,* pp. 48ff. For a somewhat modified version of the intraclass differentiation of the peasant class, see Ts. A. Stepanian and V. S. Semenov (eds.), *Problemy izmeneniia sotsial'noi struktury sovetskogo obshchestva* (Moscow, 1968), p. 137.

[21] The 1959 national census shows that 76.5 percent of all kolkhozniki did not indicate their profession. In 1965, 71 percent of all kolkhozniki belonged to Group D. P. I. Simush, "Preobrazovanie sotsial'noi prirody krest'ianstva," *Voprosy filosofii,* no. 12 (1967), p. 8. See also Simush, "Vliianie nauchno-tekhnicheskoi revoliutsii na sotsialisticheskoe selo," *ibid.,* no. 11 (1968), p. 34.

The following summary of the social characteristics of the four groups of kolkhozniki is based partly on empirical studies conducted by Soviet sociologists and partly on more general conclusions drawn from recent legal measures related to the internal organization of agricultural artels.

The income of the members of Group A is twice the income of the members of Group D. It should be remembered that we are comparing only averages and that the income of top members of Group A may be three or four times larger than the income of individual members of Group D. The remuneration for work received by Group A is closer to that received by the comparable group in the sovkhozy (representing the state enterprises) than to that received by members of Group B in the kolkhozy. Soviet sociologists generally agree that today similar professional, or functional, strata from different social classes are closer to each other than are the different strata of the same social class.[22] The growth of intraclass differences, they say, helps produce interclass similarities.

In Terpen'e, a Ukrainian village investigated by Iu. V. Arutiunian, kolkhoz members who belong to Group A have completed on the average 8.2 years of formal education; the average for Group D is 3.8 years.[23] It is significant that the average schooling of members of Group A is not equal to a high school education. That education is not as important a factor in the intraclass mobility of kolkhoz members as it is in urban employment is clearly indicated by the fact that Group B—classified as nonprofessional white-collar employees—has on the average a higher education (9.9 years of schooling) than Group A.[24] This, however, does not deny the fact that most kolkhoz chairmen have a college education. In general, education is more important for moving out of the kolkhoz than for advancing within it. In the ranks of kolkhoz intelligentsia—as Group A is often referred to— there are many persons who have had professional experience in urban employment and whose roots are not in the kolkhozy which they manage. The function of these outsiders is to help strengthen government control over kolkhoz activities by neutralizing the natural tendency of kolkhozy to develop a degree of community isolation from the broader society and to minimize informal relations engendered by community sentiment.

Differences in the income from work in kolkhozy are expressed concretely in the differences in standards and comforts of living. In Terpen'e, for example, all houses belonging to Group A families have wooden floors; 30 percent of the houses belonging to Group D families have dirt floors. Forty-seven percent of Group A families and 16 percent of Group D families live in houses with stone—rather than clay—walls. While in Group

[22] Stepanian and Semenov, p. 142.
[23] Arutiunian, *Opyt,* p. 63.
[24] *Ibid.*

D there are still families whose houses have straw roofs, in Group A all houses have tile roofs.[25]

Since the early 1950's, the election of kolkhoz chairmen and other managing personnel has become more nominal than real. Particularly the coalescence of smaller kolkhozy into agricultural enterprises of large size has necessitated strong limitations on the elective principle of kolkhoz management. The top echelon of new managers is now made up of persons who combine professional competence with experience in bureaucratic organizations and Party work. Kolkhozniki continue to elect the managerial personnel, but selection of candidates has been taken away from them completely. Kolkhoz assemblies have become vehicles through which managerial personnel inform peasants about the current activities and plans of the kolkhoz, and it gives the peasants an institutionalized channel for expressing minor grievances and recommendations. While the government shows a great interest in the preservation of kolkhoz assemblies, it views them exclusively as instruments of social activism and public control. Deprived of any genuine attributes of authority, kolkhoz assemblies meet irregularly and in some kolkhozy exist only on paper. Emphasis at the present time is on the brigade assemblies at which routine questions pertaining to the technical organization of current assignments are the central issues.

The de facto replacement of the elective principle by the bureaucratic principle in the management of kolkhoz affairs has deprived the ordinary kolkhozniki, particularly the disproportionately large Group D, of any rights in the organization of kolkhoz authority. Their exodus from the arena of authority has given the kolkhoz a better chance to modernize its administrative and supervisory procedures. Actually, the kolkhozniki "have lost" a place in the organization of authority which they really never had: the bureaucratization of kolkhoz management means only the establishment of more direct government control over collectivized agriculture.

The four groups are also different in their life styles or subcultures. Although this kind of investigation is still in an embryonic stage, it promises to become one of the more fertile sources of information on rural life and the dynamics of the kolkhoz community. Ethnographic concern with the changing patterns of rural culture and sociological concern with social stratification—or "social structure"—are two independent currents in Soviet studies of the rural community. In order to provide a broad basis for a systematic study of the differences in the styles of peasant life, they must first become integral parts of a more general research design.

Scattered information shows that the four groups differ in reading stand-

[25] *Ibid.*, p. 66.

ards and habits, musical tastes, adherence to local customs, and the utilization of leisure. So far the study of religious behavior has received the most emphasis. The government now recognizes that religion will not disappear as a simple by-product of the accelerated secularization of culture and the rapid growth of modern technology and that there is a need for a concerted atheistic campaign. In order to design an effective campaign, the authorities are in need of accurate information on the social and psychological sources and correlates of religious behavior. In their study of rural religion, Soviet social scientists—particularly ethnographers—rely primarily on external indicators—such as the presence of icons and ritual observations of religious holidays and life-crisis events. They also distribute simple questionnaires designed to determine various types of religious activities and commitments and to establish the relative importance of doctrinal and ritual parts of the religious cultural complex. Very little has been done to penetrate the depths of religion as a world outlook.

Recent studies agree that religion is still a powerful force determining the behavior of the rural population. Empirical sociological studies of individual kolkhozy and general national estimates agree that about 35 percent of kolkhozniki are believers. A sociological study of a model kolkhoz in the Stavropol' territory showed that one-half of the peasant families celebrated both national and religious holidays.[26] A study of a village in the Kalinin region revealed that 74 percent of families displayed icons in their homes.[27] There are only a few studies which relate religious behavior to intraclass differentiation among peasants. They agree that it comes as no surprise that Group D is the mainstay of rural religion. This group has the lowest level of formal education and is more isolated from the mainstream of modern culture than any other group. It has not been effectively reached by the mass organizations which are assigned the task of directing the social and cultural energies of the rural population into officially approved channels.

Modern empirical studies show that even in Group D religious behavior does not follow a set pattern and leaves much room for variations from individual to individual and from family to family. The general tendency is to place more emphasis on religious rituals than on religious doctrines. Rituals are reaffirmations of social and moral values rather than dramatizations of specific doctrines. In general, there is a complex series of transitional stages between believers and nonbelievers. Very often family rituals are performed more in deference to family traditions than in recognition of religious duties.

---

[26] G. I. Zinchenko *et al., Kholkhoz—shkola kommunizma dlia krest'ianstva. (Kompleksnoe sotsial'noe issledovanie kolkhoza 'Rossiia.')* (Moscow, 1965), p. 238.

[27] V. A. Kartsov (ed.), *Opyt istoriko–sotsiologicheskogo izucheniia sela 'Moldino'* (Moscow, 1968), p. 347.

There are two demographic characteristics of peasant religion: the number of believers is much higher among persons over 40 years of age and among women in general. Of many possible explanations of the ties of age to religion, one is directly related to both intra- and interclass mobility. When he reaches 40 years of age, a peasant belonging to Group D has virtually no chance of professional advancement; not even exemplary behavior and consistent adherence to Communist morality would help him rise on the status ladder. Now he is no longer motivated to give external support to official values and he easily sinks into rural culture at the points where it is most isolated from the achievements of recent and mostly superficial urbanization. The relative isolation of the older members of Group D from the mass organizations entrusted with the diffusion of urban culture and the upholding of Communist morality accounts for the continuity in the preservation, elaboration, and readaptation of the religious complex.

The isolation of rural women from the avenues of urbanization is much more pronounced than the isolation of men. Much of this isolation is forced upon women: they work in the kolkhoz on assignments requiring manual labor; they are the main factor in the cultivation of family gardens; and they spend abnormally long hours in countless chores around the home. In most rural families they still bake bread and do the family washing by hand. In a typical kolkhoz, Group C—mechanical equipment operators and repairmen—does not include any women. Women are given only token positions in Group A. In an average kolkhoz, 95 percent of the working women belong to Group D. The vertical mobility of these women is virtually nonexistent. The Group D women have not been given an opportunity to break away from the traditional way of life. They are the bulwark of rural religion; in kolkhoz after kolkhoz the ratio of believing women to believing men is five to one.

The aim of the intensive study of religious behavior by Soviet ethnographers and other social scientists is not to find a magic formula for the elimination of religion as a living component of the culture of Group D peasants. It is much more realistic. The goal is to illuminate the common sources of technological conservatism and religious behavior—to understand religion as part of a larger complex hindering the psychological transformation of "peasants" into "workers." It is recognized that religion is not likely to disappear as a result of technological development, that the roots of religion are much deeper than technology can reach.[28] It is also recognized that religious behavior helps explain the fact that the organization of work in kolkhozy has lagged behind the technological advances in agriculture. The continuing debate on the advantages and disadvantages of "brigades"

[28] V. N. Shubnikov *et al., Kopanka 25 let spustiia* (Moscow, 1965), p. 124.

and "zven'ia" as the basic organizational units in collective farming shows that the kolkhoz is still in search of an effective organizational adjustment to modern agricultural technology. According to one writer, the village continues to be the arena of a strong disparity between "the rapid course of technological innovations" and "the relatively slow changes in the traditional organization of work."[29]

An important function of systematic ethnographic and sociological inquiries is to assess the role of religion as a rallying point for various types of informal groupings working against a firmer and more complete integration of the rural community into the system of consistent socialism. Equally important is the effort to contribute to a fuller understanding of the dynamics of rural society by a study of the unexpected results of planned designs for social change. As a heuristic device, intraclass differentiation promises to give the empirical study of rural religion—and rural culture in general—more depth and sociological relevance.

Although the work of modern Soviet students of the rural community has suffered from conceptual imprecision, inadequate research instruments and safeguards, and disruptive ideological commitments, it has opened valuable new vistas for empirical investigations of stratification dynamics in Soviet society. The strength of this work has been more in the accumulation of empirical data than in the clarification of the basic processes of social change.

[29] Simush, "Vliianie," p. 31.

13 : Structure and Functions of the Soviet Rural Family

Stephen P. Dunn

The present paper will deal with the Soviet peasant family[1] as a structural element in the rural scene. It will be based on data from three major geographical areas—central and northern Russia, the Baltic republics, and the Caucasus (including for present purposes the Transcaucasian republics)—with occasional sidelights from other places, such as Siberia (the Slavic-derived populations) and Central Asia.

I will not attempt to describe the Soviet peasant family in its various manifestations in ethnographic detail, since, with the exception of the Caucasus, I have already published descriptive data for the areas in question[2] and have at present nothing significant to add. Rather, I will present a generalized description and interpretation of the Soviet peasant family, both as the product of historical, political (including legislative), and social forces and as a mechanism in its own right. When I come to discuss the role of the family as a focus of ideology and the rituals which embody this role, more detailed ethnographic data will be necessary, for reasons to be specified at that point.

This investigation was supported, in part, by Department of Health, Education and Welfare grant no. RD 2607-G. I also want to acknowledge the assistance of the Louis M. Rabinowitz Foundation given through a personal grant.

[1] I use the term "family" here to denote a group of people who are socially considered as being related by blood and who live together permanently and share certain activities. My use of the term does not imply any particular structure or make-up and does not necessarily correspond to the nuclear family (parents and children) with which we are familiar in the United States.

[2] S. P. Dunn and E. Dunn, *The Peasants of Central Russia* (New York: Holt, Rinehart and Winston, 1967); S. P. Dunn, *Cultural Processes in the Baltic Area under Soviet Rule,* Research Series no. 11 (Berkeley, Calif.: Institute of International Studies, 1966).

I

The peasant family, wherever found, is typically *corporate*. By this I mean that it bears responsibilities and possesses rights as a *unit*, and that the actions of its members (sale or purchase of goods, contracting of debts, and the like) are binding upon the group unless the contrary is specified. In some cases, the head of the family is empowered to take action only as agent for the group and with its consent; in others, there is no such limitation, but the distinction need not concern us here. This type of corporate family existed both in northern and central Russia and in the Caucasus, as well as in certain other parts of Europe, particularly the Balkans. Juridically speaking, the property of the peasant family in these areas remained joint property either until the death of the last surviving member or until the voluntary dissolution of the group. Special rules governed the division of property when the family split into two or more units, which usually happened when the sons set up separate households.

The family consisted, in the ideal case, of a man, his wife, his male descendants, and their wives, as well as unmarried female descendants. Only in exceptional cases did the group include married daughters and uxorilocal (in-marrying) sons-in-law. Commonly, the family group dissolved on the father's death. In the Caucasus, however, a variant structure existed, in which several brothers lived together in one place, sharing certain activities but eating and to some extent working separately. In such cases, the quarters occupied by individual brothers and their immediate families frequently had separate entrances, or were separated by staircases or ladders. The courtyard, outbuildings, and expensive items such as wine-presses, oil-presses, ovens, and grist-mills were owned in common, while the rest of the facilities and the land were held by the individual family unit.[3] The importance of this arrangement lies in its close structural resemblance to a kolkhoz.[4]

[3] I. V. Chkoniia, "Sem'ia i semeinyi byt kolkhoznikov Gruzinskoi SSR," *Materialy po etnografii Gruzii*, no. 11 (1960), pp. 5–16; R. L. Kharadze, *Gruzinskaia semeinaia obshchina* (Tbilisi, 1960–1961).

[4] In some parts of the Caucasus, as in the Balkans, the group made up of undivided brothers holding certain property in common developed into a larger unit, centered around a "big house" and sharing only certain symbolic and ideological ties, such as the celebration of a common saint's day or (in the Caucasus) the use of the central pillar in the big house as a kind of shrine. For such larger kin units, the term *patronimiia* has been introduced by the Soviet ethnographer M. O. Kosven, *Semeinaia obshchina i patronimiia* (Moscow, 1963). Such units have given rise to entire quarters in towns, or, in some cases, entire villages, and some of them still exist in folk memory.

II

The peasant family in prerevolutionary Russia had a number of clearly defined social functions which determined its internal structure and also the structure of the society which was made up of such families. Most of the functions of the prerevolutionary family have their equivalents under Soviet conditions. In the following section, I will describe briefly the functions and structural features of the Russian peasant family, pointing out the changes over time where these are relevant. To summarize, I will consider the family as: the holder of rights; the bearer of responsibilities; the agency of child-rearing and socialization; the administrator of resources; and the focus of ideology.

The Family as Holder of Rights

To begin with, the family collectively was under tsarism, and is under the Soviet regime, the subject of important rights. Historically, the family participated in the *mir* or peasant commune and had access as a group to allotted parcels of the land held in common by the *mir*. The family might also own outright certain parcels of land which had never been in the *mir* holdings or had been purchased from it, as well as buildings, tools, livestock, and commercial establishments such as grist-mills, sawmills, or oil-presses. The family participated, through its head, in the *skhod* or village assembly which was the governing body of the *mir*.

Under Soviet conditions, the rights of which the peasant family is the subject are in certain respects even more important than under the old regime. This is true because while most major forms of property, and particularly "means of production"—i.e., those items of property which are capable of producing an income, either in cash or in kind—have been collectivized, the peasant family continues to own certain means of production within the context of the collective farm.[5] These means of production include the right to use a portion of land for growing produce; livestock within certain limits; the money or goods received by its members in

[5] The word "own" is not, strictly speaking, applicable to certain categories of things in the Soviet context. For example, land, having been nationalized, cannot be owned by anyone. However, the word reflects the actual state of affairs which involves an established right of use on certain conditions. This right of use is even to some extent heritable, since as long as the household exists as a component part of the kolkhoz, it is entitled to a private plot.

payment for work on the kolkhoz; the tools and equipment necessary to cultivate the privately held plot; and (subject to various conditions and restrictions) the right to use kolkhoz equipment for the cultivation of the private plot and kolkhoz land for the pasturing of private livestock. The family also owns its dwelling house and contents. Some of this is not peculiar to the peasant family: all Soviet families may own houses and, under certain conditions, may even derive income from them. Furthermore, families of workers living in the countryside (including those of workers on sovkhozy) may and often do hold and cultivate personal plots. However, with rare exceptions (forest wardens, lighthouse-keepers, river transport workers, and a few more) such persons do not hold these plots as a perquisite of their employment, nor are they, as far as I can determine, held collectively by the family.[6] The kolkhoz family, on the other hand, is entitled by law to a plot of land from the area held by the kolkhoz, for private cultivation, to build a house. Normally, also, it is entitled to materials and assistance for building on stipulated terms.

This brings us to a highly important structural feature of the Soviet rural family. While membership in the kolkhoz is individual, the rights which accrue from it are held by the family as a unit. Consequently, the family not only enjoys rights collectively but is collectively responsible for the behavior of its members.

The Family as Bearer of Responsibility

The collective responsibility of the family also has its historical roots. In the prerevolutionary countryside, the community as a whole was collectively responsible for the delivery of taxes of various kinds to the government, of feudal dues to the landlord, of a quota of recruits for military service, and of workmen to perform compulsory labor (technically corvée or, in Russian, *barshchina*) either for the landlord or—in the case of "state peasants"—for the state. These collective obligations were distributed by the communal assembly among the constituent households, and the head of the household was held responsible in each case. Accordingly (until the system was changed in 1906, as will be described below), no peasant was permitted to leave his domicile without the permission of the head of his household, just as no household could move without permission from the communal assembly and without finding someone to assume its share of the collective obligations.

[6] V. E. Grigorovskii and M. A. Alekseev, *Lichnoe podsobnoe khoziaistvo kolkhoznikov, rabochikh i sluzhashchikh v SSSR* (Leningrad, 1968); L. Gordon and B. Levin, "Nekotorye sotsial'no-bytovye posledstvia piatidnevki v bol'shikh i malykh gorodakh," *Voprosy ekonomiki*, no. 4 (1968), pp. 138–142.

In the first decade of the twentieth century, a concerted effort was made, through the so-called Stolypin reforms, to change the system of land tenure and social organization in the countryside. The expressed aim of these reforms was to foster the development of capitalism. In line with this, the collective responsibility of the head of the family for its members was abrogated or severely watered down, and the resettlement of peasant households out of their communities was made easier under certain conditions. Specifically, these reforms envisaged the break-up of the communal land holdings, their opening up for purchase by *individuals,* and the break-up of old villages through resettlement of peasant families to outlying homesteads (*khutora*) on privately owned plots of land. Furthermore, as the reforms were implemented, all property rights in land were to be vested in individuals rather than households or other groups.

The Stolypin reforms from the beginning encountered severe obstacles. The degree to which they were implemented varied widely from one part of the country to another, depending on the relative importance of agriculture in a technical sense.

However, what is most interesting to us as students of the Soviet family is that the 1922 land code adopted by the Soviet government (and, with certain modifications, still in effect) represents in most respects a retreat from the positions taken pursuant to the Stolypin reforms. The land code once more made the household the subject of land tenure.[7] All property owned by the household (buildings, livestock, equipment, supplies, and cash) was owned in common, and the procedures for dividing it when the household broke up or was extinguished were those traditional in the Russian countryside.

The kolkhoz family of today continues to bear collective responsibility for the behavior of its members. If they do not perform satisfactorily in the public sector of the kolkhoz, the household may be deprived of part or all of its private plot. In case of minor infractions, privileges such as the use of kolkhoz equipment for the cultivation of the private plot or of kolkhoz pasture for privately owned livestock may be withdrawn. In extreme cases, the household can even be expelled from the kolkhoz.[8]

---

[7] The land itself having been nationalized, the household could not, of course, own it, but it held the right of use and enjoyment of the produce on condition that the land be cultivated by the members of the household without the help of hired labor.

[8] The application to the household of sanctions against misbehavior by its members is subject to very significant limitations. Recent items in *Izvestiia* and other sources have been critical of the application of such sanctions, particularly where they were applied unilaterally by administrators without the approval of the full membership and where the application damaged the interests of the kolkhoz as a whole. For example, there have been cases in which experienced tractor drivers—an extremely scarce commodity in some places—have been expelled because their wives refused to

The Family as Child-Rearing and Socializing Agency

The family in the Soviet countryside, as almost everywhere else, is also a child-rearing agency. Because of historical factors and because of the nature of the Soviet system, this role of the family takes on special features. Traditionally, the Russian peasant family, as in all peasant communities the world over, supplied its children with whatever ideas and skills they needed in order to live in their communities and carry on as their parents had done. The amount of formal education available to the average peasant in prerevolutionary Russia was negligible. There were church schools which rarely went beyond the first three or four grades and which were not accessible to most peasants anyway; there were a few secular schools run by the zemstvos in the last two decades before the revolution, but this movement was not sufficiently widespread and did not continue long enough to have much practical effect.

The educative function of the family has been largely taken over in the Soviet Union (as elsewhere) by the state. I refer here to formal education—the transfer of information and skills. In the Soviet context, the effect of such education, unlike the training within the family which the prerevolutionary peasant received, is essentially to turn a person into something he is not—a farmer into a physician, an industrial worker into an engineer, and in particular, a peasant into a city-dweller. Formal education for agriculture is by and large not available in the countryside itself, and when the young peasant moves into the city, his perspectives change so sharply that his career plans are unlikely to remain the same. The agricultural schools contain very few students of peasant origin, and fewer still of their graduates will work voluntarily in the countryside.

Recent sociological studies have shown[9] that, with regard to formal education, rural young people are at a sharp disadvantage. The reasons range from such simple matters as the persistent shortage of textbooks and visual

---

work in the public economy; usually the wives were offered work as field hands (*Izvestiia*, January 29, 1969). There is no indication in the treatment of these items that the principle of collective responsibility itself is being called into question. Rather, the principle of collective responsibility may work in some cases to protect the individual.

[9] V. N. Shubkin, "Youth Starts Out in Life," *Soviet Sociology*, IV, no. 3 (Winter, 1965–1966), 3–15; V. N. Shubkin *et al.*, "Quantitative Methods in Sociological Studies of Problems of Job Placement and Choice of Occupation," *ibid.*, VII, no. 1 (Summer, 1968), 3–24; *ibid.*, no. 2 (Fall, 1968), 3–31; Murray Yanowitch and Norton Dodge, "Social Class and Education: Soviet Findings and Reactions," *Comparative Education Review*, XII, no. 3 (1968), 248–267.

aids in rural schools[10] to complex questions of psychological attitude and expectation on the part of the teachers, the students themselves, or their parents. For example, in some parts of the Baltic area[11] parents have a low opinion of formal education—a situation which is most unusual in the Soviet Union. In the case described by Kalits, this seems to be because formal education is of little or no help in handling the environment in that particular place, which is not amenable to anything except raw courage and brute muscle. If a native of Kalits' island is to make use of his formal education, he must leave the island permanently (rather than merely for sea voyages and temporary jobs on the mainland, as has been traditional), and this most islanders are very unwilling to do. The same situation prevails for very different reasons among a community of religious sectarians of Russian origin settled in Armenia and studied by Kozlova.[12] Here again, social mobility would mean mobility out of the community, and the low value placed on formal education (which would almost automatically mean social mobility) derives from an effort to maintain the separateness of the group. Finally, among many Moslem or formerly Moslem peoples, there is an established cultural tradition which says that education for women is useless and even harmful.

Where, for whatever reason, formal education is not equally available to all, the family or the peer-group is called upon to supply the deficiencies. For example, in certain areas, crafts such as carpentry, the making of containers of various kinds, and smithing were once traditional and almost universally known. They are now dying out, but one sees in the Soviet press references to measures taken or planned to revive them. For instance, in the Smolensk area, the once flourishing pottery industry carried on by family units has almost died out, although there is still a demand for its products, given the unsatisfactory state of consumer goods production and distribution. The ethnographer Bobrinskii[13] urged that the pottery industry be revived on the basis of the few families which still carry it on, and some measures have been taken to bring this about.

Thus far, we have spoken of formal education and vocational training. The inculcation of values is, of course, another matter, and one which we can hardly qualify on the basis of the Soviet sources. We know that many children are brought up by their grandparents (particularly grandmothers)

---

[10] *Uchitel'skaia gazeta*, January 28, 1969, pp. 1–2.

[11] M. Ia. Kalits, "New Features in the Life of the Peasants of Kihnu Island," *Soviet Anthropology*, I, no. 1 (Summer, 1962), 34.

[12] K. I. Kozlova, "Iz opyta izucheniia Molokan Armenii," in A. I. Klibanov *et al.* (eds.), *Konkretnye issledovaniia sovremennykh religioznykh verovanii* (Moscow, 1967), pp. 119–128.

[13] A. A. Bobrinskii, "A Contribution to the Study of the Technology of Pottery in Smolensk Oblast," *Soviet Anthropology and Archeology*, I, no. 4 (Spring, 1963), 14–26.

who, as one might expect, are old-fashioned and often religious and whose values the regime considers backward if not downright subversive. We know also that this is an unintended but logical result of the regime's desire and effort to put everyone to work, and of the iron economic necessity in most cases for both spouses to work. In the Soviet countryside, this puts an even greater strain on the family than one would normally expect. In the Soviet Union, as elsewhere, child-rearing is considered predominantly women's work, but in many parts of the Soviet countryside, unlike other places, the bulk of the labor force is also female. This is in part the result of recent demographic forces—population losses due to World War II, the "demographic echo" of the war, and the migrations produced by rapid industrialization, which in many areas is pulling males off the land at an alarming rate. However, predominance of women in the rural labor force is also partly traditional. In those areas where, because of climatic or soil conditions, agriculture has always been of secondary economic importance (for example, the Northwest, the present Vladimir and Kostroma oblasti, and the northern Volga region), women stayed on the land and farmed while men carried on seasonal occupations away from the village, such as mining, lumbering, or itinerant crafts.

We have no direct way of telling precisely what values are inculcated in the Soviet rural family, but we do know that this is a matter of extreme interest to the government. Ethnographic accounts, such as the study of Viriatino[14] and less formal pieces in the popular press, criticize the antiquated values taught in some peasant families, such as uncritical subservience to the will of elders or (in some places) a low regard for formal education. We know also that in extreme cases of religious fanaticism (as well as other conditions not involving values), the authorities may interfere by removing the right of the parents to bring up their children.[15]

[14] P. I. Kushner (ed.), *Selo Viriatino v proshlom i nastoiashchem: opyt etnograficheskogo izucheniia russkoi kolkhoznoi derevni* (*Trudy Instituta etnografii XLI*) (Moscow, 1958).

[15] The matter of deprivation of parental rights is one on which precise information is extremely scarce. The popular press occasionally carries accounts of legal actions for deprivation of parental rights on grounds of improper upbringing (questions of religion come under this heading). A more frequent cause of such action is actual abuse or neglect of the child. Western sources (for example, H. K. Geiger, *The Family in Soviet Russia* (Cambridge, Mass.: Harvard University Press, 1968), pp. 266–267) generally limit themselves to reproducing anecdotal materials from the Soviet press which do not yield a clear conception of the nature of deprivation of parental rights as a device for enforcing the values sponsored by the regime. One current interpretation of the law (see *Sel'skaia zhizn'*, June 28, 1968, p. 4) states that according to Article 19 of the law on marriage and the family, parents may be deprived of parental rights if they are alcoholics (but it would seem that this rarely happens) or drug addicts, or if they engage in amoral or antisocial behavior, or if the court decides that the child will be endangered by staying where he is. The child may be restored

The Family as Administrator of Resources

Both traditionally and at present, the peasant family in the Soviet Union is the administrator of resources, which at times and under the right conditions can be considerable. Before the revolution, the head of the peasant family had control (whether merely as agent or in his own right) of all the resources of the family, in cash or in kind. In extreme cases, such as among the Russians of the Angara region in southern Siberia, this included even the cash earnings of family members at nonagricultural jobs.[16] Such centralization of resources was a factor both of ethnic tradition and in some instances (such as the case described by Saburova) of severe natural conditions, which made a policy of consistent and controlled reinvestment of resources mandatory.[17]

The major form of investment for the prerevolutionary peasant family (and this remains true to some extent today) was the founding of a new unit. This act was governed by complex rituals and strict customary rules, which varied from place to place but which in all cases specified how much of each category of goods the new household was entitled to.

The household's control over its resources was, however, subject to one highly significant structural limitation. It did not include the earnings of women or food produced by them (for example, eggs, fowl raised for meat, and mushrooms and berries gathered in the woods). Likewise, it did not

---

to the parents if his interests require this, provided he is not an adopted child, but any such action is to be taken only by and through the court.

One is struck by the extreme vagueness and flexibility of these provisions. My general impression is that deprivation of parental rights constitutes a direct means of attack and pressure against the family, but that for a number of reasons it has been used rarely and with extreme caution. Sometimes, indeed, it is not effectively used even in cases where the question of religion enters the picture, although religiosity is usually enough to force decisive action. For example, *Sovetskaia Rossiia,* January 13, 1968, p. 4, carried an account of a little girl left by the local court of Sita *sel'sovet*, Khabarovsk oblast', in the custody of her maternal grandmother (the parents being divorced and the mother having died), even though the grandmother was a Baptist. The case is made only more striking by the fact that this was not a matter of deprivation of parental rights, strictly speaking. The decision was reversed by a higher court in Khabarovsk, which was able to prove to its satisfaction that the child was being harmed by attendance at Baptist prayer meetings which (according to the account) had a strong Pentecostal tinge.

[16] L. M. Saburova, "Nekotorye cherty obshchestvennogo i semeinogo byta russkogo naseleniia Priangar'ia v pervye gody sovetskoi vlasti (1919–1929 gg.)," *Sovetskaia etnografiia*, no. 2 (1965), pp. 28–39.

[17] J. W. Bennett, *Hutterian Brethren* (Stanford, Calif.: Stanford University Press, 1967), Chapter I, makes a similar point for the Canadian plains, where analogous conditions prevailed.

include property inherited in the female line, such as clothing, ornaments, and bed-linen. On the other hand, from the proceeds of her activities, or from her inherited property, the peasant woman was expected to clothe herself, her husband, and her children and to decorate the house or portion thereof which they occupied.

Under Soviet conditions, the peasant family remains the administrator of resources, although the categories over which it has control have been narrowed somewhat. They no longer include as a matter of course the outside earnings of members, although in places and at times where seasonal migrant labor has been common, the earnings from this have gone into the general fund.[18] The resources controlled by the Soviet peasant family consist of cash and goods received by the members for work in the kolkhoz, the proceeds from sale of livestock and livestock products and vegetables raised on the private plot,[19] and in some cases outside earnings of members. These resources do not normally include state grants, pensions, and the like supplied to persons other than the head of the family.[20] Such grants are controlled either by the person receiving them or (if support for dependent children is involved) by the immediate parent. It is interesting that the traditional separation of female income and resources from the general fund persists in the kolkhoz family. At least in some households, while the ordinary earnings of women go into the general fund, pay for jobs considered specifically feminine (e.g., school teacher, bookkeeper, veterinary assistant) is kept separate.

As in the prerevolutionary countryside, resources are allocated to new households being set up, although the extent of investment on such occa-

[18] This highly important phenomenon of the Russian and Soviet rural scene has, during the Soviet period, varied inversely with the general prosperity in the countryside. It also varies with the geographical area and the more or less permanent agricultural conditions. In most parts of northern Russia, seasonal migrant labor was an ordinary feature of the economic life of the peasantry: hence, probably, the inclusion of earnings from them in the household fund along with the proceeds of agriculture (Dunn and Dunn, *The Peasants of Central Russia*, pp. 18–20).

[19] According to one source, the average proportion of income received by the kolkhoz family from the subsidiary economy varies within the Russian Federation from 33.7 percent in the North Caucasian region to 51.1 percent in the Volga-Viatka area (Grigorovskii and Alekseev, p. 63). Unfortunately, this information is not dated, but the bulk of what is in the book appears quite recent. We know that in some smaller areas, and at earlier times, the proportion of income received by the kolkhoz family from the subsidiary economy was much higher. We also know that if one includes in the calculation not only cash income but also receipts in kind consumed by the family, the importance of the private plot increases still more.

[20] By Soviet law, the "head of the kolkhoz household" must be an active worker, but this does not apply to the head of the family in peasant customary law. This position goes either automatically to the senior male member (unless senile or completely disabled) or to the ablest member by general agreement; in the case of fatherless families, the head might be a woman, but traditionally this did not occur.

sions has been reduced. Loans and free materials (within the limits of the available supply) are usually available from the kolkhoz for the building of new houses when households divide or disaster strikes, and for the repair of old ones.

It is clear, in summary, that the resources controlled by the kolkhoz family are an important cushion against both unfavorable natural conditions and sudden changes in state policy, either of which might reduce the amount of money available for distribution as wages to the kolkhozniki. The recent introduction of a guaranteed annual minimum wage for kolkhozniki will probably reduce the importance of the resources controlled by the family, as it becomes effective. However, in most areas, this guaranteed wage is still subject to limitations—such as being tied to the profits of the kolkhoz—which sharply reduce its effect, or it has not been in existence long enough to permit prediction of the final result.

It should be noted that the social role of the family—its rights and responsibilities and the resources which it controls—is subject to wide variations from time to time, from region to region, and even between kolkhozy within the same region at the same time. These variations depend on economic factors: the availability of consumer goods in the countryside, the proportion of earnings of kolkhozniki paid out in cash, and the like. For instance, where milk is easily available, many households may not keep cows.[21] On some particularly advanced kolkhozy, where there is a smoothly running system of public catering, the private operation may be reduced to almost nothing, but this is as yet a rarity. Further, it is claimed by Soviet scholars that relations between the kolkhoz and individual kolkhozniki are becoming increasingly direct and are ceasing to be mediated through the family.[22]

The Family as Focus of Ritual and Ideology

The rights and responsibilities of the peasant family can be described in their essentials on the basis of the operation of juridical norms, whether these are made and enforced by the central government through legislation and the police power or by the force of custom within the local community.

---

[21] See A. E. Panian, "Novyi byt kolkhoznikov sela Mrgavan Artashatskogo raiona Armianskoi SSR," *Sovetskaia etnografiia*, no. 2 (1967), pp. 130–139.

[22] See L. A. Anokhina, V. Iu. Krupianskaia, and M. N. Shmeleva, "Russkoe krest'-ianstvo v osveshchenii amerikanskikh etnografov," *Sovetskaia etnografiia*, no. 1 (1969), p. 167. (This is a review article dealing, in sharply negative terms, with *The Peasants of Central Russia*.) I have no basis for judging the validity of these claims. After all, even if wages are paid directly to the family members who earned them, this says nothing about what happens to the money after it is brought home.

Likewise, the extent and nature of the peasant family's economic functions depend upon state policy, in the sense that what the state does not do for the individual, the family must. For these reasons, I have thus far concentrated on the outlines of the juridical and economic situation and presented the ethnographic data themselves in schematic form. When we come to consider other aspects of the family's role, however, such an approach is no longer appropriate or even possible. When we discuss the family as the focus of ritual and ideology,[23] we are dealing with a sphere in which the state has only very limited capacity to intervene, and the same is true to a lesser extent of child-rearing. For these reasons, I will present in the following section the ethnographic data in somewhat more detail, and point out the importance of those functions of the family which cannot be reduced to matters of law (written or customary) or state policy. I will also introduce some data not yet published in English on familial ritual among the North Caucasian and Transcaucasian peoples, and on the features of traditional and modern social structure connected with it. These data are of particular interest because of the striking vitality of Caucasian familial ritual and of many modes of behavior within the family which at least seem diametrically contrary to those sponsored and encouraged by the Soviet regime. At the conclusion of this section, I will venture a general hypothesis to explain this unusual state of affairs.

III

Along with its other functions and characteristics, the Soviet peasant family is still, as in the past, the focus of important ritual activities and ideological concerns. The rituals center mainly around the life-crises, those points in an individual's life at which he undergoes decisive changes in status: namely (in the western tradition) baptism, coming of age, marriage, and death. The rituals possess the manifest function of solemnizing the individual's change of status and the latent functions of expressing the solidarity of the family or larger kin-group—often also of the community as a whole—and of providing entertainment. This last is not, as one might think, a mere side issue, since we find that the persistence of the highly elaborate and theatrical Russian peasant wedding ritual—which in its full version takes five or six days, attracts large crowds of people, and entails considerable expenditure—

---

[23] I am here using the term "ideology" not in the sense of a codified body of doctrine ("Marxist ideology," "Roman Catholic ideology," or the like), but in the sense of a more or less cohesive body of belief by which a community orients itself with respect to the rest of the world and to its own history. This body of belief usually includes both religion and values, but is not necessarily co-terminous with either of these.

is inversely correlated with the availability of other forms of entertainment in the countryside. This in turn hinges upon matters of state policy and priorities, and it can serve as an indicator of the degree of urbanization or cultural "advance," in urban or West European terms, on the local scene.

Traditionally, marriage was preceded by a rather highly structured court-ship pattern, featuring regular meetings at which unmarried girls (and sometimes also young married women whose husbands were away) gathered, either in the home of one of their number or in premises specially rented for the purpose. They were joined by the young men of the village for singing, dancing, and conversation. This institution is called in Russian *posidelki,* or "sitting party." There were other gatherings of youth—mass promenades (called "the street") and outings to the woods to gather mush-rooms or berries—which might be considered mobile *posidelki.* In some areas, the *posidelki* was accompanied by a certain amount of socially tolerated vandalism and aggression, for example, if young men from another village tried to "crash the party." It is highly significant that where regular modern recreation facilities (movie equipment, community centers, and the like) do not yet exist, the *posidelki* survives to this day, and that as soon as such facilities are established, it immediately goes out of use. Further-more, where there are clubhouses, it has not, until recently, been the custom for married women to go there, just as they did not normally attend the *posidelki* in the past. This is changing, with the increasing prevalence of urban (or, in general, western) standards in the structure of the family, but the point here is that the village clubhouse and the *posidelki* are exact functional equivalents.

The folk rituals of Soviet peasants, like those of peasants in many other parts of the world, contain very ancient elements, the origin of which has been forgotten, in many cases, by those who carry out the ritual. Soviet social scientists call these elements (along with others) "survivals."[24] The presence of these survivals and the peculiar colorfulness and in some cases "outlandishness" of the rituals into which they enter serve to express all the more forcefully the solidarity of the local community. For example, the sometimes brutal practical jokes which are part of the complex and rowdy wedding festivities held on the Estonian island of Kihnu[25] are often directed against outsiders. That is, if you are a native of the island, you will know that if you go to a wedding, you are likely to have your clothes stolen while you are asleep or be subjected to some other indignity, and it is *de rigueur* to

[24] According to Marxist doctrine, a "survival" is something left over from a pre-vious stage of cultural and social evolution. Examples would be the pagan elements found in the beliefs of many nominally Christian or Moslem peasant communities, or elements of the wedding ritual which point to the previous existence of forms of marriage not now practiced.

[25] Dunn, *Cultural Processes,* pp. 56–59.

pay no attention to this. Under these conditions, the joke loses its point, but if the person whose clothes are stolen is an outsider—particularly one who tends, as most outsiders do, to look down somewhat on island ways— then a small but significant revenge has been taken. The same thing is true to a lesser degree of the Northwest Russian wedding ritual, which includes satirical skits and songs and a marked display of wealth.[26]

It is worth noting that much of the familial and life-crisis ritual of the Russian, Baltic, and Caucasian peasantry is entirely nonreligious in terms of ordinary Christianity or Islam. For example, the marriage was considered to begin, in Russia and Estonia, with the completion of the major cycle of folk rituals, and the church wedding, while obligatory from the state's point of view, had no juridical force as the community saw it.

With respect to the rituals of baptism and burial, a different situation obtains. Traditionally, both were under the patronage of the church, and to this day there are in Russia only two ways of being buried—with the Communist civil ceremony or with some Christian ritual. In Latvia, where the traditional religion was Protestant, a folk funeral, vaguely Norse in feeling but stripped of recognizably pagan elements, has developed.[27] This is used in most cases where the deceased was neither particularly religious, politically active, nor a high official; in general, it is not considered fitting for rank-and-file kolkhozniki to be buried with a Communist funeral. A somewhat similar situation exists in Central Asia, with regard not to the funeral itself but to a complex cycle of commemorative rituals, many of whose elements are of pre-Islamic origin. This cycle has shown considerable vitality even among people who pay no attention to traditional Islam. The rituals involved are carried on, in some cases, with at least tacit approval of the local Soviet authorities.[28] On the other hand, in most parts of rural Russia for which I have data, religious funerals are usual, except for high officials and active Communists. Since the funeral is distinctly a family occasion, this reinforces the traditional ritual system and the ideological role of the family.

An accretion of folk customs and rituals has grown up around the ceremony of baptism, much as it has around the wedding. These are ceremonial visits and a dinner (or festive breakfast) with traditional songs, standard jokes, and the like. However, the folk ceremony does not seem to have

[26] L. A. Pushkareva and M. N. Shmeleva, "Sovremennaia russkaia krest'ianskaia svad'ba," *Sovetskaia etnografiia*, no. 3 (1959), pp. 47–56; Dunn and Dunn, *The Peasants of Central Russia*, p. 102.

[27] Dunn, *Cultural Processes*, p. 60.

[28] Kh. Esbergenov, "On the Struggle against Survivals of Obsolete Customs and Rites (The Karakalpak *"As"* Memorial Feast)," *Soviet Anthropology and Archeology*, III, no. 1 (Summer, 1964), 9–20.

become as independent of the religious one as in the case of marriage. The ethnographers assert that in most cases where the folk ceremonies are held, baptism is also performed in church. One suggested reason is that this is more easily done *sub rosa* than a church wedding. In many cases, the child is taken to be baptized by a grandmother or some other older woman, at least ostensibly without the parents' knowledge.[29] Often also baptism is carried out as a kind of therapeutic measure for a sickly child ("It can't do any harm and might do some good"), or for one whose parents wish it to be socially accepted.[30]

Naturally, the government has made attempts to devise secular substitutes for the religious life-crisis ceremonies. If these efforts were successful, they would have the effect of removing the focus of ideology and ritual activity from the family and directing it toward the community or the non-kin group. However, for a number of reasons, they have not been particularly successful, at least in the countryside. A number of objections of a hygienic order have been raised to the proposed secular equivalent of baptism—the festive public registration of the infant with the local executive committee. The same ethnographer also cites a widespread feeling by parents that celebration of the birth of a child should be a small-scale household festivity.[31]

The Soviet civil wedding makes a very poor showing in the countryside in competition with the folk ritual, and in fact no great push is made for it by the government, since the folk ritual itself is nonreligious. The only real effort to change the folk ritual is directed against certain individual elements of it, which (if they were taken seriously) might seem superstitious or demeaning to the woman. Some of these elements—for example, the displaying of the bridal sheet, the beating of pots on the wedding morning (originally done to frighten away evil spirits), or the "gilding" of the couple by having coins thrown at them—are specifically refused by some couples. This is true particularly of "advanced" people—veterans of the military, active Party members, and so on. On the whole, however, the folk ritual is

[29] In a sample study of 534 families in Voronezh, it was claimed that 30 percent of the children had been baptized without the parents' knowledge (M. K. Tepliakov, "Materialy k issledovaniiu religioznosti naseleniia Voronezha i Voronezhskoi oblasti," in Klibanov *et al.,* pp. 144–152). The "blame" for this situation is placed on the activity of a large body of lay officials of the church.

[30] V. N. Basilov, "Etnograficheskoe issledovanie religioznykh verovanii sel'skogo naseleniia," in Klibanov *et al.,* pp. 152–174.

[31] See V. Ia. Kalits, "Izuchenie novykh semeinykh obriadov v Estonskoi SSR," *Sovetskaia etnografiia,* no. 4 (1965), pp. 32–42. These data relate to Estonia. It is possible that this represents in part an ethnic peculiarity. The culture of the Baltic area has in many respects a pronounced Scandinavian cast, and may include the typical Scandinavian high regard for privacy and dislike of large crowds.

popular and is praised by Soviet social scientists. It is interesting to note that the formal act of registering the marriage with the village executive committee is just as independent of the folk cycle as the church wedding used to be.

Family Ritual and Social Structure in the Caucasus

The peoples of the Caucasus, taken collectively, present a highly complex ethnographic picture which can only be outlined here. Let it suffice for our purposes to say that there are two major divisions: the North Caucasus (on the northern slope of the Great Caucasus Range) and Dagestan (to the east bordering the Caspian Sea), and the Transcaucasus (between the Great and Small Caucasus ranges and the Black Sea). These divisions correspond to marked historical and ecological differences. The peoples of the North Caucasus are, for the most part, at least nominally Moslem, and historically they practiced a combination of small-scale wooden-plow agriculture and seminomadic transhumant pastoralism.[32] The Transcaucasian peoples (except for the Azerbaidjanis, who will be omitted from this survey for lack of adequate data) are Christians of long standing, practicing intensive cash-crop agriculture (tea, citrus, sugar beets, etc.) in the lowland regions and combining agriculture and animal husbandry in the mountains.

Historically, the social structure of the North Caucasian peoples was marked by a complex and highly developed feudal order. Wide use was made of the device of fostering out children as a technique for increasing social solidarity and of the vendetta as a means of social control. However, due to the difficult terrain and the wide dispersion of plots of arable land and desirable grazing grounds, strong political units did not develop in this area, except in some parts of the Dagestani lowland. In the North Caucasus and in the more mountainous parts of Dagestan, each local community was a tiny self-governing republic, normally in a state of active or latent war with its neighbors, or forming temporary alliances with them. The same factors apparently hindered the development of large joint families such as existed in Georgia and Armenia.

The peoples of the North Caucasus had and to some extent retain a distinctive family structure characterized by very marked avoidance between affinal relatives, particularly between daughters-in-law and the husband's parents and older siblings. Avoidance was also practiced between husband and wife and between fathers and children, in the sense that a man might

---

[32] This term is applied in anthropology to a regular seasonal alternation of grazing grounds, with permanent residence established near one of the locations and only part of the population, as a rule, making the journey from one to the other.

not pay any attention to his wife or children or mention them in the presence of strangers, nor might they be mentioned in the husband's presence. The same prohibition applied to a wife with regard to her husband. The taboo against a daughter-in-law's having any contact with her elder affines could be lifted after an extended period on the initiative of the mother-in-law, through a ceremony featuring the exchange of small gifts. The converse taboo (i.e., as it applied to males) was much less severe and sooner lifted.[33]

Under modern conditions these taboos continue in effect, although some of them have been weakened. For instance, Smirnova claims that the custom of avoidance between parents and children is now ignored, except for an occasional "remote echo of these customs—a certain pretended restraint on the part of the father in his attitude toward his children in public."[34] The husband-and-wife avoidance pattern is expressed in various compromise tactics, such as going to the movies in a group rather than alone or going to a wedding together but avoiding one another while there.[35] Avoidance of elder affines—both in its physical and linguistic forms—is much more stable and is still commonly practiced in the countryside, even by educated people. For example, the parts of the avoidance pattern which are connected with the wedding cycle (seclusion and inactivity of the bride in a special room of the house for a period of two to three weeks) are observed by women of the intelligentsia—teachers, physicians, etc.—in reduced form but quite strictly within the limits of that form.[36]

North Caucasian wedding ritual is, if anything, more complex and archaic than Russian or Estonian. It contains elements which recall the customs of marriage by capture and of widespread fosterage of children that were prevalent in this area in the past. The bride and groom, for example, upon the bride's being brought to the groom's village, live for a period in the houses of persons to whom each afterwards stands in an adoptive relationship, considered equivalent to one of blood, even to the extent that the incest taboo applies to it.[37] The temporary host of the groom becomes, so

---

[33] Ia. S. Smirnova, "Avoidance Customs among the Adygei and Their Disappearance during the Soviet Era," *Soviet Anthropology and Archeology*, I, no. 2 (Fall, 1962), 31–39.

[34] *Ibid.*, p. 36.

[35] Separate recreation for husbands and wives is not peculiar to the North Caucasian peoples. It is widely found in southern and Eastern Europe, and until recently, among the Russians. What is unique in the North Caucasus is the degree to which the custom has been elaborated, ritualized, and fitted into a general pattern of affinal avoidance.

[36] Ia. S. Smirnova, "Novye cherty v adygeiskoi svad'be," *Sovetskaia etnografiia*, no. 5 (1962), pp. 30–40.

[37] See A. G. Autlev and L. I. Lavrov (eds.), *Kul'tura i byt kolkhoznogo krest'ianstva Adygeiskoi avtonomnoi oblasti* (Moscow and Leningrad, 1964), pp. 140ff., for this custom among the Adygei (historically, Circassians) both in the past and today, and M. A. Aglarov, "Forms of Marriage and Certain Features of Wedding Ceremonial among the 19th–Century Andii (Based on Field Data of 1959–1960)," *Soviet Anthro-*

to speak, the sponsor of the wedding. This custom is still practiced, although the length of the stay in the "foster father's" house has been reduced. The North Caucasian wedding in the past involved important and substantial exchanges of gifts among the parties, i.e., the bride and groom and their parents and other relatives. These exchanges remained in force until World War II and retained their economic importance but are now nominal where practiced at all. The dowry (*pridanoe*)[38] continues to be a feature of the wedding, although the ethnographers insist that it has lost its former economic importance.[39]

The North Caucasian wedding ritual proper, even as described by eye-witnesses,[40] is replete with symbolic elements which emphasize the separation of the bride from her family of orientation, i.e., the one into which she was born, and her integration into her husband's family. The most striking of these ceremonies, perhaps, is the "ransoming" of the bride whereby the guests are called upon by the *djēguako* (best man or master of ceremonies) to make cash contributions, the amounts and sources of which are publicly announced. The contributions actually go to the *djēguako* and the musicians engaged for the occasion. Presumably, this "ransom" originally represented a form of bride-price, although there is no firm ethnographic evidence to that effect.

After the wedding feast, the bride is brought in veiled and formally introduced to her husband's relatives and sometimes his neighbors as well. Following this, the veil is removed, with appropriate formalities. The bride is then considered a full member of the new family, and the avoidance taboo is lifted with respect to all except the husband's parents and immediate elder siblings. The bride's fundamental change of affiliation to her husband's family is also emphasized by the fact that a special ritual has developed for the bride's first return to her parents' house, some time after the wedding.[41] On this occasion, the bride brings back her "dowry" and

---

pology and Archeology, III, no. 4 (Spring, 1965), 51–59, for similar customs among the peoples of the Ando-Tsezian linguistic group in Dagestan. Aglarov's data are historical and not precisely dated, but since the article is based on field results from 1959 to 1960, at least some of the customs must be current or fairly recent.

[38] The question of English equivalents for such terms as this one is always vexed. The *pridanoe* is certainly not a dowry in the Western European sense, since it does not pass into the husband's possession among either the Russian or other peoples of the Soviet Union. Rather, it is intended as provision for the wife's needs while in the husband's house. One might say "trousseau," except that the *pridanoe*, particularly nowadays, contains items not usually included in trousseaus in the West (such as sewing machines, furniture, or even bicycles).

[39] G. A. Sergeeva, "Field Work in Dagestan in 1959," *Soviet Anthropology and Archeology*, I, no. 2 (Fall, 1962), 57–63.

[40] Smirnova, "Novye cherty v adygeiskoi svad'be."

[41] Compare J. K. Campbell's description of a similar custom for the Sarakatsani mountaineers of Greece in *Honor, Family and Patronage* (Oxford: Clarendon Press,

presents from her parents to her in-laws, the amount and nature of which become a matter of considerable interest.

As one might expect, the Soviet authorities, ethnographers, and writers in the local popular press regard many features of the North Caucasian wedding ritual with jaundiced eyes. Typical are the remarks of a writer in a local newspaper quoted by Smirnova.

> There is much good in the wedding ritual of the Shapsugs [a self-designation of one local group of the Adygei], but also much that is backward and humiliating for a young girl. According to old custom, she can't tell her parents about the day set for her marriage. Unfortunately, this is still true today. . . . But a particularly embarrassing ritual is performed after the feast [i.e., on the wedding day].
>
> Recently I attended the wedding of the son of Shikhret Baus, a member of the "First of May" kolkhoz. After the dinner I "saw" the bride. As music began to play, she was brought into the circle by her girl friends, with her face covered. She was suffocating under a cloth, which covered her down to her knees, couldn't see where she was going, and didn't know what was happening around her. The master of ceremonies announced, "The bride is asking you to ransom her. . . ." A large sum was collected, approximately 2,000 rubles. Two questions arise. Is it necessary to "sell" the bride in this way? Why should the money go into the pockets of the master of ceremonies and the musicians? And if we must agree to the "sale" of the bride, wouldn't it be better to consider the money as a present to the young couple "for setting up housekeeping?" . . . Usually the groom's relatives take all the [bride's] things, and if they aren't enough, the bride is criticized. For about six months or a year, the bride does not see her parents. This is because of their presents. Gossip begins on this basis, and parents who can't buy good presents are criticized. Sometimes this leads to the divorce of the newlyweds.[42]

Information on current small-scale social structure among the Transcaucasian peoples is extremely scarce, at least in generally accessible languages. The few items available indicate that the social pattern is broadly the same as in the North Caucasus, except that the nature of economic operations in Georgia would seem to make the physical avoidance taboo extremely difficult to implement. Panian describes for the Armenians an avoidance taboo similar in all important respects to the North Caucasian one, and still in force, at least partially. Finally, we should note that in

1964). Panian, p. 138, notes the persistence of the same custom among the Armenians but appears to miss the ethnographic point, since he comments: "Nowadays when the bride can see a relative at any time, this custom has lost its previous significance, but nevertheless it continues stubbornly to be observed."

[42] Smirnova, "Novye cherty v adygeiskoi svad'be." Quoted from a translation made by Mrs. Liudmilla Olsen and edited by me for a volume of readings in Soviet ethnography, now being prepared for publication.

many isolated mountainous districts social customs apparently have remained virtually unchanged since the period preceding intensive contact with the Russians.[43]

What are we to make of all this rather exotic material? It seems clear that certain parts of the country—of which the North Caucasus is surely one—have simply been forgotten when it comes to setting priorities, sending out agitation teams, building schools, and the like. We may assume that except in certain areas where considerable deposits of oil, coal, and natural gas have been found, the potential economic benefits derivable from culture change have not seemed to justify the effort and expense involved. In Dagestan, for instance, much of the population is simply inaccessible to normal means of communication since, for historical reasons, it is concentrated on the steep mountain slopes and in gorges, while the level areas are relatively sparsely settled.[44] Since the family is in any case normally a stable unit highly resistant to direct outside influence, we would expect familial ritual and internal organization to be particularly conservative in a context where the degree of outside influence was sharply limited, as it is here, by economic or physical factors.

IV

In summarizing our data, we can draw the picture in broad strokes as follows:

Because it is the subject of collective rights and the bearer of collective responsibilities, the Soviet peasant family intervenes as a connecting structural link between the state and the individual in a way in which the urban

[43] See I. I. Datunashvili, "Materialy k kharakteristike sovremennogo sostoianiia religioznosti v Belokanskom, Zakatal'skom i Kakhskom raionakh (Azerbaidzhanskaia SSR)," in Klibanov *et al.*, pp. 187–194. The people involved here are a group of Islamized Georgians called Ingiloitsy living in Azerbaidjan. They are apparently still convinced Moslems. The Moslem clergy (much more numerous than those officially registered as mullahs) enjoy the open or tacit support of the community, including even those persons who are atheists by conviction. Old customs such as polygamy and the levirate (i.e., marriage with the deceased husband's brother) are practiced in concealed form, and girls are given in marriage according to the will of the parents, without consultation or appeal. This is apparently one of the most isolated and culturally conservative ethnic groups in the country, although some other mountain settlements in Dagestan or in the North Caucasus might run a close second.

[44] See M. M. Ikhilov, "Staryi i novyi Kurush," *Sovetskaia etnografiia,* no. 4 (1963), pp. 166–172. The economic disadvantages of such a settlement pattern are obvious, since the bulk of the arable land is in the plains. In some districts, efforts have been made to resettle entire communities from their mountain homes to more accessible locations, but the ethnographic data indicate that this campaign has met with considerable active or passive resistance as well as with the expectable technical difficulties.

family, for lack of these characteristics, is not equipped to do, either in the Soviet Union or in the West. Further, the Soviet peasant family *locates* the individual within the community, gives him a place to stand. It shares this function to some degree with the family in any society, but in the Soviet case, the function is expressed through elaborate, archaic, and highly colorful rituals which continue to this day to make a deep impression on the consciousness of individuals. In like fashion, the Soviet rural family shares the educative, socializing, and enculturating functions of families everywhere, but because of the uneven distribution of educational opportunity and the continuing underdevelopment of the Soviet countryside, these functions are more important for the Soviet rural family than for its counterparts elsewhere.

If the Soviet rural resident can still be called a peasant, despite all the physical and social transformations of the last hundred years—and I believe that he can—it is largely because he remains a member, both structurally and ideologically, *first* of his family unit and only then of the larger community or the state.

14 ❖ The Importance of Religion in the Soviet Rural Community

Ethel Dunn

In this paper I shall be dealing with the functions of religion in the Soviet rural community, both historically and at present. I will try to explain why religion has been an important issue and remains so today, theoretically and practically.

I. A. Kryvelev,[1] toward the end of a discussion of 20 years of field research, says: "It is common among our propagandists, and not uncommon in the literature, to find the term 'superstition' used only in the narrow sense. . . .[2] [T]here is no fundamental line of demarcation between religion and superstition. Both are founded on belief in the supernatural. Of course, the upholders of religion have an interest in upholding the idea of separating the latter from its cruder manifestations [in order to assert] the 'loftiness' of the religious ideology. It is therefore desirable to avoid this differentiation in terms."

I think Kryvelev, who undoubtedly considers himself a good Marxist, assumes that superstition is the unorganized or underground aspect of religion, religion being advanced only on a relative scale stretching from antiquity to today. To a certain extent, I would agree, because religion in the Soviet Union, both historically and at present, is part of the state struc-

This investigation was supported, in part, by Department of Health, Education and Welfare grant no. RD 2607-G. Thanks are also due the Louis M. Rabinowitz Foundation for its support during a crucial period, to Angelo Cosmides of San Francisco for calling my attention to some of the data, to Stephen P. Dunn, who taught me how to look for meaning, and—since this work has been in progress since 1960—to Fordham University's Institute of Contemporary Russian Studies and the University of California's Center for Slavic and East European Studies.

[1] I. A. Kryvelev, "Overcoming the Vestiges of Religion in the Lives of the People of the USSR," *Soviet Anthropology and Archeology*, I, no. 2 (Fall, 1962), 20.

[2] To cover what Kryvelev calls "household superstitions: belief in signs, in fortune-telling, in the evil eye . . . in witchcraft and sorcery. . . ."

ture and has evolved in parallel with the evolution of the state. Therefore, religion and superstition are the same phenomenon at different historical stages. However, I would argue that it is a fundamental weakness of Soviet studies of religion that they do not admit that at a certain stage in history, the character of religion and superstition changed. "Superstition" became a "survival"[3] and religion a basic human need, capable of nonritualized expression. I consider the Soviet Revolution of extreme importance to the *development* of religion in Russia in this sense.

My studies have led me to hypothesize that the Leninist policy on religion is genetically connected with Soviet nationality policy. M. I. Shakhnovich[4] makes clear that the Leninist policy on religion evolved at a time when disillusionment with established religion (in context, Russian Orthodoxy) was combined with attempts at renovation and a search for new religions, primarily "sciences" of society. Lenin apparently felt that his best chance for success lay in presenting his views as something altogether new, having nothing in common with religion. At the same time, he was very well aware that in Russia religion was equated with nationality and way of life, and he beat down attempts in his own faction to follow the lead of European Marxists, who held that religion was a private matter. Lenin conceded that religion should be a private matter in the eyes of the state, but not of the Party. Some Soviet authors (for example, Cherniak)[5] consider Stalin's extension of this principle to include political control of religion by whatever means necessary, including relative indulgence of the Orthodox Church, a distortion of Leninist religious policy. It seems to me that Lenin originally intended to extend the tsarist policy to all nationalities, to transform it by removing religion, leaving nationality and way of life—cultural autonomy and freedom for all ethnic groups—within very strict limits. Both Lenin and Stalin acted as politics dictated, however, and in context this meant tight control of sectarians.

I

Before considering the present situation, I would like to present a brief outline of the relative positions of Russian Orthodoxy and sectarianism[6]

[3] P. P. Kampars and N. M. Zakovich, *Sovetskaia grazhdanskaia obriadnost'* (Moscow, 1967), pp. 128–129, say: "A survival is not simply the old in the new, but something old which is obsolescent and is historically doomed to die."
[4] M. I. Shakhnovich, *Lenin i problemy ateizma: kritika religii v trudakh V. I. Lenina* (Moscow and Leningrad, 1961).
[5] V. A. Cherniak, *O preodolenii religioznykh perezhitkov: opyt konkretno-sotsiologicheskogo issledovaniia po materialam Alma-Atinskoi oblasti* (Alma-Ata, 1965), p. 135.
[6] Historically and at present, the term *sektantstvo* was applied to a wide range of

under tsarism. As Murav'ev and Dmitriev note, "Religion was the dominant ideology."[7] When we examine the legal literature dealing with sectarians, we see that this appraisal is not merely the empty bluster of contemporary (antireligious) propagandists, but a concise summary of 200 years of history. P. I. Mel'nikov,[8] in a report describing the situation of sectarians around 1857,[9] notes that the persecutions of *raskol'niki* in the first half of the eighteenth century (which were essentially economic and political) were so severe that, between the years 1716 and 1762, seven-eighths of the population of Nizhnii Novgorod (for example) had fled the country, taking their monies with them. By an *ukaz* dated December 14, 1762, the Empress Catherine invited the *raskol'niki* to return (as part of a policy, we should note, of opening frontier areas to settlement by financially sound foreigners). "The number of resettled *raskol'niki* was significant," writes Mel'nikov, "because in calling them back to the Fatherland [to settle in the Novorossiisk area], the government, besides forgiving them, gave them permission to wear beards and to go in the dress which had not been assigned, gave them the right to choose the kind of life that they wished."[10]

Mel'nikov's remark, in context, helps to clarify one puzzling aspect of the tension between the Old Belief and Russian Orthodoxy. It is generally conceded that the Old Belief, in distinction from the various sects, was almost entirely a Great Russian movement. Yet from a juridical point of view, Russian Orthodoxy and Russian nationality were virtually synonymous. A. M. Bobrishchev-Pushkin explains it thus: "Russian [religious]

---

non-Orthodox Christian groups, ranging from the Old Belief through Baptism. In this paper, "sectarianism" will include some forms of the Old Belief, since tsarist legal literature deliberately blended the terms *raskol* and *sektantstvo*. Culturally, there is a line of descent.

[7] E. F. Murav'ev and Iu. V. Dmitriev, "Concreteness in the Study and Overcoming the Vestiges of Religion," *Soviet Anthropology and Archeology*, I, no. 2 (Fall, 1962), 10.

[8] P. I. Mel'nikov, "Zapiska o russkom raskole," in V. Kel'siev (comp.), *Sbornik pravitel'stvennykh svedenii o raskol'nikakh* (London, 1860), I, 167–198.

[9] According to Kel'siev, I, 173–220, a secret committee was set up in 1853 to study the sectarian problem with a view to neutralizing the effect of Austrian concessions to Old Believers in Belokrinitsa. A first step was obviously to formalize the juridical position of sectarians in the empire, which, since the schism in the seventeenth century, had been set forth almost entirely by imperial decree. The secret committees had (since their inception in 1825) made a number of attempts to minimize the participation of the Orthodox Church, since there was an obvious conflict of interest between the political needs of the Russian state and the church's desire for religious purity. In 1855, the committees began to work directly with the church, which apparently retained until the 1917 revolution the right to decide what was a dangerous sect. A foreword to the second edition of *Sobranie postanovlenii po chasti raskola* (St. Petersburg, 1875) makes the interesting comment that much of the book's contents had never before been published, not even in *Polnoe sobranie zakonov* or *Svod zakonov*.

[10] Mel'nikov, p. 182.

toleration is not based on the principle of legal toleration; it is a national toleration. . . . [O]ur law supposes that among us it is not the person who believes but some sort of national spiritual whole: a people, a nation, a tribe. . . . Each heretic denying the truth of the state church unwillingly denies the state itself."[11]

To put the matter in its simplest form: the state, guided by its ideological arm, Russian Orthodoxy, regarded all non-Orthodox religious bodies (in this context, sectarians) as actual or potential subversives, dangerous enough to exile to the remotest corners of the Russian empire, at specified distances from Russian Orthodox populations and often among hostile non-Christian groups where their presence would serve a dual purpose (social isolation and economic development).[12] One sees, reading the documents, that the state used its dissidents to good effect, and in Siberia, the Far East, the Caucasus, and the Trancaucasus was forced to remove most of the economic restrictions on Molokans, Dukhobors, and other so-called "dangerous sects." By 1898, for instance, the economic power of sectarian settlers was sufficiently established for the Minister of Finance to suggest that special privileges be granted to sectarian groups for settling in the Maritime Province; according to his data there were already 20,000 Molokans, Dukhobors, and other sectarians in the Amur region, part of whom had come as exiles, but many had come of their own free will, attracted by the relative religious liberty. In either case, settlement had cost the government nothing.[13]

Sectarian influence on the agricultural development of the Russian empire

[11] A. M. Bobrishchev-Pushkin, *Sud i raskol'niki-sektanty* (St. Petersburg, 1902), pp. 6, 7, 10. As further proof of this we may note that the conduct of foreign faiths on Russian soil was supervised by the Ministry of Internal Affairs, as were the rules of conversion from one faith to another. The forms of registration of Old Believer and sectarian communities in the supposed liberalization of the law in 1906 were approved by the Ministry of Internal Affairs, collaborating with the Ministry of Justice. Complaints on this score as well as on the conduct of community leaders were heard in the First Department of the Senate (*Polnoe sobranie zakonov Rossiskoi imperii*, 1906: 28424). In rendering its decisions, the Senate very often relied on expert testimony—by the Orthodox Church.
[12] One was undoubtedly to make them as miserable as possible. Compare the rules for settling sectarian populations in the Transcaucasus in 1834 (*Sobranie postanovlenii*, p. 334 with V. D. Bonch-Bruevich's (*Materialy k istorii i izucheniiu russkogo sektantstva*, Issue 6: *Presledovanie baptistov evangelicheskoi sekty* (Christchurch, Hants, England, 1902), pp. 30–31) description of life in the Armenian village of Giriusy. The 1834 directive suggested that populations be deliberately mixed for disharmony: Popovtsy Old Believers who held to the strict observance of rules should be neighbors of Dukhobors who held no rules at all.
[13] See *Sbornik postanovlenii po chasti raskola 1875–1904 g. vkliuchitel'no* (St. Petersburg, 1905), p. 199; also M. M. Shmulevich, "K voprosu o dvizhenii naseleniia russkogo krest'ianstva v zapadnom Zabaikal'e v pervoi polovine XIX veka," *Kul'tura i byt narodov Buriatii* (*Etnograficheskii sbornik*), no. 4 (1965), pp. 137–138.

deserves special study. For our purposes it is sufficient to note that by the 1890's, sectarian religious communities occupied large tracts of land in the southern and eastern parts of the empire and must have been perceived as a threat by the Orthodox Church for this reason if no other.[14]

Another reason for the Orthodox Church's (and the state's) distrust of sectarians was that their juridical position in the empire had made them "a state within a state," as one official put it. Sectarians, when discovered, had been exiled, isolated from Orthodox populations. Often this measure affected whole families and even whole villages. In their new places of residence, sectarians organized as best they could, and since they did not have (or refused outright) to pay for the services of the Orthodox Church, they had their own elected officials and their own schools.[15] Sectarians did not have the right to teach the law of God in these schools until 1911 (*Polnoe sobranie zakonov Rossiiskoi imperii*, April, 1911: 55045) and even then the right had one significant qualification. Such teachings could not go against public order, and in most cases it was the local police or priest who decided what was contrary to public order. Appeal was possible, but the process was long, involved, and costly to peasants who might have to appear in courts some distance from their homes precisely during the harvest season.

There was another limitation on the idea of religious toleration on a national basis as described by my sources, and one which is of great significance to our study of religion in the Soviet rural community. Religious toleration did not extend to Baptists, except those of German origin. Difficulties with this principle could be observed as early as 1865 because of a group theologically related to Baptists but southern Russian in origin, the Shtundisty. Which group actually came first in Russia is of interest to

[14] See A. I. Klibanov, "Sovremennoe sektantstvo v Tambovskoi oblasti (po materialam ekspeditsii Instituta istorii Akademii Nauk v 1959 g.)" *Voprosy istorii religii i ateizma* (hereafter *Voprosy*), VIII (1960), 59–100; N. V. Shelgunov, *Sochineniia N. V. Shelgunova*, 3rd ed. (St. Petersburg, n.d.), III, 190; A. Vvedenskii, *Bor'ba s sektantstvom* (Odessa, 1914), p. 288. The increase in Orthodox Church landholdings between 1887 and 1905 in European Russia—300,000 desiatina (0.4 percent of the total) in 1905 against 200,000 (0.2 percent) in 1877—seems almost insignificant by comparison (Shakhnovich, pp. 300–301). Even the impressive figures cited by I. P. Tsamerian *et al., Stroitel'stvo kommunizma i preodolenie religioznykh perezhitkov* (Moscow, 1966), p. 8, do not exclude the possibility that the Orthodox Church was hard-pressed economically. In 1914, there were 77,767 Orthodox churches and 1,025 monasteries with 117,915 priests and 94,629 monks and postulants, "numerous enterprises...millions of desiatina of land...capital amounting to 69,869,000 rubles."

[15] The extent to which administrative and cultural matters were really in the hands of sectarians depended on whether the sectarian population constituted a majority in the region. Wherever possible there was an Orthodox "supervisor," but by the late nineteenth century sectarians were free to live as they chose, with one significant exception: if the Orthodox Church was strong enough to enter the area, the sectarians went under, as if they had no rights.

the history of ideas and the ways in which knowledge is disseminated in peasant groups. We should note only that there is considerable disagreement and confusion in the literature, and that the confusion was deliberately compounded by the state, which wished the situation of sectarians kept as much of a secret as possible. Baptists had been legalized by a law of 1879, but the Shtundisty were classified as an especially dangerous sect, and a law of 1894, which supposedly established guidelines for distinguishing the two, actually forced judges to decide questions of theology for political ends. The 1906 law governing the setting up of Old Believer and sectarian communities, while seemingly much more liberal than previous legislation, had one very large loophole: control was exercised at the local level by authorities who were free to use their discretion to forbid anything which might be contrary to public order.

I have gone into these matters in what may seem disproportionate detail for a study of the contemporary scene because I believe that the situation in tsarist Russia has been ignored by most students of Soviet religious policy. We are faced under both regimes with the question: why are all believers, but especially sectarians, considered dangerous? The answer, to paraphrase Bobrishchev-Pushkin,[16] is that the man who denies the dominant ideology denies the state itself. This attitude did not change with the revolution, although to a greater or lesser degree the early Bolsheviks tried to enlist the sectarians on their side. I have already gone into some of these problems elsewhere[17] and I do not see how I can improve on Bociurkiw's[18] masterful summary of church-state relations in the USSR. The significance of this legislation for our purposes is two-fold. First, the Orthodox Church was, ideologically speaking, "disenfranchised" by the revolution, although the Orthodox Church retained more privileges than other groups. Second, the position of sectarians has been steadily reverting to the one which obtained under tsarism. There are a few modest exceptions, which I shall discuss when I describe the socio-ethnographic picture of sectarians given in recent Soviet work. To run ahead somewhat, the slight signs of change I see are only logical, but they are ignored by such competent researchers as Bourdeaux,[19] and they could easily be aborted if the state decided that its security would be threatened by any liberalization of policy.

From 1928 until now, the state has had the direction of cultural change

[16] Bobrishchev-Pushkin, p. 10.

[17] Stephen P. Dunn and Ethel Dunn, "Religion as an Instrument of Culture Change: The Problem of the Sects in the Soviet Union," *Slavic Review*, XXIII, no. 3 (1964), 459–478.

[18] Bohdan R. Bociurkiw, "Church-State Relations in the USSR," *Survey*, no. 66 (1968), pp. 4–32.

[19] Michael Bourdeaux, *Religious Ferment in Russia: Protestant Opposition to Soviet Religious Policy* (New York: St. Martin's Press, 1968).

under its control. Religious organizations or persons may not collect funds for purposes other than the running of the church itself. Children may not receive public instruction in religion, although they may be instructed "in a private manner." Rothenberg[20] has tried to discover what is meant by "in a private manner," and concludes that the law is deliberately vague. It might be taken to mean within the family, except that Bourdeaux makes a good case for the view that any man with, say, five children who decided that they and their cousins should receive religious education could conceivably be imprisoned and deprived of parental rights under Soviet law. Rothenberg is quite right to point out that early Soviet legislation was much more liberal. Ryndziunskii[21] says that Old Believer populations looked upon Bolshevik attempts to remove icons and the law of God from the schools as religious persecution. In one small town in Nizhegorod guberniia in November, 1918, the peasants opted for the teaching of the law of God in the school, and the Committee of the Poor appropriated money for this purpose. The incident indicates the presence of a fairly firm public opinion running counter to the ideology the Bolsheviks wished to establish, and it is interesting that the demand for the right to teach the law of God in the schools has cropped up again, led, according to Bourdeaux, by Baptist action groups (*Initsiativniki*) but also pressed by Adventists and Pentecostalists.[22] This demand is perceived by the state as a dangerous anachronism, inasmuch as it would restore the political scene to its pre-Bolshevik status. In 1914, 40 percent of the primary schools were under the Orthodox Church and the teaching of the law of God was obligatory in all the others. Even higher educational institutions were not exempt from the requirement: a student did not receive his diploma until he had completed a certain number of hours of theology.[23] Before the revolution the dominant ideology was Russian Orthodoxy. After the revolution Marxism was substituted, and legislation intended to protect the individual from religious fanaticism was used to prevent the believer from fulfilling his desire to convince others. The believer, on the other hand, is factually unprotected from the harassment of the Marxist agitator, no matter how unsophisticated his argument, be-

[20] Joshua Rothenberg, "The Legal Aspects of Religious Education in the Soviet Union," *Comparative Education Review* (February, 1968), pp. 68–75.

[21] P. G. Ryndziunskii, "Bor'ba za preodolenie religioznykh vliianii v sovetskoi shkole (1917–1919 gg.)," *Voprosy*, III (1955), 76–79.

[22] Bourdeaux, pp. 125–127.

[23] It would be interesting to compare the number of hours of theology with the present requirement for the study of Marxism or scientific atheism. See L. I. Emeliiakh, "Iz istorii antiklerikalizma i ateizma krest'ian v 1905–1907 gg.," *Ezhegodnik Muzeia istorii religii i ateizma* (hereafter *Ezhegodnik*), III (1959), 281. My impression is that the time is the same, and that today's student fulfills the requirement just as mechanically.

cause the believer represents the last remnant of political opposition to the regime.

Most western students of the religious situation in the USSR, when they consider this proposition at all, reject it out of hand as a kind of national paranoia. Fletcher,[24] however, thinks that the Communist Party and the Baptist movement have somewhat the same appeal to certain kinds of people and that "the dynamics of the Baptist movement parallel the dynamics of the Party, and the Baptists thus represent a potential competitor to communism."[25] Klibanov[26] gives some basis for considering religious bodies political opponents. The Orthodox Church lost considerable influence and wealth in the revolution, though less than other groups. I have tried to indicate that the sectarians were in a rather special position before the revolution, but their actual degree of political organization demands further study. It is one thing for a prominent Baptist to found a political party.[27] To claim the support of all Baptists in all parts of the tsarist empire is quite another. Recent Soviet studies indicate that the amount of political opposition on the part of *kulaki* or large landowners must have varied widely from region to region, and when it occurred must have come from people who considered themselves betrayed.[28] The interesting question is: how many peasants remain in "political opposition expressed in religious form"? In

[24] William C. Fletcher, "Protestant Influences on the Outlook of the Soviet Citizen Today," in William C. Fletcher and Anthony J. Strover (eds.), *Religion and the Search for New Ideals in the USSR* (New York: Praeger, 1967), pp. 81–82.

[25] Although I share his hope that a more pluralistic society would give Baptists (and all religious bodies) more freedom, I do not agree with him that one joins the Baptist movement "only when one is willing to renounce any hope for education, responsibility, prominence or active participation of any significance at all in society." In rural communities, where the main strength of Baptism lies, willing renunciation is the least important motivation, as I shall indicate later on.

[26] Klibanov, "Sovremennoe sektantstvo."

[27] A. I. Klibanov, "The Dissident Denominations in the Past and Today," *Soviet Sociology*, III, no. 4 (Spring, 1965), 51.

[28] P. A. Efimov, "O preodolenii baptizma v SSSR v 1923–1929 gg.," *Ezhegodnik*, VI (1962), 164, indicates that in 1924–1926, the percentage of *kulaki* varied widely in Baptist or Evangelical Christian communities from 1–2 percent in Voronezh guberniia to 13.9 percent in Poltava guberniia, but he admits his data are incomplete. Careful research would probably show that if land allotment is the criterion for deciding who is or is not a *kulak*, different standards were applicable in different places. B. F. Krest'-ianinov, *Mennonity (Biblioteka sovremennoi religii)* (Moscow, 1967), p. 59, provides the following table in percentages as of 1925 for Omsk guberniia:

Sect	Kulaki	Seredniaki	Bedniaki
Mennonites	10	30	60
Baptists	7	30	63
Seventh-Day Adventists	2	27	71
Molokans	5	25	70
Evangelical Christians	3	40	57

order to answer this question, we must know the ways in which Soviet attitudes and approaches to religion have changed or remained the same, or if the data themselves have changed. Let us now consider Soviet ethnographic and sociological studies of the Russian peasant and his attitudes toward religion.

II

It is popularly supposed that most Russian peasants, even at the time of the revolution, were Orthodox. Formally, this was probably true of the communities studied by Fenomenov, Leper, Kushner, and Anokhina and Shmeleva.[29] However, the practices described by Fenomenov[30] do in fact have more in common with "superstition" than with religion—i.e., they are predominantly pre-Christian—even though the priest participates. Let us consider some of the ceremonies connected with peasant activities as described by Fenomenov.[31]

In the spring and fall, before the beginning of sowing, the whole family gathers for prayer. A lamp is lit and a special communion wafer is laid on the table before the icon. All kneel. The master of the house reads the Virgin Prayer, stands up, lays the communion wafer and a little seed in a bast basket, and goes out to sow, followed by the whole family except for very small children. Before they go out, the oven tongs are propped against the oven door. In the field each member of the household throws out one handful of seed. When the family returns to the house, they remove the oven tongs.

The driving of cattle to pasture is accompanied by special rites. In the spring, on St. George's Day, the herdsman and the priest make a circuit of the herd, the priest in front with the cross and holy water, the herdsman behind with icon in one hand, axe in the other. In Fenomenov's village in Novgorod guberniia, where the herdsman is regarded as a sorcerer, there is no priest and the villagers circle their own stock three times with an icon, a willow switch, a candle, and a sieve in their hands. An egg is rolled up to

[29] M. Ia. Fenomenov, *Sovremennaia derevnia* (2 vols., Moscow and Leningrad, 1925); E. R. Leper, "Lomka byta i mirovozreniia pod vliianiem kollektivizatsii otstaloi derevni," in *Trud i byt v kolkhozakh* (*Trudy Instituta po izucheniiu narodov SSSR*), I (1931), 73–118; P. I. Kushner (ed.), *Selo Viriatino v proshlom i nastoiashchem: opyt etnograficheskogo izucheniia russkoi kolkhoznoi derevni* (Moscow, 1958); L. A. Anokhina and M. N. Shmeleva, *Kul'tura i byt kolkhoznikov Kalininskoi oblasti* (Moscow, 1964).

[30] Fenomenov, pp. 79, 103.

[31] I am indebted to Stephen P. Dunn for the use of his notes on Fenomenov and Leper.

the horses and the stock is driven to the edge of town. The herdsman makes three circuits of the herd. After the third, guns are fired and the horses are let go. "I have heard," writes Fenomenov, "that yet another circuit is necessary—a magical one. If the herdsman doesn't want the cows to scatter, he has to go to an expert sorcerer and make the circuit with him. But the only ones who do not know how to make the circuit are little boys, who are never valued as herdsmen. The old herdsmen themselves 'know the word' and make the circuit themselves."[32]

Apparently as a protection against the herdsman, there is a ceremony in the master's yard before driving the cattle to pasture: the wife circles the yard carrying the icon of St. George and a bundle of provisions—a *kulich,* a pine stump, eggs. The master follows, carrying an axe and a stone. The stock is gathered in the middle of the yard and they go around it three times, widdershins. Each time the master knocks the stone against the butt of the axe so that sparks fly. Then the axe and the stone are buried in the manure pile at the gate and the stock is driven out. The axe is dug up again after three days, but the stone is left. The *kulich* is given to the neighbors to eat; the eggs and the pine stump are given to the herdsman. Fenomenov says that this procedure is common to the Russian North in general.

The group of peasants studied by Leper in the northernmost raion of Leningrad oblast' were also formally Orthodox, although on the basis of Aptekman's work,[33] I am inclined to doubt her statement that there were no sectarians in the region. The picture obtained from rather scanty data bears a remarkable similarity to what is observed by present-day Soviet ethnographers and sociologists: those parts of the Orthodox religion which are difficult to fulfill were dying out, and those parts which did the peasant no harm (as he saw it) survived. Church weddings were rare, but christening and burial rituals remained intact, and the village as a whole still observed the traditional holidays peculiar to it. At the time of Leper's study, the village contained a sorcerer (probably a folk healer, since people came to him to be treated). Leper said that the sorcerer's second son also practiced sorcery with icons, but she does not elaborate. Icons remained hanging in most homes, but in some the attitude toward them was very casual. Leper repeats an attitude toward the church which has since become a commonplace: "You have a theater, but where shall we go?"[34]

The material presented by Anokhina and Shmeleva[35] slips in and out of focus, perhaps because this is a regional study and peasant religious phe-

[32] Fenomenov, p. 104.
[33] D. M. Aptekman, "K kharakteristike sovremennogo sostoianiia religioznogo trezvenichestva," in A. I. Klibanov *et al.* (eds.), *Konkretnye issledovaniia sovremennykh religioznykh verovanii* (Moscow, 1967), pp. 174–187.
[34] Leper, p. 110.
[35] Anokhina and Shmeleva, pp. 236–270.

nomena do not lend themselves to convincing generalizations. With the possible exception of Old Believer populations in the forest zones of Kalinin oblast' (only referred to in passing), religious observance seemed to be of two sorts, familial and communal; in both cases, the actual participation of the Orthodox Church was minimal, and remains so today. It is interesting that the communal festivities described illustrate the thesis that most people were out to have a good time and mostly did what was expected of them. For instance, there was a holiday for making beer, during which people from other villages were free to come, even if the master of the house was unknown. The formula "Let me sit on your bench" required the master to dispense beer as a form of hospitality.

I have already described in some detail whatever religious observance was reported by Kushner for Viriatino village, Tambov oblast',[36] and will therefore stress here only the marked connection, on the communal side, with the peasant agricultural calendar, and the fact that religious observance in Viriatino was carried on within the family and without a priest, for the most part. Klibanov[37] reported a wide variety of sects in the past in Tambov oblast'—Khlysty, Skoptsy, Molokans, Dukhobors, Subbotniki. Each of the sects had, in Soviet terms, a historical reason for being, and the decline of these old Russian sects may be accounted for by the rise of new ones, primarily the True Orthodox Christians, the True Orthodox Church, and the Baptists. The strongest religious influence in Viriatino itself is the Molchal'niki, an extremist wing of the True Orthodox Christians,[38] which some Soviet researchers consider an Orthodox sect.[39] The fact that a "sect" can have, so to speak, a subsect, is a problem I will leave for others. Mitrokhin[40] has devoted some attention to the fragmentation of sects in the

[36] Kushner; Stephen P. Dunn and Ethel Dunn, *The Peasants of Central Russia* (New York: Holt, Rinehart and Winston, 1967), pp. 27–29, 94–106.

[37] Klibanov, "Sovremennoe sektantstvo," pp. 59–100.

[38] Z. A. Nikol'skaia, "K kharakteristike techeniia tak-nazyvaemykh istinno-pravoslavnykh khristian," *Voprosy,* IX (1961), 161–188.

[39] In view of the sect's political history (it was embroiled in the organizational and ideological disorders of the 1920's within the Orthodox Church and went underground in the 1930's and 1940's), it may be of some significance that the main strength of this movement in Tambov oblast' came from *edinolichniki*—farmers who refused to join collectives and either moved to cities or settled in the suburbs as artisan–craftsmen; they made up the main membership of the True Orthodox Christians when the churches were reopened. It is also interesting that, according to Z. A. Iankova, "O nekotorykh metodakh konkretno-sotsial'nogo izucheniia religii (*Iz opyta Riazanskoi ekspeditsii Instituta istorii Akademii Nauk SSSR*)," in Klibanov *et al.,* *Konkretnye,* pp. 111–119, the True Orthodox Christians in Riazan oblast' are now attending Orthodox churches for the major Orthodox holidays of Christmas, Trinity, and Easter.

[40] L. N. Mitrokhin, "Education in Atheism and Methodology of Studying the Survival of Religious Beliefs," *Soviet Sociology,* I, no. 1 (Summer, 1962), 31.

past and declares that the fact that this fragmentation and shifting still continue deserves further study. Koretskii's[41] article contains historical evidence in support of the theory that sects fragmented as social differentiation within them became more prominent. The growth of the Baptists in Tambov oblast' was mostly at the expense of the Molokans and proceeded very rapidly between 1880 and 1915.[42] The growth of the Baptists in the postwar years (1945–1948) is attributed to superior organization (the old Russian sects have none). Bograd[43] indicates that class distinctions are still keenly felt. The Baptists appeared in Michurinsk raion after World War I. According to one informant in the village of Ranino, those who were richer than the Baptists laughed at them, saying, "The non-people [*bezliud'e*] have found themselves a new God."[44] In the village of Malo-Lavrovo, 130 people who called themselves Christian Sabbatarians formed a commune in 1926. Although they believed in Christ, the New Testament, baptism, breadbreaking, and keeping the Sabbath, like the Adventists, religion was secondary. The commune broke apart in 1930 after dissension among the leadership. One of the former leaders denied that the sect was Adventist: ". . . Among the Adventists are the intelligentsia, engineers, doctors. But among us, simple peasants, direct from the plow."

Much of the Soviet work in the early 1960's (which essentially brings into the open work which has been in progress for some time) lacks clarity in a way which is not easy to pinpoint. Works on central Russia repeat over and over again that the main membership among sectarian groups are aged, illiterate, or semiliterate females, for the most part either housewives, ordinary kolkhoz members, or workers in various service trades. Why, then, the

[41] V. I. Koretskii, "Ocherki istorii religioznogo sektantstva na Tambovshchina," *Voprosy*, IX (1961), 35–76.
[42] I. A. Malakhova, "Religioznoe sektantstvo v Tambovskoi oblasti v posleoktiabr'skoi period i v nashi dni," *ibid.*, pp. 77–112.
[43] E. Ia. Bograd, "Opyt izucheniia sovremennogo sektantstva v Michurinskom raione," *ibid.*, pp. 113–143.
[44] Apparently the class composition of registered Baptist communities has changed, perhaps as a result of artificial measures, e.g., a 1960 decision to list as members of the community only those who regularly attended services. In Riazan oblast', this automatically excluded many peasants from outlying raions who were accustomed to attending services in town. N. S. Zlobin, "Sovremennyi baptizm i ego ideologiia," *ibid.*, XI (1963), 76, says that it is difficult to know the actual number of Baptists because of the many unregistered communities. In May, 1961, a Presbyter Boldin was removed from his post by the Oblast' Plenipotentiary for the Affairs of Religious Cults, apparently because he had been preaching to unregistered communities. In October, 1961, Boldin's community was deprived of its registered status (temporarily, Zlobin says), but Boldin and others continued to read (p. 105). How much of this is known to local citizens is not stated. Zlobin asked an Orthodox woman whether she would ever contemplate joining the Baptists, and she said she would not because she was a real villager (p. 102n).

concern over the state of sectarian groups? It would seem, as Fletcher[45] asserts, that these people are not in a position to influence anything, that the Communist Party has all the political power there is. For a long time, in fact, Soviet studies contented themselves with proving that believers were anomalies in the Soviet Union, that religion had become the preserve of women with few interests outside their homes. If one attempts to compare the percentage of women in the industrial labor force, in the cultural sphere, in the agricultural labor force, in the local and republican soviets as well as the Supreme Soviet, one will find reason for the official concern. Women in the USSR represent a depressed caste, and their representation in religious communities correlates fairly well with their place in the larger society, judged by age, education, and social position. More is at stake in this research than that the nature of the sectarian movement has changed, because the change has not been uniform. For years Soviet sources said that sectarian groups were attempting to attract youth, but the statistics in these articles contradicted the accusations. Recent studies indicate that the sociologist has to bear in mind not only the age and sexual composition of the communities but the economic character of the regions in which they are situated as well.

The first of my sources to document in any depth the charge that sectarians were making a big push to attract youth was Aleksandrovich, Kandaurov, and Nemirovskii,[46] and inasmuch as they used mostly raion and oblast' newspapers, I thought that perhaps the situation had been somewhat blown out of proportion. However, Serdobol'skaia[47] writes: ". . . in the society of EKhB [Evangelical Christian-Baptists] in 1960–1961 [those baptized] at younger than 30 years of age were not less than 15%, and the number of young believers by 1962 reached 15–17% of the total number of members in the community. . . ."[48] [I]n Novosibirsk in 1962, among those entering the community 31% are youth. One observes approximately the same thing in communities of Baptists in Kemerovo, Prokop'evsk in Kemerovo Oblast', Maikop of Krasnodar Krai, etc."

Cherniak is even more explicit. Hers is a thorough study of Baptism and Russian Orthodoxy in Alma-Ata oblast', and her attitude toward religion is hard-line. She considers religion the only legally existing ideology con-

[45] Fletcher, pp. 81–82.

[46] I. A. Aleksandrovich, G. E. Kandaurov, and A. I. Nemirovskii, "Sektantstvo v Voronezhskoi oblasti i rabota po ego preodoleniiu," *Ezhegodnik*, V (1961), 68.

[47] L. A. Serdobol'skaia, "Reaktsionnaia sushchnost' ideologii sovremennogo baptizma," *ibid.*, VII (1963), 115.

[48] *Ibid.*, pp. 120–121, also documents a certain drift toward "extremism" among this group, expressed by a tendency on the one hand toward Pentecostalism and on the other toward politically subversive acts, such as distributing illegal religious literature.

trary to the Soviet system permitted today and believes that the continued existence of religious bodies is exploited by opponents of the Soviet Union.[49] Yet her grasp of the issues and problems involved mark her as one of the best students of the sociology of religion in the Soviet Union today. Her data show that there is a marked difference between the effect of the Orthodox Church and of Baptism. Among the Orthodox, church affairs are mostly in the hands of elderly people who view the work as a socially useful retirement activity. Yet, "Conversation with the elder of the Orthodox Church in the city of Talgar showed that he had a very confused notion of religion. He said frankly that if he had been helped to get a pension, he would refuse to work in the church."[50] No doubt Cherniak exaggerates mercenary motives, but they must play a considerable role in the disputes among the leadership of both churches, though the Orthodox Church obviously has more money to spend and, in the cities, spends it on its choirs and the services of its church elders and priests. The situation among the Baptists is much more complex. The appeal of Orthodoxy to the population is a traditional one, rarely calling for personal sacrifice or contemplation. Baptism in Alma-Ata oblast' has a long history of militant awareness, and Cherniak considers it no accident that nearly every presbyter serving in Alma-Ata has had 40 years of service to Baptism.[51] Likewise, the governing bodies (*dvadtsatki*) of the two registered Baptist churches in Alma-Ata contain relatively few women (one in the First community and four in the Second). The *dvadtsatok* among the Baptists differs from the Orthodox in this respect as well as in the larger number of people involved; in the First community 67 percent were baptized before 1940, and in the Second community 70 percent. They are also better educated than their Orthodox counterparts: 32 percent in the First community and 35 percent in the Second have incomplete secondary education. The executive committee of these Baptist groups, the so-called Brotherly Council, is composed of people all over the age of 60, with more than 40 years of service. Two in this group have attained only primary education, the remainder have incomplete secondary education.

Cherniak's more detailed study[52] gives some reason to suppose that this situation has given rise to a generation conflict, with sexual overtones, though this latter aspect is certainly muted. In 1963, 77 percent of the membership of the First Alma-Ata community and 76 percent of the Second were female. There is a better balance of men and women in Kazakhstan than

[49] Cherniak, *O preodolenii*, pp. 7–8.
[50] *Ibid.*, pp. 44–45.
[51] V. A. Cherniak, "O demograficheskikh osobennostiakh obshchin EKhB g. Alma-Aty i Alma-Atinskoi oblasti," in Klibanov *et al., Konkretnye*, p. 214.
[52] Cherniak, *O preodolenii*.

in some other regions of the USSR, and thus only 35 percent of the women in the First Alma-Ata community were single; only 13.6 percent have secondary and incomplete secondary education, 66 percent are semiliterate, and 11 percent are illiterate.[53] In Kazakhstan as a whole, the under-30 age group in Baptist communities is strikingly large, 43 percent, and 33 percent in the two Alma-Ata communities as of 1962. It is also interesting that as of the 1959 census, 54.6 percent of the population was under 25.[54] In 1959, 60 percent of those newly accepted into Baptist communities in Kazakhstan came from Baptist families and, in 1962, the number had risen to 72 percent. These figures must relate to rural communities, inasmuch as the percentage of those from Baptist families in the two Alma-Ata communities had dropped markedly by 1962. The more youthful composition of the Baptist communities is reflected also in occupations: in the First community 34.6 percent are working and in the Second, 28 percent. In the First Alma-Ata community, of 168 white-collar workers, only 67 have a specialty. In the Second community, of 144 white-collar workers, 39 were without a specialty, and of 170 blue-collar workers, 57 had no specialty.[55] Apparently, Baptists are not exempt from demographic pressures. In some cases they have been known to come to Alma-Ata in order to live in an active church community. Kapparov and Cherniak report, based on a study of the Alma-Ata heavy machine–building plant: "There are cases (especially among sectarians) in which believers change their place of work with particular frequency with the aim of expanding their opportunities for propaganda."[56] Cherniak[57] says that sectarians are especially active where women predominate. In the Alma-Ata embroidery plant "Dzhetysu" women were 85.3 percent of the staff and 82 percent of these had little education. Since political work at the factory was nonexistent, sectarians formed a group of nine for "agitation"

[53] These figures apparently conceal a lower level of educational achievement among women generally which becomes much more pronounced in the over-55 age group (*ibid.,* p. 172).

[54] By way of comparison, Cherniak says that in Tambov oblast', in the city of Michurin, only 6 percent of the Baptists were younger than 40, and in the city of Elets, Lipetsk oblast', 7 percent (*ibid.,* p. 72, n. 8).

[55] *Ibid.,* p. 72. How typical this is may be judged from Cherniak's statistics on the share of women in the labor force in Kazakhstan. They make up 40 percent of the total; by occupation: 37 percent of the physical labor is done by women, 49 percent of the mental labor, 20 percent of the work in public organizations (Party, Komsomol, trade unions, cooperatives), 35 percent of the engineers and technicians, 60 percent of the scientific workers and educators, and 63 percent of the cultural workers. On the other hand, only 54.8 percent of the women of working age are employed in the public sector; 48.6 percent of those who are not working have small children, but 32.9 percent of women who have children older than 14 are also not working. In Alma-Ata oblast', 35.1 percent are not working (*ibid.,* p. 172)

[56] D. A. Kapparov and V. A. Cherniak, "O prichinakh i usloviiakh zhivuchesti religioznykh perezhitkov," *Voprosy filosofii,* no. 6 (1967), p. 67.

[57] Cherniak, *O preodolenii,* p. 72.

in the factory. Of those entering the group, with one exception, all were under 35 years of age. All lived on the edge of town.

Cherniak says of these Baptists: "Many of them are engaged in the sale of their own agricultural produce and often produce purchased from others on the city markets. Thus, while being city-dwellers, they are in fact apart from the real influence of the city and its culture."[58] This social isolation is perhaps the most significant single fact about contemporary sectarianism, and it is not peculiar to Alma-Ata. Essentially the same point is made by Aptekman[59] regarding the inhabitants of the settlement of Mikhailovka, Leningrad oblast'. These people are Trezvenniki, a temperance sect which owes something to the ideas of L. N. Tolstoi but more to an eccentric named Churikov. Eighty percent of the inhabitants of Mikhailovka have less than four grades of schooling; 70 percent are housewives or are handicapped. Most of their living comes from the produce of their private plots (most people still have a land allotment of 0.2–0.3 hectare), the rental of summer quarters, and by cottage industry. There are a few industrial workers, mostly service personnel. These people, Aptekman says, are outside the influence of a large organized collective. Cherniak,[60] too, says that believers are essentially an unorganized part of the population, although it seems clear that this is meant to indicate the difficulties of influencing sectarians on an official level. She thinks that the trade unions could break down these barriers by educating the person in his work, by raising his skill level, and by gradually changing his worldview. However, she notes that trade unions have been rather inconsistent in their attitude: at the Issyk fruit wine factory the local committee extended an invitation to one sectarian to join the trade union while simultaneously preparing to expel another girl because she was a sectarian.[61]

Cherniak obviously believes that the time has come, so to speak, to lift the quarantine on sectarians, to look at their situation, and to realize that the human organism is influenced as much by the psychological as by the material. In this regard she says that some Party workers have made a grave mistake in telling believers that they may believe what they choose as long as they don't congregate together; this, in fact, only drives the sickness deeper.[62]

[58] *Ibid.*, p. 73. One would think that the temptation for these Baptists to club together in an effort to package and market their produce would be overwhelming, especially in view of deficiencies in the Soviet network. The "fresh produce crisis" remains chronic in all parts of the country, especially agricultural areas, and recent changes in agricultural policy do not seem to have made much difference. Private initiative of this sort would probably be treated as an anti-Soviet crime.
[59] Aptekman, p. 177.
[60] Cherniak, *O preodolenii*, p. 177.
[61] *Ibid.*, pp. 212–213.
[62] *Ibid.*, p. 209.

Cherniak has here put her finger on the largest problem of all. The entire force of tsarist law was that sectarians might make no public show of belief, and this was why it was necessary to exile them. Soviet law has continued this tradition almost to the letter, although the exile system no longer works as it did, simply because millions of people have now been settled in areas which were previously sectarian preserves.[63]

There have been a few studies of sectarian groups in Armenia, Georgia, and the Transbaikal.[64] These studies are markedly different from those done in central Russia, apparently because pressures on the population have been less intense and "religion as a way of life" is more clearly distinguished.[65]

[63] Both the method of exile and the occupations seem to have changed. For instance, Iu. V. Gagarin, *Puti i sredstva preodoleniia religioznykh perezhitkov* (Syktyvkar, 1965) and *Evangel'skie-Khristiane-Baptisty* (Syktyvkar, 1966), says that the great majority of sectarians in the Komi ASSR live in cities. This means lumbering camps or workers' settlements, and judging from other materials at my disposal, I would think that the population is factually intermediate between worker and peasant. What the population may have been originally is somewhat obscure. Gagarin notes the arrival of a group of dekulakized persons in the 1930's, but there is no indication that they were sectarians. Rather, Gagarin's somewhat stereotyped attitude is that religion is especially attractive to this *déclassé* type because through religion he can exercise his political protest. It is true that sectarians are still being exiled for crimes of various sorts, but not, as far as I can discover, en masse. It is interesting that one legal expert, Iu. T. Mil'ko, "Nauchno-ateisticheskaia propaganda i ugolovno-pravovaia bor'ba s prestupleniiami tserkovnikov i sektantov," *Sovetskoe gosudarstvo i pravo*, no. 7 (1964), pp. 65–75, considers it a mistake to exile a sectarian offender rather than to try to rehabilitate him on the spot through atheistic propaganda, since exile only gives the sectarian the chance to spread religion in a new place.

[64] K. I. Kozlova, "Izmeneniia v religioznoi zhizni i deiatel'nosti molokanskikh obshchin," *Voprosy nauchnogo ateizma* (hereafter *VNA*), no. 2 (1966), pp. 305–321; K. I. Kozlova, "Iz opyta izucheniia Molokan Armenii," in Klibanov *et al.*, *Konkretnye*, pp. 119–128; D. M. Kogan, "O preodolenii religioznykh perezhitkov i staroobriadtsev," *Voprosy*, XII (1964), 37–43; E. G. Zolotov, "Reaktsionnyi kharakter molokanstva (Po materialam, sobrannym v 1959–1960 gg. v Gruzinskoi SSR)," *Ezhegodnik*, VI (1961), 152–159; G. I. Il'ina, "Ob izuchenii sovremennogo byta 'semeiskikh,' " *Etnograficheskii sbornik* (Ulan-Ude), no. 1 (1960), pp. 108–122; A. A. Lebedeva, "Nekotorye itogi izucheniia sem'i i semeinogo byta u russkikh Zabaikal'ia," *ibid.*, no. 3 (1962), pp. 27–37; L. E. Eliasov, "Staryi i novyi fol'klor semeiskikh Zabaikal'ia," *ibid.*, pp. 96–103.

[65] Compare, for example, the state of the Old Belief in Riazan oblast' as described by B. F. Milovidov, "Raspad staroobriadchestva v Riazanskoi oblasti," *Voprosy*, XI (1963), 126–137. As of 1961, there were only 800 Old Believers in a population of 1,444,800, and these were split into at least six factions. Some of them were said to be former *edinolichniki* who moved to suburban or urban localities during collectivization. Some were still farmers, like the inhabitants of Aleksandrovskie Vyselki, former *khutor*-dwellers who now form one of the three brigades of the Kirov kolkhoz. Their lives remain strongly traditional, not least because little has been done to change them. There is no club in Aleksandrovskie Vyselki. One senses a certain ambivalence and reserve to studies done "in the center" (see B. F. Milovidov, "Staroobriadchestvo i sotsial'nyi progress," *VNA*, no. 2 (1966), pp. 198–224) which is lacking in studies of the Semeis or Caucasian Molokans.

D. M. Kogan (see n. 64) describes the Semei Old Believers, so called because, unlike other exiles, they came in large family groups. They arrived in the Transbaikal region in the second half of the eighteenth century from Starodub and Vetka when these centers of the Old Belief were destroyed. He distinguishes them from Sibiryaks, who were Orthodox and who arrived somewhat earlier. In 1960, the Transbaikal detachment of the Institute of Ethnography studied the village of Khonkholoi, Mukhoshibir raion, Buriat ASSR. Kogan says that the village contains more than 500 households, which indicates a reasonably stable population since 1897, when a household census revealed 567 families.[66] From a Soviet point of view, the village is extremely well off: there is a club, and a new house of culture was being built. There are a school, two libraries (one in the school itself), an out-patient clinic, a hospital, a pharmacy, a kindergarten and nursery, a bakery, dining hall, and various stores and public buildings. Electrification is complete and construction of new homes continues. Kogan studied 128 families and found 53 mixed marriages, 36 of these being with Orthodox. It is interesting that many of the old superstitions survive, particularly those connected with curing the sick. For instance, to cure radiculitis (*utin*), little branches are placed on the patient's back; the sorcerer pretends to chop the branches with an axe. The patient asks, "Whom are you chopping?" The sorcerer replies, "Utin," and the response is, "Well, chop so it doesn't come back." Children are treated with water and spells, at daybreak or sunset, since it is believed that most of their illnesses are the result of fright or the evil eye. Lebedeva[67] reports that in the town of Bichura, as late as 1959, some people went to the sorcerer to be cured of toothache, even though the town had a dentist. One may, of course, assume that these practices say something about the quality of Soviet medicine, but Il'ina[68] assures us that people do go to the doctor when the spell doesn't work.

Life in these Old Believer villages remains highly traditional, even though bicycles, motorcycles, and other trappings of civilization have become fairly common. Still, women's clothes remain much what they were 100 years ago, and 17 or 18 is considered a good age for marriage. Families are still large.[69] "Young men and women working in the kolkhoz still have primary education, rarely secondary," writes Il'ina,[70] and this may explain why only relatively few families in one village she studied (15 to 20 out of 248)

[66] See A. A. Lebedeva, "Anketa kak etnograficheskii istochnik (Po materialam sploshnogo podvornogo obsledovaniia 1897 v Zabaikal'e)," *Sovetskaia etnografiia*, no. 1 (1967), p. 100.
[67] Lebedeva, "Nekotorye itogi," p. 31.
[68] See n. 64.
[69] See Lebedeva, "Anketa," p. 101.
[70] Il'ina, p. 116.

engaged in seasonal migrant labor. In 12 families, people work in a neighboring sovkhoz two or three months of the year. There are only six students away at school in this village, but in another, out of 148 families, two students were away at the veterinary school in Ulan-Ude and one was attending an agricultural school. Semeis are not excluded from social mobility, however. "Serapion Kurillovich Kiselev," Il'ina writes, "was chosen 12 times in a row to be a deputy and a member of the Presidium of the Supreme Soviet of the Buriat ASSR." His son, Georgii Serapionovich Kiselev, received advanced medical training and at the time of Il'ina's study was a Deputy Minister of Health in the Buriat ASSR.[71]

Zolotov[72] did a study of Molokan groups in the Georgian SSR. The Molokans are split into two groups, Postoiannye and Priguny, with the latter sharing some of the traits of Pentecostalism (Priguny would be translated "Jumpers"). Although the groups are mostly small, even in cities, and the membership is elderly, there appears to be a traditional reservoir for Molokan groups: the family. It is a mistake, Zolotov thinks, to assume that Molokanism is dying out. There has not been a public abjuration of faith in Georgia for 25 years (in contrast to the central regions where, forced or not, renunciation of faith happens frequently, often as a prelude to social mobility). The following very interesting details in Zolotov's article illustrate the strength of the family.

In 1959, a worker in one of the medical institutions in Tbilisi was told by her parents that it was time to marry a young Molokan whom they had selected for her. The young couple had met only once, but the groom's parents had already slaughtered a cow and prepared the wedding table. The young medical worker refused the marriage and the groom's family, distressed that all these preparations would be wasted, sent a matchmaker to a girl he had never met. The second girl agreed, in order not to shame her family. "Unfortunately," writes Zolotov, "there are still cases in which marriages in Molokan families are concluded in this manner."[73] In 1961, a young Komsomol from a Molokan family who had graduated from a medical *tekhnikum* was expelled from the Komsomol "at her own request" because she was yielding to parental pressure to marry a Molokan.

Molokan families are large. Married sons do not split off from the parental household but remain in a separate house on the family plot if the main house would be too crowded otherwise. There may be as many as

---

[71] In many years of careful reading I cannot remember ever seeing anything of the sort written of Baptists or the sons of Baptists. I am inclined to think that the difference is that the Semeis are considered an ethnic minority, whereas the Baptists are denied this status.

[72] See n. 64.

[73] Zolotov, p. 155.

four such houses on the family plot. Each evening the family gathers together for a reading of the Bible.

Molokan religious services are very simple and consist of Bible-readings and prayers. Services are held "in the sitting rooms" of ordinary houses. A table is placed in the middle, with benches along the sides. Men sit on one bench, women on another. Women are not allowed to take part in the service. At present there are two types of services: general prayers and prayers for private occasions. These include birthdays, funerals, marriages, and the naming of a child. The ceremony of naming the child includes the act of "blowing into the mouth," since it is thought that in this way the child receives the holy spirit. There is also a ceremony called "submit and be forgiven." Zolotov asked one of the workers in a factory in Tbilisi what he thought this meant, and the man replied, "This means only, submit to your father. Outside you can do what you want."

Activity among Molokan groups increased somewhat in 1953 in connection with the one hundred fiftieth anniversary of the sect's founding, including an attempt to establish one center for the sect. This was said to be on the initiative of a group in Bendery (Moldavian SSR). There was also an attempt to start a youth group in Tbilisi in 1959, but the 24-year-old man who was instrumental in the drive had little success. It is of some significance that he later joined the Pentecostalists in Rustavi.

K. I. Kozlova has apparently had an opportunity to study the Molokans of Armenia at some length and depth in two locations, the city of Dilizhan with its suburb of Novyi Dilizhan (incorporating the villages of Golovino and Papanino), and the settlement of Fioletovo, Spitakskii raion.[74] The

[74] Her methodology is of some interest. Dilizhan is a resort town, and she came to it for a month in the summers of 1963–1964, with six students. To begin with, she found that the habits of years of field work failed her in the city. They began in the homes of the local intelligentsia—people who had received higher education, who did not consider themselves believers, but whose families still attended Molokan meetings. One of her best informants was a middle-aged single woman in ill health who belonged to the Priguny sect. This woman allowed Kozlova to copy 200 songs for various occasions from her notebook, but would not be seen in Kozlova's company during meetings or at the homes of other Molokans, for fear of being ostracized (Kozlova, "Iz opyta," p. 121). Here two people wrote down conversations in a field notebook and each kept a diary of notes and observations as well. They went to the Sunday prayer meetings at which all were welcome, but they were careful to ask permission and also asked how they should dress. The Molokan presbyter did not have much authority among the population, Kozlova said, though it would be fairer to say that his authority was slipping because one son had gone away to work in the Far North and had married a non-Molokan and his two daughters had married an Azerbaidzhani and an Armenian. The attitude toward him was, "He can't put his own house in order, how can he lead us?", in spite of the fact that he had denounced his children for their actions. "He was a very cautious man and spoke unwillingly of religion," says Kozlova, who therefore stuck to ethnographic matters. Then three members of the team moved to Fioletovo, where Kozlova herself con-

settlements are in mountainous regions where there was little land for farm-ing, so that wealthy Molokans lived by sheep-herding and hauling as far away as Central Asia, and by buying up houses. Poorer people lived by crafts and seasonal migrant labor. Kozlova says, "In Molokan families it often happened that the men entered the kolkhoz and the women refused, separated out from the family, and conducted an independent economy, refusing the help of the kolkhozniki."[75] During this disagreement, a split occurred in the Molokan communities, and the new group called themselves Priguny-Maksimisty (supposedly in honor of the founder of the Molokans, Maksim Rudometkin). The Maksimisty went away to work, primarily to Erevan, where they founded a separate community. Those who remained in Fioletovo have not joined the kolkhoz to this day but are engaged in various nonagricultural aspects of production. The village is presently com-posed of three groups: 269 Priguny, 110 Postoiannye, and 55 Maksimisty, as of the beginning of 1964. There are also some recently settled Azerbai-dzhani who hold themselves somewhat apart because they do not speak Russian very well. The Priguny and Postoiannye have separate meeting houses which have been rented from fellow villagers. The Maksimisty rotate meetings from house to house. Meetings are held Saturday evening (in the case of Maksimisty) and on Sunday morning and evening. Kozlova[76] says that on Saturday houses are swept clean and people bathe. On Sunday everyone puts on clean clothes and makes a procession to the prayer meet-ing. The Maksimisty show a perference for white clothes from head to toe. Among the others, young women may be dressed in light colors, but long sleeves and a kerchief are customary, as is a long shirt for men tied at the waist with thongs. Older women wear aprons and kerchiefs of good quality and workmanship. Children do not usually attend these meetings but are, Kozlova says, constantly subjected to the religious ideology at home. Each community has a presbyter, an assistant, and several singers whose role appears to be similar to that of a cantor, inasmuch as no service would be complete without them. It is generally not considered proper for a presbyter

---

ducted interviews and two students recorded them. They stayed a month with a family of Priguny and were assisted by the local teacher who had spent more than 30 years in the village. They explained that they were studying the life of the Rus-sians, including beliefs, but they found that some people would talk to them only if they knew that what they said would not be repeated. They used the books of the local soviet for data on the 300 households and saved discussion with community leaders for last. The leader of the Postoiannye had to be approached through his deputy; the leader of the Priguny, too, was more at home with the Bible. It is interesting that the head of the Maksimisty was energetic and openly combative, saying that he was not the stuff on which the foundations of communism would be laid. Most of the information on the Maksimisty thus came from others (*ibid.*, p. 126).

[75] Kozlova, "Izmeneniia," p. 206.
[76] Kozlova, "Iz opyta," p. 125.

to accept his post until he is at least 50, but the presbyter of the Maksimisty was not yet 40 at the time of Kozlova's study. The Molokans are frequent visitors to the library and bring what they have read to their meetings for discussion. If the discussion is on a low level, this is only a reflection of their educational level.[77] Postoiannye meetings last about two hours, beginning with the reading of the Scriptures and an interpretation periodically broken by songs on old Russian motifs. Only at the end of the meeting, when the benches are cleared away and everyone is on his knees for the presbyter's prayerful requests to God, do the women begin to cry. In some the tears are genuine; in others they are the result of long practice. Among the Priguny there are still the descent of the holy spirit, the jumping, and the shaking, which, to someone who is unaccustomed to them, make a considerable assault on the nerves.[78]

The three groups differ somewhat in their attitude toward the larger society and their place in it. It is interesting that the Maksimisty, although they have the largest number of workers and are thus the most urbanized, are the most conservative. The Maksimisty will not join trade unions and refuse state subsidies because they believe that only what one has gotten with one's own hands is pleasing to God.[79] On the other hand, they have no objection to living as well as possible within that restriction. All the children of Maksimisty are in school. The majority do not join the Pioneers, but there are a few Komsomol members. The presbyter believes that his responsibility to the children ends at 16. After that, they may decide for themselves. However, Maksimisty keep a tight rein on the behavior of the community through the rituals of marriage, baptism, and burial, as in varying degrees do the Postoiannye and Priguny. The Priguny will not marry Kom-

[77]

	EDUCATION			AGE			SOCIAL STATUS[a]		
	Illit-erate	*7–10 Grades*	*4–6 Grades*	*50+*	*30–50*	*–30*	*Work-ers*	*Non-workers*[b]	*Kolkhoz-niki*
Priguny	5.5	2.5	[92][c]	42.5	40.7	16.8	32.6	5.5	60.7
Postoiannye	1.1	6.4	[92.5]	50	40	10	38.2	7.3	56.3
Maksimisty	18.1	3.6	[78.3]	34.5	23.6	41.9	45.5	52.7	

[a] These percentages do not add up and may include students, but Kozlova doesn't say.
[b] Housewives, pensioners, invalids.
[c] The bracketed figures represent what Kozlova calls "the remainder."

[78] Kozlova, "Iz opyta," p. 122, attended a prayer meeting of Priguny in Dilizhan. On this occasion the presbyter, who used his time to scold the congregation for being too worldly, shared the platform with a young man of 20. He had been blinded in an accident while a schoolboy, and his mother subsequently began to bring him to meetings and to teach him the songs and psalms. He was regarded as a future prophet, and on this occasion was seized by the spirit, lept about, and gave a long sermon. Kozlova thought him well able to play on the congregation's moods.

[79] One Maksimist from Dilizhan accepted a pension which the community demanded that he return. He refused, preferring to go to another city and live with his son.

somol members or baptize children of second marriages. Kozlova talked with a 42-year-old woman from a Priguny family who had left her first husband for another. The second marriage was also unsuccessful, but the woman, in her own words, "was forced to bear the Molokan cross for the sake of the children, in order that their lives not be tainted."[80] The Posto-iannye are more moderate, but social pressure appears very strong, especial-ly in the village.[81] Kozlova observed a Komsomol wedding in the library at Fioletovo in 1963, but the next day there was a Molokan-style wedding because the father of the groom was an assistant presbyter. If the parents have not been married this way, the child cannot be christened, and if the parents are not seen in the meeting house, there is such talk that, by the birth of the second child, they are forced to mend their ways. Kozlova reports that people who are past middle age begin to visit the meeting houses regularly, so that they can be sure of burial.[82] Young people cannot be distinguished from their contemporaries, but once they marry, Molokan tradition takes over. Kozlova says that the club is for young unmarried people, who attend dances and films. The rest of the population goes out into the hills and gathers flowers and sings both religious and popular songs. Not unexpectedly, Party and Komsomol people are few in number and rather ineffective against the forces working for community cohesion. One of these forces is the custom of mutual help. At each meeting the congrega-tion puts on the table as much as each member can afford. When 15 to 20 rubles have accumulated, the elders decide who gets it. Those considered are, of course, Molokan, but no distinction is made between Priguny or

---

[80] Kozlova, "Izmeneniia," p. 206.

[81] Increasing urbanization is at least partly responsible for the more tolerant atti-tudes. Says Kozlova, "Izmeneniia," pp. 315–316, "In the families of Postoiannye-Molokans in Dilizhan there are Party and scientific workers, teachers, engineers, etc. Believing parents react tolerantly to atheistic children having secondary and higher education. Among the Postoiannye you see more mixed marriages with other nationalities. In their homes you can see, along with the Bible, the newest phono-graph with a selection of the newest records." There are very definite limits to this toleration, however, and even historically they have had little willingness to accept new technology or even new ideas.

[82] All three groups can refuse to bury the deceased if they consider him in any sense not one of them. Kozlova, "Izmeneniia," p. 315, says that when the community refuses, the family assumes the obligation. However, she herself, while in Dilizhan, observed the funeral of a young Komsomol member who drowned while working in the virgin lands. His coffin was sent home, and custom demanded that he be prayed and sung over for two nights. After this was done, the two communities, Postoiannye and Priguny, disputed the burial. The father had been a Communist who died at the front. The grandmother was a Postoiannye, the mother a not very correct Priguny. According to the Postoiannye, burial was the obligation of the Priguny, but the presbyter refused. Public organizations intervened, and at the cemetery, orchestral music vied with psalms, and speeches from public organizations lauding the deceased and his father competed with the moralistic scoldings of the two religious communi-ties (Kozlova, "Iz opyta," pp. 122–123).

Postoiannye. The invalids, the sick, the aged, the people without families, even in Erevan, can count on this aid. This help is acknowledged by a letter of thanks which is read at the meeting. Says Kozlova, "We talked to Molokans who were not old, who related rather indifferently to faith in God but who did not wish to break finally with their community, since they knew that in case of misfortune, the community would come to their aid."[83]

III

I have described Kozlova's data in detail because her methodology differs so strikingly from most of the current sociology of religion, of which there has been a great deal, especially since 1960. It is not simply that Kozlova is an ethnographer and the others regard themselves as sociologists. Kozlova has described a people, and the others are trying to measure attitudes, using standards which no longer apply, if they ever did. Works by Andrianov, Lopatkin, and Pavliuk, Onishchenko, Eryshev, and Tepliakov,[84] to name a few, read almost exactly like the reports of tsarist researchers collected and published by Kel'siev more than a century ago (1860–1862). This is not to say that Andrianov and his colleagues have not collected some interesting information, but they have taken hundreds of pages to say something which should be the beginning of study: people attend church for a variety of reasons—for companionship, for consolation, even for culture. This being so, the fact that fewer and fewer people believe in an anthropomorphic God or can discuss their articles of faith rationally is far less important than what happens to people who cannot verbalize or act out what they believe. It is not so easy to dismiss as merely polemical the work of Serdobol'skaia, Milovidov, Filimonov, Grazhdan, and Lentin, for example.[85] One tires of the blind insistence that Marxism is somehow different from religion, that religious groups in their attempts to deal with the modern world are only seizing the opportunity to be on the side of the ultimate

[83] Kozlova, "Izmeneniia," p. 319.

[84] N. P. Andrianov, R. A. Lopatkin, and V. V. Pavliuk, *Osobennosti sovremennogo religioznogo soznaniia* (Moscow, 1966); A. S. Onishchenko, "Tendentsii izmeneniia sovremennogo religioznogo soznaniia," *VNA*, no. 2 (1966), pp. 91–109; A. A. Eryshev, "Opyt konkretno-sotsiologicheskikh issledovanii religioznosti naseleniia na Ukraine," in Klibanov *et al.*, *Konkretnye*, pp. 138–144; M. K. Tepliakov, "Materialy k issledovaniiu religioznosti naseleniia Voronezha i Voronezhskoi oblasti," in *ibid.*, pp. 144–152.

[85] L. A. Serdobol'skaia, "Reaktsionnaia sushchnost' adventizma (po materialam g. Leningrada)," *Ezhegodnik,* VI (1962), 141–157; Milovidov, "Staroobriadchestvo i sotsial'nyi progress"; E. G. Filimonov, "Traditsii religioznogo liberalizma v sovremennom baptizme," *VNA*, no. 2 (1966), pp. 243–269; V. D. Grazhdan, "Piatidesiatnichestvo i sovremennost'," *ibid.*, pp. 270–287; V. N. Lentin, "Adventisty sed'mogo dnia i nauka," *ibid.*, pp. 288–304.

right and good—communism. Still, the reason for these polemics is clear enough. In the Soviet Union the churches are the opposition, and the clergy is potentially more influential than the Party.[86] The Party affects the lives of little people only in a political sense. In spite of 52 years of cultural change, the cultural lives of many people, especially in rural localities, can only be described as impoverished. This, of course, was not intended, and since the Party is sincerely interested in the transformation of man as well as society, the Party and the regime are beginning to acknowledge that greater understanding of religion is both necessary and desirable. Thus, for example, Mitrokhin is now permitted to write:

> Religion is not simply an error of the mind, not some "incorrect" conception of this or that law of nature and society. It is a worldview, reflecting, embodying a definite attitude of man to society, a definite understanding of his place in it. Education (if, of course, we take it not from a formal point of view but as a means of assimilating socio-cultural values)—is also one of the features of the given person's connection with society. Of course, religion and semi-literacy accompany one another. But the ease of action of religion on a person is not determined by the fact that he is semi-literate but by the fact that in this case we are dealing with a man who finds himself in a definite relationship to society, and semi-literacy itself appears as one of the signs of this relationship.[87]

Klibanov[88] raises another point of great significance: the stripping away of a church hierarchy brings about, so to speak, a relapse to a pre-church (pre-Christian, pre-Islamic, pre-Buddhist) state, and ritual is mostly centered around the solidarity of the group (the family). Klibanov indicates the importance of this relapse by citing Nikol'skaia's[89] evidence of animistic, fetishistic, and magical conceptions among the Mol'chal'niki (an extremist offshoot from an Orthodox sect). The same phenomenon has been well described by Datunashvili and by Esbergenov for populations on which Islam had been superimposed; Manzhigeev and Mikhailov describe the vital-

---

[86] See, for example, the study by V. D. Kobetskii, "Metodika izucheniia chitatel'-skogo sprosa na nauchno-ateisticheskuiu literaturu," in Klibanov *et al., Konkretnye,* pp. 83–100, which suggests that the Party has been largely talking to and for itself in its atheistic propaganda. N. P. Krasnikov, "Materialy issledovaniia religioznosti i praktika nauchno-ateistcheskogo vospitaniia," in *ibid.,* pp. 129–138, shows that in many instances, Party workers did not know what caused the population's indifference to their efforts or how to combat it.

[87] L. N. Mitrokhin, "O metodologii issledovanii sovremennoi religioznosti," in *ibid.,* p. 49.

[88] A. I. Klibanov, "Nauchno-organizatsionnyi i metodicheskii opyt konkretnykh issledovanii religioznosti (po materialam tsentral'nykh oblastei RSFSR)," in *ibid.,* pp. 28–29.

[89] See n. 38.

ity of shamanism among the Transbaikal Buriats.[90] Manzhigeev's article is especially interesting because in the area he studied, Russian and Ukrainian populations also utilized the services of the shaman.

To refer back to the opening pages of this paper, the materials I have discussed also raise a very important question of theory: is Soviet nationality policy responsible at least in part for the survival of religion? Soviet students like I. A. Kryvelev[91] specifically deny that there is any connection, citing "false public opinion" as the real cause. However, I have tried to show that, at least on the village level, there is a public opinion which is dominant and often counter to the expressed aims of the regime. Even in the cities, this, so to speak, counter-Soviet ideology is rather well established, although Ol'shanskii[92] would have us believe that this is true only because of the comparatively recent rural origins of the workers involved. He found that 71 percent of his Leningrad sample and 70 percent of his Moscow sample of workers who had christened their children had grown up in rural localities. Ol'shanskii is, however, inclined to believe that in intrapersonal relationships, people tend to do what is expected of them. This is strikingly borne out by Esbergenov who says that when he did his field work in 1955 and 1956, many people declared themselves atheists and were struggling against Islam. When he returned he found that the same people were not only not struggling but were beginning to observe many of the religious customs. The alternative in a village is social ostracism. Esbergenov's informant told him that the person critical of Islam was likely to "remain outside the life of the aul. Besides that, the old people are continually saying about you that you are a bad man who honors neither himself nor the people. Finally they force you to become as they are or move out of the aul."[93]

Esbergenov himself would probably say that these villagers were misconstruing Soviet nationality policy, but there are in fact many previously Islamic groups whose Soviet descendants are equally confused and who suppose that they can be both Moslem (their "tradition") and Soviet. Eryshev's data[94] indicate that nationality is a factor in religiosity in the Ukraine,

---

[90] I. I. Datunashvili, "Materialy k kharakteristike sovremennogo sostoianiia religioznosti v Belokanskom, Zakatal'skom i Kakhskom raionakh (Azerbaidzhanskaia SSR)," in Klibanov et al., *Konkretnye*, pp. 187–194; Kh. E. Esbergenov, "Ob izuchenii religioznykh verovanii karakalpakov," in *ibid.*, pp. 202–208; I. A. Manzhigeev, "Prichiny sushchestvovaniia shamanisticheskikh perezhitkov i sposoby preodoleniia ikh," *Etnograficheskii sbornik* (Ulan-Ude), no. 3 (1962), pp. 79–86; T. M. Mikhailov, "O perezhitkakh shamanizma u buriat," *ibid.*, pp. 87–95.

[91] See n. 1.

[92] V. B. Ol'shanskii, "Sotsial'naia psikhologiia i issledovanie religioznykh verovanii," in Klibanov et al., *Konkretnye*, p. 57.

[93] Esbergenov, p. 205.

[94] See n. 84.

where Orthodoxy is rather weak and elderly, and sects of various sorts show surprising vitality both in age structure and self-renewing mechanisms (primarily education within the family group). Such outward manifestations of religiosity as survive among the Orthodox (christenings, burials, the presence of icons in the home) are perceived by the population as part of their cultural heritage. V. N. Basilov[95] says that there has been a noticeable decline in the outward, ritualized manifestations of belief and that what remains is connected with the way that people live in their family groups. In this particular region of the Altai krai, people are accustomed to going to churches a considerable distance from their homes as the occasion demands. Therefore we may say that the people's contact with organized religion is almost "by correspondence." Religion in the village of Suslovo, for example, is in the hands of old ladies who seem well aware that what they are doing may not be correct but who say that it is the best they can do without a priest. These rituals center around the "immersion" of the child or the burial of the dead. Group prayers are rare, although a group of old women gathered at the house of a fellow villager for the major holidays until she went away in 1959. Outsiders who might wish to join the group are regarded somewhat suspiciously. One senses even in Basilov's bare recitation that the spiritual life of these villagers is shockingly thin,[96] but there is not much doubt that it is traditional—a firm part of the life of the Russian peasant.

Before we can answer the question of whether Soviet nationality policy is partly responsible for the survival of religion, we would have to know for what percentage of the population religion is still a way of life, in the total community sense which it was under tsarism. So far, our data are scanty. Before the great population shifts of the last 30 years, whole villages were Muslim, Buddhist, Orthodox, or various shades of sectarian, and we know that as late as the 1920's, whole villages would convert to Baptism. This for various reasons is no longer possible, but remnants of "religion as a way of life" do exist in some places. V. A. Cherniak did a house-to-house survey of Chemolgan, Kaskelenskii raion, Alma-Ata oblast', in an attempt to find out something about the Germans.[97] She found that the settlement pattern

[95] V. N. Basilov, "Etnograficheskoe issledovanie religioznykh verovanii sel'skogo naseleniia," in Klibanov *et al., Konkretnye,* pp. 152–174.

[96] The towns of Kulunda and Barnaul are probably too distant to have much effect on this group but, according to Bourdeaux, pp. 77–83, there are active Baptist groups in these towns. In Kulunda a member of the Baptist *Initsiativniki* was tried, sentenced, and probably tortured to death in prison. N. K. Khmara was, among other things, a reformed alcoholic. It is easy to see why, if Basilov's data are typical of rural life in the area, Khmara might have been considered a dangerous man by the Soviet regime, the more so if Khmara had in any sense an alternative program.

[97] Cherniak, *O preodolenii,* p. 137. According to the 1959 census there were in the

was established in accordance with religious affiliation: Lutherans had a row of houses at the edge of the village; Catholics and Baptists occupied other rows. This pattern is repeated in other raions of the oblast' and is a reflection of the German settlers' desire to preserve their identity, which in this case was clearly both national and religious. Literate people among the German population can only read German in Gothic script, and often their only literature is the Bible. Cherniak also says, "We collected our best material when we lived in the apartments of believers. For example, you have the German Baptists who are an unregistered community in a village locality. How do they spend their free time? Evening arrives; on the streets it is dark; people have nothing to do. What do they occupy themselves with? With the Bible, a book which, as the believers say, 'is sufficient for a whole life.' Neighbors arrive, and for the whole evening they read the Bible."[98]

There are signs that, having admitted that a problem exists, the regime is trying a new approach to correct it. Much of atheistic propaganda in the past was simply an assault on the personality and ego of the believer. The new approach includes—besides more cultural facilities and entertainment for the population—dialogues between atheists and believers. On an official level theoreticians hasten to assure us that there can never be any common cause between religion and communism. On a practical level, the atheist has as much or more to learn as the believer, and the intellectual level can only improve.[99]

A word or two should be said in this connection about the drive to establish a Soviet ritual. To begin with, the question would probably not arise in a more completely secularized society, or if the regime did not feel obliged to combat religious influence. On the other hand, Kampars and Zakovich[100] make an interesting defense of the view that a society should have rituals which reflect its nature. Some not very successful attemps were made to

---

Kazakh SSR 659,751 Germans, 19,643 of them in Alma-Ata oblast' and 4,285 in Alma-Ata itself. They came from the Ukraine, Belorussia, and the Volga region.

[98] *Ibid.*, p. 211.

[99] I will cite here one very small example reported by M. Klad'ko, secretary of the Party organization of the Brest "Indposhiv" factory, in *Agitator*, no. 15 (1965), pp. 39–40. Schools were started in the factory to give the workers a chance to learn something about man and nature. Evangelical-Christian Baptists took part but at first would say little. The following exchange took place during a discussion about dreams. Sectarian Tupchik: "Do you believe in conscience [*sovest'*]?" Lecturer: "I do." Tupchik: "Have you ever seen it?" Lecturer: "No." Tupchik: "Well, just so we believe in the soul [*dusha*], though we haven't seen it." Tupchik is supported by a fellow sectarian. The lecturer explains that conscience and consciousness (*soznatel'nost'*) are the same. The Communist acts consciously. The soul is an abstract, an illusion. Now, I admit that this is a very crude discussion, but it did take place, and therein lies its importance.

[100] See n. 3.

establish Soviet rituals immediately after the revolution. Kampars and Za-kovich[101] say that the question became urgent again in the mid-1950's. L. M. Saburova[102] has made a survey of recent ethnographic literature on the subject of new rituals. The place of a ritual or a custom in the life of the people is the result of a long, complex historical past. The Soviet regime claims (with considerable justice) to have made a definite break with the past. Therefore, the problem becomes: how does the regime preserve the old custom with which the people identify, while at the same time eliminating what it considers undesirable elements and adding new ones more in keeping with the people's increased sophistication? Many popular festivals, of course, had nothing to do with Christianity or Islam but were used or adapted by religious organizations. These (from the Soviet point of view) anachronistic bodies wished to control basic social processes. The Soviet state has the same motivation, but has had, of course, less time in which to exercise this control and to put its definitive stamp on ritual and custom.

IV

It is certainly too soon to tell what will happen. As a result of long historical processes, some of which I have outlined here, the Soviet regime is deeply hostile to religion, and in spite of every effort religion remains important in the lives of people, especially in a rural community. I will, by way of summary, list some reasons for this state of affairs.

1. Historically, religion was equated with nationality and way of life.

2. Both historically and at present, religious affiliation was also a sign of political protest.

3. Currently, most believers are said to be both female and rural. In point of fact, the regime has not altered the lives of rural women to the desired or desirable degree. Rural residents have social mobility and creature comforts in almost exact proportion to their ability to leave the rural community. This is least possible for women. I believe, however, that women belong to religious groups not so much out of protest, but simply in order to have social intercourse with people with problems similar to their own (this point is also made by Iu. F. Borunkov).[103]

---

[101] Kampars and Zakovich, p. 31.

[102] L. M. Saburova, "Literatura o novykh obriadakh i prazdnikakh za 1963–1966 gg. (Osnovnye voprosy i tendentsii izucheniia)," *Sovetskaia etnografiia*, no. 5 (1967), pp. 173–181; see also E. G. Filimonov, "Problemy konkretno-sotsiologicheskikh issledovanii religioznosti v sovetskoi literature 1961–1966 gg. (Kritiko-bibliografi-cheskii obzor)," in Klibanov *et al., Konkretnye*, pp. 217–242.

[103] Iu. F. Borunkov, "Ob izuchenii struktury religioznogo soznaniia," in Klibanov *et al., Konkretnye*, p. 104.

4. A certain element of protest does exist, however. The rural scene has changed much less rapidly than the cities, but some cities are, culturally speaking, not much better off than rural areas.

5. The regime fears that discontented elements, for lack of alternative political models, will unite behind the churches and overthrow the regime. I do not consider it likely, but the fear itself is firmly enough based in the history of religious movements in Russia. Only time will tell whether the knowledge gained by recent sociological studies and others undoubtedly in progress will allow the regime to overcome its fear and to permit ordinary people both more liberty and more creative expression.

15 : The Contemporary Countryside in Soviet Literature: A Search for New Values

Gleb Žekulín

The purpose of this essay is to discuss Soviet prose literature of the contemporary countryside and to consider, in particular, interest in moral values.

After a brief critical review of western works on Russian literature since Stalin, an attempt is made to distinguish the main characteristics of the literature of the early 1960's (Part I). This is followed by an investigation of the intellectual climate in the late 1950's and early 1960's, which suggests that a search for new values is the main preoccupation of the period (Part II). There follows a discussion of the emergence of the "new" literature and the establishment of countryside fiction as a particular genre with a strongly affirmative character. V. Belov's novella *The Carpenter's Stories* is used to illustrate the discussion (Part III). Part IV provides a summary and critique of V. Chalmaev's theoretical article, which represents an attempt to give the countryside prose an ideological foundation. In conclusion, an evaluation of the genre and of its success is attempted.

I

It would be a truism to say that the death of Stalin marked the end of an era and that from then on, important, even radical changes have been occurring in the political, economic, and social life of the Soviet Union.

All translations from non-English languages in the text and in the notes are by the author.

The arts and literature in particular have been subjected to the same process of modification, though much less has been said about it. The reason for this is the following. In the arts, as in no other field of human endeavor, Soviet ideologists and theoreticians have claimed that the highest possible, and therefore the final, stage of development was reached when the method of socialist realism, as the only acceptable and permissible mode of artistic creation, was formulated in 1934[1] and reaffirmed by Zhdanov in 1946.[2] Since then, the definition was repeated with some changes of wording but none of substance in 1954.[3] Then, during the "crisis years" of 1956–1959, the term "partyness" (*partiinost'*) was brought into the formula[4] and has since become perhaps the most important single element in the specifications of this "artistic method." The formula was slightly reworded again in 1959[5] and enlarged by explicit introduction of the principle of *partiinost'* as one of its main tenets. It was reconfirmed in 1967.[6] This effectively prevented any open questioning not only of the validity of the formula but, more important, of the validity of the concept itself. Thus, on the surface, all was and still is officially calm and serene on the so-called literary front. And, since this is so, no important theoretical work, no attempt to assess the development or to establish and define the new trends in literature since 1953 has appeared in the Soviet Union.

In fact, however, profound changes have occurred in Soviet literature since 1953. The principle of socialist realism itself has been challenged.[7]

[1] See the Rules of the Union of Soviet Writers, *Pravda*, September 2, 1934.

[2] See "O zhurnalakh 'Zvezda' i 'Leningrad,' " *Kul'tura i zhizn'*, September 21, 1946, or *Literaturnaia gazeta*, September 21, 1946.

[3] See the message of the Central Committee to the Second Writers' Congress, in *Vtoroi vsesoiuznyi s"ezd. . . . Stenograficheskii otchet* (Moscow, 1956), p. 8.

[4] In A. I. Metchenko, L. M. Poliak, and L. I. Timofeev (eds.), *Istoriia russkoi sovetskoi literatury* (Moscow, 1958), vol. I. Professor Metchenko apparently was the first to discuss, in his introduction to this volume (pp. 5–52), the term *partiinost'* in a theoretical manner and in a textbook intended for university students of Soviet literature; this discussion was an elaboration of his article "Istorizm i dogma," *Novyi mir*, no. 12 (1956), pp. 223–238. Metchenko's latest effort in this field was published in the book *Estetika segodnia (Aktual'nye problemy). Sbornik statei* (Moscow, 1968). See also, on *partiinost'*, Harold Swayze, *Political Control of Literature in the USSR, 1946–1959* (Cambridge, Mass.: Harvard University Press, 1962), pp. 8–14 and *passim*, particularly p. 260; E. J. Simmons, "The Origins of Literary Control," *Survey* (April–June, 1961), pp. 78–84; the present writer's review article "Socialist Realism," *Soviet Studies*, XI, no. 4 (April, 1960), 432–442.

[5] See the message of the Central Committee to the Third Writers' Congress, *Literaturnaia gazeta*, May 23, 1959; for *partiinost'*, see *Tretii s"ezd pisatelei SSSR. Stenograficheskii otchet* (Moscow, 1959), p. 248.

[6] See *Literaturnaia gazeta*, May 24, 1967.

[7] The best-known instance is the case of A. Siniavskii, who published abroad anonymously his article on socialist realism (*Esprit*, XXVII, no. 270 (February, 1959), 335–367). In it he states that questions about socialist realism "are being discussed in our midst where they agitate recalcitrant spirits who fall into the heresy

Western scholars were quick to notice this.[8] Their description and appraisal of what had happened were very much the same, but they differed considerably when expressing their views and prognoses regarding future trends in Soviet literature.

Harold Swayze[9] seemed (in 1962) to be indecisive but leaned toward pessimism. If a relaxation of Party controls was ever to occur, it would be due to "the growing strength of the Party and the increasing totalitarianization of Soviet society."[10] At such a future time, Swayze speculated, "the regime could then afford the luxury of a moderate cultural relaxation; it could permit its subjects access to previously forbidden ideas and imaginative experiences, since the likelihood of undesirable and unpredictable reactions by any significant number of people would be slight."[11] This pessimistic outlook presumed that the Party would in the future widen its influence over literature and, therefore, over Soviet intellectual and spiritual life and, by implication, that it would be successful in its ideological transformation of the Soviet people and thus finally succeed in forming a "new Soviet man." Today it is clear that this view was unduly grim. In spite of its efforts, the Party has not managed to win decisively the ideological war against its own people, and certainly not against the writers. Swayze's alternative suggestion, expressed more as a hope than a possibility, was, as it turned out, much more to the point: the Party would fail "to fetter the poet's muse."[12] Soviet literature of the 1960's continues to fight for its freedom to render its own view of man and its own understanding of life.

In 1961, Max Hayward, in the introduction to a collection of Soviet writings, gave a very brief survey of post-Stalin literature. He established that there was a certain regularity with which "thaws" were followed by "freezing periods."[13] Thus, the first "thaw" occurred in 1953 and was suc-

---

of doubt and criticism" (p. 355). See also the important article by A. Ovcharenko, "Sotsialisticheskii realizm i sovremennyi literaturnyi protsess," *Voprosy literatury,* no. 12 (1966), pp. 4–29, and the more interesting, from the theoretical point of view, article by Iu. Andreev, "Izuchat' fakty v ikh polnote," *ibid.,* no. 3 (1968), pp. 121–137.

[8] See, particularly, George Gibian, *Interval of Freedom; Soviet Literature during the Thaw, 1954–1959* (Minneapolis: University of Minnesota Press, 1960); the very important collection of articles in *Survey* (April–June, 1961), mainly pp. 34–55; Hugh McLean and W. N. Vickery (eds. and trans.), *The Year of Protest: 1956* (New York: Random House, 1961), a selection of works by "dissenting writers" which indicates very meaningfully the different kinds of protest against the rigidity of the Party line in literature; Swayze, pp. 83–258; Patricia Blake and Max Hayward (eds.), "Dissonant Voices in Soviet Literature," *Partisan Review,* XXVIII, nos. 3–4 (1961), particularly Max Hayward's introduction, pp. 333–362; Edward J. Brown, *Russian Literature Since the Revolution* (New York: Collier Books, 1963), pp. 238–292.

[9] Swayze, Chapter VII, "Perspectives and Prospects," pp. 261–266.

[10] *Ibid.,* p. 262.

[11] *Ibid.,* p. 263.

[12] *Ibid.,* p. 265.

[13] See Blake and Hayward, pp. 355ff.

ceeded almost immediately, in 1954, by a "frost" which lasted until the Twentieth Party Congress in February, 1956. The second thaw, though rather considerable, was of a short duration—the freezing period began shortly after the Polish and Hungarian revolutions in the autumn of 1956. The third thaw occurred after Khrushchev's speech at the Third Writers' Congress in May, 1959, and was again overtaken by frost in 1961. This conception of a see-saw type of evolution in contemporary Soviet literature is quite correct and, until now, valid. The conclusion which can be drawn from this phenomenon is either that the powers that be in the Soviet Union are undecided about how to handle the writers, or that the writers' protest against the muzzling of literature is strong and cannot now be handled with full effectiveness, at least not by the old methods. Hayward failed to mention the fact that every recurring thaw was more thorough, while every frost was less frigid. Works published during later freeze periods would have been considered overly daring during preceding thaws. This indicates perhaps that the "see-saw principle" is valid only as long as the surface of the literary scene is observed and that, in fact, the process of liberalization, which could be better described as the process of literature's liberation from Stalinist fetters, goes on continuously in the depth of Soviet intellectual and spiritual life. The opinion, for instance, of G. Baklanov,[14] who states that it is impossible to write in the old way since the publication in the USSR of Solzhenitsyn's stories, seems to support this view.

Max Hayward, in this and similar survey articles[15] (perhaps precisely because they *are* survey articles), does not attempt any fundamental prognostications about possible trends. But he establishes the existence, since the mid-1950's, of two camps in Soviet literature, the "liberal" one (represented mainly by *Novyi mir*) and the "reactionary" one (represented mainly by *Oktiabr'*).[16] This distinction, while quite acceptable terminologically if seen from the point of view of one who wants to indicate briefly and clearly that one camp consists of people who oppose the established "line" in the arts, while the other camp supports it, is nevertheless slightly misleading. Not all members of the opposition camp could be described as liberals, ideologically or intellectually. Many of them avoid—because of their particular attitudes or because they do not want to get into an open and sharp

[14] G. Baklanov's review of *Odin den' Ivana Denisovicha* in *Literaturnaia gazeta,* November 22, 1962. Baklanov's view is important as that of an author of a very mediocre war novella, *Piad' zemli,* which was officially praised as a great work of socialist realism. It ran to 23 editions and was translated into eight languages.

[15] See, e.g., his "Note on Recent Developments in the Soviet Theatre," *Cahiers du monde russe et soviétique,* VII, no. 3 (July–September, 1966), 408–413.

[16] This is, if possible, even more true today. It is quite sufficient to read, e.g., how *Novyi mir* is attacked in *Oktiabr',* no. 1 (1969), pp. 184–185, or to peruse the issues of *Literaturnaia gazeta* of July 17, 1968, p. 8, or of March 12, 1969, pp. 1, 4.

conflict with the authorities—obvious political statements. This makes it even more difficult to pigeon-hole them according to their political beliefs. It seems, therefore, that the terms "opposition camp" and "establishment camp" would better express the actual situation.

Edward J. Brown (1963) sees the trend in contemporary literature as featuring two main properties. The first is individuality, expressed as much in "content [as] in the apprehension of experience."[17] The second is simplicity; this he understands as being either contrived or genuine ideological naiveté.[18] Brown also states, and quite rightly, that to write about collective life or about builders of socialism has become almost impossible because it would almost certainly have a humorous effect on readers. Nor do writers now compose pamphlets against injustice and abuses rather than works of art.[19]

These are very astute remarks and very sensitive appraisals. But it seems that it has become possible since the publication of Brown's book to go further in assessing the new trend: the lack of ideology is in itself an ideology, and so is, for example, the apparent preoccupation with the infantilism and primitivism of certain characters in certain works, mainly in those about peasant life. The change which has occurred in the last few years in Soviet literature could, perhaps, be best understood if Kazakov's story, mentioned by Brown,[20] in which the central character is a blind dog, is taken as an example. Today, this story would have been understood as being too one-sided, too negative in its conception, as lacking any constructive suggestions concerning the values proper to contemporary man; today, Kazakov's story would probably be considered too simplistic, too facile—in other words, not serious enough.

George Gibian, in his important book (1960) on the first four years of post-Stalin literature, views this literature as being preoccupied with three main themes and, in this, being quite different from Stalinist literature.[21] The three themes are science (and, therefore, scientists, research, engineering, technology), love and sex, and villainy (negative characters). His basic assumption—an absolutely correct one when the literary process is seen from the chosen angle—is that the novelty lies in the subject matter and in the authors' attitude to it,[22] not in the creation of a new artistic method. Gibian's very thorough examination of a great number of prose works and plays (one longer poem—that of Semen Kirsanov[23]—is also

---

[17] Brown, p. 291.
[18] *Ibid.*, pp. 291–292.
[19] *Ibid.*, p. 292.
[20] *Ibid.*
[21] Gibian, pp. viii, x.
[22] *Ibid.*, p. vii.
[23] "Sem' dnei nedeli," *Novyi mir,* no. 9 (1956); see Gibian, pp. 60–63.

included in the discussion) not only proves his point but makes possible some general deductions and helps to establish some trends applicable to the literature of the 1960's.

First, it becomes clear on reading Gibian's book that while all the works which he studies could be safely described as "oppositionist," their opposition was still based on the ideologically orthodox—from the ruling Party's point of view—Communist ideal; there was, so far, no "revisionism." After the Twentieth Party Congress (February, 1956) the attacks of the oppositionists were concentrated on the cult of personality; i.e., their works became openly anti-Stalinist.[24] But even this anti-Stalinism had, as its source, the fervent and probably quite genuine wish to restore to its former glitter the Party's tarnished image. Thus, the works of Granin, Dudintsev, Zhdanov, Yashin, and even Kaverin were, in fact, pro-Party in the sense that its leading role was not challenged.

The common trend which develops from all these works is a rejection of the whole Stalinist historical period and of the results of the cult of personality. As these consequences are, however, still to be seen and felt everywhere, the literature which emerged in the 1960's necessarily became *critical* in tone.

Second, preoccupation with the individual as opposed to the collective developed into the main theme. This preoccupation, which became apparent as early as 1953,[25] developed first through the perhaps unexpected device of attacks on villains, such as Ehrenburg's character Zhuravlev,

[24] It would be interesting to speculate here on how "unprepared" Khrushchev's revelations of Stalin's misdeeds actually were. In perusing the almanac *Literaturnaia Moskva, sbornik vtoroi* (Moscow, 1956), one is struck by the fact that it was presented to the censors (euphemistically expressed by the words "sdano v nabor," a formula which is found today on the last page of *Novyi mir* alone) on October 1, 1956. Let us assume that the editorial work on this book of almost 800 pages and by 37 contributors took about a month; if so, the published material was in the hands of the editors by September 1, or about six months after Khrushchev's speech. And let us assume that some well-known opportunists, such as Nikolai Pogodin, could have written in this comparatively short time works which would correspond to the "new line" (Pogodin's three-act play *Sonet Petrarki*); or that the poets who supplied short poems could have composed them in the given time (the same applies, of course, to A. Kron's *Zametki pisatelia*, which contains a direct accusation of Stalin). But it is improbable that a very long—and good—novel by Veniamin Kaverin (*Poiski i nadezhdy*, pp. 42–291), so outspokenly anti-Stalinist, could have been conceived and written in six months. It seems that either the authors had their works ready in advance and were only waiting for an opportunity to publish them, or Khrushchev's speech was not so unexpected and "secret" after all.

[25] Vera Panova's novel *Vremena goda*, in *Novyi mir*, no. 11 (1953), pp. 3–101, and no. 12, pp. 62–158; V. Pomerantsev's article "Ob iskrennosti v literature," *ibid.*, no. 12 (1953), pp. 218–245. (The latter article—for which Tvardovskii was dismissed from his post as editor-in-chief of *Novyi mir*—is referred to in Solzhenitsyn's *Rakovyi korpus* (Paris: YMCA Press, 1968), pp. 246–248, in order to show the two attitudes to art which prevailed in the USSR between 1953 and 1956.)

Dudintsev's Drozdov, and Kaverin's Kramov, but soon turned to the positive depiction of individuals' thoughts and feelings.[26]

The resulting distinguishable trend is to portray a "loner," an alienated character, whose social value is of no importance and whose intellectual worth, therefore, is of no interest. The tendency to forego heroes of strong character and to create instead a Soviet kind of "anti-hero" becomes apparent.[27]

Third, and in close interaction with the previous two trends, a search for a new set of values began. The void, which appeared due to the—in principle—critical attitude to surrounding reality, had to be filled. Not only anti-Stalinism and anticollectivism, but also the open-eyed and unbiased observation of Soviet life over the last 40 or so years of the regime, precluded acceptability of so-called Communist ethics as a moral ideal. On looking back over the period, the only break in the darkness was the war years when, it seemed, all the good qualities of the nation came to the fore. And they did so not because of compulsion, of pressures and threats originating with the rulers, but in spite of them. The war years were, in a very real sense, the years when Russians in all walks of life recovered the sense of human dignity, of moral courage, and of dedication to an ideal.[28] When looking for the origins of this moral flowering, the writers were led to the pre-Soviet period, to the old "Mother Russia." The beginnings of this trend were very humble: it was, for example, the borrowing of artistic images from Orthodoxy, from Russian art and history,[29] or the use of archaic vocabulary and outmoded idioms and expressions. Then the real interest in old traditions and customs developed[30] and prompted a reassessment of the historical past with its spiritual and humanistic values.

[26] See, e.g., S. Aleshin's play *Odna*, in *Teatr*, no. 8 (1956).

[27] See, e.g., V. F. Tendriakov's "Troika, semerka, tuz," *Novyi mir,* no. 3 (1961), or "Sud," *ibid.;* also stories by Iurii Nagibin.

[28] This is how B. Pasternak described this moral recovery of a whole nation in *Doctor Zhivago*: ". . . the war came as breath of fresh air, an omen of deliverance, a purifying storm. . . . And when the war broke out, its real horrors, its real dangers, its menace of real death, were a blessing compared with the inhuman power of the lie, a relief because it broke the spell of the dead letter. . . . It was not only felt by men in your position, in concentration camps, but by everyone without exception, at home and at the front, and they all took a deep breath and flung themselves into the furnace of this deadly liberating struggle with real joy, with rapture . . . ; we are seeing the fruit of its [the war's] fruit, the result of its results—characters tempered by misfortune, unspoilt, heroic, ready for great, desperate, unheard-of deeds. These fabulous, astounding qualities are the moral flowering of this generation." *Doctor Zhivago*, trans. Max Hayward and Manya Harari (London: Collins and Harvill Press, 1958), p. 453.

[29] Dudintsev's *Ne khlebom edinym* . . . (1956) is interesting for this type of imagery, as Gibian, p. 59, has noted.

[30] Efim Dorosh's "Derevenskii dnevnik," in *Literaturnaia Moskva,* is particularly

Thus, there is now a distinct tendency in literature to idealize old Russia, its history, its people,[31] and to portray contemporary Russians as direct heirs to an old culture, as people who tenaciously preserve the old ways in the face of the great pressures exercised by modern life. This tendency found its best expression in the by now well-developed genre of the countryside sketch.[32]

The significance which this genre acquired had a great deal to do with the tense economic, and therefore political, situation in the country. But while attempting to establish what was wrong with the Soviet countryside, the writers of sketches were led to touch upon and to investigate the themes and problems mentioned earlier, i.e., the effects of Stalinism and the alleged superiority of the collective as opposed to the individual. Peasants were the class which had suffered most, and in the most abominable way, from Stalin's ruthless policies aimed at the transformation of Russia into a Communist Soviet Union. They formed the class which was forcibly deprived of all individual rights and freedoms and coerced into the collective mold. But because they were second-class citizens hardly distinguishable from the nineteenth-century serfs, they were affected less than any other social class by the changes in Soviet society and its new way of life. Efim Dorosh[33] was the first to emphasize certain old-fashioned qualities preserved by peasants which, in his opinion, could be used to solve the problems facing agriculture and, thus, the whole country. In stressing these qualities, and linking

---

noticeable for the author's ability to combine the traditional with the new and to come out with conclusions which gently, but definitely, emphasize the decisive part played by tradition in the make-up of contemporary peasants.

[31] See, e.g., the historical novel by V. N. Ivanov, *Chernye liudi* (Moscow, 1963), or Vladimir Soloukhin's *Pis'ma iz russkogo muzeia* (Moscow, 1967).

[32] See, e.g., this author's article "Aspects of Peasant Life as Portrayed in Contemporary Soviet Literature," *Canadian Slavic Studies*, I, no. 4 (Winter, 1967), 552–565, particularly pp. 555–561.

[33] See Efin Dorosh's "Ivan Fedoseevich" (1954), "Derevenskii dnevnik" (1956, in *Literaturnaia Moskva*), "Dozhdlivoe leto" and "Dva dnia v Raigorode" (1958), "Sukhoe leto" (1961), "Raigorod v fevrale" (1962), and "Dozhd' popolam s solntsem" (1964). The correspondent of *Literaturnaia gazeta*, Zoia Boguslavskaia, in the issue dated March 12, 1969, reports ("Budni zemli," p. 3), "This year the writer [i.e., Dorosh] will complete his 'Derevenskii dnevnik.' The publication of its concluding part, entitled 'Ivan Fedoseevich Retires,' is expected to take place in the nearest future." However, similar announcements were made by the editors of *Novyi mir* in 1966 and 1967 and, with the exception of a short extract—"Poezdka v Liubogostitsi (Iz dnevnika)," *Novyi mir*, no. 1 (1965), pp. 81–87—this chapter has not been published so far. Instead Dorosh wrote and published *Zhivoe derevo iskusstva* (Moscow, 1967), a collection of essays on theater, cinema, old painting, contemporary painters, literary works, and relics of the old Russian past. It would be futile to speculate on why Dorosh is unable to finish—or to publish—the final chapter of his countryside diary, but the question, nevertheless, remains.

with them his personal love and admiration for old traditions, architecture, and art, he started the trend of seeing in the "backward" peasant a better man than his industrial or city-dwelling counterpart.

To summarize: three tendencies or trends developed in the literature of the 1950's—anti-Stalinism, interest in the inner life of contemporary Soviet people, and interest in old culture and its values which were best preserved in the countryside. These tendencies formed, at the beginning of the 1960's, a literature very different from the literature of preceding decades.

II

Literature in the Soviet Union cannot be seen or understood in separation from the totality of Soviet life. In this respect, Soviet literature and art in general still perform, as they did in the nineteenth century, a much wider range of functions than does contemporary western art. It is possible to say that Soviet literature helps, and often substitutes for, sociological, psychological, even economic and political research and analysis.

In this wider context, to explain the appearance of the tendencies sketched briefly in the preceding pages only as the sudden and accidental liberation of literature after Stalin's death would be, of course, not just to oversimplify but also to misjudge them by underrating the vitality and strength of seemingly completely subjugated people. From the people's point of view, Stalin's death was only a signal for the release of pent-up impatience with the tutelage exercised by the Party over every aspect of Soviet life. This, again, should not be taken as meaning that this impatience was the product alone of the population's anti-Communist feelings,[34] but rather that it was the result of the wide nonacceptance, by non-Party members and by some Communists as well, of the practice of communism as it had developed in the Soviet Union since the industrialization drive and the associated collectivization. The people were perhaps prepared at first, during the years of apprenticeship to socialism, to be guided by enthusiasts who were fired by exalted ideas and believed that they knew what was right and what was wrong. They were perhaps even willing to forget their personal interests while struggling for universal happiness. But after some ten years of this, followed by four war years of unimaginable hardship, the empty clichés of *agitprop* could not satisfy them any more. The war years particularly, as mentioned earlier, changed their attitude. They had matured through this awesome experience, and they resented intensely the irritating petty bureaucrats who

[34] It is the present writer's personal belief that anti-Communist feelings are widespread among the population of the Soviet Union. This is, however, neither the place nor the time to discuss this point.

insisted on determining and directing their every step as if they were small children. This sense of maturity and the people's aspiration to become masters of their own destiny, so severely suppressed by Stalin after 1945, came to the fore after 1953 and exploded following the Twentieth Party Congress in a way never experienced since the 1920's.

The intellectual and social life of the country since 1945 has been contradictory and complex. The country achieved, during the war and the postwar years of reconstruction, a high degree of industrialization: it became capable of controlling atomic energy and was on the point of sending into space the first satellite. In this respect, the Soviet Union had reached the level of development of the most advanced countries of the West. And it had to face, therefore, the same problem of having evolved in the process into a stratified, pluralistic, fractionalized society. On the other hand, the standard of living in the Soviet Union was still among the lowest, if not actually the lowest, in Europe. In addition, it had to cope with two of its own peculiar features of life mentioned earlier: the regime, which governed through and by fear and kept millions of people in concentration camps, and the impossible situation of having almost one-half of the population in the position of second-class citizens, deprived even of the comparatively limited rights enjoyed by the rest of the population. All this made it very difficult for Soviet intellectuals—a group formed mainly of writers, scientists, and engineers—to grasp and to define the essence of their being.

Like their western counterparts, Soviet intellectuals became restless and discontented, realizing that they had lost the feeling of taking part, both as a specialized group or subgroup and as individuals, in the natural and social processes. This feeling of loss developed partly from overspecialization and a surfeit of analytical knowledge and partly from the "closed-shop method" of directing Soviet life, instituted over the years by the Party bureaucracy. The intellectuals lost what may be called their sense of the cosmic meaning of life; they became alienated from their supposedly collectively built and collectively run socialist world.

In the time-honored Russian tradition, when the feeling of dissatisfaction with the reality of Soviet life could finally come to the surface, this was first expressed not by political scientists, sociologists, psychologists, or economists but by writers and poets.[35] Among the members of this most articulate group of intellectuals the opinion became strong—again in the time-honored tradition—that man cannot live a worthwhile life if he does not protest, in a more or less direct manner, against the unsatisfactory situation. It seems that the immediate post-Stalin political leaders, who were faced with their own special problems, had no time to pay great attention to what was hap-

[35] See, e.g., O. Berggol'ts' article, "Razgovor o lirike," *Literaturnaia gazeta*, April 16, 1953, and the writings mentioned in n. 25.

pening in the arts in general and in literature in particular, and thus they made no effort to prevent the intellectual and artistic thaw from taking place.[36] There was a period of vacillation between the Twentieth Party Congress in February, 1956, which accepted the "thaw principle" through Khrushchev's so-called secret speech marking the beginning of de-Stalinization, and the Twenty-first Congress in January–February, 1959, when strong apprehensions were voiced that de-Stalinization was in danger of getting out of hand and disrupting completely the Soviet way of life. It was also a period of searching, of the question: What is it in man that forces him to be dissatisfied with the given reality? The answer, formulated in a very generalized manner, seemed to have been: "Not by bread alone" can man live.[37] Until then, Soviet man seemed to have been able to live by material values alone and was accepting the paucity of emotions which characterized his official, public life. But this attitude no longer satisfied. It became necessary to master the *inner* problems of modern man in a complex society. The "strivings and searching" which went on from 1953 onwards revealed, through a spate of works (particularly in 1956—the almanac *Literaturnaia Moskva,* vol. II, is, in this respect, a document of exceptional importance) in which the most varied aspects of Soviet life were investigated,[38] that the type of literature known in the Stalin period was rapidly becoming a thing of the past.[39] The new Soviet man, as shown in these works, was no longer able to rely on official assertions that life was simple, that everything was foreseen and, therefore, properly taken into account and planned accordingly, that victory was assured, and that the road into the future was well constructed, straight, and smooth. The old beliefs were—at least as far as intellectuals were concerned—fully destroyed.

It seems that the feeling of insecurity, almost of doom, strengthened further by the political leaders' inability to take a firm hold of the political and ideological situation in the country, led and is still leading the intellectuals to assume one of the three following positions.

Some, having lost faith, are left with the feeling that the future is of no interest at all. Without interest in the future, i.e., without an ideal, they are incapable of finding strength, or hope, or even the will and the courage for

[36] Cf. the title of Il'ia Ehrenburg's novel *Ottepel'*, Part I (1954), Part II (1956).

[37] Cf. the title of V. Dudintsev's novel *Ne khlebom edinym* ... (1956).

[38] E.g., D. Granin's "Iskateli" (1955); V. Kaverin's *Poiski i nadezhdy* (1956); A. Shtein's play *Personal'noe delo* (1956); D. Granin's "Sobstvennoe mnenie" (1956); S. Aleshin's play *Odna* (1956); A. Korneichuk's play *Kryl'ia* (1954); V. Nekrasov's *V rodnom gorode* (1954); N. Zhdanov's "Poezdka na rodinu" (1956). All these titles indicate clearly the various directions in which "those who seek" (Granin's "Iskateli") were moving.

[39] The period immediately after the Twentieth Party Congress, with all its controversial factors, is reproduced faithfully, though from a conservative, pro-establishment point of view, by V. Kochetov in his novel *Brat'ia Ershovy* (Moscow, 1960).

any kind of truly constructive attitude. This is reflected in the works of a group of writers[40] who portray characters unaware of any other kind of life than repetitious and senseless routine; or characters that have consciously limited themselves to destructive questioning of all ideals and who pursue therefore what are, in fact, only their personal, egotistic, and rather mercenary aims;[41] or, finally, characters who are simple, innocent individuals lacking the drive, aspirations, or will to take their destiny in their own hands and to make something definite, purposeful, important of their lives.[42]

Others, in their effort to recapture the former strength, the feeling of certainty, the "wholeness" of their world outlook and enthusiasm, are turning to what may be called neo-Stalinism. This, of course, is the easiest stand, one which usually has the open backing of Party leaders as well as of Party rank-and-file bureaucrats. To this group belong very many literary critics, a great number of second-rate hack writers, but few talented writers whose sincerity cannot be doubted.[43]

And others, finally, are striving to achieve a world outlook which would permit them to attain some kind of intellectual and moral security and to establish a scale of values which, in its turn, would bring some kind of order and aim into their thinking and behavior, and thus restore to them the feelings of human dignity and moral fulfillment. These intellectuals realize that Stalinism has been giving the Soviet people all this, but giving it under false pretenses, thus corrupting them morally. In rejecting Stalinism, they are forced to look for a substitute. Unable to accept the neo-Stalinist variety of socialism, and not allowed to formulate a different kind of socialism because it would immediately be branded as revisionism, they must try to find a substitute outside socialist ideologies. Their choice is further

[40] Such as Iurii Kazakov, author of "Arktur—gonchii pes" (1958), "Man'ka" (1958), "Na polustanke" (1959), and "Po doroge" (1961), in whose works nothing decisive, or even visible, happens; or Vitalii Semin, author of the novella *Semero v odnom dome,* in *Novyi mir,* no. 6 (1956), and of short stories "Asia Aleksandrovna," *ibid.,* no. 11 (1965), and "Nashi starukhi," *ibid.,* no. 9 (1966), who portrays the hopelessness of the suburban or city life and whose characters, in many ways, are automatons unable to change or even to visualize any possible change in their lives.

[41] E.g., Vasilii Aksenov, author of "Kollegi" (1961), "Zvezdnyi bilet" (1961), and "Na polputi k lune" (1962), who portrays "modern" youth interested in jazz, sports, and love, but who lead a fundamentally purposeless existence.

[42] E.g., Vladimir Tendriakov, author of such novellas and short stories as "Ukhaby" (1956), "Troika, semerka, tuz" (1961), and "Sud" (1961), where he creates anti-heroes who see that their acts are often inconsistent, sometimes even dishonorable, but who are unable to go beyond self-criticism.

[43] Among these, Vsevolod Kochetov, author of, e.g., *Sekretar' obkoma* (1961) and *Brat'ia Ershovy* (1960), whose characters, heroically conceived, defend all that is for them progressive and new in culture or production technology, who unmask bureaucrats, careerists, rumor-mongers, and slanderers of socialism, and who fight revisionists and all those who let themselves be corrupted by bourgeois imperialist propaganda and decadent pseudoculture.

limited by the traditional distrust of all Russians for what they like to call
bourgeois systems. It is, therefore, not surprising that they turn to the past
of their own people in their search for a system or ideology that would
prevent them from seeing man as a finite being strictly limited by the span
of a single life and which, in this way, would enable them to overcome the
feelings of emptiness and isolation. Their highly developed sense of his-
toricism, coupled with the satisfaction of their natural human need for continuity, helps them to find what they are looking for in the Russian peasant
who, having shed his servility and, at least partly, his formal religion, has
preserved the traditions and a set of moral values which form an acceptable
complete system.

In summary, the searchings of Soviet intellectuals, reflected in contemporary literary works, for values which could be used to substitute for the
discredited Stalinist code of ethics, led to the rediscovery of the Russian
peasant as the carrier of tradition and the guardian of the nation's moral
integrity.

III

There seems to be no doubt that the Russian peasant is the most suitable
"ideal hero" for the Soviet writer of today who finds himself in a position
of protest. In him, as in a gun-sight, cross various lines which represent the
moral and spiritual evaluations of the past and the searchings and aspirations
of the present. He is, as is no other member of the nation, in the center of
that unofficial history which comprises all the problems put aside, forgotten,
or overlooked, hushed up or deliberately ignored, left unsolved or found
insoluble, without which official history is incomplete, partial, abstract, and,
in fact, untrue.

As already mentioned,[44] an awareness of the peasant's central position
for understanding the contemporary Soviet *condition humaine* came early
to the writers. But it needed a writer of outstanding talent and of exceptionally strong convictions and moral depth to bring about, through his work,
the reorientation of literature toward the really important problems.

The first three stories by Solzhenitsyn appeared at the end of 1962 and
the beginning of 1963. To these, the fourth was added six months later.[45]
Two main questions were posed by the author in these stories. First, where,
among Soviet people, are valid and true human and moral values to be

[44] See Žekulin, "Aspects of Peasant Life," and p. 382 of this essay.
[45] *Odin den' Ivana Denisovicha, Novyi mir*, no. 11 (1962), pp. 8–74; "Sluchai
na stantsii Krechetovka" and "Matrenin dvor," *ibid.*, no. 1 (1963), pp. 9–63; "Dlia
pol'zy dela," *ibid.*, no. 7 (1963), pp. 58–90.

found? The answer is quite definite: among simple Russian peasants, as represented by Ivan Denisovich Shukhov and Matryona, and not among members of the intelligentsia, as represented by Lieutenant Zotov and school director Fyodor Mikheevich. Second, what is responsible for the unjust and unnecessary sufferings of Ivan Denisovich and Matryona, and for the lack of moral fiber in Zotov and Fyodor Mikheevich and for their inability to think and act independently? The answer, again, is quite firm and definite: Stalinism.

The impact of these four stories on Soviet literature cannot be over-estimated. They seem to have set the trend not only for all oppositionist literature but also for pro-establishment works, which were forced to defend their position and to argue their case on the plane and at the level established by Solzhenitsyn.

In the figure of Ivan Denisovich,[46] Solzhenitsyn created, for the first time in post-1945 Soviet fiction, a character who is completely at variance with the traditional Soviet hero, as represented best by N. A. Ostrovsky's Pavel Korchagin.[47] Ivan Denisovich stands for all those in the Soviet Union whose creative freedom and enthusiasm were taken away from them, but whose ability and capacity to perform acts which do not necessarily bring personal benefit or advantage were thereby not destroyed. Ivan Denisovich possesses the wisdom of the simple country man. He not only knows that the most important thing is to preserve one's own life, but he also knows *how* to preserve it: he always acts within the measure of the things and facts he has to face and in this way does not allow them to control him. While, in the special circumstances selected for him by his creator, Ivan Denisovich is physically a prisoner in a concentration camp, he remains the master of reality and, in this respect, preserves his inner freedom. It is precisely this inner freedom which gives him the strength to remain, in his fight for life, kind and compassionate, tolerant and understanding, practical and helpful—briefly, the strength to remain human.

But it was the creation of Matryona—the simple and defenseless "sister"

---

[46] A great number of articles concerning this character have been published in the Soviet Union and abroad. An important study by V. Lakshin, "Ivan Denisovich—ego druz'ia i nedrugi," *Novyi mir,* no. 1 (1964), pp. 223–245, attempts, quite successfully, to summarize different views and to draw conclusions as to the success of Solzhenitsyn's portrayal of the "new" hero. A much less successful attempt to give an overall appreciation of Shukhov (and of Matryona) was made by a Soviet critic who, under the name of D. Blagov, published a long article, "A. Solzhenitsyn i dukhovnaia missiia," in the Russian émigré journal *Grani,* no. 64 (1967), pp. 116–149, and no. 65 (1967), pp. 100–128.

[47] The main character in the novel *Kak zakalialas' stal'* (1932–1933). The Shukhov-Korchagin opposition is suggested by Miroslav Drozda in a very thoughtful chapter on Solzhenitsyn in his book *Babel, Leonov, Solzhenitsyn* (Prague, 1966), specifically pp. 147–153.

of Ivan Denisovich—which really started the trend in literature. Even more than Ivan Denisovich, she is stripped by the author of all "normal" human ambitions and aspirations. She is even deprived of the quality which helps Ivan Denisovich to survive, i.e., his knowledge of how to fend for himself. The only qualities left to her by the author are kindness and compassion, but even these are of the passive, nonaggressive variety. These two qualities, which result in Matryona's inability to do evil, distinguish her from all others and elevate her, in the eyes of Solzhenitsyn, almost to the rank of a saint: "We all lived next to her, but did not grasp the fact that she was that pious person without whom, as the saying goes, not one single hamlet can stand. Nor a town. Nor the whole of our country."[48]

Solzhenitsyn, having established the type, concerns himself in his further works mainly with Stalinism[49] and with the relationship to it of members of the intelligentsia, with the question of collective guilt, with the individual's will to survive,[50] with "moral socialism,"[51] etc. But because his novels have not been printed in the Soviet Union,[52] they do not seem to have had such a direct and immediate influence as his four stories. On the other hand, Solzhenitsyn possibly experienced some later influence of the school he helped to originate. His story "Zakhar Kalita"[53] seems to be the least *engagé* of his works and leaves the reader in a state of slight confusion about its meaning—a state unknown to the reader of his other works.

The trend started by Solzhenitsyn's stories took some time to crystallize. At first his followers were difficult to distinguish among the group of mainly younger writers indiscriminately labelled by critics as authors of "lyrical" or "countryside" prose.[54] In this group were included, by different critics, Astafev, Belov, Galkin, Evdokimov, Krutilin, Likhonosov, Narchenko, Nosov, Soloukhin, Tendriakov, Mozhaev, Sbitnev, Semnov, Roshchin,

[48] Solzhenitsyn, *Sochineniia* (Frankfurt and Moscow: "Posev," 1966), p. 231.

[49] See his *Rakovyi korpus* and, particularly, *V kruge pervom* (Paris: YMCA Press, 1969).

[50] E.g., the main character of *Rakovyi korpus* by the name of Oleg Kostoglotov.

[51] "Nravstvennyi sotsialism," as formulated by Shulubin, a character in *Rakovyi korpus,* pp. 369–373 of the cited edition.

[52] Part I of *Rakovyi korpus* was finished in 1963, Part II in 1966, and *V kruge pervom* was finished in 1964; see *Novyi zhurnal,* no. 93 (December, 1968), the section "Delo Solzhenitsyna," pp. 209–268, where the story of these two novels is given in great detail and with solid documentation. In the meantime, hand-made copies of both novels circulate in the Soviet Union.

[53] Solzhenitsyn's fifth, and so far last, work published in the Soviet Union (*Novyi mir,* no. 1 (1966), pp. 69–76).

[54] The history of this group of writers can easily be followed with the help of the so-called *polemika,* organized and published by *Literaturnaia gazeta* in 1967 and 1968. It was started by V. Kamianov's article, "Ne dobrotoi edinoi . . . ," in the issue of November 22, 1967, p. 4, and followed with nine articles. The editorial article, "Chelovek na zemle," published on April 3, 1968, gives a list of all articles and sums up the discussion in a comparatively impartial manner.

Tkachenko, Zalygin, and Shukshin. But as soon as critics began to analyze more thoroughly the works of individual writers, they realized that it was necessary to distinguish between "lyrical prose" in general and "lyrical countryside prose" in particular.[55] The common points for these two types are: presence of the narrator (the stories are usually written in the first person); fragmentation of the narrative and the resulting lack of plot; interest in nature and its poetization; concern for the individual and the resulting neglect of the communal or civic; contraposition of the rural to the urban, of the quiet and slow-moving to the noisy and fast, of the simple to the complex.

"Lyrical countryside prose" goes further, however, in that it uses these devices and adds some of its own (for instance, the attempted "complete moral unification of the artist's 'ego' with the hero"),[56] not for the purpose of finding and describing individualized human emotions and conditions but with the view to establishing a type which would embody the "primary, unparalleled goodness and strength of soul."[57] Thus, the aim of proper countryside prose is to find a true "man of the soil" who draws his moral strength and stability from the very fact that he is a peasant and does not want to be anything else. It is precisely this knowledge of "belonging"—lacking in all those who are not men of the soil—which makes the peasant the embodiment of basic "goodness and soulfulness." As an individual, he can have private weaknesses and faults. But as one who "belongs" in the countryside and on the land, he is morally and spiritually complete and therefore essentially good. His goodness, then, is neither accidental nor the result of a conscious personal effort. He is good, one is almost tempted to say, in spite of himself.

While some critics defend "countryside writers"[58] and support their moral quest, others attack them violently.[59] Summarized, the main objections are

---

[55] The first to make a clear distinction was V. Kozinov in "Tsennosti istinnye i mnimye," *Literaturnaia gazeta,* January 31, 1963, p. 5, though Larisa Kriachko in "Listy i korni," *ibid.,* November 29, 1967, mentions the two types as separate; however, she does not elaborate the point.

[56] See Kamianov.

[57] *Ibid.*

[58] E.g., Kriachko, in part; S. Shurtakov, "O glavnom cheloveke na zemle," *Literaturnaia gazeta,* December 6, 1967; Iurii Kazakov, himself author of many "lyrical" short stories (see Vera Alexandrova's article, "Voices of Youth," *Survey,* no. 36 (April–June, 1961), pp. 46–48, and also G. Gibian's "New Trends in the Novel: Kazakov, Nagibin, Voronin," *ibid.,* pp. 49–51) in "Ne dovol'no li?" *Literaturnaia gazeta,* December 27, 1967; Kozinov.

[59] Among those who took part in the discussion mentioned in n. 54 are, in addition to Kamianov, F. Levin, "Obosnovana li trevoga?" *Literaturnaia gazeta,* January 17, 1968, p. 6; V. Gusev, "O proze, derevne i tsel'nykh liudiakh," *ibid.,* February 14, 1968, p. 6; and A. Ianov, "Esli zaglianut' v budushchee," *ibid.,* February 28, 1968, p. 6. But lately almost every issue of *Literaturnaia gazeta,* as well as the periodical

that these authors tend to oversimplify their characters and to portray them as detached from relevant happenings in the life of the nation; that they idealize "old-world simpletons" and promote them almost to the rank of saints; that they propagate a kind of Christian humanism by putting "abstract moral values" higher than the Communist code of morals; that they are too interested in the "old sources" (*istoki*) of Russian culture and, either by implication or directly, reject the modern complex life of the highly specialized progressive and aggressive Soviet society; that they are no longer socialist-realist writers because they do not feel "obliged, through their whole creative and public activity, [to] take part effectively in the building of Socialism."[60]

Some of these objections are, without doubt, quite valid. The "sanctification" or "canonization" of peasants can sometimes reach ridiculous proportions.[61] So does, sometimes, the idealization of all things rural.[62] But

---

press, carries attacks on the "abstract humanism" which is allegedly propagated by countryside writers—see, e.g., V. Barshchukov's "V zashchitu istorizma," *Literaturnaia gazeta*, July 17, 1968; L. Kriachko's "Soblazny technitsizma i dukhovnost'," *ibid.*, January 22, 1969 (the author, it seems, contradicts substantially her own views as expressed earlier in *ibid.*, November 29, 1967; see ns. 55 and 58); A. Volchek's "Prezhde vsego ispolnitel'," *ibid.*, February 19, 1969; B. Finiasov's review, "... Chto-to velikoe chuia ...," *ibid.*, January 22, 1969; the leading article, "Otvetstvennost' i avtoritet kritiki," *ibid.*, March 12, 1969.

[60] See "The Constitution of the Union of Writers of the USSR," section 2, Article 2, *Tretii s"ezd pisatelei SSSR. Stenograficheskii otchet* (Moscow, 1969), p. 249.

[61] See, e.g., the characters Vlasevna and Auntie Arisha in Iu. Sbitnev's "Svoia zemlia i v gorsti mila," Arsen'evna in V. Likhonosov's "Rodnye," Grandmother Ekaterina in V. Astaf'ev's "Poslednii poklon," and especially the gallery of characters in M. Roshchin's "Dvadtsat' chetyre dnia v raiu," which describes the experience of a couple who went from the city to the countryside for their annual holiday and found "paradise" in the home of a bee-keeper. "I understood finally that [the members of the bee-keeper's family] are like saints," the sophisticated city woman confesses at the end of the story.

[62] There was another discussion in *Literaturnaia gazeta* (August 23, December 6, 1967, January 24, February 21, 1968) about the kind of house best suited for today's collective farmers, in which the old-fashioned Russian stove (*russkaia pech'*) became one of the main points of contention. B. Mozhaev, author of the well-known novella *Iz zhizni Fedora Kuz'kina* (1966), devotes, in his article "Gde komu zhit'?" (February 21, 1968), almost a whole column to the defense of this "invention of true genius" (*poistine genial'noe izobretenie*) which heats, cooks, preserves food, cures illnesses, serves as a bed, etc., etc. "Instead of abusing [the Russian stove] we ought to bow low to it, to the very ground," concludes Mozhaev. It must be noted, however, that laudatory mention of the Russian stove has been made lately in almost every countryside work. To mention only two, in V. Belov's *Plotnitskie rasskazy* and in V. Shukshin's "Iz detstva Ivana Popova" the Russian stove is an important part of the background. The poetess Iraida Ul'ianova devotes the following lines to the Russian stove in her "Rodina. Iz poemy," *Molodaia gvardiia*, no. 3 (1968), p. 39: "Prostornaia, kak russkaia dusha, / Pech' russkaia—moi zapovednik detstva, / Gde ia vnimala skazkam ne dysha ... / Pech' russkaia—ot vsekh napastei sredstvo." Solzhenitsyn, of course, mentions it in his works, even in *V kruge pervom*, p. 361.

there is no denying that it is in the countryside literature that the most characteristic features of Soviet contemporary "modern" prose are most strongly and clearly expressed. (For pro-establishment critics the term "modern" has a definitely derogatory connotation.) But, as mentioned earlier, countryside literature possesses the one feature which distinguishes it from other works of "modern" oppositionist literature, namely, that it seeks to underline—one could perhaps be more specific and say to establish and propagate—moral values which are not linked in the minds of writers with the ethical code prescribed by the official Soviet ideology.

The positive, assertive character of the countryside literature becomes discernible if the latter is compared to the rest of "modern" oppositionist prose. In works which deal with sophisticated urban life,[63] the fact of the characters' alienation is ascertained, but no attempt is made to evaluate it, to find reasons for it, or to suggest possible remedies, be it only, for instance, by contrast with other, different facts. Thus, the purely "urban" works appear to be morally neutral.

In authors who deal with semi-urban, semirural life,[64] the positive aspect

---

[63] See, e.g., B. Zolotarev's short story "Nevesta" in *Novyi mir*, no. 11 (1966), pp. 107–128. There are three characters: Emma, a spinster, embittered by her unpopularity with men and by repeated failures to find a life partner; her mother Elizaveta Ven'iaminova, whose only interest is to find a husband for her daughter; and Iurii Grigor'evich, the mother's childhood friend's son, the prospective husband. The plot is very simple: Iurii comes for a weekend visit to Emma and her mother, for a kind of a bride-show; they all try very hard to make this visit a success but realize, at the same time, that they have nothing in common, except for utter indifference to everyone and everything. The visit is not really a failure; it just does not produce any result at all: these people know that "everyone has his own life and . . . no one is in a position to help the other" (p. 115). So they part on Sunday evening, neither friends nor enemies, cold, indifferent, tragically lonely. Another attempt to break this loneliness, to find contact with at least one other person and through him, perhaps, with the world again, led nowhere. The characters are all educated people (Emma works as a secretary in a research institute, Iurii, an unsuccessful writer, as an editor in a publishing house); they read, attend concerts, go out to meet friends, know what is fashionable, but amidst all these activities they are utterly lonely. The author summarizes his story, neatly and rather cleverly, by making Emma look up in the dictionary of foreign words the meaning of the word "authentic" (*autenticheskii, autentichnyi*) which, strangely enough, is not known to this rather well-read woman. The first word she finds is "outbreeding" (*autbriding*), which the dictionary explains as "the mating of animals belonging to the same species and not blood-related to each other": this is the summary of the content of the story. The second word is the required "authentic": the heroes are, of course, not authentic, real people, but only shadows. The third word is "autism" (*autizm*), explained as "unhealthy state, symptom of schizophrenia, expressed by the patient's total absorption in his own inner emotional experiences": this is the description and the evaluation of the characters in the story (p. 127).

[64] Works representative of the semi-urban, semirural genre are those of Vitalii Semin and Viktor Likhonosov. V. Semin's novella *Semero v odnom dome,* in *Novyi mir,* no. 6 (1965), pp. 62–144, is perhaps one of the most characteristic and certainly

of their works follows from the representation of morally valuable characters of the type of Solzhenitsyn's Ivan Denisovich or Matryona, usually of the middle-aged or older generation, who have not severed their connections with rural traditions and ways of life and, therefore, have been strong enough to withstand the corrupting influence of city life. Thus, these positive characters, having not lost contact with life outside them, take an active part in it and find personal satisfaction without, however, being able to effect any changes in it or influence other people. The semi-urban, semi-rural works could, perhaps, be described as being concerned with moral problems, but in a passive way.

It is in works which deal with the collective farmer's life that a pronounced active moral element is to be found. A closer analysis of Vasilii Belov's novella, *The Carpenter's Stories*,[65] would perhaps show more clearly the characteristics of this type of literature.

On the surface, the story is about three weeks in the life of the narrator but, in fact, the content is the life story of Olyosha Smolin, an ordinary, simple, and somewhat naive, not overly clever, kind-hearted, honest, and very hard-working old peasant. The author does not evaluate the main character's personality and life directly; he just unfolds them, slowly and leisurely, by reproducing without comments old Olyosha's words and by interspersing this narrative with contrasting episodes from the life of Olyosha's contemporary and opposite—Aviner Pavlovich Kozonkov. The narrator's remi-

---

the best known of his stories. See in V. Lakshin's article "Pisatel', chitatel' i kritik. Stat'ia vtoraia," *ibid.*, no. 8 (1966), pp. 242–248, an analysis of Semin's main character Mulia; Lakshin gives a good bibliography of critical reviews of Semin's work as well. But see also his other stories, particularly "Nashi starukhi," *ibid.*, no. 9 (1966), pp. 51–53, a frighteningly true and brilliantly written "mini-story" about the loneliness of the older generation and its inability to communicate with the younger one. Mulia is a morally positive character but, as in Solzhenitsyn's Matryona, the good in her is wasted: except for the narrator, no one can appreciate the true worth of Mulia, no one is, in fact, interested in her essentially as a person. V. Likhonosov's last story "Na ulitse shirokoi," *ibid.*, no. 8 (1968), pp. 3–60, paints slowly and elaborately, with the help of extracts from her letters and of reminiscences, the portrait of the narrator's mother. The evaluation of her character is achieved in the process of actual writing, when, e.g., the narrator reproaches her for having been always too kind, too meek, too patient (pp. 43 and 59). He, of course, admires these qualities in her, as he admires the attitude to life displayed by his step-father, who is not dissimilar, in many ways, to Uncle Eroshka in L. N. Tolstoi's "Kazaki." But he also knows that the lives of these two exceptionally fine people have no influence on anything at all and that, in this respect, they are completely wasted.

[65] V. Belov, *Plotnitskie rasskazy*, in *Novyi mir*, no. 7 (1968), pp. 7–56 (further references to this work will be made in parentheses in the text). Belov is also the author of the novella *Privychnoe delo*, in *Sever*, no. 1 (1966). The main hero of this work, the collective farmer Ivan Afrikanovich, became for the critics a kind of cumulative personification of the "new" countryside hero (see, e.g., Efim Dorosh's highly commendatory review entitled, significantly, "Ivan Afrikanovich," in *Novyi mir*, no. 8 (1966), pp. 257–261).

niscences and thoughts are also introduced in a contrasting manner, so that Olyosha's character, behavior, and acts are emphasized.

The story is told in the first person, and the narrator is, to a rather great extent, identifiable in the mind of the reader with the author himself. He is, as is usual in this kind of work, of rural extraction and had the good luck to acquire a good education and the comparatively high position which goes with it. As an engineer, he had little contact with the countryside over a considerable period of time. When the time comes for him to take his yearly holiday, he decides to go to his native village where he still owns the old family cottage and where he hopes to find the peace and quiet of a simple, even primitive, life. He actually finds what he is looking for, perhaps even more: the old, friendly house with its long-forgotten noises, the village and its inhabitants, the beautiful scenery—all this makes him forget the hatred he felt for this kind of life when he was leaving the village many years ago, and it helps him realize that he is finally at home again, happy and satisfied ("At one time I hated all this with my whole heart. I swore never to return here." "I am at home . . ."; ". . . I feel foolishly happy," p. 9). However, because he lived away from the village for a long time, he feels himself to some extent a strange and foreign element there. His behavior is sometimes slightly ridiculous (for instance, when he does not see through the simple and, in their childishness, harmless practical jokes played on him by his neighbors, p. 11, or when he is unable to cope with village dogs, pp. 10, 21, 33), often clumsy (his encounters with Kozonkov's daughter, who is also on a visit in the village, pp. 25, 36, 50–51), and at times dangerously foolish (when he tries to reconcile his two old neighbors, Olyosha and Aviner, pp. 51–55). As a result, the narrator—an intelligent and sophisticated modern man—appears, in comparison with Olyosha in particular, as muddled, undecided, and unsure of himself; he lacks the experience of the true full life; he does not know how to do the really important things (he would not be able, for example, to build a house for himself without outside help, or produce food to feed himself and his family); he does not possess the ability to take life as it comes and thus to be stronger than it is (his bouts of despair because he does not succeed in his trivial plans, pp. 32, 54–55); in brief, he is inferior as a personality to old peasant Olyosha.

Olyosha's physical appearance is not very prepossessing: he is likened to a medieval pirate with a frighteningly long nose (p. 10). But the unfavorable impression which this description leaves with the reader is immediately dispelled by the narrator's memories of how Olyosha was always kind to children, played with them, made toys for them, and gave them rides in his cart (p. 10). This is the method used all though the work: to offset the outer imperfection or failing with the inner merit or virtue.

Olyosha's early childhood was unhappy and difficult. He maintains that he remembers how he was born: "I swear I remember how I was born. . . . Well, I do not remember all this, only a kind of a warm fog, a drowsiness, but still, I remember. . . . It was so interesting, all this. . . . Well, not really interesting, but it was so—you know—so noble." "Well, I was born, as Christ was, in a manger and exactly on Christmas day. Everything went all right for me at first, and then I began to get all embroiled" (p. 11). The first lesson he learned in life was that it did not pay to stick to one's natural inclinations or principles, that it put one in conflict with others. This forced him to learn how to hide his feelings and even good deeds, and to lie instead. "From then on I began to sin, and they stopped beating me. My life changed. But you know what I think, my friend? It became easier for me to live after that, but from that moment on all the muddle in my life began" (pp. 12–13).

He was taught early to work, and to work very hard. His description of how, at the age of 12, he learned to plow, is one of the most touching passages in the story: "[My father] said to me: 'Here is the land, Olyosha, and here is the plow. If you don't finish the strip by mid-day, I'll come and tear your ears right off'" (p. 17). And so he tried, though it was really beyond his strength. He finished in time, with the help of the clever horse that knew how to plow better than he did, and he collapsed from exhaustion. ". . . and tears like peas rolled from my eyes. I sat and cried. Didn't even hear how my father came, sat next to me, and then also began to cry. He put his head between his hands and 'Oh'—he said—'Olyoshka, Olyoshka' . . ." (p. 17). He greatly admired his father who never compromised with his conscience and died an honest man with nothing to conceal: "[Father] worked all his life, up to his dying hour, and the one who works like that has nothing to hide" (p. 20).

Olyosha's great love affair was an unhappy one. The girl, whom he loved from his childhood and whom he was too shy to approach in the rough manner of his companions, perished later in the days of collectivization, somewhere in the far north where she was transported with her unjustly dispossessed family. He afterwards married Nastasya, for whom he felt no love but whom he respected as a wife should be respected.

He did his apprenticeship as a carpenter in the way men in his village had always done. At the age of 13 or so he joined a group of older skilled men who left the village after harvest time, and travelled with them doing carpentry work until next harvest time. The apprenticeship was hard and the work, when he learned the trade, even harder. Olyosha does not tell anything about his life during the revolution, very little about collectivization, and nothing again about life during the war years. The reader only learns that his life during this long period of 40 years or so was difficult, mainly because of petty persecutions by Aviner. He was not actively against collectivization, but neither was he for it (pp. 45–46); he just accepted it passively. During the anti-*kulak* drive he regretted the unnecessarily hard measures applied and pitied those who were unjustly treated (p. 45).

Thus, the life of Olyosha, as narrated by himself, appears to be uneventful. There are in this narration no laments, no recriminations, no accusations, no cries of indignation, no self-pity, because the life is presented as "normal" and ordinary. And in this lies one of the main features of the new prose. The reader, who sees behind the outwardly calm, almost serene facade all the horror of this life, is led to ask himself what the causes of it are. What makes Olyosha accept it in such a quiet and composed manner? Because the social changes which occurred in the countryside are hardly mentioned at all, and certainly never emphasized, the reader is not led to look for the reasons in the social structure or in the regime established in the country. On the other hand, because the life of Olyosha is shown to have been as difficult before the revolution as after it, this life, in all its dreadfulness and painfulness, appears as a fact that has always existed and cannot be changed. The reasons, therefore, are to be found in himself. Thus, the reader is made to find and evaluate the elements or the features which form the inner strength of the hero. These are, to enumerate them again briefly, kindness, compassion, and patience. But, principally, it is the knowledge of who he is and what his place is in the order of things—hence his self-assurance and dignity.

All these features are emphasized by contrasting Olyosha to Aviner Kozonkov. Olyosha loves children (p. 10) and animals (p. 16) and cannot see them suffer unnecessarily. Aviner does not notice children (pp. 21–23) and has no feeling toward animals (pp. 16–17). Olyosha cannot see indifferently a man in trouble and deeply pities him even though the man perhaps has deserved what was coming to him (he refuses to watch how Aviner's father is publicly flogged because he pitied him, p. 18). Aviner not only watches how his father is punished but, in a kind of a perverse way, even boasts about it (p. 18). Olyosha's patience is shown in the way he endures Aviner's persecutions after the establishment of the kolkhoz (p. 46). Aviner's impatience is shown by his inability to accept things as they are and his attempt to turn them, by hook or by crook, to his personal advantage (pp. 16, 23–24, 31). Olyosha knows that he is a farmer first (learning to plow, p. 17), then a skilled carpenter. He is proud of his work which he always does to perfection (as a farmer, p. 46; as a skilled tradesman, pp. 14, 44). He is, therefore, never jealous of others, never revengeful. Aviner has never learned the craft of following the plow (pp. 17–18); he has always tried to capitalize on somebody else's work or use some trick or fraud to achieve his aim. This is why he became an activist during the collectivization drive and the right-hand man of the district executive committee's representative with whom he has terrorized the village (pp. 39–40, 53). This is also why he has always been jealous and revengeful and kept denouncing his neighbors to the authorities (pp. 15, 25). Olyosha is satisfied with what he has. His aspirations are therefore not of a material character but, rather, intellectual or spiritual (he even likes to philosophize, e.g., p. 49). Aviner's aspirations are purely materialistic and his thinking never goes beyond the finding of means to satisfy his personal physical well-being (pp. 38–39).

The basic difference between the two men is that Olyosha is a peasant and does not want to be anything else, while Aviner has only one aim in life, namely to escape "peasanthood." This is the driving force which transformed Aviner into the embodiment of evil in the village as well as in Olyosha's life. Belov expresses all this by reducing Aviner's character to the picture of his hands, with long, slim, white fingers which are not those of a peasant (pp. 14, 25).

Thus, it is by this implicit preference for him—as expressed all through the work—that one is forcefully made aware of Olyosha's moral qualities, qualities which grow into true active values and which the reader learns to admire.

The same qualities are also shown and praised, again implicitly rather than explicitly, in a short work by V. Shukshin called "From the Childhood of Ivan Popov,"[66] published only recently. There one finds kindness, expressed through love for animals (pp. 103, 106), compassion (p. 109), and the knowledge of one's place in the chain of uninterrupted events, put rather beautifully by means of the following sentence: "Anyway, the old ones know everything. They heard it from their fathers, from the grandfathers. Your grandfather tells you all sorts of stories, doesn't he? Of course he does. And so will you tell them to your children and then, perhaps, to your grandchildren . . ." (p. 105). Shukshin's stories are more openly oppositionist: the picture drawn of the Siberian village during the war is truly dreadful; propaganda clichés used by the kolkhoz chairman and the district representative in the circumstances shown by the author are frightening and show the whole absurdity of so-called Party controls.

IV

The publication, within a comparatively short time, of a number of works similar to Belov's novella, quickly drew to them—as mentioned earlier—

---

[66] V. Shukshin, "Iz detstva Ivana Popova. Rasskazy," *Novyi mir*, no. 11 (1968), pp. 98–115 (further references to this work will be made in parentheses in the text).

the attention of readers and critics. What was needed now was a theoretical article which would transform a fashionable genre into a unified trend, or perhaps even a school, by giving it literary respectability and an ideological basis. Such an article appeared in September, 1968.[67]

The author, Viktor Chalmaev, begins by dividing contemporary prose into two groups and by rejecting promptly what he calls the "modern," "dynamic," "broken-up," and, therefore, "superficial culture"[68] as spread by the works of "the Gladilins and the Aksyonovs" with their "casual, slipshod," "contemporary manner of writing."[69] He then proceeds to establish what the proper culture is, and finds many words of praise for historical novels, such as *Khmel* by A. Cherkasov, *Rus' Velikaia* by Valentin Ivanov, *Gospodin Veliky Novgorod* by D. Balashov, and, quite particularly, *Chernye liudi* by Vsevolod Nikanorovich Ivanov,[70] all of which he considers to be a "new stage in the assimilation" of Russian history which was "partly interrupted after the patriotic enthusiasm of the Great Fatherland War,"[71] and all of which, in his opinion, have managed to single out the true cultural values created in the past by the Russian people. But, unfortunately, "far removed from this wealth are, particularly, those young writers who have become pitiful victims of the unhealthy fashion for the casual contemporary manner of writing."[72]

This rather clumsy introduction (which, incidentally, is unfair to the "Gladilins and Aksyonovs," because their "manner of writing" does not

[67] Viktor Andreevich Chalmaev, "Neizbezhnost'," *Molodaia gvardiia,* no. 9 (1968), pp. 259–289. Chalmaev has been known as a literary critic for quite a while. He was for a time regular contributor to *Oktiabr'* (see, e.g., no. 10 (1964), inside cover), and he is the author of a rather orthodox book, *Mir v svete podviga. O geroicheskom pafose i khudozhestvennom novatorstve sovetskoi literatury* (Moscow, 1965). (The title speaks for itself; the chapter "Derevnia i revoliutsiia," pp. 223–240, seems to contradict what he will be saying in 1968; see particularly pp. 229–230.) He became a regular contributor to *Molodaia gvardiia.* His articles there were strongly attacked. Thus, *Literaturnaia gazeta,* July 17, 1968, p. 4, published a sharp article by Vladimir Borshchukov under the title of "V zashchitu istorizma." In it Chalmaev's thoughts on M. Gorkii's creative works, expressed in "Velikie iskaniia," *Molodaia gvardiia,* no. 3 (1968), are dismissed as unacceptable to today's Soviet literary criticism. The journal *Oktiabr',* no. 12 (1968), pp. 190–199, then published an article by Petr Strokov, "O narode–'savrasushke,' o 'zagadkakh' russkogo kharaktera i iskaniiakh 'pri svete sovesti,'" which can only be described as a denunciation of Chalmaev for his article, "Neizbezhnost'." Strokov accused Chalmaev of formulating a "consistent conception, even, perhaps, a platform" (p. 190), which could not be accepted by critics or readers. The fact that in spite of these attacks Chalmaev continues to publish, and even appears in public discussions on literary works, would appear to confirm the existence of various camps in today's Soviet literary life.
[68] Chalmaev, "Neizbezhnost'," pp. 260–262.
[69] *Ibid.,* pp. 261–262.
[70] *Ibid.,* p. 265.
[71] *Ibid.*
[72] *Ibid.*

differ substantially from that of those modern writers who are acceptable to Chalmaev) is needed by the author in order to make the first ideological proposition of his essay. Chalmaev states that it is necessary to rethink and reinterpret the role of great historical figures of the past, as well as of such important popular movements as the Great Schism (*raskol'nichestvo*) and anchoretism (*pustynnozhitel'stvo*). He sees, particularly in Patriarch Tikhon and in Protopresbyter Avvakum, the source of the moral strength and inspiration of the Russian nation: the Russian organism has, as it were, stocked for future use their "spiritual strength, fiery enthusiasm and dreams" which are still feeding the Russian people's aspirations.[73] It is Avvakum and the schismatics who particularly interest Chalmaev.[74] In Avvakum he sees combined the goodness and the yearning to save a world which is suffocating in spite and hatred, religious fanaticism and nationalism. He finds an analogy between Avvakum's antiwestern attitude and Tolstoi's rejection of western bourgeois civilization: neither can accept the transformation of the latter's temporary and clearly imperfect forms and ideas into absolutes and ideals, into a "small platform" which Russia should be allowed solely to develop.[75] Chalmaev, following this line of thinking, finishes by saying that even the serf and capitalist periods in Russian history should be seen in their correct proportions, that they are just "a small piece of wood which drifts in the wide ocean and onto which the thousand-year-long strivings of the national, perpetually self-renovating *Rus'* can never be fitted."[76]

[73] *Ibid.*, pp. 265–268.

[74] *Ibid.*, pp. 267, 269. In Chalmaev's discussion of schismatics' behavior and actions, one detail turns out to be of particular interest: he tries to justify self-immolation by fire, which the schismatics used comparatively often. He does not see in this extreme act of protest the expression of wild religious fanaticism, but explains it as a refusal to answer violence by violence: by self-immolation the schismatics "save [their enemies] from sin by surrendering not only their property but their very life" (p. 269). This, of course, was exactly the attitude taken by the Czech student, Jan Palach, who burned himself publicly in January, 1969. The coincidence of attitudes is truly remarkable. It is worth noticing also that Strokov, p. 193, singles out this justification by Chalmaev of self-immolation as an act of supreme protest for his strongest attack about a month or so before the tragic incident took place in Prague.

[75] *Ibid.*, pp. 267–270.

[76] *Ibid.*, p. 270. This brings Chalmaev to a reappreciation of the Romantic and post-Romantic period in the history of Russian ideas. He partly agrees with V. Kozhinov's views, as expressed in the latter's essay published in *Voprosy literatury*, no. 5 (1968), pp. 60–82, and entitled "K metodologii istorii russkoi literatury. O realizme 30-kh godov XIX veka." Kozhinov maintains that the 1830's (which really means the years between 1825 and 1842) were for Russia the key period, wrongly considered a "period of decadence" (pp. 62–63). He sees the culprits whose works helped to create this false opinion in Chernyshevskii and his *Ocherki gogolevskogo perioda russkoi literatury* and in Herzen and his *O razvitii revoliutsionnykh idei v Rossii*. Kozhinov rejects the view (held by A. Tseitlin and A. Lebedev as representa-

Having thus established the "sources" of Russian culture in the seventeenth century, Chalmaev turns to the contemporary scene and contemporary problems which face today's Soviet intellectuals and writers. He feels that the discussions which are taking place in literary circles about the national spirit, patriotism, and the function of countryside prose reflect the worldwide interest in concepts like "the masses," "the crowd," "the public," "the people," and in the problem of how to reconcile "necessities" and "ideals."[77] He accuses some writers and critics of rejecting, in the name of progress, the idealization of the *muzhik*; he reproaches them for unwillingness to accept the "sources"; finally, he blames them for letting "the accountants" (he means "materialists") decide problems connected with the "moral fate of the nation," with the "people's original and unique psychology" and "deep ideals of goodness." He defends, on the other hand, those writers and critics who only to the uninitiated appear as old-fashioned mystics because they try to transpose the problem of relationship with the people onto the plane of ethics, making it a question of heart, of "moral agony."[78]

In his argument with "accountants," Chalmaev rejects their contention that the countryside will not exist any more around the year 2000, that the peasants of today are keen on absorbing the civilizing influences of the city and are interested only in acquiring television sets and porcelain toilet-bowls, drinking cognac, singing modern hit songs. He maintains that it is wrong and unpatriotic to refuse "to affirm the people and their ideals," to lose faith in them, to forget that true civilization cannot exist in an "uncivilized soul" which does not possess "high spiritual necessities."[79] He further asserts that "the land, the battlefield, the Church, the wedding, and the wake" have one thing in common: for earth-bound man "they open the way into infinity, into heaven."[80] Only peasants, who work the land, who do the actual fight-

---

tives of the usual opinion, traditional since the 1960's) that for Russia there was at the time "only one way open—spiritual rapproachement with the West" (p. 67). In his counter-argument he emerges as a propagator of the "bases" or "sources" of Russian culture, which he finds in pre-Petrine Russia. This means that Kozhinov in fact, in reappraising the situation in the Russia of the mid-nineteenth century, favors Slavophilism as the movement which is willing and able to create its own, special, and original culture (pp. 67–72). Chalmaev's "Neizbezhnost' " goes further when it comes to the critique of the so-called revolutionary democrats and of late, as opposed to early, Slavophilism: in his opinion, the cultural values created by these two movements are distinguished by their "izmel' chivaiushchii ikh publitsisticheskii nalet" (p. 267), a phrase which defies translation into English.

[77] *Ibid.*, p. 274.
[78] *Ibid.*, p. 275.
[79] *Ibid.*, p. 276.
[80] *Ibid.*, p. 280.

ing on the battlefields, who have preserved the "poetic" infinite "pattern of customs and habits" which molds their entire lives, know the true meaning of living. Only their lives have not been narrowed to such an extent as to require nothing more than "bourgeois necessities" and "satisfaction with things."[81] Only they possess, through traditions inherited from generation to generation, the "bright flame of humaneness, goodness, and kindness without which, as without oxygen, it is impossible to live."[82] Today's urbanized, industrialized, and mechanized society, which believes that "things make men" and that "the satisfaction of artificially created necessities forms the personality," can learn only from peasants how to preserve the forces and the ideals which actively create valuable new forms of life.[83]

The ideological "basis" constructed by Chalmaev has obvious weaknesses. The attack to which it has been subjected in Soviet journals has been made from ideological premises and seems, to a large extent, to miss the point. To accuse Chalmaev (and, with him, the authors of countryside short fiction) of idealizing peasants as "lovers of truth," "righteous men," "meek and saintly martyrs," to accuse them of propagating " 'humanism' without backbone," "abstract 'goodness,' " the " 'philosophy' of kindheartedness," "false consolations," "boundless goodness and humaneness," "passivity and meekness," "abstract, classless positions," "moral criteria," the "belief that moral values are unchangeable and eternal,"[84] makes sense only if it is done from the strict and rigid standpoint of an orthodox Party man who firmly and sincerely believes that communism has succeeded in transforming mankind and in molding a better and new type of man. For non-Communists, this kind of criticism appears to be absurd.

But if taken in the narrow context of Russian history alone, Chalmaev's "moral humanism" can be criticized on the grounds that it repeats almost exactly the mistakes made by some Slavophiles in the nineteenth century. It puts the Russians back in the pre-Petrine period and erases all the efforts made to modernize the country. It refuses to take into consideration the changes—political, economic, technological, and, of course, social—which perpetually occur and of which there has been a great number since the reign of Peter I. It isolates the country from the outside world and strengthens belief in the messianic role of the Russian people, thus sanctioning all that goes with it, such as chauvinism, national arrogance, self-righteousness.

Chalmaev can be further criticized in that, by putting forward his

[81] *Ibid.*, pp. 279–281.

[82] *Ibid.*, p. 281.

[83] *Ibid.*, p. 287.

[84] All these expressions were taken from various articles and essays published in *Literaturnaia gazeta, Oktiabr'*, and *Voprosy literatury*; the single quotes indicate the authors' ironic attitude.

theory, he is instrumental in widening the gap—which in any case is wide enough in spite of the efforts by Communists to close it—between the intellectuals and the people. What he seems to advocate is a return to the "repenting noblemen's" feeling of guilt, to uncritical admiration for the "lesser brothers," to the "going to the people," as these phenomena were known in the second half of the nineteenth century. To attribute to peasants the function of ideological leaders of the nation as a whole is to overestimate their abilities and, at the same time, to underestimate their passivity and conservatism, which Chalmaev himself emphasizes so much. Peasants as a class, because of their forced attachment to the land and, thus, limited freedom, have never and nowhere been capable of leading a really aggressive, active, and creative society; populism as a political form has always been more utopian than practical.

Peasants could and should, of course, serve as a kind of reservoir of moral strength which would supply all other members of the nation with the power necessary for progressing and which, at the same time, would help to check and even to control the more active and creative sections of the population. And this, it seems, is really all that countryside writers would have wanted, were it not for the special circumstances in which they live today in the Soviet Union. As mentioned earlier, Stalinist excesses and the resulting total collapse of the Communist code of ethics forced intellectuals to reject the practice of this regime. This, in its turn, made them refuse to accept the modern technological urban society which they saw as the product of this practice. Having no opportunity to solve in a calm, pragmatic manner the problems which their fractionalized, pluralistic, and bureaucratized society has to face, they turn back to the last whole, unbroken society they knew—the agricultural society—and try to conceive it as the model for the future. In this they will probably not succeed, mainly for two reasons. First, it seems to be a step backward which will not help solve modern social problems that have to be solved in a modern way. Second, as long as the Communist Party rules over the country, it will never permit this type of revisionist solution, particularly not since it is bound, not being able to think outside or beyond the socialist world outlook, to see in it an especially abhorrent Maoist form of revisionism.[85] In this last respect, the Party would be right: any type of socialism—and Chalmaev, of course, claims to be a faithful socialist—which attempts to build an order that would leave the society truly monolithic and undivided would be a potential ally of Maoism.

---

[85] Loyal Soviet critics seem to be haunted by "revisionism" in literature lately. The leading article in *Literaturnaia gazeta*, March 12, 1969, "Otvetstvennost' i avtoritet kritiki" accuses some critics, such as V. Lakshin, F. Svetov, and S. Lesnevskii of no less a crime than revisionism, though the actual word is not used.

V

In conclusion, countryside prose, as it developed in the 1960's, appears to be at present the most lively and influential trend in contemporary Soviet literature. It draws its strength from the fact that it is the only trend which offers, through the rediscovery of moral values which have been preserved among peasants, a possible solution to the problems faced by the modern technological society of the Soviet Union. This solution is an alternative to the solution offered by the Party and is attractive to a considerable number of intellectuals who cannot continue to accept the ideological leadership of the Party so thoroughly discredited by Stalin, his practices, and his successors.

It is doubtful whether the countryside literature in its present form will have the strength to survive for long even if it were not attacked by pro-establishment forces. But in the short time it has been standing in the forefront of literary genres, it has demonstrated its importance. Not only has it widened the scope of Soviet literature by giving its readers a deeper insight into the lives of a previously neglected or falsely portrayed section of the Soviet population, but it has also added new dimensions to artistic investigation by centering attention on the inner, moral world.[86] In this respect, countryside literature made it impossible to write and publish the conflictless, dull, and monotonously uniform oleographic hackworks which flooded the book market only quite recently. In this way, it has raised considerably the level of creative writing. There is no doubt that, besides Solzhenitsyn, there is today a number of writers, practitioners of this genre, whose works are really worth reading for their artistic, and not just informative, value. And this will, in all probability, remain the greatest service to Soviet literature performed by the countryside prose of the 1960's.

---

[86] This is where the influence of the countryside prose has gone beyond a mere widening of the vocabulary which can be noticed in all literary genres (e.g., in Evgenii Evtushenko's latest effort, "Na krasnom snegu ussuriiskom," *Literaturnaia gazeta*, March 19, 1969, p. 12, one reads the following lines: "Ne prosto za Rus' i za veru my s vami nadenem shelomy—"; "Vladimir i Kiev, vy vidite ..."; "... udarit nabat kolokolen, / i vitiazei khvatit dlia novykh polei kulikovykh!"). As an example the works of Iosif Gerasimov can be mentioned. Gerasimov, who is the author of detective-type novels, in his earlier works, namely in *Dalekaia Vega* and *Krugi na vode*, built the main intrigue around the moral guilt of the heroes. It would be possible to define these works as "psychological detective novels." But his last novella, *Piat' dnei otdykha* (Moscow, 1968), is a pure "morality story" which has almost no plot, but instead a very thorough description of the exemplary moral behavior of a soldier on a five-day leave in Leningrad during the blockade.

Selected Bibliographies

CHAPTER 1 : Agricultural Administration in Russia from the Stolypin Land Reform to Forced Collectivization: An Interpretive Study

Baykov, A. "The Economic Development of Russia." *Economic History Review*, VII (December, 1954).

Bogdenko, M. L. "K istorii nachal'nogo etapa sploshnoi kollektivizatsii sel'skogo khoziaistva SSSR." *Voprosy istorii*, no. 5 (May, 1963).

Bronger, D. *Der Kampf um die sowjetische Agrarpolitik, 1925–1929.* Cologne: *Reichsnahrstandsverlag*, 1967.

Burov, Ia. *Derevnia na perelome.* Moscow, 1926.

Chayanov, A. V. *The Theory of Peasant Economy.* Homewood, Ill.: Richard D. Irwin, Inc., 1966.

Chernyshev, I. V. *Sel'skoe khoziaistvo dovoennoi Rossii i SSSR.* Moscow, 1926.

Danilov, V. P. "K kharakteristike obshchestvenno-politicheskoi obstanovki v sovetskoi derevne nakanune kollektivizatsii." *Istoricheskie zapiski*, LXXIX (1967).

Fenomenov, M. Ia. *Sovremennaia derevnia.* 2 vols. Moscow, 1925.

Iakovlev, Ia. A. *Bor'ba za urozhai.* 2nd ed. Moscow, 1929.

———. *Derevnia kak ona est'.* Moscow, 1924.

———. *Nasha derevnia.* Moscow, 1924.

Knipovich, B. N. *Ocherki deiatelnosti narodnogo kommissariata zemledeliia za tri goda: 1917–1920.* Moscow, 1920.

Leont'ev, A. A. *Krest'ianskoe pravo.* St. Petersburg, 1914.

Lewin, M. *La paysannerie et le pouvoir soviétique, 1928–1930.* Paris: Mouton and Co., 1966.

Materialy po perspektivnomu planu razvitiia sel'skogo i lesnogo khoziaistva, 1928/29–1932/33. Parts I and II. Moscow, 1929.

Mitrofanov, A. Kh. *Itogi chistki partii.* Moscow, 1930.

Moshkov, Iu. A. *Zernovaia problema v gody sploshnoi kollektivizatsii sel'skogo khoziaistva SSSR 1929–1932 gg.* Moscow, 1966.

Pershin, P. N. *Zemel'noe ustroistvo dorevoliutsionnoi derevni.* Moscow, 1928.

Sbornik zakonopolozhenii i rasporiazhenii po zemleustroistvu. Moscow, 1927.

Shuvaev, K. M. *Staraia i novaia derevnia.* Moscow, 1937.

Spravochnik po kolkhoznomu stroitel'stvu. Leningrad, 1931.

Spravochnik zemleustroitelia. Moscow, 1928.

Stenograficheskii otchet IV soveshchaniia zemorganov 5–12 ianvaria 1929 goda. Moscow, 1929.

Vyltsan, M. A., *et al.* "Nekotorye problemy istorii kollektivizatsii v SSSR." *Voprosy istorii*, no. 3 (March, 1965).

Weinstein, A. L. *Oblozhenie i platezhi krest'ianstva v dovoennoe i revoliutsionnoe vremia.* Moscow, 1924.

Yaney, G. L. "The Concept of the Stolypin Land Reform." *Slavic Review*, XXIII (June, 1964).

CHAPTER 2 : From Stalin to Brezhnev: Soviet Agricultural Policy in Historical Perspective

Clarke, Roger A. "Soviet Agricultural Reforms Since Khrushchev." *Soviet Studies*, XX, no. 2 (October, 1968).

Durgin, F. A., Jr. "Monetization and Policy in Soviet Agriculture Since 1952." *Soviet Studies*, XV, no. 4 (April, 1964).

Jasny, N. *Khrushchev's Crop Policy.* Glasgow: George Outram and Co., 1964.

———. *The Socialized Agriculture of the USSR.* Stanford, Calif.: Stanford University Press, 1949.

Karcz, Jerzy F. "The New Soviet Agricultural Program." *Soviet Studies*, XVII, no. 2 (October, 1965).

———. "Thoughts on the Grain Problem." *Soviet Studies*, XVIII, no. 4 (April, 1967).

——— (ed.) *Soviet and East European Agriculture.* Berkeley and Los Angeles: University of California Press, 1967.

Karcz, Jerzy F., and V. P. Timoshenko. "Soviet Agricultural Policy, 1953–1962." *Food Research Institute Studies*, IV, no. 2 (May, 1964).

Kerblay, Basile. *Les marches paysans en U.R.S.S.* The Hague: Mouton and Co., 1968.

Laird, Roy D. (ed.) *Soviet Agricultural and Peasant Affairs.* Lawrence: University of Kansas Press, 1963.

Laird, Roy D., and Edward Crowley (eds.). *Soviet Agriculture: The Permanent Crisis.* New York: Praeger, 1965.

Lewin, M. *Russian Peasants and Soviet Power.* Evanston, Ill.: Northwestern University Press, 1968.

Nimitz, Nancy. *Farm Employment in the Soviet Union, 1928–1963.* Santa Monica, Calif.: RAND Corp., 1965.

———. "The Lean Years." *Problems of Communism*, XIV, no. 3 (May–June, 1965).

———. *Soviet Government Grain Procurements, Distributions and Stocks, 1940, 1945–1963.* Santa Monica, Calif.: RAND Corp., 1964.

Nove, Alec. *Economic Rationality and Soviet Politics.* New York: Praeger, 1964.

Schiller, Otto. *Das Agrarsystem der Sowjetunion.* Tübingen, 1960.

Strauss, Erich. *Soviet Agriculture in Perspective.* New York: Praeger, 1969.

Timoshenko, Vladimir P. *Agricultural Russia and the Wheat Problem.* Stanford, Calif.: Food Research Institute, 1932.

U.S. Congress, Joint Economic Committee. *Comparisons of the United States and Soviet Economies*, Part I. Washington, D.C.: Government Printing Office, 1959. (Articles by Nancy Nimitz, Arkadius Kahan and D. Gale Johnson, and Lazar Volin.)

———. *New Directions in the Soviet Economy*, Part II–B. Washington, D.C.:

Government Printing Office, 1966. (Articles by Douglas B. Diamond, Jerzy F. Karcz, Keith Bush, Harry E. Walters, and Roger E. Neetz.)

Volin, Lazar. *A Survey of Soviet Russian Agriculture.* Washington, D.C.: U.S. Department of Agriculture, 1951.

Wädekin, Karl-Eugen. "Manpower in Soviet Agriculture: Some Post-Khrushchev Developments and Problems." *Soviet Studies,* XX, no. 3 (January, 1969).

―――. *Privatproduzenten in der sowjetischen Landwirtschaft.* Cologne: Wissenschaft und Politik, 1967.

―――. *Die sowjetischen Staatsgüter.* Wiesbaden: Otto Harrassowitz, 1969.

CHAPTER 3 : Continuity and Change in the Administration
of Soviet Agriculture Since Stalin

Brezhnev, L. I. "O khode vypolneniia reshenii XXIII s"ezda i plenumov KPSS po voprosam sel'skogo khoziaistva" (report to the October, 1968, Plenum of the Central Committee, CPSU). *Pravda,* October 31, 1968.

Karcz, Jerzy F. (ed.) *Soviet and East European Agriculture.* Berkeley and Los Angeles: University of California Press, 1967.

Khrushchev, N. S. *Stroitel'stvo kommunizma v SSSR i razvitie sel'skogo khoziaistva.* 8 vols. Moscow, 1962–1964.

Laird, Roy D. (ed.) *Soviet Agricultural and Peasant Affairs.* Lawrence: University of Kansas Press, 1963.

Ploss, Sidney I. *Conflict and Decision-Making in Soviet Russia: A Case Study of Agricultural Policy, 1953–1963.* Princeton, N.J.: Princeton University Press, 1965.

Schwarz, Solomon. "Agriculture: The Curtain Is Lifted." *Problems of Communism,* XV (March–April, 1966), 12–20.

CHAPTER 4 : The Changing Nature of the Kolkhoz Chairman

Bienstock, Gregory, Solomon M. Schwarz, and Aaron Yugow. *Management in Russian Industry and Agriculture.* Ithaca, N.Y.: Cornell University Press, 1948.

Karamelev, A. N. "Dvizhenie tridtsatitysiachnikov i ukreplenie kolkhozov." *Voprosy istorii KPSS,* no. 1 (1962), pp. 115–126.

Nove, Alec. "Peasants and Officials," in Jerzy F. Karcz (ed.), *Soviet and East European Agriculture.* Berkeley and Los Angeles: University of California Press, 1967.

CHAPTER 5 : Structural Change and the Quality of Soviet Collective
Farm Management, 1952–1966

Ballard, Allen B., Jr. "An End to Collective Farms?" *Problems of Communism,* X, no. 4 (July–August, 1961), 9–16.

Diamond, Douglas B. "Trends in Output, Inputs, and Factor Productivity in Soviet Agriculture," in U.S. Congress, Joint Economic Committee, *New Directions in the Soviet Economy.* Washington, D.C.: U.S. Government Printing Office, 1966.

Domar, Evsey D. "The Soviet Collective Farm as a Producer Cooperative." *American Economic Review,* LVI, no. 4, Part I (September, 1966), 734–757.

Dryden, Ann. "A Note on the Conversion of Collective into State Farms." *ASTE Bulletin,* VII, no. 3 (Winter, 1965), 17–19.

Durgin, Frank A., Jr. "Monetization and Policy in Soviet Agriculture Since 1952." *Soviet Studies,* XV, no. 4 (April, 1964), 381–407.

———. "Quantitative, Structural and Institutional Changes in Soviet Agriculture during the Khrushchev Era 1953–1964." *Cahiers de L'Isea* (May, 1966), pp. 111–132.

Karcz, Jerzy F. "Seven Years on the Farm: Retrospect and Prospects," in U.S. Congress, Joint Economic Committee, *New Directions in the Soviet Economy.* Washington, D.C.: U.S. Government Printing Office, 1966.

Nove, Alec. "Incentives for Peasants and Administrators," in Roy D. Laird (ed.), *Soviet Agricultural and Peasant Affairs.* Lawrence: University of Kansas Press, 1963.

Oi, Walter Y., and Elizabeth M. Clayton. "A Peasant's View of a Soviet Collective Farm." *American Economic Review,* LVIII, no. 1 (March, 1968), 37–59.

Sakoff, Alexander N. "Production Brigades: Organizational Basis of Farm Work in the U.S.S.R." FAO, *Monthly Bulletin of Agricultural Economics and Statistics,* XVII, no. 1 (January, 1968), 1–8.

Smith, R. E. F. "The Amalgamation of Collective Farms: Some Technical Aspects." *Soviet Studies,* VI, no. 1 (July, 1954), 16–32.

Stuart, Robert C. "The Conversion of Collective into State Farms: Further Note II." *ASTE Bulletin,* IX, no. 1 (Spring, 1967), 14–16.

Wright, Arthur W. "Conversion of Collective Farms into State Farms: Further Note I." *ASTE Bulletin,* IX, no. 1 (Spring, 1967), 12–14.

CHAPTER 6 : The Law of Farm-Farmer Relations

Aksenenok, G. A. *Pravovoe polozhenie sovkhozov v SSSR.* Moscow, 1960.

Bagdagiulian, V. *O stimulakh i rukovodstve sel'skokhoziaistvennogo proizvodstva.* Erevan, 1967.

Bilinsky, A. "Aktuelle Rechtsprobleme der Kolchosen." *Jahrbuch für Ostrecht,* VIII, no. 1 (1967), 21–80.

Dem'iamnenko, V. N. *Gosudarstvennoe rukovodstvo i kolkhoznaia demokratiia.* Saratov, 1968.

Demidov, S. F., et al. (eds.) *Nekotorye voprosy upravleniia sel'skokhoziaistvennym proizvodstvom.* Moscow, 1967.

Emel'ianov, A. M. (ed.) *Khozraschet i stimulirovanie v sel'skom khoziaistve.* Moscow, 1968.

Godes, A. B., A. V. Davidov, and A. M. Kalandadze. *Iuridicheskoe obsluzhivanie kolkhozov i sovkhozov.* Moscow, 1965.

Guins, G. C. "Legal Nature of Soviet Collective Farms." *Washington Law Review,* XXVI (1951), 66–86.

Kalandadze, A. M. "Kolkhoznoe pravo," in *Sorok let sovetskogo prava.* Leningrad, 1957.

———. "Pravovoe obespechenie material'noi zainteresovannosti v kolkhozakh," in *Aktual'nye problemy sovetskogo gosudarstva i prava v period stroitel'stva kommunizma*. Leningrad, 1967.

Kazantsev, N. D. (ed.) *Kolkhoznoe pravo*. Moscow, 1962.

Kaz'min, I. F. "Novoe zakonodatel'stvo ob oplate truda kolkhoznikov." *Uchenye zapiski VNIISZ*, no. 12 (1968), pp. 87–100.

Kucherov, S. "The Future of the Soviet Collective Farm." *American Slavonic and* ✓
East European Review, IXX (1960), 180–210.

Mikhalkevich, V. N. (ed.) *Kommentarii k zakonodatel'stvu o pensiiakh i poso-biiakh kolkhoznikam*. Moscow, 1967.

Nizovtsev, I. V. (gen. ed.) *Vnutrikhoziaistvennyi raschet i material'nye stimuly v kolkhozakh i sovkhozakh Gor'kovskoi oblasti*. Gorky, 1967.

Pankratov, A. S. (ed.) *Zakonodatel'stvo o proizvodstve, zagotovok i zakupkakh sel'khozproduktov*. Moscow, 1967.

Schlesinger, R. "The New Structure of Soviet Agriculture." *Soviet Studies*, X ✓
(1959), 228–251.

Semin, S. I. *Razvitie obshchestvenno-ekonomicheskikh otnoshenii v kolkhozakh*. Moscow, 1968.

Skipetrov, P. A. *Obobshchestvlenie truda i sotsialisticheskaia sobstvennost'*. Moscow, 1968.

Zinchenko, G. I., and M. K. Minin. *Ekonomicheskoe stimulirovanie i nauchnaia oranizatsiia sel'skokhoziaistvennogo truda*. Moscow, 1968.

CHAPTER 7 : The Nonagricultural Rural Sector

Wädekin, K.-E. "Handwerke, Baugewerbe und materielle Dienstleistungen in sowjetischen Dörfern." *Sowjetstudien*, no. 25 (1969), pp. 38–73.

CHAPTER 8 : Recruitment and the Quality of the Soviet
Agricultural Labor Force

Dodge, Norton T. *Women in the Soviet Economy*. Baltimore: Johns Hopkins Press, 1966.

Dodge, Norton T., and Murray Feshbach. "The Role of Women in Soviet Agriculture," in Jerzy F. Karcz (ed.), *Soviet and East European Agriculture*. Berkeley and Los Angeles: University of California Press, 1967.

Duevel, Christian. "Two Ways to Activate the Soviet Rural Intelligentsia." *Radio Liberty Dispatch*, April 8, 1968.

Dunn, Stephen P., and Ethel Dunn. *The Peasants of Central Russia*. New York: Holt, Rinehart and Winston, 1967.

Gaev, A. G. "The Kolkhoz and the Kolkhoz Worker in Soviet Literature," in Roy D. Laird and Edward L. Crowley (eds.), *Soviet Agriculture: The Permanent Crisis*. New York: Praeger, 1965.

Ianov, A. "Kostromskoi eksperiment." *Literaturnaia gazeta*, December 27, 1967.

Inkeles, Alex, and Raymond A. Bauer. *The Soviet Citizen*. Cambridge, Mass.: Harvard University Press, 1959.

Rutkevich, M. N. (ed.) *Zhiznennye plany molodezhi*. Sverdlovsk, 1966.

Salnikov, I. "Nazrevshie voprosy podgotovki sel'skokhoziaistvennykh kadrov." *Kommunist*, no. 4 (1968), pp. 53–59.

410 : *The Soviet Rural Community*

Shubkin, V. N. "Opyt ispol'zovaniia kolichestvennykh metodov v konkretnom sotsiologicheskom issledovanii voprosov trudoustroistva i vybora professii," in A. G. Aganbegian (ed.), *Kolichestvennye metody v sotsiologicheskikh issledovaniiakh.* Novosibirsk, 1964.

――――. "Molodezh' vstupaet v zhizn'." *Voprosy filosofii*, no. 5 (1965), pp. 57–70.

――――. "Nekotorye problemy adaptatsii molodezhi k trudu," in Akademiia Nauk SSSR, *Sotsial'nye issledovaniia.* Moscow, 1965.

Wädekin, Karl-Eugen. "Manpower in Soviet Agriculture: Some Post-Khrushchev Developments and Problems." *Soviet Studies*, XX, no. 3 (January, 1968), 281–304.

Yanowitch, Murray, and Norton T. Dodge. "Social Class and Education: Soviet Findings and Reactions." *Comparative Education Review*, XII, no. 3 (October, 1968), 248–267.

CHAPTER 9 : The Revolution in Soviet Farm Household Income, 1953–1967

Churakov, V. Ia., and L. I. Suvorova. *Ispol'zovanie trudovykh resursov v kolkhozakh i sovkhozakh.* Moscow, 1967.

DePauw, John W. *The Soviet Statistical System: The Continuous Sample Budget Survey.* International Population Reports Series P–95, no. 62. Washington, D.C.: U.S. Department of Commerce, 1965.

D'iachkov, G. V. *Obshchestvennoe i lichnoe v kolkhozakh.* Moscow, 1968.

Laptev, I. D., and S. I. Semin (eds.). *Rentabel'nost' i rasshirennoe vosproizvodstvo v sel'skom khoziaistve.* Moscow, 1968.

Nove, Alec. "Incentives for Peasants and Administrators," in Roy D. Laird (ed.), *Soviet Agricultural and Peasant Affairs.* Lawrence: University of Kansas Press, 1963.

Sidorova, M. "Formirovanie i metodika rascheta fonda vosproizvodstva rabochei sily v kolkhozakh." *Voprosy ekonomiki*, no. 5 (1967), pp. 44–51.

Volkov, V. F., and A. K. Malakhov. *Zarabotnaia plata i premirovanie rabotnikov sovkhozov.* Moscow, 1967.

Zaslavskaia, T. I. *Raspredelenie po trudu v kolkhozakh.* Moscow, 1966.

CHAPTER 10 : Progress on Mechanization in Soviet Agriculture

Antoshkevich, V. "Sroki sluzhby mashin i amortizatsiia v sel'skom khoziaistve." *Voprosy ekonomiki*, no. 11 (1965), pp. 64–74.

Basiuk, T. L. *Organizatsiia sotsialisticheskogo sel'skokhoziaistvennogo proizvodstva.* Rev. ed. Moscow, 1965.

――――. "Sotsialism preobrazil sel'skoe khoziaistvo." *Ekonomicheskie nauki*, no. 11 (1967), pp. 53–61.

Campbell, R. W. *The Economics of Soviet Oil and Gas.* Baltimore: Johns Hopkins Press, 1968.

DePauw, J. W. *Measures of Agricultural Employment in the USSR: 1950–1966.* International Population Reports Series P–95, no. 65. Washington, D.C.: U.S. Department of Commerce, 1968.

Dovring, F. "Soviet Farm Mechanization in Perspective." *Slavic Review*, XXV, ✔ no. 2 (June, 1966), 287–302.

Efimov, A. N., and L. Ia. Berri (eds.). *Metody planirovaniia mezhotraslevykh proportsii*. Moscow, 1965.

Komina, L. "Voprosy metodologii opredeleniia polnykh trudovykh zatrat." *Vestnik statistiki*, no. 6 (1967), pp. 42–50.

Kononenko, A. "Kompleksnaia mekhanizatsiia vozdelyvaniia zernovykh kul'tur." *Ekonomika sel'skogo khoziaistva*, no. 6 (1968), pp. 108–115.

Litvak, S. "Toplivno-energeticheskii balans SSSR i effektivnost' ispol'zovaniia energoresursov v narodnom khoziaistve." *Vestnik statistiki*, no. 1 (1968), pp. 32–41.

Schinke, E. *Die Mechanisierung landwirtschaftlicher Arbeiten in der Sowjetunion*. Wiesbaden: Harrassowitz, 1967.

Siniukov, M. I. "Voprosy ratsional'nogo ispol'zovaniia i vosproizvodstva sel'skokhoziaistvennoi tekhniki." *Izvestiia Timiriazevskoi sel'skokhoziaistvennoi akademii*, no. 6 (1966), pp. 200–208.

CHAPTER 11 : Financing the Modernization of Kolkhozy

Arutiunian, Iu. V. "Osobennosti i znachenie novogo etapa razvitiia sel'skogo khoziaistva SSSR," in *Istoriia sovetskogo krest'ianstva i kolkhoznogo stroitel'stva v SSSR*. Moscow, 1963.

Atlas, M. S., *et al. Kreditno-denezhnaia sistema SSSR*. Moscow, 1967.

Durgin, F. A., Jr. "Monetization and Policy in Soviet Agriculture Since 1952." *Soviet Studies*, XV, no. 4 (April, 1964), 375–407.

Kirillov, E. A. *Finansy kolkhozov*. Moscow, 1962.

Laptev, I. D. *Obshchestvennye fondy kolkhozov*. Moscow, 1961.

Levchuk, I. *Dolgosrochnyi sel'skokhoziaistvennyi kredit*. Moscow, 1967.

Shermenev, M. K. (ed.) *Finansy i kreditovanie sel'skokhoziaistvennykh predpriiatii*. Moscow, 1963.

Stoliarov, S. G. *O tsenakh i tsenoobrazovanii v SSSR*. Moscow, 1969.

Vainer, M. G. (ed.) *Effektivnost' kapital'nykh vlozhenii v sel'skoe khoziaistvo*. Moscow, 1963.

Zaslavskaia, T. I. *Raspredelenie po trudu v kolkhozakh*. Moscow, 1966.

CHAPTER 12 : The Peasants as a Social Class

Aleksandrova, S. E. "Orientatsiia sotsial'nykh grupp molodezhi sela na obrazovanie (po materialam sotsiologicheskogo issledovaniia)." *Vestnik Moskovskogo universiteta: filosofiia*, no. 3 (1969), pp. 63–73.

Arutiunian, Iu. V. *Opyt sotsiologicheskogo izucheniia sela*. Moscow, 1968.

Grigorovskii, V. E., and M. A. Alekseev. *Lichnoe podsobnoe khoziaistvo kolkhoznikov, rabochikh i sluzhashchikh v SSSR*. Leningrad, 1968.

Kartsov, V. A. (ed.) *Opyt istoriko-sotsiologicheskogo izucheniia sela 'Molodino.'* Moscow, 1968.

Losev, A. V., *et al.* (eds.) *Sotsial'no-ekonomicheskie preobrazovaniia v Voronezhskoi derevne*. Voronezh, 1967.

Shubnikov, V. N., *et al. Kopanka 52 let spustia.* Moscow, 1965.
Stepanian, Ts. A., and V. S. Semenov (eds.). *Klassy, sotsial'nye sloi i gruppy v SSSR.* Moscow, 1968.

CHAPTER 13 : Structure and Functions of the Soviet Rural Family

Dunn, Stephen P., and Ethel Dunn. *The Peasants of Central Russia.* New York: Holt, Rinehart and Winston, 1967.
Kushner, P. I. "O nekotorykh protsessakh proiskhodiashchikh v sovremennoi kolkhoznoi sem'e." *Sovetskaia etnografiia,* no. 3 (1956), pp. 14–24.
Maynard, John. *The Russian Peasant and Other Studies.* New York, 1962.

CHAPTER 14 : The Importance of Religion in the Soviet Rural Community

Dunn, E. "Russian Sectarianism in New Marxist Scholarship." *Slavic Review,* XXVI (1967), pp. 128–140.
Klibanov, A. I. "The Dissident Denominations in the Past and Today." *Soviet Sociology,* III, no. 4 (1965).
———. *Istoriia religioznogo sektantstva v Rossii.* Moscow, 1965.
Kolarz, W. *Religion in the Soviet Union.* New York: St. Martin's Press, 1961.

CHAPTER 15 : The Contemporary Countryside in Soviet Literature:
A Search for New Values

Brown, Edward J. *Russian Literature Since the Revolution.* New York: Collier Books, 1963.
Chalmaev, Viktor Andreevich. "Neizbezhnost'." *Molodaia gvardiia,* no. 9 (1968), pp. 259–289.
Gibian, George. *Interval of Freedom; Soviet Literature during the Thaw, 1954–1959.* Minneapolis: University of Minnesota Press, 1960.
Swayze, Harold. *Political Control of Literature in the USSR, 1946–1959.* Cambridge, Mass.: Harvard University Press, 1962.
Žekulin, Gleb. "Aspects of Peasant Life as Portrayed in Contemporary Soviet Literature." *Canadian Slavic Studies,* I, no. 4 (Winter, 1967), 552–565.
———. "Socialist Realism." *Soviet Studies,* XI, no. 4 (April, 1960), 432–442.

Index

413

About the Authors

David W. Bronson and *Constance B. Krueger* are Soviet specialists working as economists for the Central Intelligence Agency. Mr. Bronson has written, with Barbara Severin, "Recent Trends in Consumption and Disposable Money Income in the U.S.S.R.," for *New Directions in the Soviet Economy*, and "Soviet Experience with Shortening the Workweek," *Industrial and Labor Relations Review*. He received a B.A. in economics from Washington State University and an M.A. in economics from the University of California. Mrs. Krueger holds a B.S. from Georgia State College for Women.

Norton T. Dodge holds a Ph.D. in economics from Harvard University. He is a graduate of Harvard's Russian Regional Studies Program and was a Graduate Student Fellow at the Russian Research Center before going to the University of Maryland where he is associate professor of economics. He has authored *Women in the Soviet Economy: Their Role in Economic, Scientific and Technical Development* and other studies of the Soviet labor force. His research has taken him to the Soviet Union four times since 1955.

Folke Dovring is professor of land economics at the University of Illinois. Formerly he taught at Lund University in Sweden, where he received his Ph.D. He has written several books among which are *Land and Labor in Europe in the Twentieth Century*, *History as a Social Science*, and *Problems of Manpower*, as well as many scholarly articles, including "Productivity of Labor in Agricultural Production," University of Illinois, College of Agriculture Experiment Station *Bulletin*, "Soviet Farm Mechanization in Perspective," *Slavic Review*, and "Underemployment in Traditional Agriculture," *Economic Development and Cultural Change*.

Ethel Dunn received an M.A. in history from Columbia University and a Certificate of the Columbia Russian Institute in 1956. Since then she has pursued a research career in the ethnography and sociology of peasant life in the Soviet Union. With her husband Stephen Dunn, she has written *The Peasants of Central Russia*. Among her many articles are "A Slavophile Looks at the Raskol and the Sects," *Slavonic and East European Review*,

417

"Russian Sectarianism in New Marxist Scholarship," *Slavic Review*, "Sects and the Survival of Religion," *Survey*, and "Educating the Small Peoples of the Soviet North: The Limits of Culture Change," *Arctic Anthropology*.

Stephen P. Dunn holds a Ph.D. in anthropology from Columbia University. He is research director of the Highgate Road Social Science Research Station, Inc. (Berkeley, Calif.), a nonprofit corporation engaged in research in the social sciences in the Soviet Union and Eastern Europe. In addition to his research work in the field of Soviet ethnology and sociology, he edits the journals *Soviet Sociology* and *Soviet Anthropology and Archeology*. His books are *Cultural Processes in the Baltic Area under Soviet Rule* and, in collaboration with his wife Ethel Dunn, *The Peasants of Central Russia*. Also in collaboration with his wife, he has published "The Transformation of Economy and Culture of the Small Peoples of the Soviet North," *Arctic Anthropology*, "Soviet Regime and Native Culture in Central Asia and Kazakhstan: The Major Peoples," *Current Anthropology*, and "Religion as an Instrument of Culture Change in the Soviet Union: The Problem of the Sects in the Soviet Union," *Slavic Review*.

Jerry F. Hough is on the Political Economy Faculty at the University of Toronto. Before moving to Toronto he was associate professor of political science at the University of Illinois. He received a B.A., M.A., and Ph.D. from Harvard University. In addition to several articles in scholarly journals, he is author of *The Soviet Prefects*.

Jerzy F. Karcz is professor of economics at the University of Southern California at Santa Barbara. He was educated at Alliance College, Kent State University, and Columbia University, where he was affiliated with the Russian Institute. He is editor of the volume *Soviet and East European Agriculture* and author of *Soviet Agricultural Marketings and Prices, 1928–1954*. Among his many important articles are "Thoughts on the Grain Problem," "The New Soviet Agricultural Program," *Soviet Studies*, and "Seven Years on the Farm: Retrospect and Prospects," *New Directions in the Soviet Economy*.

Peter B. Maggs is professor of law at the University of Illinois. He received both his B.A. and J.D. from Harvard University. He is the co-author of two books on Soviet Law: *Disarmament Inspection under Soviet Law* and *The Soviet Legal System*.

James R. Millar is associate professor of economics at the University of Illinois. In addition to this volume, he has published several articles on the

Soviet economy in scholarly journals: "On the Merits of the Convergence Hypothesis," *Journal of Economic Issues*, "A Reformulation of A. V. Chayanov's Theory of the Peasant Economy," *Economic Development and Cultural Change*, and "Soviet Rapid Development and the Agricultural Surplus Hypothesis," *Soviet Studies*. He received his B.A. from the University of Texas and his Ph.D. in economics from Cornell University. His study of the Soviet economy has also taken him to Harvard's Russian Research Center and to the Soviet Union.

Robert F. Miller was educated at the University of Michigan and Harvard University, from which he received his Ph.D. in 1965. He is currently in the Political Science Department of the University of Illinois and has taught at Washington University in St. Louis and the State University of New York at Stony Brook. Harvard University Press has recently published his first book, *"One Hundred Thousand Tractors."* Among his articles are "A Good Kolkhoz," *Survey*, and "The Politotdel: A Lesson from the Past," *Slavic Review*.

Robert C. Stuart is on the faculty of Douglass College, Rutgers University. In addition to training in economics at the University of British Columbia and the University of Wisconsin, where he received his Ph.D., he has done research on the Soviet economy at Harvard's Russian Research Center and the Timiriazev Agricultural Academy in Moscow. He has contributed articles on Liberman and Kantorovich to the volume *Soviet Leaders* and participated in a symposium held at the University of Washington, "The Agrarian Question in the Light of Communist and Non-Communist Experience."

Alexander Vucinich is professor of sociology at the University of Illinois. After receiving his Ph.D. in sociology and cultural anthropology from Columbia University in 1950, he taught at San Jose State College until 1964, when he joined the University of Illinois Sociology Department. In addition to many articles in scholarly journals, he has published *Science in Russian Culture: A History to 1860*; *Soviet Economic Institutions: The Social Structure of Production Units*; and *The Soviet Academy of Sciences*. He is currently working on science in Soviet culture.

Karl-Eugen Wädekin teaches agricultural socio-economics of Eastern Europe at the University of Giessen, Germany. He is also co-editor of the monthly journal *Osteuropa-Wirtschaft*. He is the author of three books and some 20 articles in German on Soviet agriculture. Among his contributions to the field in English are "Soviet Agriculture and Agricultural Policy," in *Soviet Agriculture: The Permanent Crisis*, "Internal Migration and the Flight from the Land in the U.S.S.R.," *Soviet Studies*, "Private Production in Soviet Agriculture," *Problems of Communism*, "Manpower in Soviet Agriculture," *Soviet Studies*, and "Housing in the U.S.S.R.—The Countryside," *Problems of Communism.*

George L. Yaney is spending the 1969–1970 academic year as a Research Fellow at Harvard's Russian Research Center. His previous research on Russian and Soviet history has taken him to Leningrad and resulted in the publication of numerous articles including "Concept of the Stolypin Land Reform," and "Some Aspects of the Imperial Russian Government on the Eve of the First World War," *Slavic Review*, "Law, Society, and the Domestic Regime in Russia, in Historical Perspective," *American Political Science Review*, "Bureaucracy and Freedom: N. M. Korkunov's Theory of the State," *American Historical Review*, "War and the Evolution of the Russian State: A Historical Reappraisal," *South Atlantic Quarterly*, and "The Good Mayor," *Georgia Review*. He was educated at Rensselaer Polytechnic Institute, University of Colorado, and Princeton University, where he received his Ph.D. He has taught history at the College of Wooster and more recently at the University of Maryland.

Gleb Žekulin was educated in the School of Economics at the University of Prague, the Faculty of Philosophy at Charles University, Prague, and Liverpool University. He has taught Russian literature at Liverpool, Glasgow, and McGill universities, and is currently teaching at the University of Toronto. Among his articles are "Forerunner of Socialist Realism: The Novel 'What to Do?' by N. G. Chernyshevski," *Slavonic and East European Review*, "Solzhenitsyn's Four Stories," *Soviet Studies*, and "Aspects of Peasant Life as Portrayed in Contemporary Soviet Literature," *Canadian Slavic Studies.*

DATE DUE